Cicero
The Advocate

edited by

JONATHAN POWELL

and

JEREMY PATERSON

OXFORD
UNIVERSITY PRESS

OXFORD

UNIVERSITY PRESS

Great Clarendon Street, Oxford OX2 6DP

Oxford University Press is a department of the University of Oxford.
It furthers the University's objective of excellence in research, scholarship,
and education by publishing worldwide in

Oxford New York

Auckland Cape Town Dar es Salaam Hong Kong Karachi
Kuala Lumpur Madrid Melbourne Mexico City Nairobi
New Delhi Shanghai Taipei Toronto

With offices in

Argentina Austria Brazil Chile Czech Republic France Greece
Guatemala Hungary Italy Japan Poland Portugal Singapore
South Korea Switzerland Thailand Turkey Ukraine Vietnam

Oxford is a registered trade mark of Oxford University Press
in the UK and in certain other countries

Published in the United States
by Oxford University Press Inc., New York

British Library Cataloguing in Publication Data
Data available

Library of Congress Cataloging in Publication Data
Data available

Typeset by Newgen Imaging Systems (P) Ltd., Chennai, India
Printed in Great Britain
on acid-free paper by
Biddles Ltd., King's Lynn

ISBN 0–19–815280–9   978–0–19–815280–4
ISBN 0–19–929829–7 (Pbk.)   978–0–19–929829–7 (Pbk.)

1 3 5 7 9 10 8 6 4 2

PREFACE

Advocacy is a feature of most developed legal systems including, notably, those of Britain, Europe, and North America. It played a major part in the legal system of ancient Rome, and Cicero was recognized both in his own time and afterwards to have been the greatest of Roman advocates. Not only did he publish a good number of his lawcourt speeches; he was also the first practising advocate in the Western world to record his reflections on the theory and practice of oratory. Comparison of Roman advocacy with modern theory and practice can illuminate general questions about the nature of this often controversial activity, while ancient Rome can also provide practical samples of the art which, although they belong to a system in some ways alien to our own, may easily seem as striking as anything in a modern courtroom drama.

This volume follows similar lines to *Cicero the Philosopher* (ed. J. G. F. Powell, Oxford University Press, 1995). It may seem strange for the Advocate to come after the Philosopher, but scholarly research does not always move in expected directions, and the oddity might have pleased Cicero, who maintained that his philosophical studies had informed his practice as an orator. In the meantime scholarship has benefited from, inter alia, a book-length literary study of Cicero's letters, G. Hutchinson, *Cicero's Correspondence* (Oxford, 1998), and a major collection of essays on Ciceronian oratory and rhetoric, *Brill's Companion to Cicero*, ed. J. M. May (Leiden, 2002), which does not, however, focus on advocacy as such. One particular stimulus to renewed interest in Cicero as advocate was provided by John Crook's excellent book *Legal Advocacy in the Roman World* (London, 1995). But the most important reason for publishing the present collection of papers was the realization, as in the case of *Cicero the Philosopher*, that a number of scholars were for whatever reason beginning to move in the same direction, often coincidentally and from different starting points (whether historical, legal, or rhetorical), and that their work could benefit from being brought together into one volume. The editors have also been conscious of fortuitous synergies: this volume might not have been thought of if one of its editors had not happened to read some books on advocates and advocacy that had belonged to his father, who was a barrister, or if an appeal by a Newcastle colleague in 1995 for more courses suitable for Combined Honours students (without Latin or Greek) had not prompted the same editor to design courses on 'Logic and Rhetoric' and 'Cicero as Advocate'. It is equally fortuitous that the other editor happened to have kept in touch with an Oxford contemporary who was soon to be promoted to the Appeal Court Bench, and who is the author of our final chapter.

The volume is, we hope, sufficiently unified by a common conviction of the interest and importance of advocacy as an activity, and of the need to study Cicero's speeches within their original, precise historical context if one is to make any coherent sense of these texts at all. At the same time, following the principle adopted in *Cicero the Philosopher*, we have not intervened to impose an artificial orthodoxy where our contributors disagree among themselves. It should go without saying that we make no claim to cover everything: this is a field in which there is much interesting work still being done. We shall have achieved our aim if the collection succeeds in casting light on some aspects of the topic, and in stimulating further enquiry and debate.

The contributions to this volume were gathered between 1999 and 2002, some having been presented at a seminar series on Cicero held in the Classics Department at Newcastle University in 1997–8. The volume has been long in maturing, owing to pressure of other commitments, but we hope that it will after all meet expectations and that it will find readers of different kinds: we are reasonably confident that there will be something of interest not only for professional classicists and ancient historians and for students of the ancient world, but also for those with a more general interest in rhetoric, advocacy and legal history. Again as in *Cicero the Philosopher*, we have provided a substantial introduction, which may function as a survey of the main issues as well as a way into the subject for those less familiar with it. (One reviewer of the earlier volume seems to have thought this was a bad idea; we cannot quite work out why.) We have arranged the papers in two parts, the first dealing with more general themes and the second, in which some chapters are unavoidably longer and more technical than the rest, with individual speeches taken as case studies, but we are aware that this arrangement (or any other) is to some extent arbitrary; the general and the particular constantly illuminate one another. We have also provided an appendix listing Cicero's known appearances as an advocate. No attempt has been made to compile a comprehensive bibliography (readers may be referred to the useful bibliographical survey by C. P. Craig in the Brill *Companion*, pp. 503–99), but we have provided a consolidated list of works cited by our contributors, which probably covers most important work on the subject. Michael C. Alexander, *The Case for the Prosecution in the Ciceronian Era* (Ann Arbor, 2002) appeared too late to be fully taken into account. Alexander's introduction covers some of the same ground as ours; his general project of reconstructing the prosecution arguments, in cases where we have Cicero's defence speeches, may be recommended as an interesting complement to our analyses of Cicero's own strategies as advocate.

We are grateful to the University of Newcastle upon Tyne's Research Committee for financial help, to Gaby Wright for translating Chapter 13 from the original German, to Kathryn Tempest for compiling the bibliography, to Kathryn Tempest and Gábor Tahin for their work on the indexes, to Lene Rubinstein for help with the Introduction, and to Jeff and Erica Johnson for the cover design.

J. G. F. P.; J. J. P.
London and Newcastle
April 2003

CONTENTS

EDITORS AND CONTRIBUTORS

Editors:

JONATHAN POWELL was Professor of Latin in the University of Newcastle upon Tyne until 2000, and is now Professor of Latin at Royal Holloway, University of London.

JEREMY PATERSON is Senior Lecturer in Ancient History, University of Newcastle upon Tyne.

Contributors:

D. H. BERRY is Senior Lecturer in Classics, University of Leeds.

CHRISTOPHER BURNAND teaches at Abingdon School and is an editor of Greece and Rome.

CHRISTOPHER CRAIG is Professor of Classics, University of Tennessee at Knoxville.

LYNN FOTHERINGHAM is Lecturer in Classics, University of Nottingham.

JILL HARRIES is Professor of Ancient History, University of St Andrews.

JEFFREY P. JOHNSON is studying for a Ph.D. at Princeton University.

JOHN LAWS (Lord Justice Laws) is a Judge of the Court of Appeal.

D. S. LEVENE is Professor of Latin in the University of Leeds.

ANDREW LINTOTT is titular Reader in Ancient History in the University of Oxford and Fellow and Tutor in Ancient History, Worcester College.

KATHRYN LOMAS is a Research Assistant at University College, London.

ANDREW M. RIGGSBY is Professor of Classics, University of Texas at Austin.

CATHERINE STEEL is Lecturer in Classics, University of Glasgow.

WILFRIED STROH is Professor of Classical Philology, University of Munich.

MICHAEL WINTERBOTTOM was Corpus Christi Professor of Latin, University of Oxford until his retirement in 2001.

Introduction

JONATHAN POWELL AND JEREMY PATERSON

i. Approaching Cicero's Forensic Speeches

It may seem obvious when stated, though apparently it is all too easily forgotten, that the primary function of a lawcourt speech is to make the best possible case, and preferably to win.[1] Other considerations, political or literary, take second place. Competent advocates should not be found putting the desire to make a fine speech, to create great literature, to air a political point, or to advertise themselves, before the interests of the case they are pleading. Naturally, the attractiveness of an advocate's style, or a real or assumed political or moral stance, may contribute to the overall persuasive effect, but the case itself must come first.

Marcus Tullius Cicero (106–43 BC) was not merely a competent advocate. He was acknowledged as the leading Roman advocate of his time. According to Quintilian, he was said to be king of the law-courts ('regnare in iudiciis dictus est').[2] This reputation could not have been achieved and maintained without continuous success in individual cases. Cicero aimed to win, and much of the time, evidently, he did win.[3] It may seem paradoxical that we are better informed as to his rate of success in those cases where we do not have his speeches than we are in relation to the published orations. This is because, whenever a particular case is mentioned as being of importance (by Cicero or another source), the result is generally mentioned too, while in the case of some of the published speeches we have only the text to go on. Sometimes we have direct evidence for the result: thus, for example, we know from allusions elsewhere in Cicero that the defences of Roscius and of Sestius were successful. Sometimes we can deduce from the continued presence in

---

The introduction is a joint product by the two editors, with J.J.P. taking particular responsibility for § v.

[1] Quint. *Inst.* 2.17.23 puts this the other way round: 'tendit quidem ad victoriam qui dicit, sed cum bene dixit, etiamsi non vincat, id quod arte continetur effecit.' ('The orator does indeed aim to win, but when he has made a good speech, even if he does not win, he has done what the art of rhetoric requires.') A good advocate can of course make the best possible case and still lose, because sometimes the best possible case is not a very good one.

[2] Quint. *Inst.* 10.1.112.   [3] For the details, see Appendix.

Rome of Cicero's client that he was acquitted, whereas otherwise he would have been in exile: thus, for example, the defences of Caelius and Plancius were clearly successful, that of Fonteius probably so. In only two cases, in fact, is there clear evidence that Cicero published an unsuccessful speech. One was the early *Pro Vareno* (now lost, but well known to Quintilian and Pliny the Younger);[4] the other was the *Pro Milone*, which is discussed below (§ vii, p. 55).

Advocacy can easily be regarded as an ephemeral art, and it is a remarkable achievement in an advocate for his speeches still to be read and analysed after more than two thousand years. This may, however, be for reasons that have little to do with the success of his advocacy. At least from the Renaissance onwards, Cicero's speeches have been admired above all on account of their literary style (there are remarkably few references to advocacy, for example, in Zieliński's study of Cicero's influence through the centuries[5]). In modern times, they have been used as examination texts in the Latin language, as material for philological or literary analysis, as examples for the study of technical rhetoric, and as sources of evidence for Roman political and social history. In short, they have been studied from almost all possible points of view other than that of practical advocacy. In the last generation the tide has begun to turn; and those scholars who have regarded the forensic speeches in this light and have contributed to their better understanding will receive honourable mention in the following pages.[6] Outside their work, however, we may still find a reluctance to take these speeches seriously as examples of advocacy, or to judge them by standards appropriate to a real lawcourt speech,[7] rather than by the aesthetic, historical, or moral criteria which classical scholars are more used to applying to works of ancient literature. In this book we aim to put the emphasis back where we

[4] L. Varenus was apparently convicted, in the Sullan *quaestio de sicariis*, of two murders and one case of wounding. As in the *Pro Roscio*, Cicero argued that the real murderers were behind the prosecution and had tried to frame Varenus. The most plausible—perhaps the only plausible—reason for Cicero to publish this speech is that he believed in Varenus' innocence. For the evidence, see Jane W. Crawford, *M. Tullius Cicero: The Fragmentary Speeches* (Atlanta, 1994) 7–18.

[5] T. Zieliński, *Cicero im Wandel der Jahrhunderte*, 3rd edn. (Leipzig and Berlin, 1912).

[6] Particular reference should be made at this point to C. Neumeister, *Grundsätze der forensischen Rhetorik gezeigt an Gerichtsreden Ciceros* (Munich, 1964), to the work of C. J. Classen and especially his *Recht–Rhetorik–Politik* (Darmstadt, 1985), and to W. Stroh's *Taxis und Taktik: die advokatische Dispositionskunst in Ciceros Gerichtsreden* (Stuttgart, 1975), the best available book on Cicero's speeches, unfortunately not yet translated into English. On more general questions regarding advocacy in the ancient world, we are much indebted to J. A. Crook, *Legal Advocacy in the Roman World* (London, 1995), a book to which every reader of this volume should pay serious attention. Cf. also F. Wieacker, *Cicero als Advokat*, Vortrag gehalten vor der Berliner Juristischen Gesellschaft am 29. April 1964 (Berlin, 1965).

[7] For the question of whether the published speeches are in fact 'real' lawcourt speeches, see below, § vii.

believe it should be; and, to reinforce the point, we have enlisted the help of one of Her Majesty's Lords Justices of Appeal, who has provided a practical lawyer's view of Ciceronian advocacy (Chapter 15) for the reader to set beside those of the classical philologists and ancient historians.

Doubtless, few if any would claim that Cicero's forensic speeches are reliable models for the practising advocate today.[8] Romans of later generations also had doubts about them in this respect.[9] But if this is the case, it is at least interesting to try to find out why. If the methods that evidently worked spectacularly well for Cicero did not work for later Romans or do not work for us, what accounts for the difference? To put the question more formally: what hypotheses do we need to form about the nature of Republican Roman lawcourts and the advocacy that was practised in them, in order to predict that Cicero's speeches (or what we know of them) would in general be successful in achieving a verdict?

One possible kind of answer to this question involves the assumption that the Republican Roman court system worked on quite different principles from developed legal systems in modern times. In the past, the assumption might simply have been that Roman and other ancient lawcourts were primitive.[10] Recently, what is essentially a similar attitude has taken on a more subtle colouring, on account of the prevailing fashion for cultural relativism. Doubtless, one should not assume without further enquiry that the Roman notion of a lawcourt was precisely the same as that implied by the legal institutions of any given modern state. Yet this kind of approach can be taken too far for plausibility. Reading the work of some recent scholars, one might think that a Roman lawcourt was a place in which all kinds of considerations, personal, social, or political, mattered more than the legal and factual points that the court was supposed to be deciding.[11]

[8] Though some of his remarks may still be quoted with approval in modern books on advocacy.

[9] See Tacitus, *Dialogus* 20, where the leading 1st-cent. advocate Marcus Aper is made to criticize the prolixity of the *Verrines*, the *Pro Tullio* (which we have only in an incomplete form) and the *Pro Caecina*: a jury of Aper's own time, it is alleged, would not sit through speeches of that length. Aper is later made to criticize Cicero's style as utilitarian (22.4–5)–not the first criticism that would naturally occur to most modern readers.

[10] See e.g. the views quoted with scepticism by Crook, *Legal Advocacy*, 18–19, cf. 27. Crook, ibid. 6–7 cautions us against complacency about modern legal systems in comparison with that of the Romans.

[11] For example, Paul R. Swarney, 'Social Status and Social Behaviour as Criteria in Judicial Proceedings in the Late Republic', in B. Halpern and D. Hobson (ed.), *Law, Politics and Society in the Ancient Mediterranean World* (Sheffield, 1993) has argued for a view of Republican trials as contests for social status and prestige. Cf. the influential view of Athenian litigation as largely a test of political strength, stated concisely by G. M. Calhoun, *Athenian Clubs in Politics and Litigation*, Bulletin of the University of Texas 262 (Austin, Tex., 1913) 103, and revived in Anglo-American scholarship in the individualistic 1980s: see L. Rubinstein, *Litigation and Co-operation: Supporting Speakers in the Courts of Classical Athens*, Historia Einzelschriften 147 (Stuttgart, 2000) 18–20.

A particular variant of this approach involves the attempt to reassess the role of rhetoric in the courts, so that a trial is seen more as a contest of rhetorical strength than as a genuine argument about issues.[12]

Nobody, of course, denies that the outcome of a trial–in any legal system–can sometimes be affected by extraneous (especially political) issues. Equally, nobody denies that legal contests may be set in motion from ulterior motives, either personal or political,[13] and that the actual wrong alleged may be little more than a convenient peg on which to hang an attack. Evidently, in a system that relied on volunteer prosecutors, the danger of this was greater than in a modern system where criminal prosecution is the prerogative of state officials, and in which, therefore, the opportunities for private citizens to pursue vendettas through the courts are severely limited. But the point at issue here is not the degree of possible abuse of the system, but the basic question of what a lawcourt is for. The differences between the Roman system and those of modern Britain or America are indeed substantial; we shall see more of them below; but they do not, in our view, extend to a fundamental difference in the way the purpose of a lawcourt was envisaged.

As Andrew Riggsby (author of our Chapter 6) has argued in an important article, the Romans did, or at least wished to, 'believe in their verdicts'.[14] In other words, the evidence taken as a whole indicates that the *ostensible* purpose of a Roman court was the same as that of a modern one. The question put to a Roman jury was whether the accused was guilty or not; the surviving *lex repetundarum* shows that, if a guilty verdict was returned, the presiding magistrate pronounced the words 'fecisse videtur' ('it appears that he did it').[15] Why, then, has doubt arisen as to whether Republican Roman juries thought they were deciding primarily on questions of guilt or innocence? The reason is that Roman advocates regularly used arguments on apparently extraneous questions to reinforce their cases (for the use of political arguments in Cicero's lawcourt speeches cf. below, § iv). It is doubtless true that such arguments, whether about the political consequences of the decision or the character of the accused, sometimes weighed with juries. An advocate would get away with using them if the case was otherwise a good one. But a jury's decision to acquit or convict against

---

[12] Cf. below, p. 44 n. 176.

[13] Or can be made out to be; one of Cicero's favourite defence strategies is to discredit the prosecution by imputing motives of personal advantage; for example, the prosecution of Caelius by Atratinus, with Clodia's support, is represented as a personal vendetta. This strategy could not have worked to the discredit of Atratinus and his associates in a system where personal and political prestige was really paramount.

[14] A. Riggsby, 'Did the Romans Believe in their Verdicts?', *Rhetorica* 15.3 (1997) 235–52.

[15] Cf. also *Att.* 4.17.5 'Drusus, Scaurus non fecisse videntur' i.e. have been found not guilty.

the weight of the evidence would attract comment then as now.[16] Nor must we forget that the rhetoric can change according to the situation. When it is to his advantage, Cicero can also insist persuasively that the question before the court is whether the defendant is guilty as charged, and that the prosecution has failed to prove its case.[17]

Most of the lawcourt speeches Cicero published–indeed, virtually all of those which are commonly read today–are from the great public trials before the *iudicia publica* or *quaestiones*, which sat in the open air in the Forum.[18] This arena, which was both extremely public and also closely connected by mere geographical contiguity[19] with that of the Senate and the popular assemblies, created its own expectations as regards the nature of the oratory practised in the courts. Because of this, and because the material of some of these trials was intimately bound up with politics, modern scholarship has tended to play down the differences between Cicero's forensic oratory and his political speeches. 'Ciceronian oratory' has been treated largely as a homogeneous unity.[20] As we show in more detail below (§ v), the activities of the advocate and of the politician were indeed often closely intertwined; but on the other hand, Cicero could see them as distinct, and he can talk of withdrawing from politics and concentrating on the courts:

I am now conducting my life so as daily to increase people's support for me and my resources. I am not touching politics at all. I am devoting myself with all industry to my cases and forensic work, which I reckon is a fine way to win the favour not only of those who use my services but of the general public as well.[21]

---

[16] Usually in the form of allegations of bribery; conversely, Cicero in the *Pro Cluentio* can argue that a jury was *not* bribed to convict, because the defendant's guilt was so obvious that the evidence in itself would force them into a guilty verdict. Certain recorded instances of legal repartee also presuppose a background of assumptions very like ours, esp. those where the jury is said to have reached a decision because they 'believed' the witnesses on one side (*Att.* 1.16.10) or the complaint of a defendant that he did not deserve to be convicted just because of the eloquence of the prosecuting counsel (Seneca the Elder, *Contr.* 7.4.7).

[17] A good example is *Pro Roscio Amerino*, in the first part of which Cicero constantly insists on the failure of the prosecution to prove that Roscius is guilty. Nothing much is said about the virtues of Roscius as a citizen, probably because not much could be said.

[18] A rough calculation indicates that the number of people present at one of these trials, including the presiding magistrate, his attendants, the jury (*iudices*), the prosecutors, the defendant with his counsel (*patroni*) and supporters (*advocati*), those assisting counsel on either side, and the witnesses, was regularly in excess of a hundred, not counting the crowd of spectators which surrounded the court and who obviously expected to hear what was said.

[19] See A. Vasaly, *Representations: Images of the World in Ciceronian Oratory* (Berkeley, Los Angeles, and Oxford, 1993) 69–70.

[20] Most recently, James M. May (ed.), *Brill's Companion to Cicero: Oratory and Rhetoric* (Leiden, 2002) has an illuminating general chapter by May on 'Ciceronian Oratory in Context' followed by a series of chapters which divide the speeches into chronological groups–early, consular, *post reditum*, and so on. A. Vasaly in the same volume, at the beginning of her chapter on the early speeches, emphasizes that Cicero's political and 'oratorical' career 'cannot and should not be separated'.   [21] *Att.* 2.22.3.

The ancient writers on rhetoric always draw a firm distinction between forensic oratory (the *genus iudiciale*) and political oratory (the *genus deliberativum*), and while we need not trust the rhetorical theorists in everything, this distinction does at least seem to have a reasonably firm basis. A lawcourt speech called to some extent for a different approach and different argumentative techniques from a speech before the Senate or a public meeting. Furthermore, within the *genus iudiciale* there are differences of technique arising from the nature of different cases and the tribunals that heard them.[22] One can at least provisionally adopt the hypothesis that it is worth while to look for the differences within ancient practice, as well as for the common features that distinguish ancient oratory as a whole. We feel that we are justified in devoting a volume to the forensic speeches alone, not because we wish to argue that Cicero's real or essential talent was as an advocate rather than a politician,[23] or that the two aspects of his career and personality can be entirely separated, but because we believe that treating the lawcourt speeches as a distinct genre, with its own very practical purpose, will lead to a better understanding and a juster evaluation of the techniques of rhetoric and argument found in them, and of the extent to which a study of them can illuminate general issues about advocacy.

Most of those who study Cicero's forensic speeches have taken their success within the Roman court system for granted, but it is necessary to mention some possible doubts about this. Already in antiquity, an anti-Ciceronian tradition had grown up, which maintained—amid much generalized invective and insult—that Cicero's actual performance in court did not measure up to his reputation[24] (one may contrast the tradition

---

[22] Rubinstein, *Litigation and Co-operation*, also stresses the differences between public and private actions in an Athenian context.

[23] This has of course been commonly stated and probably has some truth in it, if one judges Cicero's success in the two capacities with the hindsight of history; but it is clear that Cicero himself would not have accepted it. For him, advocacy was indeed a form of service to the *res publica* and a means of acquiring popularity and fame, but he placed the greatest value on his achievements as a statesman (and also, towards the end of his life, as a writer and educator).

[24] See especially the speech put in the mouth of Fufius Calenus by Dio Cassius 46.7: 'Why, you always come to the court trembling, as if you were going to fight as a gladiator, and after uttering a few words in a meek and half-dead voice you take your departure, without having remembered a word of the speech you thought out at home before you came, and without having found anything to say on the spur of the moment ... In the trials themselves, apart from reviling and abusing other people, you are most weak and cowardly. Or do you think anyone is ignorant of the fact that you never delivered one of those wonderful speeches of yours that you have published, but wrote them all out afterwards?' (Loeb translation). This is a remarkable mélange; Cicero's nervousness is deduced from his own speeches (*Cluent.* 51, *Mil.* 1) where of course he is making good use of it for rhetorical reasons (cf. C. Loutsch, *L'Exorde dans les discours de Cicéron*, Collection Latomus 224 (Brussels, 1994) 510–12, on the 'locus a timore in exordiendo'); the idea that Cicero regularly forgot what he was going to say is deduced from a tendentious tradition about the trial

about Hortensius, whose written speeches apparently did not reflect his brilliance in court).[25] This has left its mark on the historical and biographical sources and in due course on modern scholarship, some of whose practitioners[26] have been strongly hostile to Cicero and hence uncritical of the hostile tradition. Yet it is doubtless this tradition that accounts, for example, for the common belief that Cicero failed to say anything useful at the trial of Milo. The question of the relationship of the written speeches to what Cicero actually said is discussed below: there remains the fact that Cicero published his speeches and presumably wanted them to be regarded as good examples of the orator's art.[27] If that is accepted, it must follow that it is unlikely that he would have allowed anything into the written versions that would have been obviously inappropriate in the setting of a real Republican lawcourt.

Others admit that Cicero was indeed successful, but attribute his success to questionable means; at best he has been criticized for insincerity,[28] and at worst for employing dishonest arguments to achieve a verdict at all costs. This question is discussed more fully below (§ iii); here we observe merely that talk of sincerity or insincerity runs the risk of mistaking the role of the advocate. An advocate is there to plead another's case, not his or her own. Some apparently have the gift, envied by their colleagues when it exists, of believing one hundred per cent in whatever case they happen to be arguing at the time. That aside, for advocates to be candid about their own opinions and feelings would be irrelevant, if not actually incompatible with their duty to speak on behalf of their clients. Of course, they ought still to be honest in presenting the evidence and arguments, not least because their continued success depends on the willingness of tribunals to believe what they say.

Even if it is granted that the advocate should be allowed some latitude in the pursuit of immediate persuasive success, there is in Cicero's particular

of Milo (a very special case) which has also left its mark on Plutarch; and while it is certainly true that Cicero wrote out the speeches afterwards, it does not in the least follow that they were never delivered; see further § vii below. The passage also bears a suspicious resemblance to Aeschines' attack on Demosthenes (Aeschin. 2.34–5).

[25] Cic. *Orator* 132; Quint. *Inst.* 11.3.8.

[26] Most notably, of course, the great 19th-cent. historian Theodor Mommsen, who regarded Cicero as a 'Pfuscher' (botcher or bungler) and who asserted that the publication of non-political lawcourt speeches, both by the Athenian orators and by Cicero, was 'nicht Fortschritt, sondern Unnatur und Verfall . . . ein Zeichen der Krankheit' (not a step forward, but unnatural and decadent . . . a symptom of sickness). See Mommsen's *Römische Geschichte*, 8th edn. (Berlin, 1889) iii. 619–21.   [27] See § vii below.

[28] Cf. R. G. M. Nisbet (*quem honoris causa nominamus*), 'The Speeches', in T. A. Dorey (ed.), *Cicero* (London, 1965) 47–80, at 71–2 (on *Pro Milone*): 'if an orator aspires to write something more than a showpiece for the immediate occasion, seriousness and sincerity are surely necessary . . . Humbug, however eloquent and ingenious, does not make great literature.' Do the speeches of *any* advocate claim to be 'great literature' in that sense?

case a further discouraging factor to be faced: his apparent egotism. He has been taxed, not without apparent justification, with turning his speeches into political statements on his own behalf. If true, this is at first sight disquieting: does it not show that Cicero was prone to get sidetracked from his main business as an advocate? But it is at least worth trying the hypothesis that Cicero's self-presentation was not a sign of incompetence or of all-pervading vanity, but a deliberate persuasive strategy, which he adopted because it worked in the Roman Republican system (see further Chapter 2). It should be observed also that in the context of Cicero's work as an advocate in general, those speeches in which he made a great deal of his own position (that is to say, those from the great public trials) may well have been the exception rather than the rule. In the less spectacular of his surviving speeches, such as the *Pro Quinctio* or *Pro Caecina*, there is little or no obtrusion of Cicero's personality, and this may well also have been true of many of the more ordinary cases from which the speeches do not survive.[29]

The last obstacle to be faced in approaching Cicero the advocate, and perhaps the greatest for some readers nowadays, is his style. To evaluate the style of any advocate or other public speaker involves a large measure of personal taste. Cicero has excited peculiarly strong feelings through the ages, both positive, as with those Renaissance Latinists who adopted him as their sole stylistic model, and negative, as with many people nowadays who associate the name of Cicero with an artificial, pompous and inflated style of speaking—in fact with all that is bad about 'rhetoric' as popularly conceived. As a general judgement of Cicero's forensic speeches[30] this latter impression is quite wrong, though it takes either an expert's knowledge of Latin or a translation of above-average quality to enable one to see that it is wrong. The style of the speeches is, indeed, quite sophisticated and belongs to a relatively formal register of Latin, but this is true of courtroom advocacy in most times and places including our own. Cicero himself, though he laid claim to greater sophistication than any other contemporary advocate, said that it was a great fault in an orator to depart from ordinary habits of speech.[31] There are of course particular passages in his

---

[29] Cf. below, pp. 79–80. Let us not forget, either, that egotism has not been entirely unknown among advocates in modern times, although it has tended to express itself more in professional than in political terms; how often in fact or fiction have we heard an advocate refer to his 'long career at the Bar'?

[30] It perhaps has more justification in connection with some of the political speeches.

[31] *Brutus* 321 'propter exquisitius et minime vulgare orationis genus animos hominum ad me dicendi novitate converteram'; *De Oratore* 1.12 'ut in ceteris id maxime excellat quod longissime sit ab imperitorum intellegentia sensuque diiunctum, in dicendo autem vitium vel maximum sit a vulgari genere orationis atque a consuetudine communis sensus abhorrere'. Compare Aristotle, *Rhetoric* 1404b.

speeches which would be too purple for the restrained atmosphere of a contemporary lawcourt. In his youth especially, Cicero had something of a predilection for the grand style,[32] but this must be seen against the background of the fashions of the time. There were rival and changing tastes in advocacy during Cicero's lifetime.[33] Some Roman orators contemporary with Cicero championed an austere, 'Attic' style modelled on that of Lysias, and complained that Cicero was too much influenced by the elaborate style of the Eastern Greek schools.[34] Such criticisms however date from the later period of Cicero's life, when a severer manner was coming into fashion.[35] Cicero himself adjusted his style as he matured. He himself claimed, quite sensibly, that the orator should be a master of all styles:[36] the most important point was to choose the appropriate style–for the audience,[37] for the point in the argument that one had reached, and for one's ultimate persuasive aims. Style for Cicero, at least in his lawcourt speeches, was never an end in itself but always an instrument of persuasion (see further pp. 50–1 below).

We have here set out fairly briefly a manifesto for the desirability of approaching Cicero's speeches above all as examples of practical advocacy. Many issues are raised by the attempt to understand the speeches in this way, and in the remainder of this introduction we shall explore some of them further. We make no apology for the length of the following discussion, which may serve both to provide some background and to draw together a number of points that recur throughout the present collection. These are important and complex questions, as much alive today as they have ever been.

[32] Cf. *Orator* 107; note also *Brutus* 317–27 on Cicero's rivalry with Hortensius, who was a master of the 'Asiatic' style. On the development of Cicero's style over time, see also W. R. Johnson, *Luxuriance and Economy: Cicero and the Alien Style* (Berkeley, Los Angeles, and London, 1971).

[33] Just as there were, for example, in England in the earlier part of the 20th cent. No two styles could have been more different than those of two great advocates of that period, Sir Patrick Hastings and Sir Edward Marshall Hall; the former, who preferred a comparatively simple style, was heard to employ the word 'humbug' in connection with Marshall Hall's flights of emotional oratory. In general, many speeches of counsel from trials of that period now sound very Ciceronian; the change of style towards the conversational has been largely a post-World War II development; see D. Pannick, *Advocates* (Oxford, 1992) 229.

[34] On the 'Attic–Asian controversy' see J. Wisse, 'The Intellectual Background of the Rhetorical Works', in May (ed.), *Brill's Companion*, 331–74, at 364–8; E. Narducci, '*Brutus*: The History of Roman Eloquence', in the same volume, 401–25, at 404–12, both with bibliography.

[35] Stroh in this volume observes that these criticisms may have started about the time of the *De Domo*. The main source is Tacitus, *Dialogus* 18.4–5.   [36] *Orator* 69 ff.

[37] Different styles were appropriate for different tribunals; there would naturally be more scope for grandiose oratory in addressing a large jury than in addressing a single judge. For example, the style of the *Pro Quinctio*, addressed to a single judge, is very different from that of the speech for Roscius of Ameria, though only a year or so separated the two trials; cf. A. E. Douglas, *Cicero*, Greece & Rome New Surveys in the Classics 2 (1968) 39, and more generally J. M. Kelly, *Studies in the Civil Judicature of the Roman Republic* (Oxford, 1976) 111; Crook, *Legal Advocacy*, 136.

ii. Advocacy Ancient and Modern

The presence of advocates is a fairly constant feature of legal systems nowadays, but this was not always so. The emphasis placed on the role of the advocate in the Republican Roman system, and in the modern British or American systems, is not a manifestation of a universal state of affairs: the similarities, where they have not been exaggerated, provide an interesting example of historical convergence. There have been times and places in history where advocacy has been more or less forbidden, not always for the same reasons.[38] In the the legal systems of continental Europe, whose basic procedure is an investigation by a magistrate rather than a contest of two parties as in the Anglo-Saxon common law, the role of the advocate is inevitably envisaged somewhat differently.[39]

It is useful first of all to glance at the other legal system in the Graeco-Roman world that we know most about, that of classical Athens, which was also basically adversarial in procedure. In Athens, as is well known, litigants were expected to speak for themselves. The forensic speeches of the Athenian orators may be divided into three categories. There are those delivered in person in a case in which the orator himself was one of the parties. Secondly, there are the so-called *synegoriai*, speeches made in support of one or other party in a trial.[40] The third category, the best known but the strangest from a modern point of view, consists of those speeches which were 'ghosted', for another person to deliver, by a *logographos* (= exactly 'speech-writer').[41] These speeches are usually entitled 'On behalf of . . . ', but this means not that they were spoken on the client's behalf (as in the case of an advocate's speech), but that they were composed on the client's behalf and then delivered by the client in person. If such speeches were to be successful, they naturally had to be a colourable impersonation; any attempt at rhetorical trickery would excite the suspicion of the jury and might lead to an adverse verdict. Disclaimers of rhetorical skill are commonplace,

---

[38] For example, the Constitution of the State of Carolina at first forbade advocacy as a 'base and vile thing' (Pannick, *Advocates*, 241). Advocates were not allowed in jurisdictions substantially influenced by the canon law, e.g. the notorious Star Chamber in 16th-century England. Crook, *Legal Advocacy*, 14 refers to Islamic, Chinese, and ancient Egyptian parallels.

[39] Cf. Laws's observations about the difference between the English and Continental traditions in Chapter 15.

[40] See Rubinstein, *Litigation and Co-operation*, for a revaluation of the importance of *synegoriai* in the Athenian system. Of the surviving Athenian lawcourt speeches, a third are *synegoriai* (ibid. 40–1). Cf. also Crook, *Legal Advocacy*, 32–3. The Greek word *synegoros* is used e.g. by Plutarch (*Cicero* 26.8) as a translation of the Roman *patronus* or *advocatus*. Crook (n. 6) 35 n. 24. On logography see M. Lavency, *Aspects de la logographie judiciaire attique* (Louvain, 1964).

[41] This practice was not unknown in Rome either; e.g. Quintilian, *Inst.* 3.8.50 records that Cicero wrote speeches for Pompey and others to deliver.

and indeed became a recognized topic within rhetoric itself–which thus became, and remained to some extent at least, the art of concealing art.

As is well known, Athenian trials were divided into the two categories of public procedures (*graphai* and other types of public action) and private actions (*dikai*), which corresponded at least in broad outline, though hardly in detail, to the modern categories of criminal prosecutions and civil actions. In a *dike*, the plaintiff claimed to have been wronged personally and to seek redress. In a *graphe*, any citizen who wished (*ho boulomenos*) could come forward to initiate the prosecution in the interests of the community. In the public procedure called *apophasis*, there were two stages: first a decree of impeachment was passed in the Council or the Assembly, and then prosecutors were publicly appointed, not necessarily the same as the proposer(s) of the decree, to put the case to the court. The public procedures, at least, might have offered opportunities for the growth of a class of professional or semi-professional prosecuting counsel, but Athenian feeling was against it. The notion of an independent and representative class of advocates available to conduct prosecutions, such as exists in every developed Western legal system, was quite alien to Athenian modes of thought. Whether an Athenian prosecutor acted in his own interests or in those of the City of Athens, he had to take personal responsibility. A prosecutor who appeared to be a hired mouthpiece, acting from malicious or mercenary motives, would be branded as a *sykophantes*, and there was a further discouragement to such behaviour in the threat of a penalty for failing to prove one's case: if a prosecutor failed to obtain a fifth of the votes he was liable to a large fine and loss of civil rights. It is not so clear whether a similar risk attached in practice to acting as *synegoros* in a prosecution,[42] but even so, a person who so acted would be liable to have his motives scrutinized.

Much the same applies to speeches for the defence.[43] Defendants spoke on their own behalf or were assisted by *synegoroi*, but there was a firm prohibition against a *synegoros* receiving payment, which was seen as equivalent to bribery: a hired advocate would not be believed any more than a suborned witness.[44] Often, *synegoroi* were people with a demonstrable personal connection with the litigant–usually friends or relatives, and the *Rhetorica ad Alexandrum* (1442b) notes that it is useful for *synegoroi* to claim such a connection (obviously to avoid suspicion of an ulterior and especially financial motive). However, *synegoriai* were sometimes delivered by prominent politicians who had no visible personal connection with the

---

[42] See Rubinstein, *Litigation and Co-operation*, 91 ff.   [43] Ibid. 148 ff.

[44] The law is quoted in Demosthenes 46.26 'If anyone . . . being a *synegoros* receives money in respect of legal actions, either private or public, he may be prosecuted before the *thesmothetai*'.

defendant, but were generally interested in the outcome of the case; and those who made a name as accomplished orators might be in demand for the role of *synegoros* merely on the basis that they were helping a fellow-citizen by doing what he could not do for himself.[45] This duty of supporting one's friends or fellow-citizens, rather than any conception of the independence of the advocate, accounted for the fact that *synegoroi* did not apparently share in the opprobrium of failure in court: they had done their best, and could not in the end be blamed for the fact that their friend had got into trouble. The Athenians, then, operated an adversarial system without professional advocates, though not altogether without advocacy.[46]

The Roman system shared many features of the Athenian: to align the Roman system with modern patterns of legal advocacy against that of Athens is apt to create a misleading perspective. As in Athens, there was no public prosecution service. Indeed Cicero, in the *De Legibus*, regards the publicly appointed prosecutors who figured in some Greek states as an institution without parallel at Rome, and remarks that accusers cannot be effective unless they are volunteers.[47] Prosecutors, if successful, could be rewarded,[48] just as in some Greek systems including the Athenian, while those who failed to obtain a certain proportion of the jury's votes could suffer penalties, as at Athens.[49] Malicious prosecution was further guarded against, at least from the time of Gaius Gracchus, by the *lex ne quis iudicio*

[45] See esp. Hyperides 3 *Euxen.* 11–12, where Hyperides points out that the prosecutor once made use of his services, and now the defendant has an equal right to do so. The significant point is that this needed to be argued.

[46] See further R. J. Bonner, *Lawyers and Litigants in Ancient Athens* (Chicago, 1927) 204–9; Bonner's historical reconstruction of the growth of *synegoria* is corrected by Rubinstein, *Litigation and Co-operation*, 126–7.

[47] *Leg.* 3.47. Nonetheless, there is evidence that the appointment of *patroni* was at least sometimes in the hands of the court: *lex repetundarum* 9–11 (this may have arisen from the special circumstances of *repetundae* cases in which the complainants were provincials). It obviously makes a difference whether the initiative in such appointments came from the court itself or from the prospective advocates for the prosecution; the procedure of *divinatio* clearly implies that prosecutors put themselves forward and the court merely decided between those claiming the right to prosecute when there was competition. In later times, prosecution advocates in senatorial trials could be appointed by the senate (e.g. Pliny the Younger, appointed to prosecute Baebius Massa and Marius Priscus).

[48] The *lex repetundarum* for example lays down that successful prosecutors, if non-citizens, would be rewarded with citizenship; if citizens, with exemption from military service. See further M. C. Alexander, 'Praemia in the Quaestiones of the Late Republic', *CPh* 80 (1985) 20–32; T. N. Mitchell's note on *Verr. II* 1.21 (Cicero, *Verrines* II.1, with tr. and comm. by T. N. Mitchell (Warminster, 1986) 170–1); Crook, *Legal Advocacy*, 160; D. H. Berry on *Pro Sulla* 50 (Cicero, *Pro Sulla*, ed. with introd. and comm. by D. H. Berry (Cambridge, 1996) 230–1). L. R. Taylor's theory *Party Politics in the Age of Caesar* (Berkeley, 1949), that the successful prosecutor of a senator succeeded to the latter's insignia and place in the Senate, is still a matter for debate.

[49] The *lex Remmia* (date unknown, but before 80 BC) apparently laid down penalties for malicious or mercenary prosecution; Cicero refers to it in *Rosc. Am.* 55. Extreme cases are said to have involved branding on the forehead with the letter K for *kalumniator*: ibid. 57.

circumveniretur, which is the basis of one of the issues in the *Pro Cluentio*. Roman aristocrats regularly appeared in their own defence (Cato the Elder, for example, defended himself in court many times).[50] Advocates for the defence in criminal cases, or for either side in civil actions, were forbidden to receive fees, under the *lex Cincia de donis et muneribus* passed by the tribune L. Cincius Alimentus in 204 BC.[51]

The Roman notion of the advocate differed from the Athenian in one major respect. Whereas the Athenian *synegoros* was a fellow-citizen helping a litigant on equal terms, the Roman advocate was called a *patronus*, 'patron'.[52] (The term *advocatus*, from which the modern 'advocate' is derived, was originally more general, covering also those who gave legal advice and those who merely lent their support to a litigant without speaking in court.) Romans of Cicero's time looked back to an archaic period in which every Roman citizen of lower status would be, on a reasonably permanent basis, the 'client' of an aristocratic 'patron', who would speak on his behalf in legal proceedings.[53] Plautus, *Menaechmi* 571 ff. (clearly referring to Roman customs despite the Greek setting of the play) portrays a situation in which aristocrats sought out wealthy 'clients' for their own advantage, and then regretted it when they had to defend their shady dealings in court. Long after Cicero's time, there was still an expectation that patrons would speak up for their *clientes*: in the Flavian period Martial satirises those who were not up to the job or claimed not to be.[54]

---

[50] Cf. also Cic. *Brut.* 102 on Mucius Scaevola.

[51] Payment in goods or services was not, however, forbidden, and monetary payments (up to a designated limit) were eventually allowed by the emperor Claudius, presumably as a grudging legal recognition of what was happening anyway. For the details, see Courtney on Juvenal 7.106; Crook, *Legal Advocacy*, 129–31; see also below, n. 58. When Crook assimilates the position of Roman advocates to that of English barristers who cannot legally sue for fees, he is presumably talking about the later period; the original *lex Cincia* apparently made fees not only non-recoverable but actually illegal.

[52] See W. Neuhauser, *Patronus und Orator. Eine Geschichte der Begriffe von ihren Anfängen bis in die augusteische Zeit.* Commentationes Aenipontanae 14, Innsbruck, 1958; J.-M. David, *Le Patronat judiciaire au dernier siècle de la République romaine* (Rome, 1992); Crook, *Legal Advocacy*, 122–3 and (criticizing Neuhauser) 146–9. It is perhaps no more than a curious fact that, whereas the modern lawyer's 'client' retains the name of the *cliens* but his representative is not called a 'patron', in Rome the reverse was the case: the advocate was called *patronus* but the person whom he represented was not generally called a *cliens* (unless, of course, he actually stood in a relationship of 'clientship' to his *patronus*). There is an interesting exception to this in *Fam.* 5.9 (written by Vatinius in 45 BC, recalling Cicero's past services to him): 'P. Vatinius cliens advenit qui pro se causam dicier vult'; presumably Vatinius is here playing on the notion of clientship to emphasize his gratitude. In this book we shall generally use the word 'client' in the modern sense of a person who retains a legal representative.

[53] Cf. Cic. *Mur.* 10 'civitate in qua nemini umquam infimo maiores nostri patronum deesse voluerunt' ('A community in which our ancestors desired that a patron should never be lacking for anyone, even of the lowest rank').

[54] Cf. Crook, *Legal Advocacy*, 122, referring to Martial 2.32, 8.76, 12.38.

On the other hand, it is sufficiently clear that, in the late Republic, access to a *patronus* did not depend on any restrictive notion of clientship, either in the sense of a pre-existing relationship of personal dependency, or in the sense of unequal status. A *patronus* such as Cicero made his services generally available to those who asked for them; aristocratic *patroni* could defend equally aristocratic litigants, or else would be called in to help by fellow-*patroni* on account of their rhetorical expertise (cf. p. 15, n. 56). It is clear, also, that pleading in court was no longer the prerogative of aristocrats, i.e. those who exercised patronage in the traditional sense, but was open to citizens of independent means who possessed (or professed) the required expertise.

It is often assumed that the situation in Cicero's time represented a transitional stage from the original patron–client system towards a more modern-looking system of professional or quasi-professional advocates. A simple model of evolutionary progress may, however, be misleading; it is not clear that the fundamental concept of the *patronus* had changed much in the generations immediately before Cicero. It is possible that, even in considerably earlier times, a *patronus* could be approached for help by a litigant who was not previously his 'client' in the technical sense; there is no reason to assume that rhetorical strategies were not already available for defending a comparative stranger, in parallel with those that were suitable for defending a close associate. The passing of the *lex Cincia* at the end of the third century BC (see p. 13, n. 51) certainly implies that there were already advocates offering their services for hire and that a need was felt to curb them.

However, there certainly were some relevant changes during the second century BC. Cicero himself, in the *Brutus* (106), comments that there had been a significant expansion in court business at that time. The first standing courts (*quaestiones perpetuae*) were established in 149 BC; previously all public trials had been either before the popular assembly (*iudicia populi*) or before a specially convened commission of enquiry (*quaestio*). Cicero mentions this as a factor in the growth of advocacy, and in the same passage he says that the introduction of the secret ballot in trials made advocacy all the more necessary. Greek cultural influence must also have been a factor; emphasis is usually placed on the advent of Greek rhetorical theory and knowledge of the speeches of the Athenian orators, but there is also evidence for a continuing tradition of practical advocacy in the Hellenistic world.[55] In any case, as a result of these various factors, a group of Roman aristocrats emerged whose expertise in public speaking and conducting

---

[55] Crook, *Legal Advocacy*, 34–7.

cases was recognized, and who were therefore constantly in demand as *patroni*.[56]

To what extent, then, could it be said that the *patroni* of the late Republic constituted a profession?[57] In some senses they clearly did not: for a start, advocacy was not, officially at least, a way of making a living. However, the law on this matter could apparently be circumvented as long as direct pecuniary payments were avoided; advocates were repaid for their services not only with strings of onions or bottles of second-grade olive oil (as the satirist Juvenal, in a later period, cynically represents the situation), but also in political support (*favor* and *gratia*) or by means of loans and other personal services.[58] Other factors, too, make it possible to speak (if only by way of analogy) of a Roman 'Bar': there was apparently a convention that anyone who wished to practise as a *patronus* had to be introduced at the beginning of his career by a consular,[59] and in Cicero's time at least, those who embarked on such a career might often have spent some time attached as a 'pupil' to a prominent practitioner.[60] Furthermore, the general availability of the services of the *patronus*, and his willingness to sacrifice consistency in the interests of the particular case he is arguing, provide a further indication that the Roman advocate had something in common with his modern counterpart; see Chapter 11.

On the other hand, the importance of the advocate's own personality and authority as a means of persuasion[61] speaks of a situation in which advocates could figure in the role of personal protector. This impression is strong in the *Pro Caelio*, where Cicero puts on his best avuncular manner in defending his former pupil Caelius, and more or less acts the part of a character witness as well as an advocate. When a Roman defendant happened to have a personal connection of this kind with a prominent advocate such as Cicero, it was natural to bring it into play. It is relevant that the *Pro Caelio* was not the main speech for the defence, but merely a supporting speech for a case that had already been argued by the

---

[56] Note Cic. *Brutus* 207 'Antonius qui maxime expetebatur'; 'Cotta, Sulpicius expetebantur'. Cf. also the case mentioned in *Brutus* 85 ff. (from 138 BC) in which C. Laelius, after the case had been adjourned for a further hearing, approached Ser. Galba for help 'quod is in dicendo atrocior acriorque esset'. [57] See further Crook, *Legal Advocacy*, 41–5.

[58] A notable example is the loan of two million sesterces made to Cicero by P. Sulla as repayment for his successful defence, which was used towards Cicero's purchase of his house on the Palatine. Cicero just about got away with this, but did not escape criticism; see D. Berry (ed.), *Cicero, Pro Sulla* (Cambridge, 1996) 30–1. [59] Pliny, *Ep.* 2.14.

[60] On this form of training, which bears some resemblance to pupillage at the English Bar and is often though inauthentically called *tirocinium fori*, see J. G. F. Powell's notes on *Cato Maior* 10 and *Laelius* 1. Tacitus, *Dial.* 34–5 comments on its decline and replacement by formal rhetorical training.

[61] On the advocate's own prestige as a factor that could weigh with courts, cf. J. M. Kelly, *Roman Litigation* (Oxford, 1966) ch. 2.

defendant in person; an Athenian would easily have recognized it as a *synegoria*. It is thus very different from the speech of a modern advocate representing a client.[62] The same applies to the *Pro Sestio*. Here Cicero's support of Sestius' case involves him in a wide-ranging discussion of Roman politics, which again makes perfect sense according to the principles of a *synegoria* (Cicero almost certainly had Demosthenes in mind), however baffling it may be from the point of view of ordinary modern advocacy.

It is not surprising, then, that the Roman advocate might conceptualize his role in a way rather different from the modern legal professional. To place the difference in sharper relief, it is worth taking a brief look at the very different historical development of the Bar in England.[63] The first steps towards the development of a legal profession in England were taken in the Middle Ages, when the practice grew up of authorizing an 'attorney' to represent a litigant in court. Attorneys–the precursors of modern solicitors–were qualified for this function by familiarity with legal procedures, but they had no special skills in forensic argument. This left room for the development of a separate class of professionals skilled in the marshalling of facts and the presentation of legal arguments. These officials were called first *narratores*, or in law-French *conteurs* (literally 'story-tellers'); then, as their official status became recognized, they were called *servientes* (servants [of the court]). The equivalent in Norman French was *serjeant*, hence the title–which persisted until 1877 and is familiar to readers of Dickens–of Serjeant-at-Law, applied to the most senior advocates. 'Barristers' developed at first as a lower grade in the same hierarchy. Thus the English barrister began not as a private protector or supporter, like the Roman *patronus*, but as an official of the court. In this respect, it should be noted, there is no substantive difference between common-law systems and the Roman-based systems of continental Europe: however the details may differ, the advocate is in both kinds of system a professional legal expert whose primary function (historically speaking at least) is to help the court reach its decision and whose overriding duty is not to mislead the court.

This brings us to another difference between Roman and modern advocates. It is well recognized and often pointed out that, in contrast to his

---

[62] For some analysis of the notion of 'representation' in this context see Crook, *Legal Advocacy*, 158–63. But a *patronus* could also identify himself closely with his client when the situation demanded it; cf. G. A. Kennedy, 'The Rhetoric of Advocacy in Greece and Rome', *AJP* 89 (1968) 419–36; J. M. May, 'The Rhetoric of Advocacy and Patron–Client Identification: Variation on a Theme', *AJP* 102 (1981) 308–15; J. Wisse, *Ethos and Pathos from Aristotle to Cicero* (Amsterdam, 1989) 102 n. 114.

[63] This information is summarized from T. F. T. Plucknett, *A Concise History of the Common Law* (London, 1940) 193–206.

modern counterparts, the Roman advocate was primarily an orator[64] and only in second place a lawyer. From Cicero's time onwards, prospective advocates received formal training in rhetoric, and got the law they needed *ad hoc* for each particular case. It is a matter for surprise to modern readers that it was possible for Cicero in open court to make fun of the technicalities of the law and of the jurisconsults who were the real legal specialists (*Pro Murena* 23–9). By contrast, at least until very recently, the modern legally trained English barrister was given no formal instruction in advocacy; those starting at the Bar had to rely on native wit, imitation of prominent practitioners, or the occasional helpful handbook–or, of course, on Cicero, if they happened to remember anything about him from school or university. (It is an interesting question, which cannot be gone into here, to what extent the fashion for eloquence in the English and American courts, which lasted approximately from the eighteenth to the middle of the twentieth century, was due to Ciceronian influence.)

This difference can, however, be overemphasized. Although Cicero in the *Pro Murena* (for particular rhetorical purposes) makes a sharp distinction between the vocations of orator and lawyer, and although he could make Antonius in the *De Oratore* argue that an advocate did not need to know the law, there was no foundation in reality for a clear division between advocates and jurists; the activities of pleading in court and 'responding' to consultation on legal questions could be carried out by the same people.[65] Cicero himself, though he never set himself up as a jurist, was at any rate a competent lawyer. He had studied in his youth with the great lawyers Scaevola the Augur and Scaevola the Pontifex, and he was quite at home with legal issues when they arose both in court (cf. Chapter 5) and elsewhere (one of his letters, *Fam.* 7.22, records a late-night visit to his library to clarify a legal point that had arisen over dinner, and he goes into considerable technicality on some matters of religious law in his philosophical dialogue *De Legibus*, 2.46–53). Beside the *Pro Murena* and the views attributed to Antonius, we need to set another passage of *De Oratore*, in which certain advocates are censured by Crassus for ignorance of the law relating to their cases.[66] Cicero's ideal was that the advocate should have a general grasp of legal principles, and indeed he seems to regard himself as in that respect a better lawyer than the jurisconsults who cannot see the wood for the trees. We

---

[64] It should be remarked that *formal* training in oratory through the medium of Latin became widely available at Rome only after Cicero's time; he himself received his rhetorical training entirely in Greece and through the medium of the Greek language. The first school of Latin rhetoric was opened at Rome in the late 90s BC and was closed down by order of the censor L. Crassus, who in Cicero's *De Oratore* is made to justify his action on the ground that nothing was taught there except impudence.   [65] Cf. Crook, *Legal Advocacy*, 37–41.

[66] *De Or.* 1.168 ff.

should not forget that the technicalities of the law play little part in the lives of some barristers today. A modern barrister who specializes in criminal or common-law work spends most of the time trying to establish facts; new points of law are a relative rarity except in the higher reaches of the judicial system. Indeed, there have been famous criminal law practitioners, such as Sir Edward Marshall Hall KC, who have been quite open about the short-comings in their knowledge of the law (and the tradition is perpetuated by John Mortimer in his characterization of 'Rumpole of the Bailey'). There is a familiar sound in the response of a learned Roman jurisconsult faced with a question of criminal liability: 'Nihil hoc ad ius: ad Ciceronem' ('This point has nothing to do with the law; it's a case for Cicero').[67] But Cicero himself (through Crassus in the *De Oratore*) and later Quintilian (*Inst.* 12.3.4), argued persuasively, and to some extent against Roman tradition,[68] that the advo-cate did need to know the law and would be lost without it, especially when confronted with an unexpected point in court.

It is striking, furthermore, that some important conceptual distinctions, such as the difference between questions of fact and questions of law, between law and equity, between matters which are legally relevant and those which are not, and so forth, which now form an essential basis for the study of 'law'–in fact most of the fundamental conceptual distinctions which serve to articulate legal argument–were in Cicero's time not dealt with as part of the study of the law, but rather were part of the province of rhetoric.[69] It was the orators, rather than the jurisconsults, who came across these principles in the constant search for sources of effective argu-ments. Thus the rhetorically educated orator would be trained in what we would regard as legal thinking, and could argue legal points when neces-sary, just as he could argue on any other subject that happened to be rel-evant to the case. Cicero's own ideal (expressed in the *De Oratore*) of the orator as omnicompetent–lawyer, philosopher, psychologist,[70] politician, and supremely eloquent manipulator of language, all rolled into one–was not as unrealistic as we may be inclined to assume, and indeed has its par-allel today in the kind of barrister who can 'get up' enough of any subject whatever to unmask an unreliable 'expert' witness.

---

[67] Aquillius Gallus, quoted by Cic., *Topica* 51; cf. Crook, *Legal Advocacy*, 40; 142–4.

[68] However, Quintilian is perhaps too complacent about the ease with which advocates can master the art of legal argument: he maintains that all they need in order to argue points of law is a grasp of the ordinary meanings of words and the principles of right and wrong. This hardly does justice to the level of technicality of Roman law even in his time.

[69] Cf. Cic. *Topica* 50–2 on the fact/law distinction; and note the classification of legal questions (*quaestiones legales*) in Quint. *Inst.* 3.6.61; 66 ff.

[70] The use of this word may seem anachronistic; but the rhetorical analysis of *ethos* and *pathos* (character and emotion) covers much that would nowadays be brought under the heading of psychology.

iii. Cicero and the Morality of Advocacy

There is a common view among the general public that the profession of advocate is basically a dishonest one. Advocates are assumed to defend the guilty and attack the innocent, 'according as they are paid', as Swift put it in *Gulliver's Travels*. How (the ordinary person wonders) can they argue, sometimes passionately, for causes in which they are not personally concerned, and which they may themselves believe to be bad ones? On the other hand, barristers both real and fictitious can achieve the status of popular heroes for their part in defending the basic rights to freedom of speech and of association, like Thomas Erskine in the eighteenth century,[71] or for successfully securing an acquittal against the odds, as in many picturesque murder cases in the earlier part of the twentieth century.

Modern defences of the legal profession generally concentrate on three main points: (*a*) the right of the citizen to legal representation, entailing the corresponding duty of the advocate to take on any case for which he/she is competent (the so-called 'cab-rank rule') and not to refuse a case because it seems to be a bad one; (*b*) the role of the adversarial system in ensuring that justice is done, summed up in the principle that both sides of a case must be heard before a decision is reached; (*c*) the fact that, as Lord Birkett put it, the advocate 'is bound by very strict rules of conduct and an equally strict code of honour, expressly designed to allow him to discharge his duty to the administration of justice without being false to himself or to his conscience and without failing in his duty to the community in which he lives'.[72] Such statements, common among those professionally trained in the English legal system, present an extremely high-minded view of the advocate as an instrument in the administration of justice, who subordinates all private feelings and opinions to the overriding aim of securing a fair decision. They contrast markedly with the popular caricature of the lawyer. As we approach Cicero, we are bound to enquire whether the ethos of the Roman 'Bar' was in any way comparable to this, or whether it worked on entirely different assumptions.

First, the citizen's right to representation in court. No doubt, the 'cab-rank' rule was unknown to the Romans. Yet there were other considerations that may, in a way and to a certain extent, have substituted for it. In the archaic period, at least according to Cicero,[73] there was an expectation that every citizen outside the aristocratic elite would have access to a patron. As far as Cicero's time is concerned, a certain amount may be

[71] See Lord Birkett, *Six Great Advocates* (Harmondsworth, 1961) 82–96.
[72] Birkett, ibid. 99; cf. also the chapter on 'morality' in Pannick, *Advocates*, 127–69.
[73] *Mur.* 10.

deduced about the means whereby advocates were approached by prospective clients. Advocates were of course public figures around the Forum and could be approached directly, but personal connections clearly played a part in many instances. If there was such a connection, the advocate might well feel himself to be under a strict obligation as friend or patron, and it might be very difficult if not impossible to refuse. It was quite proper for an advocate to take the initiative in offering his services to a friend, as we happen to know that Cicero did with Sestius.[74] There might alternatively be an indirect connection: an advocate might be approached on a client's behalf by an influential person or persons, such as those aristocratic figures (at first unnamed, *Rosc. Am.* 4) who approached Cicero on behalf of Sextus Roscius, or such as Pompey, who prevailed upon Cicero to defend various of his henchmen after Lucca. Under such circumstances an advocate might have–or might represent himself as having–little choice but to take on the case.[75] On the other hand, if there was no pre-existing personal connection, a prospective client's request might be cast in the form of an appeal for protection (in Latin terms, an appeal to *fides*); and to refuse such an appeal, other than for very good reasons, would do little for the advocate's image as a *patronus*. Cicero himself, in the exordium to the *Pro Rabirio*, formulated the principle that he was ready to help any Roman citizen in trouble,[76] and there was apparently a certain amount of glory to be gained from taking on cases that otherwise lacked an advocate.[77] Looking back at the end of his career, in an often cited passage of the *De Officiis* (2.51), Cicero suggests that a defence advocate should be prepared to offer his services to a guilty client; however, he adds the important qualification 'provided that the defendant is not *nefarius* and *impius*', and one wonders exactly where he would have drawn the line in practice.[78]

It may be, then, that Cicero would have taken on most cases offered to him.[79] On the other hand, he sometimes[80] felt himself bound (as in the

---

[74] Cic. *Q. Fr.* 2.3.5.

[75] Cf. also *Cluent.* 50: Cicero could not refuse any request made by the people of Aletrium: for Cicero's municipal ties see further Ch. 3.

[76] This was of course by way of self-justification for taking on the case; cf. Loutsch, *L'Exorde*, 253.

[77] One thinks again of the Roscius case: Cicero has undertaken to defend Roscius 'ne omnino desertus esset'. In a later generation, note Pliny, *Ep.* 6.29.1-2, quoting a principle laid down by Thrasea Paetus: 'suscipiendas esse causas aut amicorum aut destitutas aut ad exemplum pertinentes. Cur amicorum, non eget interpretatione. Cur destitutas? quod in illis maxime et constantia agentis et humanitas cerneretur'. Cf. Crook, *Legal Advocacy*, 123.

[78] The passage is probably to be read against the background of Cicero's well-documented habit of putting certain individuals (notably Catiline and Clodius) outside the pale of civilization; hence it is unlikely to have excluded any prospective clients in Cicero's ordinary practice as an advocate.

[79] One can only reserve judgement as to whether this is the implication of Catullus' phrase (49.7) *optimus omnium patronus*. If, as some scholars assert, it was intended to mean 'everyone's patron' and was meant satirically, it shows merely that Catullus shared the plain man's view of the advocate.

[80] Not as a matter of course: Loutsch, *L'Exorde*, 506-7.

Pro Rab. Perd., just mentioned, or the *Pro Murena*) to justify in court his decision to take on a case–something that a modern advocate should never have to do. Sometimes, too, he uses his position to claim a superior knowledge of the facts (as in *Pro Cluentio*) or as a guarantee of the client's character (as in the *Pro Caelio*). In a Roman context, it evidently helped if the jury could get the idea that the advocate had satisfied himself of the justice of the cause before taking it on. Cicero may in fact have observed something like the cab-rank rule in practice, but it was in his interests–as it would certainly not be for a modern advocate–to pretend that he was not doing so. The defence of a former personal and political enemy, as in the case of Gabinius in 54 BC, was quite possible,[81] but there was an obstacle to be overcome: there had to be a formal reconciliation, *reditus in gratiam*, before the defence could take place. In Roman eyes, an advocate's personal relations with his client were a matter of importance.

It will be asked to what extent Cicero's decision to take on a case was influenced by his own estimate of the chances of success, and whether he was ready to take cases that, in reality, held out little hope of victory. The case of Scamander mentioned in *Pro Cluentio* 49 ff. may be one such. Yet it must be remembered that Cicero, in the context of this speech, had an interest in making it appear that this case (which he lost) was more hopeless than perhaps it was in fact. In the *Pro Milone*, Cicero took on the defence in circumstances that would cause difficulty to any lawyer: Milo had boasted in public about the killing of Clodius (as we learn from Asconius' commentary). Cicero failed on that occasion. But the ability to

---

[81] Quint. *Inst.* 11.1.73, Val. Max. 4.2.4, and Dio 39.63.2–5 all comment on the fact that Cicero was defending a former enemy. Their comments are illuminatingly and characteristically different. Valerius Maximus is full of admiration for Cicero's *humanitas* in forgiving Gabinius for past wrongs. Quintilian takes the lawyer's view that it was the soundness of the case that mattered, not Cicero's past personal relations with his client (an implausible view in this case, since Gabinius was found guilty). Dio, hostile to Cicero as always, says that the episode earned him a reputation as a turncoat. From Cicero's letters we learn more: shortly before the *repetundae* trial, Gabinius had been indicted for *maiestas*. Cicero was in demand as advocate for both the prosecution and the defence. Obviously he could not do both, and he was reluctant to come down on either side; to prosecute would have offended Pompey, but at that stage he regarded the prospect of reconciliation with his former enemy (necessary in order to appear for the defence) as 'eternal infamy' (*Q. Fr.* 3.4.3). He was then requested to appear as a witness for the prosecution, in which role he duly appeared in court; but his testimony was so restrained that Gabinius not only declined to cross-examine but averred that, if acquitted, he would make it up with Cicero. This event, together with the acquittal of Gabinius at the first trial, is sufficient to explain why Cicero was ready to be reconciled with Gabinius and defend him in the second trial. Modern historians are cynical in their reading of *Rab. Post.* 19 and 33 in which Cicero defends his *reditus in gratiam* with Gabinius, assuming that in reality Cicero merely gave in to pressure from Pompey and defended Gabinius against his better judgement; but Cicero had held out against pressure from Pompey right up to the first trial. Of course it may well be that Gabinius' gesture of reconciliation was prompted by Pompey, who had been extremely anxious to engage Cicero's services as advocate in the first trial and could doubtless see that they might be required again.

turn round an apparently hopeless case was the advocate's chief glory, then as now. We seldom if ever hear explicitly of Cicero himself pulling off such a feat (the case of Ligarius may be one such: see Chapter 14), but we can read in his *De Oratore*[82] of L. Antonius' famous defence of C. Norbanus, in which he first of all had more or less to apologise for defending such an apparently guilty man, but in the end persuaded the jury that the charge of sedition was unproven.

It is only natural that we have relatively little evidence for instances in which a Roman advocate actually declined to take on a case, or for the reasons for which he might do so. One example happens to be discussed by Cicero in *Att.* 1.1. Atticus' uncle Caecilius, the alleged victim with others of a substantial fraud, approached Cicero to appear for him in a case against a certain Caninius Satyrus with a view to recovering some of the losses. But Satyrus had proved himself a useful supporter of both Cicero and his brother in their campaigns for office. Further, Satyrus was linked to the highly influential L. Domitius Ahenobarbus, whose wealth and connections could have been invaluable in the forthcoming campaign. It should be noted that Cicero avers that he would not have left Caecilius in the lurch if he had been on his own in the case; this reflects the initial social pressure on any advocate to take up any case presented to him. However, Cicero says that other advocates had already been retained and, therefore, the need for his services was not great. He pleads that common humanity prevented him from appearing against so loyal a friend as Satyrus; but he admits that a cynical commentator would reckon that his refusal was motivated by the need to avoid offending anyone during his campaign for office.

In another letter dating from the period leading up to his consulship, Cicero says that he was thinking of defending his competitor (and later enemy) Catiline on a charge of provincial maladministration, though in the event it appears that he never did.[83] In 62, P. Autronius, accused of involvement in the Catilinarian conspiracy, apparently begged Cicero to defend him; Cicero, however, refused and instead gave evidence for the prosecution.[84] Yet he did defend P. Sulla on the same charge, leading to accusations of inconsistency from the prosecutors; to which Cicero replied (*Pro Sulla* 18–19) by

---

[82] *De Oratore* 2.198. This is normally regarded as a triumph of rhetorical appeal to the emotions in the face of overwhelming evidence, but it should be noted that Antonius (according to Cicero) did in fact address himself to the facts of the case: his central argument was that the rioting which Norbanus was alleged to have led was in fact a spontaneous demonstration by the public. This is a perfectly respectable argument even by modern standards.

[83] The historian Fenestella is quoted by Asc. *In Tog. Cand.* 85 for the view that Cicero actually did defend Catiline; but as Asconius argues, if this was so, it is surprising that the point was not brought up later.

[84] Cf. D. Berry, *Pro Sulla*, introd. 10; E. S. Gruen, *The Last Generation of the Roman Republic* (Berkeley, 1974) 283.

arguing simply that he had refused to defend Autronius because he was guilty, whereas he was now defending Sulla because he was innocent. Cicero is quite open about his claim to have made up his mind about both cases before deciding whether to take them on.

Certainly Cicero countenanced the possibility that an advocate might honourably refuse a defence brief (for reasons other than that he knew the defendant to be guilty). He mentions at the beginning of *Pro Roscio* that Roscius' patrons may well have tried to secure other advocates before they reached him. Whether this is true or not, it is clearly meant to save the credit of the great men who were sitting in silence during Roscius' trial. There is also a saying of Cicero preserved, unfortunately out of context, by the historian Ammianus Marcellinus, to the effect that an advocate could 'perhaps' be forgiven for refusing a brief, but not for negligence in the defence of his client.[85] The 'perhaps' is significant: it implies that on the whole advocates were expected to undertake the cases they were offered. There might be more mundane reasons for refusing to take on a defence: Cicero could not be in two places at once[86] and 'devilling' had not been thought of; the Roman advocate had to be there in person.

A pretty good summary of this issue, illustrating both the similarities and the differences between Roman and modern practice, is to be found in Quintilian.[87] The good advocate, according to him, will not plead causes which he knows to be unjust (as Quintilian picturesquely puts it, 'he will not open up the safe haven of his eloquence to pirates');[88] if the advocate discovers in the course of his investigations that a client has no hope of success, he will give advice accordingly and not be embarrassed about refusing to take the case further. On the other hand, many good cases look unpromising at first sight: it is sometimes as hard a task to defend the innocent as it is to defend the guilty. An advocate with more work than he can cope with should give priority to those cases in which the litigants, or those who approach him on their behalf, are persons of good character; he should not make a principle either of supporting the powerful against the humble, or (worse still!) of supporting inferiors against their superiors. Ideally he should not take fees for his services, and he must not bargain with clients. But (especially if he is short of money) he will not object if clients choose to offer a token of their gratitude.

---

[85] Amm. Marc. 30.4.7 'non defendi homines sine vituperatione fortasse posse, neglegenter defendi sine scelere non posse'. There is no clue as to which lost work of Cicero this comes from. The whole context in Ammianus, a vitriolic attack on the advocates of the historian's own time, is well worth reading as a curiosity.

[86] See *Att.* 13.49.1, *Fam.* 7.24.2 for an instance: one Tigellius asked Cicero to appear for him on the same day as he was due to appear for P. Sestius in 52 BC (not the *Pro Sestio* but a later trial of Sestius on a bribery charge). Apparently Tigellius was annoyed at Cicero's refusal.

[87] *Inst. Or.* 12.7; cf. 12.1.45.   [88] D. A. Russell's translation (Loeb, 2001).

Thus far Quintilian; and there is no reason to believe that much of this had changed, in practice, since Cicero's time. But Quintilian is too worried about his ideal orator's social standing and moral character (as 'vir bonus dicendi peritus') to endorse Cicero's principle that if a fellow-citizen is on trial for life or reputation, that is a sufficient reason for defending him. It seems that there was a range of acceptable attitudes and that different Roman advocates took different lines: according to *Brutus* 207, M. Antonius was 'facilis in causis recipiendis' while Crassus was 'fastidiosior'.[89] Cicero apparently followed Antonius' lead, and his self-image, not of course always consistent but adapted to the demands of particular rhetorical contexts, was at least in this respect closer to that of the modern advocate; though it is only in the developed jurisdictions of modern Europe that the principle has been established that everyone, however guilty or disreputable, is entitled to a defence and that the advocate will suffer no loss of standing or reputation by undertaking it. Even now the principle does not hold in the United States of America, where 'a lawyer ordinarily is not obliged to accept a client whose character or cause the lawyer regards as repugnant'.[90]

If one believes the quotation in Ammianus referred to just above, Cicero evidently thought that once one had taken on a case, one was obliged to give it one's best shot: negligence in the defence of a client was unpardonable. This brings us to the second consideration mentioned near the beginning of this section: that the advocate should argue the case on his client's behalf as strongly as possible in the interests of reaching a fair decision. Here Roman thinking seems to have been to some extent in line with our own. But perhaps in reality it had less in common with that of the modern professional advocate, who believes that both sides should make the best possible case in the interests of a fair trial, than with that of some members of the general public, who believe that the courts are there to ensure that the guilty are punished. Certainly, the Roman system enjoined that prosecutors should do their job properly, and there was an offence in Roman law called *praevaricatio*, i.e. collusion by the prosecution with the defence in order to get the defendant off. When a prosecution threatened, it was apparently a popular tactic to get in first with a more friendly prosecuting counsel who would allow the defence to win; of such a kind apparently was Caecilius, the alternative prosecutor whom Cicero successfully dislodged in the *divinatio* before the Verres trial. There was evidently no legal remedy against a defence advocate who failed to represent his client

---

[89] But according to Cicero he still took the cases on.

[90] *American Bar Association Model Rules of Professional Conduct*, Comment to Rule 6.2, quoted by Pannick, *Advocates*, 137. The whole discussion of this and related issues in Pannick, ibid. 135–56, is well worth reading.

properly.[91] Cicero is alleged to have pleaded less vigorously than he could have done in the case of his former enemy Gabinius, but the allegation occurs only in Dio Cassius (46.8.1) who is strongly influenced by a tradition hostile to Cicero;[92] in any case the passage shows an underlying belief that clients in court were entitled to the best defence possible. Such a belief is, however, again likely to have rested more on the notion of an advocate's duty to his client as *patronus* than on any abstract principles regarding the virtues of the adversarial system as a means of arriving at truth (though Cicero himself was acquainted with those principles in another context, that of Academic philosophy, where it was held that argument on both sides of a question offered the best chance of getting near to the truth).[93]

But how far can an advocate go in protecting the interests of a client? Disquiet may well be caused by the statements found in Roman rhetorical theorists to the effect that truth was irrelevant to the advocate. This certainly contrasts with the modern theoretical notion that the advocate's task is part of a process of discovery of truth: the advocate's duty to the court in this regard potentially overrides even his duty to the client and the cause.[94] But Cicero could happily say in the *De Officiis* that the advocate's business was to present arguments that 'look like the truth' even if they were not true.[95] Quintilian states much the same position (6.2.5): the peculiar task of the orator is 'to bring force to bear on the judges' feelings and distract their minds from the truth'.[96] Rhetoric here appears in its bad old guise of 'making the worse cause appear the better'. But one wonders whether both Cicero and Quintilian may have been misled by the requirements of their context into a more cynical view of advocacy than they needed. Cicero does not necessarily mean that the advocate is expected to lie; modern advocates would agree that their job is to present plausible arguments on the evidence as presented, and not to try to reach an independent assessment of the truth—that is the responsibility of the judge and jury. In Quintilian's case the motive may have been the desire to advertise

---

[91] No more than there is nowadays, though the idea has been seriously discussed in recent years: Pannick, *Advocates*, 197–206.

[92] Cf. n. 17 above; cf. F. Millar, 'Some Speeches in Cassius Dio', *Mus. Helv.* 18 (1961) 11–22 esp. 15 on Dio's use of anti-Ciceronian sources. Cicero himself says 'cum . . . summo studio defenderim' (*Rab. Post.* 19).

[93] Cf. P. Smith 'How not to Write Philosophy: Did Cicero Get it Right?', in J. G. F. Powell (ed.) *Cicero the Philosopher* (Oxford, 1995) 301–23.   [94] Cf. Pannick, *Advocates*, 121.

[95] 2.51: 'patroni [est] non numquam verisimile, etiamsi minus sit verum, defendere'.

[96] Cf. Quint. *Inst.* 12.1.36. Quintilian there mentions problem cases in which, he maintains, an advocate might need to use false arguments: (*a*) when a defendant who committed a crime for honourable reasons can only be acquitted if the court is persuaded that he did not do it at all; (*b*) when the defendant is technically guilty but the community is in need of his services, e.g. as a military commander; (*c*) when there is a prospect that a guilty defendant might reform his character. We must remember in this context that the Roman penal system was uncompromising.

the art of rhetoric by drawing attention to its power over the minds of those who make the decisions.

Hence it may be more illuminating to examine the practice rather than the theory. Cicero is alleged to have said, after the Cluentius trial, that he had thrown dust in the eyes of the jury, and this is usually taken to mean that he had knowingly misled the court into acquitting a guilty defendant.[97] But perhaps, even here, Cicero should not be condemned out of his own mouth: supposing that the saying is authentic (as it may not be), it is the sort of joke that any barrister might make after winning a difficult case. Cicero is also quoted (again by Ammianus) for a more high-minded view of the matter: to corrupt a jury by eloquence is just as bad as to do so by bribery.[98] A modern barrister risks disciplinary proceedings for misleading the court; a Roman advocate only risked exposure as a liar, but even so, the drafting of parts of Cicero's lawcourt speeches shows that, while he is always ready to put a rhetorical construction on the facts that is favourable to his own case, he is quite careful not to tamper with the facts them-selves.[99] He is sometimes accused of producing a dishonest defence in the case of Milo; it might be thought that anyone could see that Milo did not kill Clodius in self-defence.[100] Yet the facts may not have been so clear at the time; it is only with the hindsight of Asconius that we think we know what 'really' happened. Cicero's counter-accusation in the *Pro Roscio* may be interpreted, if one chooses, as an attempt to fasten the blame for a mur-der on two innocent men; but the awkward question remains: why did Cicero not accuse Chrysogonus? Commentators have found this baffling, but only on the assumption that Cicero was accustomed to throw around accusations at all and sundry. Could there not be a much simpler answer—namely that Cicero did not have evidence against Chrysogonus, whereas he did have what looked like evidence against Magnus and Capito?[101] Here

---

[97] Quint. *Inst.* 2.17.21. The Latin is 'tenebras se offudisse iudicibus', which is perhaps better translated as 'left the jury in a fog'; literally 'poured darkness over the jury'. There has been some debate as to the exact feature of the *Pro Cluentio* referred to. It may refer either to the plethora of irrelevant detail near the beginning of the speech, or to the famously tricky disjunctive argument about the corruption of the *iudicium Iunianum.* Cf. Crook, *Legal Advocacy,* 139; J. Humbert, 'Comment Cicéron mystifia les juges de Cluentius', *REL* 16 (1938) 275–96.

[98] 30.4.10. Again, this is quoted entirely out of context from an unidentified work. It has been hastily attributed to the *De Republica.*

[99] This is particularly noticeable in the *Verrines,* where analysis can show that Cicero usually does not seem to go beyond the evidence: cf. as a case study Ch. 9.

[100] Cf. D. Berry, 'Cicero's Masterpiece?', *Omnibus* 25 (1993) 10.

[101] The speech for Roscius, which according to Cicero made his career, continues to be a puz-zle and a focus for debate. Considerable prominence has been given to the hypothesis that the defendant Roscius was guilty and that Cicero's counter-accusation is, consequently, a tissue of lies: see among others T. E. Kinsey, 'Cicero's case against Magnus, Capito and Chrysogonus in the Pro Sexto Roscio Amerino and its use for the historian', *L'Antiquité Classique* 49 (1980) 173–90;

we simply do not know the facts; but while we should always approach advocates' speeches with due scepticism, there is no reason to start from the assumption that the facts were not more or less as Cicero stated them. Altogether it is impossible to judge such issues in the absence of evidence from behind the scenes, of a kind which we could not expect to have at this distance of time. We shall never know what Cicero was told in conference by Roscius or Milo.[102] We have no real idea whether most of the clients that Cicero defended were guilty as charged (in the case of Cluentius it is not even absolutely clear what the precise charges were– Cicero cannot of course be blamed for this, as the charges would presumably have been stated in the indictment before the court). All we know is the court's decision–and sometimes we do not even know that (see Appendix). We do not have the evidence on which to reopen the cases.[103] But Cicero is entitled to the benefit of the doubt: 'the fact is that in no instance do we know for certain that Cicero or any of the others was alleging fact or law that he knew . . . to be false.'[104]

Before closing this section, we should touch on a further issue. Modern advocates, retained for a particular case, are supposed to be insulated by their professional position from the world outside that particular courtroom, and even from responsibility for the effects of their eloquence (this is not always observed in practice: occasionally, for example, prosecuting counsel have been known to receive death threats from convicted defendants). As already suggested, a modern lawyer does not express personal opinions, but argues a particular case from the evidence. So also did a Roman advocate, as Cicero would have us believe in a famous passage of the *Pro Cluentio* already alluded to. Yet the fact that Cicero has to argue this in the context of what is itself a lawcourt speech suggests that it was not taken for granted. Clearly a Roman advocate's opponents were only too happy to point out inconsistencies between opinions expressed in court on different occasions. Thus what seems to us like a theory of advocacy was formulated in the first instance only for the immediate purpose of getting

---

'The Case against Sextus Roscius of Ameria', ibid. 54 (1985) 188–96; 'The sale of the property of Roscius of Ameria: how illegal was it?', ibid. 57 (1988) 296–7; A. Dyck, 'Evidence and Rhetoric in Cicero's Pro Roscio Amerino: The Case Against Sex. Roscius', *CQ* 53 (2003) 235–46. On the political ramifications of the Roscius case see below, ch. 2, pp. 85–6. There Paterson argues (against the view of Kinsey and others) that the facts are best explained on the assumption that the defendant Roscius was innocent. See also Craig, *Form as Argument*, 27–45.

[102] There is no reason to suppose that Cicero did not interview his clients thoroughly while preparing the case; cf. *De Or.* 2.102. Quintilian, *Inst.* 12.8, sets out the principles of good practice on this matter, which remain the same today; cf. Crook, *Legal Advocacy*, 137.

[103] The attempt to reconstruct the arguments of the opposition is, of course, an instructive exercise: see now M. C. Alexander, *The Case for the Prosecution in the Ciceronian Era* (Ann Arbor, 2002).

[104] Crook, *Legal Advocacy*, 140.

out of an awkward situation; furthermore, Cicero can only make the point stick by asserting that he was mistaken on the previous occasion and now knows better.

In a system where personal patronage was paramount, one might suppose that an advocate would make friends of those he defended and enemies of those he opposed. Yet the Roman Republican situation was evidently more complex than this. Cicero is sometimes at pains to reject the notion that opposition in court might affect personal relations.[105] He displays a wide range of attitudes to his opponents, depending on their identity and character. A relative nonentity such as Erucius (who prosecuted in the Roscius case) could be discomfited with a minimum of trouble, while subtler methods were used to undermine the authority of a Cato or a Hortensius. Particular care was necessary when the opponent was also a friend, as for example in the treatment of Servius Sulpicius in the *Pro Murena*[106] or of Laterensis in the *Pro Plancio*. This kind of carefully measured politeness can seem reminiscent of the British convention that all advocates are 'friends' even when on opposing sides;[107] in fact it arises precisely from the need to be careful because of the absence of such a convention. In the trial of Murena, when Cicero chose ridicule as his weapon to undermine the prosecution case of Cato (then still relatively young) and Sulpicius, it is possible that some temporary offence was caused, although Cato is said to have confined himself to remarking 'What a funny consul we've got' (Plutarch, *Dem. & Cic.* 5).

Evidently, a prosecution, undertaken on private initiative as they always were, could hardly fail to be seen as a personal attack on the defendant.[108] It was for this reason, among others, that Cicero preferred defending to prosecuting; we know of only one prosecution conducted by Cicero after the

---

[105] Compare C. P. Craig, 'The Accusator as Amicus: An Original Roman Tactic of Ethical Argumentation', *TAPA* 111 (1981) 31–7; Loutsch, *L'Exorde*.

[106] *Mur.* 7–10 is particularly interesting. Servius Sulpicius had apparently complained that Cicero was neglecting the duties of friendship in opposing him and defending his rival Murena. Cicero responds that an advocate's duty is to defend anyone, 'etiam alienissimos', and that Sulpicius himself as a jurist is in the habit of giving legal advice to his friends' opponents and even to his own. Again this looks at first glance like a statement of the cab-rank rule, but Cicero again spoils it (from a modern point of view) by claiming that Murena is his friend anyway. Besides, Sulpicius could not have argued as he did if the principle enunciated by Cicero had been the whole truth of the matter. On Cicero's treatment of prosecutors see further A. D. Leeman, 'The Technique of Persuasion in Cicero's Pro Murena', *Entretiens Hardt* 28 (1982) 193–228; H. C. Gotoff, 'Cicero's Analysis of the Prosecution Speeches in the *Pro Caelio*: An Exercise in Practical Criticism', *CPh* 81 (1986) 122–32.

[107] Quintilian, *Inst.* 12.9.11 mentions the need to observe professional solidarity when dealing with the advocates of the opposing side.

[108] Cf. D. F. Epstein, *Personal Enmity in Roman Politics 218–43 BC* (London, 1987) ch. 5. One should distinguish this from the common Ciceronian defence tactic whereby prosecutors were represented as malicious and as mounting an unprovoked attack on the defendant.

Verres case (that of Munatius Plancus in 52 BC).[109] But an appearance for the defence might offer opportunities to attack the other side. It is not unknown in ancient oratory for defences to be dressed up as prosecutions and vice-versa; the counter-accusation in the *Pro Roscio Amerino* is perhaps the most obvious Ciceronian example, while in the *Pro Quinctio* where Cicero is appearing for the plaintiff, he makes it sound as much like a defence as he can and even complains at the unfairness of having to speak first.[110] Later in his career, one cannot but suspect that Cicero took on with some relish the part of the defence of Caelius that involved the rebuttal of the testimony of Clodia, and it is clear enough that enmity towards the late Clodius was a principal ingredient in Cicero's decision to take on, against all the odds, the defence of Milo. In the former speech the hostility is manifested as acerbic ridicule, in the other as jubilation over the death of Clodius. Yet it is not right to assume that Cicero used these trials merely as a convenient opportunity to strike a blow against his political or personal enemies. It was not necessarily in the best interests of his case that he should do so; this may indeed be one of the reasons why the defence of Milo failed. But the invectives are not merely gratuitous in either instance. The fact is, rather, that the cases themselves required that an attack be made on the Clodian family, and it was as well that this should be mounted by someone who already bore them a grudge. Even Cicero's enmities themselves could be turned, at least theoretically, to the advantage of his clients.

We have pointed to some similarities and differences between the Roman advocate's conception of his role and that of his modern equivalent. But the most important differences, it can be argued, lay not in the conception of advocacy itself but in the legal system within which the advocate worked. The strategies of advocates are above all conditioned by the constraints and expectations of a particular system; and it is this that we must now examine more closely.

iv. The Roman Courts

A more detailed account of the Republican court system may be found in Chapter 1. The following section is intended only to highlight the ways in which the workings of the court system impinge on the general issues we are considering.

---

[109] *Q. Fr.* 3.4.2 is illuminating on the risk of failure in prosecution: in 54 BC it had been suggested that Cicero might undertake the prosecution of Gabinius, being well known to be an enemy of his; but Cicero replies 'What? with that jury?'. In the event he merely appeared as a witness for the prosecution. See above, p. 21, n. 81.

[110] It was easier in Latin, because counsel for the plaintiff was also said *defendere causam*.

The word 'court' is conventionally used to translate the Latin *iudicium*, which means both the judicial decision on a case and the tribunal which makes the decision. A *iudicium* could consist, at one extreme, of a single judge (*iudex*, usually with a co-opted panel of advisers '*qui in consilio sunt*') appointed to decide a civil issue, or, at the other extreme, of the *comitia centuriata*, theoretically the whole Roman People in quasi-military order, which could still be convened to hear cases of high treason (*perduellio*) as in the case of Rabirius in 63. Most of Cicero's major cases were heard by a panel of 'judges' (usually *iudices*; in certain cases *recuperatores*) under the presidency of a magistrate, ranging in number from about thirty to over seventy depending on the particular statute under which the case was being tried. Normally we refer to these panels as 'juries', although the parallel with a modern jury is not exact. The criminal courts, called *quaestiones*, were set up under particular laws to try particular classes of offence. Each *quaestio* was in the care of one of the praetors of the year–who were, it will be remembered, annually elected officials, not professional judges. Lesser courts were held under the presidency of junior senators who had not yet reached the praetorship: of this kind was the panel of *recuperatores* that tried the case of Caecina.[111] Civil cases were tried, after an initial hearing before the Urban or Peregrine Praetor as the case might be, by a single judge and his *consilium*; two of Cicero's speeches (*Pro Quinctio* and *Pro Roscio Comoedo*) come from cases of this sort. There were also other tribunals, analogous to courts, in which advocacy might take place: questions of religious law were decided by the College of Pontifices, before whom Cicero once famously appeared to claim back the part of his house that Clodius had 'consecrated' (his speech on this occasion, the *De Domo*, is discussed in Chapter 13).

The Roman criminal system in general worked in two stages.[112] First there was a preliminary hearing (*postulatio*, i.e. asking for leave to prosecute) before the praetor, at which it would be decided whether there was a case to answer under the relevant law. If so, the indictment would be drawn up (*nominis delatio*), and the matter sent for trial. If not, the case would be thrown out, as happened to C. Cato's abortive attempt to prosecute Gabinius.[113] If several rival prosecutors came forward, there would be a further hearing to decide who should be allowed to bring the case (oddly called *divinatio*: see Cicero's *Divinatio in Caecilium*, his first speech in the case of Verres). The second stage was the trial itself, and it was here that the advocates were heard and the witnesses examined. A typical timescale is

---

[111] The case was a retrial, arising from a previous action for breach of a praetorian interdict.

[112] As, of course, did the civil courts, with their two-part hearing *in iure*, before the praetor, and *apud iudicem*, before the judge appointed to try the facts.   [113] *Sest.* 18, *Q.Fr.* 1.2.15.

indicated by the trial of Gabinius in 54: *postulatio* 20 September, *nominis delatio* 28 September, verdict 23 October.[114] In the criminal *quaestiones* the praetor would himself preside at the trial, though his functions were, it seems, confined to keeping order, regulating procedure, and pronouncing the judgement of the court at the end. The presiding magistrate evidently did not play an active part in proceedings in the way that a modern British judge does.

As mentioned, the praetor was not necessarily an expert in the law, and neither were the *iudices*. The *iudices* in major public trials were, however, taken from the upper ranks of Roman society. The constitution of the juries, senatorial or equestrian, was a major issue in Roman politics until the matter was settled by the *lex Aurelia Cottae* in 70 BC, which established the principle that a third of the members of a *quaestio* jury should be senators and a third equestrian; the remaining third were recruited presumably from the class immediately below the equestrians, and obscurely designated *tribuni aerarii*. Except in regard to numbers, a panel of Roman judges might be seen as more like a bench of lay magistrats than like a modern jury; from another point of view, bearing in mind the senatorial status of many of the jurors (and of all of them in the major *quaestiones* under the immediately post-Sullan system), the parallel with a committee of Parliament suggests itself. An advocate's approach would be conditioned by his knowledge of the composition of the tribunal: though some jurors might be trained in the law, the advocate could not afford to use arguments that would be misunderstood by the layman. An advocate who was himself a senator, like Cicero from 70 BC onwards, would know a proportion of the individual jurors personally and would be able to allow for what he knew of their inclinations. Before that, in the *Pro Roscio*, Cicero was evidently able to predict that the jury of Sullan senators would not wish to hear anything against Sulla himself or his politics, but might be willing to see his freedman Chrysogonus taken down a peg. Later (*Off.* 2.51) he represented this defence of Roscius as a stand against tyranny, but it was so only in a specialized advocate's sense; he took all due care not to question the legitimacy of the regime.

Though in criminal cases the law of the matter would generally have been settled before the trial, when the praetor had the responsibility of deciding whether the case could appropriately be tried under the statute which he was responsible for administering, points of law sometimes remained to be argued during the actual trial, as in the *Pro Cluentio* when the question arose whether Cluentius, as an equestrian, was liable under a statute which expressly applied to senators. If such points arose, they were

---

[114] M. Alexander, *Trials in the Late Roman Republic 149 B.C. to 50 B.C.* (Toronto, 1990) 248.

taken into consideration by the jury along with the rest of the arguments. Cicero's use of legal arguments is discussed in Chapter 5. Whether in criminal or in civil cases, the opinions of legal experts had no particular authority, and Cicero suggests in the *De Oratore* that a good advocate should be able to out-argue any jurist, however great the latter's technical knowledge.[115]

The Roman court had its procedures laid down by the statute that governed it: the number and status of the judges, the time within which a trial had to take place (allowing for the collection of evidence and so on), the time allowed for the trial itself including any mandatory adjournment (*comperendinatio*), the order in which the prosecution and defence presented their cases and the time allowed for each, the time allocated for the examination of witnesses, and other matters relating to the discipline of the court. The procedure in most cases was simple enough:[116] opening speech or speeches for the prosecution, reply by the defence, then the examination of witnesses on both sides. After this the court proceeded straight to a vote; there were no closing speeches, no summing up, no time officially allocated for deliberation. The individual judges were supposed to reach independent verdicts; indeed, judges were specifically forbidden to engage in argument (the *Lex Repetundarum* states categorically: *iudex ne quis disputet*). A simple majority was sufficient either way. This contrasts strongly with the modern British system in which the members of the jury are supposed to reach, if possible, a unanimous verdict after discussion among themselves, and have a virtually unlimited time in which to do so. In addition to 'guilty' (*condemno*) or 'not guilty' (*absolvo*) there was the opportunity to vote *non liquet*, 'not proven' as Scottish law has it.

Trials took place in the Forum in the open air and could easily attract the attention of the crowd; the ring of casual spectators (quaintly called the *corona* or 'garland') was a regular feature of Roman trials, and advocates found it as important to gain their favour as much as to gain that of the jury (Cicero uses this as an excuse[117] for his philosophical philistinism in the *Pro Murena*). There is no reason to doubt that, most of the time, a reasonable level of order was kept by the praetor, assisted by his lictors and other staff. The insufficiency of the policing arrangements became obvious

---

[115] *De Oratore* 1.180, the famous *causa Curiana* in which Crassus argued on the side of equity against Q. Scaevola the famous jurist, who as advocate for the other side had argued for strict legal interpretation. Cf. also *Mur.* 29 'vestra responsa . . . evertuntur saepe dicendo'. At any rate until very recently, the English courts have taken a similarly dismissive attitude to the opinions of academic lawyers.

[116] The procedure varied somewhat from one court to another; that of the *repetundae* court was somewhat more complex, and the special court convened to try Milo heard the witnesses first and the advocates afterwards, contrary to the usual practice. See further Ch. 1.

[117] *De Finibus* 4.74.

at the trial of Milo, where the defence had to request an armed guard;[118] but this took place at a time of unusual political tension.

Rules concerning the admissibility of particular kinds of argument or evidence were scarce. A defendant would, as a matter of course, have his whole life laid bare in tabloid detail; there were no rules against attacks on past character (cf. Chapter 6). There is no record of an advocate ever being interrupted for irrelevance.[119] Nor was there any limit on barefaced appeals to sympathy: a defendant would appear in mourning, unkempt and dirty (*sordidatus*), and would be accompanied by his family and relatives in a similar state.[120] There were similarly few rules governing the presentation of evidence. To examine slaves as witnesses one had to apply to the praetor, because this involved the official use of torture. Slaves could not be required to testify against their masters. Otherwise it was up to the parties and their advocates themselves what witnesses they brought forward–if they could persuade them to attend; there was not necessarily any compulsion or penalty for non-attendance (only the prosecution could compel witnesses to attend, up to a prescribed number and with certain exemptions; the *vadimonium*[121] was required only for defendants), hence the (at first glance odd) formulation often to be found in Cicero's speeches, 'my witnesses will say such-and-such *if* they come forward'. Witnesses, it seems, could be subjected to verbal abuse, under the guise of questioning (*interrogatio*), by opposing counsel; that this might go far beyond what is now acceptable in cross-examination may be inferred from Cicero's *In Vatinium*, although this may not be an entirely typical example. It is not perhaps surprising that some preferred to give their evidence as a written deposition, as e.g. the testimony of L. Lucceius in *Pro Caelio* 55.[122]

---

[118] Asc. *In Mil.* 40–1 C.; *Fam.* 3.10; *Att.* 9.7b.2. These passages make it quite clear that Pompey provided the guard at the request of the defence, and this casts doubt on the popular version retailed by Plutarch and Dio in which Cicero was allegedly terrified into silence by those very soldiers. It is more than likely that this notion arose from a misreading of the exordium of the speech itself.

[119] This negative fact casts doubt on statements such as that of Nisbet regarding the *Pro Sestio*, 'Such irrelevance could not have been tolerated even in a Roman court'. Cf. also Crook, *Legal Advocacy*, 140–1.

[120] This kind of appeal to sympathy is often thought of as a peculiarity of ancient courts, but in fact modern parallels can easily be cited: see Pannick, *Advocates*, 27–8, 'William F. Howe [a New York lawyer at the end of the 19th cent.] learnt this lesson well. The wife and children of the defendant would be placed in the front row of the court to gaze devotedly at the man on trial. And "if by chance a particular defendant did not have a pretty wife, fond children, or a snowy-haired mother, he was not for that reason deprived of the sympathy they might create on his behalf. Howe would supply them from the firm's large stable of professional spectators." [quotation from R. H. Rovere, *Howe and Hummel*, 1947]'. Our Newcastle colleague, Donald Hill, who has served as a Justice of the Peace, reports that although crying infants are not allowed in court, it is quite possible to deploy them outside and gain sympathy by requesting an adjournment in order to attend to their needs.   [121] Security for attendance, analogous to bail. See ch. 1, p. 65.

[122] Reference to written witness-statements are however rare in the speeches, and J. Humbert, *Les Plaidoyers écrits et les plaidoiries réelles de Cicéron* (Paris, 1925) 38–9 suggests that Lucceius' statement was a record of evidence given at a previous trial.

We know little of the way in which advocates in the Republican courts planned and prepared their cases, apart from a few incidental allusions in the speeches themselves. Cicero sometimes conducted even major cases alone, according to the 'old custom' ('vetere instituto', *Cluent.* 199): e.g. the prosecution of Verres, and the defences of Cluentius and Cornelius; in the case of Milo he was the only advocate to make a continuous speech, though he was assisted by others in the examination of witnesses. But in many of the more important cases there were several advocates on both sides.[123] The defendant might or might not decide to speak in person, as, for example, Caelius did. That the advocates on the same side made prior arrangements regarding the allocation of different parts of the case is implied by some passages,[124] and is to be expected on general grounds. Passages which imply otherwise are not always easy to interpret. When, in *Pro Caelio* 23, Cicero expresses the wish that Crassus had 'also' covered the charge of the murder of Dio, it can hardly be believed that Crassus left it out by an oversight or without prior arrangement, since closer examination of the case reveals that it must have been the most central charge. One suspects in this instance that Crassus and Cicero between them had so arranged matters that Crassus deliberately left it out in order to minimize its apparent importance, and that Cicero would then sweep it up as though it needed no further argument. This could be an efficient persuasive strategy in a system where there was no judge to remind the advocates to keep to the point, or to draw the jury's attention to gaps in the defence argument. A more difficult case is the *Pro Ligario*, discussed in Chapter 14, where it does look very much as though the advocates for Ligarius were pulling opposite ways.[125]

One thing at least is clear: the order of the advocates' speeches must have been fixed in advance, and it is a well-known fact that Cicero himself usually spoke last (cf. *Brut.* 190), so that he could make the greatest impression on the jury, particularly in the sphere of *commiseratio* (appeal to pity) in which he was acknowledged to excel. This fact also explains the apparent peculiarities of speeches such as the *Pro Caelio* which do not appear to address themselves properly to the matter in hand. In this instance, it is clear enough (*Cael.* 23) that the main defence to the charges had been completed by Caelius himself and by Crassus. Cicero had no more to do on the substantive issues, and it might well have been risky to go again over ground that had already been covered.[126]

---

[123] Cf. *Brutus* 208–9, where Cicero deplores the habits of some advocates who attend for only part of a case, and reply to speeches that they have not heard. See in general Crook, *Legal Advocacy*, 127–9.　　　　　　　　　　　　　　　　　　　[124] e.g. *Pro Caelio* 7.

[125] Pannick, *Advocates*, 17 records modern instances of this type of thing, arising from the failure of advocates to consult properly beforehand.　　　　　　　　　　　　[126] Cf. above, at n. 61.

Speeches such as this, in which irrelevance appears (but only appears) to reign supreme, are exceptions, and can be explained. In those cases where Cicero appeared as sole advocate, there is not usually any problem of this kind. In the surviving private speeches–*Pro Quinctio, Pro Roscio Comoedo, Pro Caecina*–the argument is directed entirely to the issue in the case. The same must have been true of the multitude of minor cases which Cicero fought and won during the course of his career. It may well be, in fact, that the published speeches, which were doubtless selected for rhetorical brilliance rather than for any other reason and directed at a general audience rather than a specialist legal readership, give a misleading impression in this respect, since they are likely to be those in which there was some wider issue at stake beyond the trial itself, or at least some point of interest to Roman high society. The *Pro Archia*, discussed in Chapter 12, begins with a perfectly competent piece of legal advocacy regarding Archias's entitlement to citizenship, but we remember it for its praise of poetry and humane learning, for which Cicero himself apologises as a line of argument not usually found in the courts. We remember the *Pro Caelio* for the discrediting of Clodia, the *Pro Sestio* for Cicero's own political apologia, the *Pro Murena* for his amusing attacks on Sulpicius and Cato, the *Pro Roscio* (as Cicero himself in later life remembered it) for its dramatic style and especially the description of the horrific punishment that awaited Roscius if found guilty, the *Pro Cluentio* for its exposé of municipal chicanery and its urbane delineation of the advocate's role. That these things could be said in court with such freedom (or, at least, published in speeches that purported to have been delivered in court) does, of course, show an important facet of the Roman system; but this should not blind us to the presence elsewhere in Cicero of efficient argument on the law and the facts, which any modern barrister would recognize as akin to his or her own practice. It is evident that much routine argument, examination of witnesses, procedural detail, and the like, was left out of the published versions,[127] but then there need have been no expectation that it would be included. It may in fact be Cicero's own selection of material for publication that accounts for some of the current adverse criticisms of his alleged irrelevance or capriciousness.

One must also consider the possibility that some kinds of argumentation, which would be excluded from modern courts on grounds of irrelevance, may in fact have counted as relevant in a Roman context. Two obvious categories come to mind: Cicero's dilations on his own personal interest in the case (cf. Chapter 2), and the arguments from past character which are a recurrent ingredient of speeches both for the prosecution and

---

[127] See Humbert, *Les Plaidoyers*, and cf. § vii below.

for the defence (treated in this volume from different points of view in Chapters 6 and 7). Certainly, the Republican Roman system did not have the strict standards of proof which are demanded by modern rules of evidence. Nor did it have the restrictions on references to past offences which are familiar in English criminal courts (but which are now, apparently, being eroded). It is evident from Cicero that a defence counsel had to be ready to fend off personal abuse of the defendant, as well as substantive allegations; and it can be difficult for a modern reader to take seriously Cicero's own protestations of the unimpeachable character of some of his clients. It is easy to get the impression that, in Roman courts, issues of general character were more important than the actual charges. Perhaps, however, the phenomena are better accounted for by supposing that the Roman courts were indeed interested in guilt and innocence, but that they regarded questions of general character as supremely relevant to deciding such issues. This corresponds fairly well with the plain man's view even today. The reason why the courts impose restrictions on the use of character arguments is not that they are popularly believed irrelevant, but that the lay men and women who sit on juries do think they are relevant and are therefore likely to be prejudiced by them.

Even if one allows for the above points, it can easily appear, by comparison with any sophisticated modern system, that the Roman lawcourt was something of a free-for-all. Yet the Romans themselves (if Cicero can be taken as representative) saw their system of *iudicia* as an essential part of the Republican system and an insurance against tyranny. The courts embodied the immemorial principle that a Roman citizen had the right to have his case heard by his fellow-citizens and could not be deprived of civil rights merely by the arbitrary decision of a magistrate. They were a valuable check on the government, since they afforded the only real opportunity to scrutinize a magistrate's actions after his term of office.[128] If the courts ever failed to function, it was always a sign that something was amiss with the Republic; and the orators and historians of the Empire, Quintilian, Pliny the Younger, and Tacitus,[129] looked back on the days of the Republican courts as a kind of golden age. But whatever opinion one holds of the Roman court system, one thing is certain: Cicero's speeches can only be understood in the context of the court system for which they were composed, a system which had very few if any restrictions on what the advocates on either side could say.[130]

---

[128] Caesar's crossing of the Rubicon was itself due to fear of prosecution in the courts: 'ego C. Caesar . . . condemnatus essem, nisi ab exercitu auxilium petissem'.

[129] See esp. Tac. *Dial.* 37 ff.   [130] Cf. Crook, *Legal Advocacy*, 17–18.

v. **Advocacy in Cicero's Career**

As a social class the wealthy landowners of Roman Italy were committed to a strongly developed ethic of public service for the benefit of their fellow-citizens. Just how compelling this social pressure could be is illustrated by the complaints made to Polybius by Scipio Aemilianus, one of Cicero's heroes from an earlier generation, who tried in the mid-second century BC to buck the trend (Polybius 31.23). The particular way in which Scipio found himself at odds with the Roman ethos was that 'I choose not to be an advocate in court'; he preferred to spend his time cutting a dash in the hunting field. Advocacy was just one means of voluntary service for the community, alongside the giving of legal advice in public consultations, the funding of major public works,[131] the holding of magistracies, and speaking in the senate and at public meetings, or service in the army. These activities were not mutually exclusive, and a Roman aristocrat could achieve prominence in a combination of them.[132] Cicero had little inclination for a military career, and, though clearly from a landowning family of substance, did not possess the sort of wealth which was required to make an impact as a major public donor. A career in public life with the holding of at least some of the magistracies and membership of the senate was very clearly part of Cicero's ambition and that of his family, but for a man like him from one of the towns of Central Italy, there was a need to become known more widely and win the popular favour which was essential to political success in Rome. Oratory was an obvious means of acquiring public recognition; and Cicero contends that the greatest admiration was reserved for appearances in court (*Off.* 2.49).

The choice between a career as an advocate and that of a legal expert is often taken to be a foregone conclusion for Cicero. Much of this stems from the debunking of the activities of jurists in Cicero's defence of Murena. Those who can't, become jurists!

It is not thought of as a difficult subject . . . So if you arouse my anger, despite being extremely busy, I will undertake to make myself a jurisconsult in three days . . . As they say of Greek musicians, those who cannot qualify to sing to the lyre, sing to the flute, so we see those who cannot succeed in becoming orators degenerate to the study of the law.[133]

---

[131] 'walls, dockyards, harbours, aqueducts, everything which is of service to the *res publica* . . . theatres, colonnades and new temples' were on the shopping lists of the great and the good (*Off.* 2.60).
[132] Compare the ethos of the British aristocracy in the 19th cent., who often drew comfort from Roman models. M. L. Bush, *The English Aristocracy: A Comparative Synthesis* (Manchester, 1984) and J. V. Beckett, *The Aristocracy in England 1660–1914* (Oxford, 1988).   [133] *Mur.* 28–29.

However, here is a single example of a point which will be made repeatedly in this volume; any statement by an advocate must be seen in the context of what he was trying to achieve in the speech. In this case Cicero's remarks are directed at one of Murena's prosecutors, Servius Sulpicius Rufus, who was both one of the leading legal experts of his day and had been defeated in the consular elections which occasioned the Murena trial. Elsewhere, in letters and other works, Cicero expresses his unstinting admiration for Servius Sulpicius' knowledge and expertise.[134] It was not true that specializing in giving legal *responsa* could not help to promote a public career, as Cicero argues (*Mur.* 28) ('consular dignity has never belonged to this profession and popular favour even less'). There were plenty of examples of jurisconsults who reached the consulship and even the censorship.[135] Cato the Elder was an obvious precedent for Cicero; it was claimed that his willingness to dispense legal advice to all he encountered formed the basis of his public career.[136] It would have been open to Cicero to combine advocacy with the delivery of legal opinions; the reason he gave for not doing so was that judicial opinions were time-consuming to produce and would have got in the way of the careful preparation which he devoted to his speeches.[137] Jurisprudence could be reserved for old age after an active career in the courts.[138] As we have seen above, Cicero had a good training in and knowledge of the law and was proud of it.

Cicero, then, decided to be an advocate. Training consisted in sitting at the feet of notable experts (in Cicero's case these included L. Licinius Crassus, M. Antonius, and Q. Mucius Scaevola (cf. *Off.* 1.200, *Lael.* 1), all of whom were among the key figures in Roman public life about the change of the century). Cicero would also attend the courts and listen to the speeches.[139] An advocate might expect to make his début in court in his late teens or early twenties. Q. Hortensius' first speech was at the age of 19, while Crassus' famous début in the case against Gaius Papirius Carbo came when he was 21, at a time when Cicero suggests young men were more usually winning applause for their rhetorical exercises.[140] Cicero was 25 when he appeared for Quinctius in 81 BC, where he acted as a substitute for a more experienced advocate who had initially undertaken the case.[141] His initiation may have been delayed a few years because the civil

---

[134] See *Fam.* 4.1–4, and numerous letters of commendation, *Fam.* 13.17–28a.

[135] See R. A. Bauman, *Lawyers in Republican Politics*, Münchener Beiträge zur Papyrusforschung und antiken Rechtsgeschichte 75. Heft (Munich, 1983) and B.W. Frier, *The Rise of the Roman Jurists: Studies in Cicero's Pro Caecina* (Princeton, 1985), 140 ff.   [136] Plutarch, *Cato Maior* 3.1–3.

[137] *Leg.* 1.12.   [138] *Leg.* 1.10; cf. L. Licinius Crassus in *De Or.* 1.199.

[139] *Brut.* 304 cf. Tacitus *Dial.* 34.7, 'oratorum discipulus, fori auditor, sectator iudiciorum'.

[140] On Hortensius: *Brut.* 229, 301, on Crassus: *Off.* 2.47, *Brut.* 158, cf. Quint. *Inst.* 12.6.1.

[141] *Quinct.* 3.

wars of the 80s had disrupted the court system and there were few, if any opportunities. In typical manner Cicero turned this to his advantage by declaring later that this enabled him to concentrate on his studies and 'to come fully trained to the Forum'.[142] From that moment on he was to be in constant demand in the courts, except for the times he was away from Rome. The life of an advocate consisted of 'flitting about the Forum, sticking around the courts and the praetors' tribunals, undertaking private cases of great importance and devoting oneself to cases before the centumviral court' (a court which dealt primarily with property issues), as Cicero vividly put it.[143] This busy life may well owe something to Sulla's extension of the system of *quaestiones*, which led to a huge increase in cases and hence the demand for *patroni*, as did the growing practice of using multiple speakers for the defence. There were also signs of increasing litigiousness among people, a readiness to resort to the courts to settle disputes.[144] Cicero noted that in the first two decades of the first century the courts had been dominated by half a dozen prominent advocates, but that in his day the number became much greater.[145]

As an advocate Cicero had to decide if and when to be willing to appear for the prosecution rather than the defence. The social values of the day made it possible in most cases to justify defending a client; indeed it has been argued earlier in this introduction that there was probably moral and social pressure on an advocate to take up most cases which were presented to him.[146] Prosecution was a different matter. In serious, capital cases, the outcome for the defendant could be loss of public status, property and career along with exile from Rome. Vigorous prosecution could be viewed as an unfriendly and unnecessary act.[147] A prosecutor could be viewed as 'durus' ('hard-hearted') and 'molestus' ('a pest'); a public career could be closed to them.[148] Nevertheless, appearing for the prosecution could be justified. One of the grounds which could be used throws a vivid light on life in Republican Rome. Some prosecutions were the pursuit of a vendetta between families ('ulciscendi'), as in the prosecution of C. Servilius by the two Luculli brothers because of Servilius' previous prosecution of their father.[149] But such cases were comparatively rare and hence noteworthy. The more usual justification offered for prosecution was *patrocinium* (patronage), particularly of oppressed provincials (the representation of

---

[142] *Brut.* 308–9, 311.   [143] *De Orat.* 1.173.

[144] The reasons for this are discussed by Frier, *Rise of the Roman Jurists*, 27 ff.   [145] *Brut.* 207.

[146] See above, § iii.   [147] Epstein, *Personal Enmity*, ch. 5.   [148] *Off.* 2.50.

[149] *Off.* 2.50, Plutarch, *Lucullus* 1.2, see also the cases cited by Cicero in *Div. in Caec.* 64. F. Hinard, '*Paternus inimicus*. Sur un expression de Cicéron', *Mélanges de littérature et d'épigraphie latines, d'histoire ancienne et d'archéologie: Hommages à la mémoire de Pierre Wuilleumier* (Paris, 1980), 202 ff.

non-citizens by patrons was specifically provided for in the extortion court legislation). There was also the vaguer claim that the prosecution was 'rei publicae causa' ('in the interest of the Republic'). It was a combination of these that Cicero uses to justify taking up the case against Verres.[150]

So far from avoiding prosecutions at all costs, it was felt that a spectacularly successful prosecution early in one's career, when one had less to lose in terms of established reputation, could be just what was needed. Cicero sought to explain the prosecution undertaken by M. Caelius of C. Antonius in 59 BC by citing the precedents of men, like Caelius, who in their youth sought recognition for their 'industria' by undertaking a spectacular accusation and went on to have the most distinguished careers.[151] The sort of people Cicero had in mind were likely to be L. Licinius Crassus, who prosecuted Carbo in 119 BC, P. Sulpicius Rufus' case against C. Norbanus in 95 BC, Julius Caesar's appearance as a prosecutor in 77 BC.[152] Cicero comments on the expectation that he might have launched his career in a similar way in his early speech in defence of Roscius of Ameria.[153] For him the opportunity for a spectacular prosecution came later in 70 BC with the case against Verres after a decade of establishing himself in the Forum. Cicero had much to lose and his first reaction (at least so he says) was to suggest to the Sicilian petitioners an alternative.[154]

For nearly two decades running up to his consulship in 63 BC Cicero was to be kept busy in the courts. There were breaks, as for example when he went as quaestor to Sicily (75 BC); more notably, his initial burst of activity led to the collapse of his health and he took the opportunity to escape to Greece to recuperate and to refine his rhetorical skills.[155] This serves to remind us that advocacy was a physically demanding activity.[156] Not for nothing are strong lungs and physical fitness among the requirements of a good orator.[157] In these early years among the cases which came his way were a notable cluster from the towns of Central Italy, some not far from Cicero's home in Arpinum.[158] These would help to confirm his role as a patron of such places, but because the cases all took place in Rome they helped to bring him to the notice of an audience in that city.

It is impossible to know how exceptional Cicero's commitment to the courts was in these years. When eventually he does appear on the *rostra* to deliver a political speech in support of Manilius' proposal on Pompey's command (66 BC), he felt it necessary to explain to people that his duties

---

[150] *Verr. I* 1.

[151] *Cael.* 73. Caelius more unusually was to go on to two more prominent prosecutions (*Brut.* 273, cf. Quint. *Inst.* 12.7.3, Apuleius, *Apol.* 66, *Pis.* 82 with Nisbet's note). [152] Tac. *Dial.* 34.7.

[153] *Rosc. Am.* 83. [154] *Div. in Caec.* 4. [155] *Brut.* 313.

[156] It can still be; see Pannick, *Advocates*, 30. [157] *De Or.* 1.114.

[158] On the importance of *vicinitas* see Ch. 3.

in the courts had kept him away from participating in public meetings until that moment.[159] Yet by this date Cicero had also risen to the praetorship, one step from the consulship. Cicero acknowledged that it was his appearances in court and the style of his oratory which had brought him to wide attention and formed the basis for his building popular support when he was standing for office.[160] Cicero may have seen the balance between his career at this stage in politics and his work as an advocate in much the same way as he described L. Licinius Crassus' career:

Throughout the period that his life was bound up in the hard work of campaigning for office, Crassus flourished more because of the personal services he rendered people [in court] and by the praise for his talent than by the benefits of high office or the esteem in which he was held by the Republic.[161]

Cicero continued to appear in court even when holding the consulship; advocacy was also a way of remaining in the public eye at times when one was not holding public office (cf. p. 5 above).

To accept that there is a connection between Cicero's life in the courts and his career in politics is not necessarily to concede one of the most influential interpretations of Roman public life of recent years, where it has been argued that criminal trials in the Roman Republic were essentially politics by other means.[162] So, it is claimed, the way that advocates and supporters lined up on either side in cases directly reflected their political stance and groupings. But this argument is often circular. Lacking independent evidence of political alliances, historians infer them from the side people were on in a case and the politics is then interpreted in the light of these supposed groupings, and in turn other cases in court are interpreted as reflecting these supposed political alliances. But it was always possible to justify appearing for the defence of a person whose politics one did not support.[163] In the second half of the 50s BC Cicero found himself defending both A. Gabinius and P. Vatinius, with both of whom he had quarrelled viciously and very publicly over the previous four years. Despite this, Cicero felt he had to appear for them because of the deep obligation he owed to Pompey.[164]

---

[159] *Leg. Man.* 1–2.

[160] *Brut.* 321. Indeed, Cicero argued that there was never disagreement between experts and the public over whether an orator was good or bad, precisely because the public could testify to the effects upon themselves of great oratory (*Brut.* 188–9).   [161] *De Or.* 3.7.

[162] 'To a surprisingly, perhaps alarmingly, large extent the business of politics was carried out not in the *comitia* or in the *curia*, but in the courts', E. S. Gruen, *Roman Politics and the Criminal Courts 149–78 B.C.* (Harvard, 1968), 6. Cf. Gruen, *Last Generation*, chs. 7 and 8.

[163] So M. Antonius justified his defence of the turbulent tribune, C. Norbanus, on the grounds that Norbanus had served in the army under his command and, hence, Antonius was under an obligation to come to his defence (*De Or.* 2.198).

[164] *Fam.* 1.9. On the defence of Gabinius see also above, n. 81.

In Rome as nowadays, many trials had a political dimension. Some of the alleged crimes were directly matters of public concern,[165] such as extortion, public violence, bribery and corruption (such were the cases of Verres, Cornelius, Sestius, Sulla, Milo, Ligarius, and King Deiotarus). Others took place against a background of political controversy which could be exploited or played down by the advocates to suit their purposes. So Cicero sought to depoliticize the case of Sextus Roscius of Ameria, which threatened to reopen recent wounds caused by the proscriptions.[166] On the other hand, the case against Verres came up at just the moment when there was a public debate about bribery and corruption of the juries and a proposal to change the membership of the juries. It suited Cicero to import that debate into his case by arguing that the jurors had one last chance to demonstrate their incorruptibility and concern for justice by finding Verres guilty.[167] Similarly Cicero imported the hysteria which he had largely created about Catiline into his defence of Murena in 63 BC by raising the spectre that a guilty verdict would lead to a rerun election for the consulship and the possible success of Catiline.[168]

Politics obtruded still more directly in Cicero's last major cases towards the end of his career. The speeches in defence of Q. Ligarius (46 BC) and Deiotarus, king of Galatia (45 BC) illustrate the way in which advocacy could adapt to the circumstances of dictatorship. Both Ligarius and Deiotarus were vulnerable because of their support for Pompey in the civil war. Cicero had already had to suffer the indignities of having to intercede with Caesar for him to permit Ligarius' return from exile.[169] At the moment when Caesar seemed about to grant the request, Ligarius was prosecuted in his absence by Q. Aelius Tubero, whose motive according to Cicero was a personal grudge. Caesar, exercising powers granted to him as Dictator, chose to hear the case himself in the Forum and to act as sole judge. Indeed, if there is any truth in an anecdote of Plutarch (*Caes.* 39.6–7), he was predisposed to find Ligarius guilty until he heard Cicero's speech. The outcome depended on the decision of one man who had a direct interest in the issue. This required new tactics by Cicero. Although Cicero suggested that he had a defence against the charges, in the second part of the speech he chose to plead directly for mercy from Caesar: 'I take refuge in your clemency, I seek mercy for the offence, I beg forgiveness.'[170] As Quintilian was to note,[171] this sort of plea for mercy

---

[165] A. Riggsby, *Crime and Community in Ciceronian Rome* (Austin, Tex., 1999) argues that the remit of the Roman *iudicia publica*, which we tend to translate as 'criminal courts', was not exactly 'crime' in any sense comparable to the modern one, but rather injury to the *res publica*. This is an interesting point, but the case is perhaps overstated; certainly a court like the *quaestio de sicariis et veneficis* dealt with matters that would today count as part of the criminal law.

[166] See Ch. 2.   [167] *Verr. I* 42 ff.   [168] *Mur.* 48 ff.   [169] *Fam.* 6.13 and 6.14.2.

[170] *Lig.* 30; see Ch. 14.   [171] *Inst.* 5.13.5.

(*deprecatio*) had little or no place in a normal court. Again the speech for Deiotarus, which was given in even more extreme circumstances before Caesar as sole judge but in private behind closed doors, had much the same flavour ('ignosce, ignosce, Caesar', 'forgive, forgive, Caesar').[172] The loss of liberty that came with political tyranny changed advocacy for the coming generations and illustrated once again the way in which the court and the arena of public affairs were intimately linked in Cicero's own life and career.

vi. Rhetoric, Argument, and Style

A large part of Cicero's success should no doubt be attributed to the fact that he was the first Roman orator to assimilate and ponder the theory of rhetoric in the fullest sense.[173] There can be little doubt that in this respect he was exceptional for his generation and, in a Roman context, original, at least as regards his synthesis of the different strands of Greek doctrine. A youthful work of his, the *De Inventione*, follows the standard rhetorical theory of its time in an intelligent enough manner; precocious though it may have been, this was 'Cicero's *Rhetoric*' for the Middle Ages and Renaissance. But his mature works on rhetoric–the *De Oratore*, the *Brutus*, the *Orator*, and the rather briefer *Topica* and *Partitiones Oratoriae*–display a much more broad-minded conception of what rhetoric is about, and offer the mature reflections of a senior advocate at, or after, the summit of his career.[174] Cicero's refusal to be pinned down to a merely technical notion of rhetoric, and his insistence that being an orator involves natural gifts, general intelligence and culture, and mastery of pretty well every subject and style of writing, can easily look like either a recipe for dilettantism or a manifestation of deep-seated vanity about his own accomplishment. Actually, he never suggests that he has attained the ideal, and he never underestimates the necessity for hard work. It is certainly plausible to argue that Cicero's mastery of rhetoric did, in practice, give him a clear advantage over many of his contemporaries and opponents.

But how useful are the rhetorical treatises of Cicero and others for the student of Cicero's speeches? Comparison of Cicero's practice with his own theory, and with that of others, is a long-standing academic exercise. The risk with this is that analysis after the event makes everything look

---

[172] *Deiotar.* 12

[173] Cf. D. H. Berry and Malcolm Heath, 'Oratory and Declamation', in Stanley E. Porter, *Handbook of Classical Rhetoric in the Hellenistic Period 330 B.C.–A.D. 400* (Leiden, 1997) 393–407; May, *Brill's Companion.*   [174] See May, *Brill's Companion*, chs. 11–15.

obvious and inevitable, particularly since Cicero's speeches themselves were in later generations (especially by Quintilian) taken as models of rhetorical practice, so that there is a substantial risk of circularity in the use of later rhetorical precept as a point of comparison. The real need is to understand how Cicero himself set about the process of *inventio* (finding the strategy, arguments, and lines of approach he needed) in any given case, and for this purpose, since we do not have Cicero's rough notes,[175] the only useful starting point is the speech itself, supplemented by whatever we can glean about its background from the ancient commentaries and other historical sources. However, the rhetorical treatises still at least provide a set of categories which may be useful in understanding Cicero's practice, as well as (in the case of the *De Oratore* in particular) a mine of relevant examples and anecdotes illustrating Cicero's conception of oratory and advocacy.

It has recently been argued[176] that ancient audiences (and particularly juries) would themselves have been trained in rhetoric, and would therefore have been able to spot any rhetorical techniques or tricks that an advocate such as Cicero might use. In view of the scarcity of detailed evidence as to the rhetorical accomplishments of Roman jurymen, especially during Cicero's early career when rhetorical training was not available except in Greek,[177] and in view of indications that the members of juries were not, after all, always very sophisticated[178] (not to mention the influence of the general public assembled in the *corona*, which Cicero acknowledges), this view can hardly be taken as proved. It might be objected that some of the fallacies in Cicero's speeches are too blatant to have escaped detection in this way; that might seem to be so from the point of view of a modern scholar, but it would be an acute juror indeed who could see the logical flaws in Cicero's arguments on a first hearing.

One is reminded, in this context, of the old anecdote of the juror at a country assize who, when asked whether Brougham or Scarlett was the better advocate, opted unhesitatingly for Brougham. It was then pointed out that the jury had, despite this, given all the verdicts to Scarlett; whereupon the juror answered: 'Of course; he gets all the easy cases' (or words to that effect).[179] The advocate's aim is not to be admired for his advocacy but to get verdicts; the gift of making cases seem easy is, for this purpose, more relevant than any amount of rhetorical brilliance. Cicero does this in

[175] Quintilian apparently did; *Inst.* 10.7.30–1; 4.1.69.

[176] J. E. G. Zetzel, reviewing C. P. Craig, *Form as Argument in Cicero's Speeches*, BMCR 4 (1993) 450–1.   [177] Cf. n. 43 above.

[178] Cf. e.g. Quint. *Inst.* 4.2.45, 12.10.53. The qualification to sit on the Republican juries was wealth, not culture or intelligence.

[179] M. Gilbert, *The Oxford Book of Legal Anecdotes* (Oxford, 1986) 273.

practice at least some of the time, though his inclinations were the other way; his saying about Scaurus (*Brutus* 111), that he had such natural authority when speaking that he sounded more like a witness than like an advocate, is not presented as unambiguous commendation.

The formal study of rhetoric among the Romans was still in its infancy in the early first century BC, and therefore Cicero took himself to Greece in search of rhetorical training, principally with Apollonius Molon of Rhodes. Furthermore, his studies in philosophy brought some aspects of Aristotelian and Stoic logic to his notice, which he (perhaps alone of his Roman contemporaries) perceived to be a rich source for the science of argumentation; he set out some of the fruits of these studies in the *Topica*,[180] a brief, neglected but fascinating work which applies Aristotelian theories of argument to the material of Roman law, while the dialectical procedures of division (cf. *Orator* 16) and dilemma figure much more largely in Cicero's practice than in the few sentences allotted to them in his rhetorical treatises (*Inv.* 1.44–5, 83–4; cf. *Rhet. Her.* 2.38–9; 4.52; Quint. *Inst.* 5.10.69).

Nor was this all that he derived from philosophy: his studies in the Academy had apparently involved the practice of debate on general issues, often on both sides in turn (*in utramque partem*). Cicero himself declared that he owed more to the Academy than to the rhetoricians, and we need not altogether disbelieve him.[181] We see the influence of these general debates especially in those passages which unsympathetic criticism can easily brand as digressions: on town and country in the *Pro Roscio*, on the rule of law in the *Pro Cluentio*, on the advantages of the military life in the *Pro Murena*, on the errors of youth in the *Pro Caelio*, on the unwritten law in the *Pro Milone*. These are 'commonplaces' (Gk. *koinoi topoi*, Lat. *loci communes*) in the original sense of that phrase (which started as a technical term of rhetoric), i.e. arguments on general points that can be adapted to a wide range of particular contexts, but they were not in the colloquial sense 'commonplace' or hackneyed in Cicero's time, and his treatment of them could have been highly effective in context as a means of disarming the opponent. It is often valuable for an advocate to get some measure of agreement and sympathy on matters that are not in dispute before proceeding to more contentious issues; though Cicero does not necessarily go as far in this regard as an English barrister who is on record as formally submitting to a court in 1845 that 'rain falls from time to time'.[182]

With these preliminary points out of the way, we shall proceed to a brief survey of the principles behind the composition of Cicero's speeches, with reference at each point to the ancient theory of rhetoric, as it was applied

---

[180] See the commentary by T. Reinhardt (Oxford, 2003).   [181] *Orator* 11.
[182] Serjeant Shee, quoted by Pannick, *Advocates*, 220.

to forensic oratory. This, the so-called *genus iudiciale*, was always regarded in practice by the rhetorical theorists as the most important and the most amenable to systematic analysis; the other two divisions of rhetoric, 'deliberative' (i.e., practically speaking, political) and 'epideictic' (speeches for particular occasions—festivals and funerals, etc.), need not concern us here. The techniques of rhetorical composition may be divided, following ancient theory, into three main areas, as follows:

(*a*) Structure (*dispositio*)
(*b*) Strategy (*inventio*)
(*c*) Style (*elocutio*)

The heading of 'strategy' may be divided further into the three Aristotelian categories of *logos* (argument), *ethos* (character-projection), and *pathos* (emotion).

Structure.   Rhetorical theory recommended a standard order of presentation, involving a division into *exordium* (opening section), *narratio* (narrative), *divisio* (setting out of headings for argumentation), *argumentatio* (the argument itself), *refutatio* (refutation of opposing points), *digressio* (digression: not of course mandatory, but this was the recommended place for one if there was to be one), and *peroratio* (peroration or conclusion).[183] All these are elements whose presence in a forensic speech is only to be expected. The order in which they appear is mostly a matter of simple common sense, designed above all to help the listener to follow the argument, and so too are Cicero's relatively frequent departures from the standard list of ingredients or from the standard order. The *Pro Caelio*, for example, needs no narration because the main facts at issue had already been dealt with by previous speakers. A prosecution speech often needs no distinction between narrative and argument, since the argument itself takes the form of a catalogue of misdeeds. In a defence speech it is usually not helpful to draw too sharp a distinction between *argumentatio* and *refutatio*, since defence speeches are by their very nature aimed at refuting allegations made by the prosecution. In the *Pro Cluentio*, Cicero produces a *divisio* into two sections right at the beginning, apparently reflecting a similar division in the prosecution case. Such variations are common; the standard order was merely a convenient formula, not a prescriptive rule. Cicero followed it most obviously of all in the *Pro Roscio*; it may be that, in his first major public trial at the beginning of his career, he adhered more closely to tried and tested rhetorical conventions than he was to do later on.

---

[183] The terminology varied somewhat; for more detail see H. Lausberg, *Handbook of Literary Rhetoric*, Eng. tr. M. T. Bliss, A. Jansen, and D. E. Orton; ed. D. E. Orton and R. D. Anderson (Leiden, 1998), 120 ff.

The conventional theory of rhetorical structure does, indeed, provide a handy terminology and method of analysis, and we have taken advantage of this by including chapters on narrations (Chapter 4), different elements of argumentation (Chapters 5–7), and perorations (Chapter 8). Nevertheless, as a number of our contributors also show, such analytical schemes can obscure the reality of advocacy. Advocacy is a process of persuasion, which takes place over time. An advocate cannot take for granted at the beginning that the tribunal will be sympathetic, and has to prepare the ground carefully. At the beginning of a speech,[184] he has first of all to establish his line of communication with the tribunal, and this may require not only that considerable attention should be paid to self-presentation (cf. Chapter 2), to flattery of the jury and sometimes to denigration of the opponent's motives, but may also require that the actual points at issue in the case should be initially misrepresented or obscured (it is regularly pointed out that the case is not what it seems, e.g. *Rosc. Am.*, *Cael.*, *Rab. Perd.*, *Flacc.*). Controversial or sensitive points may be made in a muted form at first, and then more openly as the advocate gains confidence; it is this, rather than a double recension of the written speech, which accounts (e.g.) for the apparent change in Cicero's attitude to Pompey in the *Pro Milone*.[185] Or the advocate may subtly plant ideas in the jury's mind, the relevance of which will only become clear later (as Quintilian pointed out).[186] The narration of the facts in a speech, as is only to be expected, is often biased in order to prepare the ground for later argumentation (cf. Chapter 4). Repetition, too, can be a vital element in the process of persuasion (cf. Chapter 10). There are limits to the extent to which Cicero's speeches will submit to the more mechanical kinds of structural analysis: the fact that in some cases several different, to all appearances equally plausible analyses can be put forward is a sure sign that the wrong question has been asked.

Argument. Both Cicero's speeches and his *De Inventione* show that, from the outset of his career, he was thoroughly at home with the rhetoricians' classification of issues (what the Greeks referred to as *staseis*; in Latin, *status*) and possible lines of argument. This formed a framework that would enable rhetoricians to be precise about what exactly it was that they were

---

[184] On exordia see Loutsch, *L'Exorde*, and S. M. Cerutti, *Cicero's Accretive Style: Rhetorical Strategies in the Exordia of the Judicial Speeches* (Lanham, Md., New York, and London, 1996).

[185] *Pace* A. M. Stone, 'Pro Milone: Cicero's Second Thoughts', *Antichthon* 14 (1980) 88–111, and D. Berry, 'Pompey's Legal Knowledge–or Lack of it: Cic. *Mil.* 70 and The Date of *Pro Milone*', *Historia* 42 (1993), 503–4. Of course the gain in confidence here may be to some extent an artefact of the written speech; we shall never know whether Cicero succeeded in making these points in court, or how, if he did, the listeners reacted to them.   [186] *Inst.* 10.1.21.

trying to argue–whether it was a question of fact (did X kill Y?), a question of law (does the law recognize this document as a valid will or not?), a question of interpretation or application (what do the words of the statute mean, and do they cover this case or not?), or a question of morality versus legality (Milo should be acquitted of the murder of Clodius because the act was beneficial to the community).

A still more distinctive feature of Cicero's advocacy is his constant use of argumentative structures derived from logic and dialectic, of which the most pervasive and spectacular is the dilemma.[187] For the present purpose, a short explanation of the dilemma form will serve as an introduction to this rather neglected, but absolutely essential feature of Cicero's oratory.

In modern colloquial usage, the word 'dilemma' often refers just to a situation in which there is a hard decision to be made. Technically, however, a dilemma is an argument of the following form:

Simple dilemma:
> *Either P or Q.*
> *If P, then X.*
> *If Q, then X.*
> *Therefore, in either case, X.*

Complex dilemma:
> *Either P or Q.*
> *If P, then X.*
> *If Q, then Y.*
> *Therefore, either X or Y.*

A dilemma has three premises and a conclusion. The first premise is *disjunctive*, in other words, it offers a choice between two alternatives. In order for the argument to work, the alternatives must exhaust the available possibilities: there must be no third alternative available. The second and third premises are *hypothetical*: in other words, they state what *would* be the case if either of the two stated alternatives were true. In a simple dilemma, the conclusions of the two hypotheticals are the same; and since we know from the first premise that either one or the other alternative must be true, we are given no choice but to accept the conclusion to which both alternatives lead.[188] A complex dilemma is one in which the two conclusions drawn are different, so that the argument ends with another disjunction which offers

---

[187] See C. P. Craig, *Form as Argument in Cicero's Speeches: A Study of Dilemma* (Atlanta 1993). For Cicero's studies in logic cf. *Brut.* 152, 309, *Orator* 113.

[188] There are also variations involving negative premises.

a choice between the two. Here is a well-known example from Cicero, which speaks for itself (*Cael.* 52, our translation):

As regards this accusation, this is my first question: whether he told Clodia for what purpose he was borrowing the money, or not. If he did not tell her, why did she give it to him? If he did tell her, she has involved herself in the guilt of being an accomplice to the crime . . . If he was as intimate with Clodia as you make out, when you say so much about his sexual appetites, of course he must have told her what he wanted the money for; but if he was not, then she cannot have given it to him. So then (*turning to address Clodia*) if Caelius told you the truth, you really have broken the bounds of decency: you knowingly gave him money for a criminal purpose. But if he did not dare to tell you what it was for, then you didn't give it to him after all.

Cicero thought of the dilemma as an invincible form of argument; certainly it served him well throughout his career, from the argument in the *Pro Roscio* (that if Roscius senior was proscribed, his killer cannot be convicted of murder, whereas if he was not proscribed, his property was sold illegally)[189] through the *Pro Caelio* and *Pro Cluentio*, to his successful two-pronged appeal to Caesar in the *Pro Ligario* (Chapter 14). Once one starts to look for dilemma structures in Cicero, they emerge everywhere. Sometimes several dilemmas are superimposed, producing an argument with multiple branches, as in *Pro Roscio Amerino* 73–8: did he do it himself or did he employ an agent? He can't have done it himself because he has an alibi. Who then was his agent? Was it a slave or a free man? If it was a free man, was he from Rome or from Ameria? If from Rome, when and where did Roscius meet him, since he had not been to Rome for many years? If from Ameria, who was it? What was the reward offered? And so on.

Ethos and pathos. By *ethos* Aristotle mostly meant the speaker's presentation of his own character (a Greek *logographos* had to be careful to ensure that the speech he wrote suited the character of the person who was to deliver it). In the world of the Roman advocate, *ethos* took on a more complex air: there was the advocate's own character, as well as that of the client, to consider; there was the opportunity for destruction of the credibility of the prosecutor or of a hostile witness; there were other persons, not necessarily present in court, whose characters bore on the case in some way and could be presented either favourably or unfavourably.[190] Recent research has explored particular aspects of ethos, such as ethnic stereotypes.[191]

[189] T. E. Kinsey, 'A Dilemma in the *Pro Roscio*', *Mnemosyne* 19 (1966) 270–1.

[190] On rhetorical ethos and pathos see Wisse, *Ethos and Pathos*; on character-projection in Cicero's speeches see J. M. May, *Trials of Character: The Eloquence of Ciceronian Ethos* (Chapel Hill, NC, and London, 1988); cf. also Ch. 6 on argument from past character as relevant to establishing guilt or innocence.

[191] Vasaly, *Representations*, 191–243 and C. Steel, *Cicero, Rhetoric, and Empire* (Oxford, 2002).

As for *pathos*, one need not labour the obvious: in the appeal to the emotions Cicero reigned supreme, and he excelled particularly in the final appeal to mercy, or *commiseratio*, which was such a regular feature of his perorations (see Chapter 8). Familiar images stick in the mind: of Caesar changing colour and dropping his papers while listening to the *Pro Ligario*, or of Milo standing unmoved while Cicero wept on his behalf to no avail. The prosecutor in the trial of Plancius attempted to make fun of Cicero's histrionics, but the attempt backfired: Cicero reproached him for frivolity over serious matters, and ended with an even more affecting and tearful peroration than usual. Even in Cicero's own time, therefore, there were opponents ready to accuse him of shedding crocodile tears; but the fashion of the time and place, and his own gifts as an advocate, were such that he was able to get away with it. One is reminded again of the great English advocate Sir Edward Marshall Hall, whose emotional appeals to juries were legendary.[192] But in the hands of a lesser practitioner, such a tactic could easily seem ludicrous.

Style. After *inventio* (the devising of arguments) and *dispositio* (structure and arrangement) the rhetoricians listed *elocutio*, which covers all aspects of the use of language: diction and vocabulary, figures of speech, sentence structure, and rhythm. Of the distinctive features of Cicero's style only a little needs to be said for the purposes of this book. In his youth he evidently learned much from the Greeks: E. Norden showed that his well-known rhythmical habits[193] were not original to him, but were to be found in the Greek rhetoric of the time, as exemplified by the inscription of Antiochus of Commagene. Naturally he studied the great Athenian orators, especially Demosthenes and Isocrates.[194] As already noted, Cicero's style developed over time, and he varied his style according to the occasion. Although his sentence structure is often elaborate (at least by modern standards), essentially he speaks ordinary Latin; a Republican lawcourt was not the place for poetically inflated diction or boldly original metaphors, as is shown by the parody of the grand style in the near-contemporary rhetorical treatise *Ad Herennium* (4.15). It is true that he has, at least in his grander moments, a predilection for rhetorical figures—parallelism, antithesis, chiasmus, tricolon, anaphora, collocations of synonyms, and so on; but this is a characteristic of oratory even in modern times.[195] These are not mere mechanical devices,

[192] Cf. Pannick, *Advocates*, 26.

[193] E. Norden, *Die Antike Kunstprosa*, 2nd edn. (Leipzig and Berlin, 1909) i.141–5; for a summary of the facts about prose rhythm see J. G. F. Powell in *OCD*³ s.v. 'prose-rhythm, Latin'.

[194] See A. Weische, *Ciceros Nachahmung der attischen Redner* (Heidelberg, 1972).

[195] For example, J. F. Kennedy's famous sentence 'Ask not what your country can do for you; ask what you can do for your country' displays antithesis, chiasmus, and anaphora, and even ends with the favourite Ciceronian cretic–trochee clausula: 'dō fŏr yōur cōuntrў'.

but effective means of articulating an argument or reinforcing a point. The degeneration of the technique is seen in Persius' description of the advocate who 'balances the charges in clean-shaven antitheses' and hopes only for applause, forgetting that his client's fate depends on him (*Satire* 1.79–91); but in Cicero, there is always a reason for the use of a rhetorical figure, however elaborate. For example, his fondness for antithesis largely grows out of his fondness for dilemma (cf. above, pp. 48–9).

Among the most effective weapons in an advocate's armoury are irony and humour.[196] Some kinds of humour may no doubt be inhibited by the tense atmosphere of a lawcourt, but ridicule of some sort is rarely absent from Cicero's speeches, and it always serves a purpose: one has only to think of the way he compares the prosecutor Erucius in the *Pro Roscio* to the geese that guarded the Capitol, the narration of the corrupt activities of Staienus et al. in the *Pro Cluentio*, the bath scene in the *Pro Caelio*, the sending up of Cato's Stoic philosophy in the *Pro Murena*, or (less well known but equally amusing) the taking apart of the words of the interdict in the *Pro Caecina*. Cicero's use of literary allusions and quotations, e.g. in the *Pro Caelio* or *Pro Archia*, has often attracted attention from literary scholars,[197] but in fact such instances are fairly unusual in the corpus of his speeches as a whole (as indeed Cicero admits in the last-mentioned speech).

A word should be added, finally, on the two remaining divisions of the ancient orator's art (besides strategy, structure, and style), which cannot be studied directly in the texts of the speeches, but can only be read about and imagined: *memoria* 'memory' and *actio* 'delivery'. The ability to conduct a case without excessive use of notes, still important in modern courts, was indispensable in the ancient world. Later Roman advocates referred to the process of preparing a case as *discere causam*–'learning the case'.[198] They were expected, in other words, to have the facts and the law at their fingertips, to be able to speak fluently and without stumbling, and to be able to adapt to the changing circumstances of the trial as it proceeded. Certain sections of a speech could be prepared more or less verbatim in advance (see next section), and memorized; but an orator had to appear to be speaking, not reciting from memory. The art of memory as applied to oratory was less a matter of remembering the words like an actor, than of remembering the substance of the arguments to be used and the order in which they were to be deployed; and for this purpose the ancient

---

[196] Cf. A. Corbeill, *Controlling Laughter: Political Humor in the Late Republic* (Princeton, 1996).
[197] Cf. K. Geffcken, *Comedy in the Pro Caelio*, Mnemosyne Suppl. 30 (Leiden, 1973).
[198] Quint. *Inst.* 12.8.

rhetoricians recommended a variety of mnemonic techniques, the favourite of which was to imagine oneself in a house, visiting each room in turn and finding the appropriate argument there. Indeed, it may have been this kind of imaginary procedure that gave rise to the technical use of the word *locus* 'place' (*topos* in Greek) to mean a 'topic' in argument.

Cicero's actual delivery we can only imagine, but it seems reasonable to suppose that it accounted for a large part of the persuasive effect. He himself is not above telling us about his own successes,[199] and there is no reason why he should not have been telling the truth; like many orators he could regard his own performances with a certain detachment. What we can be sure of is this: Cicero's delivery cannot have fallen short of what was necessary to win cases, in a world in which *actio* was often seen as all-important.

vii. The Publication of the Speeches

By Cicero's time it had long been customary for orators to circulate written versions of their speeches after the event; the corpus of the Attic orators provided a challenge to emulation (and sometimes detailed imitation) of a kind familiar from other areas of Roman literary activity, and Cicero had access to the written speeches (or what purported to be the written speeches) of a considerable number of his Roman predecessors. It seems most likely that Cicero's immediate impetus towards publication in general came from the need to make a name for himself and to gain esteem in the eyes of the literate Roman elite; we have seen that advocacy was a means of attracting attention and support in the competition for political advancement, and this could only be reinforced by the wider circulation of successful speeches.

The question of the reasons for publication has sometimes been looked in narrow or misleading terms. It has been common to emphasize political motives, and the published lawcourt speeches have often been regarded as almost equivalent to political pamphlets, intended to demonstrate and publicize support for a particular person or cause. This has been successfully argued against by W. Stroh,[200] who emphasizes instead the exemplary and didactic function: Cicero will have published his speeches (especially once he had become an established public figure) as examples of 'how to do it'. However, publication should be seen above all in its social context, and there could be several motives operating together. In the case

---

[199] e.g. *Orator* 102–8.   [200] Stroh, *Taxis und Taktik*, 50–52.

of successful speeches, Cicero will have wanted to advertise his triumphs, grateful clients may have wanted to be reminded of the eloquence of their *patronus* in their support, and the public (including fellow advocates and students of rhetoric) will have been curious to know exactly how Cicero pulled it off. There are two known instances of the publication of an unsuccessful speech: the early *Pro Vareno* (cf. p. 2, n. 4 above) and the *Pro Milone* (see below, p. 55).[201] Whether it was primarily the technique or the content of the speech that Cicero wanted to bring to the reading public's attention may well have varied from one instance to another, and this seems to be the kind of issue on which it is impossible to generalize; what can be said is that by publishing a speech Cicero laid it open to scrutiny, not only admiring but also potentially hostile.

It is often suggested nowadays that the content of the speeches was substantially 'doctored' before publication for political reasons, either by addition or by subtraction. There is, however, little or no positive evidence for this. Cicero always had the option of suppressing the speech entirely, and he often did so. In fact, the published forensic speeches are a minority of those he delivered in court, and there was evidently no automatic expectation that a speech would be published. Reasons for non-publication might vary.[202] In cases of lesser importance he might simply not bother to write the speech out for publication.[203] In some cases he might wish to dissociate himself from a cause he had just successfully pleaded, or he might be concerned to avoid further offence to the opponents and their associates, especially in connection with his rare appearances for the prosecution. The circulation of a speech could evidently be taken as reinforcement of the position taken in it. But it is not clear that any useful purpose would have been served by circulating a version with a substantially altered line of argument: too many people would have heard the real thing.

The question of the relation between Cicero's speeches as delivered and the published versions was already controversial in antiquity. Quintilian (*Inst.* 12.10.54) attempts to solve it by means of the argument that if the

---

[201] Though it is likely that, apart from these two instances, Cicero's published speeches were successful, one cannot merely assume success from the fact of publication. There might have been reasons for publishing a failed speech, such as the desire to save one's credit as an advocate or to raise public support for the rehabilitation of a convicted defendant; and it must always be remembered that written versions of speeches could be circulated without their author's consent (as e.g. in the case of the senatorial speech *In Clodium et Curionem: Att.* 3.12.12; 3.15.3). It is interesting in this connection to compare the Athenian evidence; there are quite a few unsuccessful speeches in the corpus of Attic orators, especially in cases where the speeches on both sides were preserved; see L. Rubinstein in G. Thür and F. J. Fernández Nieto (eds.), *Symposion 1999: Vorträge zur griechischen und hellenistischen Rechtsgeschichte* (Cologne, Weimar, and Vienna, 2003) 193.

[202] See the useful discussion by Jane W. Crawford, *M. Tullius Cicero: The Lost and Unpublished Orations*, Hypomnemata 80 (Göttingen, 1984) 3–21.

[203] Compare his studied and ironical modesty about the *Pro Rege Deiotaro* in *Fam.* 9.12.2.

written speeches are better than the spoken ones, Cicero should have spoken as he wrote; if the spoken ones were better, he should have written as he spoke. Such an argument may be thought superficial, but it does in fact prove one crucial point: Quintilian judged the written speeches by the same standards as he would have judged the spoken ones, i.e. those of practical forensic oratory. And if Quintilian judged them that way, it is likely that other readers of Cicero would have done so too. Hence it is unlikely that Cicero would have inserted anything into a published version which would have been either impermissible or ineffective in a real speech. This is important, because scholars have been keen to identify sections of the speeches which must allegedly be later additions for precisely those reasons. The fact is that we moderns are not entitled to rely on our prejudices as to what would or would not have worked in a Roman court. Far better to take the speeches themselves, as we have them, as evidence for what was probably said, and attempt to explain that as a deliberate persuasive strategy rather than as the result of incompetent rewriting.

We know that there was a process of 'writing up', not very different, perhaps, from the way in which modern academic papers are prepared for publication (parliamentary or forensic speeches are of course a different matter nowadays, because there is a verbatim record). Only once (in a senatorial, not a forensic context: the *Post Reditum in Senatu*)[204] did Cicero read a whole speech from a pre-prepared script. Otherwise, as Quintilian (*Inst.* 10.7.30) notes, he wrote out only the beginnings and the ends beforehand; the intervening sections would be prepared only in note form. Subsequently, Cicero would 'write up' (*conficere*) the speech on the basis of his notes and, of course, of his memory (more or less fresh) of the actual occasion; the process is referred to in (among other passages) *Tusc.* 4.55, *Cato Maior* 38, *Brutus* 91. The part played by memory should not be underestimated; as already noted, techniques of cultivating the memory were an important part of ancient rhetorical training. An advocate had not only to master the facts of the case but also plan his arguments (and some of the phrasing) in detail; and the powers of memory that enabled him to do this would also serve him in recalling any changes of tactic or improvisations that had taken place during the trial itself.

From Cicero's own *Brutus* (164), from Asconius' commentary on the lost speech *Pro Cornelio* (*In Cornelianam* 62 C.), and from a letter of Pliny (1.20), we learn that much was left out of the published versions; and the information can be corroborated from a glance at the text of the *Pro Caelio* (sect. 19) and *Pro Murena* (sect. 57), where the omission of sections is indicated by headings. This is hardly surprising: the full transcripts of

---

[204] As shown by *Planc.* 74.

proceedings in court which are nowadays published are often virtually unreadable except to legal specialists. A letter to Atticus (1.13.5) suggests that additions could be made in the published version, but this refers to a political speech, not a forensic one; in *Att.* 13.20.2 Cicero declines to make an addition to the text of the *Pro Ligario*.

The *Pro Milone* is a special case, not only because it was one of Cicero's failures, but also because a transcript of Cicero's actual performance was alleged to have survived alongside the published version.[205] Asconius' account of the trial suggests that Cicero suffered an unusual amount of interruption on that occasion (and according to the Scholia Bobiensia, the transcript reflected this).[206] Plutarch and Dio Cassius suggest that he failed to get through his speech, but as we have noted, they are probably drawing on a tradition hostile to Cicero.[207] But the puzzle remains as to why Cicero should have published this unsuccessful speech. Anti-Ciceronians, both ancient and modern, have a ready answer: Cicero was proud of the published version, although he had not, on the common view, managed to deliver it. Inevitably Dio's anecdote is quoted, about Cicero sending a copy of the finished version to the exiled Milo in Marseilles. But the anecdote is unattested earlier, and it is difficult to know what source Dio could have had for it; it is appropriate only to the historian's caricature of Cicero as a pathetic, conceited, and tactless figure; and Milo's wry reply, at least in the form in which Dio gives it, presupposes the popular version of the story, that Cicero had failed to deliver the speech at all–which is refuted by the account in Asconius. The more likely explanation of the publication of the *Pro Milone* is that an unauthorised transcript of the speech had somehow got into circulation, and that Cicero published his own version (perhaps contrary to his original intention) as a corrective. If this was his purpose, he can hardly have diverged too far from the line of defence he adopted at the trial itself.[208]

[205] Asc. *In Milonianam* 41–2; Quint. *Inst.* 4.3.17; Schol. Bob. pp. 112 and 173; Stangl. J. N. Settle, 'The Trial of Milo', *TAPA* 94 (1963) 268–80, in an otherwise illuminating article, suggests on inadequate grounds that the alleged transcript was a forgery by Cicero's opponents; but it is more likely to have been merely unauthorized and inaccurate. See now A. Dyck, *Philol.* 146 (2002) 182–5. Much the same thing may have happened as is attested later by Quintilian, *Inst.* 7.2.24: 'The other speeches circulating under my name, corrupted as they are by the negligence of the shorthand-writers who took them down to make money, have very little of me in them' (Russell's tr.).

[206] The surviving fragment (ap. Quint. *Inst.* 9.2.54 and Schol. Bob. 173 Stangl) is not to be taken as an example of Cicero being put off his stroke, tempting though it may be: Quintilian quotes it (without attribution) as an example of the deliberate rhetorical technique of *aposiopesis*, a model to follow (with a parallel from Demosthenes) and not a warning of what to avoid.

[207] Plutarch, *Cicero* 35; Dio 40.54. Cf. also p. 6, n. 24 above.

[208] Cf. B. A. Marshall, *A Historical Commentary on Asconius* (Columbia, Mo., 1985) 190–1 and id., 'Excepta oratio, the other *Pro Milone* and The Question of Shorthand', *Latomus* 46 (1987) 730–6. Humbert, *Les Plaidoyers*, suggested that the argument of the spoken *Pro Milone* must have been different to some extent from the written one, but he places too much stress on the reference to *tota oratio* in Asconius.

The other standard example of an undelivered lawcourt speech[209] is the second *Actio* against Verres. Relying mostly on the late account in the Scholia Bobiensia, received scholarly opinion has it that not a word of this was ever spoken in court. However, the scholiast represents only the received opinion of the fifth century AD, and the tradition on which he draws, though detailed, may in some respects have given rise to unreliable inferences. We cannot attach much credence to the version in Plutarch, according to which Cicero compelled a vote at the end of the first *actio*: this would hardly have been possible within the procedure of the *repetundae* court. Pliny (*Ep.* 1.20.10) refers to *Verr. II* 4 as a speech which was known to be 'only published', i.e. not delivered, hence the tradition of non-delivery was established by his time; but in the same generation Tacitus in the *Dialogus* seems to assume that the whole of the five-part second *actio* was delivered before a court, since he makes a character comment that no judge would sit through such a long speech nowadays. The question of whether there could theoretically have been a second hearing depends on the number of available days in the calendar, which Cicero himself has a rhetorical interest in minimizing; a more precise calculation may reveal that (as Plutarch failed to see) there were some days available. Whether there actually was a second hearing depends on the precise point at which Verres withdrew into exile; we should not necessarily assume that he never reappeared in court after his absence on the third day of the first hearing, and there is conflicting evidence about the way his defence was, or was not, conducted.[210] All in all, we cannot be certain that the published second *actio* does not reflect actual court proceedings more closely than has usually been thought.[211]

The best treatment of the general question in modern times is still that of J. Humbert.[212] His book, more often cited than read, is often misrepresented as arguing for wholesale revision. In fact, Humbert supports the view that the differences between the two versions of the *Pro Milone* must have been largely stylistic, and on *Pro Cluentio* he concludes 'le plaidoyer

---

[209] One speech in five sections, not five speeches. I omit discussion of the *Second Philippic* which was the text of a speech intended to be delivered in the Senate.

[210] See M. Alexander, 'Hortensius' speech in Defense of Verres', *Phoenix* 30 (1976) 46–53.

[211] Not all scholars are comfortable with the common idea that the whole second *actio* is a fiction; it is often accepted that it incorporates a good deal of the evidence for the prosecution which was presented in the first hearing; see now S. Butler, *The Hand of Cicero* (London, 2002). A not altogether successful attempt was made to argue for the possibility that the second hearing did actually take place by C. Höeg, 'The Second Pleading of the Verres Trial' in *ΔΡΑΓΜΑ Martino P. Nilsson . . . dedicatum* (Stockholm, 1939) 264–79. The question remains open. On this point J.G.F.P. is indebted to discussions with Miss Kathryn Tempest.

[212] Humbert, *Les Plaidoyers*, see esp. pp. 7 and 115. See also Stroh, *Taxis und Taktik*, 31–54; the differences between the positions of Humbert and Stroh are not as great as usually made out.

écrit reproduit fidèlement la marche de la plaidoirie réelle'. Of the notion that the speeches were largely reworked after the event for political reasons, there is little or no sign either in the evidence or in Humbert's discussion: Humbert is concerned largely with court procedure and the way it is represented, or fails to be represented, in the speeches as published.

It seems, then, not unreasonable to conclude after all that the published versions of most of Cicero's speeches do reflect, more or less, the lines of argument he adopted at the trials, and–at least as regards the beginnings and ends of the speeches, which he wrote out beforehand–the style and mode of expression as well. The speeches are not, nor do they claim to be, an exact record of proceedings in court. They omit some things which were said, and doubtless add some things which were not said, though probably nothing that was seriously out of line with the original argument. They contain no record of altercations or interruptions or cross-examinations of witnesses, and they probably amalgamate points which may have been made at different stages of the trial. But, equally, they are not mere fictional compositions written after the event. They purport to be the speeches that Cicero delivered. Treated (as was the practice of antiquity) as scripts for performance,[213] they would provide a plausible reconstruction of Cicero's pleading on each particular occasion, and there is certainly no reason why we cannot take them generically as evidence for the kinds of strategies, arguments and rhetorical techniques that Cicero would have employed in an actual court. For an advocate advertising his successes to future clients and pupils, it would make no sense to indulge in radical falsification.

It remains only to add that the speeches, once published, became standard examples of oratory–as doubtless their author wished–and that they have been in continuous circulation from that time until the present day.[214]

[213] Cf. R. G. M. Nisbet, 'The Orator and the Reader: Manipulation and Response in Cicero's Fifth Verrine', in A. J. Woodman and J. G. F. Powell (eds.) *Author and Audience in Latin Literature* (Cambridge, 1992) 1–17.

[214] On the long story of the transmission of the text of the speeches, see R. H. Rouse and M. D. Reeve, 'Cicero's Speeches', in *Texts and Transmission*, ed. L. D. Reynolds (Oxford, 1983) 54–98.

PART I

THEMES

I

Legal Procedure in Cicero's Time

ANDREW LINTOTT

i. Public and Private Law

Cicero's legal cases ranged from treason, murder, and 'public violence' to disputes about property and debt. Modern Western systems of justice differentiate criminal law from civil law in a number of ways. First, the source of the prosecution: in criminal law now a representative of the state prosecutes, in civil law the injured party or someone representing them; correspondingly, in criminal cases judgement is given in favour of the state, if the prosecution succeeds, and for the most part the penalty is paid to the state, while in civil law (leaving aside matters like costs and contempt of court) the judgement is in favour of the plaintiff in the form of compensation. Furthermore, different courts and different procedure are used for the two types of case.

In late Republican Rome, if we leave out the summary justice that seems to have been meted out by the *triumvir capitalis* to persons of inferior status, criminal prosecutions took place either before an assembly of the people with a magistrate prosecuting, or in a *quaestio perpetua*, that is, a jury-court established by statute and presided over by a magistrate with (after 70 BC) about 50–75 jurors. In the latter, prosecution was usually open to any citizen who wished and indeed, for a period in the 'extortion' or recovery court (*quaestio de repetundis*), to non-citizens. Private actions, however, were characterized by a divided procedure. Plaintiffs first had to bring their opponents before the praetor and there they either established an action with his consent by acting out a ritual dialogue or asked him for an action embodied in a *formula*. The latter began by the nomination of a judge or judges and went on to specify what had to be proved for the plaintiff's claim to succeed. The matter then passed to the nominated judge or judges, who heard the evidence and came to a decision in response to the ritualized claim or the *formula* that had been given.

Though the Romans had strikingly different procedures for civil or private cases and for criminal cases, they did not draw the line between the two types of case where we do now. Theft, for example, was treated as a private wrong to be pursued by civil action, as were assault, battery, and personal affront until Sulla's *lex de iniuriis*, except when these were undertaken by a Roman in authority at the expense of those subject to him.

ii. The Prosecutors and the Location of Courts

Modern distinguishing criteria are inappropriate in other ways. Republican Rome had no public prosecutor or prosecuting service. In trials before assemblies magistrates prosecuted. Otherwise, accusations in criminal cases were undertaken by injured parties and their representatives or, where the law allowed prosecution by anyone who wished to do so on behalf of either another party or the *populus Romanus*, by other private citizens. These would have rarely acted through pure altruism, but sought also to advance their career or to help their friends and harm their enemies by the prosecution. These motives would also be found among those appearing for the defence. Speakers in court were in this respect amateurs, and theoretically in another respect too. Although certain statutes provided for rewards for successful prosecution in the form of money or civic privilege, in general advocates were not supposed to be paid for their trouble. A *lex Cincia*, passed in the latter part of the Second Punic War, had strictly limited gifts between clients and patrons in general, apparently including a clause forbidding payment for advocacy.[1] However, grateful clients found ways of expressing their gratitude. A classic example was the loan Cicero received from his client Publius Sulla, which enabled him to buy his Palatine house.[2] A particular feature of the advocacy of Cicero and his contemporaries was the political dimension. Frequently, the cases themselves were political, being concerned with treason, electoral bribery, or something similar. On other occasions the offence may not have been political, but those involved were politically significant, as when Sextius Roscius was accused of parricide by a combination of fervent Sullan partisans. Even when there was nothing of this kind, the advocate's activity might yield political dividends by securing the future support of a particular individual or group.[3]

The courts of the Roman Republic differ from those with which we are familiar in another respect, whose importance must have been considerable but is very hard to assess–their location. This was not even the forensic milieu of the younger Pliny, who pleaded private centumviral cases under

---

[1] Cic. *Att.* 1.20.7; *Sen.* 10 (dating it to 204 BC); *De Or.* 2.286; M. Crawford (ed.), *Roman Statutes, BICS* Suppl. 64 (London, 1996) ii.741–4; *MRR* i.307.   [2] Gell. 12.12.2–4.
[3] See e.g. *Comm. Pet.* 19–29; 50–1.

the roof of the *basilica Iulia* and criminal cases in the Senate or perhaps some audience-chamber of an imperial palace or villa.[4] Criminal cases were heard in the open Forum, whether it was a magistrate prosecuting before an assembly or it was a session of one of the specially created criminal courts (*quaestiones perpetuae*). The first part of private procedure likewise took place in the Forum before the tribunal of the appropriate praetor and the subsequent hearing by a judge or jury of *recuperatores* might do so. A tribunal was simply a small platform, either permanent in stone or cement, or wooden and portable, on which the magistrate sat in his curule chair, assisted by one or two attendants.[5] This was enough in itself to establish a court, though it was supplemented by benches (*subsellia*) for the jurors, the parties to the case, and their supporters. The circle of onlookers (*corona*) either stood around or sat on something convenient, such as the Aurelian steps (whatever these exactly were) at the south-east end of the Forum.[6]

We have sufficient literary evidence to conclude that the tribunal of the chief civil magistrate, the urban praetor, was originally in the *comitium* (the small assembly area outside the senate-house) but by Cicero's time had been moved to the south-east end of the Forum near the Regia.[7] There has been speculation about the position of other tribunals, but the evidence is too unsatisfactory. It is not even certain that the tribunal used for a particular *quaestio perpetua* was always in the same place. One very probable site of one of the tribunals is the rectangular gap in the late Republican paving, which has now been converted into the 'garden' (with a fig, vine and olive).[8] A little can be deduced from Ciceronian texts about the internal layout of the court. Prosecution and defence with their respective groups of witnesses had separate seating.[9] The speaker would have stood facing the magistrate and the jury with his client behind him. The orator Caepasius, defending Oppianicus' friend Fabricius in 74 BC, called on the jury to pay due regard to (*respicite*) the fortunes and vicissitudes of human life and to the old age of Fabricius. After repeating '*respicite*' several times,

---

[4] See *Ep.* 5.9 for Pliny preparing to plead in the *basilica Iulia.*; 6.31 for his acting as Trajan's assessor in the imperial villa at Centumcellae (the 'Bagni di Traiano' at Civitavecchia).

[5] J.-M. David, *Le Patronat judiciaire au dernier siècle de la république romaine*, BEFAR 277 (Rome, 1992) 16–18, 410 ff., 464 ff.; figs. 1–8.

[6] See esp. *Clu.* 93; *Flacc.* 66, and, for the other evidence F. Coarelli, *Il foro romano: periodo repubblicano e augusteo* (Rome, 1985) 190 ff. His argument from the phrase 'built as if for a theatre' in the *Pro Cluentio* passage, however, that the *gradus Aurelii* were built specifically as an auditorium for court proceedings is insecure. Moreover, the court proceedings here are not a *repetundae* case nor even a *quaestio*, but a tribunician pursuit of a fine before an assembly. The case in *Pro Flacco* is *repetundae*, but the passage implies the prosecutor had a choice of venue.

[7] F. Coarelli, *Il foro romano: periodo repubblicano e augusteo* (Rome, 1985) 22 ff.; 166 ff.

[8] A. Claridge, *Rome: An Oxford Archaeological Guide* (Oxford, 1998) 72, 85, following C. F. Giuliani and P. Verduchi, *L'area centrale del foro romano* (Florence, 1987). The plan in David, *Le Patronat*, 44–5 is highly conjectural and over-schematic. [9] *Rosc. Am.* 104; *Flacc.* 22; *Q.Fr.* 2.4.1; *Fam.* 8.8.1.

'*respexit ipse*', he looked back himself and saw that his client had slipped away from the benches behind him.[10] The members of a jury of a *quaestio perpetua*, if bored, might walk about, chat with each other or in groups, send a slave to find out the time, or ask the president of the court for an adjournment. All this implies that the jurors had space in which to move and that the court covered a considerable area. Cicero suggests that the clipped and restrained speech of the 'Atticists' cannot command the attention of a *quaestio* audience: it would be more suitable for a praetor standing close by in the *comitium* than the occupants of the benches of a court.[11] The proceedings of the court could also be monitored from a greater distance by those on the balconies (*maeniana*) over the external porticoes of the basilicas at the side of the forum. Licinius Macer is said to have committed suicide there when he saw Cicero taking off his *toga praetexta* and realized that he was about to condemn him.[12]

As for the proceedings in private cases before a single judge (*apud iudicem*), Vitruvius in the Augustan period, when discussing the provision of public rooms in private houses, mentions the construction for nobles who hold magistracies of 'libraries and basilicas, appointed with a magnificence like those of public works, since in their homes public deliberations and private trials and arbitrations are often carried out'.[13] This is a grander style of living than would have been possible for many judges living in the cramped centre of Rome under the Republic, but the principle of holding private trials in the *iudex*'s home need not be doubted. However, this would not have applied to the deliberations of the centumviral court, and in other private cases the judge might have sought the space the Forum could provide. The imperial municipal law from Irni, which based itself on the provisions of Augustus' *lex Iulia de iudiciis privatis*, talks of 'judging in the Forum or where they agree'.[14]

iii. Civil Procedure

The first requirement was to get your opponent into court. 'If (someone) summons before the praetor (*in ius*), the man is to go. If he does not go,

---

[10] *Clu.* 58–9.

[11] *Brut.* 200, 289. I take *iudex* in the latter passage in its occasional sense of 'judicial magistrate'. We find it as a synonym for 'praetor' in the epigraphic *lex repetundarum* (lines 62–3, 79); Cicero himself offers it as an alternative to consul (*Leg.* 3.8). A civil judge would have been unlikely to hear a case in the *comitium*. This passage would then imply that the *comitium* was still used for preliminary proceedings.   [12] Val. Max. 9.12.7.

[13] Vitr. 6.5.2.

[14] *Lex Irnitana* (J. Gonzalez, *JRS* 76 (1986) 147 ff.), ch. 91, tablet XB, lines 12–13.

(the summoner) is to call to witness, then he is to take him. If he delays or drags his feet, he is to lay a hand on him.'[15] Such were the fundamental provisions for summons at the beginning of the Twelve Tables. Against recalcitrants one was permitted to use force, though this would not be effective with a more wealthy and powerful opponent; more generally, the sanction of social pressure was critical. Hence the calling to witness, which enabled Horace on one occasion to revenge himself on a bore by becoming a witness, when the latter was swept by his opponent before the praetor.[16] Even if your opponent was cooperative, once Rome had ceased to be a small face-to-face society, there was a problem in getting him to the forum at a convenient time so that the approach to the praetor could be made. This was solved by *vadimonia*, that is, promises made by the defendant to appear in the forum on a certain day at a certain time, secured by a solemn guarantee (*sponsio*) to pay a sum of money if he failed to appear (the sum was a matter of form and not the full value of the suit). We have now written records from Pompeii and Herculaneum of *vadimonia* being made in the first century AD and further records of the defendants' appearance in accordance with them.[17] One of the major issues in Cicero's defence of P. Quinctius was whether the latter had given a *vadimonium* for appearance and then welshed on it. Cicero maintains, not entirely convincingly, that Quinctius did not make the *vadimonium*, as he was away at the time, and so it was improper for the praetor Burrienus to have awarded Naevius possession of Quinctius' property on account of his failure to appear.[18]

The primary division of civil procedure into that before the praetor (*in iure*) and that before the judge (*apud iudicem*) and the different ways of setting an action in motion before the praetor have already been briefly mentioned. When undermining the credibility of the prosecutor Sulpicius Rufus in his defence of Murena Cicero makes fun of the ritual dialogue used in the *legis actio sacramento in rem*, the procedure used to claim property by solemn wager, with its 'whence you have called me from before the praetor to engage by hand, thence there I call you back', and its walking to and fro. Nevertheless, in the *De Oratore* he treats it as one of two regular ways by which property can be recovered (the other being to exploit an interdict, on which see below).[19] In fact proceedings before the *centumviri*,

---

[15] Twelve Tables (Crawford, *Roman Statutes*, ii, no. 40) I.1.   [16] Hor. *Sat.* 1.9.74–8.

[17] L. Bove, *Documenti processuali dalle Tabulae Pompeianae di Murecine* (Naples, 1979), 21–71; G. Camodeca, *L'Archivio Puteolano dei Sulpicii* (Naples, 1992), nos. 1–21; G. Pugliese Carratelli, 'Tabulae Herculanenses II', *PP* 3 (1948) 165–84, nos. XIII–XV.

[18] *Quinct.* 22–5, 52–9. For a legal requirement to provide *vadimonia* in certain circumstances see *lex agraria* (Crawford, *Roman Statutes*, no. 2), lines 34, 36; *lex Rubria de Gallia Cisalpina* (ibid. no. 28), ch. XXI, col. II, lines 21–4.

[19] *Mur.* 26–7; *De Or.* 1.41; cf. XII tab. I.11 = II.1 (Crawford, *Roman Statutes*, ii, no. 40, pp. 597–602).

the most grand and solemn civil court, could only be initiated by a *legis actio sacramento*, as Cicero would have known full well, and Cicero himself had used this procedure in his youth before another long-established panel of judges, the *decemviri stlitibus iudicandis*, when acting successfully for a woman from Arretium whose free status had been challenged.[20]

However, the usual way to set up a private lawsuit in Cicero's day was by asking the praetor for a *formula*. 'The matter at stake concerns a solemn promise (*sponsio*). Let Gaius Blossius Celadus be the *iudex*. If it appears that Gaius Marcius Saturninus ought to give Gaius Sulpicius Cinnamus (?)6,000 sesterces, which is the matter at stake, let the *iudex* C. Blossius Celadus condemn C. Marcius Saturninus to C. Sulpicius Cinnamus for 6,000 sesterces. If it does not appear, let him acquit him.' So runs a later formula found on a Pompeian tablet, laying down action for a fixed sum of money. The same sort of action was brought by C. Fannius Chaerea against Cicero's client Q. Roscius.[21] This simple action and others, for example those based on the *legis actiones sacramento* or those resulting from other *sponsiones*, were adaptations of actions that had originally been laid down in statute (*legitimae*). Other actions by *formula* had also been created by successive praetors, however—how exactly they acquired, or decided that they possessed, the right to develop the law without reference to the assembly, is still a matter of debate.[22] One important group was the actions based on *bona fides*, arising from the 'consensual' contracts, that is, those made purely *consensu*, such as buying and selling or letting and hiring (*emptio-venditio*, *locatio-conductio*) and the action over partnership, which seems to have been originally used between Naevius and Quinctius.[23] A second was *actiones in factum*, actions specifically created by the praetor to remedy an unjust state of affairs that did not fit into any other legal pigeon-hole. Such was the action created by M. Terentius Varro Lucullus in 76 BC to deal with the loss caused by gangs of armed slaves, which formed the basis of the suit by Cicero's client Tullius in 71.[24]

Finally, we should mention the actions consequent on the praetorian interdicts. The latter were orders or injunctions issued by the praetor on request, for example that confirming possession (*uti possidetis*) or that requiring restitution of someone improperly expelled by force (*unde vi*). These interdicts usually had clauses excepting possession that was defective on various grounds—if it had been obtained by force, by stealth, or on sufferance. If the interdict were complied with, there was obviously no action; if it were disobeyed, the injured party would stipulate that his

[20] Gai. 4.31,95; cf. *De Or.* 1.173; *Caec.* 96–7.
[21] Bove, *Documenti,* 106 (*Tab. Pomp.* 34); *Rosc. Com.* 10–11.
[22] A. Watson, *Law-Making in the Later Roman Republic* (Oxford, 1974), 31 ff.
[23] *Quinct.* 21–2.   [24] *Tull.* 7–11.

opponent should make a solemn promise to pay a certain sum of money, if he had disobeyed the interdict. The cases went to *recuperatores*. If successful, the plaintiff won his money, but more importantly had proved his point, i.e. that he was the rightful possessor of his property and the interdict was valid for him. This could, if necessary be the basis of a further action, if his adversary refused to concede the point. It will be seen, however, that an interdict might be not so much a way of blocking an injustice as a convenient way of creating a lawsuit in which the right to possess the property might be settled. So one party in a dispute over possession might get an interdict in his favour and arrange for his opponent to violate it formally by expelling him from the property in question.[25] This, according to Cicero, is the context of his speech for Caecina: the latter had agreed to be expelled formally from property whose ownership he had been disputing with Aebutius, but in practice the property had been occupied by armed slaves and it was only by braving weapons and threats of death that Caecina had been able to reach the place from which he was to be expelled by agreement. He then sued Aebutius, not under the normal interdict *unde vi*, but under the interdict *de vi armata*, concerning expulsions from property by armed gangs, in which there were no exceptions about defective possession (except the prior use by the plaintiff of armed gangs to acquire the property).[26]

Originally, it seems that procedure *in iure* was only separated from that before the judge or judges by the interval of a clear day (*perendinum*). Later, a 30-day interval was introduced for some cases at least by the *lex Pinaria*. In Cicero's day the rules may have been similar to those prescribed by Augustus' *lex Iulia de vi privata*, now known to us through the *lex Irnitana* (chs.90–2), whereby this interval, called *intertium*, might in fact have been much longer than the third day (the day after tomorrow).[27] It used to be thought that a hearing by a judge or judges in a private case had to be completed in a single day: the judge might request a further hearing but that entailed starting again from the beginning. However, doubts have been cast on this as a general principle.[28] Certainly, private cases were adjourned for further hearings.[29] Furthermore, Cicero twice implies that there is a time-limit: in one speech he refers to possible complaints that, if he goes on

[25] *Tull.* 20, 44, cf. 29; *Caec.* 91; *lex agraria* (Crawford, *Roman Statutes*, no. 2) line 18; A. Lintott, *Judicial Reform and Land Reform in the Roman Republic* (Cambridge, 1992) 180–1, 220–1.

[26] *Caec.* 20–3; *Fam.* vii. 13.2. The significance of the case for Roman legal history is fully discussed by B. W. Frier, *The Rise of the Roman Jurists* (Princeton, 1985).

[27] Gai. 4.15; E. Metzger, *A New Outline of the Roman Civil Trial* (Oxford, 1997) 9–87; A. Rodger, 'The *Lex Irnitana* and Procedure in the Civil Courts', *JRS* 81 (1991) 74–90.

[28] Metzger, *New Outline*, 108–22.

[29] *Caec.* 6, *Quinct.* 3, *Tull.* 6, cf. *lex repetundarum*, 47–8, *Caec.* 29; Lintott, *Judicial Reform*, 100–1, 132–3 for public cases.

speaking too long, he would not leave enough time for Hortensius, the defendant's counsel; in another he asks the defendant's counsel L. Quinctius to be succinct and leave the jury time to make up its mind.[30] However, in the first case, the reference to Hortensius' peroration cannot mean that it might be cut short by the end of the hearing, since the witnesses have not yet been called. As to the second, the rapidity required may be due to the particular time-limits imposed in trials before *recuperatores*. These were deliberately intended to be speedy: the colonial charter of Urso prescribes a time-limit of 20 days from the procedure *in iure*.[31] Moreover, in suits before *recuperatores* the number of witnesses was limited.[32]

Roman private law had been developing at a great pace in the late Republic. The quantity of innovation may have been an opportunity for the unscrupulous magistrate. This was apparently the reason for the law passed by Cicero's later client, C. Cornelius, that praetors should adhere to their published edicts.[33] Although as yet there was nothing resembling a legal profession (the most important advocates usually were pursuing a political career as well), a great deal of expertise was desirable both in the substance of the law and in procedure. Cicero complains through the persona of his mentor, L. Crassus, about the sheer incompetence of certain advocates in legal technicalities.[34] It was also a period in which legal argument was becoming complex and subtle, so that we can speak of a rise in jurisprudence as a science, if not yet as a profession.

iv. Criminal Procedure

In the late Republic criminal trials were occasionally held in the assembly. This procedure was at least as old as the Twelve Tables and had been the regular mode of prosecution in public matters during the middle Republic. A magistrate–a tribune or in non-capital cases an aedile, occasionally a quaestor–appointed a day for a first hearing and declared it to the defendant, after obtaining auspices for the assembly from the praetor. This meeting was

---

[30] *Quinct.* 34; *Tull.* 6.

[31] *Tull.* 34; *Quinct.* 58; *lex Ursonensis* (Crawford, *Roman Statutes*, no. 25) ch. 95; on trials before *recuperatores* see also *lex agr.* (ibid. no. 2), line 37–ten days to choose the jury; *s.c. Calvisianum* (*FIRA* i, no. 68. v; *SEG* ix. 8) line 134–verdict within thirty days from appointment of jury.

[32] For numbers of witnesses see *Caec.* 24–8 (10 witnesses); *lex Iulia agraria* (Crawford, *Roman Statutes*, ii, no. 54) ch. 55 (10); *lex Urs.* (ibid. i, no. 25), ch. 95 (20); *lex prov. praet.* (ibid. no. 12) Cnidos v. 28–9 (20); *edictum Venafranum* (*FIRA* i, no. 67), 65 ff. (10); *s.c. Calvis.* (ibid. no. 68) 139 ff. (5–10).

[33] *Corn. I.* frr. 37–8; Asc. 59 C; Lintott, 'Cicero on Praetors who Failed to Abide by Their Edicts', *CQ* NS 27 (1977) 184–6.   [34] *De Or.* 1. 166 ff.

a *contio*, intended for investigation (*anquisitio*) and debate rather than decision, and was followed by two others of the same kind, each after a clear day's interval. During them the trial itself occurred, speeches for the prosecution and defence were made, witnesses were called. It appears that the defence had a right of reply on each occasion, but might not be allowed much time to enjoy it. Then there was an interval of at least three market-days (*trinundinum*) before a final vote in a formally constituted assembly–the *comitia centuriata*, if the accusation was capital, the *comitia tributa*, if not. We know of one trial of this kind from Cicero's letters, that in which Clodius, while aedile in 56 BC, accused Milo of using gladiators for political violence–one which in fact never seems to have been brought to a conclusion although a date was appointed for the final vote.[35] The only surviving speech by Cicero in such a trial is that delivered in his consulship for C. Rabirius, when the latter was accused of having killed the tribune Saturninus 37 years earlier. Our knowledge of what happened in 63 BC is notoriously confused by the fact that before this prosecution Labienus and Caesar had attempted by means of a plebiscite to revive trial by the *duumviri perduellionis*, an ancient office with which was associated some supposedly archaic, and certainly grisly, formulae that ordered the *duumviri* to proceed directly to execution without proper trial. After this had been blocked by *provocatio* with Cicero's aid, Labienus proceeded to a more regular form of capital prosecution that was terminated before its completion on the day of the final vote in the *comitia centuriata*, held in the Campus Martius.[36]

The majority of Cicero's criminal cases took place in a jury-court. Some of these were courts established on a permanent basis (*quaestiones perpetuae*); other *quaestiones* were investigating tribunals set up *ad hoc* to deal with offences after they had been committed. Tribunals of this second kind, which then took the form of one or two magistrates investigating with a panel of advisers (*consilium*), had in fact been created from the early second century onwards and they had provided an important precedent for the *quaestiones perpetuae* (another was the form of trial before *recuperatores*).[37] The immediate origin of the *quaestio perpetua* was, however, the *lex Calpurnia* of 149, which set up the first permanent tribunal *de repetundis*, dealing with the recovery of money exacted improperly

[35] *Dom.* 45; *Sest.* 65; *Q.Fr.* 2.3.1–2; 6.4; Varro *LL* 6.91; Livy 25.3.13–4.11; 26.3.5–12; 43.16.11; App. *BCiv.* 1.74.132; cf. *lex Osca Bant.* (Crawford, *Roman Statutes*, no. 13), 12–18 for a similar procedure in an Italian town. For the defence receiving little time, *Rab. Perd.* 6.

[36] *Rab. Perd.* esp. 10, 12, 17, 32; Suet. *Jul.* 12; Dio 37.26–27; Gelzer *RE* 7 A.1 (1939), 870 ff.; J. L. Strachan-Davidson, *Problems of the Roman Criminal Law*, 2 vols. (Oxford, 1912) i. 188 ff.; Santalucia, 1984; id., 1998, 29 ff.

[37] Mommsen, *Röm. Strafr.* 186 ff.; Strachan-Davidson, *Problems*, i.225 ff.; W. Kunkel, *Untersuchungen zur Entwicklung des römischen Kriminalverfahrens in vorsullanischer Zeit* (Munich, 1962), 45 ff.; id., *RE* 24 (1963) 720 ff.; Lintott, 'Provocatio', *ANRW* I. 2 (1972), 253 ff.

by Romans in authority from allies and perhaps citizens also. This *quaestio de repetundis* was radically reformed by C. Gracchus or at his behest, and further changes were made by Servilius Caepio in 106, Servilius Glaucia in 104 or 101, Sulla in 81–80, until finally Julius Caesar in 59 passed the definitive law.[38] During this period the form of the *quaestio perpetua* was also adopted by legislators for trials about treason, electoral bribery, embezzlement, public violence, murder, assault and battery, forgery, and other offences.

The Quaestio de Repetundis

Most of our evidence about procedure in a *quaestio perpetua* concerns that *de repetundis*. Here there is a problem, as much of this derives from the bronze fragments from Urbino engraved with the text of a law which, according to the best view, is that devised by C. Gracchus.[39] This procedure had already been altered by the time that Cicero was a tiro in the forum in the 90s BC and was to be changed further during his forensic career. However, it is convenient to begin with the law engraved on the bronze tablet.

The fundamental provisions of this law are as follows. There was to be a permanent court, presided over by a praetor, but in which all important decisions were to be in the hands of a trial-jury of fifty: these were to be created by a process of selection and rejection from an original album of 450 men who were neither senators nor former minor magistrates nor close-relatives of senators (*lex rep.* 6, 12–26, 60, 75, 82). Prosecution was for injured parties or their representatives, though non-citizens could be given a Roman *patronus* by the praetor after the accusation had been made (ibid. 1–3, 9–12). The prosecutor summoned his opponent before the praetor, as in civil suit, but then 'denounced his name' (*nomen deferre*) (ibid. 19). If the praetor accepted the suit, there was a delay while any *patronus* was appointed and the selection of the jury took place. The prosecutor might also be granted time to collect evidence or witnesses in Italy–it seems that in this period he was expected to have those from abroad with him when he began the action. The number of prosecution witnesses was limited to forty-eight and their testimony was to be written down and deposited before the trial, together with any documentary evidence, probably with the praetor (ibid. 31–4).

---

[38] On the history of the *quaestio de repetundis* see Kunkel, *Untersuchungen*, 61 ff.; A. W. Lintott, 'The *Leges de Repetundis* and Associate Measures under the Republic', *ZSS* 98 (1981) 162–212 and *Judicial Reform and Land Reform in the Roman Republic* (Cambridge, 1992), 11 ff.; C. Venturini, *Studi sul crimen repetundarum nell' età repubblicana* (Milan, 1979).

[39] For a summary of the arguments and further references see Lintott, *Judicial Reform*, 166–9.

The procedure for the main trial is largely missing, except for a brief reference to the praetor asking questions (*lex rep.* 35), but we have enough text to reconstruct the voting procedure (ibid. 44–56). Requests for a further hearing were permissible, but those jurors who did so more than twice were to be fined. When at least two-thirds of the jury were prepared to vote, those not prepared to do so were removed. The remainder took boxwood ballots four fingers long, marked in ink with C for *condemno* on one side and A for *absolvo* on the other, obliterated the letter that they did not want–or both if they wished to record a no-vote–and then in turn cast them into a jar with their arm bare but any surviving letter covered with their fingers. A juror selected by lot then took the ballots in succession from the jar, showed each vote to the public and announced it as 'acquit', 'condemn' or 'no-vote' before passing it on to another juror who finally gave it to the praetor. If there were more 'condemn's than either 'acquit's or 'no-vote's, the defendant was condemned: otherwise he was acquitted. Provided it was not decided that the prosecution had been collusive and deliberately designed to fail, the defendant could not be tried again for any offence under this law committed before the time of the trial (ibid. 55–6). The penalty under this law was purely financial: the condemned man was required to repay double the value of what he had improperly taken. In order to decide what was owed to each injured party, the *quaestio de repetundis*, unlike other *quaestiones*, included a secondary hearing before the same jury, the estimation of damages (*litis aestumatio*) (ibid. 58–63). Meanwhile, the defendant was required to provide guarantors to the quaestor at the treasury for a sum decided by the jury or submit to the seizure of his property (ibid. 57–8). If the total sum due became available in a reasonable time, it was passed on by the treasury-quaestor to the injured parties. If not, on a day fixed in advance a distribution was made to the injured parties of sums proportional to their losses (ibid. 59–63). The money of those absent, together with any sums recovered later, was kept at the treasury for the injured parties for five years, only then reverting to the Roman people (ibid. 63–9). There were, furthermore, rewards for successful leading prosecutors in any case. Non-citizens might receive Roman citizenship, if they wished, or, if not, *provocatio* and immunity from military service and other public duty, while remaining in their own community. There were also rewards (the detail does not survive) for Roman citizens who prosecuted (ibid. 76–87).

As we can tell from brief indications in the text of this law, prosecutions in the *quaestio de repetundis* previously had had the nature of a civil suit: the procedure had been the *legis actio sacramento* (which would have required that a Roman citizen acted for a non-Roman plaintiff), and the penalty was simple repayment. This was completely transformed by the law on the bronze tablet. Certain features of this deserve to be stressed. Immensely elaborate legal machinery was incorporated into statute and the primary job of the magistrate who presided over the court was to ensure that this machinery was not only properly operated but seen to have been properly operated. Judgement was given by a big jury, clearly drawn from the equestrian order (though this definition does not survive on the bronze) but not from its upper echelons which were closely connected to senators. Prosecution was opened up to the injured parties. Lawsuits were penal and there were additional rewards for prosecutors. Thus a criminal court had been created, where judgement was delivered neither by an assembly nor by a small group of judges from the core of the elite. In this the magistrate was important, but his activities were determined strictly by the statute and he could not affect the central decisions of the court.[40]

The *quaestio de repetundis* seems to have been in due course the model for the other *quaestiones perpetuae*. However, we have hardly any detailed evidence for their workings. First, let us follow the history of the *repetundae* court into Cicero's lifetime.[41] There were changes in the composition of the jury. Servilius Caepio's law of 106 BC introduced senators to the juries, prob- ably not exclusively: in that case we would expect the *equites* with senatorial connections to have joined the Gracchan jurors in the non-senatorial part of the panel. Within a few years, senators were removed by Servilius Glaucia, but it is very likely that the most illustrious *equites* remained and so the jury was representative of the whole equestrian order.

Another important change is perhaps best ascribed to Caepio–the intro- duction of what was called *divinatio*, whereby prosecution was open to anyone who put himself forward as advocate for the plaintiff's case and, if necessary, a jury chose before the trial between competing prosecutors, as for example between Cicero and Q. Caecilius in the Verres prosecution.[42] In Cicero's day the summons before the praetor by the plaintiff (*in ius educere*) had been replaced by a demand (*postulare*) for appearance before the praetor by a prospective prosecutor, who would not actually perform the denunciation (*nominis delatio*) until he knew that he was selected to undertake the suit. This was an opportunity for established and aspiring Romans from the senatorial and equestrian orders, and it seems that the actual conduct of the prosecution by non-citizens *de facto* lapsed.

Glaucia introduced changes to the procedure also. One of these was *comperendinatio*–the division of the main trial into two apparently similar

---

[40] See Lintott, *Judicial Reform*, 16–25 and 1981, 177–85; A. N. Sherwin-White, 'The Political Ideas of C. Gracchus', *JRS* 72 (1982), 18–31.

[41] See Lintott, *Judicial Reform*, 25–9; 1981, 186–205 with further references.

[42] *Div. Caec.*; see also *Q.Fr.* 3.2.1; also *Fam.* 8.8.3 in relation to the dependent procedure, *quo ea pecunia pervenerit*, on which see below.

parts (the *litis aestumatio* remaining a third element). It is worth remembering that, when Cicero prosecuted Verres in 70 BC, although his tactics of compressing the first action led to Verres going directly into exile, all was not over: though the second part of the main trial was otiose, the *litis aestumatio*, highly complex in Verres' case, was not.[43] A second change introduced by Glaucia was the addition to the *litis aestumatio* of a clause concerning 'the man to whom that money ultimately came' (*quo ea pecunia pervenerit*). In consequence there might be a supplementary suit for money acquired illegally against someone who had been a receiver of the ill-gotten gains. Such was the suit brought against Cicero's client Rabirius Postumus for money received from Gabinius during their expedition to Egypt to restore Ptolemy Auletes.[44] A further procedural development, first attested under Glaucia's law, was the *inquisitio*. This was a tour of investigation conducted by the selected prosecutor in order to collect evidence in the province in which the accused magistrate had been operating. Such a tour might last several months, but Cicero deliberately restricted his investigation in Sicily to 50 days in order to get on with his prosecution.[45]

The crimes covered by the *quaestio de repetundis* also expanded. Whereas the law of C. Gracchus provided a means by which a man robbed by a magistrate could get (double) compensation for his loss, it is apparent that by 91 the receipt of freely given presents was an offence in this court, on the ground that these were bribes or kickbacks. According to Dio Cassius, this was the ostensible ground for the prosecution of the upright P. Rutilius Rufus in the 90s BC, and indeed he may have been technically guilty as charged (in addition to being an enemy of the tax-collectors).[46] It is obvious that such prosecutions would not be brought by the man who had given the bribe but would be undertaken by someone acting on behalf of the Roman people. This extension of the scope of the *quaestio de repetundis* allowed it to be used against jurors who received bribes. However, the original limitations on those who could be prosecuted in the court still applied. So only senators, their close relatives, and those who had been minor magistrates (and thus likely to become senators in due course) were liable. The ironical consequence was that the equestrian jurors in the court could not be prosecuted for receiving bribes. Cato's attempt to remedy this in 61 failed, thanks to opposition from Crassus and Cicero himself, and

---

[43] Plut. *Cic.* 8.4, stating that the total claimed was 3 million sesterces (in *Verr.* I 56 it is 4 million). For the continuation of *litis aestumatio* under Sulla's *lex Cornelia* see *Clu.* 116–with a tendentious view of its importance. [44] *Rab. Post.*, esp. 8 ff.; *Fam.* 8.8.2–3.

[45] *Scaur.* 23; Asc. 21 C; *Verr.* I 6, II 1.30.

[46] Dio, fr. 97,1; Athen. 4.168 D–E = Poseidonius, *FGH* 87 F27; Livy, *Per.* 70; Val. Max. 2.10.5. Other sources in *MRR* ii.8.

there is no direct evidence of this being changed by either Julius Caesar or Augustus.[47] There is also evidence that some forms of extracting or receiving money were treated as capital offences: this was certainly so under Caesar's law of 59 and may have been so under the *lex Cornelia* of Sulla. The sort of crimes envisaged here are those enumerated in the Digest–receiving a bribe to execute, imprison, or conduct a capital trial against someone.[48]

Quaestio *Procedure in the Ciceronian Period*

The statutes that set up other *quaestiones*, following the example of the Gracchan *lex de repetundis*, would probably have resembled it in various elements of procedure, in the methods of creating a jury, and in the authority conferred on the jury. The right to prosecute would have been open, as it had become in the *repetundae* court about 100 BC. Sulla revised the statutes of the existing *quaestiones*. How far this resulted in a standardization of procedure is quite uncertain. It is certain, however, that only senators were now allowed to be members of a jury in a *quaestio*, and the probability is that they were now selected for each court by a uniform procedure. We hear for the first time of numbered *decuriae* of jurors, presumably panels which contained roughly a tenth of those available. The praetor selected a *decuria* for a case, presumably excluding those that already had heavy commitments, and from this a group of potential jurors was selected by lot. These were then further reduced by a limited amount of rejection, probably done by prosecutor and defendant alternately.[49] The ensuing juries were smaller than those in the pre-Sullan period–thirty-two at the trial of Oppianicus in 74 BC and probably considerably less at Verres' trial (eight can be described as almost all the jury). One peculiarity of the period deserves mention: Oppianicus could demand open voting. This is completely at odds with Gracchan principles and suggests an attempt to re-establish the authority of powerful men.[50]

The character of the juries was completely altered by the *lex Aurelia* of 70. This introduced three albums of senators, *equites*, and 'tribunes of the

---

[47] *Clu.* 104; 153; *Rab. Post.* 16; *Att.* 1.17.8; 18.3; 2.1.8.

[48] *Clu.* 115–16; *s.c. Calvis.* (*FIRA* i, no. 68, v) 97 ff.; *Dig.* 48.11.7. For other crimes which overlapped with *maiestas*, see *Pis.* 50, 90.

[49] *Verr. II* 1.156–8; 2.79; *Schol. Gronov. Verr. I* 16 (335 St.); *Clu.* 91–2, 96. For similar allotment and rejection in the process before *recuperatores* see *s.c. Calvis.* (*FIRA* i, no. 68) 121–2; *lex prov. praet.* (Crawford, *Roman Statutes*, no. 12) Cnidos v. 16–18; *lex agr.* 37 (ibid. no. 2) with commentary in Lintott, *Judicial Reform* 241–2.

[50] *Clu.* 74–5; *Verr. I* 30. Apart from the compulsory *comperendinatio* in *repetundae* cases, it was still possible to hold a further hearing (*ampliatio*), if not enough of the jury were prepared to vote, see *Caec.* 29; *Verr. II* 1.26 and 74; *Clu.* 55.

treasury' (*tribuni aerarii*), the last being an honorific rank for people who had similar wealth to *equites* but had not been enrolled among the *equites Romani*. Cicero can assimilate them in his speeches to *equites*, and this may well be how they regarded themselves.[51] We do not know how many were enrolled in the albums under this law, though the figure of 300 from each order (hence 900 in all) has been put forward, based on the number of senatorial jurors under Pompey's later law.[52] The single law reforming the juries in all the courts probably implies that there was now, as under Sulla's legislation, a uniform system for creating a jury, by allotment of equal numbers from all three albums and then reducing them by rejection. This did not necessarily produce exactly the same number in each case: seventy voted in Gabinius' trial for *maiestas* in 54 BC; seventy, comprising twenty-two senators, twenty-three *equites*, twenty-five *tribuni aerarii*, in Scaurus' trial *de repetundis* in the same year; on the other hand only fifty voted in the trial of Procilius, apparently for some kind of murder in the *quaestio de sicariis et veneficiis*, and only fifty-six in Clodius' trial for *incestum*, for which the jury seems to have been in the end selected in the normal fashion.[53]

Vatinius attempted to modify the procedure in his tribunate of 59 BC by passing a law permitting the rejection of alternate panels of jurors—procedure which, according to Cicero, later applied to trials for electoral bribery. Then in 55 BC Crassus' *lex Licinia de sodaliciis* required the jurors to be placed in panels according to tribes: the prosecutors under that law were to select a certain number of tribes from which the defendant could make rejections until three were left. In the same year a law of Pompey's provided that the albums of jurors should be formed from only the richest members of the three orders.[54] Three years later, when Pompey created special courts *de vi* and *de ambitu* to deal with the violence and corruption that had preceded his third consulship, he drew up an even more select album. This is probably the group of '360 *iudices*, with whom Pompey used to be particularly popular', mentioned by Cicero in a letter of 49 BC.[55]

Our knowledge of procedure in most cases remains the barest outline. First came the demand (*postulare*) for the defendant's appearance before the relevant praetor or *quaesitor*—the latter were usually former aediles selected to supplement the praetors as presidents of courts, since the number of praetors available (six) was inadequate.[56] Next, in a *repetundae* case

---

[51] *Font.* 36; *Clu.* 121, 130; *Flacc.* 4 with *Schol. Bob.* 94 St.; *Flacc.* 96; *Planc.* 41; *Rab. Post.* 14. In a political context the two orders are separated by Cicero (*In Cat.* 4.15; *Rab. Perd.* 27).

[52] See the *s.c.* in *Fam.* 8.8.5; P. A. Brunt, *The Fall of the Roman Republic* (Oxford, 1988) 210.

[53] *Att.* 4.18.1; *Q.Fr.* 3.4.1; *Att.* 4.15.4; 1.16.5 and 11, cf. 2, 14.1.

[54] *Vat.* 27; *Schol. Bob.* 149–50 St.; *Planc.* 36 ff.; *Att.* 4.15.9; Asc. 17 C.

[55] Asc. 38 C; *Att.* 8.16.2.

[56] See *Q.Fr.* 3.1.15; *Fam.* 8.6.2 for *postulatio* and *nominis delatio*; on the *quaesitor* or *iudex quaestionis*, A. W. Lintott, *Violence in Republican Rome* (Oxford, 1968) 122.

the *divinatio* took place and the man selected as prosecutor was awarded a period for investigation in the province (*inquisitio*). In other courts procedure was more rapid: trial was fixed for the tenth day after the accusation had been accepted in accusations of *maiestas* and *vis*.[57] Trials in *quaestiones* seem normally to have been confined to the ten hours between the first hour and the eleventh hour each day, unless they had to be completed in one day, to judge from Caesar's later regulations for his colony at Urso.[58] There were limitations on the length of speeches in trials *de repetundis* from Sulla's time onwards at least. The law from Urso later gave four hours to the prosecutor, two to the *subscriptor* and granted the defence double the amount of time allocated to the prosecution.[59]

As in private suits before a *iudex*, the evidence was presented after the speeches on each side had been given. The testimony had to be available in writing and sealed with the seals of the jury before the trial; on one occasion Cicero had this written testimony read out during his speech, while requesting the witness to stand up.[60] The actual hearing of the witnesses must have had more of the nature of a cross-examination. Although Cicero's *In Vatinium* by its very nature cannot do justice to the form of this interrogation, it gives us some idea of its vehemence. Witnesses were expected to confine themselves to answering the questions they were asked and not to turn themselves into advocates, but did not always restrain themselves. This part of the trial might on occasion have become fiercely agonistic. This was certainly true of the *altercatio* that followed, in which prosecution and defence argued over the evidence and which constituted the last part of the case presented by each side. We only know of this from Quintilian: what might be regarded as a small fragment of the *altercatio* between Cicero and Hortensius in the Verres trial, also preserved by Quintilian, 'you should understand riddles, since you have a sphinx at home', is said actually to have occurred while Cicero was asking a witness a question.[61] Verdicts were final in a *quaestio perpetua* as in an assembly trial.

---

[57] On *inquisitio* see *Q.Fr.* 3.2.1; Asc. 19 C; on the interval before trial *Q.Fr.* 2.12.2; Asc. 59 C.

[58] *Lex Urs.* (Crawford, *Roman Statutes*, no. 25) ch. 102, lines 22–4, cf. Asc. 41 C.

[59] *Verr. I* 32; *Verr. II* 1.25; *Flacc.* 82–six hours allowed for the prosecutor's *subscriptor; lex Urs.* ch. 102.

[60] On deferment of witnesses see *Rosc. Am.* 82, 102; *Verr. I* 51; Ps. Asc. 223 St.; on written testimony *Cael.* 19–20, 66; *Flacc.* 21, cf. *lex rep.* 33–4 with commentary in Lintott, *Judicial Reform*, 126–7; *Clu.* 168. The references to testimony in Ciceronian speeches can for the most part be explained either by the two-part nature of *repetundae* trials, or by the prior deposition of testimony and its citation during the speeches, as J. Humbert *Les Plaidoyers écrits et les plaidoiries réelles de Cicéron* (Paris, 1925 [1972]), 38–66, pointed out. Note, however, that the reference in *Cael.* 55 to Lucceius' testimony under oath needs no special explanation (*contra* Humbert, 41), as written testimony was given under oath (cf. *Tabulae Herculanenses* XVI–XXV in Pugliese Carratelli, 'Tabulae Herculanenses II'). Furthermore, Triarius' *interrogatio* of all the *Sardi* (*Scaur.* 21) can hardly refer to the actual examination of witnesses in court (*contra* Humbert, *Les Plaidoyers*, 206–7).

[61] *Ad Her.* 4.47; *Q.Fr.* 2.4.1 on Vatinius; Quint. *Inst.* 6.4.1 ff. cf. 6.3.98 on *altercatio*. The doubts of Humbert (*Les Plaidoyers*, 60 ff.) about the existence of the *altercatio* in Cicero's day seem to me unjustified, given the inadequate evidence for procedure in this period.

Provocatio seems to have been specifically forbidden in the statutes establishing the courts. Both Tiberius Gracchus and Marcus Antonius proposed the introduction of appeal to an assembly from judges in a *quaestio*, but without effect. Conversely, any attempt to prosecute a man a second time on the same charge, after he had been acquitted, was liable to founder, if it was not actually illegal, as it was under the Gracchan *lex de repetundis*. The one exception to this was a case where it was proved that there had been a collusive, and therefore deliberately ineffective, prosecution—an act that the Romans termed *praevaricatio*.[62]

Special Courts

In spite of the restrictions mentioned, trials before a *quaestio* were time-consuming. In 52, when Pompey as consul set up by statute the special courts to deal with violence and electoral bribery, he deliberately compressed the timetable. The first three days of each trial were to be devoted to the hearing of witnesses and only at the end of this were the written versions of their testimonies to be sealed: this evidence was to be heard by the full panel of jurors before any rejections. Then on the fourth day, the panel was to be reduced by allotment to eighty-one (twenty-seven from each order), and the speeches were held, the prosecution being granted two hours to speak, the defence three. The vote followed on the same day, but first prosecution and defence were each to reject fifteen jurors, five from each order, leaving a voting jury of fifty-one.[63]

This is the only special court for which we have any precise evidence. Clodius' trial for sacrilege in 61 BC seems to have followed a course similar to that in the regular *quaestiones*, with the hearing of the prosecution witnesses, including Cicero, preceding the opening of the defence case. We have only bare notices of the trials of Vestal Virgins and their alleged lovers for *incestum* in 73 BC: presumably a special *quaestio* was set up.[64] Two other unusual forms of trial may be mentioned. First, the criminal hearings before Caesar as dictator, before whom Cicero delivered speeches for Ligarius and King Deiotarus. The former was little more than a plea for pardon; the latter attempted to be a forensic speech that dealt with issues of evidence. These trials took place in circumstances similar to trials before emperors *in cubiculo*. Cicero in fact complains in the prooemium of *Pro Rege Deiotaro* (5–7) that it was disconcerting to be speaking within the walls of a house (*domesticos parietes*), without the large audience that he was used to addressing in such cases and the inspiration that came from being

---

[62] On appeal see Plut. *Ti. Gr.* 16.1; Cic. *Phil.* 1.21; on *praevaricatio, lex rep.* 56 with the commentary in Lintott, *Judicial Reform*, 137–9. See also *lex rep.* 70 and the commentary, ibid. 149–50, for bans on tribunician obstruction to *quaestio* trials.   [63] Asc. 36, 39, 53 C.

[64] *Att.* 1.16.3–5; *MRR* ii.114.

able to point to the monuments of Rome and to heaven itself. The change of location had much to do with the change of the style of oratory under the Principate.[65] Finally, another unfortunate precedent for the Principate deserves to be mentioned, the hearings about the Catilinarians in the Senate and their subsequent condemnation. That they provided Augustus with some precedent for the introduction of senatorial jurisdiction is only too likely (63 BC was after all the year of his birth). However, it should be emphasized that what happened in the early hours of 3 December and on 5 December in the Senate were not trials. The meeting of 3 December may be considered an unusual example of a preliminary investigation, justified by the need to take preventive measures against the conspirators. On 5 December there was no examination of what the conspirators had actually confessed; the accused were neither present nor represented in any way; there was no judicial form to the proceedings.[66] Similar objections might be made to some of the imperial trials described by Tacitus, but that is another story.

[65] Tac. *Dial.* 39.   [66] *In Cat.* 3.8–15 and 4; *Sull.* 41–2; Sall. *Cat.* 46.5–47.4; 50.3–53.1.

2

Self-Reference in Cicero's Forensic Speeches

Jeremy Paterson

In 1792 Thomas Erskine, defending Tom Paine on a charge of seditious libel before a hostile court, turned to the jury and said, 'I will now lay aside the role of the advocate and address you as a man', to which the judge tartly replied, 'You will do nothing of the sort. The only right and licence you have to appear in this court is as an advocate.'[1] This neat distinction between the advocate and the man was not one which could be maintained in a Roman court. Consider, for example, Cicero in full flow in his defence of Roscius of Ameria (*Rosc. Am.* 143):

Verum haec omnis oratio . . . mea est, qua me uti res publica et dolor meus et istorum iniuria coegit. Sex. Roscius horum nihil indignum putat, neminem accusat, nihil de suo patrimonio queritur.

But all that I have said is in my own name; it is the Republic, my indignation, and the offence of these men which forced me to speak. Sextus Roscius feels no indignation at these acts, accuses no one, and makes no complaint about his inheritance.

Cicero 'as a man' intrudes in his court speeches to a degree which is startling to a modern audience, even to the extent of overshadowing the character and deeds of the person being defended.[2] No judge now would permit a barrister to discourse at length on his earlier career in public life, his relationship with the accused and the prosecution lawyers, or anecdotes about one's time as a magistrate in Sicily.

There could be a simple interpretation of this phenomenon. It could be argued that we are dealing with a genuine character trait of Cicero, that he was in reality self-absorbed and conceited and missed no opportunity to discourse on his favourite subject: himself. Indeed, Cicero's self-glorification

---

[1] Quoted by R. Du Cann, *The Art of the Advocate* (London, 1980) 40.
[2] A. Thierfelder, 'Über den Wert der Bemerkungen zur eigenen Person in Ciceros Prozessreden', *Gymnasium* 72 (1965) 385–415; J. Graff, *Ciceros Selbstauffassung*, Diss. (Heidelberg, 1963).

was a theme in antiquity. According to Plutarch (*Cic.* 24.1), 'he made himself an object of loathing to many, not by any wicked action, but by becoming hated by many for constantly praising and glorifying himself.'[3] Cicero himself acknowledged that the accusation had been levelled at him (*Dom.* 93): 'Since you criticize me, because you say that I have a habit of speaking too boastfully about myself, who has ever heard me speaking about myself except when forced to and out of necessity?' But the adverse comments by contemporaries on Cicero were not of a general kind about a supposed character trait, but were focused on the frequency and nature of his references to his consulship and the suppression of the so-called conspiracy of Catiline.[4] Cicero's actions in his consulship were controversial and a rich source for criticism and attack by his opponents. But Cicero's references to himself in his court speeches are found long before the events of 63 BC and were never confined to the subject of his consulship. Further, it is difficult to believe that Cicero's clients would have been happy with behaviour which in some ways might be thought to be counterproductive. The explanation for such material lies in the nature of the Roman courts and the tactics of the courtroom rather than any self-obsession on Cicero's part.

The key lies in the term 'patronus' for the advocate in the courts. Legal remedies in Rome emerged gradually in a world of self-help, where the disadvantaged turned to the wealthy and influential for help and patronage.[5] The whole point about patrons is that they have, or have access to, the wealth, power, influence and 'auctoritas', which clients lack in the defence of their interests. As the opportunity to seek redress in the courts grows, it would be surprising if the *patronus*, acting as advocate, did not seek to exploit these same advantages in the court room and the opposition did not wish to undermine them, while promoting their own influence. Advocates had neither the ability, nor usually the desire, to set aside their public persona when they addressed the courts. Indeed, the character, or alleged

---

[3] Note, however, that this theme is one of the key comparisons for Plutarch of Cicero with Demosthenes and is something of a literary construct. Demosthenes shared with Cicero a love of honour, but not his addiction to self-praise (Plut. *Dem.* Introduction 3.3–5 and *Dem. & Cic.* 2.1–3). On this see J. L. Moles, *Plutarch: Life of Cicero* (Warminster, 1988) on *Cic.* 24.1, who points out that this passage functions as a structural parallel for *Dem.* 8.1–16.4. Plutarch, *Cic.* 6.5 repeats the famous story from Cicero, *Planc.* 63–7 about Cicero's return from his quaestorship in Siciliy to discover that people did not even remember where he had been. Cicero's point was that it was better to stay in Rome if you wanted to keep in the public eye; but Plutarch has added a gloss of his own, not justified by what Cicero said, 'His surpassing delight in being praised and his excessive passion for glory remained with him always and many times threw into confusion many of his rational calculations.'

[4] See P. Petzold, *De Ciceronis detractoribus ac laudatoribus Romanis* (Leipzig, 1911) and Walter Allen Jr., 'Cicero's Conceit', *TAPA* 85 (1954) 121–44. Dio 37.38.2 and 38.12.7.

[5] Such a reconstruction of the development of Roman law is controversial. See J. M. Kelly, *Roman Litigation* (Oxford, 1966) 1–4 and 31–68.

character, of those involved, not just the parties to the case but also their advocates, was at issue (Cic. *De Or.* 2.182):

Valet igitur multum ad vincendum probari mores et instituta et facta et vitam eorum, qui agent causas, et eorum pro quibus, et item improbari adversariorum, animos eorum, apud quos agetur, conciliari quam maxime ad benevolentiam cum erga oratorem tum erga illum, pro quo dicet orator.

A powerful contribution to winning a case is the approval of the habits, principles, actions, and lives of those who are pleading the case and of those on whose behalf they appear. In the same way the lives of the opponents should meet with disapproval and the minds of those before whom the case is heard should be won over as far as possible to show good will towards the orator as well as the client on whose behalf he is speaking.

The concentration on the character (in Greek the 'ethos') of the participants had a long history in rhetoric going back at least to Aristotle (*Rhet.* 2.1.5–7 (1378ᵃ6–20)) and has been acutely analysed in recent scholarship.[6] It has interesting consequences for the conduct of any case. First, since the character of the advocate is at issue, the relationship between the *patroni* on both sides of a case was often a source of debate. Thus, the taking of a case could be presented as an unfriendly act with regard to the opposing advocates, who would claim that they had reason to presume on the other's friendship. So, for example, in the Murena case one of the prosecutors, Servius Sulpicius, claimed that Cicero 'had been forgetful of their friendship and attachment' by taking up Murena's defence (*Mur.* 7). In the Sulla case the prosecutor, L. Torquatus, represents his action as the pursuit of a family vendetta against an enemy (*inimicus*) and Cicero's intervention on Sulla's behalf as unfriendly towards him (*Sull.* 48). Cicero had a variety of defences available. The first is to acknowledge the friendship between the advocates and to present the issue as an agonizing choice between the obligations of friendship towards the opponent and friendship towards the client, and a recognition that a request to defend the honour and status of anyone who seeks your help takes precedence. So, in the Murena case, Cicero freely acknowledges the friendship of Servius Sulpicius, claims that his obligations were fulfilled by supporting Servius' campaign for the consulship, demonstrates that his friendship with Murena was close and of long standing, and finally reminds the court of his obligations as an advocate 'not to refuse my labours to protect men from dangers' (*Mur.* 7 and 8).

A second consequence of the persona of an advocate being at issue in the case was that the advocate's behaviour and statements in other cases could on occasion be raised in court. The main claim would be one of

[6] J. Wisse, *Ethos and Pathos from Aristotle to Cicero* (Amsterdam, 1989) and J. M. May, *Trials of Character: the Eloquence of Ciceronian Ethos* (Chapel Hill, NC, and London, 1988).

inconsistency. In the case of P. Sulla the prosecution accused Cicero of inconsistency in that Sulla was the only person accused of involvement in the
Catiline conspiracy that Cicero chose to defend (*Sull.* 5). Again, in the case
of Cn. Plancius the prosecutor had referred to Cicero's language and tactics
in a similar previous case, that of C. Cispius in 56 BC, where Cicero's
defence had been unsuccessful. 'We have heard all this before' is the cry
('obsoletae iam sunt preces tuae', 'your pleas are old hat' (*Planc.* 75)) and
the argument is that this sort of tactic did not work before and should not
work now. The most interesting example is when Attius, the prosecutor in
the Cluentius trial, accused Cicero of inconsistency (*Cluent.* 138) by citing
a statement by Cicero 'in some speech or other of mine' (in fact his most
famous performance in court, the first speech against Verres, but Cicero is
trying to play down the significance of the point and probably to inspire
laughter), in which he had conceded that the jury in the case of
C. Oppianicus had been bribed. In the trial of Cluentius the Oppianicus
case was again at issue and Cicero now wanted to present a very different
view of it.

Cicero's response to his lack of consistency ('constantia', *Cluent.* 141) has
a modern ring to it. He argued that the circumstances of each case were
different. In his prosecution of Verres he had to exploit all the stories going
round about corruption in the courts. 'However,' he stated, 'it is a big
mistake for anyone to suppose that they have our sworn personal views in
any speech which we make in court. All these speeches reflect the cases
and the circumstances, not the views of the men themselves or their advocates' (*Cluent.* 139). He goes on to cite a famous and witty demonstration of
this principle by his mentor, L. Licinius Crassus. Here we see a more modern principle that the advocate is in duty bound to present the best case to
be made for their client, irrespective of what the advocate has said in any
other case, being developed in a world where the question of consistency
could be raised because the advocate's persona was an issue in the court,
whether he liked it or not.

Cicero and many of his fellow-advocates would be well known to the
jurors in the court in the way that few, if any, modern advocates are. They
came with their reputations both in court and in public life already established in the minds of the jurors. This was obviously something which
could be exploited in the trial. One of the key features of a speech in a
Roman courtroom was the advocate's attempt to impose his *auctoritas* on
the proceedings. So it was acceptable to talk about oneself when appropriate. This normally meant that the issue of the standing of the advocate had
initially been raised by the opposition in an attempt to undermine the advocate's influence (*Sulla* 2: 'quantum de mea auctoritate deripuisset, tantum se
de huius praesidiis deminuturum', 'the more Torquatus can undermine my

influence, the more he will weaken the defence of this man, Sulla') and so the advocate feels forced to make a response.[7] The key issue was how to talk about oneself without crossing the boundary of arrogance and boastfulness.[8] This was a familiar topic in rhetorical theory.[9] It was always going to be a source of contention between Cicero and his opponents whether he overstepped the mark or not.

In the early stages of one's career it was possible to come up against advocates whose acknowledged *auctoritas* was significantly greater than one's own, and it was necessary in the interests of the client to find ways of countering this. In his first known appearance in court, on behalf of P. Quinctius, Cicero acknowledges the eloquence of Hortensius (the other counsel) and the potential disadvantage this brought to his case: 'the position is that I, who have little ability either as a result of experience or natural talent, am compared with a most eloquent of advocates' (*Quinct.* 2). But the purpose of this statement is soon made clear when Cicero addresses Aquilius, the judge in the case (*Quinct.* 4): 'the more numerous my disadvantages are, Aquilius, the greater should be the positive way (*meliore mente*) in which you listen to my words so that truth, weakened by so many unfavourable conditions, may at last be revived by the sense of equity of men of such distinction.' Again, at first sight Cicero's advertisement of his recent election to the aedileship in his first speech against Verres in 70 BC seems very artificial and unnecessary (*Verr.* I 36 f. cf. *Div. in Caec.* 72), but its purpose is revealed when Cicero explicitly compares his aedileship with the consulship won for the same year by Hortensius, Verres' defence counsel:

Hortensius will then be consul with supreme command and power, while I shall be aedile, that is, little more than an ordinary citizen. Yet what I am now promising to do is of such importance, so welcome and so pleasing to the people of Rome, that the consul himself must seem even less than an ordinary citizen, if that were possible, when matched against me on this issue.

Cicero is seeking to counter any influence Hortensius might have gained as a result of his recent electoral success.

---

[7] *Mur.* 2: 'since my taking up the case has been criticized, before I begin to speak on behalf of Murena, I shall say a few words on my own behalf.' *Sull.* 2: 'Since L. Torquatus . . . has thought that by violating our close relationship, he could detract from the authority of my defence, I shall link a defence of my own commitment to the case with driving away the threat to my client.'

[8] *Inv.* 1.22: 'Benevolence towards us can be won, if we speak about our deeds and duties without arrogance.' Particularly unacceptable is boasting in court about one's rhetorical abilities (*Div. in Caec.* 17).

[9] See e.g. Aristotle *NE* 4.7.1 on moderation in relation to boasting (note that Plutarch, *Comparison of Demosthenes and Cicero* 2, accuses Cicero precisely of lack of moderation in what he said) and Plut. *Mor.* 540 c, 'On how to praise oneself without causing envy'.

In order to be effective, rhetoric of this sort must rest upon a presumption that jurors had an innate sense of fairness and a resentment of justice being perverted by the unfair use of influence. As Cicero argues in part of a famous eulogy of Roman civil law (*Caec.* 73):

Quod enim est ius civile? quod neque inflecti gratia neque perfringi potentia neque adulterari pecunia possit.

What is the civil law? It is something which cannot be perverted by favours, destroyed by power, or corrupted by money.

Cicero admits that the main defence of these principles was based on public censure and public opinion (*Caec.* 69, 72). That may not in reality have been sufficient.[10] Nevertheless, the existence of this general consensus should not be ignored. Of course, it could, and did, inspire advocates to argue at every conceivable opportunity that the opposition was seeking to win by improper influence rather than the strength of their case. In the case of L. Murena in 63 BC one of the prosecutors, M. Cato, had apparently argued that Cicero should not have taken on the defence of Murena, in part because Cicero was consul at the time (*Mur.* 3). Cicero's initial answer is less than convincing (*Mur.* 5): 'It should not be so much duty calling me to defend the fortunes of a friend as the republic calling a consul to defend the safety of all', echoing the terms of the so called *senatus consultum ultimum* (the ultimate decree of the senate), which in a crisis called on the magistrates to defend the state.[11] This presumed that the safety of the state was at issue in the Murena case. Later in the speech Cicero turns the accusation of undue influence against Cato himself (*Mur.* 58 ff.), 'I fear his *auctoritas* much more than his accusation' and he goes on to make a much more subtle point that the use of influence is particularly unacceptable socially when used by a prosecutor: 'the whole people and wise and far-sighted judges in this state have always resisted the excessively great resources of a prosecutor. I do not believe that a prosecutor should bring to court absolute power, nor extraordinary influence, nor too much favour.' But he implies that such resources are acceptable when used for the defence of the weak.

A clear sign that there were sensitivities here which had to be taken into account can be seen from Suetonius' discussion (*DA* 56) of Augustus' practice as emperor in his appearances in court. When a friend of his

---

[10] See the gloomy assessment of J. M. Kelly, *Roman Litigation* (Oxford, 1966) 31–68.

[11] Earlier in 63 BC Cicero had already made a similar claim in his defence of Rabirius, where 'salus rei publicae' and 'consulare officium' (the safety of the Republic and the duties of a consul) were among the reasons Cicero took the defence (*Rab. Perd.* 2) cf. *Rosc. Am.* 143. The claim anticipates the same justification, which Augustus gave in 23 BC at the Caepio and Murena trial, when his right to appear was challenged (Dio 54.3).

was prosecuted on a charge of poisoning, Augustus went as far as to put the dilemma he was in to the Senate. The problem was that if he appeared in support of his friend, it might be thought that he was trying to shield a guilty man from the full rigour of the law; on the other hand, if he refused to appear, he might be thought to be abandoning a friend and damning him in advance. The Senate supported his appearance in court, but he chose simply to sit on the benches in silence for several hours. Commentators have often assumed that both in Roman public life and in the courts wealth and influence predominated. Indeed, they can cite the many instances of people protesting that this is just what was happening. But for these protests to have any support, then they must have rested upon some basic general presumptions about fair play and fair trials. Those with influence had to be careful in the way they sought to wield it. Too blatant a use of power could prove counterproductive, not least with jurors.

Some of these issues were in play in Cicero's first major case, the defence of Sextus Roscius of Ameria in 80 BC. The previous decade had been traumatic for those who lived through it. Civil wars had strained loyalties and had seen the confiscation of property and the killing of many prominent men for picking the wrong side. For many—and not just his partisans—Sulla's takeover as dictator represented a restoration of order and a chance to return to a sort of normality. His legislative programme was a reshaping of the Republican system to ensure a central role for his supporters. This breathing space had been won at the price of the often bloody elimination of Sulla's fiercest enemies in the proscriptions, a proceeding about which even Sulla's supporters felt somewhat queasy. One sign of a return to ordered government was the re-establishment of the courts with jurors chosen from the senatorial order which included many promoted to the senate by Sulla himself. The first trial to come before these reconstituted courts was that of Roscius for the murder of his father. It was a case which could be made to involve the proscriptions, the alleged criminal activities of Chrysogonus, a freedman close to Sulla himself, and Sulla's own actions as dictator. Indeed, Cicero was to argue (*Rosc. Am.* 2) that some mention of the state of the Republic was unavoidable. This was a minefield. The jurors, most of whom owed their position both as senators and members of the jury to Sulla, would be unlikely to return a not guilty verdict, if they thought that it would in any way be an implied criticism of Sulla and his settlement, which they supported. Indeed, this may well be what the prosecution was counting on and it presented a considerable challenge to the defence.

Scholars have made varied assessments of what lay behind the Roscius case. It used to be seen as an archetypical 'political' case with Cicero as the front man for a coalition of nobles, who either sought to bully Sulla into retirement or, more subtly as the spokesman for Sullan supporters who wanted Sulla to clean up his act and distance the new system from the distasteful aspects of the past few years.[12] But Cicero's whole tone in the speech does little to support this view. He consistently seeks to 'depoliticize' the whole trial and avoids any whisper of criticism of Sulla. On the other hand the apparent illogicality and feebleness of the prosecution case has led some even to suppose that there was collusion between prosecution and defence and that it was always intended that Roscius should get off.[13] Indeed, the prosecution was in a bind. Roscius' father's name, it was claimed, had been entered on the list of the proscribed and his property had been confiscated and sold for the benefit of those who were behind the prosecution of Sextus Roscius. The charge against the younger Roscius was organizing the murder of his father. But if Roscius Senior had genuinely been proscribed, then his killing could not be the subject of a murder case. On the other hand, if the father had not been entered on the proscription lists before they closed, then the confiscation and sale of his property, from which Chrysogonus and the prosecutors benefited, could not be justified. The most economic and plausible explanation is that the case against Roscius is as weak as Cicero represents it and that the prosecution were relying on their influence and what Cicero calls the 'iniquitas temporum' ('the inequity of the times') (*Rosc. Am.* 1) to intimidate the court and get away with a shabby scam (as Cicero himself argues in *Rosc. Am.* 28).[14]

These circumstances governed the strategy of the opening of Cicero's defence. He immediately draws the attention of the jurors to the distinguished supporters of Roscius, who, like Augustus later, chose to sit silently on the benches of the court. They were 'summi oratores hominesque nobilissimi' ('consummate orators and men of most noble birth') (*Rosc. Am.* 1). The choice of 'nobilissimi' is a careful one, for, as Cicero was to emphasize later, Sulla's propaganda with some justification represented his takeover as a victory for the cause of the nobility (*Rosc. Am.* 135). Though he does not name them here, the Metelli, the Servilii, and the Scipiones were patrons of Roscius' father (*Rosc. Am.* 15), families at the very heart of the elite. But Cicero has to deal with the obvious question. Why did not one of these act as Roscius' advocate? His answer was that given who they were, any comments about the current state of affairs would be given a wider significance than was intended (*Rosc. Am.* 2: 'multo plura dixisse,

---

[12] For the attempt to attack Sulla see the deeply flawed case presented by J. Carcopino, *Sylla ou la monarchie manquée* (Paris 1947) 147 ff. For the trial as a warning to Sulla to act properly see E. Gruen, *Roman Politics and the Criminal Courts, 149–78 B.C.* (Harvard, 1968) 265–71.

[13] R. Heinze, 'Ciceros politische Anfänge' (1909) in E. Burck (ed.), *Vom Geist des Römertums* (Darmstadt, 1960), 87–140 and W. Stroh, *Taxis und Taktik* (Stuttgart, 1975), 55–79.

[14] See the excellent discussion in C. Craig, *Form as Argument in Cicero's Speeches: A Study of Dilemma* (Atlanta, 1993) 27–45 with bibliography.

quam dixisset, putaretur'). They might be thought to be attacking Sulla. However, men like these were the principal beneficiaries of Sulla's settlement and would not wish to rock the boat. But it could also be considered counterproductive, because if any of them had spoken, they would have been inhibited in what they could say, for fear that the jurors would interpret anything said on Roscius' behalf as anti-Sullan and incline to convict him. Cicero was to claim much later that he had been a victim of a very similar situation in his defence of C. Antonius in 59 BC at a time when Pompey and Julius Caesar were dominating public life. Cicero asserted (*Dom.* 41) that in his defence of Antonius he had 'made certain complaints about the Republic, which I considered relevant to the case of my wretched client' and that as a result Caesar and Pompey, stung by what they considered to be an attack on them, had promptly facilitated the adoption of Clodius, Cicero's enemy, into a plebeian family to enable him to stand for the tribunate and initiate the attack on Cicero which drove him into exile. It is certainly possible to doubt Cicero's interpretation of all this.[15] But it is easy to see how it came about. Antonius had been an old enemy of Caesar who had prosecuted him in 76 BC and Pompey had been a vocal advocate of Antonius' recall from his province because of his mismanagement.[16] So Cicero's remarks were probably little more than the standard claim that the *potentia* of Antonius' opponents was prejudicial to his client's case. Both the cases of Antonius and of Roscius show how the courts could often be enmeshed with public life in Rome.

In contrast to the leading names who sat in court to support Roscius, Cicero's insignificance at this stage of his career meant that his defence would not be overinterpreted. The whole opening of his speech is a brilliant exploitation of the unequal *auctoritas* argument. In this case Cicero's lack of *auctoritas* is presented by him as a positive advantage, while hinting that Roscius has more distinguished supporters in the background. On the other hand reference to the 'iniquitas temporum' ('the inequity of the times') (*Rosc. Am.* 1) and an aside that 'not only the practice of pardoning, but even the custom of legal proceedings has been removed from the state' (ibid. 3) set the listener up for the exposure of the unfair use of influence by Chrysogonus, Sulla's freedman, which Cicero claims lies behind the prosecution.

The need to reassure the Sullan jurors also explains the remarkable passage of autobiography which Cicero includes in the last third of the speech, where his target is Chrysogonus. He has already carefully separated Sulla from any responsibility for the actions of his freedman (131) and now he seeks to nail any final concerns the jurors might have

---

[15] See T. N. Mitchell, *Cicero the Senior Statesman* (New Haven, 1991) 115–20.
[16] Caesar: Asconius 84 C, 92 C, and Plut. *Caes.* 4; Pompey: *Att.* 1.12.1.

that a not guilty verdict would in any way be a criticism of the Sullan regime's success (136):

> Those who know me are aware that as soon as the possibility of an agreement–something I wanted above all–could not be achieved, to the best of my limited and feeble abilities I supported most strongly the victory of those who in fact won. For who was there who did not see that men of low birth were contending with men of dignity for the highest honours. In such a contest it would have been the act of a desperate citizen not to join those whose preservation assured dignity at home and authority abroad. I rejoice and am highly delighted, gentlemen of the jury, that this has been accomplished, that each has got his status and rank restored to him. I realize that all this has been achieved with the good will of the gods, the support of the Roman people, and the counsel, command, and good fortune of Sulla. I ought not to criticize the punishment meted out to those who fought against us in every way they could. I praise the honours held by those brave men who displayed exceptional commitment in the struggle. My opinion is that the struggle was precisely to bring about what has happened and openly state that I was a devoted supporter of that party.

The passage fully commits Cicero to a Sullan interpretation of the events of the past few years. The Sullan cause is the cause of the traditional nobility of Rome. In Asia the semblance of a senate had gathered round Sulla. Many notable figures who had found life difficult in Rome in the middle of the decade because of opposition to Marius and Cinna saw the chance of revival for their careers under him.[17] Cicero is careful to endorse a Sullan view of the proscriptions, that Sulla had made every effort to come to terms with his opponents and that he persecuted only those who fought on after breaking the agreement he had made at Teanum with Scipio.[18] Cicero, like many others in the courtroom probably, had not left Rome at any point. He had gone on living and working there, not necessarily out of support for the Cinnan regime or indeed opposition to Sulla, but simply because he had no real cause to leave, however uncomfortable he might feel. Here he endorses the efforts of those in Rome, notably L. Valerius Flaccus in 85 BC, who sought to come to a settlement with Sulla to prevent the need for civil war. Of course, what Cicero's narrative entirely omits is the fact that, in common again with many others, he did not actually take up arms on Sulla's behalf at any stage. There is much here that would have resonated in the minds of many of the jurors who may well have had similar experiences. By seeking to identify himself with the jurors, Cicero reinforced the message at the heart of his defence that an acquittal of Roscius would be safe and would not be in any way disruptive

---

[17] J. Paterson, 'Politics in the Late Republic', in T. P. Wiseman (ed.), *Roman Political Life 90 B.C.–A.D. 69* (Exeter, 1985) 23–7.   [18] Appian *BC* 1.85.

of the Sullan settlement. So far from being arbitrary self-glorification or self-justification, Cicero's concentration on his own experiences is a key to his defence strategy.

Cicero's reputation in the courts grew dramatically in the 70s and 60s BC and at the same time, and not unconnected, he was successful in climbing the *cursus honorum* and in reaching the consulship in 63 BC. His actions during that year in suppressing the so-called 'conspiracy of Catiline' were a source of great controversy. There were those at the time, as Cicero admits, who felt that at the very least he had exaggerated the scale and nature of the 'conspiracy'. Then, as now, the most worrying aspect of the whole affair was that practically all the evidence, such as it was, was provided or engineered by Cicero himself. We may be dealing, as some suspected at the time, with Cicero's conspiracy against Catiline.[19] Nevertheless, Cicero had become a person to be reckoned with and his undoubted *auctoritas* was to be exploited for what it was worth in the interests of his clients. In 62 BC in a manifestly non-political case, the defence of the poet Aulus Licinius Archias, who was prosecuted for falsely claiming Roman citizenship, Cicero was always ready to remind the jury of just what he had done.[20] In praising the virtues of the study of literature, for example, he claims that 'if I had not been persuaded from my youth upwards by the teachings of many and much that I read that there is nothing to be so greatly sought after in life as praise and honour ... then I should never have withstood for the safety of you all (the jury) so many great struggles and these daily attacks from wretched criminals' (*Arch.* 14). Again near the end of his speech he emphasizes the fact that he had sponsored Archias to complete a poem about Cicero, which covered 'the actions which I took in my consulship, along with you (the jurors) to protect the safety of this city, the empire, the lives of its citizens, and the whole state' (*Arch.* 28). Nothing in the defence required these reminders of what Cicero had done as consul; but note how Cicero draws the jury into both statements (he had been working both on their behalf and in collaboration with them). Once again Cicero exploits his own experiences to persuade the jurors that his and their views are identical. A subtle exploitation of *auctoritas*.

It might be thought that the trial of Murena in 63 BC for using bribery in his election campaign for the consulship of 62 BC was more closely

---

[19] R. Seager, 'Iusta Catilinae', *Historia* 22 (1973) 240–8.

[20] Unconvincing cases have been made for there being a 'political' background to Archias' trial in the rivalry of Pompey and Lucullus (e.g. J. H. Taylor, 'Political Motives in Cicero's Defence of Archias', *AJP* 73 (1952) 62–70), but their weakness can be seen from the statement of E. S. Gruen, *The Last Generation of the Roman Republic* (Berkeley, 1974) 267–8: 'the implicit political struggle is, of course, ignored.' Indeed it is, because it did not exist.

involved in the politics of 63 BC and so, indeed, Cicero seeks to make it. The trial came at a significant point in the events of that year after Catiline had left Rome but before the exposure of the conspirators on 3 December. The lull had raised suspicions in people's minds that Cicero may have exaggerated the dangers and it may be that the prosecution chose this as the best moment to bring the case to trial, when questions could be raised about Cicero's conduct as consul. In reality the Murena case had little to do with the so-called conspiracy, but the prosecution had to face the fact that Cicero would exploit his actions and *auctoritas* as consul in defence of Murena in an obvious way by arguing that the successful prosecution of Murena would mean that Rome would start the year without one consul at a dangerous moment in its history, while his acquittal would ensure the continued stability which Cicero's vigilance had brought the state. Therefore it becomes essential for the prosecutors to undermine Cicero's standing, which they do by the time-honoured technique of claiming that Cicero's position as consul put him at an unfair advantage. Cicero had to find a response which on the one hand exploited for all it was worth his current position and influence, while at the same time refuting the prosecution's claims of *arrogantia*. So the speech opens with Cicero himself at the forefront reminding the jury of one of the duties as consul, when he announced Murena's election as consul and prayed that (*Mur.* 1):

ea res *mihi*, fidei magistratuique *meo*, populo plebique Romanae bene atque feliciter eveniret (this event might turn out well and happily for myself, for people's trust in me, for my magistracy, for the people and plebs of Rome).

Later in the speech come reminders of just who Cicero is (*Mur.* 86, 'By my authority as consul I exhort you' and 90, 'I, as consul, commend this man, a consul, to you, members of the jury').

Cicero also seizes on the need to offer an explanation for Murena's success in the election by replaying his own role in undermining Catiline's campaign (*Mur.* 51–3). He goes on to argue that the acquittal of Murena would help him as consul in his defence of the Republic. He exploits the air of uncertainty, suspicion and terror, which he himself had largely created, to suggest that the conspirators are still around in the city (*Mur.* 78, 'intus, intus, inquam, est equus Troianus', 'the Trojan horse is within the walls. Within the walls, I say') and that it would be playing into their hands to leave Rome without two consuls in January 62 BC. Cicero's justification for concentrating on himself and his actions as consul was the standard one that the prosecution had made it an issue in the first place; but he then goes on to rebut the charge that the speech was a vehicle for his own political campaign against Catiline (*Mur.* 2):

Before I begin to speak for L. Murena, I shall say a few words on my own behalf, not because at this time the defence of my own duties is more important to me than the defence of this man's wellbeing, but because when my actions are approved by you then I may be able with greater authority to fend off the attacks of his enemies on this man's honour, reputation and all his possessions.

To modern eyes this looks like a classic case of Cicero eating his cake and having it. But the argument must have had some plausibility in the eyes of the jury. The prosecution had sought to undermine Cicero's standing; a defence of his *auctoritas* was to be expected, indeed required. Of course, Cicero was aware that he was in danger of overstepping a boundary and alienating the jury by using his position to pressurize them. As often he tries to defuse this with ironic wit, when he appeals to the jury, 'Listen, listen to a consul (I'll not put it any more arrogantly, but just say this), to a consul who spends every moment of every day and night thinking about the Republic' (*Mur.* 78).

Cicero carries this approach a dramatic stage further in his defence of P. Sulla in 62 BC, where Cicero practically stands foursquare in front of his client and turns the spotlight on himself. It was successful in this case and was to become a key tactic in later speeches. Right from the start it is Cicero's standing which is at stake. He admits that he sees the case as a chance to demonstrate his *lenitas* and *misericordia*, after the circumstances of the consulship had forced him to be tough and fierce (*Sull.* 1). And at the very end of the speech he appeals to the jurors to join him in repelling the false reputation he had gained for cruelty by his execution of the conspirators. A good third of the whole speech is about Cicero and his actions and behaviour. Once again Cicero can justify himself with the fact that the prosecution had raised his standing in the first place ('Torquatus attacked me throughout his speech') and Torquatus' purpose that 'he wanted to rob my defence of its *auctoritas*' (*Sull.* 35). This prosecution strategy was an obvious one in the circumstances. In one way the revelation in December of a group of conspirators had been a godsend to Cicero. It enabled him to claim that his warnings about a widespread conspiracy had been right all along. But the execution of those conspirators, albeit after a Senate vote, was extremely dubious in legal terms. Further there continued to be disquiet about the fact that so much of the 'evidence' about the conspiracy originated with Cicero himself. Concern about Cicero's dominant role was widespread and found a voice in the attacks from the incoming tribunes, Q. Metellus Nepos and L. Calpurnius Bestia. Their accusation that Cicero had behaved tyrannically, that his consulship had constituted a *regnum*, was taken up by Torquatus (*Sull.* 21). He also exploits the concern about the nature of the evidence (*Sull.* 21, 'Those against whom you give evidence are condemned; the man you defend hopes to go free') and Cicero's apparent inconsistency in only defending Sulla out of all those accused of involvement in the conspiracy (*Sull.* 10, 'You gave evidence against Autronius; you defend Sulla'). Since Cicero's position is crucial, Torquatus could not avoid attempting to undermine it. This explains why he directed his fire at Cicero and not the other defence counsel (*Sull.* 3). It also makes it inevitable that Cicero would have to defend himself, if his defence of Sulla was to succeed. To the dispassionate critic Cicero does not succeed. Early in the speech he claims that he 'will use his *auctoritas* moderately and would not use it at all, had Torquatus not forced him to do so' (*Sull.* 10). But a later passage is hardly a case of moderation (*Sull.* 33): 'I as consul ... by my plans, by my efforts, at risk of my life ... saved the state from ruin.' This is a reassertion of his authority. Further his only real contribution comes when he swears on oath that as consul he had no evidence against Sulla (*Sull.* 86). Cicero is not just advocate, but leading witness, and would like to be judge and jury as well. But in the end the strategy succeeded.

The defence of Sestius in 56 BC is even more startling with Sestius reduced to a bit part, while Cicero holds centre stage throughout. Indeed Cicero claims that the case was really about himself ('P. Sestius est reus non suo, sed meo nomine', 'Sestius is accused not in his own name but in mine', *Sest.* 31). In part Cicero's justification is that the principal charge against Sestius was his use of armed force during his tribunate to counter opposition to Cicero's recall from exile. It is interesting to note that Cicero speaks as though those attending the trial were expecting him to talk about himself: 'I will lay out today, members of the jury, a complete account of my actions and plans. I will not disappoint your enormous desire to hear me nor that of this huge crowd, greater than I ever remember attending a trial before' (*Sest.* 36). But there are unexpected sides to this. In the opening Cicero undertakes to review in conventional manner Sestius' background and career (*Sest.* 5); but even here the agenda is set by Cicero's career rather than by that of Sestius. After brief remarks about Sestius' family Cicero turns to matters of more importance ('the dignity of the Republic', 7), namely the year of Cicero's consulship when Sestius was a quaestor. It is Sestius' role in helping against the Catilinarians which is emphasized (8–12). Surprising in one way is the fact that this account of 63 BC is so restrained with little emphasis on Cicero's own actions. Cicero has learned his lesson and does not want to reopen the controversial aspects of 63 BC which had led to his exile in 58 BC. Cicero then hastens over Sestius' time as quaestor in the province of Macedonia in order to get to Sestius' tribunate of 57 BC, where again Cicero is in the forefront (14: 'since P. Sestius did nothing in his tribunate but support my reputation and case'). Then on the thinnest of excuses the central part of Cicero's speech is taken up not with the events of 57 BC when Sestius was tribune, but with the events of 58 BC when Cicero went into exile, which had little direct relevance to Sestius. When it comes, Cicero's justification is that Sestius in his tribunate had healed the wounds inflicted on the Republic in the previous year (31). Cicero was exploiting the wave of support which had led to his recall in the interests of his client (147: 'If you wanted me to be saved, then you should protect those, by whose efforts you got me back'). It needs to be remembered that other advocates had spoken in support of Sestius before Cicero and one of them, Hortensius, had dealt in detail with the charge (3). Something different was expected of Cicero and this explains the nature and tenor of his speech. In an age of multiple advocates it is difficult to judge Cicero's contribution when we do not know how he fitted in with the other advocates.

It might be thought that the Sestius case, like that of Sulla, was exceptional in that they both inevitably involved the interests of Cicero himself. However, Cicero deploys much the same strategy in his defence in 54 BC of Gnaeus Plancius on a charge of electoral corruption. The case had little real political significance or direct involvement of Cicero's interests in any way. Behind the prosecution was M. Juventius Laterensis who had been beaten in the elections for aedile in 55 BC by Plancius and took it badly. Once again we see Cicero putting himself at the centre of the case, playing on the sympathy which his exile had inspired. So he claims at the outset that the opportunity to defend Plancius was welcome, because of 'the notable and exceptional loyalty he had shown in preserving my safety' (*Planc.* 1), recalling the protection and help which Plancius had provided as quaestor in Macedonia where he supported Cicero through the dark days of his exile. Cicero goes on to imply that the prosecution was motivated by enmity and dislike of him–an implausible charge, since Cicero could not deny that Juventius had also been a supporter of his case (*Planc.* 86). The purpose of this was to alienate the prosecution from the jury, whose sympathies Cicero claimed because they included those who had supported Cicero's recall. Cicero sets this up at the outset (2) in preparation for the final section of the speech where Cicero discourses at length on his experiences in exile and those who might have helped him (86 ff.), in particular Plancius. This then leads directly into the peroration where Cicero's fate is linked directly to Plancius, when Cicero expresses the hope that the jury members will show the same determination in saving Plancius, which they showed in rescuing Cicero (104).

Cicero was also able to take his identification with Plancius further. As men of equestrian birth, the first in their families to seek public office, they both faced, or claimed to face, the resentment of better-born or better-connected rivals. So Cicero was able to use his own career as a model to explain Plancius' achievements. Cicero concedes that in the matter of birth Juventius had the better of Plancius, 'but to no greater extent than I was bettered by my competitors for the other magistracies and especially for the consulship' (*Planc.* 18). In stating that Plancius had obtained his posts by the route which 'always lies open to men born of our equestrian status' (17), Cicero is drawing in the sympathies of the jury, on which men of equestrian status predominated. Cicero was also able to cite his own experience as quaestor to undermine one of the prosecution claims. His anecdote became famous, in which he vividly tells how, after a successful quaestorship in Sicily, it was brought home to him on his return that people had hardly noticed that he was not in Rome. A witty tale told against himself (*Planc.* 64).

Cicero could have chosen other lines of defence. He justifies the concentration on himself in the usual way by claiming that the prosecution had started it by attacking him (*Planc.* 3 and 58). Again, as in the other cases, where Cicero highlights himself, he has to refute the suggestion that he was making overweening use of his *auctoritas*. So he is careful to state (3) that 'I do not presume that Plancius by his services to me is entitled to freedom from prosecution', whereas in fact large parts of his speech are directed to just that end. Similarly, while Cicero notes his own role in the campaign for Plancius' election, he goes out of his way to play down his influence (24).

The defence of Plancius shows just how far Cicero had travelled from the young advocate in the cases of Quinctius and of Roscius of Ameria, where he had to counter the greater influence of his opponents, to the wholehearted exploitation of his *auctoritas* in the defence of Sestius and of Plancius.

This aspect of Cicero's advocacy has no modern parallel. It was not prompted by overpowering vanity on Cicero's part, but was a response to the nature of advocacy in Rome and its origins in patronage, where the influence of the patron was at the heart of the system. Further, although contemporary politics intrude frequently in these cases, it is not because they are simply politics conducted by other means.[21] Not all advocates had significant public careers, but those who had would certainly exploit the

---

[21] The whole tenor of my argument is somewhat different from Ann Vasaly, 'Cicero's early speeches', in J. M. May (ed.), *Brill's Companion to Cicero: Oratory and Rhetoric* (Leiden, 2002) 71–111. She sees Cicero as 'crafting a public image' and claims that 'Cicero made use even of his earliest speeches to appear as more than simply an advocate speaking in defence of a particular client' (98). My contention remains that in his court speeches Cicero's primary concern at all times was the interests of his clients.

influence they had gained. Equally the other side in any case had to devise ways of undermining that influence in the eyes of the jury, so leaving the way open for Cicero, and others in defence cases, to claim that they had no choice but to discuss themselves, because the prosecution had done it first. In concentrating on himself, Cicero never forgot what he was about, which was to win the case for his client. His strategies should be interpreted in light of the fact that courts in Rome breathed the air of the Roman Forum.

0   50   100 miles

0   80   160 km

Arretium

Volaterrae

Interamnia

Ameria

Tarquinii

Rome

Aletrium

Tusculum   Sora   Larinum

Arpinum   Atina

Aquinum   Venafrum

Allifae

Atella

3

A Volscian Mafia? Cicero and his Italian Clients in the Forensic Speeches

Kathryn Lomas

Ego mehercule et illi et omnibus municipibus duas esse censeo patrias, unam naturae, alteram civitatis ... sed necesse est caritate eam praestare, qua rei publicae nomen universae civitatis est; pro qua mori et cui nos totos dedere et in qua nostra omnia ponere et quasi consecrare debemus. dulcis autem non multo secus est ea, quae genuit, quam illa, quae excepit. itaque ego hanc meam esse patriam prorsus numquam negabo, dum illa sit maior, haec in ea contineatur.

all men from the *municipia* have two *patriae*, one by birth and one by citizenship ... But that which is the common citizenship must stand first in our affection in the name of the state; for it is our duty to die for this and to give ourselves completely, to consecrate ourselves and offer up everything we have. But that into which we were born is not less sweet to us than into which we were adopted. And so I will never deny that this [i.e. Arpinum] is my *patria*, although the other [i.e. Rome] is greater, and includes this one within it.

(Cicero, *De Legibus* 2.5)

This passage from the *De Legibus* sums up the essential dilemma of the Italian nobility in the first century BC. In the aftermath of the bitter Social War between Rome and the Italians, ending in the extension of Roman citizenship to all Italians, the competing claims of existing local loyalties and the new demands made by integration into the Roman State, created an intense debate amongst the Italian nobility about the nature of regional identity and how to reconcile this with the profound changes in the

This chapter was originally delivered as part of the 'Cicero the Advocate' seminar series at the University of Newcastle upon Tyne, and subsequently as a paper to the Northumberland and Durham Classical Association. I would like to thank Mr J. J. Paterson, Prof. J. G. F. Powell, and Prof. T. J. Cornell for their comments on various aspects of this chapter.

relationship of Italian states to Rome. Cicero was deeply and personally engaged with this; his home city–Arpinum–was a Volscian community in southern Latium which was granted Roman citizenship in 188 BC.[1] His family was highly placed. According to Plutarch, he was descended from the Volscian king Tullus[2]; his grandfather and father were leading men in Arpinum and the family had close senatorial connections (notably with Aemilius Scaurus and L. Crassus) but Cicero was the first to pursue a political career at Rome rather than Arpinum.[3] As a result, he was deeply concerned with the contemporary debate about how to reconcile a commitment to one's own city with a career which required increasing integration into the Roman elite. Indeed, it has become a commonplace of Ciceronian scholarship that Cicero's Italian origins, and the tension between these and his identification with the Roman elite, fundamentally colour his writings and world-view, and that Italians occupy an important role in his works. However, the reality is considerably more complex and nowhere more so than in the legal speeches. The most striking thing about Cicero's works is not the prominence of Italians, even in those speeches where the Italian background is most vital to his conduct of the case, but their relatively low level of visibility.[4] Nevertheless, the forensic speeches in which Cicero defends men of municipal origin cast an important light on Italian identity in the mid-first century BC and, conversely, the municipal background of the defendants is important to our understanding of these speeches. This chapter will examine two interconnected themes: first, what do we know about the Italians who were defended by Cicero or otherwise appear prominently in his legal speeches, their background and the munici-palities from which they originated, and Cicero's connections with them? Second, how are they characterized in the speeches, what role do they play, and what does this tell us about Roman and Italian identity in the generation after the Social War? The principal focus will be on the *Pro Roscio Amerino*, the *Pro Cluentio*, the *Pro Caecina*, the *Pro Caelio*, and the *Pro Plancio*, all of which have municipal Italy as an essential part of their background. They are not by any means the only speeches which have an Italian dimension, but they are the works which bring this most to the fore, and between them they allow us to explore a wide range of Italian communities in this era and an equally wide range of relationships between the elites of these communities and Rome.

---

[1] Volscian origins: Plut. *Cic.* 1, Strab. 5.3.10; *civitas sine suffragio*, 303 BC: Livy 10.1.3, Festus 262L; *civitas optimo iure*, 188 BC: Livy 38.36.7. [2] Plut. *Cic.* 1.
[3] D. Stockton, *Cicero: A Political Biography* (Oxford, 1971) 1–7; C. Nicolet, 'Arpinum, Aemilius Scaurus et les Tullii Cicerones' *REL* 45 (1967) 276–304; E. D. Rawson, 'L. Crassus and Cicero: The Formation of a Statesman', *Roman Culture and Society. Collected Papers* (Oxford, 1991) 16–33. On the politics of Cicero's family in Arpinum, see Val. Max. 6.9.14, Cic. *Leg.* 3.36, T. P. Wiseman, *New Men in the Roman Senate* (Oxford, 1971) 30–3, 55. [4] See below, pp. 114–16 and n. 93.

All of the major protagonists in this sequence of speeches are men (and to a lesser extent women) of municipal background, but the majority are equally well embedded in the upper echelons of Roman society—all of them wealthy, although many were of equestrian rather than senatorial rank. Given the high social profile which they seem to have enjoyed, both in their own communities and at Rome, one must assume that as with Cicero's friend Atticus, this was from choice rather than economic necessity.[5] However, they illustrate a wide range of experiences, ambitions, and opportunities for members of the Italian elite in this period of history.

Caelius and Interamnia

One of the highest-profile Italians defended by Cicero was his friend and client M. Caelius Rufus, prosecuted *de vi* in 56 BC. He was born *c*.88/7 BC, probably at Interamnia Praetuttiorum in the northern Apennines.[6] His family were of equestrian rank but Caelius himself was following a senatorial career at Rome, as the first of his family to make the transition from regional to Roman politics.[7] Cicero makes great play with his origins as part of the defence case, in reply to the prosecution's charge that Caelius' municipal and equestrian background was a mark against him and that he was disapproved of by the municipality of Interamnia. He stresses the depth of local support for Caelius and makes reference to a retinue of notables and senators from the region who allegedly turn up in Rome to support him during his trial.[8]

Interamnia itself was on the border between Picenum and eastern Samnium, on a major route of communication. It was the major settlement of the Praetuttii, a small *ethnos* whose territory bordered onto Picenum proper and which was culturally and linguistically closely related to the

[5] Wiseman, *New Men*; T. P. Wiseman, '*Domi Nobiles* and the Roman Cultural Elite', in M. Cébeillac-Gervasioni, (ed.), *Les 'Bourgeoisies' municipales italiennes aux IIme et Iere siècles av. J.-C.* (Paris, 1983) 299–307; U. Laffi, 'I senati locali nell'Italia repubblicana', in M. Cébeillac-Gervasioni (ed.), *Les 'Bourgeoisies' municipales italiennes aux IIme et Iere siècles av. J.-C.* (Paris, 1983) 59–74.

[6] There are some textual problems with Cic. *Cael.* 3, and the name of his home city is corrupted. Interamnia is, however, the most plausible reconstruction and usually accepted as the home-town of Caelius.

[7] *Cael.* 3–5, 9–10; T. R. S. Broughton, *The Magistrates of the Roman Republic* (New York, 1952) 235, 248–9.

[8] *Cael.* 5, 'idemque nunc lectissimos viros et nostri ordinis et equites Romanos cum legatione ad hoc iudicium et cum gravissima atque ornatissima laudatione miserunt' ('and these same people have now sent most distinguished men from our Order and the equites as a delegation to this court to offer a most weighty and eloquent commendation of him').

Picenes.[9] Interamnia was inhabited well before the Roman conquest, as attested by Iron Age inhumation burials, mostly on the west side of the city and traces of Praetuttian settlement within the area of the later Roman city, as well as fifth-century inscriptions in the south Picene language found in the surrounding area.[10] The territory of the Praetuttii came under Roman control *c.*290 BC and was enrolled in the tribe Velina in 241,[11] but as with many communities in this region of Italy, its urban development took place relatively late. A gradual process of urbanization began during the second century BC, following devastation of the region during the Hannibalic War, but Interamnia retained the status of *conciliabulum*–in other words not an autonomous urban community–until the Social war.[12] According to Frontinus, it became a *municipium* immediately after the Social War[13] but was heavily penalized by Sulla, who founded a veteran colony there, having been on the wrong side in either the Social or Civil Wars.[14] The existence of the colony has been a matter of debate, but there is epigraphic evidence to support the assertions of Florus and the *Gromatici*. However, the community may have retained dual status–that of *municipium* and that of *colonia*–until a considerably later date, as implied by an inscription of the early empire.[15]

In the first century BC, Interamnia was a community in a state of transition. The foundation of the colony created all sorts of structural and constitutional complexities. The pre-municipal magistrates–the *octoviri*–remained the main magistrates of the city, along with the more Roman-sounding Praetors, although later inscriptions make reference to a more conventional *cursus* headed by *duoviri*.[16] Colonization may also have created a fair amount of social and political tension as well. The potentially divisive effects of such a foundation–in this case the colony at Pompeii–are graphically portrayed in the *Pro Sulla*.[17] Caelius' father must have been both politically astute and a supporter of the Sullan regime, since he retained his estates and was able to fund his son's senatorial career at Rome. In addition to

---

[9] Pliny *NH* 3.13.110, 112; Ptol. 3.1.58; Steph. Byz. s.v., Πραιτετία; G. J. Bradley and K. Lomas 'Regio V: Introduction', in T. J. Cornell and K. Lomas (eds.) *Cities and Urbanism in Ancient Italy: An Archaeological Encyclopaedia* (Leiden, forthcoming).

[10] E. Giammarco, 'Per la storia linguistica di Interamna e di Teate', *Abruzzo* 21 (1983) 159–68.

[11] Livy 10.10.12–11.8; Florus 1.10.15; *CIL* 9.5065, 5074.

[12] Livy 22.9.5, 27.43.10; Polyb. 3.88.3; Frontin. 18; B. Campbell, *The Writings of the Roman Land-Surveyors* (London, 2000) 66–7 and 355.

[13] Frontin. 18; Campbell, *The Writings of the Roman Land-Surveyors*, 66–7 and 355.

[14] Florus 2.9; Gromat. 226.5; 255.1; 259.1

[15] *CIL* 9.5074 (= I² 1903a–b) makes reference to the people of Interamnia as 'municipi et coloniai municipibus coloneis incoleis'. On the phenomenon of dual status, see A. Degrassi, 'Quattuorviri in colonie Romane e in municipi retti da duoviri', *Mem. Linc.* 8.2 (1950) 281–344; L. Migliorati. 'Municipes et coloni. Note di urbanistica teramana', *Arch. Class.* 28 (1976) 242–56.

[16] *CIL* 9.5067 (Octoviri), 5073 (praetors), 5144 (duoviri).

[17] Cic. *Sulla* 60–62; D. H. Berry, *Cicero Pro P. Sulla Oratio* (Cambridge, 1996) 35–6, 250–7; T. P. Wiseman, 'Cicero *Pro Sulla* 61–2' *LCM* ii (1977) 21–2.

the political disruption and administrative changes of the post-Social
War era, Interamnia underwent a major phase of urbanization, although this
seems to have been a slow process, which started in the early second century
and continued into the Augustan era. The city was clearly flourishing–
several sources cite Interamnia as an important wine-growing area, and the
large amount of public building in progress in the middle years of the century
attests to an affluent and dynamic community.[18] The precise layout of the
city is impossible to recover and most buildings are fragmentary, but there
may have been two distinct zones–an eastern one which corresponds to
the original settlement, and a western one which has been identified with the
Sullan colony. Baths of the first century BC and a temple of Hercules built
in 55 BC are epigraphically attested, and deposits of architectural terracottas
dating to the second and first centuries BC provide further evidence of lavish
public or private structures. A number of opulent private houses provide
evidence of the wealth of the city's elite at this date.[19] The so-called Domus
del Leone was a large house of Ciceronian date (possibly mid-first century
BC), located close to the forum and richly decorated with marble and with
mosaic pavement. Another large private house, of similar date although in
a much less complete state of preservation, has been found close to the
cathedral,[20] but most other structures (e.g. the theatre, amphitheatre, and
more baths) date to the Augustan era or the first century AD. Despite
its scrappy nature, the archaeological evidence suggests that Interamnia was
a dynamic community in the Ciceronian era, in the process of making the
transition into a Romanized city. The nature of elite society there, and the
level of contact with Rome, is less easy to assess. There were clearly wealthy
and prominent families, as demonstrated by the lavish private houses, but it
is difficult to imagine that the group of local senators and *equites* who came
to Rome to support Caelius, as Cicero claims, would have been large. The
number of equestrian families from the city is impossible to guess at, but the
number of senators at this date was probably small. Apart from Caelius
himself, only Manlius Maltinius has been identified as a possible senator
from Interamnia, and his provenance is not entirely certain.[21] Another senatorial family–the Poppaei–produced two consuls (cos. and cos. suff. AD 9)–
but its rise to prominence was rather later, under Augustus. The likelihood
is, therefore, that the elite of Interamnia was flourishing but may have comprised a fairly small number of families.

---

[18] Pliny *NH* 14.67.1, 75.8; Sil. It. 15.568; W. Mazzitti, *Teramo archeologica. Ripertorio di monumenti* (Teramo, 1983).

[19] *CIL* 9.5074–75 (baths), 9.5052 (temple of Hercules); H. Jouffroy, *La Construction publique en Italie et dans L'Afrique romain* (Strasbourg, 1986) 34, 53; F. Savini, 'Teramo. Scavi nel teatro romano' *NSc* 6.2 (1929) 391–402.

[20] A. and G. Cingoli, *Da Interamnia a Teramo* (Teramo, 1978).

[21] Wiseman, *New Men*, no. 246.

Plancius and Atina

In some respects, the background of Cn. Plancius was socially similar to that of Caelius. He was the son of an *eques* and *publicanus* from Atina in southern Latium, and was seeking to make a political career at Rome, also the first generation of his family to do so. He served in Africa, Crete, and Macedonia as military tribune and then as quaestor, held the tribunate in 56 and was elected aedile in 55/4 BC after which he was prosecuted on a charge of electoral bribery by M. Juventius Laterensis of Tusculum, one of the unsuccessful candidates.[22] Politically, he was a Pompeian supporter, had close connections with C. Sentius Saturninus also from Atina, and was related to Scribonia, later wife of Octavian.[23]

His home town, Atina, was a Volscian settlement in origin, dominating the valley of the River Melfi and overlooking the Via Appia. By the fourth century BC, it was a settlement of some significance and was in the forefront of the conflict between Samnites (by whom it was occupied during the fourth century) and Rome.[24] Atina was captured by Rome in 290 BC and its status between 290 and 89 BC is uncertain. Coarelli suggests that the city may have received *civitas sine suffragio* at some point, and full citizenship in the second century BC, but this is not entirely certain.[25] Bafflingly, Cicero describes the city as a *praefectura*, a term most usually applied to communities which were not fully urbanized, although elsewhere he refers to it as a *municipium*, and also as an *oppidum*, or small town.[26] Since it seems likely that Atina was an urban settlement by this date, it is most likely to have been a *municipium* of the tribe Teretina, and is known to have had a Romanized duoviral constitution, unlike some other cities of this region which retained the traditional form of government by three aediles–a fact which Cicero records with local pride.[27] A number of elite families from Atina were politically successful at Rome during the first century BC. As well as Plancius, there are two other *gentes* from Atina, the Arruntii (L. Arruntius L.f. consul in 22 BC, and the Sentii

---

[22] *Planc.* 21–4, 26–8, 77, 99; *Q.Fr.* 2.13, 3.1; Schol. Bob. 142, 153. Plancius had assisted Cicero during his exile, *Att.* 3.14, 3.22; *Fam.* 14.1.

[23] The Sentii had made an impact at Rome earlier than the Plancii. C. Sentius was consul in 19 BC, but his father had been praetor in 94 BC. A. Licordari, 'Ascesa al senato e rapporti con i territori d'origine Italia: Regio I (Latium)', *Epigrafia e ordine senatorio* (Rome, 1982) 23–4.

[24] E. T. Salmon, *Samnium and the Samnites* (Cambridge, 1965) 253, 271–8.

[25] F. Coarelli, *Lazio* (Bari, 1982) 226. There is no certain evidence for this, but the hypothesis is plausible. Neighbouring cities, including Arpinum, Fundi, Formiae, and Cumae, all had their status upgraded from *civitas sine suffragio* to *civitas optimo iure* in the 180s BC (Livy 38.36.7).

[26] *Planc.* 21.

[27] Cic. *Fam.* 3.11; *CIL* 10.6105, 6108 (Formiae), 10.6233–5, 6238–9, 6242 (Fundi), 10.5680–83 (Arpinum).

(C. Sentius, C.f., aed. *c.*97, pr. urb. 94; L. Sentius C.f., monetalis 105 BC).[28] Two further families, the Tettii and the Helvii, also rose to senatorial rank under Augustus.[29] All of these *gentes* seem to have been more successful than Plancius at maintaining a high profile in the city. The only other member of the *gens Plancia* attested at Atina is Plancia, mother of the *duumvir* L. Postumius Rufus.[30] Cicero's assertion[31] that Atina rallied around Plancius because his political success at Rome was rare amongst the elite of the city is not borne out by the number of local families which were clearly on the way up the social and political ladder.

Atina was clearly a flourishing community during the late Republic and early Empire but large parts of the ancient city have been destroyed and evidence for its development is mainly epigraphic. There was large-scale public building in the first century BC, but much of this is slightly later than the Ciceronian era and was largely the result of Atinates who forged careers at Rome in the Civil War period or under Augustus. There are a substantial number of building inscriptions and dedications to patrons of the city, demonstrating a high level of euergetic and civic activity and access to a substantial network of patronage. L. Arruntius, the consul of 22 BC, was responsible for reconstructing much of the layout of the city, undertaking the building or repair of streets, footpaths, and drains.[32] The forum pecuarium was built (together with further road repairs), at the expense of two *duoviri*.[33] Other inscriptions commemorate patrons of the city and local benefactors but offer fewer details of the nature of the benefactions. There are few archaeological remains. Parts of the city wall survive, built of polygonal masonry with later rebuilding and refacing in *opus incertum* probably undertaken during the middle of the first century BC.[34] Outside the city there was a sanctuary of the Italic goddess Mefitis, identified by a Latin inscription and a votive deposit of terracotta figurines,[35] and a late Republican villa has been found at Vicalvi, in the territory of Atina.[36] Economically, much of the city's wealth was agrarian,

---

[28] Arruntii: Wiseman, *New Men*, no. 41, Licordari, 'Ascesa al senato', 23; *ILS* 5349; Sentii: Wiseman, *New Men*, nos. 387, 388, Licordari, 'Ascesa al senato', 24, R. Syme, 'Senators, Tribes and Towns', *Historia* 13 (1964) 105–24. Wiseman also lists M. Petreius, who served under Pompey 55–49 BC, and P. Tettius Rufus, who reached the praetorship under Augustus, as senators from Atina (Wiseman, *New Men*, nos. 314, 425, 426), although the origins of the Petreii are not certain. See also O. Salomies, 'Senatori oriundi del Lazio', in H. Solin (ed.), *Studi storico-epigrafici sul Lazio Antico* (Rome, 1996) 43–7, who includes the Tillii and the Rubrenii in the list of 1st-cent. BC senators from Atina.

[29] Licordari, 'Ascesa al senato', 24.   [30] *CIL* 10.5075.   [31] *Planc.* 22–3.

[32] *CIL* 10.5055.   [33] *CIL* 10.5074.

[34] E. Beranger and A. Sorrentino, *La cinta muraria di Atina* (Sora, 1980); Jouffroy, *Construction publique*, 18.

[35] *CIL* 10.5047; S. Aurigemma and G. Scaccia Scarafoni, *NSc* (1950), 108–15; Coarelli, *Lazio*, 228. The terracottas indicate that the sanctuary dated to at least the 4th cent. BC but the inscription seems to indicate that it was still in use in the late Republic.   [36] Coarelli, *Lazio*, 229.

with an emphasis on pastoralism. Atina was located on a network of *tratturi*, or drove roads, as well as on the major arterial routes, and the existence of a specialist *forum pecuarium* for the sale of sheep suggests that it exploited this and developed into an important centre for marketing livestock.[37]

Roscius and Ameria

Ameria was a flourishing Umbrian municipium, located in the Tiber valley, and 56 km north of Rome. Cato gives the unlikely foundation date of 1124 BC, but the earliest physical evidence dates to the fourth century BC. It was ethnically on the border between Umbria and Etruria, and pre-Roman inscriptions use both languages.[38] Relatively little is known of its urban development, but the site appears to have been inhabited since at least the fifth century BC, and to have been fortified with massive walls at the end of the fourth century. Most of the remains of Roman buildings—both private houses and presumed public buildings—are fragmentary and appear to date to the Principate rather than the Ciceronian period.[39] However, the Latin epigraphy from the city (again, mainly of imperial date) indicates a flourishing community, with evidence of an alimentary scheme and numerous other benefactions.[40] It also confirms the long-term prominence of the Roscii, the family of Cicero's client. Roscii are found in inscriptions from the city from the late Republic until well into the Empire and their social level ranges from holders of civic office to the freedmen and freed-women of the family.[41] However, unlike Atina and Interamnia, it seems to have lacked families which were promoted to senatorial rank.[42] The region's economy was buoyant. Ameria controlled a fertile territory and was a noted fruit-growing area, probably supplying the Roman

---

[37] *CIL* 10.5074.

[38] fr. 49 P (= Pliny *HN* 3.114); E. Vetter, *Handbuch der Italischen Dialekte* (Heidelberg, 1953) 229; M. Gaggiotti, et al., *Umbria-Marche* (Bari, 1980) 18–20, 30–4; G. Bradley, *Ancient Umbria. State, Culture and Identity in Central Italy from the Iron Age to the Augustan Era* (Oxford, 2000) 177, 208–9.

[39] G. Mancini, 'Amelia', *NSc* (1920), 15 ff.; A. Di Tomassi, *Guida di Amelia* (Terni, 1936); Gaggiotti et al., *Umbria-Marche*. 30–4.   [40] CIL 11.4345–565.

[41] *CIL* 11.4397 (Roscius C.f); 11.4398 (thesaurus paid for by T. Roscius T. f., IVvir); 4349 (possibly a fake–restoration of Temple of Mars by L. Roscius); 4379 (Sex. Roscius, served in Leg. III); 4370 (L. Roscius L. f., served with Leg. II Hispaniae); 4399 (T. Roscius T. f. Capito and T. Venedius T. f. Roscius, IVviri); 4428, 4494, 4511–16 (epitaphs of Roscii, mostly freedmen and women).

[42] M. Gaggiotti and L. Sensi, 'Ascesa al senato e rapporti con i territori d'origine Italia: Regio VI (Umbria)', *Epigrafie e ordine senatorio*, ii (Rome, 1981) 248.

market and therefore a lucrative activity. Numerous villas have been identified in the territory of the city.[43]

Cicero's client, Sextus Roscius, was the son of a leading citizen of Ameria, also called Sextus Roscius, who had been murdered in Rome. He was prosecuted for parricide by Chrysogonus in 80 BC, probably to prevent him reclaiming family estates which had been confiscated.[44] The Roscius case has a rather different social background from that of the *Pro Plancio* and the *Pro Caelio*. Whereas Plancius and Caelius were first-generation senators, translating their local status and family wealth into political careers, the *Pro Roscio* has its social roots in pre-Social War Italy. Roscius the elder was an Italian grandee of an older type, with a house in Rome and very highly placed social connections but no apparent ambition to pursue a senatorial career. He is defined by Cicero in terms of three categories–his importance within Ameria (pre-eminent), his importance within the region (pre-eminent), and his importance in Rome (*hospes* of the Metelli, Scipiones, and Servilii).[45] More to the point, this was not just the formal obligation of *hospitium*, which could at one level be a variant on *clientela*; he seems to have been on personal terms with these families, and his son was eventually taken in by Metellus' sister until the court case was resolved.[46] Intriguingly, Roscius' close connections with Roman nobility had included Sulla, and he was clearly a Sullan partisan–Cicero describes him as a vehement supporter who indulged in what sounds like somewhat triumphalist behaviour and was frequently seen in Rome during the proscriptions.[47] He was also indubitably rich, owning thirteen estates close to the Tiber. The size of these estates and their implication for the social and economic status of the Roscii has been much discussed, perhaps most

[43] Plin. *NH* 2.148, 15.50–59; Columella 5.10.19; Virg. *Georg.* 1.265; Cato *Agr.* 11.5; Strabo *Geog.* 5.2.10. Di Tomassi, *Guida di Amelia*; Gaggiotti, *Umbria-Marche*, 20. On elite agrarian production, see N. Purcell, 'The Roman Villa and the Landscape of Production', in T. J. Cornell and K. Lomas (ed.) *Urban Society in Roman Italy* (London, 1995) 151–79, and on the food supply of the city of Rome, see N. Morley, *Metropolis and Hinterland: The City of Rome and the Italian Economy, 200 B.C.–A.D. 200* (Cambridge, 1996).

[44] *Rosc. Am.* 18–19; on the dating of the prosecution and subsequent speech, see T. Kinsey, 'The Dates of the Pro Roscio Amerino and the Pro Quinctio', *Mnemosyne* 20 (1967) 61–7.

[45] *Rosc. Am.* 1–16; J. M. May, *Trials of Character: The Eloquence of Ciceronian Ethos* (Chapel Hill NC, 1988) 21–30 on Cicero's constructions of character and invoking of *ethos* in the Roscius case.

[46] *Rosc. Am.* 27. *Hospitium* and *clientela* could shade into one another, but *hospitium* did not of itself imply a patron-client relationship and is usually couched in terms of social equality. Wiseman, *New Men*, 33–7.

[47] *Rosc. Am.* 16. 'Posteaquam victoria constituta est ab armisque recessimus, cum proscriberentur homines atque ex omni regione caperentur ii, qui adversarii fuisse putabantur, erat ille Romae frequens atque in foro et in ore omnium cotidie versabantur, magis ut exultare victoria nobilitatis videretur quam timere' ('After victory had been won and we had moved away from war, when men were being proscribed and arrested in every quarter, he frequented Rome and showed himself in the forum in view of everyone every day, and he seemed rather to be exulting in the victory of the nobles than fearing').

fully by Rawson,[48] who argues that this did not represent an unduly large amount of wealth. Although it is difficult to quantify what thirteen estates in this area would yield, we do know that it was a rich area with an economy based on market gardening. This would have been a profitable occupation, particularly in the Tiber valley, which had good communications with Rome and was close enough to supply the Roman market. Cicero's stress on the fact that the farms were adjacent to the Tiber suggests that they were prime property, well placed to export their produce down the Tiber to Rome for the lucrative city market.[49] Whatever the case, Roscius must have been a man of considerable substance if he was able to rub shoulders with the Metelli and Scipiones and swagger his way through the Sullan dictatorship, but neither he nor his sons seem to have aimed to translate social status into Roman office.

Caecina, Volaterrae, and Tarquinii

Aulus Caecina was prosecuted in an inheritance case in 69 BC. The Caecinae, were long-standing friends and clients of Cicero and there are frequent references to them in his letters.[50] Caecina's son was a close friend of Cicero, and was noted both as an orator and for his training, acquired from father, in the traditional Etruscan discipline of augury.[51] The *gens* was enormously important in northern Etruria. It had been one of the most influential families in the region for centuries, attested by Etruscan tombs which carry the name *Ceicna* (=Caecina), which continued to be prominent well into the Roman period. Inscriptions from Volaterrae attest numerous *Caecinae* and their freedmen and women.[52] The Caecinae attained senatorial rank, although there is some doubt over the date at which this occurred, which is unusual since there are few other senatorial families from Volaterrae. The only other example cited by Wiseman is C. Curtius.[53] The

[48] E. D. Rawson, 'The Ciceronian aristocracy and its Properties', in M. I. Finley (ed.), *Studies in Roman Property* (Cambridge, 1976) 85–102 (repr. in *Roman Culture and Society. Collected Papers* (Oxford 1991) 204–22). The term *fundus*, which Cicero uses to described the Roscius estates, does not carry any particular implications about the size of the land-holdings.

[49] On transport of goods in Roman Italy, see Morley, *Metropolis and Hinterland*; R. M. Laurence, *The Roads of Roman Italy: Mobility and Cultural Change* (London, 2000).

[50] *Fam* 6.5–6.9, 13.66, *Att.* 11.7. On Cicero's patronage of Volaterrae more generally, see *Att.* 1.19, *Fam.* 13.4–13.5.   [51] Cic. *Fam.* 6.9.1, 6.6.3.

[52] *CIL* 11.1743, 1760–8.

[53] Wiseman, *New Men*, no. 148, adlected by Caesar in 45 (Cic. *Fam.* 13.5.2) following damage to his family under Sulla. Wiseman speculates that he could be the son of the Curtius proscribed in 82 BC and mentioned by Cicero in *Rosc. Am.* 90. Senatorial Caecinae include A. Caecina, the friend of Cicero and Octavian (Cic. *Att.* 16.8.2), and A. Caecina Severus, cos. suff. 1 BC.

most notable feature of Volaterrae's elite is its high level of stability and continuity. The *gentes* prominent in the late Republic and Augustan era–*Caecinae, Carrinates, Volasennae,* and *Arminii*–are also represented under their Etruscan names (*Ceicna, Carinas, Velusna,* and *Armni*) in the funerary epigraphy of the Etruscan city.[54] Further to this, recent research on social structure and landholdings in the *Ager Volaterranus* indicates that little changed in Roman Etruria. Patterns of landholdings and land-use remained remarkably stable, a continuity of social status, landownership, and economic activity which perhaps indicates that the local elite was relatively immune to Roman influence.[55] The other key characters who feature in the *Pro Caecina,* Fulcinius and Caesennia of Tarquinii, were also people of rank whose families are represented in the later epigraphy of their city. A L. Fulcinius is known to have been a senator before 139 BC,[56] and there is also evidence for Caesennius Lento, who was a legate of Caesar in Spain in 44 and G. Tarquitius Priscus, quaestor 81, legate of Sertorius in 76–72.[57]

Volaterrae was one of the most important cities in northern Etruria. It was inhabited from the seventh century BC but its heyday was the fourth century, a period at which it seems to have expanded rapidly, and had a rich material culture as represented in its funerary monuments, buildings, and output of alabaster urns.[58] It continued to flourish after the Roman conquest of the region until the rise of Sulla, with evidence of a prosperous territory and a high density of rural settlement. There are also signs of substantial public building activity, in the form of two new or refurbished temples on the acropolis. In the 80s BC, however, the city supported Marius and one of its leading men–C. Carrinas–was a Marian general.[59] As a result it was besieged by Sulla and subjected to a loss of territory, and also a loss of civic status which forms part of the technical argument of Caecina's inheritance case.[60] Laws to settle Roman colonists on the confiscated lands were introduced

---

[54] *TLE*² 285, *CIE* 18–42 (Caicna); M. Torelli, 'La situazione in Etruria', in *Epigrafia e ordine senatorio,* ii (Rome, 1981) 283–4 (Carrinates and Volasennae); for the immediate antecendents of Caecina and the career of the man himself, see P. Hohti, 'Aulus Caecina the Volaterran: Romanization of an Etruscan', in P. Bruun (ed.), *Studies in the Romanization of Etruria* (Rome, 1975) 414–21.

[55] See, most recently N. Terrenato, '"Tam Firmum Municipium": The Romanization of Volaterrae and its Cultural Implications', *JRS* 88 (1998) 94–114.

[56] The mother of Marius was a Fulcinia, giving a direct Arpinate connection with the case, if Wiseman's speculation (*New Men,* 55) that she belonged to the Tarquinian *gens* Fulcinia is correct.

[57] *CIL* 11.3392, 3415–17; Wiseman, *New Men,* nos. 82, 420; Torelli, 'La situazione in Etruria', 275–99.

[58] F.-H. Pairault, *Recherches sur quelques séries d'urnes de Volterra à représentations mythologiques,* Collection de l'École Française de Rome 12 (Rome, 1972); F. Glinister, 'Volaterrae', in T. J. Cornell and K. Lomas (eds.), *Cities and Urbanism in Ancient Italy: An Archaeological Encyclopaedia* (Leiden, forthcoming). On the economy more generally, see Pliny *NH* 11.37.197; Sen., *Nat. Q.* 2.39; Cic., *Quinct.* 6.24; Strabo 1.1.   [59] Wiseman, *New Men,* no. 105; Dio 51.21.6; Val. Max. 7.8.3.

[60] Cic. *Caecin.* 95–104.

in 63 and 60 BC, but were defeated on both occasions, and the land distributions did not proceed until 45 BC.[61] Cicero was instrumental in deterring at least one of the earlier attempts at colonization, and also interceded to protect Volaterran landholdings from the Caesarian land distribution of 45.[62] Volaterrae seems to have undergone a recovery later in the first century. There was a large amount of public building after the Civil War, much of it paid for by Caecina Severus and several less exalted local notables, and the entire monumental centre of the city closely echoes the development of the fora in Rome under Augustus.[63] Despite this apparently high level of Romanization, however, the most notable feature of Volaterrae is the extent to which there is social, cultural, and economic continuity between the Etruscan and Roman city. Patterns of farming–and consequently landownership–remained centred on small farms and very few villas are found in the territory,[64] and social hierarchies remain dominated by the same elite families which were prominent in the Etruscan era. It is perhaps significant that the most visibly Roman element of the city–the forum, which is usually a central feature or urban topography–is isolated outside the walls of the city.

Cluentius, Oppianicus, and Larinum

The notorious Cluentius case is a highly convoluted tale of accusation and counter-accusation involving elite families of several cities in central and southern Italy. A. Cluentius Habitus, a leading citizen of Larinum, accused his stepfather Oppianicus of attempted poisoning and he was duly convicted, but the case was reopened by his son, who charged Cluentius with murder in 66 BC. The complexity is increased because it involved several families from Larinum and elsewhere.[65]

---

[61] The date of the colony at Volaterrae is uncertain. Some sources attribute colonial status to Caesar (Lib. Col. 214.10–13; W. H. Harris, *Rome in Etruria and Umbria* (Oxford, 1971) 55–60); but the earliest definite evidence that it was a colonia is Julio-Claudian (*AE* 1994. 612).

[62] Cic. *Fam.* 13.4; Harris, *Rome in Etruria and Umbria*, 246; Terrenato, 'The Romanization of Volaterrae', 106–7.

[63] Jouffroy, *La Construction publique*, 99; P. Inghirami, 'Il teatro romano di Volterra', *Rassegna Volterrana* 40–1 (1977) 31–47. A fragmentary inscription (*AE* 1957, 220) reveals that the builders of the new complex were A. Caecina Severus, who held the consulship in the reign of Augustus, and G. Caecina Largus.

[64] Argued strongly by N. Terrenato and A. Saggin, 'Ricognizioni archeologiche nel territorio di Volterra. La pianura costiera', *Arch. Class.* 46 (1994), 465–82; Terrenato, 'The Romanization of Volaterrae'.

[65] The full list of families implicated includes Cluentii, Sassii, Oppianici, Aurii, Magii, Vibii (all from Larinum), and the Fabricii from Aletrium. The familial relationships of the *Pro Cluentio* are explored in P. Moreau, 'Structures de parenté et alliance à Larinum', in Cébelliac-Gervasioni S.V., *Les Bourgeoisies municipales*, 99–123.

Larinum was an Apulian city, 32 km south-east of modern Termoli, but its ethnicity is disputed by ancient authors who attribute its foundation to several different peoples of south-east Italy.[66] Most scholars identify it as culturally Oscan but the complexity of the issue is shown by the city's bronze coinage. One issue (*c.*268 BC) is Campanian in type, with a head of Apollo and the Greek legend ΛΑΡΙΝΩΝ, while the second group (*c.*250 BC) is of Apulian type with an Oscan legend, and the third group (*c.*217 BC) uses the Roman uncial standard but with an Oscan inscription.[67] Traditionally, it was assumed that the urbanization of Larinum, as of many other Oscan settlements, largely post-dated the Roman conquest but recent excavation shows that there was a substantial pre-Roman city on the site, developing between the fourth and second centuries BC.[68] It probably entered the orbit of Rome during the Samnite wars and was a Roman ally until its revolt on the outbreak of the Social War in 90 BC.[69] After the war it became a Roman *municipium*, and features in accounts of the Civil Wars as supporting Pompey.[70] There is a substantial amount of Latin epigraphy from Larinum, most of it funerary.[71] Of the families involved in the *Pro Cluentio*, there is no trace of the Aurii or the Magii but the Cluentii were still present during the Empire, as attested by the epitaphs of the freedwoman Cluentia Cypare, wife of the Augustalis Gn. Petronius Restitutus, and Cluentius Priscianus, possibly also a freedman. There is also an epitaph of the mid-first century BC, of Didia Decumana, daughter of Barbus, set up by her daughters Oppianica and Billiena.[72] The most direct epigraphic evidence for Larinum in the period after the Social War, however, is a fragmentary text which appears to be a dedication to Sulla, naming him as patron of the city.[73] Torelli cites parallels from Fundi, Sutri, Alba Fucens, and Clusium, as well as from Delos and elsewhere in the eastern Mediterranean, and suggests that it may be a consequence of Oppianicus' take-over of Larinum on behalf of Sulla and the ensuing local proscriptions.[74] Only one senatorial family is attested–the Vibii, which appears in the *Pro Cluentio* as an important local family, and which rose to senatorial

[66] Pliny *N.H.* 3.105, Ptol. 3.1.65; Mela 2.66; Steph. Byz. Larinates; *Lib. Col.* 260.

[67] B. V. Head, *Historia Nummorum*, 2nd edn. (Oxford, 1911) 28–9.

[68] J. A. Lloyd, 'Pentri, Frentani and the beginnings of urbanisation (c. 500–80 BC)', in G. Barker (ed.), *A Mediterranean Valley: Landscape Archaeology and* Annales *History in the Biferno Valley* (London, 1995) 181–212; A. Di Niro, *Necropoli archaiche di Termoli e Larino* (Termoli 1981). Finds include a temple of the 3rd cent. BC, together with a votive deposit of coins, black-glaze pottery and figurines of Hellenistic type.　　　　[69] Salmon, *Samnium and the Samnites*, 386–93.

[70] Social war, App. *BC* 1.52; Pompeian sympathies, Cic. *Att.* 7.12; Caes. *BC* 1.23.

[71] N. Stelluti, *Epigrafi di Larino e la bassa Frentania* (Campobasso, 1997).

[72] *CIL* 9.742 (Cluentia Cypare), 9.754 (Cluentius Priscianus), 9.751 (Oppianica).

[73] M. Torelli, 'Una nuova iscrizione di Silla da Larino', *Athenaeum* NS 51 (1973) 336–54. 'L. Cornelio L.F. Sullae Felici, dictatori, patrono' ['To L. Cornelius Sulla Felix, Dictator, patron'].

[74] Torelli, ibid. On proscriptions at Larinum, Cic. *Cluent.* 25.

rank during the reign of Augustus.[75] Unfortunately, little archaeological evidence of the Ciceronian city has survived,[76] but it is known to have been a flourishing community in the early Empire, and may have been a city of some significance in the era of Cluentius.

Italian Identity in the Forensic Speeches

Cicero's Italian associates are, therefore, many and various in their career patterns, social background, and relationship with Rome. They include both senatorial contemporaries and men who retained their equestrian rank but who were nevertheless major players in Rome and in Italy as a whole, not just their own localities. They are clearly just a small sample of Cicero's municipal case-load: other speeches such as the defence of an Arretine woman who had lost her citizen status after Sulla penalized Etruria,[77] have not survived, but assuming that we can take the extant list of Italian defendants as broadly typical, municipal notables seem to fall into two categories. Some, like Caelius, Plancius, and Cicero himself, who were pursuing social promotion and political prominence at Rome—gaining membership of the Senate and standing for office at Rome. Others—like Roscius, Cluentius and Oppianicus—were wealthy and socially prominent, interacting with the highest levels of the Roman elite, but without seeking to gain senatorial status and political power in Rome. It is all too easy, given the bias of our evidence towards the Roman viewpoint, to think of the history of the first century BC as a linear process of convergence, by which the Italian nobility sought entry *en masse* into the senatorial order, but it is clear that political integration was only one of several paths open to Italian nobles. Their response to Rome was not uniform, and could be influenced by a wide range of factors such as family history and existing social contacts with senatorial families, business interests, and a huge variety of local considerations. Some—like the Roscii—maintained social contacts with highly placed senatorial families, and even intermarried with the Roman elite, but preferred to give priority to their local status rather than compete for Roman office.[78] This is by no means an indication of lower status or of lack of engagement with Rome. The mere fact

---

[75] A. Vibius Habitus, cos. suff. AD 8; G. Vibius Postumus, cos. suff. AD 5 (*CIL* 9.730, *AE* 1966. 74; Wiseman, *New Men*, nos. 259, 488, 491); cf. Cic. *Cluent* 25 and 165 for Vibii at Larinum.

[76] De Felice, E., *Larinum,* Forma Italiae 36 (Florence, 1994).   [77] *Caecin.* 97.

[78] For an earlier example of this phenomenon, cf. Cicero's grandfather, who was berated by Aemilius Scaurus for actively rejecting a political career at Rome in favour of remaining in Arpinum (Cic. *Leg.* 3.36).

of enjoying marriage connections, *hospitium*, and a range of other social relationships with senatorial families gives an indication of their importance and influence.[79] Viewed from the Roman perspective, there was an intense level of political interest in the recently enfranchised Italians by Roman aristocrats, who were faced with the need to find ways of engaging with and exploiting this vast new electorate; but at the same time there was considerable hostility to Italians, whose presence increased competition for office.[80] Under the circumstances, it is not surprising that both groups may have been ambivalent about each other.

Cicero has sometimes been assumed to have a general interest in, and affinity with, the Italian nobility and to have had a greater willingness to represent municipal clients because of his own background. However, both the distribution of his personal municipal contacts and the way in which he characterizes Italians in his speeches suggests a more complicated pattern and a more specific focus. Examination of the ways in which he defines the status and identity of the Italian defendants is revealing on this point.

The most important factor, both for Cicero himself and for his clients and their associates, is not a blanket identification with the municipal elites *per se*, but with a specific local group. The bond between Cicero and his Italian defendants is not general municipal origin, but the specific claims of *vicinitas*–local loyalties–and/or personal contact.[81] The importance of the ties of local loyalties and allegiances is stressed in numerous different contexts, and in ways which indicate that it was rather different from ties of patronage, although there are clearly areas of overlap. *Vicinitas* is, for instance, an important factor in establishing the social identity, status, and moral credentials of a municipal notable for the jury. Cicero uses the prominence of Roscius in three levels of activity and status–municipal, regional, and Roman–as a way of indicating his standing.[82] Extra kudos is clearly gained because the defendant is prominent in all three fields. In the same way, the support allegedly given to Plancius and Caelius by their respective *vicini* is cited as evidence of both their high social standing and their moral good character. In his defence of Rabirius Postumus, Cicero emphasizes the unusually high level of support in Campania and Apulia by indicating that it is so widespread that it cannot be accounted for just by *vicinitas*, but draws in people from a wider area.[83]

---

[79] Wiseman, *New Men*, 33–52.

[80] [Sallust] *Cic.* 3–5. E. Gabba, 'Le città italiche del I sec. a.C. e la politica', *Rivista Storica Italiana* 93 (1986) 653–63 (reprinted in Gabba, *Italia Romana*, Como, 1998). See also J. H. D'Arms, 'Upper Class Attitudes towards *viri municipales* and their Towns in the Early Roman Empire', *Athenaeum* 62 (1984) 440–67, who identifies the increased pressure on the Roman elite as giving rise to some hostility towards the Italians.   [81] Wiseman, *New Men*, 33–40.

[82] Most strikingly in *Rosc. Am.* 15–18, but see also *Planc.* 22–3 and, in the different context of a letter to L. Lucceius, *Fam.* 5.15.2.   [83] *Planc.* 22–23, *Cael.* 5, *Rab. Perd.* 8.

The importance of ties of *vicinitas* can perhaps be seen most strikingly in the Plancius case. At several key points in his defence, Cicero stresses the support derived from the people of Atina and the surrounding communities as an integral part of his argument for Plancius' good character and popularity. Further to this, he lays great emphasis on his own Arpinate origins and therefore the fact that he himself is speaking as a *vicinus* of Plancius.[84]

Omnia, quae dico de Plancio, dico expertus in nobis. Sumus enim finitimi Atinatibus ... Nemo Arpinas non Plancio studuit, nemo Soranus, nemo Casinas, nemo Aquinas. Totus ille tractus celeberrimus, Venafranus, Allifanus, tota denique nostra illa aspera, et montuosa, et fidelis, et simplex, et fautrix suorum regio, se huius honore ornari, se augeri dignitate arbitrabatur. Iisdemque nunc ex municipiis adsunt equites Romani publice, cum testimonio: nec minore nunc sunt sollicitudine, quam tum erant studio.

Everything that I say about Plancius, I say from experience. For we [i.e. the people of Arpinum] are neighbours of the people of Atina.... There was no one at Arpinum, at Sora, at Casinum, at Aquinum, but was Plancius' adherent. Thickly-populated districts of Venafrum and Allifae, and, in a word, all our rugged countryside, which holds among its hills hearts loyal and unaffected and staunchly true to the bond of kinship, counted my clients distinction an honour, his promotion a compliment, to itself. Roman knights have come from these same townships and are here today to present their official testimony, and the suspense they feel for Plancius now is only equalled by their zeal for him then. (*Pro Plancio* 21–2)

This passage indicates in particular the emotive power of *vicinitas*. Plancius is not just supported by people from Atina, for instance, but also by those from Sora, Arpinum, Casinum, Aquinum, Venafrum, and Allifae–in other words a significant area of southern Latium. Plancius is presented as a pillar of his community who draws demonstrations of loyalty from it, and from the region as a whole. Despite this, the relationship between Italian nobles and their municipalities was not straightforward. Cicero elsewhere implies that the Plancii were large-scale municipal patrons who were using their influence on behalf of their city, despite the fact that he also says that Plancius was almost exclusively based in Rome.[85] He clearly derived substantial status from his locality, but apparently from a distance.

The emphasis on the power of *vicinitas* and the paramount importance of local contacts is unsurprising, if looked at in the wider context of the history of ancient Italy. Strong regional networks of contacts between cities within a region, and between locally prominent families are the norm rather than the exception. The wide range of contacts of the Caecinae

---

[84] *Planc.* 1–40, 20–24, 72.

[85] *Planc.* 45–48 (Plancii as local patrons), 67 (Plancius as based in Rome).

provide a striking example, since inscriptions mentioning Caecinae are found at Clusium, Tarquinii, Volsinii, and other major Etruscan centres, and the Caecina case itself involves disputes over property at Tarquinii as well as Volaterrae.[86] Conversely, there was frequently intense local rivalry for status between individuals and cities within a region, something which is well documented as a key factor in both the internal politics and external relations of cities in ancient Italy and which could sometimes flare into open warfare.[87] Local connections were by no means an automatic guarantee of support, either from one's region or one's own municipality.[88]

Vicinitas in general is an important element in Cicero's defence of municipal clients, but more specifically can be seen as a direct influence on Cicero himself, his choice of cases, and the way he relates to other Italians. His ties with the region around Arpinum clearly inform his acceptance and conduct of certain cases. This is perhaps most apparent in the *Pro Plancio*, in which he explicitly acknowledges his interest as a *vicinus* of Plancius, but is also found in other contexts. His initial connection with the unsavoury Cluentius case came through a local connection with his region. He was persuaded to represent the Fabricii of Aletrium, who were implicated in some of the many ramifications of the case, because a deputation of the citizens of Aletrium, which is in the same region as Arpinum, called upon him as a *vicinus* to represent the Fabricius brothers.[89] Significantly, he dropped the case when it came to court a second time, because the *municipium* of Aletrium had formally withdrawn support from the Fabricii, who were now deemed to be a liability to the good name of the city.[90]

Despite this strong sense of his ties of *vicinitas* with southern Latium, there is also an ambivalence towards his connections with Arpinum which is perceptible in much of Cicero's writing. He clearly took his local roots and his obligations as patron of the city very seriously indeed. The extract from the *De Legibus* quoted above demonstrates the strength of his feeling, as well as his recognition of the tensions posed by it, and there are also some practical demonstrations of his support for his home town. In 46 BC, he tried to intervene on behalf of the *municipium* of Arpinum to expedite collection of some rents owing on land owned by the city, and his reasons for doing so are instructive.[91] First, there is the consideration of patronage

---

[86] Hohti, *The Romanization of Etruria*, 414–16; M. Torelli, 'Senatori etruschi della tarda repubblica e dell'impero', *Dialoghi d'Archeologia* 3 (1969) 220–310.

[87] Tacitus records riots and open war caused by rivalry between Pompeii and Nuceria (*Ann.* 14.17), and between Capua and Puteoli (*Hist.* 3.57), and a 1st-cent. AD graffito (*ILS* 6443c) strikingly expresses hostility against the people of Pompeii and Pithecusae.

[88] For example, the three leading families of Arpinum—the Marii, Gratidii and Tullii Cicerones— were all closely connected by marriage, but there may have been a political rift between the Marii and Gratidii on the one hand and the Tullii. Rawson, *Roman Culture and Society*, 16–33.

[89] *Cluent.* 46–49.   [90] *Cluent.* 57.   [91] Cic. *Fam.* 13.11.

and the need to earn the favour both of leading Arpinates, and of the city as a community. More specifically, Cicero is attempting to engineer the election of his son, his nephew, and M. Caesius, the son of a friend, as aediles, commenting approvingly on the survival of this traditional magistracy.[92] A year later, in 45 BC, he was attempting to do the same for the neighbouring city of Atella, citing the ties of *vicinitas* and patronage as the reason.[93] The implication of this is that the local networks of obligations and contacts amongst the south Latin cities–the 'Volscian mafia' of the title–retain an important place in Cicero's world-view, despite his years in Rome. However, his degree of engagement with other cities and other parts of Italy, except where he has strong personal contacts through friends or clients such as Caecina, seem to be much less prominent. We know, for instance, that Cicero owned numerous estates throughout Italy and was patron of a number of cities, including Locri in the far South, but we hear little of any real engagement with communities outside southern Latium and the Bay of Naples, with the exception of Volaterrae.[94] This emphasis on his home area can also be seen in works other than the forensic speeches. Cicero's letters of recommendation and interventions on behalf of Italian communities or individuals also reflect the same bias, with the vast majority concerned with the same relatively small area–southern Latium, the Bay of Naples, and Volaterrae.[95]

With the exception of the points where Cicero's Arpinate background gives him a local interest and obligations, the most notable thing about Cicero's speeches is the extent to which any particular Italian emphasis is missing. Except where factual issues connected with the case are at stake, there is very little reference to the municipal background of his clients. Italians–Plancius, the Roscii, Oppianicus, Caecina, etc.–are defined primarily by their status at Rome. The emphasis is on their role as *publicanus* (father of Plancius), associate of Roman *gentes* (Roscius), equestrian (most of the protagonists in the *Pro Caecina* and *Pro Cluentio*), or their senatorial credentials (Caelius and Plancius). Since most Italian notables were either senators or equites, Italian origins are often subsumed into their Roman status or only mentioned tangentially. Even close associates of Cicero, and frequent correspondents–Cluvius of Puteoli, for instance–rarely have their home city referred to, even in private correspondence. This is despite the

---

[92] 'is enim magistratus in nostro municipio nec alius ullus creari solet' ('in our city, it is the custom to appoint this chief magistracy and no other'). [93] Cic. *Fam.* 13.7.
[94] On the close relationship between Cicero and Volaterrae, see *Att.* 1.19, *Fam.* 13.4–5; E. D. Rawson, 'Caesar, Etruria and the *disciplina Etrusca*', *JRS* 68 (1978) 132–52 (repr. in Rawson, *Roman Culture and Society*, 290–323). For a list of Cicero's villas and estates, *Att.* 1.4, 2.4, 9.9, 11.4, 11.13, 12.1, 12.9, 12.44, 13.47a, 15.2; D'Arms, *The Romans on The Bay of Naples*, 171 ff.
[95] E. Deniaux, *Clientèles et pouvoir à l'époque de Cicéron* (Rome, 1993) 70.

fact that the juries before which these speeches would have been delivered may have included a substantial Italian element. At this date, Roman juries were composed of one-third senators, one-third *equites*, and one-third *tribuni aerarii*, a group of equestrian status. Since the equestrian order now contained a substantial number of Italians, it cannot be assumed that this emphasis on Roman at the expense of Italian identity was designed simply to play to the preconceptions of an all-Roman jury.

Where the Italians are invoked, it is usually as an anonymous mass who appear in support of their local notable and whose presence acts as a form of moral validation, both for the defendant and–in some senses–for Cicero himself.[96] The ranks of local notables who allegedly turn up to support Plancius, Caelius, and Rabirius are there as a form of character reference, providing a clean-cut old fashioned Italian morality, implicitly as a contrast with the *mores* of Rome.[97] The role of the municipality in these speeches is to provide a source of support for a client, or a source of moral *topoi* for Cicero to exploit. The younger Roscius, for instance, is described as devoted to his home town, hardly leaving his family estates even to venture into Ameria and spending almost no time in Rome, as a proof of his moral rectitude.[98] The virtuous Aletrians in the *Pro Cluentio* are used as a pious counterweight to the moral dubiousness of Oppianicus, Sassia, and the Fabricii.[99] The Atinates are used as guarantors of Plancius' good character, but nevertheless the city is described rather pejoratively as an 'oppidum'–a little town–where behaviour at the Games gets distinctly rustic.[100] Cicero also plays with the idea that the further a place is from Rome, the more wholesome it is–a variant on the urban *versus* rural *topos*, in which *artificium* and dissimulation are associated with Rome and the regions around it–including Tusculum, the home town of Plancius' opponent Laterensis–while moral virtue is associated with the smaller city of Atina. Cicero also exploits this type of moral *topos* as part of his use of *ethos* as a device designed to sway the jury not just by establishing the defendant's good character but also by establishing Cicero's own persona.[101] The Italians in the speeches, therefore, are very much there to prove a moral and rhetorical point–to be innocent, moral, and virtuous rustics in contrast to the urban cynicism and corruption of Cicero's opponents, or to provide moral support during the trial itself.

This ambiguity and tension between Roman and local identity is to be expected, not just because of the partial nature of forensic oratory, but also because of the profound changes in notions of identity and elite behaviour in the years after the Social War. The pull of *vicinitas* and local loyalties is

---

[96] *Cael.* 5, *Planc.* 19–22.   [97] *Rab. Perd.* 8, *Cael.* 5, *Planc.* 19–22, *Cluent.* 197–8.
[98] *Rosc. Am.* 26, 39–40.   [99] *Cluent.* 46, 57.   [100] *Planc.* 30.
[101] May, *Trials of character*, 23–31, 105–9, 117–22.

still very strong, even for those, such as Cicero himself, who spent much of their lives in Rome, and is not, at this date, necessarily weaker than the impulse to integrate with the senatorial elite at Rome. Some areas of Italy are notably conservative in their social and economic structures and behaviour, and correspondingly lacking in elite integration with Rome. The elder Roscius and the younger Plancius represent contrasting models of elite behaviour in this era. Roscius is clearly a major figure, but very much in a traditional manner—a regional baron who has close social and personal ties with the highest levels of Roman society, but does not apparently aspire to join the senatorial order. Plancius, on the other hand, comes from a very similar social background—the son of a leading *eques* with a high public profile at Rome—but seeks to become part of the Roman elite rather than staying within that of Atina. The relative paucity of overt references to Italianness, even in the context of friends and clients of Cicero who are of municipal origin, is a further pointer to these tensions surrounding identity. Cicero himself in the *De Legibus* debates aloud the issue of his identity as a Roman and an Arpinate, but his coyness when it comes to other comment may be due to a desire to foster a sense of *Romanitas*. Nevertheless, it is clear that the forensic speeches strongly reflect this dual identity. Cicero, as well as his clients, remains caught up in a powerful web of regional loyalties and obligations, while at the same time striving to emphasize an overriding Roman identity. It is well beyond the scope of a single chapter to undertake a comprehensive study of Italian identity in Cicero's speeches, but even a brief survey of the evidence indicates that they frequently reflect the tension between Roman and regional identity which is such a strong element of this transitional period of Italian history.

4

Reading Cicero's Narratives

D. S. LEVENE

Ancient rhetorical theorists recommended that the typical forensic speech should contain a section known as the *narratio*: this was the part that normally followed the preliminary discussion–the *exordium*–and set out the facts of the case prior to a full discussion of the issues.[1] The *narratio*, so defined, is thus not precisely identical to 'narrative' in its modern sense: any part of a Ciceronian speech may contain something that a modern scholar would call 'narrative'.[2] Nevertheless, in this chapter I shall be limiting my discussion to the *narratio* as defined by the ancient theorists. The boundaries of the *narratio* were themselves not always clearly defined in practice (see further below); but even in these problematic cases there is often a clear core narrative at the appropriate point; and it is on this that I shall concentrate. I shall, however, for reasons that will appear shortly, also be looking at the *exordium*, and the ways in which this provides (or fails to provide) a context for the narrative that follows.[3]

Citations in this chapter from the Greek rhetoricians are according to the pagination of L. Spengel, *Rhetores Graeci* (Leipzig, 1853). Versions of this chapter have been delivered to meetings at the Institute of Classical Studies in London, Corpus Christi College, Oxford, Newcastle University, Pennsylvania State University, New York University, Princeton University, University of California, Berkeley, and University of Oregon. I should like to thank those present for a great deal of stimulating discussion. In addition Jane Chaplin, Chris Kraus, Andrew Laird, John Moles, Jonathan Powell, and Tony Woodman have read and commented extensively on earlier drafts, and I should like to thank them for their extremely useful contributions.

[1] e.g. *Rhet. Her.* 1.12–16; Cic. *De Or.* 2.326–30; Quint. *Inst.* 4.2.

[2] Modern writers regularly apply the term 'narrative' to any text with an underlying 'story': the defining feature separating narrative from non-narrative literature is above all the presentation of chronologically sequenced events. See e.g. P. Ricoeur, *Time and Narrative* (Chicago, 1984), esp. i. 52–87; also S. Rimmon-Kenan, *Narrative Fiction: Contemporary Poetics* (London, 1983) 14–15. For modern views of narrative as applied to ancient literature, see *The Oxford Classical Dictionary*, 3rd edn. (Oxford, 1996), s.v. *narrative, narration*.

[3] For a more general theoretical discussion of some of the issues that I shall be raising here, see N. E. Enkvist, 'On the Interpretability of Texts in General and of Literary Texts in Particular', in R. D. Sell (ed.), *Literary Pragmatics* (London, 1991) 1–25.

i

In 1925 Jules Humbert published a famous monograph,[4] arguing that the surviving published versions of Cicero's speeches bear very little resemblance to the words that he spoke on the day: the whole form of the speech, according to Humbert, would have been substantially transformed for publication, with, for example, two or more speeches combined into one. Though Humbert's thesis did not achieve universal acceptance, it (or a less radical version of it) gained a number of distinguished followers.[5] Not until fifty years later were fundamental arguments against it presented by Wilfried Stroh.[6] Stroh argued against Humbert's reconstructions of the original trials, and of the evidence that he claimed to have discovered for those trials within the published speeches; but, more importantly, he also argued that the very nature of Cicero's publication of his speeches was such as to preclude a Humbertian analysis. They were published (Stroh claimed), often for use in education, to be read as speeches that *could* have been delivered (even if in fact they did receive some alteration). So they are not going to be, as Humbert had argued, products that by their very nature bear little resemblance to anything that might have been said in court. Stroh's conclusion:

Die Übereinstimmung der gesprochenen mit der geschriebenen Rede mag in einem gewissen Maß Fiktion sein; aber wenn wir rhetorisch richtig interpretieren wollen, dann haben wir–so paradox es klingt–diese Fiktion als Wirklichkeit zu nehmen.

The agreement of the spoken and the written speech may to a certain extent be a fiction; but if we want to interpret them correctly rhetorically, then we must–paradoxical as it may sound–take this fiction for fact.[7]

This conclusion provides the basis for Stroh's own analysis of Cicero's persuasive techniques: and it has become a standard premise for many other scholars in the area–Classen, for example, or Vasaly–who, as a result, are prepared to examine even speeches, like the Second Actio Verrines, that were never actually delivered, as rhetorical products designed to persuade their constructed 'original audience'.[8] On Stroh's view the distinction between the reading audience and the hearers of a speech is irrelevant,

---

[4] J. Humbert, *Les Plaidoyers écrits et les plaidoiries réelles de Cicéron* (Paris, 1925).

[5] e.g. W. Kroll, 'Ciceros Rede für Plancius', *RhM* 86 (1937) 127–39 at 136–7; A. Michel, *Rhétorique et philosophie chez Cicéron* (Paris, 1960) 386–9; A. E. Douglas, *M. Tulli Ciceronis Brutus* (Oxford, 1966) 78–9. [6] W. Stroh, *Taxis und Taktik* (Stuttgart, 1975) 31–54.

[7] Ibid. 54.

[8] C. J. Classen, *Recht, Rhetorik, Politik* (Darmstadt, 1985); A. Vasaly, *Representations: Images of the World in Ciceronian Oratory* (Berkeley, 1993).

because even ancient readers would have read it as a transcript of a spoken work. One can therefore unproblematically examine its relationship to the 'internal' audience, those assumed to be hearing it, and effectively ignore the readers altogether.[9]

Stroh's account of the publication of Cicero's speeches is not, of course, the whole story: in particular it seems reasonable to argue that for some speeches, at any rate, Cicero's aims in publication were more strongly political than Stroh would appear to allow.[10] Nevertheless, the evidence does suggest that he is correct to identify students of rhetoric as a primary component of the intended audience (see further below, 138–9), and hence to see the intended ancient readers examining the published work in order to determine its rhetorical effect upon its presumed hearers. Stroh's conclusion that the relationship of the speech to its readers is fundamentally irrelevant to its interpretation would, one might feel, follow from this quite naturally.

But in at least one respect such elision of the written speech into the spoken may not be quite so straightforward: namely in narrative. For the understanding of narratives will often depend on more than is presented within the text itself. A narrative where an audience is acquainted with various pieces of background information may appear fundamentally different from one where the audience does not have this knowledge. If a person is named, or an event is referred to which the audience is assumed already to know, that reference may seem straightforward. If, on the other hand, the audience does not know the person or event in question, the reference can appear highly obscure and allusive.[11]

---

[9] This is the basic approach, for example, of the one extensive published study of Ciceronian narrative: D. Berger, *Cicero als Erzähler* (Frankfurt am Main, 1978), esp. 14–18. For a short sketch of a different approach, closer to what I shall be doing in this chapter, see M. Fuhrmann, 'Mündlichkeit und fiktive Mündlichkeit in den von Cicero veröffentlichen Reden', in G. Vogt-Spira (ed.), *Strukturen der Mündlichkeit in der römischen Literatur* (Tübingen, 1990) 53–62. Likewise even Berger (*Cicero als Erzähler*, 68–193, esp. 68–70, 79–84, 161–5) in her extended analysis of the Second Actio Verrines does argue that those speeches reveal their intended audience as an audience of readers. Compare R. L. Enos, *The Literate Mode of Cicero's Legal Rhetoric* (Carbondale, Ill., 1988), who examines the relationship between the oral mode of the original address and the 'stylized recreations' (89) for a literate audience, arguing that fictional elements are introduced into the written speech to give an impression of their original oral immediacy (esp. 86–93): he sees the original oral speeches as 'acts of rhetoric', but the subsequent published speeches as 'rhetorical interpretations . . . aesthetically contrived pieces of discourse' (92). Cf. also (more briefly) R. G. M. Nisbet, 'The Orator and the Reader: Manipulation and Response in Cicero's Fifth Verrine', in A. J. Woodman and J. G. F. Powell (eds.), *Author and Audience in Latin Literature* (Cambridge, 1992) 1–17 (esp. 1–2, 17) (=*Collected Papers in Latin Literature*, ed. S. J. Harrison (Oxford, 1995) 362–80).

[10] Cf. J. Crawford, *M. Tullius Cicero: The Lost and Unpublished Orations* (Göttingen, 1984) 3–16; E. Narducci, *Cicerone e l'eloquenza romana* (Rome, 1997), 164–9.

[11] Cf. N. E. Enkvist, 'Connexity, Interpretability, Universes of Discourse', in S. Allén (ed.), *Possible Worlds in Humanities, Arts and Sciences* (Berlin, 1989) 162–86 (esp. 163–9). This point is recognized by Classen, *Recht, Rhetorik, Politik*, 6–7; but he simply takes it as evidence that Cicero may have

The relevance of this to Cicero will be clear. His forensic speeches were delivered in the course of trials, with himself often speaking last. The hearers, by the time that Cicero came to speak, would already be acquainted with a good deal of the background to the case, provided by the previous speakers. When the case is closely involved with current political events (as Cicero's published forensic speeches often are), for those there on the day such events will form the contemporary backdrop: they will not need to be told, say, that a certain person is consul. But the readers are in a very different position. More often than not, they will have access to nothing else that was said, and Cicero's speech will provide their sole information about the circumstances of the trial. Moreover, the political background is evanescent: much that was common knowledge at the time may be forgotten later, and, even if it is remembered, it will not necessarily be associated with chance allusions in the speech.

So under such circumstances the reader's view of the narrative can be fundamentally different from that of the original hearers. Nor, it might seem, can such a reader easily achieve an appreciation of the hearer's position, as Stroh's approach would appear to require: without substantial research, one cannot simply have the access to information which was available at the time; and without that information, it may not be possible even to identify which allusions are obscure and which straightforward, what is old information being re-presented and what is new information being introduced for the first time—issues which may be central to understanding what is going on in the narrative. In short, a speech that was straightforward when delivered may require a complex hermeneutic approach to read.

None of this necessarily suggests that Cicero altered any given speech for publication. But, even if he did not alter it, in publishing it he could hardly have failed to be aware of the position of those who were to read it; were it to be the case that much of the speech was utterly incomprehensible to a reader (to take an extreme example), its intended effect, whether pedagogic or political, could hardly fail to be diminished. It is therefore worthwhile to examine how the narrative of a Ciceronian speech would have appeared to an ancient reader. This of course chiefly involves an analysis of the *narratio*; but, as I indicated at the start, the *exordium* is also important to consider. For a reader reading the speech in isolation, in the manner I have outlined, the *exordium* is likely to provide the first indications of the circumstances of the case. In treating Cicero's forensic speeches, I shall therefore be examining not only the narratives

added some background information or otherwise made alterations in publishing the speech: it does not affect his basic analysis, which still fundamentally depends on the speech being interpreted solely in the context of its assumed hearers.

themselves, but also to what extent the reader, in reading the narrative, is expected to employ information provided by the *exordium*. I shall be seeking to answer two basic questions: (1) how far, if at all, reliance on the speech alone rather than on the general background available to the original hearers means that the narrative has a different effect; and (2) whether in the light of this it is actually possible, as Stroh's analysis requires, for a reader to reconstruct—or construct—the effect of the speech upon those hearers.

One preliminary matter, however, still needs to be considered. It may appear that to speak uncomplicatedly about 'the information available to Cicero's audience', whether that audience is the original hearers of the speech at the trial or those reading the speech subsequently, is to over-simplify an extremely complex issue. Audiences, as is well known, are rarely monolithic: many different levels of knowledge may be comprised within them. The hearers at a Roman trial would include not merely the jury, whose verdict would decide the issue, but typically also numerous bystanders, whose reaction to the speech might be influential in setting the atmosphere in which the trial was judged, but who would not necessarily have attended the whole trial.[12] Likewise, readers might include at least some individuals who would come to the speech with considerable aware-ness of the circumstances of the case, perhaps through direct personal knowledge, or even conceivably through having made an extensive historical study of the background.

Nevertheless, for the purposes of this discussion it is legitimate and indeed necessary to focus upon just one subset of hearers and one subset of readers. This chapter is examining a particular claim of Stroh's: that speeches would typically be published to be read by students and others interested in rhetoric, and they would be read with the purpose of appre-ciating their rhetorical effect.[13] Stroh's argument depends upon accepting this group as the primary (though not of course the only) readers that the orator had in mind when publishing his speech; it is that which provides his justification for his own basic methodology, the examination of the rhetorical effect of these speeches upon the assumed original hearers. In addressing Stroh's position, therefore, I assume a level of knowledge such as would typically be possessed by a student of rhetoric reading the speech, in so far as we can know this from Quintilian and elsewhere (see further below, 139–41).

Likewise, the hearers who are under consideration here may legiti-mately be assumed to be relatively homogeneous. While it is certainly

---

[12] On the multiple audiences at a Roman trial, and the consequent balancing act necessary in a speech at that trial, see Enos, *The Literate Mode*, 48–51.   [13] Stroh, *Taxis und Taktik*, 52–4.

true that all sorts of people might be present at a trial, and that their differing reactions might well matter in a general way, it is undeniable that
Cicero's forensic speeches are at least ostensibly addressed to the jury
alone. Moreover, the overwhelming tendency of Latin rhetorical theory is
to focus almost exclusively on persuading that jury, and constructing the
detail of one's speech with the jury in mind. Acknowledgements of the
importance of the wider circle of listeners are surprisingly rare. The most
famous example is Cicero, *Brut.* 192, where Brutus says that he is unable
to speak in a court unless he carries the crowd as well as the judges with
him. This, however, appears in the specific context of an attempt by
Cicero to prove that popular judgement, and not the opinion of expert
critics, is the essential criterion for oratorical quality;[14] elsewhere in
Brutus, as in his other rhetorical works, Cicero's assumption appears to be
that it is the jury alone at whom a forensic speech is aimed.[15] Pliny, *Ep.*
1.20.12–13, defending the practice of giving lengthy speeches, suggests
that not all of the audience will be convinced by the same arguments (and
thus it is necessary for the orator to include as wide a variety as possible);
but this passage appears to be talking about different temperaments,
rather than different levels of knowledge,[16] and moreover about variation
within the jury rather than differences between the jury and the
bystanders. And Quintilian *Inst.* 4.2.22, talking specifically about narrative,
is especially revealing: when repeating information from earlier in the
case, the speaker's real object is to influence the judges by providing them
with the facts appropriately slanted, but he should cover up this object
with a *pretence* ('simulemus') that he is providing information for a

---

[14] Compare Tacitus, *Dialogus* 34.4, where the responses of bystanders to a speech is used by
Messala to show how orators in the Republic were able to train themselves to meet all varieties
of taste; cf. also *Dialogus* 39.4 for the orator's need of a big audience if he is going to speak to the
grandest standard. Neither of these passages, however, suggests that anything in the speech would
be there *specifically* to appeal to those bystanders.

[15] Note e.g. *Brut.* 200, where it is the attention paid to the orator *by the jury* that is the test of
his success (the word *iudices* is used twice). *Brut.* 165 is also relevant (likewise 178): Cicero distin-
guishes skill in speaking at *iudicia* from that at *contiones*, and refers to the latter alone as *popularis
dictio*. At *Fin.* 4.74 Cicero explains to Cato that the attack on the latter's Stoicism in *Pro Murena*
was because 'apud imperitos tum illa dicta sunt, aliquid etiam coronae datum' ('at that time
the audience of the speech was untrained [sc. in philosophy], and something was even given to
the crowd'); but this has an apologetic function, to justify Cicero's more serious treatment in *De
Finibus* of the same points of which he was so dismissive in *Murena*. Moreover, the 'etiam' may be
significant–it implies that, whatever orators may have done in practice, such a focus on the crowd
was not seen by a Roman readership as a normal feature of forensic oratory.

[16] Pliny, *Ep.* 1.20.12: 'aliud alios movet ac plerumque parvae res maximas trahunt. varia sunt
hominum iudicia, variae voluntates. inde qui eandem causam simul audierunt, saepe diversum,
interdum idem sed ex diversis animi motibus sentiunt' ('Different things affect different people, and
often small things have great consequences. Men have different judgements, and different wishes.
Hence people who have simultaneously heard the same case often have different responses, or
sometimes the same response but from different influences on the mind').

replacement judge or explaining matters to bystanders (see further n. 20 below).

Thus the ancient reader would read the speech under the assumption that the hearers of the speech were the jury: it is the effect of the speech on the jury that, on Stroh's argument, such readers would be seeking to reconstruct. The jury would at the very least be expected to have heard all of the previous arguments in the case and, coming as they did from a fairly uniform upper-class background, could be assumed to have a fair amount of political and historical information in common.

ii

I have selected passages from three speeches, illustrating between them a range of issues: *Pro Sexto Roscio Amerino, Pro Sestio,* and *Pro Balbo*. I shall begin with the last of the three to be delivered: *Pro Balbo* has the simplest narrative, but a narrative, as we shall see, of an unusual form, which allows the issues to be presented fairly starkly. The speech was delivered in late 56 BC, in defence of Caesar's lieutenant L. Cornelius Balbus, a Spaniard who had acquired Roman citizenship from Pompey in 72. He was prosecuted for claiming citizenship illegally. The case is one of a number that Cicero undertook at the behest of the triumvirs at this time: Cicero spoke last, after Pompey and Crassus. Balbus was acquitted.

Pro Balbo allows us to begin by raising a basic question: how does the reader even know that he is about to read a forensic speech? If the title 'Pro Balbo' was there to be read, that would have given him a strong hint, of course; but an epideictic speech, for example, could in theory stand under the same title. In practice, however, there is no problem. Every surviving Ciceronian forensic speech, except two, begins with a direct address to the judge or judges by name:[17] the word 'iudices', or the name of the individual judge, appears within the first couple of lines, conveniently indicating to the reader precisely what sort of speech he is concerned with.[18] This may simply be a convenient coincidence; there are, after all, good rhetorical reasons for addressing the judges directly in an *exordium*.[19]

---

[17] I exclude from consideration *In Vatinium*, which is addressed to Vatinius himself (though it does, interestingly, refer in the first sentence to his *testimonium*, which may perform a similar function); it is moreover a speech in a unique form, and it is not clear how far it even purports to represent what was said at the trial (see Quint. *Inst.* 5.7.6, and Stroh, *Taxis und Taktik*, 48–50, with bibliography). I also exclude *Pro Roscio Comoedo* and *Pro Fonteio*, the openings of which are lost.

[18] Cf. Fuhrmann, 'Mündlichkeit und fictive Mündlichkeit', 56.

[19] See e.g. *Rhet. Her.* 1.6, 1.8; Cicero, *Inv.* 1.22, *De Or.* 2.322–4, *Part. Or.* 28; Quint. *Inst* 4.1.5, 4.1.16–22; cf. C. Loutsch, *L'Exorde dans les discours de Cicéron* (Brussels, 1994) 38–9, 529–34.

But the two exceptions are revealing: *Pro Balbo* is one, *Pro Caecina* the other:

si auctoritates patronorum in iudiciis valent, ab amplissimis viris L. Corneli causa defensa est.

If the authority of barristers is effective in trials, Lucius Cornelius' case has been defended by most distinguished men. (*Balb.* 1)

si, quantum in agro locisque desertis audacia potest, tantum in foro atque in iudiciis impudentia valeret, non minus nunc in causa cederet A. Caecina Sex. Aebuti impudentiae, quam tum in vi facienda cessit audaciae.

If sheer effrontery were as effective in the forum and in trials as recklessness can be in the countryside and in lonely places, Aulus Caecina would now give way in this dispute to the effrontery of Sextus Aebutius, just as then in creating violence he gave way to his recklessness. (*Caec.* 1)

In both cases the phrase *in iudiciis* appears in the first sentence. Here rhetorical theory provides no explanation: this phrase conveniently signals the circumstances of the speech for the readers, which must leave us with a nagging suspicion that the sentences containing it were written for their benefit. However that may be, *Pro Balbo*, like every other Cicero speech, signals its forensic nature from the start for a reader coming to it cold. For the original hearers, the phrase is less pointed, a formal nod towards their known position rather than an essential provider of information.

Along similar lines, the opening sentence of *Pro Balbo* also indicates to the reader that Cicero is speaking last. In this respect his practice is less consistent. Most of his speeches refer eventually to the other advocates in the case; but it is unusual for him to mention the fact so early. The argument of the speech, of course, explains this: flattery of Pompey, in particular, is to play a major part in his case for Balbus (he will be claiming that Pompey's grant of citizenship could not have been illegal), and this passage provides an early pointer to that line of defence. But at the same time another clue has been provided about the circumstances of the delivery of the speech; the reader can store up the significant information, even while recognizing that the rhetorical importance lies elsewhere. Pompey is named at 2: the effect is similar. Crassus, who is less central to the case, is not named until 17, though the existence of a third defence counsel apart from Cicero and Pompey is implicit in the plurals of the opening sentence.

The fact that Balbus is indebted to Pompey and Crassus–but not to Cicero–is also introduced in 1 (at this point, of course, neither Pompey nor Crassus has yet been named): 'nam ceteris a quibus est defensus hunc debere plurimum video; ego quantum ei debeam, alio loco' ('for I see that this man here is greatly in debt to the others who have defended him; how great my own debt is to him will appear elsewhere'). This, too, can be regarded as information for the reader to store up; but there is a significant difference from what we have seen so far. Cicero's own debt to Balbus, we are told, will be discussed later; but the reference to Balbus' debt to his–as yet unnamed–defenders is more of a problem. Is it a reminder of something that the original audience knew from the rest of the case, or would they, too, regard it as an obscure allusion? The distinction is vital if one is to appreciate fully the rhetorical effect: yet nothing in the words makes it clear. I shall call this an 'undetermined allusion': because, from the point of view of the reader attempting (in best Stroh fashion) to appreciate the rhetoric of the case, it is as yet an open question: the reader cannot determine the impact of the allusion on the original hearers.

What is the case actually about? In 2, Cicero describes Pompey's earlier speech:

nihil enim umquam audivi quod mihi de iure subtilius dici videretur, nihil memoria maiore de exemplis, nihil peritius de foederibus, nihil inlustriore auctoritate de bellis, nihil de re publica gravius, nihil de ipso modestius.

For I have never heard any speech that seemed to me more minute concerning the law, more extensive in recalling precedents, more learned concerning treaties, of more shining authority concerning wars, more serious about the state, more restrained about himself.

This is (to extend my earlier terminology) a 'determined allusion': an allusion to something that the original hearers would by definition know. It gives the reader further clues: an important political case, with international aspects, and one moreover that involves Pompey himself. This last may even hint to the reader that the earlier reference to Balbus' debt to Pompey may after all be information that the hearers possessed: his reading of the speech may thus be seen to involve him in revision of his judgements of the earlier section.

Chapter 4 provides a more complex problem:

Cn. Pompeio, qui sui facti, sui iudici, sui benefici voluit me esse, ut apud eosdem vos, iudices, nuper in alia causa fuerim, et praedicatorem et actorem.

Gnaeus Pompeius, who has desired that before you, gentlemen of the jury, the same people before whom I recently appeared in another case, I should act as both publicist and advocate of his deed, his judgement, and his generosity.

This is another 'determined allusion': the reference is obscure to the reader, but he infers that the hearers will know what is meant. But earlier determined allusions have concerned matters that are clearly important to the speech and are going to be discussed later: here the role of the allusion to the hearers is less clear. Not only will they, unlike the reader, understand what Cicero is referring to; they will also be in a better position to appreciate its relevance. A reader may guess that it is not essential to the rhetorical effect of the speech to recognize the precise allusion; but he can hardly be sure.

In 5, the topic of the case is focused more closely:

ac mihi quidem hoc dignum re publica videtur, hoc deberi huius excellentis viri praestantissimae gloriae, hoc proprium esse vestri offici, hoc satis esse causae ut, quod fecisse Cn. Pompeium constet, id omnes ei licuisse concedant. nam verius nihil est quam quod hesterno die dixit ipse, ita L. Cornelium de fortunis omnibus dimicare ut nullius in delicti crimen vocaretur. non enim furatus esse civitatem, non genus suum ementitus, non in aliquo impudenti mendacio delituisse, non inrepsisse in censum dicitur: unum obicitur, natum esse Gadibus, quod negat nemo.

And indeed to me at least it seems worthy of the state, and owed to the outstanding glory of this worthy man, and appropriate to your duty, and a suffi-cient plea, that what it is accepted that Gnaeus Pompeius did, everyone should grant that he was permitted to do. For nothing is truer than what he himself said yesterday, that Lucius Cornelius is battling for his very existence, without being charged with any crime. No one claims that he stole the citizenship, that he mis-represented his family background, that he concealed himself in some shameful falsehood, that he sneaked into the censorial roll. The one and only objection is that he was born at Cadiz—and no one denies it.

The trial concerns something that Pompey did, the legality of which is questioned. This appears to be a 'determined allusion', one that the hearers are presumed to have understood; it is followed immediately by a refer-ence to Pompey's speech, in which he himself is supposed to have addressed the subject. The very next sentence provides us with the key: the case is about Balbus' claim to citizenship. By now the reader can have pieced together many of the clues: Balbus is in Pompey's debt because of something Pompey did; the legality of what Pompey did is at the heart of the case; the case concerns Balbus' acquisition of the citizenship. Other things are still left unexplained. The third defence counsel is still unknown, and Balbus is apparently in his debt too; nor are the grand political, diplo-matic and military overtones yet clear. Still, light is starting to dawn.

Where does the *exordium* in *Pro Balbo* end and the narrative begin? There is no clear break, as there is in many speeches; but the facts of the case are now presented by Cicero (5–6):

cetera accusator fatetur, hunc in Hispania durissimo bello cum Q. Metello, cum C. Memmio et in classe et in exercitu fuisse; ut Pompeius in Hispaniam venerit Memmiumque habere quaestorem coeperit, numquam a Memmio discessisse, Carthagine esse obsessum, acerrimis illis proeliis et maximis, Sucroensi et Turiensi, interfuisse, cum Pompeio ad extremum belli tempus fuisse. haec sunt propria Corneli, pietas in rem publicam nostram, labor, adsiduitas, dimicatio, virtus digna summo imperatore, spes pro periculis praemiorum; praemia quidem ipsa non sunt in eius facto qui adeptus est, sed in eius qui dedit. donatus igitur ob eas causas a Cn. Pompeio civitate. id accusator non negat, sed reprehendit.

Everything else is admitted by the prosecutor: that he was in Spain during an exceptionally tough campaign under Quintus Metellus and Gaius Memmius in the navy and the army; that when Pompeius came to Spain and first took Memmius as his quaestor, he never left Memmius; that he was besieged at New Carthage; that he participated in those great and fierce battles at the Sucro and the Turia, that he was with Pompeius right up to the end of the war. Cornelius' personal qualities are these: loyalty to our state, effort, industry, fighting, courage worthy of the greatest general, and expectation of rewards that would equal his perils. But rewards depend not on the actions of him who earned them, but of him who granted them. So he was for these reasons granted citizenship by Pompeius. The prosecutor does not deny this, but he criticizes it.

Unusually, Cicero introduces the facts in indirect speech, repeating what has, he claims, already been said by the prosecutor. The point is, apparently, that these facts are not in dispute. However, they are, albeit in indirect speech, nevertheless presented by Cicero in a manner not unlike that of a traditional *narratio*. They are presented in chronological order, in a paratactic style. But it might seem that the significance of that narrative to the reader is fundamentally different from its significance to a listener. For a reader, these events are being introduced for the first time: for a listener, they merely constitute a brief reminder of something that has already been heard. In effect, the whole narrative comprises one long 'determined allusion'.

Does this matter? By the end of the passage, after all, although not all of the allusions of the exordium are yet clear, nor is the precise nature of the prosecution case, nevertheless the main features of the case have fallen into place. Is the difference between learning these details for the first time and hearing them repeated actually significant for the reader's understanding? A case could be made for its being relatively unimportant. It is striking that the complex hermeneutics required earlier now seem to be absent: when one is faced with a simple chronological sequence of events, as we are here, they are so readily comprehensible that the difference between a first reading and a second hearing appears a somewhat formal and trivial one.[20]

---

[20] It was controversial in ancient rhetorical theory whether it was necessary for the defence counsel to include a *narratio* if the facts were already familiar to the jury from the earlier speeches. Cicero himself consistently held that it was unnecessary (*Inv.* 1.30, *De Or.* 2.330, *Part. Or.* 15); cf. Aristotle, *Rh.* 1417ᵃ8–12; *contra* Apollodorus, cited in Seneca, *Con.* 2.1.36. Quintilian agrees in principle (*Inst.* 4.2.4–8), but then at 4.2.20–3 presents a more nuanced account: one might do so, for example, in order to provide one's own slant on the case. If so, it is necessary, he holds, to season it with reminders to the judges that they already know what he is describing (cf. L. Calboli Montefusco, *Exordium Narratio Epilogus* (Bologna, 1988) 39–40). The implication of both of these positions is that the main effect of an exact repetition would be weariness, not that it would of itself provide a different view of the case.

If the prosecution speech had itself indeed narrated a similar sequence of events in a similarly straightforward manner, it would indeed seem that the difference would be slight. But are we entitled to assume that this was in fact the way in which the prosecution *did* handle it? Were it the case that, for example, the prosecution's narrative had focused on an entirely different set of events, or had treated them in such a way as to be barely recognizable in Cicero's summary here, the hearer would have the difficulty of relating Cicero's apparently straightforward account of the prosecution speech to what the prosecution speaker had in fact said. One needs only read the opposing speeches of Demosthenes and Aeschines on the Embassy and the Crown[21] in order to appreciate that a narrative that is apparently easily comprehensible in its own right may become considerably more opaque when one attempts to relate it to the competing narrative to which it is responding, especially when, as here, the events in question took place a good twenty years before the trial, and so could not necessarily be assumed to form part of the hearer's immediate experience.

It is of course true that the speech itself implicitly addresses this point. The very way in which Cicero handles the narrative indicates to the reader that the detail of the matters to which it refers is inessential to the case. Cicero says that this was all said by the prosecutor and that it forms no part of the case against Balbus. The corollary would seem to be that the details are going to be irrelevant to Cicero's defence, as is in fact the case. The reader is therefore invited to accept the narrative as a simple chronological account of events, in which the allusions to things outside his knowledge in no way hinder his understanding the general effect of Cicero's speech. However, this is only partly true in the event that the prosecution *had* handled the matter differently from the way that Cicero indicates. It is certainly the case that, even were that so, the reader, like the hearer, is aware that the bulk of the speech remains unaffected by the matters set out here; but the effect of straightforward simplicity that we find in this paragraph would be potentially undermined.

I shall leave *Pro Balbo* at this point, where the narrative (such as it is) has come to an end, although much of the case, from the reader's point of view, remains to be determined. What precisely is the problem about Balbus' citizenship? Who is the mysterious 'other defender'? What is the nature of Balbus' debt to him? What is Cicero's own relationship to Pompey? Specifically, what was the 'earlier case' where he spoke on his behalf? The first two of these questions will be answered by the end of the speech; the others remain unanswered throughout.

---

[21] The Embassy: Demosthenes 19 and Aeschines 2. The Crown: Aeschines 3 and Demosthenes 18.

Before moving on, however, let me summarize the position. We have seen two types of allusion to events outside the reader's knowledge: 'determined allusions', where it is clear from the manner of the allusion that the hearers comprehended the reference; and 'undetermined allusions', where it is possible that the point was equally obscure to the original hearers. The reader is gradually able, by piecing together the information derived from some of these, to reconstruct the case. The one 'undetermined allusion' is partially clarified later, when we learn that the case concerns Balbus' debt to Pompey; and the same information allows us to realize that it was information that the hearers in fact possessed—in fact, it is seen in retrospect as a 'determined allusion' after all. But the reference was also to Crassus, and that part remains 'undetermined', and its role in the case unclear. So too some other 'determined' allusions remain unclear to the reader: he never learns about them, and is never in a position to gauge their relevance. This relatively simple speech requires considerable ingenuity on the part of the reader to unravel, and the success of that unravelling is far from sure.

iii

Pro Roscio Amerino was Cicero's first *causa publica*, delivered under Sulla in 80 BC, and involved the defence of a young man on a charge of parricide. As Cicero presents it, the father had in fact been murdered by two of his other relatives, who were in partnership with one of Sulla's freedmen called Chrysogonus, who arranged for him to be proscribed posthumously so that they could acquire his property. They then had the son prosecuted for parricide, in order to secure their title to the estate. Cicero, the sole speaker for the defence, obtained Roscius' acquittal.

The *narratio* of *Pro Roscio Amerino* runs from 15 to 30; and it narrates the story in a fashion which, on the face of things, could hardly be clearer. The story of Roscius' family background, and the events before and after the father's death, are told apparently in chronological order,[22] with all requisite information apparently present. But there is one place where it might seem that the clarity breaks down. Near the start Cicero cannot resist, it seems, a pathetic reminder of his client's hapless position (15):

ex suis omnibus commodis hoc solum filio reliquit; nam patrimonium domestici praedones vi ereptum possident, fama et vita innocentis ab hospitibus amicisque paternis defenditur.

[22] See however Stroh, *Taxis und Taktik*, 58–9 for Cicero's manipulation of the real chronology in this section.

From all his advantages he [sc. Roscius senior] left only this one [sc. friendship with great families] to his son: for household bandits have taken his inheritance by force and control it, while the guiltless man's reputation and life are defended by his father's hosts and friends.

What precisely does a reader take 'patrimonium domestici praedones . . . possident' to refer to? That Roscius has lost his property was explicitly stated at 6: but at that point the only current possessor mentioned was Chrysogonus: 'duobus milibus nummum sese dicit emisse adulescens vel potentissimus hoc tempore nostrae civitatis, L. Cornelius Chrysogonus' ('the person who claims that he bought [Roscius' property] for 2,000 sesterces is a young man, currently quite the most powerful in our community, Lucius Cornelius Chrysogonus'). From this alone, one might conceivably even conclude that Chrysogonus was connected with Roscius' *domus*. The only other clues came directly before the *narratio* began, in 13: a reference to the possession of Roscius' property by those who accuse him: 'accusant ei qui in fortunas huius invaserunt . . . accusant ei quibus occidi patrem Sex. Rosci bono fuit . . . accusant ei qui hunc ipsum iugulare summe cupierunt' ('the prosecutors are those who laid hands on this man's property . . . who profited by the killing of Sextus Roscius' father . . . who desired above all to murder the defendant himself').

On general grounds the reader might assume that those speaking for the prosecution–so far unnamed–do not include Chrysogonus; for a man called 'L. Cornelius Chrysogonus' to be conducting a prosecution in 80 BC would be unusual.[23] It would not, however, be impossible, as the career of the contemporary rhetorician M'. Otacilius Pitholaus shows;[24] and Chrysogonus is described as 'potentissimus hoc tempore nostrae civitatis'. At the very least the reader would have to keep open the possibility that Chrysogonus was himself the person referred to in 13 and 15, and that he was one of the prosecutors–especially in view of *dicit* and *postulat* in 6, which would seem (at least on the face of things) to imply that Chrysogonus was one of those speaking before the jury. But for the moment it remains uncertain to whom 'domestici praedones' refers: the identity of the prosecutors is unknown to the reader, as is the identity of the possessors of Roscius' property. Yet it appears to be an allusion to something that matters to the speech.

---

[23] Cf. Loutsch, *L'Exorde*, 153 (following Schol. Gronov. p. 303,17 (Stangl)), who suggests that Cicero's reference to Chrysogonus by his full names (an unusual mode of reference in the speeches) is specifically in order to draw attention to his servile origins.

[24] According to Suetonius, *Gram.* 27, Pitholaus, a freedman, acted as *subscriptor* in a prosecution. See R. A. Kaster, *C. Suetonius Tranquillus: De Grammaticis et Rhetoribus* (Oxford, 1995) 297–301, esp. 299–300 on his role in this prosecution. On the social status of prosecutors more generally, see J.-M. David, *Le Patronat judiciaire au dernier siècle de la république romaine* (Rome, 1992) 525–47.

Now, a very sharp reader when he reached chapter 15 *might* put two and two together and conclude that some relatives of Roscius are both involved in the prosecution and in possession of some of Roscius' property. But he could hardly conclude this with any confidence; and, in consequence, this must appear an 'undetermined allusion'—one where it is unclear to the reader whether the reference is something that would be comprehensible to the hearers. If the 'domestic bandits' are the actual speakers for the prosecution, at least part of the matter is likely to be clear to the hearers, as they will already know that Roscius' relatives have spoken. If the 'domestic bandits' are not the prosecutors, it is possible that they would be as much in the dark as the reader. The reader can hardly view this part of the narrative as anything but obscure; nor can he readily reconstruct the effect upon the hearers.

Within a short time, however, the allusion is—up to a point—explained (17):

erant ei inimicitiae cum duobus Rosciis Amerinis, quorum alterum sedere in accusatorum subselliis video, alterum tria huiusce praedia possidere audio . . . duo isti sunt T. Roscii, quorum alteri Capitoni cognomen est, ipse qui adest Magnus vocatur.

He [sc. Roscius senior] had a feud with two Roscii of Ameria, one of whom I see on the prosecution benches, the other of whom I hear owns three of the defendant's farms . . . two Titi Roscii, one surnamed Capito, the other, who is here, called Magnus.

Cicero now makes it clear that there are two relatives of Roscius, one, Magnus, who is involved with the prosecution, and another, Capito, who has taken over part of the property. But the explanation is still not complete, because the clear impression has been given earlier that one and the same person both was involved in the prosecution and possessed the property. At 21 Cicero clarifies further: 'in reliquas omnis fortunas iste T. Roscius nomine Chrysogoni, quem ad modum ipse dicit, impetum facit' ('all his remaining property Titus Roscius there, as he himself says, seized in the name of Chrysogonus'). Chrysogonus' possession has already been outlined in the *exordium*; but is this acting as Chrysogonus' agent what was meant by 'the accusers possessing the property'? It is still unclear. At 23 Cicero adds further information:

iste T. Roscius, vir optimus, procurator Chrysogoni, Ameriam venit, in praedia huius invadit . . . ipse amplissimae pecuniae fit dominus . . . multa palam domum suam auferebat, plura clam de medio removebat.

Titus Roscius there, that excellent man, Chrysogonus' agent, came to Ameria, seized this man's farms . . . he himself took control of a large amount of money . . . he openly took away much to his own house, and secretly removed more from the scene.

This is presumably a reference to Magnus. There is the slight complication that *both* villainous Roscii have the *praenomen* Titus; but the *iste*, and the fact that we have already been told that the Roscius in court has been acting on Chrysogonus' behalf, at last make it fairly certain that one of those involved in the prosecution is both a relative of the defendant and the current owner of part of the estate. It is still, however, possible that Chrysogonus, who is known to possess part of the property, is one of those referred to as the accusers in 13; not until 60 is it made clear that Chrysogonus is not present at the trial at all, and thus cannot be directly participating in the prosecution.

Does this mean that, as with some of the references in *Pro Balbo*, the reader is able to understand in retrospect that the supposed 'undetermined allusion' is in fact an allusion to something that the hearers already knew? Unfortunately not, for, even if we assume that the reader is capable in retrospect of applying his new knowledge to all the previous occasions where matters beyond his ken were introduced (and that involves considerably more complex deductive reasoning than did the comparable portions of *Pro Balbo*), the precise level of the hearers' knowledge at the appropriate points in the speech is still far from clear. The reader can deduce from 28 (cf. also 58) that the prosecution did not make any mention of the sale of the property: 'de bonorum venditione et de ista societate verbum esse facturum neminem' ('[Roscius' enemies said] that no one would mention a word about the sale of the property or that association').[25] This, however, refers to the (allegedly) illegal act of sale described in 23; but it is not clear that the silence extended to any mention at all of the current ownership: on the contrary, the phrase 'quem ad modum ipse dicit' in 21 appears to suggest that some such reference might have been made. Moreover, it is unclear whom precisely the hearers would identify as the 'accusers' in 13 and as the 'domestici praedones' in 15. If Magnus was one of the prosecution speakers, then the identification would be relatively straightforward; but he may well have only been present as an adviser to the main prosecutor, Erucius,[26] in which case the identification would depend on how earlier speeches had dealt with him. Likewise, it later transpires that Capito may come forward as a witness (84), but the possibility of the hearers identifying him with these villains alluded to by Cicero will depend entirely on the precise form that the prosecution's account of him had taken. These matters could have been instantly comprehensible to the hearers, or they could have involved the hearers themselves in complex hermeneutic activity comparable to the reader's

---

[25] C. P. Craig, *Form as Argument in Cicero's Speeches* (Atlanta, 1993) 29–30.
[26] Cf. Stroh, *Taxis und Taktik*, 56–7.

own. The reader, in reconstructing the effect of the speech à la Stroh, simply cannot tell.

iv

Pro Sestio, like *Pro Balbo*, was delivered in 56 BC, but early in the year. Cicero had returned from exile in late 57; Sestius, one of the tribunes of 57, had been involved in campaigning for his recall. He was prosecuted for employing violence in the course of his campaign; and he was defended by Crassus, Hortensius, Calvus, and Cicero himself. Cicero spoke last, and centred his defence as much on his own conduct as on Sestius'. Sestius was acquitted.

Pro Sestio has one of the longest narratives of all Cicero's surviving speeches. It begins at 6 and, according to some, continues right up until chapter 96, when Cicero launches into his famous account of his political programme, though perhaps the clearest break appears in 77; that is the point at which the chronological presentation of events essentially breaks down, and Cicero addresses directly the arguments of the prosecution. However, such a division between narrative and argument perhaps makes less sense in *Pro Sestio* than in many speeches, because much of the narrative, especially in its later stages, involves arguments aimed at defending Cicero's own conduct in increasingly heightened language, though the opening part is relatively simple; moreover, the last part of the speech, in the course of the argument, includes an extended narration describing Cicero's return from exile (128–31).[27] But, even if the distinction is not regarded as entirely straightforward, the opening chapters, up to 14, where Cicero leaves the specific situation of Sestius in order to discourse more widely upon the political background, unquestionably stands solidly on the *narratio* end of the continuum.

Cicero is at this point relating Sestius' earlier political career, and, as with *Pro Roscio Amerino*, does so broadly in chronological sequence. Very shortly, however, we reach a potentially awkward area: Cicero's account of Sestius' behaviour during the Catilinarian conspiracy (8). Catiline is not mentioned by name until 12, and Cicero's consulship then is simply assumed; but this is less of a difficulty, because that fairly basic information can reasonably be thought of as familiar to readers and hearers alike.

---

[27] On the structure of *Pro Sestio* and the interplay between narrative and argument in the speech, see E. Évrard, 'Le *Pro Sestio* de Cicéron: un leurre', in *Filologia e forme letterarie: studi offerti a Francesco della Corte*, ii (Urbino, n.d.) 223–34.

But the handling of Cicero's colleague Antonius is much more of a
problem:

quaestor hic C. Antoni, conlegae mei, iudices, fuit sorte, sed societate consiliorum
meus. impedior non nullius offici, ut ego interpretor, religione quo minus exponam
quam multa P. Sestius, cum esset cum conlega meo, senserit, ad me detulerit, quanto
ante providerit. atque ego de Antonio nihil dico praeter unum: numquam illum illo
summo timore ac periculo civitatis neque communem metum omnium nec pro-
priam non nullorum de ipso suspicionem aut infitiando tollere aut dissimulando
sedare voluisse.

He [sc. Sestius], judges, by lot became quaestor to Gaius Antonius, my colleague;
but by sharing in my counsels he was mine. My scruples of a certain duty that I feel
I owe prevent me from explaining how many things Publius Sestius learned, when
he was with my colleague, how much information he brought to me, how much
foresight he showed. And I shall only say one thing about Antonius: at that time
of the utmost fear and peril to the state, amid the common fear of everybody and
the particular suspicions of some people about him, he never was willing either to
remove that fear by denial or quiet it by deceit.

Antonius was now in exile, and his alleged participation in the conspiracy
seems to have been a major factor in his condemnation, even if it did not
form part of the formal charge against him.[28] So much may have been
assumed as public knowledge, even for a reader; but Cicero, who had
(unsuccessfully) defended Antonius, seems here to be assuming that
Antonius was innocent but that at the same time he needed watching: this
more or less corresponds to the position that Cicero adopts towards
Antonius in other writings after the trial.[29] But how oblique and obscure
would it appear to the hearers? If they could be assumed to have followed
closely the history of Cicero's relationship with and attitude towards his
former colleague, it would be very clear; if not, it would come across as
a dark hint of unspecified involvement. Even if a reader happened himself
to be aware of the situation, how could he, without knowing the hearers'
precise situation, assess the effect of this passage upon them? Once again,
this appears to be an 'undetermined allusion'; one that depends not on the
previous speeches in the trial, but on the hearers' general state of political
awareness.

  One may also observe a standard rhetorical device that is on display in
this narration: *praeteritio* (or *occultatio*), the art of mentioning something
by saying that one is not going to mention it. When speaking of Sestius'
(allegedly) distinguished career, Cicero twice uses this technique.[30] He

---

[28] R. G. Austin, *M. Tulli Ciceronis Pro M. Caelio Oratio*, 2nd edn. (Oxford, 1952) 156–7; E. S. Gruen,
'The Trial of C. Antonius', *Latomus* 32 (1973) 301–10.   [29] *Flac.* 95, *Pis.* 5, *Cael.* 74.
   [30] *Sest.* 7: 'possum multa de liberalitate, de domesticis officiis, de tribunatu militari, de provinciali
in eo magistratu abstinentia; sed mihi ante oculos obversatur rei publicae dignitas, quae me ad sese

was, let us remember, the fourth speaker for the defence: had no one discussed this already? Cicero nowhere tells us; but it makes a difference, because it is clear that *praeteritio* in a narrative will have a different effect depending on whether it is a passing reminder of something already set out in detail or forms the sole source of knowledge for the hearers (see further below, 145).

Another interesting point is the insertion of two documents into the narrative, a Capuan decree commending Sestius, and Cicero's letter summoning him to Rome:

recita, quaeso, L. Sesti, quid decrerint Capuae decuriones, ut iam puerilis tua vox possit aliquid significare inimicis vestris, quidnam, cum se conroborarit, effectura esse videatur. DECURIONUM DECRETA . . . recito memoriam perfuncti periculi, praedicationem amplissimi benefici, vocem offici praesentis, testimonium praeteriti temporis.

Lucius Sestius, recite, I pray, what the decurions of Capua decreed, so that now your childlike voice can indicate to your enemies what it seems likely to accomplish when it strengthens. THE DECREES OF THE DECURIONS. I recite a record of danger undergone, a declaration of the utmost benefit received, words of present obligation, a witness to times past. (*Sest.* 10)

ut illius temporis atrocitatem recordari possitis, audite litteras et vestram memoriam ad timoris praeteriti cogitationem excitate. LITTERAE CICERONIS CONSULIS.

So that you can remember the horror of that time, hear the letter, and rouse your memory to think of the fear that is past. LETTER OF CICERO AS CONSUL. (*Sest.* 11)

Reference is made to these documents, and hints are given as to something of their contents; but the documents themselves are not quoted. This is, once again, a 'determined allusion', but of a rather different sort: not merely an allusion to something that the hearers obviously know and the reader does not, but an allusion to what is in effect part of Cicero's speech to which the reader has no access. But, very conveniently, Cicero includes in his speech explicit reference to what the quotation of these documents is supposed to accomplish: with the first we are told that it will set out Sestius' services to Capua; we are also told that Sestius' son–a young son, in case we did not know–is the person reading it out. With the second, we

rapit, haec minora relinquere hortatur' ('I can say much of his generosity, of his private services, of his military tribuneship, of his incorruptibility in those official duties; but I have always before my eyes the dignity of the State, which pulls me towards it, and encourages me to leave these lesser matters'). *Sest.* 13: 'hunc igitur animum attulit ad tribunatum P. Sestius, ut quaesturam Macedoniae relinquam et aliquando ad haec propiora veniam; quamquam non est omittenda singularis illa integritas provincialis . . . verum haec ita praetereamus ut tamen intuentes et respectantes relinquamus' ('So this was the attitude which Publius Sestius brought to his tribuneship, if I may leave aside his quaestorship in Macedonia and come at last to these more recent events; though I should not omit his unique incorruptibility in his province . . . but let us pass this over, though watching and looking back at it as we take our leave').

are told that it is to remind the audience of 'illius temporis atrocitatem', and to remind them of 'timoris praeteriti cogitationem'. This latter, at any rate, is genuinely a plausible reason for his introduction of the letter, given that rhetorical theory suggested vividness–ἐνάργεια/*evidentia*–as a prime virtue of narratives.[31] True, it is not unknown for Cicero to include in his speeches explicit references to his purpose in speaking a particular way, but one might regard it as suspiciously coincidental to have two in such quick succession in connection with these documents to which the reader has no other access: this express pointer to their rhetorical effect is at best largely superfluous for the hearers; for the reader it is essential. Yet, even with these pointers, how can the reader assess the precise effect of the documents upon the hearers? Do they, for example, foreshadow other aspects of the case? He cannot tell; all he can do is take Cicero's silence on the matter as implying that they do not.

Finally, Cicero comes to Sestius' tribunate. He has already said in the *exordium* (3) that he would be going over ground already covered by Hortensius: 'a Q. Hortensio . . . causa est P. Sesti perorata' ('Publius Sestius' case has been argued through by Quintus Hortensius'). He repeats that here (14):

de quo quidem tribunatu . . . dictum est a Q. Hortensio . . . sed tamen, quoniam tribunatus totus P. Sesti nihil aliud nisi meum nomen causamque sustinuit, necessario mihi de isdem rebus esse arbitror si non subtilius disputandum, at certe dolentius deplorandum. qua in oratione si asperius in quosdam homines invehi vellem, quis non concederet ut eos, quorum sceleris furore violatus essem, vocis libertate perstringerem? sed agam moderate . . . neque quemquam offendet oratio mea nisi qui se ita obtulerit ut in eum non invasisse sed incucurisse videamur.

Quintus Hortensius has spoken about this tribuneship at least . . . but since the whole tribuneship of Publius Sestius supported nothing other than my name and my cause, I think it essential to speak of the same matters, if not arguing too finely, at any rate complaining more bitterly. And if in this speech I should want to attack certain people more harshly, who wouldn't allow me use my freedom of speech to wound those whose lunatic crimes assaulted me? But I shall conduct the case moderately . . . and my speech will hurt no one, unless he has put himself forward in such a way that I seem not to have attacked him but to have run into him.

Who are these enemies? Of course, Cicero's enmity with Clodius was notorious, and doubtless most readers would appreciate that the reference is to him, especially if they recalled Sestius' own battles with Clodius on Cicero's behalf. But would Gabinius and Piso be identified as obvious enemies of Cicero? He regarded them as such after his return, but Piso's

---

[31] e.g. Quint. *Inst.* 4.2.64, 4.2.123–4, 8.3.61–2; see H. Lausberg, *Handbuch der literarischen Rhetorik* (Munich, 1960) 185–6. On the significance of ἐνάργεια in oratory more generally see Vasaly, *Representations*, 89–104.

behaviour towards him in the run-up to his exile does not appear to have been straightforwardly hostile, and Cicero had actually supported Gabinius in his speech *Pro Lege Manilia*.[32] Could the readers understand these references as pointing towards future attacks on these figures in particular? A reader who was very knowledgeable might; the same reader might connect to the same people the references in the *exordium* to the recent disasters of the state (1–2, 5), although the implication there that the same people are behind the prosecution of Sestius would make the connection with Gabinius and Piso that much harder to draw.

Of course, by the end of the speech it will be clear whom Cicero is attacking. But how can the reader tell whether it would have been clear to the hearers? That would depend, once again, on their precise knowledge of the political situation, and furthermore on how closely the earlier speeches dealt with these particular events. It might appear from the context in 14 that Hortensius discussed this, as Cicero's attack on these figures is said to be in the course of his repetition of Hortensius' points. But Hortensius' speech is said to have dealt with Sestius' tribunate; while the events concerning Gabinius and Piso were essentially related to their consulship the previous year. This is, in short, another 'undetermined allusion': it is impossible for the reader to determine what role they had previously played in the case, and hence to understand whether the original hearers would have seen this as an obscure reference to what was yet to come, or as a transparent reference to known features of the events.

V

What general conclusions can be drawn from these speeches? The questions I was seeking to answer (above, 121) were: (1) how far, if at all, one's reliance on the speech alone rather than on the general background available to the original hearers means that the narrative has a different effect; and (2) whether in the light of this it is actually possible, as Stroh's analysis requires, for a reader to reconstruct–or construct–the effect of the speech upon the hearers.

With (1), the fact that a lot of information appears in the *exordium*, combined with the fact that the *narratio* is told in a straightforward chronological style, means that the effect of the *narratio* on a reader is not altogether dissimilar to that on the listener, even if the *exordium* had a radically different effect, requiring complex deductive powers in the reader,

---

[32] Cf. also *Q. Fr.* 1.4.4: Cicero is clearly there *surprised* by the consuls' failure to support him.

but not of the listener. But, even so, the *narratio* is not invariably transparent, and I showed various examples of key parts that are far from clear to the reader, sometimes requiring deductions on his part which are at best only partially mirrored by those of the listener.

But what of (2), the most important question of all? Is it actually possible, as Stroh requires, for the reader to reconstruct the effect of the speech upon the hearers? One point might make such a reconstruction appear easier. I have been tacitly assuming throughout that the reader is reading the speech for the first time. But we have no reason to limit our analyses purely to first readings. On a second reading, much of what was previously obscure to the reader may become clear; in particular, some of the 'determined allusions', references to matters that he knows the listeners know, but of which he is himself unaware, he too will learn later. It might be thought that, at any rate on a second reading, he will have assimilated much of the required information, and so will be in a position to assess the effect of the speech upon the hearers.

This will work up to a point; but there are three clear reasons why it can at best be only a partial answer. (i) The process of reconstructing information can, as we have seen, be very complex; whether even an alert reader can not merely acquire the information, but can always assimilate it to the point where he will be able to call on it when required in re-reading the text must be doubtful. (ii) Not all 'determined allusions' *are* ultimately explained; and with those that are not, even if one recognizes that the reference is to things that the hearers were supposed to know, gauging the precise effect on those hearers is not always going to be possible. And, most important (iii): there are also 'undetermined allusions', including allusions in the narrative itself, where, even if it later becomes possible to understand what was being referred to, it is impossible to tell from the speech whether the original hearers understood the reference at the time.[33] Without that information, the reader is quite unable to reconstruct the effect of the speech on the hearers; in which case we can hardly sustain the idea that reading the speech as a transcript of the spoken word may unproblematically enable one to appreciate the effect of the spoken word.

This conclusion, however, causes further problems of its own. The evidence, as I said (above, 119), suggests that Stroh's position does actually represent the way in which the Romans themselves saw the purpose of publishing and reading speeches.[34] The general assumption is that

---

[33] The same point may be made with regard to the possibility that readers might obtain information from other published sources, such as hypotheses or commentaries: even where such sources existed (and they could not be *assumed* to exist), the information supplied would not as a rule allow one to determine what the hearers knew *at that point* in the speech. See further below, 140–1.

[34] See Stroh, *Taxis und Taktik*, 52–4.

speeches are indeed to be read as transcripts of the spoken word, and most sources do not seem to find such a manner of reading in any way awkward. Quintilian, for example, concludes that there are no material differences between written speeches and their spoken counterparts (*Inst.* 12.10.49–57):[35] moreover, even those against whom Quintilian here is arguing appear to be claiming only that written speeches, which are likely to be studied by a trained audience, require especial polish,[36] not that there are more fundamental problems arising from the fact of their being read out of context. Cicero himself indicates that the intended audience of his published speeches is students of his rhetorical technique;[37] he implies that the same is true of the speeches of his predecessors.[38] The idea that one would study examples of great oratory in order to learn rhetorical technique is standard among the Roman theorists: Quintilian in particular continually recommends and quotes passages from Cicero as providing useful models for the aspiring orator,[39] and the underlying assumption seems to be that one was indeed expected to read them to assess their effect upon the original hearers.

It is true that there is also some evidence within rhetorical theory that the reading of speeches, as opposed to hearing them, was seen by the Romans as potentially problematic. One area that might on the face of things appear important is the question of delivery. The central importance of the speaker's actual manner of delivery was a commonplace of rhetorical criticism: it was a regular view that even a speech which looked poor on the page could be rescued by an outstanding delivery.[40] Reading a speech would naturally mean that one would miss the performative aspect, which was available to the original hearers.[41]

However, this is less relevant to the questions being discussed here than one might have expected. The text of a speech was still regularly seen as having a rhetorical effect that was essentially autonomous and independent of its delivery: the theorists do not give any weight to the idea that it might have different effects on the audience as a result of being delivered

---

[35] Also Plin. *Ep.* 1.20.9–10: esp. 1.20.9: 'est enim oratio actionis exemplar et quasi ἀρχέτυπον' ('for a [written] speech is the model and as it were *archetype* of the delivered version'); and this applies, according to Pliny, even to speeches (like the *Verrines*) that were never actually delivered.

[36] Compare Cicero, *Brut.* 92–3, which explains that some orators' written versions pale by comparison with their spoken originals because of their lack of proper training, which means that they cannot capture the speech in writing once the actual occasion has passed. Cf. Narducci, *Cicerone*, 162.   [37] *Att.* 2.1.3, 4.2.2; *Q. fr.* 3.1.11; *Brut.* 123.

[38] *Brut.* 92, 122, 126, 127, 164.   [39] Cf. also *Rhet. Her.* 4.78; Cic. *De Or.* 2.90–2.

[40] e.g. Cic. *De Or.* 3.213, *Orat.* 56; Quint. *Inst.* 11.3.5–9; *contra*, *Rhet. Her.* 3.19.

[41] Differences between hearing and reading are discussed in some detail by Quint. *Inst.* 10.1.16–19, essentially in terms of the greater immediacy of the former, as against the opportunities for more objective criticism provided by the latter.

in different ways.[42] When the relationship between text and delivery is considered, the assumption is that a proper delivery will simply reinforce rhetorical effects that are already present in the text: this is especially clear at Quint. *Inst.* 11.3.47–51, where he describes in detail the tone of voice that would be used for the opening of *Pro Milone*, and 11.3.108–10, where he sets out the gestures for the opening of *Pro Ligario*.[43] The weight allotted to delivery does not, therefore, provide any reason to suggest that reading a text in order to determine the rhetorical effect on the hearers was seen as a problematic activity.

But there is also material that might appear to be more directly focused on the issues under consideration here. Quint. *Inst.* 10.1.20–23 is especially interesting: he recommends specifically that the whole work should be read twice; he says that it is useful to get some knowledge of the *causas*, and that, where possible, one should read the speeches on both sides of the case. At 2.5.7 he makes a similar point: before pupils begin to study a speech, the teacher should explain the case to them, 'nam sic clarius quae dicentur intelligi poterunt' ('for thus what is going to be said will be able to be understood more clearly'). The existence of commentaries like Asconius', much of which is precisely occupied with elucidating references for the reader, tends to the same point: people were aware that there were difficulties if they read speeches but possessed only the information contained within those speeches.

But, at the same time, Quintilian's prescriptions, even while showing some awareness that there might be a problem, hardly solve that problem. While in an ideal situation one might seek to read other speeches from the case, or learn about the *causa*, often those other speeches will not have been published, and sufficiently detailed information about the *causa* will not be available. Moreover, the orator publishing his speech could hardly assume that readers would in practice have access to these, even had they *been* published, given the haphazard nature of much ancient book-distribution.

What is more, not all of Quintilian's advice, looked at carefully, is in fact as closely addressed to solving this problem as might have appeared initially. In particular, when dealing with 'reading other speeches from the case', he makes no distinction between speeches that were actually delivered as part

---

[42] For a similar point see R. Webb, 'Imagination and the Arousal of the Emotions in Graeco-Roman Rhetoric', in S. M. Braund and C. Gill (eds.), *The Passions in Roman Thought and Literature* (Cambridge, 1997) 112–27 at 113.

[43] Cf. also Cic. *Part. Or.* 25; Quint. *Inst.* 11.3.96–7, 11.3.161–76. Slightly different is Cic. *Brut.* 141 (of Antonius): 'gestus erat non verba exprimens, sed cum sententiis congruens' ('his gestures were not expressing words, but fitting his opinions'), which seems to reject the very precise match between word and gesture advocated by Quintilian, but does not suggest that these 'opinions' are fundamentally different from those already discernible in the text of the speech.

of the case and those published purely as declamatory exercises, like Brutus' *Pro Milone*; the point seems to be to assess other possible ways of handling the same material, rather than to provide the reader with background information. And, most importantly, the re-reading of the speech is said to be so that one can appreciate where an orator 'praeparat, dissimulat, insidiatur' (10.1.21), insinuating hints which may appear irrelevant for the moment but which will be important in the context of the speech as a whole. But with 'undetermined allusions', the whole problem is that, even in retrospect, one actually cannot tell whether or not this *is* something that Cicero is cunningly insinuating, or whether it is simply a straightforward reminder of something that the hearers already knew: such information about the level of the audience's knowledge does not as a rule even emerge from hypotheses or commentaries (cf. above, n. 33). So if Quintilian shows a certain awareness of the problems inherent in reading speeches, his 'solution' does not go very far towards actually solving them. Therefore we are still faced with the question: in the light of these difficulties, how is it that speeches were expected to be read as rhetorical products, if a proper reconstruction of their full rhetorical effect was not a viable possibility?

vi

If speeches were indeed intended to be read in didactic contexts, the readers would be operating with a certain awareness of rhetorical theory; and an examination of how the theories treat narratives may be helpful. There are various extended discussions in the theoretical texts; but a standard feature is that three canonical qualities were regarded as essential: narratives should be brief, clear, and plausible.[44] Clarity was often treated from a stylistic standpoint (and as such was not associated solely with the narrative),[45] but many of our texts indicate that it also involved arranging a series of events in such a way that they should appear transparent.[46] Yet

---

[44] e.g *Rh. Al.* 1438ª22; *Rhet. Her.* 1.14–17; Cic. *Inv.* 1.19, *De Or.* 2.83, 2.326–30, *Orat.* 122, *Part. Or.* 31–2, *Top.* 97; Quint. *Inst.* 4.2.31 (attributing the doctrine to Isocrates); Anon. Seg. 436,13–14 (Spengel). See Lausberg, *Handbuch*, 168–9; Calboli Montefusco, *Exordium*, 65–9.

[45] e.g. Aristotle, *Rh.* 1404ᵇ2–3; *Rh. Al.* 1438ª32–ᵇ24; *Rhet. Her.* 4.17; Cic. *De Or.* 1.144; Quint. *Inst.* 1.5.1, 1.6.41, 8.2.1, 8.2.12–16, 8.2.22–4. See Lausberg, *Handbuch*, 284–6; Calboli Montefusco, *Exordium*, 69–70.

[46] e.g. *Rhet. Her.* 1.15 (Cic. *Inv.* 1.29 is almost identical): 'rem dilucide narrabimus si ut quicquid primum gestum erit ita primum exponemus, et rerum ac temporum ordinem conservabimus ut gestae res erunt, aut ut potuisse geri videbuntur: hic erit considerandum ne quid perturbate, ne quid contorte, ne quid nove dicamus, ne quam in aliam rem transeamus' ('we will narrate the matter clearly if we first set out whatever is done first, and preserve the order of events and times just as things are done, or seem capable of being done: we must take thought here to ensure that

this would appear to be violated, from the reader's standpoint, by allusions to matters outside his, and perhaps also the hearer's, knowledge.

However, we may argue that it is precisely *because* theorists regarded clarity as a prime virtue of narratives that readers will have assumed that the narrative exemplified that virtue.[47] There is in any case a tendency to use the *exordium* to deal with many of the most awkward hermeneutic problems (above, 137–8); and, as for the remaining undetermined allusions within the narrative itself, the automatic response is likely to be to interpret the passage in such a way that it conforms to the expectations of rhetorical correctness. Such an approach is encouraged by the treatment of 'clarity' by the Roman theorists. The sort of obscure allusion under discussion in this chapter is nowhere referred to directly as a fault in this context. It is perhaps sometimes there implicitly, as at Quint. *Inst.* 4.2.36 (above, n. 46), where a narrative is said to achieve clarity by being 'distincta rebus personis temporibus locis causis' ('marked out by events, persons, times, places, and causes'). But Quintilian does not, as he does in so many other contexts, explicitly criticize speeches for referring to matters unknown to the hearer. A consequence is that the trained reader is less likely to have his attention drawn to obscure allusions as a problematic area; it follows that he will read them as, from the hearer's standpoint, straightforward, and detach his own response and his own failure to understand the nature of the case from the hearer's assumed response, even though he has no precise evidence from which to determine the latter.

The paradox of this conclusion is apparent. The object of reading speeches is to train oneself rhetorically by studying models and seeing how the great masters handled the matter. But when it appears that the great master might have acted other than according to precept, the rule, so far from being modified, is preserved by the presumption that he in fact observed it.[48]

Now, this might not seem an unreasonable presumption; after all, Cicero *was* generally considered to be a great master, and so it might seem fair to

we say nothing jumbled, nothing awkward, nothing new, that we do not switch to another topic'). Also Cic. *De Or.* 2.329: 'erit autem perspicua narratio . . . si ordine temporum servato' ('the narrative will be clear . . . if the chronological order is preserved'). Cf. also *Rh. Al.* 1438ª28–33, Anon. Seg. 438,2–4 (Spengel). Quintilian is slightly more nuanced: he accepts chronological order as the general rule (*Inst.* 4.2.87; cf. also 10.7.6), but accepts that this may be violated for the sake of clarity itself–if the narrative will be clearer by following some other arrangement (4.2.83). His general principle (4.2.36) is that the narrative will be clear if 'distincta rebus personis temporibus locis causis' ('marked out by events, persons, times, places, and causes'). See Lausberg, *Handbuch*, 177–9.

[47] Cf. Enkvist, 'On the Interpretability of Texts', for a discussion of the way in which texts are understood via processes of inference derived from the reader's prior theoretical suppositions.

[48] Note Quint. *Inst.* 10.1.24–7, advocating that even when a speech may appear faulty, one should judge it charitably, and assume that the orator knew what he was doing.

assume that he did indeed obey the rules, which were, after all, supposedly devised for the sake of rhetorical effectiveness.[49] But it is not in fact clear that in practice obscure references in the course of a narration would invariably be rhetorically ineffective. Certainly in the case of *Pro Roscio Amerino*, for example, dark hints that various people involved with the prosecution had benefited in not fully specified ways would appear to enhance one of Cicero's main lines of defence–presenting the jury with a hidden conspiracy with links to the reins of power.[50] And, if we turn from Roman theorists to Greek, we do indeed find rhetoricians who explicitly allowed exceptions to the rule of clarity: notably the pragmatic school of Theodorus of Gadara (Quint. *Inst.* 4.2.32).[51] Theodorus lived slightly after Cicero, but it is striking that Quintilian, normally himself pragmatically inclined, does not adopt this flexibility, and his refutation is brief and dogmatic (4.2.64–5): even if the facts are against one, he says, it is better to have a clear (and false) narrative than an obscure one. And this runs against Quintilian's normal practice; far more commonly he emphasises the possibilities of exceptions to rules.[52] Cicero, too, spends a great deal of time demonstrating that general rules may be broken for the sake of rhetorical effectiveness. Yet in the matter of 'clarity of narration', no such exceptions are noted by either him or Quintilian. Narratives are to be clear; no other discussion, apparently, is needed.[53]

Why should this be? Why should theorists of rhetorical narrative not reflect all the practical possibilities of that rhetorical narrative? The answer lies in the fact that this requirement of 'clarity' is not simply derived from dispassionate observation of what makes an effective speech. Much ancient rhetorical theory is caught up in an attempt to reconcile two essentially incompatible standpoints: (1) the idea that the fundamental standard for rhetorical correctness is the ability to persuade an audience, and (2) the establishment of objective canons of critical taste–with the concomitant problem of how these can represent the most effective

---

[49] In particular, note Quintilian's admiration for Cicero: he cites his speeches vastly more often than those of any other orator, and explicitly refers to him as, if not perfect from a strict philosophical standpoint (*Inst.* 12.1.19–21, 12.10.12–13; cf. also 10.2.9, 10.2.15), nevertheless the finest orator of all in practice (10.1.105–12, 10.2.25).

[50] See Berger, *Cicero als Erzähler*, 33–41, esp. 39–40.

[51] Cf. also Quint. *Inst.* 8.2.18. On Theodorus see G. M. A. Grube, 'Theodorus of Gadara', *AJP* 80 (1959) 337–65. Likewise Anon. Seg. suggests that disordering the narrative is sometimes desirable even at the cost of clarity (445,3–8 (Spengel)), and argues that a speaker may legitimately employ obscurity in order to deceive the jurors (438,22–4 (Spengel)).

[52] See especially Quint. *Inst.* 2.13.1–17; cf. D. L. Clark, *Rhetoric in Greco-Roman Education* (New York, 1957) 116–17.

[53] Note in particular Quint. *Inst.* 4.2.44–5: discussing the three virtues of brevity, clarity, and plausibility, he implicitly treats clarity as paramount, arguing that even brevity should be sacrificed if it leads to obscurity; also *Rh. Al.* 1438^{a}39–61, Cic. *De Or.* 2.328.

means of persuading an audience that does not happen to share those standards of taste.[54]

In the case of clarity in narratives, while as a general rule it was seen as having pragmatic value,[55] it was also closely bound up with the establishment of objective standards. The reason is that the question was not simply an aesthetic one: the notion of a clear, straightforward mode of presentation had, for the Greeks and Romans, strong moral overtones. The orator's ability to persuade through deceit had been a problematic area for rhetoric since its earliest days.[56] Certain theorists responded to this by advocating the adoption of a straightforward and unadorned rhetoric, which would persuade in a morally sound manner, by pure presentation of truth: this approach is associated above all with the Stoics, who regarded clarity as one of the primary virtues of a speaker,[57] and appear to have done so on essentially moral grounds.[58] Of course, the Stoics were unusual in their willingness to allow their concern for truth to control their theory throughout. But the association of clear and plain language with morality is attested much more widely, even among those who are not setting up truth as an ostensible aim.[59] For example, the Roman Atticists of the

[54] On this tension in ancient rhetorical theory, see H. M. DeWitt, 'Quo Virtus: The Concept of Propriety in Ancient Literary Criticism', unpub. diss. (Oxford, 1987) 181–336.

[55] e.g. *Rh. Al.* 1428ª23; Cic. *De Or.* 2.329; Quint. *Inst.* 4.2.38. See J. D. O'Banion, 'Narration and Argumentation: Quintilian on *narratio* as the heart of rhetorical thinking', *Rhetorica* 5 (1987) 325–51 at 346–7.

[56] Cf. D. S. Levene, 'God and Man in the Classical Latin Panegyric', *PCPS* 43 (1997) 66–103 at 93–9; more generally G. Fey, *Das ethische Dilemma der Rhetorik in der Theorie der Antike und der Neuzeit* (Stuttgart, 1990).

[57] See Diogenes Laertius 7.59: C. Atherton, 'Hand over Fist: The Failure of Stoic Rhetoric', *CQ* 38 (1988) 392–427, argues that this applies to rhetorical and philosophical speech alike, as the Stoics did not distinguish the two. Moreover, Cicero, *De Or.* 3.66 (cf. also *De Or.* 2.159 and *Brut.* 119–20) appears to identify Stoic rhetoric with (a poor version of) the plain style alone (Atherton, 'Hand over Fist', 401–4)–the style primarily associated with narrative, in which clarity was seen as a fundamental necessity (above, 141–2). True, in Cicero's view their style was 'obscurum'–lacking clarity–but this is a partisan judgement against their lack of success, rather than a denial that clarity was among their aims; and Cicero was prepared to concede clarity to the Stoics Panaetius (*Fin.* 4.79) and Cato (*Fin.* 3.19)–though admittedly he elsewhere attributes Cato's rhetorical excellence to his use of non-Stoic rhetorical teachers (*Brut.* 118–19: see A. D. Leeman, *Orationis Ratio* (Amsterdam, 1963) 204–5). Plutarch, *Stoic. Rep.* 1047 B quotes Chrysippus as permitting ἀσάφεια, but it is not clear to what precisely this referred (the context in Plutarch is a discussion of hiatus); also cf. Atherton, 'Hand over Fist', 422–3, who suggests that Chrysippus may have been not actively recommending lack of clarity, but regarding it as a venial fault providing the speaker is well-intentioned.

[58] For the moral underpinnings to Stoic rhetorical theory, see G. A. Kennedy, *The Art of Persuasion in Greece* (Princeton, 1963) 292–3; on the specific importance to them of straightforward truth-telling in general and clarity in particular see Atherton, 'Hand over Fist', 407–11, 423–7. On philosophical problems with the Stoic notion of clarity more generally, see C. Atherton, *The Stoics on Ambiguity* (Cambridge, 1993), 87–92.

[59] Note that even the Stoics were prepared to allow their ideal sage to use plausible-sounding language to deceive–though this was not seen as the sage's deceit, but was the weakness of others assenting to false impressions (Quint. *Inst.* 12.1.38; Plut. *Stoic. Rep.* 1055 F, 1056 A, 1057 C: see Atherton, 'Hand over Fist', 424–6).

mid-first century BC, who advocated a not dissimilar manner of oratory, criticized their opponents in terms which had a strongly moral cast: they accused them of 'oriental' effeminacy and redundancy, as opposed to their own appropriately 'masculine' plainness and simplicity.[60] The focus of the attack was primarily stylistic; but in this area style regularly shades into content,[61] and the desire for clear and simple language was linked inevitably to a desire for clear and comprehensible content.

Most theorists, of course, such as Cicero and Quintilian, opposed such attitudes to rhetoric in their full-blown form. Nevertheless they did not escape their influence. In particular, even though rejecting plain and unadorned rhetoric as the sole standard for oratory in general,[62] it was commonplace to accept it for narrative,[63] and, while the overt reasoning for this move tended to be on the grounds of rhetorical effectiveness,[64] the moral overtones associated with this approach are also implicit in various parts of their discussion.[65] To offer objections, and to suggest occasions when clarity of narrative might be thought undesirable, would be potentially to concede moral ground to their opponents: it would appear to imply that even the *appearance* of moral straightforwardness was inessential, and hence suggest rhetoric to be a corrupt art persuading a corrupt audience. At Rome in particular, where moral simplicity formed part of the traditional cultural self-image, a positive portrayal of rhetoric is likely to be one that has incorporated such an image within its theory, and ignored or downplayed the alternatives.[66] And given that the theory was presented in such a manner, a person who read speeches for rhetorical training, with rhetorical theory foremost in his mind, would accordingly be liable to construct his reading in a manner exemplifying the theory.

Indeed, in other areas too one may argue that rhetorical theory governs the reading of the speech. Thus, in *Pro Sestio*, what looks like a clear *praeteritio* is, in the absence of other indications, likely to be read precisely as an example of a standard *praeteritio*, introducing information previously unknown to the audience (above, 134–5).[67] There may also be an

---

[60] Cf. Cic. *Brut.* 51; Quint. *Inst.* 8 pr. 17–22, 12.10.12, 12.10.16–26; Tac. *Dial.* 18.5. See DeWitt, 'Quo Virtus', 252–4.   [61] See in particular Cicero, *De Or.* 3.19; Quint. *Inst.* 8.2.22–4.

[62] Note, however, the related commonplace that the orator, to be effective, must appear to be speaking artlessly: see e.g. Aristotle, *Rh.* 1404[b]18–25; *Rhet. Her.* 4.10; Quint. *Inst.* 4.1.9, 4.2.57, 4.2.125–7, 8.3.2, 9.3.102, 12.9.5–6. See Fey, *Das ethische Dilemma*, 97–8.

[63] e.g. Cic. *Orat.* 124; Quint. *Inst.* 12.10.59. Note also O'Banion, 'Narration and Argumentation', arguing that the *narratio* is the part of the speech on which the effectiveness of the whole depends.

[64] e.g. Quint. *Inst.* 4.2.38–9; see O'Banion, 'Narration and Argumentation', 346–7.

[65] For examples of positive moral language associated with the quality of clarity in particular see e.g. Cic. *De Or.* 1.229, *Orat.* 20; Quint. *Inst.* 2.3.9, 8.2.1–2, 11.3.30.

[66] Cf. Cic. *De Or.* 2.153.

[67] That this was the normal assumption underlying the *praeteritio* is clear from *Rh. Al.* 1438[b]4–6; *Rhet. Her.* 4.37; cf. Quint. *Inst.* 9.2.75. See Lausberg, *Handbuch*, 436–7.

assumption (above, 135–6) that material to which one does not have access is inessential to the case, or at least that one is given all the information necessary to comprehend its effect, even if one does not understand the reference precisely. These assumptions *may* be correct (especially if the speech has on occasion been reworked for publication with the aim of providing the reader with the extra information necessary for his comprehension). But it is important to see that this is not something for which there is evidence: this is simply a construct of the speech's effect erected on the basis of one's theoretical preconceptions.

So my conclusion is a very complex one. We have Cicero's speeches, speeches that *may* (though we, like the original readers, cannot always tell for sure) have employed complexities and flexibilities in his narratives in order to enhance his case. But the reader has problems of his own in interpreting the speech, and so will approach it through preconceptions derived from a rhetorical theory that is itself only partly connected to the pragmatics of rhetoric: for rhetorical theory has its own agenda, governed by its role as not merely the teacher, but the defender of rhetoric within Roman culture.

To return to Stroh's words: 'The agreement of the spoken and the written speech may to a certain extent be a fiction; but if we want to interpret them correctly rhetorically, then we must–paradoxical as it may sound–take this fiction for fact.' From the standpoint of the reader, my ultimate conclusion is exactly the reverse of Stroh's. Cicero's written speech may indeed exactly correspond to the words spoken–though I have shown one or two areas where alterations look highly probable. But, even if they are in fact the same, the ancient reading process in effect created of Cicero's narrative a construct derived from rhetorical theory, that may bear only partial resemblance to the actual effect of the original. Even if written and spoken *were* the same, if we wish to understand the two, then we must–paradoxical as it may sound–take that fact as fiction.

5

Cicero and the Law

JILL HARRIES

'The laws of nature are somewhat removed from the perceptions of the crowd,' wrote the young Cicero.[1] This was true; it was never expedient for an advocate to appear intellectual when addressing his public in the Forum.[2] However, Cicero the advocate had intellectual preoccupations which he shared with Cicero the philosopher. In his theorizing on advocacy, Cicero drew on his practical experience in the courts. Conversely, in his handling of law in all its forms before his public audiences, Cicero addressed himself to an underlying 'iuris consensus', agreed social assumptions on law and rights, which he had argued, in loftier vein, in the *De Republica* was necessary for the formation of a *populus* and for the very existence of a *res publica*.[3]

The 'consensus' on law was expressed in part through the various forms of written law and their modification in response to social change. Written law was finite, in that it was written, but *ius* did not consist only of what was written. The 'consensus' also rested on social and legal concepts such as *aequitas* (proportional fairness), and *consuetudo* (custom), and these too were legitimate matters for legal disputation. This meant that 'legal' argumentation could be based both narrowly on technicalities, and more broadly on legal principle and social (or popular) perception. For example, legal arguments in the narrow sense could be offered on the definition of unlawful violence (*Pro Caecina, Pro Tullio*) or the operation of *societas* (*Pro Roscio Comoedio*). But *maiestas minuta* was (and remained) profoundly problematic.

---

[1] *Inv.* 2.67, 'naturae iura . . . a vulgari intellegentia remotiora sunt'.

[2] *De Or.* 2.4; Cicero comments of L. Licinius Crassus that he wanted the reputation of being a man who looked down on (Greek) learning, while Antonius preferred to be thought never to have studied anything at all. See E. Rawson, 'Lucius Crassus and Cicero: The Formation of a Statesman', *Proceedings of the Cambridge Philological Society* NS 17 (1971) 75–88 = *Roman Culture and Society*, ed. F. Millar (Oxford, 1991) 125–48 at 21 on Crassus, an optimate who used popular language.

[3] *Rep.* 1.39. On the legal framework of the argument, see M. Schofield, 'Cicero's Definition of Res Publica', in J. G. F. Powell (ed.), *Cicero the Philosopher* (Oxford, 1995) 63–84 at 82. For a broader discussion, see J. Coleman, *A History of Political Thought: From Ancient Greece to Early Christianity* (Oxford, 2000) 275–84.

Was an action against a tribune an affront to the *maiestas* of the Roman people, or lawful, as Cicero argued in the *Pro Cornelio*, if undertaken for the public good? How was the public good (and with it the legal definition of treason) to be assessed, if not by the *iudices*, assisted by the partly 'legal' and partly 'political' arguments of the eloquent advocate?

Cicero's appreciation of the 'popular' base of law, both in his imaginary *res publica* and the real one, formed the practical and theoretical framework for his use of law-related argument as an advocate. But how good a lawyer was he? He did not claim to be well grounded in the finer points of law; expert jurisprudents, such as his friends Servius Sulpicius or Trebatius, were there to be consulted (and occasionally insulted as well).[4] However, it does not follow from this that Cicero's knowledge and understanding of law and the laws should be dismissed as 'superficial'.[5] Such a verdict does scant justice to the seriousness not only of his philosophical analysis of law but also his reflections on the theory and practice of legal advocacy and the place of legal science within it. It also ignores the difficulty experienced by observers and practitioners at the time and since, of defining what the law was, and whether it could be 'known'.

It will be argued here that Cicero's use of law as an advocate is best explained in terms of three factors: first, the nature of public pleading; second, the many uncertainties and obscurities inherent in the multifarious nature of Roman law in the first century BC, which allowed space for genuine dispute; and third, Cicero's contention, expressed most fully in the *De Oratore* of 55 BC, that knowledge of law *per se* was less important than eloquence in the winning of cases. Finally, we shall see from analysis of Cicero's speech on the disputed citizenship of L. Cornelius Balbus in 56 how his eloquent exploitation of legal obscurity before a patriotic audience worked in practice.

In the Forum

The law-courts in the Roman Forum of the late Republic were a battleground:

for in these the effectiveness (*vis*) of a pleader is commonly judged by the unqualified (*imperiti*) on the basis of a triumphant outcome; here you are confronted by

---

[4] As at *Pro Murena* 19–30; for jurists' limitations, see A. Watson, 'Limits of Juristic Decision in the Late Roman Republic', *ANRW* I.2 (1972) 215–25.

[5] e.g. by P. Stein, 'The Place of Sulpicius Rufus in the Development of Roman Legal Science', in O. Behrends et al. (eds.), *Festschrift F. Wieacker* (Göttingen, 1978) 175–84.

an armed opponent who must be both struck down and driven back; here often he who will be master of the result is alienated and irritated, or is even a friend to your opponent and an enemy to you.[6]

The courts were intensely adversarial, as courts under many systems were and are, but also more than usually public. Such public buildings and open spaces in the Roman Forum as were adapted to the purpose with space and seating might be full of courts, in which cases were heard before juries of varying sizes, or a single judge.[7] Proceedings were witnessed by a ring of onlookers (*corona*), whose goodwill also had to be conciliated. With or without crowds, law-courts were 'theatres', where every advocate was expected to be another Roscius, with the inconvenient proviso that allowance might be made for Roscius to have an off-day, whereas the unfortunate advocate was granted no such toleration.[8]

To communicate with so varied, and perhaps vociferous, an audience, the advocate was obliged to use 'popular' language, to win the crowd.[9] He and others could measure his effectiveness by the outward signs of the jury's and the crowd's behaviour. Thus Cicero, reflecting on the behaviour of *iudices*, noted that good speakers held the attention of their audience, who showed interest, enthusiasm, and emotion as required, while the bad orator was confronted by *iudices* who yawned, gossiped to each other, wandered about, asked the time and pleaded for adjournments.[10] Even those charged with making judicial decisions would share the 'vulgi opinio', popular view,[11] when they came to decide their verdict.

The open and unregulated nature of public hearings carried obvious dangers. Anyone could set himself up as an advocate. Part of the scene in the Forum were the bad lawyers, 'flitting about', touting for cases; these were bad because they were ignorant of basic points of law and unwilling to go to the trouble of preparing their cases properly,[12] yet plausible enough to persuade unfortunate clients into employing their disreputable services. The structure of the political career-ladder encouraged the proliferation of irresponsible amateurs; successful prosecutions were a way of attracting popular attention and were therefore a route to the top. Legal

---

[6] *De Or.* 2.72, cf. 1.157 for Forum as battleground, complete with combatants, camps, dust, and shouting.

[7] cf Cic. *Verr.* II 5.143–4; *Pro Flacco* 59. On political topography of Roman Forum, see A. Vasaly, *Representations: Images of the World in Ciceronian Oratory* (Berkeley, Calif., 1993) 34–5; F. Millar, *The Crowd in the Late Republic*, Jerome Lectures 22 (Ann Arbor, Mich., 1998) 39–45.

[8] *De Or.* 1.124. On the other hand, Roscius had problems finding the perfect pupil (ibid. 129).

[9] Repeatedly emphasized, e.g. *De Or.* 1.12, 80, 94, 108, 221; 2.154–9, 178, 186, 205–12 (emotional appeals); cf. *Verr.* I 18–19, the *iudices* will follow the *existimatio* of the people.

[10] *Brutus* 200.

[11] *Topica* 73; for all this as subversion of justice, see C. J. Classen, 'Cicero, the Laws, and the Law-Courts', *Latomus* 37 (1978) 579–619.   [12] *De Or.* 1.173; 2.101.

hacks canvassing for clients in the Forum, surrounded by a group of friends would have been visually indistinguishable from aspiring politicians canvassing for votes; 'upright and with nose in the air, keen and alert in expression and manner, looking from side to side, they wander the forum with a great crowd (*caterva*) in tow.'[13] Indeed, the advocate and the politician could have been the same person.

Even where reputable advocates were employed, who knew what they were doing and put the proper effort into their cases,[14] the structure of the courts themselves encouraged the exploitation of emotion and ignorance; in the *quaestiones perpetuae, iudices* were not chosen for their expertise in law, and there was no president to provide an impartial summing up of the advocates' arguments. In the Centumviral Court, which convened to hear cases of civil property and inheritance law, (and from which Cicero derived many of his precedents), there were one hundred judges, of varying expertise, to be swayed. In cases presided over by a single judge, the outcome would depend on the view taken by the judge and perhaps his *consilium* and his *assessors*; these might appear the least open to emotional manipulation, but Cicero never advances any argument to suggest that a different style of pleading should be used in such cases, presumably because single judges had their prejudices and intellectual blind-spots too.

Given Cicero's talent for emotive distractions and the congenial surroundings for its exercise afforded by the Roman courts, we might expect legal argumentation not to rate highly in Cicero's priorities. That he accorded it the attention he did says much about his forensic technique and his intellectual approach in general to questions of law. In addition, it suggests that at least some of his casual audience in the Forum expected to hear legal argument and to be influenced by it.[15] Exploitation of emotion could have worn thin, especially as regular attenders at court occasions would have become streetwise over time. Legally-minded advocates on the other side could have put the emotively waffling Cicero at a disadvantage, if he was not prepared to engage in legal disputation too. Moreover, as we have seen, consideration of law in many aspects and on many levels was a central part of Cicero's thinking and although his philosophical treatment of law is irrelevant to the present purpose, his rejection of the

[13] *De Or.* 1.173; 2.184.

[14] Cf. Antonius' description of his preparation of cases in *De Or.* 2.102 ff., which describes detailed briefing by the client in private; consideration of strong points in the argument and points at issue; and performance in court, using proof, winning favour, and manipulation of emotion in the required direction.

[15] Missing speeches by other advocates, e.g. supporting Caelius and Balbus in 56, may have contained more solid legal fare than Cicero provides for either case; he was often put last, to have maximum emotional impact. For legal argumentation on the passing of legislation, see M. H. Crawford (ed.), *Roman Statutes* (London, 1996), i. 11.

kind of narrow legalism practised by the jurists (and, in a distinctively archaizing way, by Caesar), was consistent with his practice as a forensic orator. Mastering the small print was a useful ad hoc tool; control of the nature of law itself gave the orator far greater scope to convince his adjudicators that his version of the law was the way the law ought to be.

It should be clear from what has been said already of Cicero's connection of the issue of legal expertise with forensic effectiveness that a study of Cicero's techniques of legal argumentation as evidenced in the speeches cannot be carried out in isolation from his theoretical discussions of the subject. As he frequently insisted, it was his practice (*usus*) which informed his theory.[16] People who theorized on a topic without having experience of it were as useless as civilians who told generals what to do; as the exiled Hannibal said, having sat through the philosopher Phormio's lecture on generalship, 'he had seen many old men suffering from dementia, but none as dotty as Phormio'.[17] Therefore we will look first at Cicero's theory of what the forensic orator had to do to conduct his case most effectively, before turning to how this theory was applied by Cicero in court.

'Knowing' Law

The first book of Cicero's *De Oratore*, written in 55 BC but set in the year 91, is partly taken up with a *disputatio* between L. Licinius Crassus, consul in 95, and M. Antonius, on the extent of the *iuris scientia*, knowledge of the law, required of the advocate. Each adopts a slightly extreme position. Crassus requires of the advocate as near total knowledge of all disciplines, law included, as is practically possible, while Antonius urges the advisability of delegating to experts, pointing out that eloquence is essential for the advocate, whereas knowledge is not. Cicero's resolution of the controversy is expressed *in propria persona* early in Book 2, when he appears to follow Crassus' line, that 'no one could have ever flourished or excelled in eloquence without training in speaking and moreover a knowledge of all subjects', of which law was one.[18] On the other hand, in a different context, he could also concede Antonius' argument on the general desirability of expert advice;[19] one could know a lot, but not everything.

However, 'knowing' the law was itself a problematic concept. What was there to know? Legal textbooks down to the present define Roman law in

---

[16] *De Or.* 1.5, 105, 145; all making explicit what is implied throughout by Cicero's use of real cases as *exempla*. [17] *De Or.* 2.75.
[18] *De Or.* 2.5.   [19] e.g. *Balb.* 45, see below, p. 162.

terms of what was written down, the *lex scripta*. But, as every Roman schoolboy knew from his rhetorical exercises,[20] in a given theoretical case, arguments could be advanced for written law, on the one hand, and, on the other, the case for proportional fairness, or *aequitas*. Knowing law was further complicated by a third element, custom, or *consuetudo*. Customary law could be discussed in legal terms, but 'custom' was also a matter of usage in society as a whole, which could impinge on social assumptions about history or the *mos maiorum*, which were politically loaded ideas. The history of law, like the history of religion, was bound up with Roman conceptions of their identity, which rested on constant reworkings of their past. Similarly concepts of 'fairness' depended on what was socially acceptable. Therefore, because forensic argumentation on law deployed terms which also carried extra-legal baggage, it followed that some legal arguments advanced in court rested on material, particularly precedents, that derived from history or depended for their effect on extra-legal considerations.

It was, then, this blurring of the frontiers of what strict law was that provides part of the explanation for Cicero's practice as an advocate when handling legal questions. He did not introduce apparently non-legal material (only) to mislead; knowledge of *ius* in the strict sense could only be a subset of the knowledge required of the advocate, who had to relate to daily experience as much as to legal technicality. Separating *ius* from its social matrix was not easy. Did it follow that 'law' could not be defined at all?

Definitions

Contrary to the doubts expressed above, Cicero believed that definition of *ius* could be attempted. To start with, there were a number of basic types; the 'law of the citizen' (*ius civile*), which Cicero in youth defined as custom written down as statute;[21] the pontifical 'sacred law' hallowed by antiquity, and what passed for international law, labelled for internal use by the Romans as the 'ius fetiale' but also described by Cicero as the 'ius commune', under which peoples could deal with each other. Also, law was defined in terms of its sources. In the 80s, the young Cicero of the *De Inventione* had produced a conventional list, glossing his reflections on *leges* with reflections on the laws of nature and a definition of custom as being what was sanctioned by antiquity and general popular agreement.[22] In 55, Cicero's 'Antonius' defined *iuris scientia* as expertise in statutes (*leges*) and custom (*consuetudo*), along with the ability to give advice, conduct a lawsuit, and safeguard a client; his exemplary (and pre-91) jurisconsults included Sextus

---

[20] *De Or.* 1.244, 'alius scriptum, alius aequitatem defendere docentur'. Cf. ibid. 2.100 with example of such an exercise.   [21] *Inv.* 2.64.
[22] Ibid. 65–8.

Aelius, Manius Manilius and P. Mucius Scaevola.[23] In his *Topica* addressed to the young equestrian jurist, C. Trebatius Testa, in the troubled summer of 44, Cicero offered, as an example of the method of arranging argument known as *partitio*, a textbook definition of the *ius civile*, as consisting of the 'content of statutes (*leges*), resolutions of the Senate (*senatus consulta*), judicial decisions (*res iudicatae*), the authority of the jurists, the edicts of the magistrates, custom and equity'.[24]

In the first century, the volume of written law available, though often highly specialized, was still manageable. The volume of Roman statute law was tiny,[25] while senatorial decrees had something of an *ad hoc* nature, and were not, under the Republic, universally binding. The Praetor's Edict, the *ius honorarium*, grew over the years with successive annual revisions by the praetors to form the framework of civil law, enabling the Praetor to issue *formulae* defining what was the point at issue in lawsuits and referring them on to a judge to determine the facts. Edicts by other magistrates enabled the law to be administered in the relevant sphere of authority, including in the provinces. And, while jurisprudence was a growth industry by the late second century, the eighteen books of the Pontiff Scaevola's *ius civile* hardly compare in terms of size with the blockbusters of the imperial jurists; Ulpian, the most prolific, was the author of no less than three hundred volumes, mostly written at presumably break-neck speed in the reign of Caracalla (AD 211–217).[26]

Although Cicero claimed that he knew only as much law as he needed to get by as an orator (while conversely Servius Sulpicius had only as much eloquence as he needed to present his jurisprudence in court), knowledge of law in its most technical and occasionally even pedantic sense, was part of his culture. He had learned the Twelve Tables by heart as a boy; at Rome, he had sat at the feet of Q. Mucius Scaevola the Augur in the late 90s; subsequently he was a student of the younger Q. Mucius, the Pontifex.[27] For both, Cicero retained a lifelong admiration. His use of legal precedents and authorities is frequent and deceptively casual, and happened even on social occasions, as in this recollection of a somewhat inebriated dispute with the young *eques* and legal expert, C. Trebatius Testa:

You made fun of me yesterday, over a drink or two, for saying that it was a disputed point whether an action for theft is available to an heir in respect of a theft

---

[23] *De Or.* 1.212. It is a tribute to Cicero's care over chronological authenticity that Antonius' canon did not include either of the contemporary Scaevolae, the Augur, or the Pontiff. Aelius and Manilius were favourite jurists of Cicero, who crop up elsewhere. [24] *Topica* 28.

[25] Cf. Crassus' comment at *De Or.* 1.192, praising the public accessibility of law and the fact that it is contained in 'not many volumes'. Contrast Antonius (ibid. 246) on the unattractiveness of law and the arrogance of its practitioners.

[26] For what survives of Ulpian, mostly preserved as extracts in Justinian's *Digest*, see O. Lenel, *Palingenesia Iuris* (Leipzig, 1889) ii. 379–1200. [27] *De Amicitia* 1.

committed before. So when I got home, though late and rather intoxicated, I noted the relevant section and am forwarding you a copy. You will find that the view, which, you claimed, had never been held by anybody, was in fact the opinion of Sextus Aelius, Manius Manilius, and M. Brutus, but for my part I agree with Scaevola and Testa.[28]

That Cicero could engage in such discussions at will is symptomatic of a legal culture which took mastery of the sources of law in its stride. Although Cicero could set up a slightly exaggerated debate in the *De Oratore* on the merits of a legal education as contrasted with the superior desirability of eloquence, this was in fact a false contrast. Cicero's own practice in the courts shows that he appreciated the need for both.

The argument that legal knowledge was possible could also be expressed in the negative. Bad advocates, who did not know, or could not be bothered with, legal technicalities and the principles of the *ius civile* let their clients down. Such were the late second-century consular *patroni* Hypsaeus and Gnaeus Octavius who pleaded on opposite sides at inordinate length before the praetor in a case involving guardianship; because neither knew the law, including the Law of the Twelve Tables, properly, they both risked winning the case for the other side.[29] Cicero/Crassus also castigated an erroneous plea in a debt case heard before the praetor Q. Pompeius, and careless drafting of a servitude concerning light in a contract of sale.[30] Such charlatans were both impudent in themselves and dangerous to their clients:

> to show off to the Centumviral Court about such matters as the rights of long use (*usucapio*), guardianship (*tutela*), kinship by clan (*gentilitas*) or paternal descent (*agnatio*), changes in shore-lines, formation of islands by rivers, disputes about pledges (*nexum*), transfers of property (*mancipia*) rights relating to partition-walls and light and rain-drips, the validity and invalidity of wills, and countless other matters, without any knowledge whatever of what is his own and what is another's, or even the difference between a citizen and a foreigner, is a mark of real cheek.[31]

Another, related form of incompetence was not to understand enough to engage with disputes involving the legal thinking underlying the *ius civile*. What was to happen in a case, which actually came before the Centumviral Court, where a father had written a will mistakenly assuming that his son was dead, only for the lost son to return and claim his inheritance?

Certainly, in that case the question concerned the *ius civile*, as to whether a son could be disinherited from his father's property, when his father had not instituted him as heir in his will, nor had he disinherited him by name.[32]

---

[28] *Fam.* 7.22.   [29] *De Or.* 1.166–7.   [30] Ibid. 168–9 (debt); 179 (servitude).
[31] Ibid. 173.
[32] Ibid. 175. The rule on wills was that sons-in-power had to be disinherited by name; daughters could be excluded by a general clause.

The same could be argued for whether a freedman's legacy should pass to a family by lineal or clan descent; or the law of clientship involving a foreign exile subject to protection by a patron; or the obligations of a vendor to reveal defects in his property prior to the agreement of sale. Knowledge of the rights of the citizen, of slaves and freedmen, and of the married and their heirs, also were necessary for the successful advocate.[33] But what did *iuris scientia* contribute to winning the battles of the courts?

Knowledge versus *Eloquence*

To know the sources and have mastery of the written law did not guarantee victory in the courts. Too much, as we have seen, was in dispute for an outcome to be certain. In a system which gave equity and custom weight equal, if not superior, to written law, and privileged the popular will, as mediated through *iudices*, the eloquent advocate had a free hand. As indicated above, Crassus' line on the need for the orator to be an expert was part of a broader contention advanced in the *De Oratore* that the perfect speaker required a broad education in every discipline. This was not merely a theoretical desideratum. In court advocacy, the use of *exempla* drawn not only from law but also from history and from life helped to obscure the boundary between what was strictly legal argument and what was not. History, in other words, could be the basis of legal decision. It was this cultural ambiguity which justified Crassus' statement that an orator required to know about history as well as about law:

> (he) must learn thoroughly the *ius civile*, he must have knowledge of the statutes, he must know all about ancient history (*antiquitas*), the custom of the Senate, the regulation of the *res publica*, the institutions of our allies, treaties, agreements, the cause of empire must be understood.[34]

As we shall see, Pompey's grant of citizenship to Balbus was justified in terms of numerous precedents, consisting of the grants made by great men in the past, notably the popular hero, Marius. These, as they entailed extension of the *civitas*, were 'legal' in a sense, but Cicero's technique in their presentation was to emphasize the *auctoritas* of the donors rather than the exact circumstances of the grants.[35]

But precedents were a grey area not only because they could be historical (or even literary) as well as legal, but also because arguments from precedents could be combined with arguments by analogy (*similitudines*), which also did not require to be based on the *ius civile*. The effect of this was to further

---

[33] *De Or.* 1.184.

[34] Cf. *De Or.* 1.18 that the orator must remember the whole of ancient history (*omnis antiquitas*) and the power of precedent (*exemplorumque vis*), as well as knowledge of law and statutes.

[35] *Balbo* 46–50.

subvert the written word and strengthen the hands of the champions of *aequitas* against the *lex scripta*. The argument advanced, in a provocatively extreme form, by M. Antonius, that what an advocate needed above all was eloquence, and that he therefore did not need to devote special study to the law at all, is partly based on a narrow definition of knowledge as specialist rather than general. Antonius' notion of eloquence in fact did require knowledge, but not strictly legal knowledge. Therefore he could, for argumentative purposes, exploit the range of arguments based on precedent and analogy open to the advocate. It was paradoxically Crassus whom Cicero/Antonius saluted as the master of that technique in the famous 'causa Curiana', when Crassus adduced examples 'both from statutes and from *senatus consulta*, and from life and everyday speech, where, if we followed the words rather than the spirit, we would achieve nothing'.[36]

Yet even Crassus could be outdone, as when challenged over a legal decision issued to a client by the versatile Servius Sulpicius Galba:

Galba playfully and with a wide range of and numerous illustrations brought forward many arguments from analogy, and made many points against strict law (*ius*) and in favour of equity; and Crassus ... took refuge with legal authorities (*auctores*) pointing out that what he had said was in the books of his brother P. Mucius (Scaevola) and in the commentaries of Sextus Aelius (on the Twelve Tables), yet he conceded that Galba's contention seemed to him plausible and close to the truth.[37]

Can the large measure of uncertainty present in law be ascribed to the primitive state of law at Rome? The fact that the formal system of Roman law was still at an early stage of development, compared with the sophistication to come, would not in itself have created larger areas of disputed law. Legal systems are the product of the society which created them; some societies, including that of early Rome, functioned very well with very little of what we would recognize as positive law at all. Conversely, elaborate systems of written law with multiple remedies create new problems of their own. However, the challenge for Roman law in the first century was to cope with the combined impact of an expanding empire and the influx of Greek ideas on, among other things, methods of argumentation and analysis of systems, including systems of law. It was not coincidence that both Cicero and Caesar had ideas about codification and systematization of law.[38] Orators and jurists alike found new things to dispute about, and new ways of expressing legal disagreement.

[36] *De Or.* 1.243. On the causa Curiana see also ibid. 1.180; 2.24, 221–2; *Brutus* 145; 197–8; *Top.* 44.
[37] *De Or.* 1.240.
[38] Cicero's ideal law-code was set out in *De Legibus* 2 and 3; for ideas on arrangement of laws using Greek principles, *De Or.* 1.186–9. For Caesar's alleged codification project see Suetonius, *Divus Julius* 44.2.

The impact on first-century Rome of cultural and social change compounded the difficulties deriving from the fact that no legal system, even a highly developed one, can encompass every possible eventuality. As has been argued, the limitations of the *lex scripta* were openly acknowledged and left many of the complexities of people's dealings with each other open to the interpretations supplied by those who could claim consistency with the nebulous, but nevertheless crucial, authority of custom and equity. Advocates worked in the wide disputed space between the limited guidance offered by written authorities and the amorphous provisions of *aequitas* and *consuetudo*. Cicero's aim as advocate was to lay claim to that disputed legal space through eloquent advocacy designed to win his case by convincing *iudices* of what he thought the law should be.

Could this result in changes to the written law itself? Certainly, a by-product of the techniques used by the advocate to win was that a verdict could legitimize a disputed definition of an offence, even if it did not receive formal recognition as a precedent. A prominent example of this, which was to have a long history, was the law on *maiestas*, and how the offence we know as treason was to be defined. Cicero's Antonius recalled his method of defending Norbanus against the accusation of *maiestas* brought by Sulpicus under Saturninus' treason law:

'For I conceded most of the changes levelled by my opponent there, but I said that he was not guilty of *maiestas minuta*, and the whole of that case depended on the definition of that word under the Lex Appuleia.'[39]

Cicero's recollection of Antonius' method may also have been reinforced by his own use of a similar line of argument, when defending the tribune Cornelius on the same charge: Cornelius' reading out of his bill after the interposition of a tribunician veto was not *maiestas minuta* as it did not damage the *maiestas* either of the tribunate or of the Roman people.[40] In both cases, the fates of the defendants hinged on the definition of a word, and the ability of the competing advocates to convince the adjudicators that their definition was correct. Such cases did not necessarily create precedents, but, where they did, their accumulated effect was to enable redefinition of offences, not by legislative fiat, but through the courts.

To summarize thus far, what was in fact at issue in the *De Oratore* was not whether advocates should know the law or not, but what was the balance to be struck between knowledge and eloquence. Legal knowledge was one part of the eloquent advocate's armoury but it was not the only one, nor would it necessarily prove the most effective. Cicero's practice

---

[39] *De Or.* 2.107, cf. 109.
[40] Asconius 71.17 C.; J. W. Crawford, *M. Tullius Cicero: The Fragmentary Speeches. An Edition with Commentary* (Atlanta, 1994) 67–86.

was to use law, even when it was certain, only as one of his methods to achieve victory. If law was not on his side, he had other weapons, in which he took great pride. His techniques of obfuscation included his fooling the judges over the charge against Cluentius in 66,[41] and, twenty years later, he recollected his defeat of the advocate M. Calidius, who had all the weight of written and oral evidence on his side, but was confounded by the theatricality of Cicero's use of emotion and gesture.[42] On occasion, he could be openly contemptuous of those, like Servius Sulpicius Rufus, who based their arguments on the detail of law, dismissing their technique as pedantry, which was unlikely either to sway a court or further its possessor's political ambitions.[43] In politer mode, too, he drew a clear distinction between the jurist who in a case of a disputed sale would ask technical questions about the transfer, and the forensic orator who would play on emotions, 'make the dumb speak and raise the dead, to stir things up'.[44] There was no doubt in his mind as to which would prevail.

'Knowing the law' through personal study or guidance from experts was a necessary prerequisite for success. But 'knowing' was not just a matter of learning the rules, because the law did not consist of rules. Too many areas of uncertainty existed and where dispute occurred the outcome would depend not on who knew most, because certain knowledge might not be possible, but who could put forward the most persuasive case, relying not only on authorities in the strict sense but also on the more debatable clout of history, precedent and analogy, the creation of red herrings, and the generation of probably irrelevant emotions. Given Cicero's respect for emotion as a determinant of outcome and his confidence in his own powers of generating feeling at the expense of rational argument, the attention he paid to legal argumentation is surprising. That he did so, at least when he thought he had a case, suggests that Roman *iudicia* could still assess legal argument intelligently, despite the distractions caused by emotive advocates and the often rowdy environment in which they worked.

Using Law: The *Pro Balbo*

After a brief period of heady independence in the early months of 56, Cicero was hauled into line by the 'Three', Pompey, Caesar, and Crassus, and, as public demonstration of his new docility, he championed various

---

[41] Quint. *Inst.* 2.17.21.   [42] *Brutus* 277.
[43] *Mur.* 19–30; this argument was designed to alienate the sympathies of the *iudices* from legal pedants (and philosophers) and did not reflect Cicero's respect for Servius, which is often expressed elsewhere.   [44] *Topica* 45.

causes and clients favoured by the controlling powers.[45] These included his defence in that year of Pompey's grant of citizenship to L. Cornelius Balbus of Gades, now Caesar's client; the grant was challenged before an unknown court by another Gaditane, on the grounds that Pompey had unwittingly granted citizenship to a man from a *civitas*, which had not 'given consent'. The defenders of the grant, apart from Cicero, who spoke last, were M. Licinius Crassus and Pompey himself.

The speech is of extraordinary interest for what it says about Roman views of citizenship grants, as well as its political background.[46] Less often noticed is that the methods used by Cicero have very little to do with undisputed law, still less with written law, because he was functioning in an area of law, the evolving *ius commune*, which still relied heavily on custom, as might be expected, given that there was no international body able to impose its will, apart from Rome itself. Some law of this kind was to be found in the text of treaties, and the main points at issue raised by the prosecution derived from a treaty text of over twenty years previously, and were responded to by Cicero with a virtuoso display of semantic sophistication. But Cicero also relied heavily on assertions of customary usage with regard to citizenship and on the use of *exempla*, meaning both legal precedents and inspiring historical examples. Considerations of personality, notably the unengaging public profile of Balbus, were also discussed by Cicero but for purposes of analysis of legal argumentation may be left on one side; as Cicero was to reflect, a year later, whatever the personalities of a case, all cases could ultimately be reduced to debate on an issue of legal principle.[47]

Cases in Roman civil law often turned on the interpretation of texts, for example of wills, where much play could be made with the wording as against the intention of a testator. The case of Balbus was argued in terms of the text of a treaty. The case of the *accusator* rested on fine points in (or not in) a treaty which defined the legal relationship of Gades with Rome. This had been agreed by the Senate in 78, as part of its strategy in dealing with the threat from Sertorius.[48] According to Cicero *iuris periti* had felt the need to regularize a relationship between the cities 'said to' have been inaugurated by a treaty negotiated with Gades by a Roman centurion in 206, but which, before 78, had in fact depended on the *fides* of the Gaditani, the *iustitia* of the Romans and *vetustas*, antiquity.

---

[45] T. N. Mitchell, *Cicero: The Senior Statesman* (New Haven, 1991) 186 claims that Cicero 'happily' undertook the case of Balbus. This may be doubted.
[46] On political trials of the 50s, see E. Gruen, *The Last Generation of the Roman Republic* (Berkeley, Calif., 1968) 46–50. [47] *De Or.* 2.130–45.
[48] *Balb.* 34. This is consistent with a general juristic urge to regularize unwritten and customary arrangements.

This document, which, it should be remembered, was not designed to meet the needs of a Balbus or a Pompey, was central to the cases on both sides. Consequently, their argumentation had to depend on the precise wording of a treaty constructed for an entirely different purpose. If the treaty did say anything about citizenship, as some treaties did, it is amazing that neither learned counsel quoted it, suggesting that questions of *civitas* were not in the minds of the drafters at the time. In the apparent absence of anything directly material to the case, it was not only knowledge which was required of the advocates but creativity. Each had to construct a case about citizenship, relying on a document which may have had nothing whatever to say about the issue of citizenship. Not surprisingly, each side relied heavily on what was not in the document. The *accusator* claimed that the provisions of the treaty did not 'give consent', whereas there were other treaties with Gallic and Illyrian tribes which explicitly withheld it (therefore Balbus could not be granted citizenship); Cicero's counter-argument was that it did not withhold consent either (as the Gallic treaties did), therefore 'where there is no saving clause, admission then must be lawful'.[49] The accuser also maintained that the treaty was subject to an exemption clause 'if there be anything sacrosanct', in the Lex Gellia Cornelia, which had empowered Pompey to make his grant.[50] This was scornfully dismissed: the issue of sacrosanctity was irrelevant because the treaty had not been voted by the Roman people, who were custodians of 'sacrosanctity'. And any notion that the Gaditani were empowered to decide such things for themselves (if they had) was nullified by further semantic exercises on Cicero's part; the treaty stated 'let them uphold the greatness (*maiestas*) of the Roman people in a friendly way', using the imperative (*conservanto*) and stating that the relationship was 'friendly' (*comiter*) but not 'mutual' (*communiter*). The people of Gades might be friends, but they were also, under Cicero's, and the Roman, reading of the *ius commune*, clients. Therefore, as there was nothing to prevent him in the treaty, and, even if there were, the Romans could do as they liked, Pompey's grant under the statute should stand.

The nub of the case, as Cicero represented it, was the question of consent: no one, according to the prosecution, from a people bound to the Romans by treaty could acquire Roman citizenship, unless that people had given consent.[51] Not so, according to Balbus' advocate. First, there was the objection, learnedly discussed, that the provision applied both to federate

---

[49] *Balb.* 32–3.

[50] On the difficult textual and legal problems of this passage, see E. Badian, 'E.H.N.I.R.', *Mus. Helv.* 45 (1988) 203–17; my thanks to Christopher Smith for this reference.

[51] *Balb.* 8.19, 'negat ex foederato populo quemquam potuisse, nisi is populus fundus factus esset, in hanc civitatem venire.'

and to free cities; this served to subvert the prosecutor's claim to understand the law and to establish Cicero's superior knowledge. Second, there was a general statement about intention (*ratio* and *sententia*): the object had been to allow Latin and allied states to adopt Roman statutes into their laws, and, if they became bedded down over time, to allow them to be part of the recipient's legal system. And finally there was the support of precedents for adoption of Roman statutes by Latins, which included the *lex Furia* on wills in 183 and the notorious *lex Voconia*, which prevented the institution of wealthy women as heirs and restricted their right to receive legacies. More recently, the *lex Julia* of 90 offered citizenship on the basis that those peoples who did not 'give consent' would not receive the citizenship; Naples and Heraclea took advantage of this provision to abide by their existing treaties. So it followed that the force (*vis*) of the *lex Julia* was that states became 'consenting' because of what the Romans thought, not of their own volition; that assertion of inequality was also to apply to the situation of Gades under the treaty of 78. Only at this point is there mention of the written word, the 'terminology' (*verbum*) of the law. The rest of the argument depends on assertions of principle and the uses of precedent.

That Cicero was not entirely happy with the textual situation with regard to the treaty is suggested by his rapid shift to what he asserted was the real point of the case, the Roman legal situation with regard to citizenship in general. Cicero's general argument concerning the nature of citizenship was based on the practice of the Romans, when considering donations of *civitas*, and was backed, again by precedent. No one, Cicero insisted, could change his citizenship against his will,[52] and no one could be prevented from so doing, if he wished, provided that his new state was ready to adopt him. Therefore, if the people of Gades voted that a Roman citizen could become a citizen of Gades, he would have the right to take up the offer, and no treaty would debar him from exchanging the citizenship of Rome for that of Gades. By analogy, therefore, a citizen of Gades could become a citizen of Rome.[53]

Exempla from the past added weight to the orator's history of the Roman *civitas*. Numerous famous ancient Romans who changed *civitas* by attachment (*dicatio*), the substitution of the citizenship of the receiving city for the Roman citizenship, were invoked;[54] the orator's knowledge of ancient history was deployed to add weight to his account and distract from the awkward little technicality, now virtually forgotten. And change of citizenship could also come about through *postliminium*, the right of subsequent return, which enabled Roman prisoners of war, whose civil rights were suspended during their period away, to have their citizenship

---

[52] Cf. *Caecin.* 95–100; *Dom.* 77.   [53] *Balb.* 29.   [54] Ibid. 28.

restored on their return. More difficulties in the law of *postliminium* could be generated by too much travel; in, probably, the mid-second century, the Greek freedman, Gnaeus Publicius Menander, accompanied a Roman delegation back to his native Greece, having first acquired the protection of a statute stating that if Publicius went back to his home in Greece and then returned to Rome, he would still be a Roman citizen.[55]

Textual analysis, arguments from customary practice on the nature of the Roman citizenship, and the use of *exempla* together provided the semblance of a cogent case. Yet we do not, and cannot, know from Cicero how impressive the opposing case may have been. What is beyond dispute is that Balbus had the political heavyweights on his side and that it was up to Cicero, the last of the three speakers, to drive that point home. This he did by depicting Pompey in the unusual role of a legal authority:

> For I have never heard ever what seemed to me a more acute speech on the point of law, nothing with a greater recollection of precedents, nothing more expert on treaties, nothing with more brilliant authority on wars, nothing of greater weight on the state.[56]

The same theme was picked up later, in connection with the interpretation of treaties (a further indication that Cicero's refutation of the *accusator* was not beyond challenge). Now the argument was that the actions of all previous generals (especially Marius, but also Sulla, Pompeius Strabo, and others) who had conferred citizenship had created binding legal precedents, which had never been successfully challenged. It was those who had held *imperium* who were best qualified (he said) to interpret treaties, military law and international law.[57] Such generals, Cicero maintained, were on a par with lawyers, whose expertise in their own fields gave them preference in all forms of consultation. For example, reminisced the orator, his mentor Q. Mucius Scaevola the Augur would refer clients who consulted him about mortgages to the expert guidance of the brokers Furius and Cascellius, while he himself would consult one Marcus Tugio on water-rights, rather than his friend the eminent jurist, C. Aquilius Gallus. On this analogy, generals were the best lawyers on treaties and on all the 'law' of peace and war. It was irrelevant that the comparison may have been unsound, if taken literally; even generals acted in legal matters with the advice of *consilia*. But in terms of authority, Cicero's point stood. What his case came down to was a simple question; whom to believe?

---

[55] At *Digest* 49.15.5, Pomponius' commentary on Scaevola cites the Menander precedent, suggesting Scaevola's 18-book *De Iure Civili* may have been Cicero's source for this precedent, and perhaps the whole discussion.

[56] *Balb.* 1.2. For Pompey as legal exponent of Caesar's *lex agraria* in 59, see Plut. *Pompey* 47; Dio *RH* 38.4–5. On *auctoritas* of Pompey on Cicero's return from exile see *Pro Sestio* 107–8.

[57] *Balb.* 45.

Finally, Cicero in his peroration acknowledged explicitly what had been implicit throughout, that the law could be disputed, and that, even if the law was clear, the court had the power to change it. The judges had a choice. They could go along with the famous names and precedents already cited: better to be honourably wrong with them than be schooled by the prosecution.[58] Alternatively, if they believed they had to decide about a clear point of law, they should not so act as to pass any innovative resolution about a matter so sanctioned by antiquity (*in re tam inveterata*). The power of custom and precedent could not lightly be set aside.

Conclusion

This analysis of the speech for Balbus has, inevitably, been selective in focusing on the legal or quasi-legal arguments, without taking account of Cicero's emotive digressions designed to create sympathy for Balbus, enthusiasm for past and present Roman greatness, and excuses advanced for acting as advocate for the creature of the triumvirs, all of which were integral parts of his strategy to convince an inexpert and sceptical public of the rightness of his case. In Cicero's representation of the case, the wording of the treaty, custom, precedent, and the authority of Balbus' patron and backers, all should have guaranteed his victory.

Was Balbus' case justified? The reader of Cicero should be cautious in making a judgement, given that we do not have the other speeches in the case. Perhaps it is a question which is not worth asking; the protagonists themselves may not have been sure of the answer. With law, as we have seen, in a state of constant tension between advocates of written law and *aequitas*, and juries buffeted by competing authorities, eloquent and misleading orators, and the manifold distractions of a crowded Forum, Cicero himself could not always have been certain whether his presentation of his case would convince his *iudices*. As his 'Crassus' observed of his own experience, good advocates are always nervous.[59]

---

[58] Ibid. 64, 'ne utilius vobis et honestius sit illis ducibus errare quam hoc magistro erudiri'. This suggests the prosecution did have a technical case.   [59] *De Or.* 1.119–21.

6

The Rhetoric of Character in the Roman Courts

Andrew M. Riggsby

This chapter considers three problems in Roman (primarily Ciceronian) oratory and rhetoric surrounding the notion of 'character'. The first is the question of how forensic oratory was constrained by external notions of character; this is inextricably tied to a debate of long standing whether antiquity understood a person's character to be 'fixed'. I argue that the evidence is best accounted for if we see oratorical practice as being informed by such a view. The second section shows that awareness of this view of character can also aid our understanding of the overall function of the Roman criminal courts; the differing roles of personality in those courts and our own do not indicate fundamentally different roles for the two institutions. Finally, and more tentatively, I suggest that oratorical practice, shaped by this view of character, in turn affected the reception of the Aristotelian theory of ethos.

i. The Rhetoric of Character

It is sometimes asserted that in antiquity an individual's 'character'[1] was assumed to be fixed or static throughout adult life.[2] This idea is taken as a given by a recent study of oratorical ethos. It is also used to ground

I would like to thank Chris Craig, Michael Gagarin, Gwyn Morgan, and the editors for useful comments on earlier versions of this chapter.

[1] This word does not translate any single Latin term. It corresponds variously to *ingenium, natura, animus,* and occasionally *voluntas.* See also n. 9 below.

[2] Recently and sustainedly J. M. May, *Trials of Character: The Eloquence of Ciceronian Ethos* (Chapel Hill, NC, 1988) 6, 16, 22, 75, 163; further examples are collected by A. Hands, 'Postremo suo tantum ingenio utebatur', *CQ* 24 (1974) 312–17, 312 nn. 1–4, 315 n. 1; C. J. Gill, 'The Question of Character Development: Plutarch and Tacitus', *CQ* 33 (1983) 469–87, 469 nn. 2–3, 475 n. 43, 484 n. 94; and A. J. Woodman, 'Tacitus' Obituary of Tiberius', *CQ* 39 (1989) 197–205, n. 5.

interpretation of various figures depicted in ancient historians and bio-graphers. A set of studies by Hands, Gill, and Woodman (see n. 2) has questioned the assumption of a fixed character from several different angles.[3] While this work has made some important points, it goes too far in asserting that ancient writers 'knew' that character is not fixed.[4] For the most part we will be interested in folk models of character, that is the implicit models or metaphors, through which individuals understand the conduct of daily life. Unlike philosophical or scientific models, these folk theories are not articulated in any single text, but can be reconstructed from the scattered evidence. So, for instance, someone who says 'he's just like that' evinces a belief in character (though quite possibly a limited or qualified one), even if he does not articulate it.

One promising source of evidence on this issue, already touched on by Hands (*CQ* 24 (1974) 313), is ancient rhetorical theory. While casting light on the general psychological issues, rhetoric is of course particularly relevant to the study of actual oratory. These two types of evidence present differing methodological problems. Oratory occasionally provides clear statements of the fixity of character, like *Pro Sulla* 79:

Valeat ad poenam et ad salutem vita plurimum, quam solam videtis per se ex sua natura facillime perspici, subito flecti fingique non posse.[5]

---

[3] While once, and perhaps still, orthodoxy, the static view has never been held universally; cf. W. Allen (ed.), *Tacitus: The Annals, Books I–VI* (Boston, 1890) xiv–xix; K. Nipperdey (ed.), *P. Cornelius Tacitus* (Berlin, 1915) 446; and R. Häussler, *Tacitus und das historische Bewußtsein* (Heidelberg, 1965) 268, 324.

[4] By sketching out a model of what 'character' is and how it affects behaviour, I want to sep-arate the various questions that have heretofore been mutually entangled. Let us define 'charac-ter' as a set of dispositions to perform certain stereotypical actions. Character is thus distinct from, say, reason in that the latter is a more general faculty. It does not lead one to specific kinds of action, but rather determines a method for deciding on courses of action. Character is also analytically distinct from (though potentially related to) emotions, which are primarily internal states, not directly connected to courses of action. Nothing in this model requires that character (even if it exists) be inherited; belief in inherited behavioural characteristics logically implies belief in character (whether or not fixed), but the reverse does not necessarily hold true. It is also logi-cally possible that character could be flexible only at certain periods of one's life–say youth or old age. Gill, 'The Question of Character Development', anticipated to some extent by R. M. Ogilvie, *A Commentary on Livy, Books 1–5* (Oxford, 1965) 463, has shown that for many Romans a person's education and upbringing could, in principle and within limits, affect his adult character. But even this flexibility seems to have been limited and not always to have been taken seriously. It must be emphasized that what follows is meant as a particular psychological model or at most a set of models. I do not claim that its constructs and distinctions are necessarily useful or even valid for all psychologies.

[5] And compare largely identical formulations at *Inv.* 2.36 and *Sul.* 69, neither with a qualifier like *subito*; a similar idea in somewhat different form at *Clu.* 70; *Flac.* 100: 'annui temporis criminationem omnis aetas L. Flacci et perpetua vita defendet.' This last should probably be taken as another example of this argument, rather than an appeal to the value of Flaccus' good service to the state over time as outweighing any particular crimes of one year (thus May, *Trials of Character*, 100). Cicero does go on to make the latter argument, but the sentence quoted comes at the end of

A man's life should be especially relevant to his conviction or acquittal. You all see that this alone because of its nature can be spotted easily and cannot be quickly turned or refashioned.

However, it is quite possible that such assertions could be tendentious and *ad hoc*. Clearly, a speech constitutes poor evidence for its author's beliefs; it may, as we shall see, be better evidence for those of his audience. (And in this particular passage, one would have to guess how important *subito* is to Cicero's argument; elsewhere in similar contexts he does not add the qualifier.) In any case, the logic of his sustained practice will be more important than occasional explicit pronouncements. Rhetorical theory is less subject to such occasional bias, but it is at an additional remove from the broader public opinion we hope to understand. Two considerations may reduce concern over these methodological problems. One is that having complementary types of evidence can help. Rhetoric and oratory are far from independent of each other, but together they do show that this view of character is not a simple genre feature.[6] Thus the methods recommended do seem acceptable to a mass audience. Concrete examples follow below. As for oratory itself, we should remember that jurors were not *tabulae rasae*. A strategy, no matter how flattering a light it might cast on one's client, is of no value if it conflicts too strongly with the jurors' preconceptions about the case or about the world in general (cf. *De Or.* 2.186–7, *Clu.* 17). Discussions of human nature are precisely the kind of area in which one would expect an advocate to have the least freedom to operate. Of necessity we are all, as Giddens points out,[7] amateur social scientists. In particular, one could not function in daily life without a view, articulate or not, of character or its absence. The possibility of multiple or even conflicting views will be considered below.

To begin our examination of ancient texts, then, let us turn to the discussion of arguments from character at *De Inventione* 2.32–7. (As so often there is a passage of the *Rhetorica ad Herennium* (2.5) which is essentially the same in content, arrangement, and even wording. For one valuable discrepancy, see below.) Immediately after a section on arguments from motive, Cicero stresses the importance of having both types of argument

a lengthy discussion of the value of various types of evidence. The following sentence (beginning with *Et*) then introduces the new topic. Thus while this version of the evidentiary argument makes for a smooth transition to the balance of interest argument, it is likely to be taken in the epistemological sense when read in the order of delivery.

[6] One reader worried that there might be some circularity at this point, that oratory is used to prove a theory of character which is then used to explain the same oratory. My view of the argument is that the working hypothesis (Roman belief in fixity of character) is deduced from neither oratory nor rhetoric, but accounts for the practice of both.

[7] A. Giddens, *The Constitution of Society* (Berkeley, Calif., 1984) 27.

(motive and character) available in all cases:[8]

Nam causa facti parum firmitudinis habet, nisi animus eius qui insimulatur in eam suspicionem adducitur uti a tali culpa non videatur abhorruisse. Ut enim animum alicuius improbare nihil attinet, cum causa quare peccaret non intercessit, sic causam peccati intercedere leve est si animus nulli minus honestae rationi affinis ostenditur. (*Inv.* 2.32)

For a motive is hardly powerful enough unless the mind of the accused is placed under suspicion that it would not have recoiled from such a misdeed. Just as it does no good to attack someone's character when there is no motive, so it is pointless to introduce a motive if his character is not shown to be susceptible to wrongdoing.

Cicero then offers to both prosecution and defence ranked lists of arguments from character, beginning with the strongest. The orator is to apply, in each particular case, the best argument which the facts (as generally accepted) will allow. The arguments for the prosecution are as follows:

Prosecution Arguments
   P1: Defendant was convicted of same crime previously (*Inv.* 2.32).
   P2: Defendant suspected of same crime previously (§ 32).
   P3: Defendant convicted or suspected of a similar crime under similar circumstances (§ 32).
   P4: Defendant convicted of other crimes (§ 33).
   P5: Defendant has concealed his true character; some crime must be the first (§ 33).
   P6: In the absence of information you may omit this argument, but explain why you have done so (§ 34).

Those for the defence are these:

Defence Arguments (it is not clear that a relative ranking of D2–4 is to be understood)
   D1: Defendant has lived a pure and good life (*Inv.* 2.35–6; there are many elaborations on this basic argument).
   D2: Defendant has been slandered (§ 37).
   D3: Defendant's past actions were due to *imprudentia, necessitudo, persuasio,* or *adulescentia* (§ 37).
   D4: Defendant's character flaws are not conducive to the crime in question (§ 37).
   D5: 'Negare oportebit de vita eius et de moribus quaeri, sed de eo crimine quo de arguatur' (§ 37; on the interpretation of this, see below).

---

[8] Cicero's other mentions of *inventio* are highly abbreviated; they recommend the argument from character in similar, but slightly less emphatic terms (*Part. Or.* 34–5, *De Or.* 2.182; *Or.* 45–6).

To analyse these data we need to distinguish two potentially independent issues within the general idea of fixity of character. First, we may ask about the extent to which one's character may change over time. The explicit claim of *Sul.* 79 (quoted above) would allow for slow change; *Sul.* 69 and *Inv.* 2.36 apparently none at all. Then we may ask how close is the link between 'character' and action.[9] That is, is character an absolute determinant of action or is it just a general propensity? The explicit requirement of *Inv.* 2.32 for arguments from character assumes both high fixity and a close link. Such a close link allows the inference of character from the *ante acta vita*; the combination allows the inference from this character back to other, similar, actions at different times:

Actions (general) → Character → Actions (specific)

Let me give one example of the entire derivation in practice:

Ipsum illum Autronium, quoniam eius nomen finitimum maxime est huius periculo et crimini, non sua vita ac natura convicit? Semper audax, petulans, libidinosus; quem in stuprorum defensionibus non solum verbis uti improbissimis solitum esse scimus verum etiam pugnis et calcibus, quem exturbare homines ex possessionibus, caedem facere vicinorum, spoliare fana sociorum, comitatu et armis disturbare iudicia, in bonis rebus omnis contemnere, in malis pugnare contra bonos, non rei publicae cedere, non fortunae ipsi succumbere. Huius si causa non manifestissimis rebus teneretur, tamen eum mores ipsius ac vita convinceret. (*Sul.* 71)

Wasn't Autronius convicted by his own life and character, a man whose name is intimately connected with the accusation against my client? He was always bold, petulant, and a creature of his desires. We know that in defence of his sex crimes he was accustomed to use not only words but also his fists and feet. He cast men from their possessions, slaughtered his neighbours, despoiled allied shrines, broke up trials with an armed gang, held all men in contempt in good times, fought against the good in bad times, did not defer to the Republic, did not give in to fortune itself. If he had not been caught red-handed, his life and habits would still have convicted him.

Autronius was given over to antisocial behaviour (*exturbare, caedem facere, spoliare*, etc.), therefore he was of vicious character (*semper audax, petulans, libidinosus*), and so was clearly a member of the Catilinarian conspiracy. (Let me also note another point about this particular passage. A belief that character predicts action tends to increase the burden of proof for the prosecution, who must prove multiple crimes, not one. One might suspect then, that the Ciceronian corpus, composed almost entirely of defences, would show a bias in favour of this view of character. Aside from his use in character inference in the *Verrines*, note how Cicero creates that problem for

[9] This distinction corresponds to that between *ingenium* (or *natura*) on the one hand, and *mores* (or *vita*) on the other. See H. Hoffmann, 'Morum tempora diversa', *Gymnasium* 75 (1968), 220–50.

himself in *Pro Sulla*. Autronius is certainly an easy target, but that Cicero would raise the issue still suggests that the 'problem', such as it was, was unavoidable.[10])

We should note that linkage is strong, but not absolute: actions may be compelled by necessity, they may be calculated to conceal character, or they may have been chosen out of foolishness or persuasion (D3). Presumably the problem in the latter two cases is that the subject may mean well (or ill), but not know how to achieve it. Nonetheless, the underlying assumption seems to be that the character-action link is strong.[11]

We can also find support for the idea of fixity of character over most of one's lifespan. The only argument which presupposes a change is the youth defence (D3), but we have already noted this exception; if anything is fixed, it is adult character. What is important, however, is the lack of any other argument which depends on changeability of character. Hands (*CQ* 24 (1974) 313) has claimed that this passage argues against a concept of fixed character because it provides arguments both for those with favourable past lives and for those with unfavourable ones. But we must look at the arguments in more detail. When the 'facts' are against you, the one response not allowed is 'So what?' One may argue that the so-called facts are actually slander, that linkage is not absolute (above), or that a more (or less) precise division of 'character' is called for (i.e. that your client has character flaws (e.g. *ira*), but not ones conducive to the crime at hand (e.g. *furtum*)). But one does not have the option of saying that one's client has changed. There is no rhetoric of redemption. That would have been a far simpler and so presumably better claim, had orators and rhetoricians actually had a free hand in this matter. Their avoidance of the obvious suggests that they did not.

To confirm this we need to look carefully at option D5: deny that there is a question *de vita et de moribus*. This makes no claims and requires no presuppositions about character. The apparent denial of the relevance of character could, however, be motivated by an alternative view that it was not predictive. I would suggest that Cicero's phrasing does not articulate an argument about the logical relevance of character, but the legal relevance of past action. Cicero asks the advocate to exploit an ambiguity in the expression *quaerere (de)*; it means (among other things) both 'ask about something'

---

[10] But why, if belief in predictive character is widespread, does Cicero argue for it at all here? I read this passage as an instance of *amplificatio* in the form of an expansive treatment of a strong point in the argument. Cf. the powerful (but probably irrelevant) arguments for the principle of self-defence in *Mil.* 7–11.

[11] F. S. Halliwell, 'The Tradition of Greek Conceptions of Character', in C. Pelling (ed.), *Characterization and Individuality in Greek Literature* (Oxford, 1990) 52–4, makes a similar argument for what I call 'strong linkage' on the basis of Attic oratory.

and 'make something the subject of a judicial inquiry (*quaestio*)'.[12] Thus on one level the advocate can (more or less truthfully) claim the traditional last resort of the defence—the *status translativus* (*Inv.* 2.57–61)—the claim that the court of record does not have jurisdiction (over the past actions in this instance). At the same time the same words imply (much more tendentiously) that character is not relevant at all. This normally unpalatable implication is difficult for the audience to resist because of the high plausibility of the stricter reading. Note also that *crimen* more often refers to the accusation than the offence itself. This makes it more likely that *de eo crimine quo de arguatur* makes a procedural point. This interpretation is supported by the corresponding sentence in the *Rhetorica ad Herennium* (2.5), one of the few places in that passage which is phrased significantly differently from that in *De Inventione*:

Dicat non se de moribus eius apud censores, sed de criminibus adversariorum apud iudices dicere.

Let him say that he is not speaking before the censors about morals, but before jurors about the opposition's criminal accusations.

Here the translative force of the argument is made explicit.[13] The parallel structure of the two passages means that this should be able to stand as a gloss for Cicero's more ambiguous Latin. So the strategies suggested by *De Inventione* strongly presuppose that the audience will expect and respond to arguments about the defendant's past life. These arguments in turn presuppose that some component of the defendant, fixed over time, guides all his actions.

These conclusions on the fixity of character and the strength of the character–action link, based on rhetorical theory, can now be compared to Cicero's oratorical practice. Consider the strategies from the above list used in his surviving criminal court speeches:

Cicero's Ethical Strategies (for more detail, see Appendix)
  Pro Roscio: D1 (*passim*); Roscius is a dull but honest rustic; he has no history of past crimes.
  In Verrem: P2 (*Verr. I* 10–12); In his earlier offices Verres is 'known' to have robbed the public treasury and despoiled temples (though no previous convictions are known or alluded to).

---

[12] e.g. *Mur.* 67, *Cael.* 25, 70, *Mil.* 8, 14, 15, 31, *Rosc. Am.* 119; the *lex Cornelia de sicariis et veneficiis* quoted at *Clu.* 148; *OLD*, s.v. *quaero* 10a,b.

[13] Even if one does not accept this precise interpretation, one can still note the extreme disfavour with which the argument is treated. It is not offered as an option for the prosecution at all. The concealment/first time argument (P5) is applicable in even the worst case, and is apparently always superior to the argument that character is irrelevant (for instance, because it is changeable), if this is what *non quaeri* means. Cf. also n. 18 below for another, looser parallel in Quintilian.

Pro Fonteio: D1 (§§ 5, 37–40); Fonteius is of unimpeachable and well-attested character; he has no history of crime.

Pro Cluentio: D2 (§§ 19, 133, 167, 196–8); Cluentius' well-attested good character is besmirched only by misinterpretation and by long-standing false rumour (*invidia*).

Pro C. Rabirio: D2 (§§ 7–9); the prosecution's attacks on Rabirius' character are *ad hoc* fictions.

Pro Murena: D2 (§§ 11–14); the prosecution's attacks on Murena's character are *ad hoc* fictions.

Pro Sulla: D2 (§§ 1, 69, 72–5, 78–80); the only possible mark on Sulla's good character is his *ambitus* conviction which was unjustified.

Pro Flacco: D1 (frag. Med.; §§ 6–8); Flaccus' good character is uncontested; he has no history of bad actions.

Pro Sestio: D1 (§§ 7–13 and *passim*); Sestius is a noble and patriotic figure; not only is his past free of blemishes, it provides positive evidence of good character.

Pro Caelio: D3 (§§ 42, 48 and *passim*); Caelius may have committed certain youthful indiscretions, but he is and will continue to be generally a useful citizen.

Pro Plancio: D2 (§§ 27–31, 33–5, 61); Plancius' alleged crimes are not real (nor would they be crimes if they were).

Pro Rabirio Postumo: D3 (§§ 1–2, 22–9); Rabirius is a good man who has done some foolish things.

Pro Milone: D1 (§ 61 and *passim*); Milo is of upright character, as is shown especially by his struggles against Clodius.

Before we consider the import of these facts, a few words about the rigidity of the scheme will be in order. Any formal typology, even (especially?) one derived from ancient rhetorical theory, is likely to oversimplify Ciceronian oratorical practice. While the schema used here accurately reflects the range of arguments Cicero uses, it gives an incorrect impression that rigid distinctions can be drawn between the various strategies within that range. I note here three rhetorical moves which frequently make it hard to distinguish individual strategies (for peculiarities of individual speeches see Appendix). First, we must take account of Alexander's contention that the Roman relative of the idea of 'double jeopardy' insulated a defendant from a second prosecution on a given charge for *any* violation of that law which had taken place before the first prosecution.[14] Thus a responsible prosecutor would bring up all conceivable violations of the given law during the trial. For this reason, many old charges, which

---

[14] M. C. Alexander, 'Repetition of Prosecution, and the Scope of Prosecutions, in the Standing Criminal Courts of the Late Republic', *CA* 1 (1982) 141–66.

seem like extraneous ethical attacks to us, may have been in some sense 'real' charges. For instance, the bulk of *Pro Cluentio* deals with the events surrounding the bribery-filled *iudicium Iunianum* rather than the charges of poisoning clearly justiciable under the *lex Cornelia de sicariis et veneficiis*. While there were probably good legal arguments to suggest Cluentius would not be liable for these events (at least not under the homicide law), the very fact that it was a debatable issue would demand the prosecution's (and so the defence's) attention. Thus we may question the sincerity of Cicero's repeated claims (§§ 1, 3, 5, 7, etc.) that this line of attack was based on mere *invidia*, i.e. an attempt to prove something about Cluentius' character, rather than a particular crime within the jurisdiction of the court. Though most obvious in *Pro Cluentio*, this difficulty in distinguishing character attacks from 'real' charges is general. The difficulty is aggravated by the second move: where Cicero from time to time refutes or rejects prosecution accounts of his client's character (D2), then announces that there are in fact no reasons to suspect that character (D1; e.g. *Mur.* 14). Thus a claim that there were no prosecution attacks on his client's character (e.g. *Font.* 40), does not prove that apparent criticism of the defendant's *ante acta vita* elsewhere in the speech is, in fact, directed against violations of the relevant statute. The third move is somewhat less common. *Inv.* 2.35 suggests that a defendant's previous services to the state may be offered as positive proof of good character (D1). Yet there are places (e.g. *Flac.* 98–9) where service to the state (actual or prospective) is fairly clearly offered to *counter-balance* guilt, not to disprove it, and there are also places (e.g. *Mil.* 72–103) where the purported service and the purported crime are the same act. In such cases the assertion of public service would itself be a defence under the *status qualitatis* (*Inv.* 2.62–71). On balance the defendant's behaviour has been praiseworthy, and so he should be spared. In some cases the force of such praise is (probably intentionally) unclear. We might note here that in making the latter two moves, Cicero is cheating 'up' the scale. That is, he tries to appropriate the force of the best (D1) argument where it is not strictly appropriate to the facts even as he himself presents them.

Whatever the details of the typology, however, Cicero always makes a character argument based on past actions, like those recommended in *De Inventione*. This argument may not be central to the speech or even extensive, but it is always present, which confirms that there was a strong expectation of this kind of argument. Such an expectation would be strange unless the defendant is assumed to have a character that is stable over time (thus making selectively chosen past actions relevant) and strongly enough determinant of action that sound inferences can be drawn in both directions. (For discussion of another possibility, see § II below.) As in rhetorical theory, the only case where even potential change of character is admitted is that of *adulescentia (pro Caelio)*. And only once is a break in linkage (concerning *stultitia*) invoked (*Pro Rabirio Postumo*).[15] It is important to note that this analysis does not require us to evaluate the truth of Cicero's particular assertions (e.g. the good character of his individual clients). All we need observe is that he evidently felt compelled to adopt such a strategy of praise. And there is a further parallel between theory and practice. The ranked options of *Inv.* 2.32–7 show a preference for a simple notion of character (good or bad) to a more complicated one (involving a number of distinct, potentially independent appetites). The speeches show this preference even more strongly, and the devices discussed in the previous paragraph to enhance arguments from past life reinforce that preference. In fact, Cicero never offers the defence that his client has existing but irrelevant character flaws. This is particularly striking in the defence of P. Sulla. During his trial for *vis* in 62 BC, his actual earlier conviction on a charge of *ambitus* in 65 is represented as malicious slander rather than as irrelevant to an accusation of violence: 'cum communi ambitionis invidia tum singulari Autroni odio' (*Sul.* 1).[16]

After Cicero there is an unfortunate lacuna in our Latin sources for rhetorical theory, but at the end of that gap is the extensive treatise of Quintilian.[17] Quintilian's approach to character is similar, but not identical to Cicero's. At 5.10.23–31 he describes arguments *a persona*; listed are a variety of categories (e.g. age, nationality, sex, *animi natura*) which can be used to predict actions. Finally he suggests:

Spectantur ante acta dictaque; ex praeteritis enim aestimari solent praesentia (5.10.28).

Previous words and deeds are scrutinized, for the present is customarily judged on the basis of the past.

Quintilian assumes the more complicated, multi-parameter version of character here (*animi natura*, § 27), and shows more concern for its various sources (again: age, nationality, etc.). However, the underlying assumptions about character fixity remain largely the same, and their predictive value is made explicit. Quintilian then returns to the topic in his discussion of issues of fact (*coniectura*), and particularly those based on past time (7.2.27–35). Here he presents most of the same advice as is found in *De Inventione*. The accuser must show faults in the defendant, preferably ones that bear a direct relation to the accusation (§ 28). He

---

[15] Arguably, the defence of Caelius does this as well. Youth is both the quasi-exogenous cause of Caelius' misbehaviour and a transient condition. [16] See also Appendix.

[17] We have, of course, rhetorical raw material (the *exempla* of Valerius Maximus) and finished product (the declamations of the elder Seneca), but no theoretical handbooks.

even repeats the argument that 'there must be a first time' (§ 33). The defence must deny or diminish these attacks. If this is impossible, then the defendant's faults should be shown to be the 'wrong' ones, such as prodigality in a case of theft (§ 29). If this fails, the last line of defence is *non de hoc quaeri* (§ 30), the same argument as in *De Inventione*.[18] Quintilian does at least conceive of the possibility that a defendant's past life will be so spotless that the prosecution will not even bring it up. This may represent a change in popular attitudes over time or Quintilian's own pragmatic resistance to absolute rules. In any case the justification of such an omission is that supposedly it allows the jurors to believe that you have a valid argument, and have simply chosen not to use it in the face of an over-abundance of direct evidence (§ 34). What is fatal is to reveal that you do not really have a character argument. Under Quintilian's scheme it is not absolutely necessary to win the character argument, but it is crucial not to lose it. His precepts, like Cicero's, presuppose an audience expectation of discussion of the defendant's past life, which in turn presupposes a 'character' which is fixed over time and largely determines its possessor's actions.

The claim has been made, as recently by Berry, that this view of character was just a rhetorical trick, invoked only when useful.[19] An orator certainly could and would take up any position of advantage, but nothing would be gained by contradicting an audience's beliefs. Anything could be said about a matter on which the audience was indifferent or ignorant—e.g. Cicero's reception on his return from Sicily (*Planc.* 64–5) or the goings-on in Chrysogonus' house (*Rosc. Am.* 133–4). I would suggest again that a person without views on character would not be able to function. One might imagine, however, an audience that had multiple and potentially contradictory views available. Someone today might, on different occasions, hold both that 'people don't change' and that 'you can never really know anyone'. If Roman audiences were similarly broad-minded, orators would presumably have taken advantage of that. Yet, as we have seen, they do not appeal to change in character. Cicero's clients have never 'reformed'. Arguments from silence are never certain, but we have quite a number of Ciceronian speeches. Moreover, practical oratory insists even more on fixity of character than theoretical rhetoric. Character argument is constrained from the outside, most plausibly by public belief.

---

[18] This provides an additional argument for the reading of *Inv.* 2.37 proposed above. If the orator is in fact being urged to claim that past actions have no predictive value and so are irrelevant, it is odd that Cicero and Quintilian would use the *same* oblique periphrasis to express the same idea.

[19] D. H. Berry, *Cicero Pro P. Sulla Oratio*, Cambridge Classical Texts and Commentaries 30 (Cambridge, 1996) 275.

ii. Character and the Courts

So far we have used the study of rhetoric and oratory to illuminate Roman psychological views. This section will attempt to read in the reverse direction–to show how an account of psychological presuppositions should affect our understanding both of oratorical practice and of rhetorical theory. In particular, it will be suggested that we must reconsider the status of the distinction between argument about the charge and argument about character. This modern distinction has been wrongly imposed on the Romans, but the anachronism sometimes has been concealed by reference to Aristotelian theory that, as we will see, is not applicable at Rome.

It has long been observed that Roman courts allowed and seem even to have demanded discussion of matters that would be excluded as irrelevant and/or prejudicial in an Anglo-American court. High on the list are the character, reputation, and past life of the defendant. A century ago this could be adduced as proof of the corruption or primitiveness of the Roman courts.

Prof. Ramsey well remarks, 'the moral feeling which prevailed in a Roman court of justice was entirely at variance with the principles which rule our own . . . ' There was no professionally trained judge to sift the evidence in a summing-up. The praetors were changed from year to year, and merely acted as chairmen of the Courts. With such presidents, no wonder that irrelevant considerations often were the most powerful in determining a verdict.[20]

Today more neutral, culturalist explanations of the difference are likely to be preferred. So, perhaps, the Roman public courts are to be seen as deciding general fitness for membership in the community, in the fashion of Athenian ostracism.[21] In principle such cultural explanations are in some respects attractive.[22] Too close an identification of superficially similar institutions can certainly be misleading. For instance, Robinson warns against a casual equation of the Urban Praetor with an English Lord Chancellor;[23] Nippel points out the dangers of seeing in the *tresviri capitales* a primitive police force.[24] Yet we must ask carefully and in individual cases just which institutions are different and in what respects. I have argued elsewhere that much of Cicero's supposedly irrelevant material can be seen as thematically tied to the various charges, so long as the offences are

---

[20] W. Heitland, *M. T. Ciceronis Oratio Pro Murena* (London, 1876) 116, 117.

[21] For examples of such views, see A. Riggsby, 'Did the Romans Believe in their Verdicts?', *Rhetorica* 15.3 (1997) 235–52.

[22] They do not, however, square well with Roman descriptions and prescriptions for how their courts work; see Riggsby, 'Did the Romans Believe in their Verdicts?'

[23] O. Robinson, *The Sources of Roman Law* (London, 1997) 79.

[24] W. Nippel, *Public Order in Ancient Rome* (Cambridge, 1995) 22–6.

properly understood.[25] For instance, Plancius' personal ties to Cicero obviously do not disprove bribery or collusion in modern terms, but they can be made relevant to a charge of *ambitus*. Cicero's treatment of Caelius as a youth would be merely a bid for sympathy in an assault trial, but has real significance against a charge of *vis*. Offences differ between systems, but that does not mean the courts necessarily do. Here I want to make a slightly different point. Accounts of a person's character (most commonly but not necessarily that of the defendant) clearly count as evidence of guilt or innocence in a Roman court. While Anglo-American courts discourage that kind of evidence, it is largely for much narrower reasons than is sometimes suggested and those reasons lie largely outside the cultural categories of 'court' and 'iudicium'.

I begin, with apologies for a small paradox that will be resolved quickly, by noting an argument from a political, not a forensic speech. Cicero's *Pro Lege Manilia* explicitly makes the kind of inferences I have been discussing. Past actions are manifestations of a fixed and determining character from which one can then predict other actions of the same person. (There is also an argument about reputation here, which may be ignored for present purposes.) Cicero does not work through the whole chain at once, but the individual parts are quite clear. He notes that the Romans need a general who will do certain things, and in particular one who will not use his command as an opportunity to enrich himself at the expense of Roman subjects and allies (§ 66). That is, he says more summarily earlier, the Romans need a general who is characterized by *temperantia* (§ 64). But Cicero had already 'proved' that Pompey possessed the required *temperantia* (as well as other virtues). His past actions in similar circumstances had proved that this was part of his character (§ 40). Consider his *temperantia* in other matters. Where do you think he got his famous and incredible swiftness? It wasn't the outstanding strength of his rowers or secret techniques of his pilots or some new winds that brought him so swiftly into the furthest lands, but the things which usually delay others have not slowed him. Greed did not call him from his fixed course to some loot, not lust to pleasure, nor pleasant scenes to their enjoyment, nor some noble city to sightseeing, nor even the labour itself to rest. Finally, he decided he must not even stop to see the statues and paintings and other works of art in Greek cities which the others feel are there for the taking. This is a virtual textbook example of the argument from past life. Suppose one were to hear such claims being made by or on behalf of a would-be president or prime minister. This argument, or at least its logic, would be remarkable only for its banality. The premises or the sufficiency of virtue without technical skill

[25] A. Riggsby, *Crime and Community in Ciceronian Rome* (Austin, Tex., 1999).

might be suspect, but the character point remains instantly comprehensible. On the surface this might be taken to argue for one of the interpretations of the Roman courts that I am trying to contest here. If Roman forensic and deliberative oratory use the same kinds of reasoning, does that not constitute one more piece of evidence that Roman criminal trials were simply politics 'by other means' or, less ambitiously, that it at least shows that the Roman courts are somehow a different context from modern ones? Again, however, we must ask whether the differences should be explained at the highest level of abstraction (court vs. non-court).

In fact, I suggest, the distinction lies elsewhere. We may begin by noting that the fact-versus-character distinction is not airtight in modern courts. For instance, the general rule in my own jurisdiction, the state of Texas, is:

Character evidence generally. Evidence of a person's character or a trait of his character is not admissible for the purpose of proving that he acted in conformity therewith on a particular occasion, except . . . (Rule of Criminal Evidence 404a).

The exceptions are several. First, note that the general rule excludes this evidence for the purpose of making the kinds of inferences we have been discussing, but not for all purposes.[26] Second, the explicit exceptions include 'evidence of a pertinent trait of his character offered by an accused, or by the prosecution to rebut the same' or 'evidence of the character of a witness' (RCrE 404a1, 3). Moreover, specific past acts may not be introduced for purposes of inferring 'act[ing] in conformity', but *may be used* to show many other things, including 'proof of motive, opportunity, intent, preparation, plan, knowledge, identity, or absence of mistake or accident' (RCrE 404b). Finally, 'Evidence of the habit of a person . . . is relevant to prove that the conduct of the person . . . on a particular occasion was in conformity with the habit' (RCrE 406). Character evidence, then, is not to be used to make inferences as to the central question of whether the defendant committed the crime or not, but it may be used to judge subordinate issues. And in fact it may be used to decide that central question if the defence raises the issue first. Character evidence is not simply considered irrelevant. If this were so, it would not be admitted in so many circumstances. Instead, this pattern develops out of the high and biased standard of proof of the criminal courts. Conviction requires proof 'beyond a reasonable doubt'. Character evidence is simply not reliable enough (in the eyes of contemporary law) to be the basis for that judgement. Telling here is the defence's option to introduce the character issue. Character argument is allowed to raise doubts (though it may fail to do so), but not to settle them.

---

[26] Evidence offered simply as character assassination, not bearing on these or similar issues, would be excluded on general grounds of irrelevance (RCrE 402).

The Roman situation differs in at least three striking respects. First, as I argued in the first section, there appears to have been widespread belief in the predictive power of character as revealed in past actions. The more fixed and determinative of action character is, the greater its value as evidence. Second, the abstract standards of proof of the Roman courts were very different from ours. While there is some dispute in the secondary literature over the details, it is clear that the notion of 'burden of proof' was weakly if at all developed. And even if the notion was developed, it seems to have been a matter of civil, not criminal law. Roman defendants were not protected by a high standard of proof. Thus if character arguments were construed as being even fairly accurate, they would have been an attractive source of proof. The similarity to the *comitia* (or to a modern election) is in willingness to accept merely probable conclusions.

Third, psychological inference under the model we have been discussing is considerably simpler than under modern, scientific theories. Roman courts, we noted, not only allowed character inference, but seem to have demanded it. There are narrow circumstances where our system does the same: the invocation of expert psychological testimony to issues of unusual mental states (such as the kind of insanity needed to avoid criminal liability). These experts draw their information about the defendant not from any experience of the crime, but from interviews and case histories—a general evaluation of the defendant's tendencies (character) on the basis of his general life, which in turn is used to infer the likelihood of specific action in a specific case. The need for specialist testimony is natural in light of contemporary psychological assumptions. Personality is complex and relatively unpredictable, and so is not in general susceptible to sure enough reasoning for judicial purposes. In the limited cases in which it is required, only specially trained and certified experts can provide it. Romans' different psychological assumptions produce a different situation in the courtroom. If character varies little, the need for expert knowledge decreases. Moreover, character is defined in fairly simple terms—good and bad or perhaps susceptibility to certain basic emotions—and so no experts are required. Jurors can be confident of their own ability to make psychological judgements.

It might be argued, however, that character fixity—even if it were a genuine and widespread belief—is not really the crux of the matter. Perhaps it is just the demonstrably greater interest at Anglo-American courts in the 'fair' use of evidence. There is certainly some truth to this, but we need to unpack what the unfairness of character argument might consist of. Unreliability is certainly an issue, but perhaps not the most important one. It is also the case that character cannot be tied to specific cases. No criminal checks to see whether there is someone more black-hearted nearby who would be more inclined to a planned offence than himself. Yet the same could be said of arguments about motive, which are admissible (RCrE 404b). It should also be noted that the rules on the (in)admissibility of character evidence do not invoke a balancing test (appropriate if prejudice were at issue), but a situational one. Even shocking character evidence is admissible as long as its purpose is acceptable.[27]

iii. Character and the Theory of Ethos

Finally, I want to look at a potentially deeper connection between oratory and rhetoric. I will suggest that the practical importance of inference-from-character has a bearing on a long-standing issue in rhetorical theory– the reception of the Aristotelian notion of ethos. Aristotle's *Rhetoric* (1355^{b}35–1356^{a}4) claims that the orator has at his disposal a variety of *pisteis*, 'reasons for belief'. These are categorized as either 'non-technical' (roughly 'types of evidence') or 'technical' (roughly 'types of persuasion'). The latter type is further subdivided into three forms: logos, ethos, and pathos.[28] These refer respectively to logical argument (inductive and deductive), display of the speaker's (who is normally the litigant as well) character, and creating emotional responses in the audience. Roman rhetoric preserves a considerable portion of this Aristotelian framework, if only indirectly. For instance, Quintilian recalls the Aristotelian categories of technical and non-technical reasons for belief. The latter is given many of its standard subdivisions: torture, oaths, document, etc. Yet the subdivisions of technical persuasion are substantially reshaped. First of all, as in most post-Aristotelian rhetorics, the roles of ethos and pathos are greatly reduced relative to that of logos.[29] G. Kennedy has said of the original three-way distinction 'Cicero appreciated it, but did not succeed in re-establishing it. Quintilian thinks that knowledge of the case, conveyed by rational argument, is the fundamental thing.'[30] Furthermore, the terms are sometimes redefined. 'Ethical' strategies are those that are designed to evoke mild emotions in the hearer, while 'pathetic' ones produce strong ones. In the course of redefinition, the distinction becomes confused, perhaps in Cicero,

---

[27] There is a balancing test for relevancy in general (RCrE 403), but rules dealing specifically with character operate on a different basis.

[28] I use these terms in a modern, technical sense as types of argument, for both Latin and Greek authors and regardless of whether they were originally meant as techical terms.

[29] In Quintilian, see *Inst.* 6.2.8–24; cf. F. Solmsen, 'Aristotle and Cicero on the Orator's Playing upon the Feelings', *CPh* 33 (1938) 394–6.   [30] G. A. Kennedy, *Quintilian* (New York, 1969), 68.

certainly in Quintilian.[31] Thus the original category of ethos is not merely reduced but eliminated, for the old version of pathos encompasses the new versions of pathos *and* ethos. This reduction of the role of ethos is particularly striking since 'character' is generally agreed to be more important in Roman oratory than in Athenian.

This problem should lead us to consider a little more carefully the details of the redefinition of ethos. Wisse (*Ethos and Pathos*, 240–1) has shown that Cicero offers a version in *De Oratore* (esp. 2.182–4) which is actually intermediate between the Aristotelian and Quintilianic versions. The division in this work corresponding to Aristotelian ethos is defined both by a source in character drawing and a (mild) emotional effect. This puts ethos in direct competition with pathos, which is defined solely in terms of its emotional effect. The hybrid definition of ethos may be connected to another development noted by Wisse. Aristotle's version is perhaps best seen as ' "rational" ethos'–that is, persuasion by making the speaker appear to be competent and trustworthy (32–4). This can be addressed adequately by the character-oriented definition. Cicero, like most later authors, is more interested in 'ethos "of sympathy" '. This is the establishment of an emotional bond between speaker and audience. This obviously necessitates inclusion of emotion in the definition of ethos. But this does not so much solve the problem as redescribe it. Why move to an ethos of sympathy? One reason could be connected to a famous difference in the context of Roman forensic oratory. The Roman, but not the Athenian, litigant was generally represented by an advocate. When advocate and party are separated, the notion of self-presentation that makes up Aristotle's ethos can reasonably be applied to either. Hence it slides over to a notion of character presentation. At the same time, the presentation of the advocate becomes less theoretically interesting as his influence (in the Roman context) depends more on external prestige. As Kennedy points out, advocacy makes for a wider range of emotional strategies than speaking for one's self.[32] Trustworthiness may be the point in one case, but in the next the advocate may offer a paternalistic defence of a problematic defendant or a legalistic defence of an admittedly shifty one. Such, for instance, are Cicero's defences of Caelius and Rabirius Postumus. To the extent that the custom of advocacy did eventually reshape the rhetorical tradition, it would have been to the detriment of Aristotelian ethos. Unfortunately for the current question, ethos seems to

---

[31] E. Fantham, 'Ciceronian *conciliare* and Aristotelian Ethos', *Phoenix* 27 (1973) 262–75; J. Wisse, *Ethos and Pathos from Aristotle to Cicero* (Amsterdam, 1989) 241. For a more positive interpretation of Ciceronian 'confusion' see L. Calboli Montefusco, 'Cicerone, De oratore: la doppia funzione dell'ethos dell'oratore', *Rhetorica* 10 (1992) 245–59.

[32] G. A. Kennedy, 'The Rhetoric of Advocacy in Greece and Rome', *AJP* 89 (1968) 419–36.

have taken on its diminished position well before the rhetorical tradition had managed to theorize advocacy at all well.[33]

While ethos was squeezed to some extent by pathos, let me suggest that there was pressure from the other direction as well. If for Cicero ethos was character-driven, then it would have been a close relative of the logical arguments from character that I have been discussing in this paper. This can be shown directly by the fact that the rhetorical passages cited above all appear in the context of inferential argument, along with such topics as motive, opportunity, time, and, consequence. To the extent that inference from character was particularly important to the Romans, it could have had the somewhat surprising result of reducing the importance of ethos in rhetorical theory. That is, character-presentation in general, which could plausibly have been considered under that rubric, was instead seen primarily as a species of logos. This may not, however, have been a particularly Roman phenomenon. Greek orators certainly make the same kinds of inference (cf. n. 13). Thus there may have been pressure from the very beginning on the Aristotelian notion of ethos. The practice of advocacy, which puts more characters in play in any given speech, may have increased this pressure even before a *theory* of advocacy was developed. This story or any of its kind is, of necessity, rather speculative. Nonetheless it coheres well with the facts of oratorical practice and rhetorical theory it aims to connect.

If I am right to suggest that fixity of character was a broadly held psychological theory rather than a disposable rhetorical prop, then we would expect it to have effects across boundaries of genre and across the internal divisions of formal rhetoric. I hope to have shown that there is good reason (at least within the limits set by the texts examined here) to accept that there are such effects and to retain belief in an appropriately tailored theory of the prominent role of 'character' in the theory and practice of Roman oratory.

Appendix: Ethical Strategies

In this appendix I give fuller information about the ethical strategies of Cicero's various criminal courts speeches as they relate to the question of character. I also give very selective references to the secondary literature, primarily to May, *Trials*

---

[33] Wisse, *Ethos and Pathos*, 89. He also (88, 94) notes pedagogical reasons for changes in the place of *inventio* in rhetoric which would have aided the promotion of logos against both of its competitors, but (as he points out) this change in *inventio* seems to presuppose the demotion of ethos and pathos.

of Character. While wide-ranging, May's book is primarily interested in the orator's own ethos. Thus I cite (in reduced form) only passages concerned specifically with the defendant.

Pro Roscio: D1 (*passim*); Roscius is a dull but honest rustic; he has no history of past crimes. Nearly the entire speech is devoted to showing that Roscius is this sort of rustic, while his opponents (Capito, Magnus, Chrysogonus, and Erucius) are greedy, daring city folk and thus more likely to have committed the crime themselves.[34]

In Verrem: P2 (*Verr. I* 10–12); In his earlier offices Verres is 'known' to have robbed the public treasury and despoiled temples (though no previous convictions are known or alluded to). Note that Cicero claims precedents throughout Verres' life not only for the particular offence for which he was on trial (*pecunia capta*), but of the subsidiary accusations such as cruelty and impiety. Thus the ethical attack is both synchronic and diachronic. That is, earlier actions prove the likelihood of later ones, and general immorality proves the likelihood of contemporary criminality. See May, *Trials of Character*, 38–40, 46.

Pro Fonteio: D1 (§§ 5, 37–40); Fonteius is of unimpeachable and well-attested character; he has no history of crime. Cicero adds the *amplificationes* that Fonteius has previously shown his honesty in an office which involved handling public funds and so could not have the *avaritia* necessary to justify a *repetundae* charge (§ 5) and that no charge has even been offered against his client's character (§ 40, cf. *Inv.* 2.36). If we take this last assertion literally, then the charges against him in the lacunose beginning of the speech (§§ 1–6) must be taken as potential instances of *repetundae*, not (as usually) as subsidiary character assassination (cf. above).

Pro Cluentio: D2 (§§ 19, 133, 167, 196–8); Cluentius' well-attested good character is besmirched only by misinterpretation and by long-standing false rumour (*invidia*). As discussed above (p. 173), it is hard to tell whether the long narrative of the *iudicium Iunianum* and its prequels and sequels (§§ 9–142) should be related to a charge under the *lex Cornelia de sicariis et veneficiis*; if not then most of the speech is devoted to proving Cluentius' good character by clearing him of past wrong-doing.[35]

Pro C. Rabirio: D2 (§§ 7–9); the prosecution's attacks on Rabirius' character are *ad hoc* fictions, calculated to eat up Cicero's short allotted time (§ 9). Here the praise of Rabirius' services to the state is fairly clearly part of the defence proper, not amplification of a general assertion of good character (cf. above).

Pro Murena: D2 (§§ 11–14); the prosecution's attacks on Murena's character are *ad hoc* fictions. After refuting aspersions on Murena's character, Cicero seems to claim the stronger (D1) position that his client's past is spotless: 'Nihil igitur in vitam L. Murenae dici potest . . . Nondum enim nostris laudibus . . . sed prope inimicorum confessione virum bonum atque integrum hominem defendimus' (§ 14). Also the

---

[34] See A. Vasaly, 'The Masks of Rhetoric: Cicero's *Pro Roscio Amerino*', *Rhetorica* 3 (1985), 1–20; *Representations: Images of the World in Ciceronian Oratory* (Berkeley, Los Angeles, and Oxford, 1993) 157–72; and May, *Trials of Character*, 22–31.

[35] For a full discussion of the depiction of Cluentius' ethos, see J. Kirby, *The Rhetoric of Cicero's* Pro Cluentio (Amsterdam, 1990) 31–8.

contentio dignitatis (§§ 15–53) common to *ambitus* trials inevitably addresses to some extent the character and past life of the defendant. See May, *Trials of Character*, 60–4, 68.

Pro Sulla: D2 (§§ 1, 69, 72–5, 78–80); the only possible mark on Sulla's good character is his *ambitus* conviction which was unjustified. Late in the speech (§ 73), Cicero hints at a fall-back to the argument (D4) that Sulla's proven character flaw (*ambitus*) amounted to overzealousness to save the state, a problem not conducive to revolution (*vis*). He does not, however, make this argument explicit. 'Quam [cupiditatem] si nemo alius habuit in consulatu petendo, cupidior iudicatus est hic fuisse quam ceteri; sin etiam in aliis non nullis fuit iste consulatus amor, fortuna in hoc fuit fortasse gravior quam in ceteris'. See May, *Trials of Character*, 74–6.

Pro Flacco: D1 (frag. Med.; §§ 6–8); Flaccus' good character is uncontested; he has no history of bad actions. As in the *pro Fonteio*, Cicero claims the defendant's general probity, then particularly notes his past honesty in dealing with public funds (§§ 6–7, cf. *Inv.* 2.35), and hence his lack of *avaritia*. He also notes his great services to the state (§§ 101–4, cf. *Inv.* 2.35), but it is not clear whether this represents the *amplificatio* suggested by *De Inventione*. The prosecution seems (fr. Med.) to have tried to use the *non quaeri* attack. See May, *Trials of Character*, 80–1, 84–5.

Pro Sestio: D1 (§§ 7–13 and *passim*); Sestius is a noble and patriotic figure; not only is his past free of blemishes, it provides positive evidence of good character. Cicero claims that Sestius' life and character will be the focus of the speech (§ 5): 'Sed quoniam singulis criminibus ceteri responderunt, dicam ego de omni statu P. Sesti, de genere vitae, de natura, de moribus, de incredibili amore in bonos, de studio conservandae salutis communis atque oti'. Given this announcement the body of the speech has (as is often noted) precious little to say about Sestius himself and a great deal about the political situation of the early 50s. Cicero does use Sestius' services to the state as (among other things) amplification of the D1 strategy of asserting good character (§§ 1–2, 144–5, cf. *Inv.* 2.35). See May, *Trials of Character*, 90–1, 99.

Pro Caelio: D3 (§§ 42, 48 and *passim*); Caelius may have committed certain youthful indiscretions, but he is and will continue to be generally a useful citizen. Most of this speech is devoted to delineating the various characters in terms similar to the stock characters of Roman comedy, including Caelius as the *adulescens* and Cicero as the indulgent father.[36]

Pro Plancio: D2 (§§ 27–31, 33–5, 61); Plancius' alleged crimes are not real (nor would they be crimes if they were). As in the *Pro Murena*, the *contentio dignitatis* (§§ 17–18, 51, 58–60) incidentally touches on similar issues. See May, *Trials of Character*, 117, 119–20, 122.

Pro Rabiro Postumo: D3 (§§ 1–2, 22–9); Rabirius is a good man who has done some foolish things. Rabirius' particular foolishness is said to have consisted mainly in making himself subject to the whims of a foreign king, thus the defence of *stultitia* is combined with that of *necessitudo* (*Inv.* 2.37). For example, of Rabirius' taking up the post of dioecetes and concomitant eastern clothing in order to

---

[36] See K. Geffcken, *Comedy in the Pro Caelio*, Mnemosyne Suppl. 30 (Leiden, 1973), and May, *Trials of Character*, 106, 108–9, 115–16.

recover his investment Cicero says: 'Odiosum negotium Postumo videbatur, sed erat nulla omnino recusatio' (§ 28).

Pro Milone: D1 (§ 61 and *passim*); Milo is of upright character, as is shown especially by his struggles against Clodius. Cicero spends a lot of time discussing Milo's political correctness, but only in § 61 does he put it in a more general context of virtue. The discussion of Milo's character in this speech is very diffuse and nearly always interwoven with his interaction with Clodius. For those who believe that the extant *pro Milone* was composed by the addition of material to the original with little other editing,[37] this section is in part of the speech likely to have been in the original. Service to the state is invoked (§§ 6, 30, 72–103; cf. *Inv.* 2.35), but the point of the argument is unclear; the first reference seems to be in support of a claim of good character, but the others constitute defence on the specific charge (cf. above). See May, *Trials of Character* 129–40, especially 137–9.

Pro Scauro: D1? (frr. b, f); Cicero seems to have claimed the virtue of Scaurus (and of his entire family). The speech is highly fragmentary and it is hard to tell exactly what Cicero's ethical strategy was. There are several fragments (c, d, e Clark) which appear to refer to 'unjust' prosecutions of Scaurus' father (Asc. 20.24–5C). These may be comparanda for the present trial or for earlier trials which the prosecutions had used to blacken Scaurus' character via his ancestry.

---

[37] e.g. A. M. Stone, 'Pro Milone: Cicero's Second Thoughts', *Antichthon* 14 (1980) 88–111.

7

Audience Expectations, Invective, and Proof

CHRISTOPHER CRAIG

Non timeo, iudices, ne odio mearum inimicitiarum inflammatus libentius haec in illum evomere videar quam verius.

I do not fear, gentlemen of the jury, lest inflamed by the hatred of my personal enmities I may seem to hurl these charges at him with more *verve* than veracity.

(*Mil.* 78b)

Thus Cicero, in the midst of one of the most sustained passages of savage invective preserved among his speeches (*Mil.* 72–91). The orator is defending his friend Milo, who has been accused of seditious violence for murdering Cicero's enemy Clodius. His purpose here is to show that, even if Milo had murdered Clodius, he should still be acquitted because the removal of Clodius was in the best interests of the *res publica*. Cicero's assertion of veracity, in the midst of a torrent of invective asserting that Clodius was murderous, rapacious, sacrilegious, unsparing of his own family, guilty of incest with his sister, hateful to the gods, and a clear and present danger to the continued survival of the Roman state, nicely underscores the problem of audience perceptions of invective in Ciceronian oratory. Why does Cicero feel the need for this assertion? Does the audience expect exuberant *ad hominem* attacks not to be true? If they do not, then what is the relationship of *ad hominem* attacks to factually probative argument? In what follows, I will address these questions by analysing Cicero's speech for Milo as a case study of Cicero's use of invective in a judicial speech.[1]

---

[1] In this essay, the terms '*ad hominem* attack', '*ad hominem* argument', and 'invective' are used interchangeably. I do not use *ad hominem* in the narrow Lockean sense of the demonstration that the speaker's position contradicts his or her previously espoused principles. For a review of the terminological confusions that have plagued the study of *ad hominem* argument, see D. Walton, *Ad Hominem Arguments* (Tuscaloosa, 1998).

Since the answers to all of these questions depend upon our understanding of the Roman juries' expectations for the content and uses of *ad
hominem* attacks, we must first establish those expectations. As a general
rule, Cicero's juries are educated in public speaking,[2] so that we can
recover their expectations from instructional manuals on rhetoric as well
as from the practice of the Greek and Roman orators whose speeches they
studied or witnessed. Having documented these varied and potentially
conflicting expectations for *ad hominem* argument, we will turn to an analysis of the ways in which Cicero addresses them in *pro Milone*.

i. Expectations for Content of *ad hominem* Attacks

Rhetorical Theory

Two contemporary textbooks, the anonymous *Rhetorica ad Herennium* and
Cicero's own youthful *De Inventione*, give a fair representation of the rhetorical expectations that the formally educated jurors would bring to a speech.[3]
The young Cicero, at *Inv.* 1.34–6, gives for arguments from character
(*ex persona*) a set of topics that are so comprehensive that they embrace
almost anything that one could say about a given individual.[4] These *loci* will
produce arguments about the defendant's character in a judicial consideration of a question of fact (*Inv.* 2.28–31). But the praise or blame of an
individual, while required in this judicial context, is the proper province of a
different *genus causarum*, the *genus demonstrativum*, or epideictic, and Cicero's
brief discussion of this *genus* (*Inv.* 2.177–8) seems to urge use of exactly the
same *loci* in a free-standing speech of praise or blame that he has already

---

[2] For the composition of the juries and the workings of the *quaestiones publicae*, see A. H. M. Jones,
The Criminal Courts of the Roman Republic and Principate (Oxford, 1976); A. H. J. Greenidge, *The Legal
Procedure of Cicero's Time* (Oxford, 1901); A. Riggsby, *Crime and Community in Ciceronian Rome*
(Austin, Tex., 1999).

[3] G. A. Kennedy, *The Art of Rhetoric in the Roman World* (Princeton, 1972) 106–8 gives an
overview and comparison of *Inv.* and *Rhet. Her.* For their textbook status see M. L. Clarke, *Rhetoric
at Rome*, rev. D. H., Berry, 3rd edn. (London and New York, 1996). In what follows, I use the Loeb
edition of H. M. Hubbell (1976) for *Inv.* and that of H. Caplan (1954) for *Rhet. Her.*

[4] (1) *nomen* (name); (2) *natura* (nature, including, but not limited to: gender, ethnic group, country, kinship, age; physical appearance, strength and quickness, intelligence, memory; affability,
modesty, patience and their opposites); (3) *victus* (manner of life, including upbringing, teachers,
friends, occupation, financial management and home life); (4) *fortuna* (fortune, including status as
slave or free, rich or poor, private citizen or officeholder, and if the latter, whether he acquired the
position justly, is successful, is famous, or the opposites; what sort of children he has. If the target
is dead, what was the manner of death? (5) *habitus* (habit); (6) *affectio* (emotional reactions),
(7) *studium* (interest or devotion to a pursuit such as philosophy, poetry, geometry, or literature);
(8) consilium (deliberate plan to do or not do something); (9–11) *facta, casus, orationes* (what he
did, what happened to him, what he said, treated by Cicero as a group).

enumerated for a judicial speech. Similar to Cicero's discussion of epideictic, but much fuller in its description and prescribed ordering of *loci*, is the treatment in the *Rhetorica ad Herennium* (3.10–15), which is the most concise theoretical account of the rhetoric of praise and blame from the Ciceronian age. Here the very broad *loci* of praise are listed in order, and we are told that for censure one simply says the opposite. These *loci* are grouped into advantages coming from three sources: (1) the external elements of birth, education, wealth, kinds of power, glorious achievements, citizenship or national origin, and friendships, (2) the physical attributes of speed and quickness, strength, good looks, and health, and (3) the *virtutes animi*, which are the four cardinal virtues. The point of a speech of praise is to demonstrate the presence of the cardinal virtues, and the point of a *vituperatio* is to demonstrate their opposites. If an invective shows that its target lacks prudence, justice, courage, and self-restraint, then it is successful by this standard, irrespective of the individual content *loci* used (*Rhet. Her.* 3.13; 15). For our purposes, there are two points to note about these treatments. First, the specific content *loci* of invective, both in the *Rhetorica ad Herennium* and especially in *De Inventione*, are so broad that they are virtually ubiquitous. Second, a rhetorically educated audience will have a clear expectation that the rhetoric of praise and blame, formally conceived, is appropriate in any speech of the judicial or deliberative genus as well (*Rhet. Her.* 3.15).

Loci of Invective in Greek and Roman Practice

It is almost impossible to say anything about an individual that cannot be included in the *loci* given by the Auctor ad Herennium or by Cicero. But in Greek and Roman practice, there is a much clearer delineation of the specific content *loci* that an audience will expect a formal invective to contain. While any speech that demonstrates in its target the opposites of the four cardinal virtues is an invective in the broadest sense, the use of these *loci*, already established when Cicero began his public life, might arouse in the educated audience a connoisseur's appreciation for familiar themes effectively used; the audience will expect such *loci* when a speaker is pronouncing an invective, and will be urged to perceive as invective a speech where these traditional *loci* occur. For this study, I have chosen to focus upon these *loci* rather than to take account of all of the various themes that Cicero repeats in attacking his enemies.[5] I have done so to obtain the most

---

[5] Thus I have not simply adopted the collections of invective *loci* noted by I. Opelt, *Die lateinischen Schimpfwörter und verwandte sprachliche Erscheinungen: eine Typologie* (Heidelberg, 1965) 129–64, or G. Achard, *Pratique rhétorique et idéologie politique dans les discours "optimates" de Cicéron* (Leiden, 1981) 186–355, since they use Cicero's speeches as a principal source for *loci* regardless of their occurrence in the earlier tradition. That said, there is a very substantial overlap between the established *loci* that we will identify and those listed by Opelt and Achard.

unambiguous examples of *loci* that would evoke in an educated audience the sense that an invective as formal exercise was being delivered.

These conventional *loci* of invective have already been carefully documented. Nisbet, in an appendix to his commentary on *In Pisonem*, offered a list of such *loci* based in part upon the *topoi* of invective that Süss had located in the practice of the Greek orators that occur in *In Pisonem*, and that are further shown to be literary or conventional by their recurrence in the pseudo-Sallustian *invectiva in Ciceronem* or the speech of Fufius Calenus at Dio 46.1–28. Later, Merrill collected Cicero's invective *loci* that have antecedents in Roman oratory. So, by combining the sets of *loci* offered by Nisbet, Süss, and Merrill, one can arrive at a working list of practical *loci*, all with antecedents in Greek and Roman practice, that Cicero's educated and experienced hearers might expect an orator to use in *vituperatio*.[6] With some merging of equivalent categories from these three sources, we arrive at a list of seventeen conventional *loci* of invective established in Greek and Roman practice by Cicero's time. Keyed to the *Oratio in Pisonem*, a relatively pure exercise in the invective genre delivered in the Senate,[7] these *loci* are:

embarrassing family origin	here covering Nisbet's three topics of (i) father a slave (§ 1. *Syrum*) (ii) barbarian origin (Piso's grandfather a Gaul., fr. 9 n.) (iii) ancestor's menial occupation (Piso's grandfather an auctioneer, fr. 9 n.; Piso's father a wartime profiteer dealing in leather, § 87)
unworthy of one's family	§§ 53 and 62

---

[6] See R. G. M. Nisbet, *M. Tulli Ciceronis in L. Calpurnium Pisonem Oratio* (Oxford, 1961), 192–7; W. Süss, *Ethos: Studien zur älteren griechischen Rhetorik* (Leipzig, 1910; repr. Aalen 1975) 245–62; N. W. Merrill, *Cicero and Early Roman Invective*, Ph.D. diss. (University of Cincinnati, 1975) 203–4. Excluding attacks specifically concerning Piso's Epicureanism, Nisbet documents the following eleven literary or conventional *loci*: (1) father a slave; (2) barbarian origin; (3) ancestor's menial occupation; (4) unworthy of one's family; (5) physical appearance; (6) eccentricity of dress; (7) gluttony and drunkenness; (8) hypocrisy for appearing virtuous; (9) avarice, possibly linked with prodigality; (10) taking bribes; (11) pretentiousness. From Süss's work, add also: (1) sexual misconduct; (2) hostility to family (*misophilia*); (3) cowardice in war; (4) squandering of one's patrimony. I omit one of Süss's other *loci*, a sullen appearance indicating a hatred of mankind, because I have seen no clear examples of it in Roman invective through Cicero's time. Finally, Merrill's traditional Roman loci are: (1) Aspiring to *regnum* or tyranny–associated with *vis, libido, superbia* and *crudelitas* (following J. R. Dunkle, 'The Greek Tyrant and Roman Political Invective of the Late Republic', *TAPA* 98 (1967) 157–71); (2) sexual misconduct and effeminacy; (3) cruelty to citizens and allies; (4) plunder of private and public property; (5) drunkenness; (6) inept oratorical delivery; (7) baseness of birth.

[7] See the introduction of Nisbet, *In Pisonem*, and the narrative commentary of S. Koster, *Die Invektive in der griechischen und römischen Literatur*, Beiträge zur klassischen Philologie 99 (Meisenheim an Glan, 1980) 210–81.

physical appearance	§ 1
eccentricity of dress	13.6 n; 92.3 n.
gluttony and drunkenness, possibly leading to acts of *crudelitas* and *libido*	§§ 13, 22, 42, 66
hypocrisy for appearing virtuous	fr. 18; § 1
avarice, possibly linked with prodigality	fr. 9; §§ 24, 66
taking bribes	§§ 83, 84, 87
pretentiousness	1.16 n. (eyebrows); §§ 22, 68 ('Graeci') philosophical pretensions (*passim*)
sexual misconduct	§§ 70, 86
hostility to family (*misophilia*)	No example
cowardice in war	No example
squandering of one's patrimony/ financial embarrassment	No example
aspiring to *regnum* or tyranny, associated with *vis, libido, superbia,* and *crudelitas* (cf. Dunkle, cited n. 5)	§ 24
cruelty to citizens and allies	§ 88, M. Baebius; also §§ 83–4, deaths of Plator and Pleuratus
plunder of private and public property	§ 85, Temple of Jupiter Urios
oratorical ineptitude	No example

The total for *In Pisonem* is 13 out of 17. Cicero's *Second Philippic*, the Ciceronian invective *par excellence*, will serve as another example.[8] In that speech, the orator has a more pressing political agenda, but that agenda can best be served by personal attack on Antonius (C. P. Craig, *Form as Argument in Cicero's Speeches: A Study of Dilemma* (Atlanta, 1993) 147–55). The speech contains an even greater variety and abundance of the different conventional *loci* of formal invective than does *In Pisonem* (15 of 17): (*Note*: The instances under a given *locus* are not necessarily exhaustive.)

embarrassing family origin	No example, but cf. §§ 3 and 90 (Antonius' children are the grandchildren of a freedman) and 14 (Antonius' stepfather was a Catilinarian)

---

[8] The most famous Ciceronian invective must be the *First Catilinarian*. In its use of invective *loci*, as in so much else, that speech is atypical. I hope to demonstrate elsewhere that the orator has good reasons to be relatively sparing with the formal *loci* of invective against Catiline.

unworthy of one's family	§ 42 (contrast with M. Antonius the orator)
physical appearance	§ 63
eccentricity of dress	§§ 76 (Gallic dress); 86 and 111 (naked)
gluttony and drunkenness	§§ 6, 31, 62–3, and 75 (with vomiting); 77, 81, 84, 87, 104–5
hypocrisy for appearing virtuous	No example
avarice, possibly linked with prodigality	§§ 40–1, 50, 62, 64–5, 103, 111
taking bribes	§§ 92–6, 97
pretentiousness	§ 70 ('Et consul et Antonius')
unacceptable sexual conduct	§§ 6, cf. 20, 58, and 61 (Volumnia); 44–5 (Curio), 48, 50, 62, 86, 99, 105
hostility to family (*misophilia*)	§§ 56, 98, 99
cowardice in war	§§ 71, 74–5, 78
squandering of one's patrimony/ financial embarrassment	§§ 36, 37, 42, 44, 48, 50, 62, 71–4, 78, 103
aspiring to *regnum* or tyranny, associated with *vis, libido, superbia, crudelitas,* and *avaritia* (cf. Dunkle, cited n. 5)	§§ 35, 87, 117
cruelty to citizens and allies	§ 71
plunder of private or public property	§§ 66–9 (Pompeius' house) *et passim*
oratorical ineptitude	§§ 8–9, 18, 19, 20, 25, 28, 29, 30, 31–2, 42, 43

It seems reasonable to infer that the insistent use of these *loci* is a hallmark of invective as formally conceived, and would invoke in the audience certain invective expectations. We may now turn to the exact nature of those expectations for each type of speech, judicial, epideictic, and deliberative. We will see that all of these sets of expectations are important for understanding audience expectations for invective in a Ciceronian judicial speech.

ii. Audience Expectations for the Use of Invective

Judicial Oratory

Role of ad hominem *Attacks in Hellenistic Rhetorical Theory.* The central role of the jury's judgement of the defendant's character, and thus of the role of *ad hominem* argument in the jury's deliberations, is underscored by the teachings of *De Inventione* and the *Rhetorica ad Herennium*. *Ad hominem* attacks may be used in the exordium (*Inv.* 1.22; *Rhet. Her.* 1.8) and in the *indignatio* of the peroration (*Inv.* 1.98–105, esp. 100, 105; cf. *Rhet. Her.* 2.47–9), and must be used in the *argumentatio* of any question of fact. If a person is accused of a crime, and the defence denies that the defendant committed the act, it is not enough for the prosecutor to show motive and opportunity. He must also show that the defendant's character is consonant with the commission of the crime. If he cannot establish any link between the defendant's character and a predisposition to commit the crime, he should still adduce any negative character evidence available, since everything that impugns the defendant's character thereby weakens the defence. (*Inv.* 2.32–7; cf. *Rhet. Her.* 2.5).

Ad hominem *Attacks in Judicial Oratory in Roman Practice.* In keeping with the teaching of Hellenistic rhetoric, it is clear from Cicero's extant speeches that one important factor in helping the jury to reach their verdict is their sense of the character of the accused; while the defence must assure the jurors of the defendant's relatively high moral character, the prosecution must do the opposite.[9] This expectation is so strong that the prosecution's failure to make allegations that we might consider slanderously defamatory can be taken as a clear sign of the weakness of their case. So, in his defence of Fonteius on a charge of misgovernment in Gaul in 69, Cicero can expostulate:

Ecquis umquam reus, praesertim in hac vitae ratione versatus in honoribus petendis, in potestatibus, in imperiis gerendis, sic accusatus est, ut nullum probrum, nullum facinus, nulla turpitudo, quae a lubidine aut a petulantia aut ab audacia nata esset, ab accusatore obiceretur, si non vera, at certe ficta cum aliqua ratione ac suspicione?

Was ever any defendant, especially one involved in this way of life, in seeking offices, in positions of power, in managing commands, accused in such a way that no vice, no crime, no disgrace which had arisen from lust or from meanness or from temerity was adduced by the prosecutor, *if not as a true charge, yet certainly as one fabricated with some plausibility of suspicion?* (My emphases; *Font.* 37. See the whole passage through § 40).

After adducing examples of the most upright Romans who had been falsely vilified in court in this way, the orator points out that the prosecutors of Fonteius have apparently been unable to make a single allegation about Fonteius' character. Their failure to do this (which we might think decorous restraint) is a clear argument for Fonteius' innocence.

[9] See D. H. Berry, *Cicero Pro P. Sulla Oratio*, Cambridge Classical Texts and Commentaries 30 (Cambridge, 1996) 273 and on *Sull.* 69.10 for useful discussion and thorough documentation of *argumenta ex persona* in the judicial speeches.

The fact that these plausible *ad hominem* arguments are to be expected allows Cicero to draw useful conclusions not only from their absence but also from their presence. So in the defense of Murena, the orator can fend off the attack on the defendant's character in part exactly because it is expected, and so can be dismissed as *pro forma*.

Intellego, iudices, tris totius accusationis partis fuisse, et earum unam in reprehensione vitae, alteram in contentione dignitatis, tertiam in criminibus ambitus esse versatam. Atque harum trium partium prima illa quae gravissima debebat esse ita fuit infirma et levis ut illos lex magis quaedam accusatoria quam vera male dicendi facultas de vita L. Murenae dicere aliquid coegerit.

I understand, gentlemen of the jury, that there were three parts of the accusation, and that of these one was concerned with censure of his life, the second with a comparison of the candidates' prestige, the third with the charges of electoral bribery. And of these three parts that first, which ought to have been the most substantial, was so weak and inconsequential that some standard rule (*lex*) of prosecuting, rather than a true capacity for speaking ill about the life of L. Murena, forced them to say something. (*Mur.* 11)

In short, Cicero's opponents are unsurprisingly damned if they do and damned if they don't use *ad hominem* attacks. In either case, Cicero's criticism is founded in the accepted expectation that such attacks are, even as *De Inventione* dictates, essential for a prosecution in a question of fact, and that such attacks, while not necessarily true, must be at least plausible allegations rather than patent falsehoods.

Free-Standing, Formal Invective

Cicero's educated audience may properly expect any or all of the invective *loci*, not only in a pure invective, but in any judicial speech which treats a question of fact, and so expects a portrayal of the defendant's character. But there is a fundamental difference in the audience expectations for the formal invective and the judicial speech that might have these *loci* in common. We have seen that, in a judicial speech concerning a question of fact, *ad hominem* attacks against the defendant must be at least plausible because their value is essentially probative concerning the target's capacity for criminal behaviour. But what truth value can be attached to formal invective outside the courts? It is after all part of a larger arena of social expression in which it can be argued that a speaker, and thus a rhetorically educated audience, are not at all concerned with the plausibility, much less the actual validity, of specific assertions. R. Syme gives the classic statement of this position:

In the allegation of disgusting immorality, degrading pursuits and ignoble origins the Roman politician knew no compunction or limit. Hence the alarming picture of contemporary society revealed by oratory, invective and lampoon.

Crime, vice and corruption in the last age of the Republic are embodied in types as perfect of their kind as are the civic and moral paragons of early days; which is fitting, for the evil and the good are both the fabrication of skilled literary artists. (*The Roman Revolution* (Oxford, 1939) 149)

Similarly Nisbet (*In Pisonem*, 193), noting the long tradition of invective in Greek literature and Roman practice, concludes that, 'Under these circumstances, it is not surprising that Roman invective often shows more regard for literary convention than for historical truth.'

Recently, A. Corbeill (*Controlling Laughter: Political Humor in The Late Republic* (Princeton, 1996)), in an innovative and important study of Ciceronian invective, has taken a somewhat different view. Corbeill's project is to demonstrate that invective, broadly conceived, is a tool of public humiliation that labels its target as other, and in so doing clarifies and affirms the specific values of the community of Rome's ruling elite. His principal concern is with the mechanisms whereby the target's physical appearance is made to resonate with specific Roman prejudices, and with Roman assumptions about the correlation of physical appearance with character, to accomplish this excluding and defining task. Corbeill (*Controlling Laughter*, 5) seems to insist that the Roman audience believed the content of invectives. This insistence is reflected in his analyses of individual Ciceronian invective passages, where he assumes that the audience must believe the negative characterization of the target in order for the invective to be persuasive.

A. M. Riggsby ('Did The Romans Believe in their Verdicts?', *Rhetorica* 15.3 (1997) 235–51; esp. 247–8) offers a more flexible assumption about what invective demands that the audience believe about the target. He argues from the exchange between Cicero and Clodius recorded at *Att.* 1.16.10[10] that in invective in the Senate, as opposed to the law courts, Romans are primarily involved in a zero-sum game of prestige. Making an invective attack upon an opponent directly to the opponent's face is a manner of insult that increases the attacker's prestige at the expense of the target, regardless of the audience's perception of the veracity of the specific allegation; in this arena, the truth is largely irrelevant.[11]

I believe that Riggsby's hypothesis, which agrees with Syme and Nisbet in virtually dismissing the relevance of truth value in free-standing, formal

[10] While this is an exchange in the senate rather than a continuous speech, its tone and venue make it a valid example. It is worth noting that formal invective seems more at home in the Senate, and that on topics for which speeches before both Senate and people exist, invective is more prominent before a senatorial audience. See the analyses of D. Mack, *Senatsreden und Volksreden bei Cicero* (Würzburg, 1937; repr. Hildesheim, 1967). I am indebted to Prof. R. Kallet-Marx for helpful discussion of this point.

[11] For a much broader inference about the value of truth in Ciceronian oratory based upon this passage, see H. C. Gotoff, *HSCP* 95 (1993) 288–313.

invective, requires only slight adjustment. While invective charges need not be perceived as true, invective charges that are perceived as true have a deeper impact on the audience. So, in the passage Riggsby cites (*Att.* 1.16.10),[12] Clodius' charge that Cicero has been to Baiae (and thus is a pretentious social climber and a voluptuary) is false. Cicero does not deny the charge, but simply counter-attacks. Similarly Clodius' accusation that Cicero is acting like a tyrant brings only counter-attack. Clodius' reference to Cicero's new house on the Palatine (implying pretentiousness and perhaps avarice, since the financing that Cicero had obtained after procuring P. Sulla's acquittal was no longer secret),[13] likewise meets with a simple counter-attack. But Clodius' charge that the jury in the Bona Dea trial did not believe Cicero is supported by the stark fact of Clodius' acquittal. So it demands a counter-attack that demonstrates as well that the charge is not true.

In short, while the truth of specific allegations is not of primary importance in the social function of invective, Corbeill is right to assume that perceived truth of allegations is a wellspring of invective power. Rather than saying that the truth of invective allegations is irrelevant, we may more accurately say that it is of secondary importance.

As we have already seen, Riggsby's distinction between judicial and other contexts is also critical. Corbeill's assumption of the credibility of invective attacks is grounded in his sensible conviction that Romans would not base legal and political decisions on arguments that they only partially believed. But in non-judicial contexts, what is more important in the milieu of Rome's extremely personalized politics is the fact of humiliation rather than the specific content of the insult. Only in the arenas where determinations

---

[12] 'Surgit pulchellus puer, obicit mihi me ad Baias fuisse. falsum, sed tamen "quid? hoc simile est" inquam quasi in operto dicas fuisse. "quid" inquit homini Arpinati cum aquis calidis?" "narra" inquam patrono tuo, "qui Arpinatis aquas concupivit" (nosti enim Marianas). "quousque" inquit "hunc regem feremus?" "regem appellas" inquam, "cum Rex tui mentionem nullam fecerit?"–ille autem Regis hereditatem spe devorarat. "domum" inquit "emisti." "putes" inquam "dicere 'iudices emisti.'" "iuranti" inquit tibi "non crediderunt." "mihi vero" inquam "xxv iudices crediderunt, xxxi, quoniam nummos ante acceperunt, tibi nihil crediderunt." magnis clamoribus adflictus conticuit et concidit.' ('Our little Beauty gets on his feet and accuses me of having been at Baiae–not true, but anyhow, "well," I reply, "is that like saying I intruded on the Mysteries?" "What business has an Arpinum man with the waters?" "Tell that to your counsel," I retorted; "he has been keen enough to get certain of them that belonged to an Arpinum man" (you know Marius' place of course). "How long", cried he, "are we going to put up with this king?" "You talk about kings," I answered, "when Rex didn't have a word to say about you?" (he had hoped to have the squandering of Rex's money). "So you've bought a house," said he. I rejoined, "One might think he was saying that I had bought a jury." "They didn't credit you on oath." "On the contrary twenty-five jurymen gave *me* credit and thirty-one gave *you* none–they got their money in advance!" The roars of applause were too much for him and he collapsed into silence.' (Text and tr. Bailey (1965) 156–9.)

[13] See Berry, *Cicero Pro P. Sulla Oratio*, 31.

of fact are of primary importance, most specifically in the courts, must invective flow within the narrower banks of plausibility.[14]

Invective in Deliberative Arguments

There is a final consideration in our understanding of the expectations that *ad hominem* arguments arouse in Cicero's juries. Invective arguments, even if taken as part of a strategy of humiliation with uncertain factual grounding, may still be probative in another sphere, that of deliberative oratory (*Inv.* 2.156b–76; somewhat differently *Rhet. Her.* 3.2–9). What is the most advantageous course for the polity to take, where advantage may be defined in terms first of honour then expediency then convenience (*Inv.*), or alternatively of security and/or honour (*Rhet. Her.*)? In the *Second Philippic*, for example, Cicero shows that it is not advantageous to maintain Antonius as a leader either of the state or even of his own supporters. He does so not only by his emphasis upon Antonius' ineptitude and host of personal failings,[15] but also by the very fact that he can make Antonius the object of such attacks, however factually grounded.

This sphere of argument is worth noting in a consideration of the role of invective in judicial oratory because the judicial pleadings in the high-profile and often strongly politicized cases for which Cicero's speeches are preserved easily admit of arguments that are not merely concerned with the justice of past acts, but also with what is most advantageous for the state. This is seen perhaps most clearly in trials for seditious violence (*vis*). Here the double basis for the charge is that the defendant committed a violent act and that that act was *contra rem publicam*.[16] The notion that an act is or is not *contra rem publicam* can lead directly to a debate about what is in the best interest of the Republic, a fundamentally deliberative issue nestled within a judicial proceeding. Even in the rhetorical textbooks, there is

[14] A hybrid case, in which the humiliating function of invective can coalesce with the probative function of *ad hominem* judicial argument, is the discrediting of witnesses, especially in a highly politicized atmosphere where a question of fact is not the principal issue. In *In Vatinium*, which purports to be an interrogation of a witness in a criminal trial (see L. G. Pocock, *A Commentary on Cicero In Vatinium* (London, 1926; repr. Amsterdam, 1967)), Cicero levels attacks that may be true, as the observation of Vatinius' physical appearance (*Vat.* 4, 10, 39), or tendentious, as that his physical appearance bespeaks an evil nature (Corbeill, *Controlling Laughter*, 49–55), or spitefully fanciful, as that he had beaten his own mother (*Vat.* 11). Whatever their veracity, all work for the different but complementary functions of humiliating and discrediting the witness.

[15] The theoretical treatments of deliberative and invective overlap substantially in a deliberative speech about determining who will lead the state, since the central deliberative locus of honour is keyed to demonstrating the extent to which a decision reflects the four cardinal virtues, while the central goal of *vituperatio* is keyed in a negative way to those same virtues.

[16] See A. W. Lintott, *Violence in Republican Rome*, 2nd edn. (Oxford, 1968) 107–24; Riggsby, *Crime and Community*, 79–119.

a space for such arguments in judicial oratory; one subspecies of the status of quality, *comparatio* (*Inv.* 2.72–3; *Rhet. Her.* 2.21–2), based purely on what is advantageous, argues that an act which could not be countenanced in itself may be justified by an ensuing positive result.

These arguments about what constitutes the best interest of the republic, whether they are carried on primarily in the Senate, in *contiones*, or in the courts, are easily cast in personal terms.[17] Using Ciceronian speeches, judicial and otherwise, from 63 through April of 56, plus *pro Milone* and the *Philippics*, Achard (*Pratique rhétorique*, 186–355) has identified the *loci* of invective which Cicero uses in espousing an optimate ideology. These do not comprise ideologically explicit attacks in the familiar modern sense, in which tax-and-spend, bleeding-heart liberals trade jibes with heartless, greedy conservatives. Rather opponents are simply demonized with all the resources at the orator's disposal,[18] and so the prevenient *loci* of invective that we have seen become the *loci* of political debate. But the special emphases of these *loci*, whether of aiming at tyranny, *crudelitas*, plunder, or the rest, tend to consist in their specific charges of actions that disrupt the public peace, subvert public religion, undermine the social order, and directly threaten the lives and property of citizens.[19] This complex of themes goes back to the treatment of Catiline and is repeated in the *Post Reditum* speeches.

The plausibility required of each of these themes will of course depend upon individual persuasive contexts. Generally, to the extent that the audience is made to perceive the target as a source of danger, these themes are probative, and their truth value is primary. For example, in the defence of Sestius on a charge of *vis*, Cicero's vivid description of Clodius' savage attack on Cicero's supporters in the Forum (*Sest.* 75–7), which would fall

---

[17] The most extreme case of such personalizing is in Cicero's speeches after his return from exile. J. M. May, (*Trials of Character: The Eloquence of Ciceronian Ethos* (Chapel Hill, NC, and London, 1988) 94 and n. 18) collects the passages in which the orator simply equates the republic with himself. Conversely, his opponents become not only public enemies, but as May ('Cicero and the Beasts', *Syllecta Classica* 7 (1996) 143–53) notes, subhuman monsters.

[18] For the morally laden terms that Cicero uses to contrast his fellow *optimates* with *populares*, *boni vs. improbi*, etc., see J. Hellegouarc'h *Le Vocabulaire latin des relations et des partis politiques sous la république*, 2nd edn. (Paris, 1972: 484–541).

[19] Achard's list of *loci*, with six principal subdivisions, is framed both more elaborately and differently from the seventeen prevenient conventional loci of invective that we have identified. Still, there is substantial overlap. As noted above (n. 5) I have not simply adopted his list because my concern is with the audience expectations that Cicero's jury will bring to *Pro Milone*, and Achard uses *Pro Milone* and the *Philippics* to define his set of *loci*. Further, some of his *loci* are defined too broadly to be analytically useful. His *dissimulatio*, for example, (260–8) can mean anything from Catilinarian treachery to a politician's lack of complete disclosure. That said, one may fairly wonder whether Cicero had trained his audiences, by the time of his defence of Milo, to treat some of these charges, especially *furor* (239–47 and 519), and disrespect for the gods and their rites (306–11 s.v. *impietas*) as expected *loci* of formal invective. Since the expectations that these themes might arouse are arguable, I have chosen not to consider them on a par with the prevenient conventional *loci*.

under the traditional invective *locus* of *crudelitas*, is probative of the idea that it was Cicero's enemies rather than his supporters who acted *contra rem publicam*, so violence against them was justified. To carry this probative burden, Cicero's description of Clodian *crudelitas* must be plausible.

But to the extent that the audience does not perceive the target's behaviour as a danger, these themes can be part of an act of humiliation in a zero-sum game of prestige, and their truth value is secondary. So, for example, Cicero's passing allusions in *Pro Sestio* to the rumour that Clodius was his sister's lover (*Sest.* 16, 39, 116), while part of a coherent portrait of Clodius as a violent man with no respect for Roman values, need not be taken at face value in order to make Cicero's case. They are invective grace notes. In a judicial speech concerned with a question of quality rather than a question of fact, it is the depiction of the target as a *dangerous* monster with no regard for what Romans hold sacred that is probative as a justification for extra-legal action for the good of the state.

In summary the educated jury that we should imagine for Cicero's speech for Milo would have this array of varied and perhaps contradictory expectations: (1) In judging a question of fact in a judicial speech, *ad hominem* argument is necessary for proof of the charge, and must be convincing, or at least plausible. (2) *Ad hominem* argument apart from a judicial question of fact is a means of humiliating political opponents in a zero-sum game of prestige, and need not be factually convincing or plausible. (3) In judging a deliberative question, including political questions embedded in a judicial speech, *ad hominem* argument is to be expected, and must be convincing or at least plausible if it is to lead to a direct course of action. But it may otherwise have a simple function of humiliating one's enemies, for which the truth value of the allegation is secondary.

iii. *Pro Milone*

Now let us focus upon the speech for Milo in order to examine the ways in which a Roman jury's expectations for invective's role in arguing for guilt in past acts, for relative status in the public sphere, and for the best course for the state in political deliberations, are reflected in Cicero's use of *ad hominem* argument in a judicial speech. Since we know that the *pro Milone* we have is not the speech that Cicero delivered, and since it is a speech for the defence, rather than a prosecution speech that requires *ad hominem* attack, the choice of this speech may seem to require some justification. I choose it for these reasons: (1) I accept the notion that, if this speech does not represent what Cicero actually said, it still stands as a representation, albeit a fictive representation, of an oral persuasive process before a given audience in specific circumstances. Following the broad rationale of Wilfried Stroh for the published speeches, it can be read as such a representation without disputing that the published version pursues an agenda that goes beyond seeking Milo's acquittal.[20] (2) The *ad hominem* attacks mandated in judicial oratory are in the province of the prosecutor. Among Ciceronian speeches, we will expect to find them only in his sole extant prosecution speeches, the *Verrines*, or in speeches which defend his client by accusing someone else, and thus allow Cicero to invoke the *ad hominem* attacks expected of a prosecutor in the course of his defence. The tactic of accusing the adversary, which Quintilian will style *antikategoria* or *mutua accusatio* (*Inst.* 3.10.4; 7.2.9), can be seen most notably in *Pro Roscio Amerino, Pro Cluentio, Pro Sestio*, and *Pro Milone*. Of these speeches, *Pro Milone* offers the most extensive attack upon an invective target whom Cicero also attacks elsewhere. So this speech offers the clearest sense of the range of invective *loci* that the orator might choose as effective, or omit as unhelpful, in a specific judicial oration.

Let us establish that prevenient range of formal invective *loci* at the outset. There is one topic that Cicero cannot use against Clodius under any circumstances. The *novus homo* from Arpinum cannot very well criticize the scion of one of Rome's most illustrious patrician families on the basis of family origin. Cowardice in war shows more promise, but Cicero, who will himself remain virtually devoid of military distinction until 51 BC, elects not to use it. Drunkenness finds only a glancing allusion (*Har. Resp.* 55). Cicero finds an opportunity to level every other invective *locus* at Clodius in a fully developed way, either in the speeches following his return from exile in 57 or in the unpublished invective *In Clodium et Curionem* of 61, of which a few fragments have come down to us (J. W. Crawford, *M. Tullius Cicero: The Fragmentary Speeches. An Edition with Commentary*, APA American Classical Studies, 2nd edn. (Atlanta, 1994) 227–63). For the more common *loci*, those of aspiring to tyranny, cruelty and plunder, I have not multiplied citations; the following list is illustrative rather than exhaustive.

embarrassing family origin	No example.
unworthy of one's family	*Clod.* F 20 Cr (Turin palimpsest and *Schol. Bob.* 88.31–2 St, q.v.) 'Quo loco ita fuit caecus, ut facile appareret vidisse eum quod fas non fuisset' ('In this place he was so

---

[20] W. Stroh, *Taxis und Taktik. Die advokatische Dispositionskunst in Ciceros Gerichtsreden* (Stuttgart, 1975) 31–54, esp. 51–4. Most recently, A. R. Dyck, 'Narrative Obfuscation, Philosophical *Topoi*, and Tragic Patterning in Cicero's *Pro Milone*', *HSCP* 98 (1998) 219–41, esp. 221–2, while not endorsing Stroh, effectively practises this approach.

	blind, that it was clear that he had seen a thing which had not been religiously proper');[21] *Clod.* F 23 Cr (Turin palimpsest); *Clod.* F 24 Cr (=*Schol. Bob.* 89.29–30 St) 'sed, credo, postquam speculum tibi allatum est, longo te a pulchris abesse sensisti' ('But, I believe, after a mirror was brought you, you realized that you were far removed from the beautiful');[22] *Dom.* 105; *Har. Resp.* 26–7, 38.
physical appearance	*Clod.* F 21 Cr (Turin palimpsest), *Clod.* F 24 Cr (=*Schol. Bob.* 89.29–30 St) (both referring to Clodius' female self-presentation at the Bona Dea.)
eccentricity of dress	*Clod.* FF 21, 22, 23 Cr (Turin palimpsest); *Har. Resp.* 44 (both passages refer in exquisite detail to Clodius' female apparel at the Bona Dea.)
gluttony and drunkenness, possibly leading to acts of cruelty and *libido*	*Har. Resp.* 55 'Est quidem ille plenus vini, stupri, somni' ('That man is indeed full of wine, debauchery, sleep').
hypocrisy for appearing virtuous	*Har. Resp.* 8 and 12 and 14 (Clodius as champion of religious scruples).
avarice, possibly linked with prodigality	*Clod.* F 23 Cr (=*Schol. Bob.* 86, 32 St, q.v.); *Dom.* 23–4, 115–16, 129; *Sest.* 66.
taking bribes	*Dom.* 23–4, 129; *Sest.* 84; *Har. Resp.* 1, 28–9, 42.
pretentiousness	*Clod.* F 19 Cr 'Primum homo durus ac priscus invectus est in eos qui mense Aprili apud Baias essent et aquis calidis uterentur. quid cum hoc homine nobis tam tristi ac severo?' etc. ('First the harsh and old-fashioned fellow inveighed against those who were at Baiae in the month of April and enjoyed the waters. What can we do with a person so stern and strict?') This is obviously ironic. Also *Har. Resp.* 8 and 12 and 14 (Clodius as

---

[21] As the Bobbio Scholiast notes, 'caecus' [blind] is a reference to Clodius most famous ancestor. Achard, *Pratique rhétorique*, 245, notes that 'caecus' in the mental sense is only used of Clodius in Ciceronian invective; it always carries the reminder that Clodius is unworthy of his ancestor.

[22] 'pulcher' [beautiful] is the designation of Clodius' branch of the Claudian family, so his appearance in women's garb uses the adjective both in its literal sense and in reference to his deviance from the standards of his family.

unacceptable sexual conduct	champion of religious scruples) as above, s.v. 'hypocrisy . . . '
	Clod. F 5 Cr (= *Schol. Bob.* 86.23 St, q.v.) (Bona Dea with effeminacy), *Clod.* FF 21–4 Cr (Bona Dea with effeminacy, see 'physical appearance' and 'eccentricity of dress' above), *Clod.* F28 Cr (incest or Bona Dea); *Dom.* 26 (incest–double meaning of 'fratricida, sororicida'), 36 (Clodius' adoptive father was his *puer delicatus*), 92 (incest), 118 and 134–5 and 139 (allusions to sexual relations of Clodius with the mother-in-law of L. Pinarius Natta, the pontifex who consecrated Cicero's home site), 139 (Bona Dea; man for every woman and woman for every man); *Sest.* 16–17 (incest), 39 (incest and Bona Dea), 116 (incest and Bona Dea, with effeminacy); *Har. Resp.* 4 and 8 (Bona Dea), 9 (incest), 39 (incest and Bona Dea), 42 (homosexual prostitution, incest, sexual object for pirates and barbarians) 59 (homosexual prostitution, incest); *Cael.* 32 and 36 (incest implied); *Prov. Cons.* 24 (Bona Dea); *Pis.* 65 (Piso may dine with Clodius, his love).
hostility to family (*misophilia*)	*Dom.* 26, 35 (Clodius' adoption); *Har. Resp.* 57 (Clodius' adoption).
cowardice in war	No example.
squandering of one's patrimony/financial embarrassment	*Clod.* FF 9, 10, 11, 12 Cr (= *Schol. Bob.* 87.4, 87.7, 87.11, 87.14 St, q.v.).
aspiring to *regnum* or tyranny	(associated with *vis, libido, superbia* and *crudelitas*). *Dom.* 24, 68, 110, 129–31, 137; *Sest.* 34, 42; *Har. Resp.* 54–5.
cruelty to citizens and allies	*Dom.* 6, 12, 14, 23, 26, 42, 43, 45, 58–9, 61, 67, 115, 128, 129, 131; *Sest.* 75–8, 84–5, 95 *et passim; Har. Resp.* 6, 30, 34, 35, 42, 49, 58.
plunder of private and public property	*Dom.* 13, 20, 24, 51, 60, 107, 122, 147 *et passim;* Sest. 39, 95 *et passim; Har. Resp.* 30, 39, 42, 58, 59 *et passim.*
oratorical ineptitude	*Clod.* F 20 Cr (Turin Palimpsest); *Dom.* 2 and 76, and cf. 40; *Har. Resp.* 8.

These fifteen *loci* comprise a broad range of possibilities for highly recognizable and expected *ad hominem* attack that Cicero has used against Clodius when he was alive, and that the educated and experienced jury might expect the orator to use again at need. (To read the speech is to be assured that *nihil nisi bonum de mortuis* was not a constraining principle.) Careful attention to the *Pro Milone* will show the way in which audience expectations for the arguments in this judicial context inform Cicero's use of these invective *loci.*[23]

The circumstances of the speech, largely known from the invaluable testimony of Asconius (30–56 C), are too familiar to require detailed rehearsal.[24] Because of various political and religious obstructions, the year 52 opened before consuls and praetors could be elected. The entourages of the venerable enemies Clodius, a candidate for the praetorship, and Milo, who was standing for the consulship, accidentally met on the Appian way on 18 January. A mêlée ensued and Clodius, wounded, went to earth in a roadside inn. Milo ordered him dragged from the inn and killed (31–2 C). Amidst rioting, the senate specifically decreed that the events on the Appian Way and their aftermath were *contra rem publicam*. To bring stability to the city, Pompeius was prevailed upon to serve as sole consul. In that role, he promulgated the legislation that established a special court for seditious violence (*vis*), with a special procedure, to try cases arising from the acts that the Senate had labelled *contra rem publicam*. This tribunal might not unreasonably be thought a kangaroo court designed specifically to convict Milo (36 C). Cicero was the sole patronus, and pled in a forum surrounded by Pompeius' soldiers. He failed, and Milo withdrew into exile. Subsequently the orator published the *pro Milone* that we have (41–2 C). The argumentation of our speech seems to differ from the failed delivered version. In that version, Cicero had pled that Milo was acting in self-defence. In our version, he apparently added the *extra causam* argument (§§ 72–91) that, even if Milo had killed Clodius, he should be acquitted because the killing of Clodius promoted the common good.[25]

The structure of the speech is given in Table 7.1. This structure follows that of A. C. Clark (ed.) *M. Tulli Ciceronis Pro T. Annio Milone ad indices oratio* (Oxford 1895) xlix–lvii, who keys each section to the rhetorical precepts of

---

[23] For a more comprehensive analysis of the speech, see most recently Dyck, 'Narrative Obfuscation', with lit. Of the works he cites, see esp. C. Neumeister, *Grundsätze de forenischen Rhetorik, gezeigt an Gerichtsredan Ciceros* (Munich, 1964) 82–129; May, *Trials of Character*, 129–40.

[24] For a thorough narrative consideration of these events, see A. W. Lintott, 'Cicero and Milo', *JRS* 64 (1974) 62–75. See also B. A. Marshall, *A Historical Commentary on Asconius* (Columbia, Mo., 1985). For issues of chronology, J. Ruebel 'The Trial of Milo in 52 B.C.: A Chronological Study', *TAPA* 109 (1979) 231–49.

[25] The best argued speculation on the relationship between the content of the spoken and published orations is A. M. Stone, '*Pro Milone*: Cicero's Second Thoughts', *Antichthon* 14 (1980) 88–111, with lit. For a radically different view of the evidence, see Marshall, *A Historical Commentary*.

Table 7.1 *Structure of 'Pro Milone'*

	Unworthy of family	Avarice	Sex	Hostile to family	Tyranny	Crudelitas	Plunder
Exordium (1–6)						3	3
Prevenient prejudices (7–22)							
(a) The self-confessed killer is condemned (7–11)							
(b) The Senate ruled Milo's action *contra rem publicam* (12–14)			13			18, 19, 20	17
(c) Pompey has condemned Milo (15–22)	17, 18						
Narration (24–29)							
Projects and character of Clodius (24–26)						24, 25, 26	
Circumstances of the action (27–29)						31	
Framing of question at issue (30–31)							
Argumentation (32–71)							
From motive (32–34)							
From character (35–41)					35	37, 38, 40, 41	

Section						
Comparison of Milo and Clodius (41–43)				43		
Transition to circumstances (44)					52	50
From the circumstances (45–56)		55				
Commonplace on interrogation of slaves (57–60)		59				
Inference: Milo innocent (61–63)						
Commonplace against rumors (64–66)						
Appeal to Pompey (67–71)						
Extra causam (72–91)		73, 74, 75, 76				
If Milo had killed Clodius, he should go free because Clodius' death a public benefit (72–81)		72, 73, 76	75	76, 80	73, 77	73, 74, 75, 76
The gods responsible for Clodius' death (83–91)	86	85, 87, 89		87, 89	87	87, 89
Peroration (92–105)			95	103		95

Source: A. C. Clark (ed.), *M. Tulli Ciceronis Pro T. Annio Milone ad iudices oratio* (Oxford, 1895), pp. xlix–lvii.

the *Rhetorica ad Herennium*. While *pro Milone* certainly represents a unified persuasive process,[26] Cicero uses two different staseis. The first is the conjectural stasis, the question of fact (§§ 30–66; v. esp. *Inv.* 2.14–51; *Rhet. Her.* 2.3–12). Against the prosecution's false charge that Milo had laid an ambush for Clodius, Cicero argues the equally false position that Clodius laid an ambush for Milo. Thus Milo's killing of Clodius was self-defence. This plea might be viewed as a status of quality (He was responsible for Clodius' death, but his action was justified), or perhaps better as a status of definition (He was responsible for Clodius' death, but it was not murder, and thus not seditious violence). In any event, the plea, and the arguments used to support it, are finally rooted in the question of fact, *utrum utri insidias fecerit* ('who laid the ambush for whom', § 31) Cicero thus constructs a comparison of the mutually exclusive alternatives that Milo or Clodius planned the ambush. In this question of fact both Cicero and his audience would expect to hear probative *ad hominem* arguments characterizing Clodius' as the sort of person who would commit such a crime.

The *extra causam* section (72–91) argues a *comparatio*, the subspecies of the stasis of quality that Clodius' death confers an overriding benefit (*Inv.* 2.72–3; *Rhet. Her.* 2.21–2). This line becomes vigorously explicit in sections 79–83a, in which Cicero argues that the jurors, and Pompey himself, would not want to bring Clodius back to life even if they could, that Clodius was a tyrant, and thus that if Milo had killed him (as he did not), the defendant would rightfully boast of the deed. In terms of the charge of *vis*, this argument maintains that the killer of Clodius acted *pro re publica*, and thus must be innocent. Since the Senate had expressly decreed that the murder of Clodius was *contra rem publicam*, this argument can only be introduced as a hypothetical *obiter dictum*.[27] It is nonetheless central to Cicero's answer to the charge. The audience would here properly expect *ad hominem* arguments in support of the deliberative proposition that Clodius was so dangerous that his death was in the best interest of the state. These arguments, although explicitly labelled *extra causam*, are probative and so must be plausible.

Within this structure, the *loci* of invective formally conceived, as means of playing a zero-sum game of public humiliation in which truth value is secondary, have no clear place. So it is perhaps to be expected that the variety of established *loci* of invective in *Pro Milone* is substantially less than in *In Pisonem* or the *Second Philippic*:

embarrassing family origin	No example.
unworthy of one's family	*Mil.* 17, 18, 86.
physical appearance	No example.

---

[26] Neumeister, *Grundsätze*, 82–129.   [27] Thus correctly Stone, '*Pro Milone*', 90–1.

eccentricity of dress	No example.
gluttony and drunkenness, possibly leading to acts of cruelty and *libido*	*No developed example*, but v. *Mil.* 56 'adde inscitiam pransi, poti, oscitantis ducis' ('add the witlessness of a well-fed, well-oiled, yawning leader').
hypocrisy for appearing virtuous	No example.
avarice, possibly linked with prodigality	*Mil.* 73–6, in horrific detail.
taking bribes	No example.
pretentiousness	No example.
unacceptable sexual conduct	*Mil.* 13 'de illo incesto stupro' ('concerning that unholy copulation'), 55 (Clodius usually accompanied by prostitutes; Clodius a woman against men), 59, 72–3, 73, 76, 85 'omni nefario stupro' ('with every wicked copulation'), 87, 89 (Clodius effeminate attacker of a real man).
hostility to family (*misophilia*)	*Mil.* 75–6.
cowardice in war	No example, cf. *Mil.* 41.
squandering of one's patrimony/financial embarrassment	No example.
aspiring to *regnum* or tyranny	(associated with *vis, libido, superbia*, and *crudelitas*) *Mil.* 35, 43, 76, 80, 87, 89.
cruelty to citizens and allies	*Mil.* 3 'P. Clodii furor rapinis et incendiis et omnibus exitiis publicis' ('the frenzy of Publius Clodius with pillaging, burnings, and all public ruination'), 18 (murder of M. Papirius and attempted murder of Pompey), 19–20 (multiple attempts to murder Cicero), 24 (plan to savage the state), 25 (announced intention to murder Milo) 26 (murderous intention and prediction that Milo would be dead in three days), 31 (Milo attacked by Clodius in the past), 37 (attack on Hortensius, death of C. Vibienus, plot to kill Cicero, plot to kill Pompey, murder of Papirius, more recent attempt to murder Cicero), 38 (wounding of Sestius, attack on Q. Fabricius and the slaughter in the forum in January of 57,

attack on the house of Lucius Caecilius), 40 (Clodius' attack on Pompey in February of 56), 41 (how many times did Clodius use violence!), 52 (Clodius had an inveterate habit of violence and had predicted that Milo would die), 73, 77, 87 (Clodius oppressed the republic, harried the senate, banished Cicero, burned his house, and persecuted his wife and children, plotted to murder Pompey, orchestrated the murder of both magistrates and private citizens, burned Quintus Cicero's house, etc.)

plunder of private and public property

Mil. 3 'P. Clodii furor rapinis et incendiis et omnibus exitiis publicis' 'the frenzy of Publius Clodius with pillaging, burnings, and all public ruination') 17 'proinde quasi Appius ille Caecus viam muniverit, non qua populus uteretur, sed ubi impune sui posteri latrocinarentur!' ('As if Appius the Blind had built his Way not so that the people might use it, but so that his descendants could practise banditry there with impunity!'), 50 (if Clodius had been killed at night, all Etruria would be under suspicion because of his depredations there), 73–5 (General remarks and half a dozen specific examples of victims of Clodius' depredations), 76 (plan to seize the Republic with a slave army), 78 (no one's property would have been safe had Clodius lived), 87 (Clodius believed that he would be able to seize the property of anyone), 89 (Clodius would have seized everything), 95 'plebem et infimam multitudinem, quae P. Clodio duce fortunis vestris imminebat' ('the plebeians and the crowd of the poor, who were threatening your fortunes with Publius Clodius as their leader').

oratorical ineptitude

No example.

Again, Cicero's persuasive strategy is to depict Clodius as both an inveterate murderer who laid the ambush for Milo and as a monster whose death is a benefit to the state. Invective *loci* that do not lend themselves to this probative strategy, but would merely serve to insult his dead enemy, simply disappear. Thus Cicero here has nothing to say about Clodius' effeminate deportment at the Bona Dea, about his correct and detailed feminine garb on that occasion, about the pedestrian wickedness of taking bribes, about his pretentious posture of moral superiority, about his financial vicissitudes, or about his oratorical ineptitude.

Of the *loci* that Cicero does use, aspiring to tyranny is closely linked with cruelty towards the persons of individuals and with plunder of public and private property, and this plunder is of course evidence of avarice. The one of these associated *loci* which is most germane for the question of fact is the demonstration of cruelty, which includes the predisposition to murder. This is then the *locus* that Hellenistic rhetoric (*Inv.* 2.32) demands receive the greatest attention in the *ad hominem* arguments concerning the question of fact. Accordingly, as Table 7.1 and the list above demonstrate, instances of that murderous predisposition are far more common in Cicero's treatment of the question of fact in the first part of the speech than in his treatment of the issue of quality in secs. 72–91. That said, the entire cluster of *loci* of aiming at tyranny, cruelty, plunder, and avarice is far more highly concentrated in secs. 72–91 than in the rest of the speech. This is exactly what we would expect, given that these sections attempt to demonstrate the overriding benefit of Clodius' death.

The other three *loci* that Cicero uses, unworthiness of one's family, unacceptable sexual conduct, and hostility to one's own family, do not form such a conventional cluster. To understand how these *loci* are integrated into the argument, it will be useful to note some of the specific contexts in which they arise:

The first two of the three occurrences of the notion that Clodius is unworthy of his family (*Mil.* 17, 18, 86) come in the course of Cicero's complaint that the creation of a special court *de vi* to try this case was unnecessary; Clodius was no more important a decedent than other Romans whose deaths had not triggered special laws or special courts. In an apparent direct response to the prosecution's emotional argument that Clodius had died among the monuments of his ancestors on the Appian Way which his own ancestor, Appius Claudius Caecus, had built, Cicero remarks:

proinde quasi Appius ille Caecus viam muniverit, non qua populus uteretur, sed ubi impune sui posteri latrocinarentur!

Indeed, as if Appius the Blind built the road not so that the people might use it, but as a place where his descendants might commit robbery with impunity! (*Mil.* 17).

Itaque in eadem ista Appia via cum ornatissimum equitem Romanum P. Clodius
M. Papirium occidisset, non fuit illud facinus puniendum; homo enim nobilis in
suis monumentis equitem Romanum occiderat.

And so on this same Appian Way when Publius Clodius had killed Marcus
Papirius, a most distinguished Roman knight, that crime was not to be punished;
for a person of noble birth had, among his own monuments, killed a Roman
knight. (*Mil.* 18).

Cicero then goes on to amplify the murder of Marcus Papirius. The idea
that Clodius is unworthy of his family is here at once a direct response to
a prosecution argument, a part of the argument that the special court is
unnecessary, and, most important, a way of emphasizing the most powerful probative *locus* of character for the question of fact. Clodius manifested
crudelitas; he had already established himself as a murderer. Cicero's
restraint and selectivity become even clearer when we compare this
response emphasizing Clodius' cruelty and brigandage with the instances of
the *locus* of unworthiness of one's family that we have seen in Cicero's earlier speeches. In these Clodius departed from the ways of Appius the Blind
primarily through his behaviour at the Bona Dea, and perhaps through his
relations with his sister.

The broad range of Cicero's earlier attacks on Clodius' unacceptable
sexual conduct is documented above. The contexts in which such attacks
occur in this speech are again illuminating. We find at *Mil.* 13, the beginning of Cicero's complaint that there was no need for this specially constituted court:

cuius enim de illo incesto stupro iudicium decernendi senatui potestas esset erepta,
de eius interitu quis potest credere senatum iudicium novum constituendum
putasse?

The power of sitting in judgement concerning his famous sacrilegious copulation
had been snatched away from the Senate. Who can believe that the Senate
thought a new court had to be established concerning his death?

Cicero's heavy-handed allusion to the Bona Dea scandal in his argument
emphasizes the public and religious consequences of Clodius' sexual mis-
adventures rather than their mechanics or private social dimension. This
theme is more appropriate than is that of incest for showing that Clodius is
a danger to the state, and so will resonate more effectively with the later
argument of the stasis of quality. The only other references to Clodius' sexual misconduct before the *extra causam* section of the speech are two passing mentions, in section 55, where Cicero notes that Clodius on the decisive
day was not accompanied by his usual prostitutes and effeminates, and in
section 59, when Cicero treats the interrogation of Clodius' slaves by his
brother Appius. This is likewise an allusion to the Bona Dea scandal. In the

extra causam section itself, there are two more references to the Bona Dea, at *Mil.* 72 ('cuius nefandum adulterium in pulvinaribus sanctissimis nobilissimae feminae comprehenderunt' whose unholy adultery they apprehended on the most sacred couches of a most noble lady') and *Mil.* 87 ('polluerat stupro sanctissimas religiones' 'he had polluted with copulation the most sacred rites'). Of the remaining four references to sexual misconduct, all in the *extra causam* section, two are very general references: *Mil.* 76, 'eum cui nihil umquam nefas fuit nec in facinore nec in libidine' ('him to whom nothing was ever unholy neither in crime nor in lust'); *Mil.* 85, 'omni nefario stupro' ('with every unspeakable copulation'), and one looks to the sort of sexual violence that Clodius would have practised on the jurors' wives and children had he lived (*Mil.* 76). There is only one reference in the speech to Clodius' alleged incest with one of his sisters, in this case with Clodia Luculli: *Mil.* 73, 'eum quem cum sorore germana nefarium stuprum fecisse L. Lucullus iuratus se quaestionibus habitis dixit comperisse' ('Lucius Lucullus, under oath, said that he had discovered through interrogation of slaves that he [sc. Clodius] had committed unspeakable copulation with his own sister'.

The clustering of allusions to unacceptable sexual conduct in the *extra causam* section makes sense, because the theme here is to prove the general notion that Clodius is a monster whose death is a benefit to the state. At the same time, this theme, like all of the vilification of Clodius that Cicero undertakes in arguing the stasis of quality, buttresses as well the argument in the question of fact; if he is the sort of person who would be guilty of one enormity, he could more easily be guilty of another.

The complete neglect of the charge that Clodius had been a *puer delicatus* is sensible; that is hardly the behaviour of a murderous monster. The relative neglect of the incest theme in favour of the Bona Dea affair is likewise understandable, since breach of the *pax deorum* is the more dangerous to the polity. The actual treatment of the Bona Dea stands in stark contrast to the fragments that we have of *In Clodium et Curionem*, a formal invective, which contains material Cicero delivered in the Senate in May of 61 in the aftermath of Clodius' scandalous acquittal on the charge of sacrilege arising from the Bona Dea affair. While in *Pro Milone* Clodius must be shown to be a monster whose death was necessary for Rome's salvation, in the earlier invective, Cicero was concerned to rally the senate in the face of the stunning acquittal of Clodius, and to do so by making his adversary appear ridiculous and impotent to his face. So the capture of Clodius in women's clothing (esp. *Clod.* FF. 21–4 Cr) had received special attention. To take one example:

tune, cum vincirentur pedes fasciis, cum calautica capiti accommodaretur, cum vix manicatam tunicam in lacertos induceres, cum strophio accurate praecingerere, in tam longo spatio numquam te Appi Claudi nepotem esse recordatus es?

Did you, when your feet were being shod in slippers, when the lady's headdress was being fitted to your head, when you were scarcely pulling the long-sleeved tunic over your upper arms, when you were being fitted with a brassiere, in so long a time did your never remember that you were a descendant of Appius Claudius? (From *Clod.* F 23 Cr (Turin Palimpsest))

Such a description can have no place in *pro Milone*. There, while the notion of effeminacy is not wholly absent, it finds only two brief mentions, and only in the context of explaining how Clodius could have plotted to murder Milo and yet been killed himself (*Mil.* 55, 'mulier inciderat in viros' ('a woman, he had fallen upon men'); 89 'ut homo effeminatus fortissimum virum conaretur occidere' ('that an effeminate person tried to kill a very brave man').

The last of our seven traditional *loci* of Greek and Roman invective that we find in *Pro Milone* is that of hostility to family, woven into a depiction of Clodius as the avaricious despoiler of all in sections 75–6:

qui Appium fratrem, hominem mihi coniunctum fidissima gratia, absentem de possessione fundi deiecit; qui parietem sic per vestibulum sororis instituit ducere, sic agere fundamenta ut sororem non modo vestibulo privaret sed omni aditu et limine. quamquam haec quidem iam tolerabilia videbantur, etsi aequabiliter in rem publicam, in privatos, in longinquos, in propinquos, in alienos, in suos inruebat

He who expelled his absent brother Appius, a man joined to me by the most faithful kindness, from possession of a farm, he who built a wall through his sister's forecourt, who constructed his foundations in such a way that he deprived her forecourt not only of light but of access and an entry way. Although these things at any rate then seemed tolerable, although he was attacking equally the republic, private citizens, distant acquaintances, close relations, strangers, his own people

This *locus* is thus a grace note within the themes of avarice and plunder which occur almost exclusively in Cicero's pleading of the qualitative status of the speech in sections 72–91.

In summary, this analysis demonstrates the way in which Cicero uses the traditional material of invective in a highly selective and disciplined way that subordinates the invective goal of humiliating an enemy to the need to make arguments of probative value in a judicial context. Cicero excludes *loci* that he had earlier used against Clodius in different contexts, even though these could more richly portray his old enemy as despicable. He does so because the content of these *loci* would distract from the probative picture that he wants to paint of Clodius as murderer and monster. Clodius would hardly be made more fearsome by vivid description of his effeminate deportment at the Bona Dea, or about his correct and detailed women's garb on that occasion. His pretentious posture of moral superiority, so mercilessly attacked in *In Clodium et Curionem* and in *De Haruspicum Responso*, would here make him too morally aware and too subtle for the portrait that Cicero wants to paint. Financial embarrassment might likewise place Clodius in a position of relative weakness, and so might detract from his horrific and monstrous aspect. Similarly, the taking of bribes, while sordid, is hardly good monster material. Finally, illustrations of oratorical ineptitude would be more spitefully gratifying than apt for characterising the walking enormity who is the Clodius of our speech.

Of the *loci* used, the most important for the question of fact is the most broadly distributed throughout the speech, that of Clodius' *crudelitas*; he had a predisposition and an explicit intent towards murderous violence. The *loci* that cluster with *crudelitas*, namely aiming at tyranny, plunder, and avarice, are largely grouped in the torrent of abuse that characterises Clodius as a monster in the issue of quality in sections 72–91. Unworthiness of family is woven into *crudelitas*, as hostility to family is a grace note in the characterisation of cruelty and avaricious plunder. Even sexual misconduct, an easy target, is focused upon the sacrilege of the Bona Dea, and thus upon the harm that Clodius has done to the public religious life of the community, rather than upon the theme of Clodius' alleged incest with his sisters or his youthful career as a *puer delicatus*. Further, the Bona Dea scandal is deliberately treated with an emphasis that makes Clodius seem dangerous rather than ridiculous. And in the one mention of incest, Cicero adduces the sworn testimony of Lucullus, and so emphasises the judicial context and distances the tone from one of free-standing, formal invective.

Finally, we may note the pressure exerted on Cicero by the fact that the generous use of invective *loci* risks making his speech converge upon formal invective, and so moving the audience to perceive it as an exercise in which veracity, or plausibility, is not a primary concern. This leads us back to the quotation with which we began. At the very place where the *loci* of invective are most thickly clustered, forming a veritable torrent of abuse in the *extra causam* section (72–91), the orator feels the need explicitly to assert that he is telling the truth (78b). That assertion of Cicero's veracity underscores the tension between the necessity for probative argument in a judicial speech and the necessity to incorporate into that argument the *loci* of a genre in which the truth of allegations is of only secondary importance.[28]

---

[28] For helpful discussion and other kindnesses, I must thank Andrew Riggsby, Anthony Corbeill, and (last, but not least) the editors. Errors are my own.

8

Perorations

MICHAEL WINTERBOTTOM

Prehistory

The peroration[1] was the last part of an oration, and typically proem, narrative, and proofs would have preceded it. This articulation of a speech had been canonical for centuries before the time of Cicero. It is made clear, for didactic purposes, throughout a display oration by the sophist Gorgias,[2] in which the hero Palamedes defends himself before his peers on a charge of betraying the Greek army to the Trojans. Towards the end (33), he says: 'It remains to speak to you, judges, about yourselves; then I shall cease my defence.' The necessary indication of the approaching end is unsubtly given. But: 'When a trial takes place in a popular court, appeal to pity, prayers, and the intercession of friends are of service; but before you, the first of the Greeks, it is not right to try to persuade you by invoking the help of friends, or by prayers or appeals to pity.' Similarly, in 37, he says in the last words of the speech that 'to recall briefly what has been argued earlier at length is reasonable before a "low" jury; but the first of the Greeks should not be asked to pay attention or to remember what has been said'. These disclaimers show that Gorgias was well aware, and expected his pupils to be well aware, that the ordinary rhetorical teaching was that a peroration should contain two elements, emotional appeal and recapitulation. Palamedes avoids the usual methods only because of the high rank of his judges.

But equally significant is what Palamedes *does* say. He prefaces two parallel sections (28–32 and 33–6) by saying that he will speak 'to you, judges, about me' and then 'to you about yourselves'. Gorgias would have regarded

I am most grateful to Professor Donald Russell and to Dr Catherine Steel for commenting on a draft of this chapter, and to Professor Russell for permitting me to make use of his translation of Quintilian (Loeb Classical Library, 2001) in advance of publication.

[1] Called *conclusio* and *peroratio* by Latin writers, who also naturalize the Greek term as *epilogus*.
[2] *Palamedes*. Printed e.g. in Diels–Kranz, *Die Fragmente der Vorsokratiker*, ii.294–303. Date uncertain, but Gorgias died *c.*380 BC.

these two sections taken together as forming the peroration. In the first, Palamedes dilates on his own excellent character[3] and his services to the Greeks. In the second, he warns the judges that if they convict him unjustly, they will destroy their reputations for ever. 'On you depends the outcome of the trial. No mistake could be more important than one made here. If you give an unjust verdict, you will not merely be wronging me and my parents; you will have it on your consciences that you have done something ungodly, unjust, unlawful, in killing an ally, one who is of use to you, a benefactor of Greece, a Greek though you are yourselves Greek, for no provable crime and with no plausible motive' (36). Of course, whatever Palamedes may say, there is some appeal to the emotions in both passages,[4] and the last words cited have some flavour of recapitulation. But Gorgias is showing his pupils that there is more to an epilogue than recapitulation and emotional appeal arising out of the specific case. There is, or may be, need both to emphasize the general character of the defendant and to stress to the judges that their own interests are involved in the outcome of the trial.

When, centuries later, around 80 BC, Cicero came to write his youthful *De Inventione*,[5] he passed on from some Greek source the recommendation assumed in the *Palamedes*, that a peroration should contain a recapitulation and arousal of pity. His schema only becomes tripartite because anger is given equal weight with pity. The logical step was to produce a twofold scheme, where recapitulation was balanced by arousal of emotion in general; and that is what we find in Cicero's later *Partitiones Oratoriae*, as well as in later writers like Quintilian. I shall not go into the complications of rhetorical theory on this matter,[6] as I intend to discuss Cicero's actual perorations without much attention to the precepts he or others laid down for them. It is, however, worth bearing in mind that the rhetoricians often talk of 'amplification' in this area. They are not consistent in their use of the word, and there is much overlap with the arousal of anger. But the idea that the peroration did well to widen the focus,[7] to put the case in a fuller

---

[3] The topic has been briefly alluded to at 15 in the treatment of the conjectural arguments.

[4] In the first, note esp. 28 'I beg you, then . . .'; see below, pp. 224–6.

[5] 1.98; cf. the contemporary *Ad Herennium* 2.47, where Caplan's notes in the Loeb edn. will be found very helpful. See further *Part. Orat.* 52; Quint. *Inst.* 6.1.1. There is much more detail in H. Lausberg, *Handbook of Literary Rhetoric* (Leiden, 1998) §§ 431–42; R. Volkmann, *Die Rhetorik der Griechen und Römer in systematischer Uebersicht*, 2nd edn. (Leipzig, 1885; repr. Hildesheim, 1963) 262–84 remains valuable.

[6] Nor shall I point out in the speeches examples of the *loci* listed in the *De Inventione* (1.101–5 arousing anger, 106–9 arousing pity). See e.g. D. H. Berry's notes on *Sull.* 88–91 (*Cicero Pro P. Sulla Oratio*, Cambridge, 1996) and T. B. L. Webster (ed.) *M. Tulli Ciceronis Pro L. Flacco Oratio* (Oxford, 1931), p. xix.

[7] Cf. the suggestive gloss of Webster, ibid.: 'transference of the discourse from the particular to the general.'

context, will be helpful. We have seen Gorgias' Palamedes doing that, and we will find Cicero often doing it too.

The Beginning of the End

Many a restive audience has taken heart at the utterance of the blessed word 'finally'. We have seen Palamedes saying 'then I shall cease my defence'. And a peroration in Cicero may politely announce its coming. It is natural that the announcement should ring out loud and clear in the *Pro Milone*, a speech that was worked up for publication after a less than successful *actio*. Cicero took the opportunity to make it, amongst other things, a model for the aspiring student.[8] So: 'I have now said quite enough about the case, and have perhaps strayed too far outside it. What remains except for me to beg and beseech you, judges, to accord this most brave of men the pity for which he is not himself asking . . . ?' (92). This brief transition, while alluding to the preceding passage *extra causam* (Milo's killing of Clodius was for the good of the state), also establishes the strategy of the peroration: it is Cicero, not the stoical or brutish Milo, who is to shed the tears. The turn to address to the judges, who are to make their decision after the speech is over, is characteristic. So is the tone of supplication, and the allusion to the arousal of pity. No one could doubt that the peroration was beginning.

Even in this case, which looks so cut and dried,[9] it is to be observed that the long preceding section *extra causam* could be seen as parallel to the account of Palamedes' services which Gorgias seemed to include in his peroration. In the *Pro Quinctio* the orator announces the end of the speech *after* the recapitulation.[10] It will be more profitable to look at what in other speeches *follows* a clear indication that the end is nigh. In the *Pro Caelio* the words that herald the peroration precede a summary of Caelius' career,[11] putting it in the best light possible; only after that do we have the final emotional

---

[8] The articulation of the whole speech is pedantically marked. It is characteristic that *incipientem* ('beginning') appears in the second line, and 'sed finis sit' ('but let there be an end') in the last line but six.

[9] I owe much to Lynn Fotheringham's insistence, in many discussions, that marking the structure of Ciceronian orations is not a task to be lightly undertaken.

[10] 91 'Nunc causa perorata res ipsa . . . cogere videtur ut te . . . obsecret . . . P. Quinctius' ('The case itself has been pleaded through; now it seems to make it imperative that Publius Quinctius should beseech you').

[11] 70 'Dicta est a me causa, iudices, et perorata' ('I have spoken the case, judges, and pleaded it through'). The last word is not (I suppose) to be regarded as a sort of didactic pun. Cf. *Quinct.* 91 (cited in n. 10), *Font.* 37. The account of Caelius' career may be thought of as a kind of recapitulation, in the sense that it corresponds to the defence of Caelius against the criticisms of the accusers starting at 3.

appeal to the judges to save the man (77–80). In the *Pro Plancio*[12] the indicator precedes a statement (that becomes highly emotional) of Plancius' services (not to the state but) to Cicero. In the *Pro Sestio*, the indicator demands that we should regard the address of exhortation to the youth of Rome as part of the peroration. In both speeches critics have delayed the conclusion until the call to pity proper. These cases may help us to identify the start of the peroration where there is no indicator to help us. In the *Pro Cluentio*, for instance, Peterson[13] marked the conclusion as starting at 195, while himself admitting that its first sentence is closely tied up with the one that precedes. We should think rather of marking the break at 188, where Cicero starts on a summary of the misdeeds of Sassia which may well be taken as recapitulation, and which is self-consciously introduced by a reference back to the start of the narration. In the *Pro Flacco*,[14] there is a very marked change from detail to general principles at 94. In the *Pro Rabirio Postumo* we should look to 41, where a wide-ranging encomium of Caesar takes over from details of the case. In these places we see perorations starting with widely different kinds of what Cicero will have counted as amplification. In other places where there is no indicator, we are not helped either by any great change of topic or tone. Leeman,[15] placing the start of the epilogue of the *Pro Murena* at 83, himself points to elements of pathos in the preceding appeal to Cato and to the judges; and the crucial point that the defendant must be acquitted so that there will be two consuls on 1 January is made with all power in that passage. Again, in the *Pro Sulla*, Berry well remarks that 'from § 69 an emotional climax is gradually built up, culminating in the grand *conclusio* of §§ 86–93'. The sudden change of tone in the *Pro Caelio*, when Cicero goes straight from the droll scene in the baths to the epilogue, 'leaving the case quite suddenly,

---

[12] *Planc.* 95 'nunc venio ad illud extremum' ('Now I come to that final point'); Holden puts the break at 100. *Sest.* 136: 'sed ut extremum habeat aliquid oratio mea, et ut ego ante dicendi finem faciam quam vos me tam attente audiendi' ('But so that my oration may have some end, and so that I stop speaking before you stop listening to me so attentively'); P. MacKendrick, *The Speeches of Cicero: Context, Law, Rhetoric* (London, 1995) 204 puts the break at 144, admittedly strongly marked as closural: 'plura etiam dicere parantem horum aspectus . . . repressit' ('I was going on to say yet more, but the sight of these people held me back').

[13] See his edition of the speech (London, 1899), pp. lv and 260–1. In 188 'principio orationis meae' ('at the start of my speech') refers back to 12.

[14] 'sed quid ego de epistulis Falcidi aut de Androne Sextilio aut de Deciani censu tam diu disputo, de salute omnium nostrum, . . . de summa re publica taceo?' ('But why do I go on so long about the letters of Falcidius and Sextilius Andro and the census of Decianus, but say nothing of the safety of us all . . . and the highest interests of the state?'); cf. *Dom.* 142 'revocate iam animos vestros ab hac subtili nostra disputatione ad universam rem publicam' ('bring back your minds now from this subtle analysis of mine to the state as a whole').

[15] *Entretiens Hardt* 28 (1982) 224. For the importance of 1 January see Quint. *Inst.* 6.1.35; Cicero is, significantly, returning to a point made early on in the speech, at 4. J. Adamietz (*Marcus Tullius Cicero Pro Murena* (Darmstadt, 1989), p. 238) rightly calls the section 78–83a 'related in sense' to what follows. On *Sull.*, Berry, p. 48.

wrapped in mystery, with the jury rocking in inextinguishable laughter' (Austin on 70–80) is highly unusual. We should not feel that the start of a peroration is always to be precisely pinned down.

Recapitulation

Cicero once said that recapitulation is less often needed in defence cases than in accusation.[16] It certainly plays an undemonstrative part in his own (mostly defence) speeches. He soon learnt to do better than the bald point by point summary found in the early *Pro Quinctio*,[17] where five whole sections (86–90) retail the heads almost dispassionately. He is already doing better in the last lines of the *Pro Caecina* (104). And he had after all given readers of the *De Inventione* hints as to how to avoid suspicion and boredom by varying the approach.[18] In the mighty last paragraph of the Fifth Verrine he uses the invocation of one god after another to recall to the judges the shrines that Verres has ransacked. When this degree of subtlety is being employed, the Greek term *anamnesis*, 'reminding', is more appropriate than 'recapitulation'. The rhetorical question of *Rosc. Am.* 152, comparing the accuser and the defendant, in no way grates; but it deftly summarizes a main contention of the speech. In *Sull.* 86–7 a solemn oath introduces an effective restatement of the crucial part that the orator himself plays in the proof of Sulla's innocence. And when it came to the point it was not always the formal arguments that were going to have the greatest effect on the judges. The *Pro Murena* ends with words (90) that give a final expression of the main theme of the speech: the state is in danger, and Murena is the man to lead it to safety. That is, in its way, 'recapitulation'.

Pity: Making a Scene

Those last lines of the *Pro Murena* spoke of the 'conspiracy now shaking the Republic', and the orator had been much concerned in this speech to arouse fear in his audience. There was room in the peroration for all kinds of emotion: Cicero lists fifteen in the *Orator* (131). But he stresses there

---

[16] *Part. Orat.* 59–60 (though contrast Quint. *Inst.* 6.1.8).

[17] The laborious variety of the verbs ('I have shown . . . I have told you . . . I have demonstrated . .' etc.) does not much help.

[18] 1.98–100. For the use of 'figures' to vary the impact, see e.g. Quint. *Inst.* 6.1.2–4, singling out for praise *Verr.* 5.136 as well as the invocation of 184–9; Anon. Seg. 221.

(130) that he was a past master in the field of pity: others would leave to him the last of a series of speeches, so that the judges would vote under the sway of his pathetic appeals. This was connected with his almost constant practice of avoiding accusations; for, says the *Partitiones Oratoriae* in its simple way,[19] it is for the accuser to make the judge angry, but for the defence counsel to make him feel pity. How does Cicero do it?

Quintilian[20] notes that orators could produce tears by actions as well as by words. He does not mention Cicero in this context, and some of the (accuser's) ploys he talks of sound un-Ciceronian:[21] showing a bloody sword, bones taken from wounds, blood-stained clothes; unbinding wounds; exhibiting a picture of the act complained of. Still, Cicero is not above forwarding the defence of Rabirius by pointing to 'these scars full on his face which he received when fighting for the state'[22] (just as in the same case Cicero's colleague Hortensius spoke of 'my scars', no doubt in a speech put into Rabirius' mouth). As to what Quintilian calls the 'established practice'[23] of 'bringing forward the defendants themselves unkempt and unsightly, together with their children and parents', Cicero follows in the footsteps of orators both Athenian and Roman. He represents Cluentius' wicked mother overjoyed to see the sight of the man's 'shabbiness and mourning and unkemptness' (*Cluent.* 192). But, as Quintilian may imply, the disarray could extend to friends and relations brought in to add to the pathos. Near the end of the speech for Sestius (144–5), Cicero represents himself as halted in his tracks by the sight not only of Sestius himself but of his young son ('looking at me with eyes full of tears'), Milo 'in a defendant's shabby clothes', Lentulus 'in this pitifully unkempt and shabby state'; and, in sum, the disarray of all these excellent persons.[24]

[19] 14–15, with some qualification in 58. I say little about the arousal of anger in Cicero's perorations. But his tendency to turn defence into attack means that *indignatio* is not lacking. See for instance his assaults on Naevius in *Quinct.* (e.g. 94), on Chrysogonus in *Rosc. Am.* (e.g. 146–7), and on the Gauls in *Font.* (e.g. 30–2). Conversely, the peroration of *Verr.* 5 merges pathos with anger (for Cicero thinks of himself as defending the Sicilians by prosecuting Verres).

[20] *Inst.* 6.1.30–32; for the sword cf. 48.

[21] It may be remarked that Quintilian mentions (*Inst.* 6.1.49) two instances of Cicero combating such methods when employed by others (including a preserved passage, *Rab. Perd.* 25).

[22] 36, '*hasce* ore adverso pro re publica cicatrices'. For Hortensius see H. Malcovati, *Oratorum Romanorum Fragmenta*, 4th edn. (Turin, 1976) 322. Add Quint. *Inst.* 6.1.21.

[23] Quint. *Inst.* 6.1.30 ('institutum'). Documented (for children) by Berry on *Sull.* 88 line 14. Cf. also Asconius § 18 Clark, p. 23 Stangl: 'ipse quoque Scaurus dixit pro se ac magnopere iudices movit et squalore et lacrimis et aedilitatis effusae memoria ac favore populari ac praecipue paternae auctoritatis recordatione' ('Scaurus too spoke in his own defence, and greatly influenced the judges by his unkemptness, his tears, the memory of his lavish aedileship, his popularity with the people, and especially the recollection of his father's authority'). That reminds us that it was not only Cicero who used these methods at this period.

[24] This exhibition, it should be added, Cicero represents as being put on not for Sestius, but 'for me and me only' (145; cf. 146 'iis quos meo nomine sordidatos videtis', 'those whom you see shabbily clothed for my sake'). The whole of 144–7 aims to arouse pity for Cicero as much as for Sestius.

Here they were then, actually in court, looking grubby. Relatives were preferred, the closer the better. Apparently it worked. 'Many in judging have forgiven the sins of children because they pity their parents', remarks Cicero in the *Pro Cluentio* (195). Caelius' father was present to support his son's case: 'Keep before your eyes as well the afflicted father here, bowed down with age: Caelius is his only son, his prop and stay.... Never let it be thought that you have flung aside an old man whose hopes are well-nigh done..' (79–80, tr. Austin). His public show of grief would have been the more effective (and necessary) considering that Cicero has told us earlier that the accusers had made the father part of the charge against the son, as being insufficiently high-ranking, and as having been ill-treated by him (3). He might have been angry with his son in the past: now, at least he is ready to help save him. Even defunct parents can be employed. Murena's father was dead,[25] but rates a mention in the epilogue (especially as his son had served under him in the East); his mother seems not to be in court, but Cicero pictures her as one of the people to whom Murena would not be able to turn if he is convicted (so too his brother, still in Transalpine Gaul). Children were excellent, though potentially dangerous,[26] pawns in the game. Cicero tells us in the *Orator* (131) how he 'carried a baby in his arms during a peroration,[27] and in another case filled the Forum with lamentation by raising a small child in the air'. Best of all, perhaps, a sister who is a Vestal Virgin. The fortunate brother was Fonteius.[28] The girl 'holds her brother in her embrace',[29] and implores the protection of the Roman people on his behalf. Cicero warns of a danger: her tears may put out the sacred fire. She holds out to the judges 'her suppliant hands, the same which she holds out to the immortal gods on your behalf'. She shares the last words of the speech with the frightful Gauls.

All this is (in Quintilian's terms) action, though of course complementing rather than taking the place of the words without which we would not know of them at all. The virgin is apparently there in person, embracing her brother and weeping as the orator describes, even choreographs, her actions. The words, here as elsewhere, dwell much on weeping, and it is

---

[25] See *Mur.* 90 (his *imago* had been mentioned in 88). For his son's service under him in Asia, see 11–12; for the mother, 88; for the brother, 89. For another dead father, *Font.* 41, 48.

[26] See Quint. *Inst.* 6.1.41, 46–7. But even an old man could cause problems: *Cluent.* 57–9, recalled by Quint. *Inst.* 6.1.41.

[27] Cf. Quint. *Inst.* 6.1.47: words spoken 'to a corpulent litigant, whose opponent, a child, had been paraded round the judges by his advocate: "What am I to do? *I* can't tote you around." ' More children of various ages: *Sull.* 88; *Flacc.* 106; *Sest.* 144, 146.

[28] He also has a mother: *Font.* 46. For the sister, 46–9.

[29] 46 'complexa teneat'. There is much talk of *complexus* on these occasions. See e.g. *Font.* 46; *Sest.* 146; *Planc.* 99, 100, 102; G.O. Hutchinson, *Cicero's Correspondence* (Oxford, 1998) 30 n. 5. Add Quint. *Inst.* 6.1.42.

not to be imagined that the tears failed to flow. The orator would himself often oblige. But others followed suit. Milo,[30] unwilling to play the game, is unusual. A typical, if extreme, tableau ends the speech for Plancius (104): 'I am prevented from saying more by your tears'[31] (those of the president of the court) 'and yours, members of the jury, not merely mine, which give me sudden hope amid all my fears that you will act to save him as you acted in saving me, for these your tears remind me of those you so often and so profusely shed for me.' Such an ending is the more striking considering that we learned earlier in the speech (83) that the accuser had reminded the jury of Cicero's habit of arousing pity, and had even suggested that Cicero had set exile as the penalty in his law on bribery precisely in order to make his epilogues the more effective.

In the *Pro Fonteio*, we saw, the virgin holds out suppliant hands. There is much talk elsewhere of supplication,[32] and it would be interesting to know if it went beyond gestures with the hand. At another passage of the same speech (41) it is purely metaphorical: Cicero lists things that 'supplicate' for the defendant, including his ancient family and his career. Again, Cicero seems to draw back from making Caelius' father fall down before the judges: 'Here he is, gentlemen, a suppliant for your compassion, subservient to your power; see him prostrate before you—I will not say, prostrate at your feet, but before your instincts, your sensibilities' (*Cael.* 79, tr. Austin). Cicero goes on: 'raise him up',[33] but he probably did not need this attention literally, any more than did Cluentius when Cicero asks his judges (*Cluent.* 200) to 'raise up now at last this your suppliant'. That a full physical supplication was not unknown to Romans is implied by a scene in the *Pro Quinctio* (96–7), where Quinctius is described as lying 'for a long time' prostrate at the feet of Naevius' friends, beseeching them by the immortal gods, or again taking Naevius' hand[34] in tears and begging him by the ashes of his dead brother. But we cannot be sure that such scenes were enacted, or even physically possible, in the conditions of a court in the Ciceronian period. Under the Empire Quintilian is not averse to 'lying prostrate and embracing the knees', where the circumstances make this appropriate, though he characteristically points out the dangers of saying things like 'he stretches out towards your knees his suppliant hands' where nothing of the sort is happening.[35]

---

[30] See the remarks of Quintilian, *Inst.* 6.1.24–5, 27.

[31] On the delivery of such words (parallels in Hutchinson, *Cicero's Correspondence*, 32 n. 8), see Quint. *Inst.* 11.3.173 (on *Mil.* 105).   [32] Even of a young child at *Flacc.* 106.

[33] *sustentate*; the word for 'raise' in *Cluent.* 200 is *levate* (cf. 202 *sublevatis*; *Arch.* 31, 'humanitate vestra levatus': 'raised up by your kindness'). All three verbs are regularly used metaphorically.

[34] 'manum . . . in propinquorum bonis proscribendis exercitatam' ('took the hand so practised in seizing the property of his relations'). Cicero perhaps recalls a supreme moment in Homer (*Iliad* 24.477–9).

[35] *Inst.* 6.1.34 and 42. Discussing gesture in supplicatory passages, though, Quintilian only refers to the use of hands (11.3.86, 114–15). 9.4.11 is not concerned with oratory.

It would seem then that Ciceronian talk of supplication is part of the quasi-religious language that will be discussed below, rather than a stage direction for extravagant appeals to the judges. But the importance of what the ancients called *actio* (which covered a wide range of non-verbal topics) in epilogues, as in all other parts of a speech, cannot be ignored. Quintilian concentrates in particular on the voice: the peroration, when it aims to arouse emotion, needs a tone suitable to the emotion concerned; for instance (11.3.170), pity requires 'inflections of voice and a tearful sweetness, which is both most likely to touch the heart and also very natural: you find bereaved parents and widows lamenting in a kind of singing tone at the actual funeral' (tr. Russell). Here, as so often, oratory aims to give an artistic version of what nature produces unaided.

Pity: 'I Beg You'

That brings us back from actions to words. The orator has to ensure that he speaks words he can best act,[36] as well as that he accompanies his words with effective *actio*. Some words recur obsessively in perorations. Cognates of *miser* are especially prominent. The defendant is wretched, and therefore deserves the pity of the judges. Thus Fonteius is 'misero atque innocenti' (*Font.* 45, 'pitiful and innocent'), and his *miseriae* move the people of Narbo (46). But his relatives are to be pitied too, his mother (46, 'lectissimae miserrimaeque feminae': 'a woman most distinguished and most pitiful'), and, of course, his Vestal sister (47, 'cui miserae quod praesidium, quod solacium reliquum est hoc amisso?': 'poor thing, what protection, what solace is left to her if she loses him?'). Then there is the orator himself.[37] In the speech for Milo, Cicero exclaims 'o me miserum, o me infelicem!' [38] (102, 'how pitiful and unfortunate I am!') at the thought that he whom Milo had saved might not be able to save Milo; for, as we shall see, the orator is an important personage in his own right in these last passages of a speech. A little later it is Rome that deserves pity if it loses such

---

[36] Note the references to drama in Quintilian's account of the epilogue: *Inst.* 6.1.26, 49 ('scenes' of melodramatic displays in court); add 6.2.35, part of the (Ciceronian) topic on the need for an orator to be moved if he is to move others.

[37] Cf., divertingly, *Cluent.* 199, where Cicero asks the judges to bear in mind that a single woman is opposing 'the trouble taken by all these people, and, together with that, the burden I have borne in pleading this case from start to finish quite alone, in the old manner'.

[38] For exclamations with 'o' cf. (besides *Mil.* 94) e.g. *Planc.* 99 'o acerbam . . . o rem . . . o reliquos', *Sull.* 91 (five repetitions). Generally Doreen Innes and Michael Winterbottom, *Sopatros the Rhetor* (London, 1988) 10 and 11 (the 'ὦ style'); more will be found in that vicinity relevant to our topic, especially on the Greek front, which I have had largely to neglect here. Exclamation, like *geminatio* (below, n. 62), is typical of the *elocutio* of the emotive grand style appropriate to a peroration.

a citizen (105). Similarly, it is not only Murena who is pitiful (*Mur.* 88, 'quo se miser vertet?': 'where will the wretched man turn?'); the whole picture painted by Cicero is calculated to call for the judges' pity (90, 'quae si acerba, si misera, si luctuosa sunt, si alienissima a mansuetudine et misericordia vestra, iudices': 'if all this is bitter, pitiful, grievous, quite alien from your kindness and sense of pity, judges'). For the *miser* suffering *miseriae* the imperative is obvious: *miseremini*.[39]

'Your kindness and sense of pity.' In Athens there had been an altar to Pity,[40] symbolizing the mercy that the citizens traditionally showed towards the oppressed, and orators could appeal in its name. In Rome, one had to hope that the judges would feel the same fine sentiment. Cicero usually refers to their fairness, humanity, and clemency as a fact to be assumed.[41] When, defending Rabirius Postumus (45), he says: 'you who, I am confident, are entirely fair', that strikes a note of doubt confirmed in the next section ('but if you now choose to forget your kindness'). Again, in the speech for Roscius of Ameria (150), he speaks of the judges' 'former goodness and pity': 'If that is still there, we can yet be saved; but if the cruelty now at large in the state has made your hearts too harder and more relentless (but surely that cannot be), then all is up.' Such ploys may merely be part of the process of manipulating the judges; but they remind us that a jury could not always be relied upon to be sympathetic.

Whatever their bias, the judges were all-important.[42] The defendant comes to them as though to the gods,[43] for they have, for the moment, a godlike power of life and death, or at least the making or breaking of a career. He flees to them as to a 'refuge'.[44] He comes, literally or metaphorically, on bended knee.[45] It is appropriate, then, that orators should employ

---

[39] Used in triple anaphora in the last words (106) of the *Pro Flacco*.

[40] See my note on [Quintilian,] *Decl. Min.* 292.3.

[41] *aequitas*: *Cluent.* 202 'you who are fair (*aequi*) to all', a theme of the epilogue of that speech (cf. 199–200), taking up the proem 5–7. *humanitas*: *Balb.* 62. *misericordia*: *Cael.* 79; Cicero reminds the judges of their own fathers (another (cf. n. 34) parallel with Homeric pathos: *Iliad* 24.486). *Sull.* 87 ('I am as capable of feeling pity (*misericors*), judges, as you') has a special point, for Cicero had argued that he was cruel only to be kind during the conspiracy; cf. 92 'in your kindness (*mansuetudo*) and humanity'. All of this was (hoped to be) part of the *natura* of the judges: *Quinct.* 91, 'that you should act in accordance with your nature and your good will (*bonitas*)'; *Cluent.* 200.

[42] *Mur.* 83 'huiusce rei potestas omnis in vobis sita est' ('all the power in this matter resides in you'), picking up 2, cited in the next note; *Cluent.* 200 (*soli*); *Dom.* 142 (*solis*).

[43] *Cluent.* 195 ('quosdam alios deos', 'other "gods" ', picking up the reference to actual gods in 194); cf. *Mur.* 2 ('cum omnis deorum immortalium potestas aut translata sit ad vos aut certe communicata vobiscum', 'since all the power of the immortal gods has been transferred to you or at least shared with you'). Cf. *Lig.* 38, 'homines enim ad deos nulla re propius accedunt quam salutem hominibus dando' ('for men nowhere come nearer to the gods than in giving men their safety'), pointed in a speech addressed to Caesar.

[44] *Rosc. Am.* 150, *Mur.* 87 (and, in a proem, *Cluent.* 7). For flight see *Quinct.* 98, *Sull.* 88 ('supplex ad vos, iudices, confugit', 'he flees as a suppliant to you, judges').

[45] Some have connected *supplex* with *(sub)plicare*, 'bend'.

towards judges the language that one might use in addressing the gods. 'Qua re oro obtestorque vos, iudices' ('Wherefore I implore and beseech you, judges').[46] The words may be attributed to the client: 'orat vos Habitus, iudices, et flens obsecrat' ('Cluentius, judges, implores and tearfully entreats you'),[47] or to a relative: 'hic vos orat, iudices, parvus' ('this small boy implores you, judges').[48] Cicero tells the judges that he strives for the acquittal of Plancius (*Planc.* 102) 'not with money, ... not with authority, not with influence, but with *prayers*,[49] with tears, with pity', and joins with the anxious father in those prayers: 'we two fathers pray on behalf of one son.' It hardly needs to be demonstrated that such vocabulary is redolent of religious usage.[50]

It is natural then that Cicero should, where he can, bring his cases into closer relation with the divine. This is not true only of perorations. He starts his speech for Murena in this way (and the handbooks remind us that prologue and epilogue share much in the way of tone and topic).[51] He had prayed to the gods when announcing the election of Murena to the consulship, and he now prays both to them and to the judges that Murena may keep the office. This is balanced in the epilogue by separate mentions of Jupiter (88) and the rites of Juno Sospita, in which consuls played a role (90). I have already mentioned the final paragraph of the Fifth Verrine. Similarly, in the peroration of the *De Domo* Cicero addresses the gods (144 'te, Capitoline, ... teque, Iuno Regina, et te ... Minerva ... precor atque quaeso ... vosque ... patrii penates ... obtestor ...': 'You Capitoline Jupiter ... and you Queen Juno ... and you Minerva ... I beg and beseech ... and I implore you, the family gods of our fathers') before rounding off the speech with entreaty

---

[46] *Cael.* 78. Similar phrases (also employing *obsecro*) in *Rab. Perd.* 35 (adding *hortor*), *Mur.* 86, *Sest.* 147, *Planc.* 104 (addressed to the president of the court), *Rab. Post.* 46, *Mil.* 105.

[47] *Cluent.* 201. Similarly *Quinct.* 91 (also 99), *Rab. Perd.* 37, *Mur.* 87 (soon after use of the first person); add *Rosc.* 144 (Roscius to Chrysogonus).

[48] *Sull.* 89. Similarly *Flacc.* 106, *Planc.* 102.

[49] Note Cicero's treatment of Fonteius' Vestal sister (*Font.* 46) 'quae pro vobis ... tot annos in dis immortalibus *placandis* occupata est ut ea nunc pro salute sua fratrisque sui animos vestros *placare* possit' ('who has been occupied for so many years placating the immortal gods on your behalf that she can now placate your minds to win her safety and that of her brother'); cf. her prayers to the gods in 48, to the judges in 49.

[50] Cf. too the ambivalence of the concept of *fides*. See R. Heinze, '*Fides*', in E. Burck (ed.), *Vom Geist des Römertums*, 3rd edn. (Stuttgart, 1960) 70–3. In Cicero e.g. *Verr.* 5.172, *Font.* 40 and 46, *Caec.* 103 ('in vestra fide ac *religione*', 'in your sense of loyalty and duty'), *Mur.* 86 'vestram fidem obtestatur' ('he implores your protection', looking back to 2), *Arch.* 31.

[51] Quintilian is very conscious of the common ground between the two: see *Inst.* 4.1.13–14, 28; 6.1.9, 12–13, 51; 6.2.20. See also Anon. Seg. 19–20, 27. But both stress that the epilogue is more emotional. We have already seen examples of an epilogue picking up the prologue, something that helps to give a satisfying sense of closure (see nn. 41 (where a good deal more could have been said about echoes of the proem in the epilogue of *Cluent.*), 42, and 50); see also below, nn. 53 and 63. Notes 11, 15, 43, and 44 are also relevant.

to the high priests who will decide the case: 'quaeso obtestorque vos, pontifices, . . .' (147 'I beseech and implore you, priests, [to restore me to my
house]'). Gods and judges are put on much the same level, and talked to or
about in comparable terms.

Widening: 'To Speak to You, Judges, About Yourselves'

Gorgias made Palamedes warn his judges of the dangers they would run if
they came to an unjust decision (*Palam.* 35–6). We have seen Cicero very
concerned to make the judges pity his client. Nor is he above flattering
them.[52] But he will also, like Palamedes, stress to them the significance of
their own role. The importance of the case is deduced from the ramifying
consequences of the judges' verdict.[53] Even a minor case may be asserted
to be of wider import: Caecina is said to bring to the judges 'a cause of significance to all' (103). That of Roscius of Ameria is widened to cover the
rights of the sons of the proscribed in general (152). As for the judges of
Verres, 'all Roman citizens, present or absent, . . . think that . . . their whole
liberty is concerned in your votes' (5.172); 'today the eyes of everyone are
upon each and every one of us' (175).

   But the case may be important to the judges in a different sense. As
Quintilian remarks (*Inst.* 6.1.13), 'Cicero says in his accusation of Verres that
the bad reputation of the courts can be positively mended if the defendant
is found guilty'; and we find Cicero threatening the judges that the wrong
decision will cause a change in the composition of the courts.[54] Again,
special circumstances about the present panel may be alluded to. The last
words of *Pro Milone* stress not only the wisdom of the judges but the fact
that Pompey chose them (105). Cicero openly implies in the last section of
the speech for Sulla (93) that some procedural device had been used to
produce a jury inclined to vote against the defendant. He asks them to
show by their impartial acquittal of Sulla that they are not the sort of jury
that his opponents had intended. Again, an individual judge of particular
interest may be mentioned.[55] In the *Pro Archia*, the very last words (32)

---

[52] Thus *Mur.* 83: they are 'the most honourable and the most wise of men, chosen from the
most distinguished orders'.

[53] *Mur.* 83–4 ('you hold and steer the whole state in this case . . . in this case you will vote not
about the salvation of Murena alone, but about your own salvation'); similarly *Flacc.* 94 ('the highest interests of the state') and 99 (a long list of the things at stake); *Sest.* 147. The importance of
the law *de vi* is stressed in *Cael.* 70 for a different reason: Caelius is being charged under a law
grotesquely out of proportion to the circumstances. This takes up the topic of the proem (1).

[54] *Verr.* 5.177–8. Quintilian is referring to *Verr.* I. 43.

[55] Cf. also the personal appeal to Flavus in *Planc.* 104.

point to the fact that the president is the orator's brother Quintus, who more than most should listen respectfully to his arguments. In defending Cluentius, Cicero, naming various supporters of his case, turns 'with a greater sense of embarrassment' to another individual, Publius Volumnius, 'for you are a judge in the case of Cluentius' (198).

Widening: Friends and Services

Palamedes rejected 'the help of friends' as a means of swaying the judges; but his paragraph 'concerning myself' (28–32) expatiated on the blame-lessness of his previous life and on the benefits he had done mankind. Cicero, who (as we shall see) elaborates on the good character and good deeds of his clients where he can, cannot afford not to bolster his treatment of those topics by employing their friends; their favour is in effect part of his evidence.

It was heartening when the client's townspeople rallied round. They added to the spectacle that we have seen to attend the epilogue.[56] Cicero asks the judges not to allow the cruelty of Cluentius' mother to prevail, on the grounds ('incredibly enough, but what I am going to say is quite true') that 'all the able-bodied men of Larinum are in Rome to give Cluentius their support, so far as they can, in his grave danger by their enthusiasm and by their large numbers' (195). The town, he goes on, is left to be defended by women and children; the men are here because they know that the judges will be pronouncing not just on the fate of one citizen of their town but on the prestige of the whole place. Their views are given expression in a formal way, by the reading of a *laudatio* of the client in court;[57] while it is recited, Cicero asks those who have brought it to rise from their seats (196). Their tears are mentioned (197). He also lists individual supporters (198). In the last section of the speech, the judges are urged to 'restore Cluentius to his *municipium*, give him back to the friends, neighbours and guest-friends whose enthusiastic support you can see with your own eyes' (202).

Cluentius' life, 'lived most honourably' (195), is, Cicero implies, what these massed persons of Larinum are witnessing to. They witness, further, to his assiduous public spirit in his home town (196). Good character and public service here, as often, went together. For a more retiring citizen, one had to be content with vague expressions of virtue: 'a man of unique

---

[56] And not only of course that. Cf. *Mur.* 90: 'concede this to the honourable town of Lanuvium, which you have seen here during the whole of the case, in large numbers and in mourning.'
[57] See A. H. J. Greenidge, *The Legal Procedure of Cicero's Time* (London, 1901) 490–1.

propriety, known virtue and tested loyalty' (*Caec.* 104). But many of Cicero's clients moved on the public stage, and allusion needed to be made to their official record. When Cicero asks (*Mur.* 88) where the wretched Murena will turn, he does so in order to mention not merely his mother, but his service in Asia and Transalpine Gaul (89). With a figure of still greater panache, Cicero pictures the Gauls 'virtually in arms' to press their charges against Fonteius. Against them Cicero arrays 'strong forces' to resist a barbaric attack (*Font.* 44–6). There is Macedonia, saved by the counsel and action of Fonteius; there is Further Spain, which has sent *laudationes* in his support; there are 'auxiliary troops' from Gaul itself, including the whole *civitas* of Massilia, saved by Fonteius, and Narbo, whose siege he lifted, not to speak of 'all the tax-collectors, farmers, cattle-breeders and other traders' from the province.

But others presented greater problems. Speaking for Caelius, Cicero makes the best he can of things like the youthful accusations of his elders and betters.[58] Cicero's promise that in future Caelius will mend his ways and bear rich fruit for the state is a substitute for pointing to such fruit in the past.[59] Again, the main service of Milo, in Cicero's eyes, had been to rescue him from exile, and he does not suppress that (100, 102–3). But Cicero attributes to Milo claims to wider service, partly in direct speech (94, 98), partly in reported (95–7). Milo turns out to be a bulwark of the state.[60] Others might have thought him no better than the man he killed.

In other speeches Cicero talks of his client's services not to the state but to other people. Thus loyal attentions to Caesar are affirmed in the speech for Balbus.[61] But a recurring theme is a client's services to Cicero, especially in helping in his return from exile: help not, perhaps, in Cicero's eyes to be distinguished from services to the state. He says he wishes to pay back to Rabirius Postumus the tears he had shed for Cicero (*Rab. Post.* 47), and he does so by dwelling emotionally on Rabirius' help to him when he left Italy. Indeed, he at times gives the impression that the judges are honour bound themselves to repay what he owes to a client. He says he had promised Plancius that he would, if he was restored to his country, make recompense

---

[58] Note e.g. 74 'Would that his desire for glory had carried him in other directions!' This treatment of Caelius' record late in the speech is not unlike that of Sulla's in *Sull.* 69–79, to the placing of which Cicero himself calls attention in 69. Compare too what was said of the *Palamedes* in n. 3.

[59] The last words (80): 'You more than all others shall reap a rich and lasting fruit from all his exertions and his toils' (tr. Austin). One might connect this passage with Quintilian's report (1.6.29) that 'Caelius seeks to prove that he is *homo frugi*, not because he is abstemious (he could not even pretend to be that), but because he is useful, that is "fruitful" to many' (tr. Russell). For another promise, see the last words of *Mur.* (90).   [60] Cf. *Sest.* 144.

[61] *Balb.* 63. But Cicero goes on (64) to stress Caesar's own services to the state.

in person; if he did not, 'these men, these,[62] would in my stead provide the full reward for all your labours' (*Planc.* 101). And the theme is elaborated in the remainder of the speech. Similarly, it is made part of the pathos of the peroration of the speech for Milo that the man who helped bring Cicero back to Rome is himself to be driven out of Rome (94, 102); and of the speech for Flaccus that Cicero had promised to preserve his *dignitas* because of what he had done to save the state (106, cf. 103).

This is perhaps only a particular facet of the way in which Cicero uses his own authority to help his clients. 'I beg and ask you,' he says to the judges at the end of the speech for C. Rabirius (*Rab. Perd.* 38), 'to regard this my defence as being what loyalty asks when a friend is in danger, and what the safety of the state requires from a consul.' Cicero's guarantee for the future behaviour of Caelius is premised on the condition 'if *I* have myself done my duty by the state' (*Cael.* 77). He asks for the acquittal of Murena 'in view of my extreme and well-known concern for the state, and of my authority as consul' (*Mur.* 86).[63]

'Wherefore, Save ...'

The way the judges should vote is commonly presented as the logical consequence of what has been said and done to persuade them. Cicero may accordingly use phrases like 'this being so' or 'wherefore' to introduce his exhortation to them to act as he wishes;[64] there follows a request or, more peremptorily, an imperative. The defendant needs to be saved.[65] The impending fate is not death, but death may be brought in nevertheless. Contemplating the idea of Cluentius being found guilty, Cicero hints that his client will find it difficult to go on living, and there is talk of a burial elsewhere than in ancestral tombs (*Cluent.* 201).[66] He deplores the prospect

---

[62] For the emotional *geminatio* cf. e.g. *Planc.* 98 'audi, audi', 100 'vi me, vi', 101 'memini enim, memini'; and generally my note on [Quintilian,] *Decl. Min.* 325.15.

[63] Cf. also 90: 'quem ego vobis ... consul consulem, iudices, ita commendo' ('I as consul commend him as consul to you, judges'). All this takes up themes of the proem. The matter of Cicero's self-presentation in perorations (and elsewhere) is a large topic that cannot be treated here.

[64] *quae cum ita sint*: *Mur.* 86, *Arch.* 32; *quapropter*: *Caec.* 104 (followed by a statement of Caecina's qualities), *Dom.* 147; *qua re*: *Arch.* 31, *Cael.* 78. Cf. *quam ob rem* in *Sull.* 86, followed by solemn affirmation, on oath. Similarly, in deliberative oratory (not so very different from forensic), e.g. *Leg. Manil.* 69, 'quae cum ita sint, C. Manili, ... tuam ... sententiam laudo' ('This being so, Gaius Manilius, I praise your opinion'); *in Clod. et Cur.* p. 451 Schoell, 'quam ob rem, patres conscripti, erigite animos' ('wherefore, fathers, be encouraged').

[65] *conservate*: *Cluent.* 202, *Mur.* 90, *Arch.* 31, *Cael.* 77 (cf. 80); cf. *Sest.* 147 ('ut ... conservetis'), *Planc.* 104 ('ut ... conserves'), *Mil.* 104 'conservandum virum'.

[66] So also e.g. *Rab. Perd.* 37, *Sull.* 89 (with Berry ad loc.).

that Milo will have no burial place in Italy (*Mil.* 104). That was to turn the screw of the pathos; but exile was indeed a harsh penalty, at least for a sensitive soul like Cicero. Or the defendant should be 'reserved',[67] for what they may yet do for the state. But whatever the formula, the judges are, at this final stage of the speech, more than ever before at the forefront of the orator's mind. 'On the epilogue depends the state of mind in which the judge retires to consider his verdict; there is nothing more we shall be able to say' (Quintilian 6.1.10).

[67] *Font.* 42 'ad dubia rei publicae tempora reservandum' ('to be kept for crises of the state'); *Flacc.* 106 (the last words: 'rei publicae reservate', 'keep for the state').

Part II

Case Studies

9

Being Economical with the Truth: What Really Happened at Lampsacus?

CATHERINE STEEL

In Verrem II 1.63–7

(63) Lampsacus, gentlemen, is a town on the Hellespont, and one of the most distinguished towns in the province of Asia. The Lampsacenes themselves are extremely dutiful towards Roman citizens of all kinds, and are also particularly quiet and restrained in their behaviour: they are exceptionally inclined to the Greek habit of absolute leisure in place of any sort of violent disturbance.

Verres had insisted to Dolabella that he should send him on an embassy to King Nicomedes and King Sadalas, motivated more by the opportunities for personal gain that the journey would afford than by any pressing public interest. It so happened that his route took him to Lampsacus with damaging and indeed practically fatal consequences for the city. He was installed at the house of a man called Ianitor, and his entourage were lodged with other hosts. As was his habit, and as his criminal lusts urged him to do, he immediately instructed his entourage, who were an unspeakably wicked group, to look around and see whether there was any girl or woman who might justify his staying on in Lampsacus.

(64) Among Verres' entourage was a man called Rubrius, who was an apt servant of his lust and had a remarkable capacity to find this sort of thing out wherever he went. He brought back the news that there was a man called Philodamus, easily one of the town's leading citizens in terms of his birth, career, wealth, and reputation, who had an outstandingly attractive daughter, who lived with him because she had no husband. However, she was thought to be extremely virtuous and chaste. When Verres heard this he was so on fire, despite never having seen her or even having heard about her from someone who had seen her, that he immediately said that he wanted to move to Philodamus'. His host Ianitor had no suspicion of what was going on and because he was afraid that *he* had done something to

I am very grateful to Michael Winterbottom, Robin Osborne, Jonathan Powell, and Jeremy Paterson who read and improved earlier versions of this chapter.

annoy Verres began to do his utmost to keep him. Given that Verres could not find an excuse to leave Ianitor he set about developing another strategy to accomplish the seduction. He said that Rubrius, his darling, his aide and confidant in every kind of situation, was not lodged in sufficient comfort and should be moved to Philodamus'.

(65) When this message was given to Philodamus, he did not know what disaster was now threatening him and his children. Nonetheless he went to see Verres, and explained that this wasn't part of his obligations: when he fulfilled his duties in playing host to Romans, he expected to have praetors or consuls as his guests and not a legate's hanger-on. Wrapped up in his one desire, Verres paid no attention to Philodamus' justified complaint, and gave orders that he should be forced to lodge Rubrius, although he had no obligations so to do. When Philodamus had failed to uphold his rights he tried hard to maintain his own civilized standards of behaviour. Given that he had always been considered to be particularly welcoming and friendly towards us, he didn't want to make it seem that Rubrius himself was an unwelcome guest. He arranged a dinner party of lavish splendour (he was one of the most hospitable people in his community), and asked Rubrius to decide who was invited, keeping just a space for himself, if Rubrius didn't mind. He even sent his son, a very promising young man, out to dinner with a relative. (66) Rubrius invited the entourage and Verres told them all what they must do. They arrived early and took their places. Conversation sprang up and someone suggested that they drink in the Greek fashion. Philodamus encouraged them, toasts were drunk in larger measures, and there was a buzz of talk and laughter around the room. Once Rubrius thought that things had hotted up nicely, he said, 'Come on, Philodamus, why don't you ask your daughter to come in and join us?'. Philodamus was a highly respectable father, already of advanced years: he was horrified by this unprincipled request. Rubrius insisted. So Philodamus, simply to make some reply, said that it wasn't a Greek custom for women to take part in men's dinner-parties. At this, different people around the room cried out: 'This simply isn't on; bring her in.' At the same time Rubrius told his slaves to shut the doors and to take up positions at the exit.

(67) When Philodamus understood that the purpose of this was a violent attack on his daughter he summoned his own slaves, and told them to ignore him and preserve his daughter, and to send someone to tell his son of this private catastrophe. Meanwhile, there were disturbances all over the house. Philodamus, a leading citizen and an honourable man, was buffeted between the slaves of Rubrius and his own in his own house; it was every man for himself; and finally he was drenched with boiling water by Rubrius himself. When the son was told about this he immediately raced home in a state of panic, to save his father's life and his sister's chastity. As soon as they heard what was going on the Lampsacenes gathered at the house with the same intention, although it was the middle of the night: they were stirred up equally by Philodamus' standing and the scale of the offence. Cornelius, Verres' bodyguard, who had been stationed with Verres' slaves by Rubrius as though on guard to carry the woman off, was killed, several of the slaves were wounded, and Rubrius himself was hurt in the mêlée. When Verres saw what a huge disturbance his desire had caused, he desired to run away somehow, if he could.

(63) Oppidum est in Hellesponto Lampsacum, iudices, in primis Asiae provinciae clarum et nobile; homines autem ipsi Lampsaceni cum summe in omnis civis Romanos officiosi, tum praeterea maxime sedati et quieti, prope praeter ceteros ad summum Graecorum otium potius quam ad ullam vim aut tumultum adcommodati.

Accidit, cum iste ad Cn. Dolabellam efflagitasset ut se ad regem Nicomedem regemque Sadalam mitteret, cumque iter hoc sibi magis ad quaestum suum quam ad rei publicae tempus adcommodatum depoposcisset, ut illo itinere veniret Lampsacum cum magna calamitate et prope pernicie civitatis. Deducitur iste ad Ianitorem quendam hospitem, comitesque eius item apud ceteros hospites conlocantur. Ut mos erat istius, atque ut eum suae libidines flagitiosae facere admonebant, statim negotium dat illis suis comitibus, nequissimis turpissimisque hominibus, uti videant et investigent ecqua virgo sit aut mulier digna quam ob rem ipse Lampsaci diutius commoraretur.

(64) Erat comes eius Rubrius quidam, homo factus ad istius libidines, qui miro artificio, quocumque venerat, haec investigare omnia solebat. Is ad eum rem istam defert, Philodamum esse quendam, genere, honore, copiis, existimatione facile principem Lampsacenorum; eius esse filiam, quae cum patre habitaret propterea quod virum non haberet, mulierem eximia pulchritudine; sed eam summa integritate pudicitiaque existimari. Homo, ut haec audivit, sic exarsit ad id quod non modo ipse numquam viderat, sed ne audierat quidem ab eo qui ipse vidisset, ut statim ad Philodamum migrare se diceret velle. Hospes Ianitor, qui nihil suspicaretur, veritus ne quid in ipso se offenderetur, hominem summa vi retinere coepit. Iste qui hospitis relinquendi causam reperire non posset, alia sibi ratione viam munire ad stuprum coepit; Rubrium, delicias suas, in omnibus eius modi rebus adiutorem suum et conscium, parum laute deversari dicit; ad Philodamum deduci iubet.

(65) Quod ubi est Philodamo nuntiatum, tametsi erat ignarus quantum sibi ac liberis suis iam tum mali constitueretur, tamen ad istum venit; ostendit munus illud suum non esse; se, cum suae partes essent hospitum recipiendorum, tum ipsos tamen praetores et consules, non legatorum adseculas, recipere solere. Iste, qui una cupiditate raperetur, totum illius postulatum causamque neglexit; per vim ad eum, qui recipere non debebat, Rubrium deduci imperavit. Hic Philodamus, posteaquam ius suum obtinere non potuit, ut humanitatem consuetudinemque suam retineret laborabat. Homo, qui semper hospitalissimus amicissimusque nostrorum hominum existimatus esset, noluit videri ipsum illum Rubrium invitus domum suam recepisse; magnifice et ornate, ut erat in primis inter suos copiosus, convivium comparat; rogat Rubrium ut quos ei commodum sit invitet, locum sibi soli si videatur, relinquat; etiam filium suum, lectissimum adulescentem, foras ad propinquum suum quendam mittit ad cenam. (66) Rubrius istius comites invitat; eos omnis Verres certiores facit quid opus esset. Mature veniunt, discumbitur. Fit sermo inter eos, et invitatio ut Graeco more biberetur; hortatur hospes, poscunt maioribus poculis, celebratur omnium sermone laetitiaque convivium. Posteaquam satis calere res Rubrio visa est, 'Quaeso,' inquit, 'Philodame, cur ad nos filiam tuam non intro vocari iubes?' Homo, qui et summa gravitate et iam id aetatis et parens esset, obstipuit hominis improbi dicto. Instare Rubrius. Tum ille, ut aliquid responderet, negavit moris esse Graecorum ut in convivio virorum accumberent mulieres. Hic tum alius ex alia parte, 'Enim vero

ferendum hoc quidem non est; vocetur mulier!' Et simul servis suis Rubrius ut ianuam clauderent et ipsi ad foris adsisterent imperat.

(67) Quod ubi ille intellexit, id agi atque id parari ut filiae suae vis adferretur, servos suos ad se vocat; his imperat ut se ipsum neglegant, filiam defendant; excurrat aliquis qui hoc tantum domestici mali filio nuntiet. Clamor interea fit tota domo; inter servos Rubri atque hospitis iactatur domi suae vir primarius et homo honestissimus; pro se quisque manus adfert; aqua denique ferventi a Rubrio ipso Philodamus perfunditur. Haec ubi filio nuntiata sunt, statim exanimatus ad aedis contendit, ut et vitae patris et pudicitiae sororis succurreret; omnes eodem animo Lampsaceni, simul ut hoc audierunt, quod eos cum Philodami dignitas tum iniuriae magnitudo movebat, ad aedis noctu convenerunt. Hic lictor istius Cornelius, qui cum eius servis erat a Rubrio quasi in praesidio ad auferendam mulierem conlocatus, occiditur; servi non nulli vulnerantur; ipse Rubrius in turba sauciatur. Iste, qui sua cupiditate tantos tumultus concitatos videret, cupere aliqua evolare, si posset. (*Verr. II* 1.63–7)[1]

So Cicero begins his account of a particularly sordid episode in Verres' career: the attempted kidnap and rape of a Lampsacene noblewoman, which was followed by a riot by the outraged Lampsacenes in which Verres was almost burned alive, and by a trial rigged by Verres which led to the judicial murder of Philodamus and his son.[2] Such at least is how Cicero presents and interprets his evidence, and his account has been accepted in its essentials by those who have considered this passage.[3] My purpose in this chapter is to challenge that consensus by arguing that none of the evidence which Cicero cites points conclusively to the interpretation he offers, and that other explanations of what happened can be constructed on the basis of the facts he does give.[4] Cicero is not, in this prosecution speech, presenting an objective historical account, but making the best possible case for Verres' guilt.

It seems clear that Cicero wishes his readers to see the events at Lampsacus as a tightly unified whole, where the banquet is followed on the one hand by the justified but abortive attempt by the citizens of Lampsacus to punish Verres, and the unjust but successful attempt by Verres to punish

---

[1] The text is that of the OCT.   [2] *Verr. II* 1.63–85.

[3] See esp. M. Fuhrmann, 'Tecniche Narrative nella Seconda Orazione contro Verre', *Ciceroniana, Atti del IV Colloquium Tullianum* 27–42 (Rome, 1980); P. Fabbri, 'De humanitate Ciceronis erga Provinciales in Verris crimine Lampsaceno describendo', *Atti del I congresso internazionale di studi Ciceroniani* (Rome, 1961); D. Magie, *Roman Rule in Asia Minor*, 2 vols. (Princeton, 1950) 247–8; M. Sartre, *L'Asie Mineure et l'Anatolie d'Alexandre à Dioclétien* (Paris, 1995) 150.

[4] Cicero's information about the whole episode was likely to be quite thorough. The military tribune whom he mentions in §71 as one of his sources, Gaius Varro, was his cousin and near-contemporary, and Cicero probably heard about the events at Lampsacus and the trial of Philodamus on Varro's return from the East. Varro is said to have got his information directly from Philodamus (71.21–3), and so Cicero's material probably had an inherent bias against Verres.

Philodamus and his son.[5] Thus the episode does not simply demonstrate Verres' viciousness but is also a case of unfinished business: Verres has not yet been punished, and it falls to the jury so to do. Cicero is explicit:

Do you hope that you will find a refuge here? You are making a mistake: The reason that they [sc. the citizens of Lampsacus] allowed you to get away alive was not so that you could find peace here, but so that you might get your deserts.[6]

One of the arguments of this chapter is that Cicero's presentation is misleading in setting up the connections, and that the conviction of Philodamus and the riot of the Lampsacenes should be seen as two separate incidents, related only by virtue of having their origins in the death of the lictor Cornelius.

The Banquet

The interpretation of the nature of the banquet and of Verres' culpability depends crucially on the issue of Verres' presence or absence on this occasion. It is important to note that Cicero never says that Verres was there, and his whole argument to implicate Verres in the attempted kidnap depends upon statements about Verres' thoughts and *intentions* and not his actions.

The reader becomes alerted to Verres' possible absence during the description of the preparation for the banquet. In response to Philodamus' *carte blanche* about the guest-list, 'Rubrius invited the entourage and Verres told them all what they must do. They arrived early and took their places' (66). Far from being evidence that Verres was himself a guest, the very fact that Cicero does not make it clear here that Verres was present indicates that he was not there.[7] Cicero would not neglect the opportunity to show Verres at this banquet: quite apart from his role in the supposed kidnap, allegations of misbehaviour in sympotic contexts are a recurring feature of Cicero's invective against Verres elsewhere in the *Verrines*, and against his other forensic opponents and political enemies.[8] But if Verres was not

---

[5] Quintilian provides support for this view, inasmuch as he treats the passage as a *narratio* with its own peroration (4.2.2; 6.1.54).

[6] 82.23–5: 'hic tibi perfugium speras futurum? Erras: ut huc incideres, non ut hic conquiesceres, illi te vivum exire passi sunt.'

[7] *Pace* Fuhrmann, 'Tecniche Narrative', 27: 'Questi [sc. Philodamus] diede un banchetto in onore dell'ospite e die suoi amici; fra gli invitati figurava anche Verre.' ('He gave a banquet in honour of his guest and his friends; Verres too was among those invited.')

[8] e.g. *Verr. II* 5.31; *Pis.* 21–2; *Phil.* 2.63–7; cf. A. Corbeill, *Controlling Laughter: Political Humor in the Late Republic* (Princeton, 1996) 128–43.

present he cannot have been responsible for many of the details of the banquet. The request that Philodamus' daughter attend may have been pre-arranged, but it hardly seems credible that Verres would have briefed Rubrius about boiling water, or have indicated that the evening should end with a fatality, let alone the death of one of his lictors. Nonetheless, the unwary reader may be trapped by Cicero's comment at the end of his narration: 'when Verres saw what a huge disturbance his lust had caused, he wanted to run away somehow, if he could.'[9] Cicero is not saying something obviously false, and the alert reader will see that he must mean that Verres wished that he were no longer in Lampsacus. But it is very easy to be misled into thinking that Cicero means Verres wanted to escape from the actual scene of the riot.

Of course, Verres' absence does not in itself guarantee his innocence. It is possible that Verres wanted to lay hands on Philodamus' daughter, was behind Rubrius' efforts to kidnap the woman, and was absent from a well-justified fear of violence and a desire to keep his involvement secret. Cicero's account suggests this interpretation: Verres gives instructions to those of his entourage who do attend (see above), and the alleged reason for the dead lictor's presence is so that he can organize the kidnap (67).

Close examination of the narrative shows how the compelling picture which Cicero constructs of Verres' attitudes and desires depends upon insinuation. Early in the narrative, Verres' arrival in Lampsacus is said to take place 'with damaging and indeed practically fatal consequences for the city' (63). Readers are warned to expect the worst, and are prepared to accept his tendentious account of various changes in accommodation which follows. So pervasive and consistent is the hostile gloss in Cicero's description that it is very difficult for the reader to consider more innocent explanations.

Verres' first acts, once he is lodged with Ianitor, are described thus: 'As was his habit, and as his criminal lusts urged him to do, he immediately instructed his entourage, who were an unspeakably perverted group, to look around and see whether there was any girl or woman who might justify his staying on in Lampsacus' (63). The classification of Verres and his followers as deeply wicked leads us as readers to expect them to act in character throughout the episode. Cicero also obliquely asserts his own knowledge of Verres' habits. Armed with this 'knowledge', readers are then more likely to believe Cicero's interpretation of any particular action by Verres and not seek alternative explanations: as so often in the *Verrines*, Cicero assumes Verres' guilt, while ostensibly proving it.

[9] 67.8–10: 'Iste, qui sua cupiditate tantos tumultus concitatos videret, cupere aliqua evolare, si posset.'

Cicero then sets up Rubrius as the particular confidant and aide to Verres, and it becomes natural for a reader to accept that Rubrius' movements and actions will be devoted to Verres' ends. Just as Cicero is able to talk about Verres' habits, so with Rubrius: he 'had a remarkable capacity to find this sort of thing out [sc. women whom Verres might find attractive] wherever he went'. Cicero then describes, in a way which his preparation makes entirely plausible, how Rubrius finds out about and tells Verres about the daughter of Philodamus. By this point the reader believes that Verres is obsessed with sex and that Rubrius is his close confidant, and so Cicero's account of the change of lodgings and the reason for it becomes entirely plausible.[10] The fact that both Ianitor and Philodamus are unhappy about the proposed changes serves to demonstrate Verres' callous indifference to the welfare of the provincials.[11]

Cicero's persuasive creation of an atmosphere of unbridled lust helps to conceal the fact that he does not point to any evidence for his account. He merely states that it was Verres' habit to look for attractive women, and that Rubrius helped him so to do. Even the business of the lodgings becomes much less convincing on closer examination. We have only Cicero's word for Verres' attempt to move from Ianitor's house to Philodamus', as no action resulted. Likewise, we must rely on Cicero's interpretation to believe that Verres tried to get Rubrius moved to Philodamus' house because he himself could not go. Other explanations are possible. Perhaps the comfort of Rubrius' lodgings, which Cicero puts forward as a pretext, was a genuine issue. Or we may even question whether there was a *change* of lodging involved: Rubrius could have been sent to Philodamus as part of the original dispositions. (Cicero does not give any name to Rubrius' putative first host). It is also worth observing that Philodamus' behaviour corresponds to that which Cicero has earlier

[10] The relationship between Verres and Rubrius, which is central to this whole episode, serves also to prepare readers for the importance throughout the second *actio* of Verres' various henchmen, particularly Timarchides and Apronius. These are both signs of the corruption of Verres' regime in Sicily and indications of his personal viciousness (Corbeill, *Controlling Laughter*, 91–5, 106–12). There are hints of the possibility of a personal dimension here, especially in Cicero's report of Verres' words to Ianitor, explaining why Rubrius had to move: 'that Rubrius, his darling, his aide and confidant in every kind of situation, was not lodged in sufficient comfort' (64). This sentence contains an interesting problem of focalization: whose is the parenthesis? Is this markedly colloquial phrase, *delicias suas*, simply Cicero's description of Rubrius? Or does Cicero want us to think that Verres is so far gone in shamelessness that he could reveal such a liaison to a provincial?

[11] Officials abroad regularly abused their rights to lodging and entertainment: the *lex Iulia* of 59 laid down strict limits to what could be demanded, and Cicero in his letters from Cilicia draws frequent attention to his adherence to this law (*Att.* 5.10.2, 14.2, 15.2, 16.3, 17.2). It is the mark of the bad magistrate not to be satisfied with his welcome. Compare the disgust of the consul's wife at the baths in Teanum Sidicinum (Gaius Gracchus, fr. 48 Malcovati) and Postumius' anger at his welcome by the Praenestines (Livy 42.1.6–12).

(63) said to be characteristic of the Lampsacenes in general. Philodamus' sense of his own value picks up on the town's description as *clarum et nobile*, and his ultimately generous behaviour is what we expect from a member of a community which is 'extremely dutiful towards the Romans'.

The account of the banquet itself also deserves careful scrutiny. Cicero implies that it is an event on a large scale: Philodamus, who is 'one of the most hospitable of men' 'prepares a banquet on a splendidly lavish scale',[12] and Rubrius, given *carte blanche* by Philodamus, invites 'that man's entourage'. The implication is that all the Romans attend, which supports the statement that the alleged attempted rape was carefully planned and that Verres briefed everyone beforehand. Yet we have grounds to query this impression. If, as I suggest, Verres was not present at this banquet (and therefore presumably not invited), then it seems unlikely that it could have been on a very large scale. We should perhaps think rather in terms of Rubrius inviting some of his friends. The initial absence of Philodamus' son, which Cicero ascribes to an order by Philodamus so that Rubrius and his friends are not disturbed, could also have another explanation: Philodamus' son had better things to do than have dinner with some unimportant Romans.

It is also possible to avoid having to interpret Rubrius' disastrous request for Philodamus' daughter to join the party as the beginning of a kidnap. As Philodamus points out, it was not the practice for Greek women to attend dinner-parties, and on Cicero's telling the reader is to interpret the fact that Rubrius ignores this aspect of Greek behaviour as a small example of the contempt for the Greeks which is revealed on a much larger scale in the kidnap attempt itself. Yet if we ignore the context which Cicero has set up, Philodamus' remark points to another interpretation of Rubrius' request. The corollary to Philodamus' remark is that it was a Roman habit for women to be present at these events.[13] It is, therefore, possible that Rubrius simply did not understand how offensive and inappropriate his request was, and that the incident was a cultural misunderstanding and not the start of a premeditated attack.[14] But Cicero makes it difficult for readers to

---

[12] 65.4–6: magnifice et ornate . . . convivium comparat.

[13] Cf. Nepos, *Lives* Preface 6. What was Philodamus' daughter's marital position? We are told that she had no husband and so was living in her father's house (64); but that could mean widowhood, and she is never called a *virgo*.

[14] Nothing is known about Rubrius apart from what emerges in this passage; but given his position, as part of the entourage of a legate, it is probable that he was a young man who was in the provinces, quite possibly for the first time, to gain experience as a preliminary to a political career (cf. D. C. Braund, '*Cohors*. The Governor and his Entourage in the Self-Image of The Roman Republic', in R. Laurence and J. Berry (eds.), *Cultural Identity in The Roman Empire* (London, 1998)). Ignorance about Greek customs is not improbable: and even if he did know that his request was offensive, that knowledge could easily, under the circumstances, have been obscured by alcohol.

think in these terms, because Rubrius' request is told as part of a carefully planned assault on the woman.

A final issue about the dinner party, or at least its aftermath, is the presence of the lictor Cornelius. Cicero says that he was 'stationed there with Verres' slaves by Rubrius as though on guard to carry the woman off' (67). Apart from supporting the planned nature of the operation, this can also be taken as an indication of Verres' unfitness for his duties, since he uses his official bodyguard in order to carry out his sordid sexual intrigues.[15] But it is possible to suggest another scenario which would explain why Cornelius became involved in the brawl. He may have been summoned once the fight began. There was time for a message to be sent to Philodamus' son and for him to return, and for *omnes Lampsaceni* to gather at Philodamus' house: there was surely also time for one of Rubrius' slaves to run back to Ianitor's house and explain to Verres that there was a problem. The dispatch of a lictor would under the circumstances be a sensible response.[16] We may even want to query the scale of the brawl, inasmuch as it is possible to imagine, for example, that things calmed down, but then revived when Philodamus' son returned and found Cornelius the lictor, the symbol of Roman authority, seeking to impose order.[17]

It is of course impossible to know what happened at Lampsacus when Verres visited. But we can offer an alternative to Cicero's interpretation. Verres arrives at Lampsacus while on a legitimate embassy to the kings Nicomedes and Sadales.[18] During his brief stay, there are some problems with the lodgings of one of his subordinates, Rubrius, which are resolved satisfactorily. At a banquet at his new lodging, Rubrius, either because he does not know what appropriate behaviour is or because he is drunk (or indeed from a combination of the two), makes a suggestion about his host's daughter that is badly received. A fight breaks out; Verres is told, and sends his bodyguard to help to extract Rubrius, but the bodyguard is killed. This is a sordid story, but not one which reflects badly on Verres personally.

[15] As a legate on official business, Verres would have had two lictors with him (T. Mommsen, *Römisches Staatsrecht*, 3rd edn. (Leipzig, 1887) 386–7).

[16] It is also worth considering whether Cornelius could have been a guest at Philodamus' dinner party, and thus present from the start, although without any orders from Verres. N. Purcell, 'The Apparitores: A Study in Social Mobility', *PBSR* 51 (1983) 125–73, demonstrates that *apparitores* came from a sufficiently wide range of origins to make this conceivable. This hypothesis is attractive inasmuch as it would accord with Cicero's presentation of events elsewhere in the narrative, which is misleading but not mendacious.

[17] For the physical presence of lictors, see A. J. Marshall, 'Symbols and Showmanship in Roman Public Life: The Fasces', *Phoenix* 38 (1984) 120–41.

[18] Verres' embassy is not recorded in any other sources, and it is impossible to know exactly what its aims were. But, given the delicate situation of the whole region following the first Mithridatic War, we do not have to follow Cicero in his suggestion that there was no pressing public interest which could justify the embassy (63.22–4).

This is not to argue that the events at Lampsacus are unproblematic. Even the revised version of events which I am advocating raises serious issues about imperial government and the standards of behaviour to be expected from Romans on official business in the provinces. If Romans act like conquerors, demanding hospitality and imposing their authority while ignoring the sensibilities of their subjects, they will on occasion provoke open hostility.[19] One of the consequences of Cicero's ascribing what happened to Verres' viciousness is that the potentially much wider problems inherent within the system of administration are obscured.

The Aftermath

Cicero's account of the affair at Lampsacus does not end with Verres' wish to run away. The following morning there is a meeting of the Lampsacene assembly, which is followed by a march on the house where Verres is staying (68). The desire of the people to roast Verres alive is averted only by the pleas of the Roman expatriate community in the town (69), and Cicero then draws a contrast between Verres and a Roman governor called Hadrianus, who did actually suffer this fate: Verres was more fortunate, although his offences were much greater (70–1), and the conviction of Philodamus and his son do not detract from his crimes (70–2). This leads into a description of the trial (72–6), in which Cicero emphasizes the role played by Dolabella, the governor to whom Verres was attached; then (77) he addresses Dolabella directly to exclaim that his wrongdoing in helping Verres have Philodamus and his son convicted makes Cicero unable to pity his fate now (Dolabella was in exile). Cicero then returns to the attack on Verres by the Lampsacenes and dilates on its full horror (78–82), and concludes by arguing that Verres' own actions show how unjust he was to attempt to incriminate Philodamus and son: he gave evidence in which he ascribed the blame to two other Lampsacenes. His failure to pursue the real culprits is ironically presented by Cicero as a further fault.

The purpose of this elaboration is to show how the effects of Verres' actions spread beyond those immediately involved to encompass both the whole of the town of Lampsacus and the structures of Roman government in Asia Minor. Any doubts that a reader might have about the global seriousness of a brawl at a dinner party are swept away as Cicero shows how this led to rioting and a gross miscarriage of justice. Moreover, Cicero

---

[19] Cf. J. S. Richardson, 'The Administration of the Empire', *CAH* 9, 2nd edn. (Cambridge, 1994) 572–84.

increases the injustice of Verres' actions by linking the riot closely to the trial. He presents the riot as an indication of the support of the Lampsacenes as a whole for Philodamus' attempt the previous night to save his daughter. Since their riot is presented as a reasonable response to what Verres did, the reader's sense of injustice when Philodamus and his son are convicted is increased. And Cicero makes explicit the point that their conviction does not mean that Verres' actions were justified: the most that it shows is that they were involved in the homicide.[20]

Cicero begins his justification of the Lampsacene riot at the very beginning of his account, with his brief sketch of the Lampsacenes' character. He draws attention to their distinction, their dutifulness towards Romans, and their tendency to quiet behaviour. Each of these qualities has a particular resonance within the context of Roman anxieties about 'typical' Greek behaviour. The description of the city itself as *clarum et nobile* may be meant to indicate that it is not democratic, and therefore not in thrall to the lower classes. The Lampsacenes' quiet and restrained behaviour shows that they do not in general go in for dangerous and destabilizing political activity. It is worth comparing how Cicero denigrates the Greeks of Asia Minor in his speech *Pro Flacco*. There, he emphasizes how dangerously prone they are to democratic, and rhetorical, excess.[21] The Lampsacenes are contrasted with this stereotype to suggest that they are ideal Greeks, from a Roman point of view. A reader will be on their side from the start.

The Lampsacenes' normal behaviour also takes on a particular relevance in the discussion of what they actually *do* in response to Verres.[22] Cicero was faced with a considerable challenge in making his readers approve of a riot by Greeks against a Roman: under normal circumstances this would be regarded with considerable alarm. His tactic is to emphasize the enormity of the provocation, while showing how the Lampsacenes still acted with self-restraint.

Lampsacene self-restraint is first apparent in the conduct of the assembly. Whatever excesses Greeks in general may indulge in, this particular community discusses its affairs in an orderly manner and without rowdiness. The decision to march on Verres' house is one that is supported by everybody. Their willingness to draw back from lynching Verres and listen to the pleas of the Roman business community confirms their moderation, as well as their ultimate good will towards Rome. Against this background the fact that they almost murdered a Roman legate appears quite extraordinary, and it is

---

[20] 72.5–6: 'It is clear to me that Nero's verdict does not acquit you of wrong-doing, but rather that they are found guilty of homicide' ('in quo video Neronis iudicio non te absolutum esse improbitatis, sed illos damnatos esse caedis').

[21] *Flacc.* 18–20; cf. A. Vasaly, *Representations: Images of the World in Ciceronian Oratory* (Berkeley, Calif., 1993) 198–205.   [22] Cf. Fuhrmann, 'Techniche Narrative'.

clear that Cicero wants to stress this paradox by juxtaposing their deliberations with their violence (69.20–4):

Given that this was the general opinion, and that everyone spoke for the motion in accordance with their feelings of outrage, everyone set out for the house where the man was staying; they began to batter down the door with rocks, to attack it with weapons, to pile up wood and faggots around it and to set light to them.[23]

Even an abortive lynching is an impressive demonstration of disaffection from a friendly community.

When Cicero returns to the riot in 78–82, he picks up these ideas and uses this picture of a people driven beyond what they can bear as evidence to reinforce the full horror of Verres' actions. In order to resist Verres, the Lampsacenes did things which count as war and would under normal circumstances be requited by war:

Did the state of Lampsacus try to make war on the Roman people? Was their intention to revolt from our territories and jurisdiction? Because I see myself and understand from what I have read and heard about, that if a state damages a legate of the Roman people to the slightest extent (quite apart from putting him under siege and attacking him in large numbers with fire and weapons and hand-to-hand violence) then, if that state does not make public reparation, it is normal for war to be declared and waged upon it.[24]

The answer to the rhetorical questions is, on the surface, 'no': the Lampsacenes were driven to extremes not by any hostility against Rome in general, but by the insupportable behaviour of Verres. Given their exceptionally tranquil nature, the fact that they were willing to fight Rome is a stunning indication of their outrage. But if a reader contemplates the possibility of the answer 'yes', there is a further, more disturbing, resonance to Cicero's talk of rebellion, which he does not make explicit but could hardly escape his readers. Asia Minor had indeed recently been the location of a serious and prolonged rebellion, instigated by Mithridates, which Sulla had brought under control only some five years previously. In a wider context, Cicero is suggesting that Verres' irresponsible behaviour came close to taking the lid off the problems of this region.

By establishing the Lampsacenes as exceptionally loyal right at the start of the whole episode, Cicero can perform the astonishing task of making

---

[23] 69.20–3: 'haec cum omnes sentirent, et cum in eam rationem pro suo quisque sensu ac dolore loqueretur, omnes ad eam domum in qua iste deversabatur profecti sunt; caedere ianuam saxis, instare ferro, ligna et sarmenta circumdare ignemque subicere coeperunt.'

[24] 79.3–9: 'bellumne populo Romano Lampsacena civitas facere conabatur? deficere ab imperio ac nomine nostro volebat? video enim et ex iis quae legi et audivi intellego, in qua civitate non modo legatus populi Romani circumsessus, non modo igni, ferro, manu, copiis oppugnatus, sed aliqua ex parte violatus sit, nisi publice satis factum sit, ei civitate bellum indici atque inferri solere.'

an attack on a Roman by a subject people a matter of reproach for the Roman rather than the subjects. But it would probably have been difficult for him to accomplish this had the Lampsacenes in fact taken their violent intentions to a fatal conclusion. As things are, their restraint shows that they are ultimately well disposed; and it also means that it is up to the hypothetical jury to complete the Lampsacenes' work:

Nothing would have moderated the Lampsacenes' feelings against Verres if they had not believed that he would meet with appropriate punishment at Rome. Even though they had received an injury of such a kind for which they could not get adequate recompense by any legal means, they preferred to trust their wrongs to our legal code and courts rather than give way to their sense of outrage.[25]

Cicero does not spell out what the Lampsacenes might do if Verres is acquitted. This is not simply because the Lampsacenes were actually going to do nothing if the Roman whose behaviour allegedly led to a riot ten years earlier was not found guilty of extortion in Sicily. Verres had of course by now gone into exile: this passage is an indication of Cicero's desire, in the *Verrines*, to reassure the public that Verres' self-inflicted punishment was deserved.

There are strong grounds for believing that Cicero's account of the riot is seriously misleading. These emerge most clearly if one considers matters from the point of view of the Lampsacenes themselves. They woke up, on the morning after the banquet, to face an alarming problem: a dead lictor. Roman reprisals against the whole city must have been at least conceivable.[26] If that were the situation, then the purpose of the assembly may not have been to work out a strategy of revenge on Verres. Their concern could rather be to avoid facing reprisals themselves.

It is worth considering more closely what the assembly decided. Cicero summarizes as follows:

There was no reason for fearing, if the Lampsacenes had taken violent revenge on him for his horrible crime, that the Senate and people of Rome would think that their state should be punished; but if a legate of the Roman people dealt with allies and foreign states in such a way that they could not keep the chastity of their

---

[25] 82.9–14: 'Lampsacenos in istum numquam ulla res mitigasset nisi eum poenas Romae daturum credidissent: etsi talem acceperant iniuriam, quam nulla lege satis digne persequi possent, tamen incommoda sua nostris committere legibus et iudiciis quam dolori suo permittere maluerunt.'

[26] Sulla's intrusive reforms in Asia Minor after the first Mithridatic War were a recent reminder of Roman willingness to get involved in the internal matters of Greek cities, and a close parallel to Lampsacus is provided by the murder of a Roman garrison commander at Chaeronea in the 80s, and the community's subsequent anxiety about Roman reprisals: see Plutarch, *Life of Cimon* 1–2 and J. Ma, 'Black Hunter Variations', *PCPhS* 40 (1994) 49–80, esp. 62–3. Compare also Augustus' reaction at Cyzicus in 20 BC: he took away the city's freedom after some Romans had been killed in a riot (Dio 54.7.6.).

children safe from his lust, then anything was worth suffering rather than living in circumstances of such deplorable violence.[27]

This seems at first sight to confirm Cicero's earlier narrative describing a serious outrage, and suggest that the Lampsacenes were very hostile to Verres. But there are reasons why one could challenge that interpretation. In the first place, it was very much in the interests of the Lampsacenes to emphasize the enormity of the Roman offence. The most effective justification for Philodamus' killing of a lictor would be a carefully planned assault on his daughter, such as Cicero described. No less than Cicero, the Lampsacenes had strong motives for concealing the possibility that Rubrius' actions were the product of a horrible drunken mistake. On the other hand, the further step in Cicero's account, which is the involvement of Verres, was not something that the Lampsacenes would wish to suggest. Instead, they needed to persuade him not to punish the community as a whole. Their implicit threat of action if Verres, the legate, now takes reprisals for actions in protecting children, is cast in terms of 'allies and foreign states'. This suggests that the concern of the assembly, not surprisingly, is the interests of the whole community and not what may happen to Philodamus.[28]

It may then be possible to reject Cicero's implication that the assembly was a call for community revenge which found an immediate outlet in the riot. Cicero himself points to an alternative and plausible explanation for what happened towards the end of his account, when he attacks Verres for not pursuing the people who were really guilty of the assault (83). To support this, he quotes briefly from a letter which Verres wrote to Nero, the governor of the province of Asia (83.2–4):

'A letter of Gaius Verres to Nero. Themistagoras and Thessalus.' You say that Themistagoras and Thessalus stirred up the people.[29]

The role of this pair in causing the riot is worth further consideration. Our knowledge of the internal politics of Lampsacus at this time is practically non-existent, but it seems not unreasonable to assume that how to deal

---

[27] 68.16–20: 'non esse metuendum, si istius nefarium scelus Lampsaceni ulti vi manuque essent, ne senatus populusque Romanus in eam civitatem animadvertendum putaret; quodsi hoc iure legati populi Romani in socios nationesque exteras uterentur, ut pudicitiam liberorum servare ab eorum libidine tutam non liceret, quidvis esse perpeti satius quam in tanta vi atque acerbitate versari.'

[28] In the description of the assembly's deliberations I have translated the conditional clause ('si istius nefarium scelus Lampsaceni ulti vi manuque essent') as though it related to the past, that is, the death of the lictor. The pluperfect subjunctive could also represent an original future perfect original, (as Greenwood translates for the Loeb edition), and in this case the sentence would be looking towards future vengeance and thus implying that the assembly was already contemplating staging a riot. The ambiguity is uncharacteristic, and I suspect that Cicero was trying to mislead the careless reader without having openly to give a false account of the Lampsacenes' deliberations.

[29] 83.2–4: 'EPISTULA C. VERRIS AD NERONEM. THEMISTAGORAS ET THESSALUS–. Themistagoram et Thessalum scribis populum concitasse.'

with Roman power was an issue which caused dissension among active politicians.[30] Moreover, there were strong specific grounds for hostility to Rome in Lampsacus in 80 BC. Although Lampsacus itself had not joined Mithridates, it did have to make some contribution to the sum of 20,000 talents which Sulla demanded from the province of Asia as a whole, and it is hard to imagine that this was not a source of resentment. A possible scenario to explain the riot would be along the lines that a number of leading Lampsacenes went from the assembly to Ianitor's house in order to present to Verres the feelings of the community and to seek assurances that there would be no reprisals against Lampsacus as a whole. They were accompanied by their fellow-citizens, and when they reached Ianitor's, Themistagoras and Thessalus took this opportunity to pursue their own agenda by urging an attack on the Romans. It is after all very likely indeed that Rubrius (who could hardly have stayed on with Philodamus) had returned to Verres' lodgings after the disaster of the previous evening. Rubrius' presence would be a provocation; if, as I suggested above, the Lampsacene assembly for its own protection emphasized Rubrius' wrongdoing the previous evening, the crowd once stirred up by Themistagoras and Thessalus may have been after Rubrius and not Verres at all.

This is of course speculative. What Cicero's reference to Themistagoras and Thessalus does allow one to say with some confidence is that more was involved in the riot than spontaneous outrage at the events of the previous evening. And by setting the riot in a political context, it is also possible to give a more sympathetic interpretation to Verres' failure to prosecute Themistagoras and Thessalus. Instead of being an attempt to cover up a miscarriage of justice, it can be seen as the act of a sensible politician, who did not wish further to inflame anti-Roman feeling in the province.

What my reconstruction has so far failed to account for is the trial and execution of Philodamus and his son. Cicero describes this in deeply emotive and pathetic terms, as an event which should elicit the pity of the jurors, and, as I discussed above, gave it an extended treatment. As ever in this case, the facts from which Cicero builds his stunning narrative are not necessarily unfavourable to Verres.

The account of the trial is presented to the reader as something that will provoke pity:

Listen, please, gentlemen of the jury, and at last pity our allies and show that they can depend on you for some protection.[31]

[30] See e.g. the evidence collected in G. E. M. de Ste-Croix; *The Class Struggle in the Ancient Greek World* (London, 1981) 306–8 and 518–37.

[31] 72.7–9: 'audite, quaeso, iudices, et aliquando miserimini sociorum et ostendite aliquid iis in vestra fide praesidi esse oportere.'

and Cicero then sets up the problem which Verres faced:

Because it seemed to the whole of Asia that Verres' so-called bodyguard (in reality the instrument of his disgusting lust) had met a fitting end, Verres was extremely worried that Philodamus might be acquitted by Nero's court.[32]

This is followed by a description of what Verres did to counter the problem. He insisted that Dolabella should leave his province, Cilicia, and travel into Asia to take a hand in the trial (72). When Dolabella arrived, he in turn applied pressure on the governor of Asia, Gaius Nero, to try the case himself, and also packed Nero's advisory council with his own subordinates, and with Romans who were owed money by Greek cities and who would be prepared to do Verres a favour in return for his help in extracting the debts. Moreover, Dolabella used his influence in the area to stop any Roman from defending Philodamus, and found a complaisant prosecutor from among Lampsacus' creditors by offering the services of his lictors as debt-collectors (73). Cicero uses his description of Dolabella's actions to suggest that there were two reasons why Philodamus did not get a fair trial: he could find no one to defend him, and the body of men who judged him were prejudiced.

The lack of an advocate is ascribed to fear on the part of those who might have defended him:

He, wretched man, had been unable to find anyone to act as his counsel. Which Roman, after all, would not be put off by Dolabella's influence, and which Greek by his violence and authority?[33]

It may be more useful to see the absence of a defence advocate as a structural problem rather than the result of an individual's behaviour. No provincial would wish to provoke the Roman overlords when there was no case to argue; similarly, if a conviction was almost inevitable, there would be no prospect for a Roman of acquiring useful influence.[34] There is no need to think that either Verres or Dolabella had to take action to deter possible advocates.

Although Cicero ascribes the composition of the advisory council to Dolabella's machinations, it is difficult to see what choice Nero had. It was standard practice for a governor to use both his entourage and the local Roman community, as Nero does here. Indeed, Verres is strongly criticized

---

[32] 72.9–12: 'quod toti Asiae iure occisus videbatur istius ille verbo lictor, re vera minister improbissimae cupiditatis, pertimuit iste ne Philodamus Neronis iudicio liberaretur.'

[33] 74.26–9: 'ille miser defensorem reperire neminem poterat; quis enim esset aut togatus, qui Dolabellae gratia, aut Graecus, qui eiusdem vi et imperio non moveretur?'

[34] It is striking that Cicero makes no attempt to question the guilt of Philodamus and his son.

by Cicero later in the second *actio* for using only his own companions on his *consilium* in Sicily.[35] And, given the extent to which the cities were in debt in this period,[36] it would probably have been difficult for Nero to find any Romans of suitable standing who were *not* creditors of the Greeks. Dolabella's interference in the case may not be suspicious either. Verres was his legate and Rubrius could ultimately have been attached to Dolabella and not Verres. The trial was a matter of interest to Dolabella.

It seems likely that Philodamus and his son did not get a fair trial, even if the verdict was not unjust. But this was not necessarily because Verres tried to rig the trial. The Roman administration of justice would have great difficulty under any circumstances of trying a Greek accused of murdering a Roman. Undertaking the defence, particularly in a case where the evidence against the accused was very strong, carried with it strong political implications, and a panel of judges composed exclusively of Romans would tend to be prejudiced in favour of the fellow-citizen. As elsewhere in this episode, accusations of individual wickedness take the place of and conceal more general structural problems. But it is also worth noting that events at Lampsacus were not referred back to Rome, as happened in similar cases of sedition and uprising in the provinces.[37] Cicero suggests, in §§ 84–5, that this is further evidence of a cover up; it could equally be taken to show that the riot was not particularly serious and that the death of the lictor Cornelius had been dealt with adequately by the trial and conviction of Philodamus and his son.

What then can we say about what happened at Lampsacus? A young and inexperienced Roman behaves offensively at a party and in the fight which follows the lictor who is sent to extract him is killed; the following morning a public assembly debates its response and appeals to Verres not to take action against the community as a whole. However, the people are stirred up by two anti-Roman politicians and transform themselves into a lynch-mob looking for the young Roman; but, in the end, this attack fails to come to much. At a subsequent trial, the man who held the banquet and his son are convicted of the murder of the lictor and are executed. Verres' actions seem to have been limited to one or two quite sensible initiatives: the possible dispatch of Cornelius the lictor to bring Rubrius home (though that back-fired) and the decision not to pursue Themistagoras and Thessalus.

---

[35] *Verr. II* 5.114.

[36] For the extent of indebtedness, see D. Magie, *Roman Rule in Asia Minor*, 2 vols. (Princeton, 1950) 232–58.

[37] A. W. Lintott *Imperium Romanum: Politics and Administration* (London, 1993) 66.

Conclusions

The first and clearest point is that there is no evidence to suggest that Verres' actions during and after the affray at Lampsacus were anything other than those of an upright and conscientious provincial official. So far from being a monster of depravity, he seems to have acted with sense and humanity. In terms of convincing scholars, the *Verrines* are perhaps Cicero's finest achievement; astonishingly few have suggested that Verres was other than he is painted.[38] It is surely time for an evaluation of his guilt as a whole.

Cicero's handling of the Lampsacus episode also throws important light on his forensic technique in general and on the specific tactics he employs in prosecuting Verres. Despite the unquestioning faith that has for the most part been placed in Cicero's account, we can expect at least part of his original readership to have been more critical. Although Verres' advocates had not had the opportunity to present a formal defence, one imagines that the circumstances leading up to the trial had been fully discussed.[39] Cicero's readers would have approached the second *actio* as a version of events, eager to explore Cicero's manipulation of the 'facts'. And it seems quite clear that Cicero wanted this kind of critical attitude to his written speeches. His famous remark about confusing the jurors at the trial of Cluentius is not only a boast about his skill, but also an encouragement for people to go and see how it was done by reading the *Pro Cluentio*.[40] Cicero was regarded as a great orator not simply because he could rouse people's emotions: his masterly handling of evidence was as important, and this can only be appreciated by a critical reading.

One of the paradoxes, however, about reading the Lampsacus episode closely is that it becomes much more difficult to explain its presence. On a naive view, all is clear: an indication of Verres' criminality which contributes to his developing characterization. As we have seen, closer attention shows how evanescent this picture is. An adequate explanation for this may simply be that Cicero's account of the events at Lampsacus are a splendid example of his virtuosity, precisely because of the disparity between fact and presentation. But one can offer another reason in terms of the relationship between the first speech of the second hearing and the other four.

---

[38] A notable exception is G. Martorana, 'La *Venus* di Verre e le Verrine', *Kokalos* 25 (1979 [1981] 73–103).

[39] So, for example, at the dinner-party during the trial thrown by Sisenna about which Cicero is scathing (*Verr. II* 4.33–4).

[40] Quintilian *Inst. Or.* 2.17.21: 'Cicero, cum se tenebras offudisse iudicibus in causa Cluenti gloriatus est . . .' That Quintilian cites it indicates that the remark had some canonical status, though Cicero may not have intended that when he made it.

In the fifth speech Cicero considers Verres' achievements as a military commander in Sicily, including a long and emotive account of an attack, by pirates, on the harbour at Syracuse which Verres' incompetence had made possible.[41] According to Cicero, the first response of the Roman citizens at Syracuse to this disaster was to march on the governor's house, and when Verres came out to them, their response was such as to make him fear a replay of events at Lampsacus.[42]

Although Cicero's account of these events is brilliantly impassioned,[43] he does not describe any actual violence and says instead that the crowd restrained themselves and went off to prepare the defence of the city. The reference to events at Lampsacus serves to obscure this anti-climax by reminding readers of a precedent for Verres' capacity to rouse the hostility of those with whom he comes into official contact; and in turn, it is the need to provide supporting evidence which leads Cicero to work so hard to create his highly tendentious version of events at Lampsacus.

From this perspective, the Lampsacus episode is not simply a self-contained example of Cicero's skill in manipulating evidence, but part of a strategy to orchestrate the vast amount of material against Verres so that it is comprehensible and effective for the reader. And in addition to one particular instance of foreshadowing, this passage contributes to the creation of the relationship which Cicero sets up between Roman and provincial. Cicero pulls off the astonishing feat of presenting Roman provincial government as completely, and convincingly, corrupt and oppressive. The standard practice of a governor taking advice from a *consilium* composed of his entourage and locally based Roman citizens becomes part of the conspiracy of injustice against Philodamus (§ 73), and the riot of Lampsacenes, when faced with no official provocation whatsoever, can only be an indication of the personal failings of Verres (§ 70). This episode helps readers to develop the sympathy for the provincials, and disgust at Verres, which are essential if the rest of the second *actio* is to work. Of course the picture he is creating is deeply subversive of Roman views of themselves as just imperialists: it is only neutralized by Cicero's focus on individuals, on Verres and Dolabella. But once one has exonerated Verres, one is left with potentially explosive thoughts on provincial government. In this respect, Cicero's cleverness has perhaps led him further than he intended.

---

[41] *Verr. II* 5.80–100.   [42] *Verr. II* 5.93.10–94.18.

[43] See R. G. M. Nisbet, 'The Orator and the Reader: Manipulation and response in Cicero's Fifth Verrine', in A. J. Woodman and J. G. F. Powell (eds.), *Author and Audience in Latin Literature* (Cambridge, 1992) 1–17; repr. in his *Collected Papers on Latin Literature*, ed. S. J. Harrison (Oxford, 1995) 362–80.

10

Repetition and Unity in a Civil Law Speech: The Pro Caecina

Lynn Fotheringham

i. Introduction: The Advocate at Civil Law

Although the fame of 'Cicero the Advocate' rests largely on his speeches for the defence in politically charged criminal cases, a volume with this title is a fitting place to examine one of his civil law speeches. This paper will focus on the *Pro Caecina* in an attempt to analyse the relationship between Cicero's speech and the complicated civil law suit to which it was tailored. A key to the analysis will be found in the structure of the speech, investigated through the repetitions of words and themes which unify the many arguments employed.

An approach centred on the structure of the speech forces a close engagement with the text. Earlier structural analyses provide a starting point, and insights from rhetorical theory and discourse analysis may be applied. Cicero's selection and ordering of material provide clues to his strategy, which must be deciphered before the text can be safely used as evidence for either the background of the case itself or the socio-legal context.

The principle of examining structure in order to understand strategy is put into practice by W. Stroh, *Taxis und Taktik. Die advokatische Dispositionskunst in Ciceros Gerichtsreden* (Stuttgart, 1975); his rhetorical analysis of the speech is nevertheless inevitably dependent on existing legal scholarship. Structural analysis is a minor element of B. W. Frier's *The Rise of the Roman Jurists: Studies in Cicero's* Pro Caecina (Princeton, 1985), which, although it is situated within the legal historical tradition, has done much to make the text accessible to those whose interests lie outside the Civil Law. My disagreements with Stroh and Frier in no way imply that I am unaware of

Thanks are due to (in alphabetical order) Christopher Pelling, Jonathan Powell, John Richardson, and Catherine Steel, for reading, listening, and encouraging at various times. Jeremy Paterson's editorial guidance was detailed and constructive.

my enormous debt to their work. But while legal historians have long used the *Pro Caecina* as evidence for the contemporary wording of the relevant interdict,[1] and while Frier looks beyond the strictly legal to issues as diverse as social conflict in Etruria and the emergence of the juristic profession as a whole, the relationship between the text and the case remains in need of illumination.

The most striking feature of the *Pro Caecina* is that the speech, like the suit in which it was delivered, is complicated in the extreme. An anecdote which sheds light on the multiplication of arguments in this ancient text is cited by a scholar of modern law, R. A. Ferguson, arguing that 'advocacy leads to a natural proliferation of stories at trial':

The defendant says that he never borrowed any pot; and that he used it carefully; also, that the pot was broken and useless when he borrowed it; also, that he borrowed the pot of somebody not the plaintiff; also, that the pot in question was the defendant's own pot; also that the plaintiff never owned any pot, iron or other; also that the defendant never had any pot whatsoever.   ('Untold Stories in The Law', in P. Brooks and P. Gewirtz (eds.), *Law's Stories: Narrative and Rhetoric in The Law* (New Haven, 1996) 84–7)

In Cicero's speeches, the combination of apparently incompatible 'stories' or arguments is one of the clues seized on as evidence that the published text is departing from the originally delivered speech. Ferguson's anecdote, however, reminds us that multiple arguments occur in courtroom speeches themselves; far from being a clue to later recension, they are a typical feature of adversarial advocacy.

Another striking feature of the speech is its use of legalistic quibbling arguments. A tendency to reduce its complicated arguments to a single and very minor concern goes back to Cicero himself:

tota mihi causa pro Caecina de verbis interdicti fuit: res involutas definiendo explicavimus, ius civile laudavimus, verba ambigua distinximus.

The whole of my case *Pro Caecina* concerned the words of the interdict: I untangled intricate problems by clear definitions, I praised the civil law, I made a choice among the different meanings of doubtful words.   (*Or.* 102)[2]

---

[1] See O. Lenel, *Das Edictum Perpetuum. Ein Versuch zu seiner Wiederherstellung* (Leipzig, 1927) 467.

[2] This judgement of Cicero's on the speech has had considerable influence. C. Middleton, *The Life of Marcus Tullius Cicero* (London, 1810) 131, who describes the speech as depending on 'a subtle point of law', quotes *Or.* 102, but only as far as 'explicavimus', omitting the 'laus iuris ciuilis' altogether. J. H. Freese, *M. Tulli Ciceronis Pro L. Murena Oratio ad Iudices* (London and New York, 1894) 69, commenting on *Mur.* 25, states that 'the dispute [in the *Pro Caecina*] turns upon the difference between "deicere" and "eicere"'. A. Haury, *L'Ironie et l'humour chez Cicéron* (Leiden, 1955) 123–4, attributes to the legalistic genre the absence of irony and humour from this speech, although P. Gotzes, *De Ciceronis Tribus Generibus Dicendi in Orationibus pro A. Caecina, de imperio Cn. Pompeii, pro Rabirio perduellionis reo adhibitis* (Rostock, 1914) demonstrates the presence of humour.

If the later rhetorical work and not the speech itself were extant, we would think that Cicero's argument had been based on the letter of the law; in the speech itself, however, he claims that it is based on the spirit.[3] This discrepancy can be attributed partly to the polemic going on in the later work, and partly to contemporary perceptions of legal discourse which affect Cicero's presentation in both works.

In the *Orator* Cicero is using the traditional 'Three Style Theory' of the rhetoricians to undermine his critics' polar opposition between the florid 'Asianist' and a more restrained 'Atticist' style: he argues that the best orators must not use either a high-flown or a low-key style, nor even something in the middle, all the time.[4] The argument has two stages: first that the style of a good orator varies across his œuvre; second that style also varies within individual speeches. Each stage is illustrated with three examples from Cicero's own work:

is erit igitur eloquens, ut idem illud iteremus, qui poterit parva summisse, modica temperate, magna graviter dicere. *tota mihi causa pro Caecina de verbis interdicti fuit: res involutas definiendo explicavimus, ius civile laudavimus, verba ambigua distinximus.* fuit ornandus in Manilia lege Pompeius: temperata oratione ornandi copiam persecuti sumus. ius omne retinendae maiestatis Rabiri causa continebatur: ergo in ea omni genere amplificationis exarsimus. ‖ at haec interdum temperanda et varianda sunt. quod igitur in Accusationis non reperitur genus, quod in Habiti, quod in Corneli, quod in plurimis nostris defensionibus?

[Stage 1] So, to repeat, the eloquent man will be he who is capable of speaking in a restrained manner of little things, in a controlled manner of moderate things, and in a weighty manner of great things. *The whole of my case for Caecina concerned the words of the interdict: I untangled intricate problems by clear definitions, I praised the civil law, I made a choice among the different meanings of doubtful words.* The honour of Pompey was to be enhanced in the speech *Pro Lege Manilia:* I controlled my speech and sought enough and more than enough honour. The entire law preserving the sovereignty of the state was involved in the case *Pro Rabirio Perduellionis:* therefore I blazed forth in that case with all manner of embellishment. ‖ [Stage 2] But these things must be modified and varied from time to time. Which style of speaking, then, is absent from my *In Verrem*, my *Pro Cluentio* or *Pro Cornelio*, or the bulk of my defence speeches?   (*Or.* 101–3)

---

[3] The conflict between the spirit and letter of the law ('voluntas' vs. 'verbum' or 'scriptum' vs. 'sententia' in Latin) was well known to rhetorical theorists (see e.g. *Inv.* 1.17, 2.116–43; *Her.* 1.19). In the *Pro Caecina* it is repeated frequently, in the repetition of the contrast of 'verbum' with 'res' (40, 49, 51, 58, 77) or 'aequitas' (37, 49, 58, 66–7, 77, 81, 84, 104).

[4] There is a wide range of terminology for all three styles in Greek and Latin. 'Plain' is a poor translation for the style described as 'tenuis, subtilis, summissus' and so on; hence 'low-key'. The basic outline of the three styles in the *Orator* can be found at 75–99, where Cicero, to disarm his 'Atticist' critics, devotes far more space to the 'low-key' style than to the other two, and admits that one who is only ever grandiloquent seems to be a madman.

This polemical presentation does not do justice to the variety evident within the speeches chosen to illustrate the first stage; the *Pro Caecina* is no more uniformly low-key than it is wholly based on quibbling arguments.[5] But it is not insignificant that a civil law speech is chosen to represent the low-key style, or that it is described for this purpose as being predominantly concerned with the most legalistic type of discourse. This characterization is influenced by a contemporary stereotype of the way legalistic argument is conducted by legal experts (jurists), and of the way it should be conducted by the *patroni* (advocates, who were not in principle legal experts, but orators) who act in civil suits.[6]

Earlier in the *Orator*, Cicero has taken care to link civil lawsuits and the low-key style:

quam enim indecorum est de stillicidiis, cum apud unum iudicem dicas, amplissimis verbis et locis uti communibus?

For how inappropriate would it be to use the most elaborate words and commonplaces when you are conducting a rainwater case in front of a single judge? (*Or.* 72)[7]

The link between the civil law discourse of the jurists and the practice of quibbling over the definition of words is part of the polemic in the *Pro Murena*:

in omni denique iure civili aequitatem reliquerunt, verba ipsa tenuerunt, ut, quia in alicuius libris exempli causa id nomen invenerant, putarunt omnis mulieres quae coemptionem facerent 'Gaias' vocari. iam illud mihi quidem mirum videri solet, tot homines, tam ingeniosos, post tot annos etiam nunc statuere non potuisse utrum 'diem tertium' an 'perendinum', 'iudicem' an 'arbitrum', 'rem' an 'litem' dici oporteret.

In the entire civil law, they [= jurists] have in the end abandoned equity and clung on to the words themselves, with the result that they have come to the conclusion that all women who undertake the *coemptio* form of marriage are called 'Gaia',

---

[5] In an investigation of the three speeches named in Stage 1, Gotzes, *De Ciceronis Tribus Generibus Dicendi*, identified a number of linguistic features associated with each of the three styles; he includes the use of legal language as a marker of low-key style. H. M. Hubbell, 'Cicero on Styles of Oratory', *YCS* 19 (1966) 171–86, on the other hand, argues that there is no statistical evidence for the 'Three Style Theory'. But his conclusion that Cicero was a poor literary critic takes no account of the polemic which underlies the *Orator* characterization; while Gotzes' work, which does not ignore the more high-flown passages of the *Pro Caecina*, illustrates the importance of subject-matter in the perception of style.

[6] See B. Nicholas, *An Introduction to Roman Law* (Oxford, 1962) 28–9, for the traditional account of the differentiation between jurists and orators; J. A. Crook, *Legal Advocacy in the Roman World* (London, 1995) 37–46, for a reassessment; K. Hopkins *Conquerors and Slaves* (Cambridge, 1978) 80–9, for a sociological treatment.

[7] The wording of L. Laurand's synopsis of the speech (*Cicéron* (Paris, 1933) 22), specifically echoes *Or.* 72.

because they found the name used as an example in somebody-or-other's books. Now that indeed always seems amazing to me, that so many men, equipped with such intelligence, have not been able, even now after so many years, to decide whether we should say 'the third day' or 'the day after tomorrow'; 'judge' or 'arbitrator'; 'case' or 'suit'. (*Mur.* 27)

In the *Pro Murena*, Cicero is attacking Servius Sulpicius Rufus' claim that, as a jurist, he deserves the consulship; the orator is ranked above the jurist in political importance partly on the grounds of his ability to rise above such trivialities. In the *Orator* Cicero argues that he can deal with trivialities in an appropriately low-key fashion, as well as being able to use a high-flown style when that is appropriate. To demonstrate this he selects a speech of his own which was part of a civil law suit, and which contained some quibbling arguments.

The typically legal, low-key style of the *Pro Caecina* is enlivened by more high-flown passages of which the *Orator* polemic can take no account; the typically legalistic quibbling on which that polemic relies is underplayed in the speech itself by Cicero's repeated emphasis on the spirit of the law. The speech, in fact, argues from both spirit and letter, and this potential contradiction may in part be explained by the contemporary negative response to letter-of-the-law arguments exploited to such effect in the *Pro Murena*: even where Cicero uses them, he must detach himself from them. But Ferguson's anecdote also contributes to the explanation: advocacy leads to multiple and potentially incompatible arguments.

The combination of incompatible arguments in the *Pro Caecina*, then, is not something that needs to be explained away, but something we may expect to have existed in his opponents' speeches as well. When Cicero seizes upon inconsistencies in his opponents' combinations of arguments, we may deduce that they were playing the same game as he; perhaps they did not play it so well. The combination of arguments and the steps taken to unify them provide the key to the strategy, not the identification of a single central argument.

The perceived need to identify a central argument undermines the analyses of both Stroh and Frier. Stroh argues that because Cicero attacks his opposite number Piso for the quibbling on which his own argument relies, he misrepresents his own case. Stroh's analyis is based on G. Nicosia, *Studi sulla 'Deiectio'* (Milan, 1965), who identifies the essential basis of Cicero's complicated case in a single quibble which is also a misrepresentation of the law. Frier, on the other hand, denies that Cicero was misrepresenting the law, on the grounds that the law at this stage was not sufficiently stable to be misrepresented. His own analysis, following a hint from J. Humbert, *Les Plaidoyers écrits et les plaidoiries réelles de Cicéron* (Paris, 1925) 252, seeks to reconstruct the history of the case by assigning different arguments to the three different hearings known to have taken place. He therefore seeks to identify the argument which was the most important at the final hearing.

These identifications fail to take account of the aspect of adversarial advocacy raised by Ferguson. In the anecdote about the pot, although the defendant's arguments as listed are contradictory, this is not true of the plaintiff's arguments which they answer: he borrowed a pot; he used it carelessly; the pot was in good condition to start with; it was my pot . . . Advocates may prefer a contradictory set of responses to leaving any argument unanswered. And even if certain arguments appear to have been dealt with at earlier hearings, to leave them unanswered at the final hearing may run the risk of seeing them subsequently resurrected by the opposition. The advocate must instead seek a way of combining all the necessary arguments into a unified whole. Repetition of key themes would seem an appropriate way of unifying them, and repetition pervades the *Pro Caecina*.[8]

This case, then, required a strategy which allowed the combination of a large number of arguments, some of them perhaps raised at different points in the development of the suit, some of them potentially incompatible. This paper argues that Cicero developed such a strategy, that if a single argument emerges from the speech as the most important that is because he wished it to and not because it was the legal crux of the case, and that this argument exploits contemporary prejudices about civil law discourse. There is no need to invoke later rewriting; the speech, despite its bewildering number of arguments, is a unity, and an excellent example of the advocate at civil law.

ii. The Arguments in the Case

This particular civil law suit concerned an estate at Tarquinii, once the property of one Marcus Fulcinius, and adjoining an estate which formed part of his wife Caesennia's dowry. On his death, Fulcinius' estate passed to the couple's son, and on the son's death, to a Publius Caesennius, who auctioned it (see Fig. 10.1 for family tree). This information comes from the opening of Cicero's *narratio* (*Caecin.* 10–12); Frier (pp. 4–27) provides a fascinating and detailed exposition of the historical context and implications.

---

[8] Gotzes identifies repetition as a feature of the speech, which he suggests is used for clarity. This is a feature of the low-key style; repetition for ornament is a feature of the middle style.

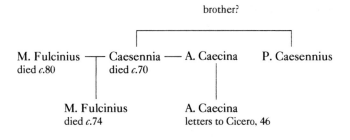

FIGURE 10.1. *Family tree*

Much of this is background, irrelevant in legal terms to the suit conducted later; Cicero himself admits that his account begins at a very early stage in the story (10), leading Frier to see it as an intrusion from an earlier speech into the published version of the final one (p. 117). C. Damon on the other hand suggests (in *The Mask of the Parasite: A Pathology of Roman Patronage* (Ann Arbor, Mich., 1997) 222–35) that these details are included in order to demonstrate the probability that Caesennia would wish to purchase the estate at auction: it had belonged to her husband and then to her son, and it adjoined an estate of her own. To this observation it can be added that the presentation of Fulcinius' family as upright citizens is reinforced by the description of their involvement in normal and honourable legal activity such as dowry-transactions and wills.[9]

Caesennia's friend, Aebutius, and her second husband, Caecina, disagreed over who had bought the estate at the auction. Aebutius made the bid and handed over the money; both the seller, Caesennius, and the banker, Phormio, attested to this fact (27), and Cicero did not dispute it. On Caecina's behalf, however, he contended that Aebutius had been acting as Caesennia's agent in this transaction, that she had paid him the money for it later, and that the estate therefore belonged to her, passing to Caecina on her death (13–17). This dispute over the ownership of the estate is presented by Cicero as the last resort of a man who had already attempted to undermine Caecina's inheritance in other ways (18–19). The presentation of Aebutius as excessively litigious contrasts both with

---

[9] J.-M. David, *Le Patronat judiciaire au dernier siècle de la république romaine* (Rome, 1992) 53 n. 8, 196 n. 94, points out the importance of the fact that Aebutius is described as having no familial connection with Caesennia; this description too is pointed by the contrast with her actual family.

the characterization of Fulcinius' family, and with the claim that Caecina himself would have preferred never to be embroiled in a law suit (23).

Despite Cicero's downplaying of the ownership issue, disagreement over the auction may have been the origin of the dispute. Ownership of the estate was not, however, relevant to the interdict under which the dispute was being judged, and the change in focus needs to be explained. It appears that a ritual eviction (*deductio*) was a preliminary to hearings on disputed ownership. According to Cicero, Caecina and Aebutius agreed that Aebutius would 'evict' Caecina from the estate with a show of violence, but on the day he instead used real violence to prevent Caecina from even entering the property. This gave Caecina an excuse to ask the praetor for the interdict *de vi armata* (on armed violence), which concerned possession (or rather dispossession) instead of ownership (18–23):

VNDE TV SEX. AEBVTI AVT FAMILIA AVT PROCVRATOR TVVS A. CAECINAM AVT FAMILIAM AVT PROCVRATOREM ILLIVS VI HOMINIBVS COACTIS ARMATISVE DEIECISTI, EO RESTITVAS.

Sextus Aebutius, you should restore Aulus Caecina to the place from which you or your bailiff or your household threw out him or his bailiff or his household, by means of force and men you had summoned and provided with arms.

This changed the course of the dispute, focusing attention on the events of the *deductio* rather than on the original disagreement.

In Roman law, the fact of X's ownership was not a defence against the complaint that X had violently dispossessed Y.[10] Cicero goes one step further and argues that even possession was not relevant under the *de vi armata*, on the grounds that possession is not explicitly mentioned in the wording (90–3). This quibble is the argument identified by Nicosia and Stroh as the crux of Cicero's case and a misrepresentation of the law. But though the imperial jurists came to a directly opposite interpretation of this interdict, Frier (pp. 171–83, with bibliography) claims that the argument, however ludicrous it may seem, was worth running in the late republic, when the interpretation was not yet fixed.[11] Cicero, moreover, combines this quibbling argument with the claim that Caecina did have possession (94–5), and, for that matter, ownership. The identification of 90–3 as the central argument of the case is a lawyer's analysis, concerned primarily with the interdict and its interpretation. Other factors were at play in Cicero's construction of the argument.

Regardless of the legal position, ownership has an obvious moral relevance: if Aebutius had no claim to own the estate in the first place, his

[10] See Nicholas, *An Introduction to Roman Law*, 109.
[11] In this Frier has some support from P. Birks, Review of Frier, *Oxford Journal of Legal Studies* 7 (1987) 444–53.

TABLE 10.1. *The arguments of Piso and Cicero's replies*

Piso's arguments[a]	Cicero's replies
(1) That the terms of the interdict did not apply to this case.	*Caecin.* 35–40, 49–50, 82–89 ('deicere'); 41–48 ('vis')
(2) That the interdict required 'possession' on the part of the person ejected.	*Caecin.* 90–93
(3) That Caecina did not 'possess'.	*Caecin.* 94–95
(4) That Caecina's 'possession' was in any case impossible, if it was based on inheritance, on account of the disabilities inflicted on his *civitas* Volaterrae, which prevented his being an heir.	*Caecin.* 95–103
(5) Facts were adduced which went to prove Aebutius' ownership.	*Caecin.* 13–17, 27
(6) A suggestion was made, perhaps by the *recuperatores*, that some other form of action might have been brought.	*Caecin.* 4–10, 32–40

Note:
[a] A. H. J. Greenidge, *The Legal Procedure of Cicero's Time* (Oxford, 1901) 562–3.

violent attempt to keep a grip on it is difficult to defend. On the other hand, if Caecina had no claim, his actions become suspect. Cicero's presentation and that of Aebutius' *patronus*, Piso, would have mirrored one another in this respect. Both would have wished to demonstrate that their client owned the estate, as well as demonstrating that the interdict vindicated their client's actions. Since the board of *recuperatores* selected to judge the case were not necessarily legal experts, any more than the *patroni* themselves, they may have been open to persuasion based on other than strictly legal arguments.[12] Both *patroni* must have worked to combine their arguments effectively, in the manner of adversarial advocacy.

Table 10.1 shows the multiplicity of Piso's arguments, identified by Greenidge (*The Legal Procedure of Cicero's Time*, 556–68) as requiring an answer from Cicero by the time of the final hearing. Although these are deduced from Cicero's extant speech, the order in which Greenidge presents them is not Cicero's (as indicated by the second column); the analysis is based on legal principles. Cicero, of course, is not analysing but synthesizing the arguments, creating a particular impression of their interrelationship in the minds of the *recuperatores*.

As in the anecdote about the pot, the effect of the combined arguments varies, depending on who is speaking. Argument (2) and argument (3), when used by Piso in an attack on Caecina's possession, are interdependent, but by choosing to reply to both Cicero ends up with two arguments of which one or the other is superfluous: Caecina did not need possession, but he had it anyway. Cicero is careful to draw attention to this superfluity (94), and thus to his apparently

---

[12] Quint. *Inst.* 7.5.3 recommends discussing ownership despite its irrelevance.

complete demolition of Piso's case. But Piso is also using arguments which are strictly superfluous, thus mirroring Cicero's strategy: if he proves argument (3), he does not need argument (4), which is the one attributed by Cicero to an earlier stage in Aebutius' attempts to manipulate the law against Caecina. Argument (4), however, is also relevant to argument (5), since Caecina, if he had been disbarred from inheriting, could no more own the estate than he could possess it. And argument (5) is legally irrelevant. Both advocates bring as many arguments to bear as possible, sometimes resulting in a superfluity which can be described as 'having the cake and eating it too'.

The order of arguments in Greenidge's list does reflect Cicero's presentation in one respect: argument (1) is the one presented by Cicero as the most important in Piso's case. In particular, Piso's apparent claim that the term 'deicere' did not apply to Aebutius' actions, because Caecina had not reached the estate, is rebutted repeatedly throughout the speech. This repetition works as a unifying force on the many and different arguments that need to be combined, as well as creating the strong impression that it is Piso's case which is based on a quibble, encapsulated in the phrase '*reieci, non deieci*' (I threw you *back*, I did not throw you *out*). There is no need to believe that this argument really was as important to Piso's case as Cicero makes it out to be; it serves Cicero's purpose to do so because, although he is able to present language-based arguments against it, he is also able to present his own case as being based, in contrast, on the spirit of the law. He thus exploits the kind of prejudice against letter-of-the-law arguments evidenced in the *Pro Murena*, while using these arguments himself.

Table 10.1 also demonstrates that a large part of the speech is not covered by Cicero's replies to these six arguments, although 51–64 can be included in argument (1). Two more elements of Piso's case can be added: the testimony of witnesses; and a claim that Cicero's case relied too much on the arguments of a particular jurisconsult. The witnesses are dealt with immediately after the *narratio* (23–31); Cicero claims that they support his view of what happened during the *deductio*. The influence on Cicero's argument of the jurisconsult Gaius Aquilius Gallus is defended at 65–79. The issue serves three functions. It allows Cicero to raise the tone by including high-flown passages on the preservation of the civil law itself, which men such as Gallus uphold (70, 73–6). It affords an opportunity to accuse Piso of contradicting himself, on the grounds that he both attacks and relies on juristic opinion (67–9). And it enables Cicero to dissociate himself from one of the quibbling arguments which support his own case, which he attributes to an unnamed jurisconsult supposedly consulted by Piso. He thus excuses his own use of quibbles while attacking Piso's, without appearing to contradict himself.

The defence of jurists and of the law, which is omitted from Greenidge's legal analysis, has no direct bearing on the interpretation of the interdict. But in terms of Cicero's rhetorical synthesis, intended for hearers who were not academic lawyers, these passages are important because of the contribution they make to his self-presentation. He, like his client, is a man concerned only with what is fair and equitable, who has been dragged down to the level of verbal quibbling by the unscrupulous actions and arguments of Aebutius and Piso.[13] To understand the synthesis of arguments requires the tools of rhetoric and discourse analysis as well as those of law.

iii. Investigating the Structure of the Argument

Analyses of Ciceronian structure tend to be heavily influenced by ancient rhetorical theory and based on content extrapolated from its expression. Despite Stroh's emphasis on the interrelationship of structure and strategy, little detailed work has been done on the way the speeches are structured from the point of view of their language. A typical analysis consists of a diagram or paraphrase of the text, labelled according to the rhetorical *partes orationis* (the parts of the speech).[14] The number and names of the *partes orationis* vary, but the following list of four is standard: *exordium, narratio, argumentatio, peroratio* (introduction, statement of facts, argumentation, conclusion). The most obvious flaw in this sequence is the lack of guidelines for subdividing the *argumentatio*, generally the longest part of the speech, and for present purposes the most interesting.[15] The *Pro Caecina* has an *exordium* (1–10), *narratio* (10–23), and *peroratio* (103–4); this leaves 23–102 for the *argumentatio*, which must be further subdivided.

Commentators subdivide the *argumentationes* as they subdivide the speeches, by identifying and labelling passages within the text, in the end providing a summary of the content with section-numbers attached. The resulting impression of discrete passages dealing with separable arguments is influenced by our familiarity with modern written texts, divided into

---

[13] For a discussion of Cicero's exploitation of the relatively recent legal concept of equity in this speech, see G. Ciulei, *L'Équité chez Cicéron* (Amsterdam, 1972) 53–61.

[14] Examples may be found in P. MacKendrick, *The Speeches of Cicero: Context, Law, Rhetoric* (London, 1995), who presents summary paraphrases of twenty-three speeches in a style familiar from many a commentary, and reprints the elaborate tabular analysis of the *Pro Milone* by F. P. Donnelly, *Cicero's Milo: A Rhetorical Commentary* (New York, 1935).

[15] The rhetoricians sometimes divide the *argumentatio* into arguments affirming the speaker's claims and arguments rebutting those of the other side (*confirmatio* and *confutatio*). But this distinction may be more useful in conceptual than in structural terms: MacKendrick is only able to separate the affirmation from the rebuttal in four or five speeches.

TABLE 10.2. *A comparison of two structural analyses of the speech*

	Stroh (1975)		Frier (1985)		
exordium	1–10		1–9		
narratio	10–23		10–23		
de testibus	23–31		23–31		
partitio	none		32		
de actione	31–40		32–40	⎫	
de vi	41–50		41–8	⎪	
de verbis	51–64		49–64	⎬ de re 32–85	
de iuris consultis	65–78	(de iure civili 67-77)	65–79	⎪	
de interdicto	79–89	(de verbo 86-9)	79–85	⎭	
			86–9	⎫	
de possessione	90–5		90–3	⎬ de verbo 86–95	
			94–5	⎭	
de civitate	95–103		95–102		
peroratio	104		103–4		

separate paragraphs and chapters, but an orally delivered speech may not have been perceived as a succession of discrete arguments. If one of the reasons for the difficulty of the *Pro Caecina* is the sheer number of arguments it contains, another is the fact that the arguments are not always clearly differentiated. I have adopted the term 'gliding transition', used by Brink in relation to Horace's *Ars Poetica*, for those passages in a text where the subject-matter has clearly changed but the moment of change cannot be clearly pinpointed.[16]

Gliding transitions may be detected by comparing the subdivisions of the *argumentatio* made by Stroh (pp. 92–100) and Frier (pp. 115–16), presented in Table 10.2; the argument labels are based on their paraphrases.[17] The

[16] C. O. Brink, *Horace on Poetry*, i: *Prolegomena to The Literary Epistles* (Cambridge, 1963). For paragraphing in antiquity, see M. B. Parkes, *Pause and Effect: An Introduction to the History of Punctuation in the West* (Aldershot, 1992) 10, 66, with bibliography. For the section- and chapter-numbers in Cicero's text, see J. Glucker 'Chapter and Verse in Cicero', *Grazer Beiträge* 11 (1984) 103–12, who is dismissive of their importance. The numerators, however, were responding to the text, and blatant disagreements often indicate gliding transitions.

[17] After the *exordium* and *narratio* comes a discussion of the witnesses (*de testibus*), an argument that the correct legal action has been brought (*de actione*), a defence of the claim that violence took place (*de vi*), and a lengthy discussion on the interpretation of words (*de verbis*). At 64 Cicero turns to the jurisconsults (*de iuris consultis*) with digressions on the law in general (*de iure ciuili*), culminating in a final rejection of Piso's interpretation of the interdict (*de interdicto*). At 90 he discusses the possession of the disputed estate (*de possessione*), and at 95 the problem of Caecina's citizenship (*de civitate*). The fourth column of the table is due to Frier's division of the *argumentatio* into two main sections, the *de re* and *de verbo*, which he then further subdivides.

table shows broad agreement; the minor discrepancies demonstrate that Frier is not simply following his predecessor. The decision as to whether, for example, the *narratio* begins at the end of 9 or in the middle of 10, must be based on an examination of the text, though neither scholar justifies his decisions with reference to the language at these points. These minor disagreements suggest, however, that points of transition are not always easy to identify. Gliding transitions can be used as clues to the strategy of the text because they blur the difference between one argument and the next, giving the impression that the two are closely connected.

Here insights may be gained from both ancient rhetorical theory and modern discourse analysis. Those who work in this area of linguistics emphasize the difficulty of making explicit the intuitive understanding that the subject-matter has changed, such as that shared so frequently by Stroh and Frier. Seeking an explanation based on language rather than content, which may be subjectively assessed, discourse analysts stress that clear-cut rules are impossible to establish,[18] but point to a range of linguistic practices which may be used to mark 'topic-shift'. One is the 'topic-sentence', in which a new topic is actually mentioned.[19]

A version of the topic-sentence, in which something is explicitly stated to be the new topic, is included by some ancient rhetoricians in their lists of *partes orationis*.[20] The *propositio* can be a statement of the essential disagreement between the two sides, but the term is also applied to a statement which introduces a new argument in the course of the speech, something like a chapter-heading in a modern book. The *partitio* is a summary of the arguments to come, something like a table of contents; it is sometimes a list of all the *propositiones*.[21] The question of whether the *Pro Caecina* contains a *partitio* is the only disagreement with Stroh explicitly acknowledged by Frier, perhaps drawn to his attention because ancient rhetorical theorists disagreed over whether every speech should contain one. Quintilian (*Inst.* 4.4.2, 4.5.4) argues that these clear markers of structure are not always desirable; when they are missing, it is obviously harder to establish where one argument or topic ends and another begins.

The study of topic may also be approached from an analysis of vocabulary; verbal repetition within a passage gives it unity and detaches it from

[18] See e.g. G. Brown and G. Yule, *Discourse Analysis* (Cambridge, 1983) ch. 3, esp. 68–73, 94–100; M. Hoey, *Patterns of Lexis in Text* (Oxford, 1991) esp. 118–23; M. McCarthy, *Discourse Analysis for Language Teachers* (Cambridge, 1991) ch. 3, 64–87.

[19] The word 'topic' is used here as a synonym for subject-matter, not in the traditional rhetorical sense of common-place ('locus communis').

[20] Although Quintilian (*Inst.* 3.9.1–3; 4.4.1–4.5.28) denies these two *partes orationis* their place in the list, his discussion is useful and his terminology convenient.

[21] The *Pro Murena* is the clearest example; the wording of the tripartite *partitio* (11) is repeated later in the three *propositiones* (11, 14, 54).

TABLE 10.3. *The most frequently repeated words in four passages*

23–30 'de testibus' (710 words)	32–40 'de actione' (991 words)	41–8 'de vi' (696 words)	51–64 'de verbis' (1450 words)
dicere (23)	AGERE (18)	VIS (26)	VERBUM (30)
TESTIS (18)	*arma* (16)	facere (14)	res (24)
arma (10)	ius (16)	*arma* (11)	*arma* (22)
Caecina (10)	res (16)	dicere (10)	*homo* (20)
Aebutius (9)	dicere (15)	*homo* (10)	deicere (15)
homo (8)	*homo* (12)	fuga (9)	unus (15)
	deicere (11)	videre (8)	
	interdicere (10)	manus (7)	
	omnis (10)		

the surrounding context, and the repeated words contribute to the listeners' sense of topic. On the other hand, repetition of words and themes can be used to unify the whole text. Investigating repetitions within and across topics serves two functions: to justify the structural analysis reached and to contribute to an understanding of Cicero's synthesis.

Table 10.2 shows more agreement as to topic in *Pro Caecina* 23–64 than in what follows, when Cicero reaches the topic of jurisconsults. If, as suggested above, Cicero is here attempting to combine a number of arguments, to dissociate himself from some of the ones he is using, and to accuse Piso of self-contradiction while escaping the same charge himself, it is not surprising that transitions begin to be blurred. But the use of topic-sentences and vocabulary patterns in the analysis of structure can be more easily illustrated by examining the passages where the divisions are more clear-cut.

Statistics on repetition in *Caecin.* 23–64 support both the divisions and the labels of Table 10.2. Table 10.3 shows the most frequently repeated words in the four arguments.[22] The word already identified as a label for the topic (printed in capitals), is the most frequently occurring word in three of the four: *agere* (to take action) in the 'de actione'; *vis* (violence) in the 'de vi'; *verbum* (word) in the 'de verbis'. The exception is *dicere* (to speak) in the 'de testibus', which is however closely associated with *testis* (witness). Some of the other high frequencies can also be explained by reference to topic. The frequency of *ius* (law) in the 'de actione' is appropriate

---

[22] Since there is disagreement between Stroh and Frier over whether 31 and 49–50 go more closely with what precedes or with what follows, they are omitted from the investigation. The words appearing in the table all occur at least once per hundred words within the passage in question (the figure in brackets is the number of occurrences). Prepositions, pronouns, the copula, etc. are all omitted from the count, since these are always among the most frequent words in a text, but provide little information on the topic. Obvious cognates, such as *agere* and *actio*, are counted as the same word. The study of the vocabulary of the speech was made possible by the provision of an electronic text from the Oxford Text Archive (http://ota.ahds.ac.uk).

to the debate on legal action; the apparently colourless word *facere* (to make or do) occurs in the 'de ui' in the repeated statement *vis facta est* (violence was committed); the frequency of *res* in 51–64 is due to a repeated antithesis between *res* and *verbum*.

The four words used as labels do not appear in the other columns: *agere*, for example, ceases to occur in 41–8, where *vis* acquires a frequency it did not have before. In contrast to these rising and falling concentrations, which suggest that the passages are separate arguments, the most evenly distributed words across the four arguments are *arma* (arms) and *homo* (man), marked in italic. The phrase 'homines armati' is a quotation from the interdict, frequently repeated in order to reinforce the impression that the interdict does apply to the events of the *deductio*. These repetitions unite passages which are otherwise distinct from the point of view of vocabulary.

A topic-sentence containing the most frequent word can be found for each of the four arguments. These confirm the assignation of topic, but cannot establish the precise point of topic-shift, because even in the case of the two arguments where the point of topic-shift is not in dispute, the topic-sentence is not the first sentence of the argument. For example, the *narratio* closes with the words 'hac de sponsione uobis iudicandum est' at 23.[23] In what follows the generalizing tone makes it clear that the statement of facts is over. But the explicit statement that witness testimony is the next topic comes only after a number of transitional comments:[24]

hac de sponsione vobis iudicandum est. ‖ maxime fuit optandum Caecinae, recuperatores, ut controversiae nihil haberet, secundo loco ut ne cum tam improbo homine, tertio ut cum tam stulto haberet. etenim non minus nos stultitia illius sublevat quam laedit improbitas. improbus fuit, quod homines coegit, armavit, coactis armatisque vim fecit. laesit in eo Caecinam, sublevat ibidem; nam in eas ipsas res quas improbissime fecit *testimonia* sumpsit et eis in causa *testimoniis* utitur. itaque mihi certum est, recuperatores, ante quam ad meam defensionem meosque *testis* venio, illius uti confessione et *testimoniis*.

It is concerning this legal wager that you are to make a judgement. ‖ For Caecina, gentlemen, it was most to be wished that he would not be involved in any kind of dispute at all; secondly, not with such an unscrupulous man; thirdly, that any dispute in which he was involved might be with such a stupid man. And indeed his stupidity assists us no less than his unscrupulousness injures us. He was unscrupulous inasmuch as he summoned and armed a band of men, and committed an act of violence with the men he had summoned and armed. In this he injured Caecina, but at the same time he assists us, for he collected *witness-statements* to those very things which he had done with the utmost unscrupulousness, and he is using those

[23] This is confirmed by Quint. *Inst.* 4.2.132.
[24] This passage echoes the opening of the speech by repeating the generalizing tone and the characterization of Aebutius as *improbus*; this kind of repetition, as well as unifying the speech, reinforces the sense that this is the opening of the *argumentatio*.

witness-statements in this case. And so I have decided, gentlemen, to use that man's admission and *witness-statements* before I come to my defence speech and my *witnesses*. (23–4)

It would not be appropriate to separate these transitional comments from a 'de testibus' beginning with the first sentence which contains the word 'testimonia'; the words 'in eo' (in this) indicate the close connection of this sentence to what goes before.

A similar point can be made about the opening of the 'de vi,' which is introduced by a three-part quotation of Piso's argument. The word *vis* itself does not occur in the first quote, but in the second:

'queramur,' inquit, 'licet; tamen hoc interdicto Aebutius non tenetur.' quid ita? 'quod *vis* Caecinae facta non est.' . . . 'nemo,' inquit, 'occisus est neque saucius factus.'

'We may complain,' he says, 'that's allowed. Nevertheless Aebutius is not constrained by this interdict.' Why so? 'Because *violence* was not committed against Caecina.' . . . 'Nobody,' says he, 'was killed or made to suffer injury.' (41)

Once again, the sentence which contains the word *vis* is postponed. In the 'de actione' and the 'de verbis', where the points of transition are disputed, the topic-sentence containing the words *actio* or *verba* cannot be seen as indicating precisely where the topic begins.

The shift from the 'de testibus' to the 'de actione' is a gliding transition consisting of the following sequence of sentences (30–2):

(*a*) quid huic tu homini facias? nonne concedas interdum ut excusatione summae stultitiae summae improbitatis odium deprecetur?

(*b*) utrum, recuperatores, his *testibus* non credidistis, cum quid liqueret non habuistis? at controversia non erat quin verum dicerent.

(*c*) an in coacta multitudine, in armis, in telis, in praesenti metu mortis perspicuoque periculo caedis dubium uobis fuit inesse vis aliqua videretur necne? quibus igitur in rebus vis intellegi potest, si in his non intellegetur?

(*d*) an vero illa defensio vobis praeclara visa est: 'non deieci, sed obstiti; non enim sum passus in fundum ingredi, sed armatos homines opposui, ut intellegeres, si in fundo pedem posuisses, statim tibi esse pereundum?' quid ais? is qui armis proterritus, fugatus, pulsus est, non videtur esse deiectus?

(*e*) posterius de verbo videbimus; nunc rem ipsam ponamus quam illi non negant et eius rei ius *actionemque* quaeramus.

(*a*) What are you to do with such a man? Should you not concede that he beg pardon from time to time, on the grounds of extreme stupidity, for the hatred aroused by his extreme unscrupulousness?

(*b*) Well, gentlemen, did you not believe these *witnesses*, when you adjourned without decision? But the dispute was not over whether they were speaking the truth.

(*c*) Or was there some doubt in your minds as to whether or not some sort of violence seemed to exist, in the summoning of a band of men, in arms, in weapons, in the present fear of death and the evident danger of slaughter? In what things, then, can violence be understood to exist, if it is not to be understood in these?

(*d*) Or indeed did that defence seem to you to be evident: 'I did not throw you out, but I stood in your way; for I did not allow you to enter the farm, but I put armed men in your way, so that you would understand that if you put a foot on to the farm, you would immediately be destroyed'? What are you saying? Does the man not seem to be 'thrown out' who is terrified away by arms, put to flight and ejected?

(*e*) Later we will see about the word, but for now let us put up for inspection the thing itself which they themselves do not deny and let us seek the legal *action* appropriate to this matter.

In terms of content, Cicero moves here from the last of Piso's ten witnesses (*a*), to the witnesses in general (*b*),[25] then immediately proposes an alternative *controversia* to the assessment of the witnesses. This shifts the emphasis to the definition of violence, anticipating the 'de vi' (*c*). Another definitional argument anticipates discussions of *deicere* at various points in the speech (*d*). Formally, all of these points are presented as questions, and it is difficult to put a clear break into the sequence of alternative questions introduced by the particles 'utrum ... an ... an ...', although in (*b*) the topic is still the witnesses and by (*d*) it has become 'deicere'.

The antithesis between *res* and *verbum* in (*e*) is the potential *partitio*, which appears to imply that the two topics will be discussed separately. The sentence is closely connected to the preceding argument, and the *verbum* in question is most naturally taken as *deicere*. The second part of the sentence serves as a *propositio* for the argument which follows; 'ius actionemque' encapsulates the discussion of appropriate legal activity.[26] It is difficult to believe that a strong break would have been heard before this sentence; it is also closely linked by verbal repetition to what follows.[27] The transition glides.

Stroh denies that this sentence is the *partitio* of the speech, but suggests that the words 'posterius de verbo videbimus' refer to an argument about the interdict's use of the word 'unde' at 86–9, Cicero's ultimate answer to Piso's 'reieci, non deieci' argument. Frier accepts that this is the argument referred to, but to reinstate this sentence as the *partitio* he must argue that a shift fundamental to the structure of the speech, from a discussion of *res*

[25] Words from the opening of the 'de testibus' (*improbitas, stultitia*) are repeated in (*a*), which may be seen as ring composition, a sign that the topic is coming to an end; (*b*) contains the last occurrence of *testes* for a while.

[26] Although the individual words are frequent in the argument, this collocation is not repeated until 40, marking the end of the 'de actione' as it marks the beginning.

[27] Two verbs are repeated: 'nunc rem ipsam *ponamus* quam illi non *negant* et eius rei ius actionemque quaeramus. est haec res *posita* quae ab aduersario non *negatur*' (*Caecin.* 32).

to a discussion of *verbum*, takes place at this point. In fact the *res–verbum* antithesis occurs many times in the course of the speech, in repeated declarations that Cicero is championing the spirit of the law (40, 49, 51, 58, 77); it is difficult to believe that the *recuperatores* would have continued to wait until 86 for a major structural shift from one topic to the other. If 'posterius de verbo videbimus' must refer to a specific passage, a better case can be made for 49–64 *de verbis*.

The opening of this argument is another point of disagreement, though the topic of what follows (*verba*) is not. Frier puts the break at the beginning of 49, Stroh at the beginning of 51; both breaks have possible topic-sentences:

iam *vim* factam negare non potes; *deiectus* quem ad modum sit, qui non accesserit, id quaeritur.

Now you cannot deny that *violence* was committed; what is under discussion is how someone who did not get to a place can be *thrown out.* (49)

an hoc dubium est quin neque *verborum* tanta copia sit non modo in nostra lingua, quae dicitur esse inops, sed ne in alia quidem ulla, res ut omnes suis certis ac propriis vocabulis nominentur

Or is there any doubt that there is not a sufficient supply of *words*, not only in our language, which is said to be without resources, but even in any other, to provide all objects with their own correct names   (51)

Frier's choice emphasizes a particular word, *deicere*, which dominates the discussion in 49–50; Stroh's emphasizes words in general. Cicero returns to the words of the interdict at 55 ('hoc ipsum *interdictum* quo de agitur consideremus'), and to *deicere* at 64 ('venio nunc ad illum tuum: "non *deieci*; non enim sivi accedere" ').

The antithesis between *vis* and *deicere* in Frier's topic-sentence is not an indication that this discussion is still part of the 'de vi'; sentences at points of topic-shift often look backwards as well as forwards.[28] Vocabulary analysis indicates a change in emphasis at 49. The word *deicere* has dropped out of sight since the opening of the 'de vi,' appearing only once at 47; *vis* fades from view after 49, appearing only once in connection with *detrusus*. These distributions support the claim that the topic is shifting, but they cannot decide the issue of where the break should be positioned. As for Stroh's topic-sentence, it is the third in a series of questions, the second two introduced by the particles 'an ... an ... '.[29] There is a shift from specific to

---

[28] The gerundive *iudicandum* in the final sentence of the *narratio* is picked up in the following *optandum*; the first word in the 'de vi,' *queramur*, refers to Cicero's 'complaint' at the end of the 'de actione.'

[29] Although there is no *utrum*, this is reminiscent of the sequence of questions used in the glide from the 'de testibus' to the 'de actione'; *an* (see *OLD* s.v.), can be used to introduce alternative questions without a preceding *utrum*.

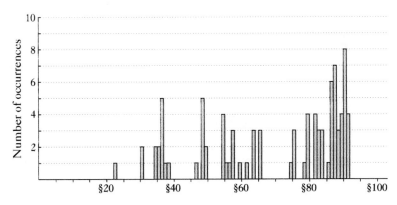

FIGURE 10.2. *The distribution of* deicere

general at 51, but it would probably not have seemed to be a marked break in oral delivery.

A case can be made, based on the language of the text, to support Frier's identification of 49–64 as a unit which opens and closes with discussions of *deicere* (49–50 and 64). But the choice between the two analyses misses a larger point about Cicero's synthesis of arguments. Figure 10.2 shows the distribution of the important word *deicere* throughout the *argumentatio*. There is substantial discussion of the term in the 'de actione'; it fades from sight in the 'de vi' and in the general discussion of words, but reappears well before 64; after 66 it fades from view as Cicero turns to general legal issues, but it is repeated still more emphatically in the verbal arguments which resume at 79. So 49–64 cannot be singled out as being uniquely concerned with the word *deicere*.

Many of these repetitions are explicit discussions of the word's meaning and implications. Cicero mentions the 'reieci, non deieci' argument at the beginning and end of the 'de testibus' (24, 31), but explicitly attacks it in the 'de actione' by means of a *reductio ad absurdum* based on a hypothetical parallel situation:

quaero, si te hodie domum tuam redeuntem coacti homines et armati non modo limine tectoque aedium tuarum sed primo aditu vestibuloque prohibuerint, quid acturus sis.

I ask you, if while you were returning home today, men summoned together and armed should keep you away not only from the threshold and the interior of your house, but from the very approach and entrance-hall, what action would you take? (35)

The flaw in the parallel is that Piso is described as being *reiectus* from his own house, of which he presumably has both ownership and possession.

Cicero conveniently ignores the fact that Caecina's ownership and possession were both disputed by Aebutius. A second attack at 50 is another *reductio ad absurdum*, an over-interpretation of the prefix *de-* (literally 'down'); the interdict should only apply to evictions which take place on hillsides! At 64, after several absurd definitions of other words from the interdict, Cicero claims none are as absurd as 'reieci, non deieci'.

The repeated rebuttal of 'reieci, non deieci' presents the other arguments in the case as mere digressions: that Piso's witnesses support Cicero's own argument; that no other appropriate action could have been brought by Caecina; that the dispute over whether real violence took place is only a quibble. It is natural to be suspicious of Cicero's presentation here. It may be doubted whether the witnesses testified to anything other than coming out in support of Aebutius' claim to ownership of the estate, a form of self-help widely tolerated in Roman law. That Cicero spends part of the *exordium* refuting the suggestion that another action should have been brought implies that this suggestion was more of a problem than he pretends in the 'de actione'. Perhaps the issue of whether or not violence took place was also more of a problem than he admits, leading the *recuperatores* to query the very use of this interdict.[30] If so, it would be to his advantage to subordinate other queries about the interdict to the obviously quibbling objection to *deicere*.

Cicero's strategy was to take the arguments which might have been seen as crucial and turn them into incidental asides from what he constantly presents as the main theme. Once the structure of the speech is seen as something other than a succession of discrete topics with clearly marked transitions, the repeated rebuttal of 'reieci, non deieci' can be seen to do more than unify the multiple arguments which had arisen during this complicated case. It is also a key element of Cicero's strategy to present the letter-of-the-law arguments as more important to Piso's case than to his own.

iv. The Climax of the Strategy and the Unity of the Text

The remainder of the *argumentatio* can be dealt with in two parts: the complex of arguments on jurists, the law and the interdict (65–95); and the *de civitate*. The latter is in many ways separate from the rest of the *argumentatio*. In 65–95 the topic-shifts come quickly, reflected by more subdivisions in

---

[30] Birks, *Oxford Journal of Legal Studies* 7 (1987), 452 suggests that violence may have been 'deliberately provoked' by Caecina's supporters.

Stroh's analysis, and shorter passages in Frier's. Cicero is moving towards a climax. A few topic-sentences will illustrate the succession of arguments, whose combination is so important to the speech.

Piso seems to have attacked Cicero's reliance on the advice of a particular jurist:

atque illud in tota defensione tua mihi maxime mirum videbatur, te dicere *iuris consultorum* auctoritati obtemperari non oportere

And in the entirety of your defence, what seemed the most amazing to me was your claim that it is not necessary to pay attention to the authoritative opinions of the *jurisconsults*. (65)

Cicero turns this into an attack on the civil law itself:

nam qui *ius civile* contemnendum putat, is vincula revellit non modo iudiciorum sed etiam utilitatis vitaeque communis.

For he who thinks the *civil law* should be despised loosens the bonds which hold together not only the courts but also the common interest and life. (70)

He then returns to the jurisconsults by naming his own adviser, Gaius Aquilius Gallus, in mid-77.

Piso's unnamed adviser ('vester iste auctor') is brought up in mid-79. This is the mysterious figure who provides Cicero with the quibbling argument that even if Caecina was *reiectus* from the estate, he was *deiectus* from the road outside the estate:

Aebutius autem qui fatetur aliquo ex loco deiectum esse Caecinam, is quoniam se restituisse dixit, necesse est male fecerit sponsionem.

But it must be the case that Aebutius, who admits that he cast Caecina out of some place, has made a bad legal wager, since he claimed that he had restored him. (80)

At 86 Cicero presents his final verbal argument against '*reieci*, non *deieci*', which focuses on the word 'unde' in the interdict: since 'unde' can mean both 'ex quo loco' (out of which place) and 'a quo loco' (away from each place), '*unde deiecisti*' cannot be interpreted as excluding '*a* quo loco *reiecisti*'. Cicero once again dissociates himself from the quibbling in which he is indulging, this time by claiming that it is not he who is being over-clever by finding a new interpretation, but the *maiores* (elders) who were wise in drafting a document that could not be pinned to a single interpretation.

Finally at 90 he turns to the issue of possession, but continues to quibble:

exoritur hic iam obrutis rebus omnibus et perditis illa defensio, eum deici posse qui tum *possideat*, qui non *possideat*, nullo modo posse.

At this point, now that the whole of your case is in ruins, you come up with the defence that he who has *possession* can be 'thrown out'; he who does not have *possession* can in no way be 'thrown out'.

Cicero responds by arguing that since possession is not mentioned in the interdict, it is not relevant to it. But in a shift from quibbling to a more equitable stance, he also triumphantly proclaims that Caecina has possession in any case.

atque ego in hoc Caecinam non defendo; *possedit enim Caecina*, recuperatores.

But I am not defending Caecina in this manner, *for Caecina did have possession*, gentlemen. (94)

Cicero is here arguing a case on two separate grounds, one of which is strictly and explicitly unnecessary, in the manner of advocates.

In the last of the digressions Cicero broadens the focus to the jurists and law, before returning to what has been repeatedly represented as the principal argument: 'reieci, non deieci'. The rapid succession of arguments, all verbal, all associated with someone other than Cicero, is followed by a brief but confident final claim that the argument about possession is irrelevant in any case. This must have reinforced the impression, so important to Cicero's presentation, that Piso's case depended on irrelevant quibbling. To the legal historian, the speed with which the possession argument is dismissed is suspicious, especially because in terms of the interdict it is the most important. And suspicion is appropriate; in Piso's presentation, 'reieci, non deieci' may not have been separate from the possession argument at all.[31]

Frier's suggestion that 86–95 constitute an argument *de verbo* can be dismissed; Cicero has been arguing *de verbo* since the first attack on 'reieci, non deieci' in the argument *de actione*. The argument about 'unde' is no more verbal than the argument about *de-* in 50. The so-called *partitio* makes a distinction more important to the strategy than to the structure of the speech.

So Cicero has his cake and eats it too: he provides arguments based on the letter of the law, but he makes it clear that his case is based in the spirit. It is more than likely that Piso was playing the same game. The analysis that the dispute centred on the distinction between *deicere* and *reicere* is correct, not because this ridiculous quibble was the central legal issue, but because Cicero's victory depended on giving the impression that this ridiculous quibble was what Piso wished to be the central legal issue.

How does the final argument of the speech, the 'de civitate', fit into the strategy? This is the most politically charged argument in the speech, a recapitulation of Cicero's argument in an earlier case that citizenship rights could not be taken away from the people of such communities as

---

[31] So Birks, ibid. 452–3, noting that Piso needed to 'peg his policy argument [i.e. the possession argument] to the text of the interdict'.

Arretium and Volaterrae.[32] Frier argues that this issue was not important in the final hearing of the case, and that Cicero must have chosen, when he published the speech, to combine it with arguments from the later stages of the case, because of its political interest. This suggestion begs a number of questions about publication practice, including the question of what attracted the speech-reading public. It seems unlikely that potential readers with no legal interests would have made their way through several complicated arguments in order to reach Cicero's views on disenfranchisement at the end.

The legality of Sulla's action in depriving certain Italian communities of full citizen rights was debated long after the *Pro Caecina*.[33] Cicero's claim that it had been settled by the earlier case in which he had spoken is disingenuous, though it reinforces the sense of his own authority: precedent, though it could be used as an argument, was not binding in Roman law. The question needed to be addressed once it had been raised, whether by Aebutius or Piso, at any stage in the argument. And in fact we have only Cicero's word for it that the argument was raised early on and abandoned. This is stated in the *narratio* (18), implying that only someone as litigious as Aebutius would make such a ridiculous accusation.

This connection between the *narratio* and the 'de civitate' points to a structural reason for seeing the latter as an original part of the final speech. These two passages, both of which Frier suggests were reinserted for publication, frame the long and varied central argument on *deicere* and provide ring composition.[34] Their apparent separateness from that argument need not be counted against them; the repetition towards the end of themes from the *narratio* serves as a unifying element in the speech. At the same time, the relegation of this issue to a position outside the central argument is another way of making it appear unimportant. It was unimportant from a legal point of view, but one more argument may be used to demonstrate its importance to Cicero's presentation.

One question, the auction of the estate, is not raised after the *narratio* except very briefly in the 'de testibus'. It is clear that on this question, which bears on the legally irrelevant but nevertheless potentially important

[32] For the speech on the Arretine woman, see J. W. Crawford, *Marcus Tullius Cicero: The Lost and Unpublished Orations* (Göttingen, 1984) 33–4 with bibliography.

[33] See Frier, *The Rise of the Roman Jurists*, 101.

[34] This effect is reinforced by verbal repetition: *calamitatem* (18); *calamitate* (95). In both the *narratio* and the 'de civitate' Cicero apologizes for leaving out material which he might have included: *praetermittam* (11); *praetereo* (101). This creates the impression that he has a superfluity of facts and arguments to back up his case, while suggesting that he has no wish to waste his hearers' time. The characters of Caecina and Aebutius are brought more vividly to life in the *exordium* and *narratio*, and then in the 'de civitate' and *peroratio*, than they are in the central argument. This too contributes to the ring composition effect.

issue of ownership, Cicero was short of evidence. Having dealt with the interdict in the way that he wishes, he selects with great care the issue with which he will end the argument. It is not an issue to which evidence is relevant. It is one which allows him to claim, for what it is worth, that precedent is on his side. It also lends itself to some climactic praise of Caecina's character. It is an excellent issue with which to distract the *recuperatores* from the possibility that Caecina had no right to the estate in the first place.

This analysis of the arguments of the speech has taken into account their expression as well as their subject-matter, and in particular the repetition of particular arguments and the impression they are likely to have made on the *recuperatores*. The analysis of verbal repetition made possible by modern technology has been used to back up earlier structural analyses, while the observation of repeated key-words in topic-sentences has refined them. By expanding the focus from the legalities of the interdict's interpretation to contemporary perceptions of these legalities, it has demonstrated that the extant *Pro Caecina* is a structural and strategic unity which could have functioned as the final speech for the plaintiff in this case. The integration of these approaches suggests that the study of a stylistic feature such as repetition can have important implications for the broader study of the speeches of Cicero the Advocate.

11

The Advocate as a Professional: The Role of the Patronus in Cicero's Pro Cluentio

CHRISTOPHER BURNAND

Sed errat vehementer, si quis in orationibus nostris quas in iudiciis habuimus auctoritates nostras consignatas se habere arbitratur. omnes enim illae causarum ac temporum sunt, non hominum ipsorum aut patronorum. nam si causae ipsae pro se loqui possent, nemo adhiberet oratorem. nunc adhibemur ut ea dicamus, non quae auctoritate nostra constituantur sed quae ex re ipsa causaque ducantur.

If anyone thinks that the speeches we make in the law courts represent an authentic record of our personal opinions, he is very wrong. All such speeches reflect particular cases and circumstances, not the personal opinions of the advocates themselves. If cases could speak for themselves, no one would employ an advocate. But as they cannot, we are called in to make speeches, which express not our own individual opinions, but whatever the actual facts of the case suggest.[1]

In this way Cicero depicts his role as an advocate while defending Cluentius in 66 BC. The advocate is presented as a semi-professional pleader who employs only his rhetorical skill in order to win his client's case. The description has a strikingly modern ring to it, and bears comparison with the account of the modern advocate's duty as set out by David Pannick: 'He earns his living propounding views to which he does not necessarily subscribe, and which are sometimes anathema to him, on

A version of this chapter was first delivered at the 1998 Triennial Conference of the Hellenic and Roman Societies in Cambridge, and I am most grateful to the audience on that occasion for a lively discussion. I am also indebted to Katherine Clarke, Michael Comber, Liz Irwin, Chris Pelling, Greg Woolf, and the editors for their full and helpful comments on various earlier drafts.

[1] Cic. *Clu.* 139.

behalf of clients whose conduct may not interest him, will often offend him, and can occasionally cause him outrage.'[2]

However this modern and quasi-professional portrait of the Roman advocate sits uneasily with another version which depicts the pleader in the Roman Forum as, primarily, a *patronus* speaking on behalf of a *cliens*.[3] Kennedy is explicit about the original link between advocacy and patronage: 'The system (of advocacy) was an extension of the patron–client relationship of the earlier republic.'[4] According to this approach the advocates, who were usually members of the political elite, were expanding their assistance towards their *clientes* into the realm of the courts. But they also began to speak as advocates on behalf of a broader group of supporters or friends,[5] on whose behalf they could deploy their own authority as important figures, just as they might help them at other times in canvassing for magisterial office.

This is a theme which has attracted a lot of attention since Kennedy's article of 1968, in which he highlighted the important effect that the practice of advocacy had upon Roman forensic speeches.[6] May has emphasized this use of transferred authority as a technique of persuasion which Cicero favoured throughout his career,[7] and even David, who has traced the development of a new, more popular style of oratory, has seen this development as merely offering a broader scope to traditional patronage: 'Même aux niveaux les plus modestes des procédures privés, la plupart de ceux qui plaidaient appartenaient déjà à l'aristocratie sénatoriale et ne faisaient que prolonger par l'assistance judiciaire l'exercice d'une relation

---

[2] D. Pannick, *Advocates* (Oxford, 1992) 1. He also quotes Lord Macmillan: '[The advocate is there to] present to the court all that can be said on behalf of his client's case, all that his client would have said for himself if he had possessed the requisite skill and knowledge' (H. P. Macmillan, 'The Ethics of Advocacy', in *Law and Other Things* (Cambridge, 1937) 181).

[3] In this chapter, for the sake of clarity, I use the Latin terms *patronus* and *cliens* to refer to the ties of traditional Roman patronage, reserving the English 'client' for the man represented in court by an advocate.

[4] G. Kennedy, *The Art of Rhetoric in the Roman World* (Princeton, 1972) 13. This development has been traced in detail in W. Neuhauser's lexicographical study, *Patronus und Orator* (Innsbruck, 1958) 19–64. He argues that the original obligation for the *patronus* to speak for his client in court developed into a looser bond where mutual interest was uppermost.

[5] The continued use of the term *patronus* for the Roman advocate seems to be a linguistic survival from the earlier period, and does not mean that we should see the relationship between advocate and client as parallel to that between *patronus* and *cliens*, although Crook suggests that the use of this terminology may continue to colour the relationship even under the Empire (J. A. Crook, *Legal Advocacy in the Roman World* (London, 1995) 122–3).

[6] G. Kennedy, 'The Rhetoric of Advocacy in Greece and Rome', *AJP* 89 (1968) 419–36.

[7] J. May, 'The Rhetoric of Advocacy and Patron-Client Identification: Variation on a Theme', *AJP* 102 (1981) 308–15. At p. 309 he states, 'By identifying himself with his clients and their causes with his cause, Cicero bestows upon their defences a measure of his own authority.' He pursued this line more comprehensively in *Trials of Character: The Eloquence of Ciceronian Ethos* (Chapel Hill, NC, 1988).

de patronat qu'ils s'étaient gagnée ailleurs' ('Even at the most modest levels of private cases, the majority of pleaders already belonged to the senatorial aristocracy and were doing nothing other than extend by judicial
assistance the exercise of a patronal relationship which they had won in
another way').[8]

These two perspectives on the practice of Roman advocacy are not
immediately reconcilable. In this chapter I do not intend to suggest that
either perspective is wrong. Rather, both views were adopted in various
circumstances, even by Cicero himself. Indeed, this fluid approach towards
the advocate's role seems to stem from the very fact that there was no generally agreed consensus upon its precise nature: it was open to a constant
process of renegotiation and redefinition between the advocate and the
court.[9] I concentrate on the image of the advocate as a professional, as
painted by Cicero in his defence of Cluentius, since this is the perspective
which has been less recognized. I argue that Cicero could exploit the fact
that, as an advocate who appeared regularly in the Roman courts, he was
able to advertise his faithful loyalty to the practice of the Roman law, and
hence to legal government. However, I begin by reviewing the traditional
view of advocacy as a branch of patronage, with particular reference to the
Pro Caelio.

This view is immediately suggested by the frequent use of the word
patronus of a defence advocate, and Cicero's own dialogue on oratory written in 55 BC, the *De Oratore*, is explicit about the importance of the patron's
personal qualities. One of the interlocutors, Marcus Antonius, sets out the
ways in which the forensic speaker should attempt to win the favour of his
audience on behalf of his client: 'valet igitur multum ad vincendum probari
mores et instituta et facta et vitam eorum, qui agent causas, et eorum, pro
quibus, et item improbari adversariorum' ('Therefore an important factor
in winning is for the characters, principles, deeds and course of life, both
of those who are to plead cases and of their clients, to be approved, and
conversely for those of their opponents to be criticized').[10] This is a clear
statement that the character and achievements of the speaker might be as
important in the conduct of a case as those of the person who was directly
concerned.

This is an alien idea for us, accustomed as we are to contemporary legal
advocacy–a modern jury would be rather surprised if a barrister was to
adduce his own achievements and good character on behalf of his client.
However this approach fits well with the idea that Roman advocacy

---

[8] J. M. David, *Le Patronat judiciaire au dernier siècle de la république romaine* (Rome, 1992) 656.
[9] But it should be noted that even the understanding of the modern advocate's role is under-
going a constant evolution through time.   [10] Cic. *De Or.* 2.182.

evolved out of the system of patronage: the *patronus* reminds the court of his own achievements, so that they might look favourably upon his protégé's case.

In the *De Oratore* Cicero makes Antonius go on to give an example of this type of advocacy, in which he describes his defence of Gaius Norbanus, previously Antonius' quaestor, against the charge of *maiestas*:

> Nothing could more deeply disgrace my reputation, or cause me more bitter sorrow, than that I, who was on many occasions considered to have been the saviour of complete strangers so long as they were citizens, had been unable to help my own friend. I asked the judges, should they see me affected by just and loyal grief, to excuse it in the light of my age, career and achievements.[11]

Antonius mentions his own *honores* and *res gestae* ostensibly as part of a plea to excuse his conduct in choosing to defend a slightly dubious client. But this tactful reference to his own achievements will have served to remind the jurors of their, and Rome's, debt to himself: the implication is that Norbanus, as a friend and man who served under Antonius, deserved special consideration.[12]

Although Cicero never rivalled Antonius' military achievements, once he had attained a leading role in Roman politics, he was able to exploit a similar technique in defence of his own clients. His speech on behalf of Marcus Caelius Rufus in 56 BC offers perhaps the best example of such pleading. Kennedy aptly describes Cicero's persona in this speech as that of 'the dignified consular, the saviour of the republic, the wise mentor of the young at Rome'.[13] At the start of the speech Cicero asserts that he himself has risen to his present pre-eminence from the same modest, municipal background as Caelius.[14] And Cicero can assure the court that they need have no worries about Caelius' education at Rome, because he had been entrusted to the care of Marcus Crassus and Cicero himself.[15] Cicero's paternal response to the prosecution charges that Caelius is a wastrel is that he is only a young man letting off some steam, and he is prepared to vouch personally for his future good faith towards the *res publica*.

---

[11] *De Or.* 2.200–1.

[12] An apparent counter-example is offered by Cic. *Mur.* 58–9. Here Cicero claims that Scipio Africanus' prosecution of Lucius Cotta was unsuccessful precisely because of the excessive prestige of the former, as a man who had been twice consul and had been responsible for the destruction of both Numantia and Carthage: 'The very wise men who at that time judged that case were unwilling for anyone to be condemned in such a way that they might seem to have been crushed by the excessive strength of an opponent.' However Cicero adduces this illustration as part of his attempt to undermine Cato's own authority as the prosecutor of Murena in the present case, and the jury's impulse to acquit stems from a fear that Scipio's authority would influence them.

[13] Kennedy, 'The Rhetoric of Advocacy', 432.   [14] Cic. *Cael.* 6.   [15] Ibid. 9.

Conservate igitur rei publicae, iudices, civem bonarum artium, bonarum partium, bonorum virorum. promitto hoc vobis et rei publicae spondeo, si modo nos ipsi rei publicae satis fecimus, numquam hunc a nostris rationibus seiunctum fore.

Therefore, men of the jury, preserve for the state a citizen who is talented, loyal and an optimate. I promise you this and I can assure the state on oath that, if I myself have served it well, he too will never cease to follow our political ideas.[16]

This sentence encapsulates the traditional view of the advocate as patron: just as Cicero has served the state well, so will his protégé, Caelius.[17] But it would be wrong even here to take Cicero's picture of his own role too literally. On this particular occasion it suits his case to present himself as a respected member of the elite, who has exercised some restraining influence upon a defendant accused of numerous youthful indiscretions, perhaps in the mould of the traditional *patronus* guiding his protégé's early career. By presenting himself as a father-figure, Cicero offers himself as a much needed character witness for his own client.

Yet even in this speech Cicero asserts Caelius' good character partly on the basis of Caelius' own practice in the Roman courts. As specific examples there are the prosecutions which the latter has conducted against Gaius Antonius and Lucius Calpurnius: Cicero argues that these cases can be considered hostages, or tokens, for Caelius' future goodwill towards the state.[18] But on a more general level Cicero asks the court to consider the whole lifestyle of the young legal practitioner. He assures the court, as one who knows, that such rhetorical skill as Caelius has displayed cannot be achieved without the most strenuous hard work: 'obterendae sunt omnes voluptates, relinquenda studia delectationis, ludus, iocus, convivium, sermo paene est familiarium deserendus' ('Every pleasure has to be renounced, all relaxation, fun, amusement, every party refused, even conversation with friends has to be almost abandoned').[19] The life of the orator which Cicero depicts in this passage demands round the clock activity and utter devotion to the life of the Forum and the courts. We can doubt, as perhaps the jury did, whether Caelius really imposed such a self-denying ordinance, but the important point is that Cicero thinks it feasible to present to the court such a pseudo-professional portrait of the orator. Indeed, in the *Brutus*, Cicero was to claim for himself a similarly diligent and exhausting training in the world of the Forum, when his days and nights were devoted to listening to others, practising declamation, and preparing and conducting real cases in the courts.[20]

---

[16] Ibid. 77.

[17] It is important to emphasize that Cicero was only adopting this role for the purpose of making his case: Caelius had clearly not been subject to Cicero's influence for some time.

[18] *Cael.* 78.   [19] Ibid. 46.

[20] Cic. *Brut.* 308–21. Throughout this section Cicero emphasizes the unceasing nature of his training.

This image of disciplined forensic activity is far removed from that of a *patronus* simply standing up and using his own authority to vouch for his client. Cicero himself ascribed the proliferation of advocacy at Rome to the introduction of the secret ballot for public trials in 137 BC.[21] David has preferred to ascribe the development of a more professional style of pleading to the *populares*, from Gaius Gracchus onwards, who sought to use a new kind of forceful and emotional oratory to appeal to the broader Roman public.[22] Whatever the historical causation, come the age of Cicero, Roman advocacy had become an all-consuming pursuit, where the rhetorical ability of the pleader might play as important a role as that of the authority contributed by a traditional patron, a change which would have radically altered the daily practice of justice in the Roman courts.

As I have noted above, David sees this development as merely offering an extension of the traditional form of patronage. However David himself demonstrates that Cicero seems to have undertaken all but two of his known cases before 64 BC, not as the result of any personal ties with the client, but because he was sought out, presumably as an up-and-coming talent.[23] This does not of course mean that Cicero was not winning his briefs through his own contacts, as young barristers do today, but it emphasizes how, as a *novus homo*, he could exploit his well-rehearsed rhetorical talents to flourish in the world of the Forum.

The speech which Cicero made on behalf of Cluentius offers an important window onto this semi-professional world. The background to this trial is complicated, and I present here a simplified outline. Aulus Cluentius Habitus was a knight from Larinum, a town 125 miles east of Rome. In 74 BC he had successfully prosecuted his stepfather Statius Abbius Oppianicus on the charge of attempting to murder him, that is Cluentius himself, with poison. This trial became notorious for the suspicion that bribery of the jurors had been carried out by both prosecution and defence. Two years later Oppianicus himself had died, and later still in 66 BC Oppianicus' own son, also called Oppianicus, charged Cluentius with the poisoning of his stepfather and two other figures.[24] However, according to Cicero, the prosecution passed very briefly over the actual charge of the alleged poisoning and devoted the bulk of its efforts to the earlier trial, alleging that Cluentius had committed 'judicial murder' against Oppianicus Senior by bribing the jury. As a result Cicero's defence speech is similarly weighted, and he only deals directly with the charge of the stepfather's murder and other poisonings in a very small proportion of the speech.

---

[21] Cic. *Brut.* 106.   [22] David, *Le Patronat judiciaire*, 553–6.   [23] Ibid. 224.
[24] Henceforth I refer to the father as Oppianicus Senior, and to his son as Oppianicus Junior.

What is immediately striking upon reading the speech is that the world which it depicts is a world where advocates dominate the courts. Apart from Cicero as speaker for the defence, Titus Attius had conducted the prosecution on behalf of Oppianicus Junior. In the earlier trial of Oppianicus Senior, the tribune Lucius Quinctius had been the defence advocate, whilst Publius Cannutius had conducted the prosecution.[25] But Cicero refers to several other trials in the course of his speech, and we find as advocates two sets of brothers, the Caepasii and the Cominii, as well as further appearances by Cannutius and Cicero himself.[26]

Cicero refers to all these men in the *Brutus*, a dialogue on the history of Roman advocacy, and it is clear that, with the exception of Lucius Quinctius, they all came from a non-senatorial background.[27] Whilst most of them remained *equites*, the two Caepasii showed what could be achieved by hard work, albeit on a less spectacular scale than Cicero himself:

> To the same age belonged the brothers Gaius and Lucius Caepasius, who with great effort, though newcomers and unknown, swiftly reached the quaestorship, with a style of speaking that was provincial and without form.[28]

Although Cicero is equally dismissive of their rhetorical ability in the *Pro Cluentio*, these men seem to have pursued what amounted to a career at the Bar, offering their services to any man who applied for their help, calling them 'industrious men, who believe that they should count any opportunity for speaking as a compliment and an asset'.[29] The pressures of continuous work in the Roman courts are well illustrated by a passage of the *De Oratore*.[30] Here Cicero makes Antonius criticize advocates who are keen to advertise the popularity of their services by taking on too many cases at the same time, and who therefore fail to master the facts of the different cases successfully: better to concentrate on one case at a time, and ensure that you conduct each case satisfactorily.

Such a system is far removed from that of the traditional *patronus*: the rhetorical skill of advocates and their regular presence in the courts must

---

[25] On Quinctius acting as defence advocate for Oppianicus Senior see *Clu.* 74; on Cannutius prosecuting on behalf of Cluentius see *Clu.* 29.

[26] Cannutius prosecutes Oppianicus' accomplices, Scamander and Gaius Fabricius, on behalf of Cluentius (*Clu.* 50, 58); Cicero appears as defence advocate for Scamander (*Clu.* 50), and in 69 BC for the aedile's clerk, Decimus Matrinius (*Clu.* 126); Gaius and Lucius Caepasius defend Gaius Fabricius (*Clu.* 57); Publius and Lucius Cominius prosecute Gaius Aelius Staienus, one of the jurors in the trial of Oppianicus Senior (*Clu.* 100). In addition, there is a reference to a man called Ennius, whom Cicero accuses of specializing in false prosecutions. In bringing these Cicero envisages him employing the services of an advocate (*Clu.* 163).

[27] Cannutius (*Brut.* 205); the Caepasii (*Brut.* 242); Attius (*Brut.* 271); Quinctius (*Brut.* 223); Publius Cominius (*Brut.* 271).   [28] *Brut.* 242.

[29] *Clu.* 57.   [30] *De Or.* 2.101.

have revolutionized Roman legal practice. These changes will have offered new opportunities to the advocates with regard to the arguments which they might employ, and Cicero's own speech provides ample evidence of these changes.

One of the most important themes of the speech as a whole is Cicero's insistence that a law-court must maintain different standards of evidence and proof from those practised by speakers in public meetings. The jurors must abandon any preconceived notions which they might have of the case as a result of such harangues. While stories of bribery at the trial of Oppianicus may have abounded in common rumours, a court must base its decision on solid evidence: 'illa definitio iudiciorum aequorum quae nobis a maioribus tradita est retineatur, ut in iudiciis et sine invidia culpa plectatur et sine culpa invidia ponatur' ('That definition of a fair trial which was handed down to us by our ancestors is something to which we should adhere: in a trial, guilt must be punished when there is no prejudice, and if there is no guilt, then prejudice must be set aside').[31] As a culmination to this purple passage, Cicero refers to the court, and his own role within it, as offering Cluentius a haven and refuge from ill-fortune.[32] This appeal must have carried particular weight coming from a regular court pleader.

But this was a sensitive issue for Cicero since in his speech against Verres he had denounced the corruption of the senatorial courts, and Attius, the prosecutor in the present trial, had quoted a particularly embarrassing assertion from that speech:

The Roman people will learn from me how it is . . . that a senator has been found, who, when he was a judge in one and the same case (the trial of Oppianicus Senior), received money from the defendant to divide up among the judges, and from the accuser, that he should condemn the defendant.[33]

This poses a notable difficulty for Cicero in the present case, since while he admits that bribery had occurred in the trial of Oppianicus Senior, he is insistent that the bribery was attempted by Oppianicus, and he is extremely careful to avoid any mention of the possibility that both the prosecution and the defence were attempting to subvert the course of justice.[34] Although he admits the problem of his own inconsistency, Cicero is

---

[31] *Clu.* 5.

[32] *Clu.* 7: 'quam ob rem magna me spes tenet, si quae sunt in causa explicare atque omnia dicendo consequi potuero, hunc locum consessumque vestrum, quem illi horribilem A. Cluentio ac formidolosum fore putaverunt, eum tandem eius fortunae miserae multumque iactatae portum ac perfugium futurum' ('Therefore I have great hope, if I can explain the facts of the case and deal with each of them in the course of my speech, that this court and you, its judges, which his prosecutors thought would bring terror and dread to Cluentius, will at last offer a haven and refuge from the storms which have long assailed his fortunes').   [33] Cic. *Verr. I* 38–9.

[34] *Clu.* 64.

nevertheless bullish in his dismissal of this attack. It is here, in the passage quoted at the start of the chapter, that he insists that an advocate's job was not to advance his own personal opinions, but those arguments which best support his client's case.[35]

Once more it is apparent that Cicero is deploying this argument to suit the particular circumstances of the case. On this occasion he is trying to explain the inconsistency of his own pronouncements, but it remains significant that he can express the advocate's duties in this way. For he presents the job of the pleader as distinct from his own personal authority: his task is merely to put the particular case which he is making in the best possible way, and so he can set out contradictory arguments in different cases. As I noted above, this approaches very closely the role expected of a modern advocate.

Cicero has already painted a similar picture earlier in the speech. For he had to suffer a second embarrassment in this case, having previously acted as the unsuccessful defence counsel for the freedman Scamander who was supposed to have purchased the poison for Oppianicus Senior's attempt upon Cluentius' life. Of course, now that Cicero is speaking for Cluentius it is in his interest to admit that Scamander's case was weak, but it is significant that he can say that his duty was to make the best possible case for Scamander, though he himself had little faith in his own arguments.[36] Again there is a close parallel with the role of the modern advocate: 'The advocate is entitled to take all possible points, bad as well as good. He has no right "to set himself up as a judge of his client's case".'[37]

Particularly noteworthy is Cicero's description of his own anxieties at speaking: 'Whenever I get up to speak I seem to be on trial myself, not only for my ability but for my integrity and dutifulness as well.'[38] His two concerns are that he should be talented enough to put his case well, and that he should be dutiful enough towards his client to employ the full range of

[35] This is not to say that Cicero does not want his own authority and affable character to carry some weight with the jurors in the present trial, a point which Nisbet made in describing Cicero's 'easy and confiding manner' (R. G. M. Nisbet, 'The Speeches', in T. A. Dorey (ed.), *Cicero* (London, 1965) 59): it is in this vein that he admits his own earlier error in following popular prejudice against Cluentius. However this does not detract from the significance of Cicero's earlier assertion, and Cicero's admission of his own error serves to reinforce the idea that the advocate's own opinion is not very important.

[36] *Clu.* 51. Compare also his description of the advocate's role at *Off.* 2.51: 'In lawsuits, a judge should always pursue the truth, but an advocate should sometimes defend what looks like the truth, even if it is not strictly true.' We might also compare Cicero's later pride in winning Cluentius' acquittal in the present case through deception of the jurors (Quint. *Inst.* 2.17.21). Quintilian refers to the matter in his discussion of how it is possible for the orator to persuade his audience with bad arguments while himself remaining unpersuaded.

[37] Pannick, *Advocates*, 92–3, quoting T. Humphreys, *Criminal Days* (London, 1946) 105.

[38] *Clu.* 51.

those talents. That is, he is concerned with his professional authority as an advocate, not so much with the personal authority which he might display as *patronus* on behalf of his *cliens*.

Even in the present trial, he is prepared to distance himself from his client, Cluentius.[39] He does this in order to raise a point of law which, so he alleges, Cluentius had asked him to avoid as a dishonourable argument. The point was that Cluentius could not legally be accused of the judicial murder of Oppianicus Senior since he was an *eques*, while the law held only senators responsible under this charge.[40] Cicero asserts that he has restrained himself from this line out of deference towards his client's wishes, but, as a matter of personal pride, he is not prepared altogether to drop arguments over the legal minutiae: 'I think it essential for my own interests to make clear that I have not been overcome by Attius upon any of the issues.'[41] Again it is obvious that Cicero, by emphasizing his independence, is trying to have the best of both worlds: he can use the argument, while maintaining his client's good honour. However it is important that he can talk about his own reputation as an independent performer, irrespective of his ties to the client.[42]

This separation also meant that the advocate could make the plea that he owed a broader allegiance than the obvious one towards his client. Cicero makes this clear when he again justifies his introduction of legal niceties to the case:

hic nunc est quiddam quod ad me pertineat, de quo ante dixi, quod ego populo Romano praestare debeam, quoniam is meae vitae status est ut omnis mihi cura et opera posita sit in hominum periculis defendendis.

[39] This is another favourite technique of Cicero's advocacy, since it enables him to use arguments which might not reflect creditably on his clients. So in his defence of Sextus Roscius of Ameria, he claims that he is attacking the freedman Chrysogonus in a personal capacity, and against the wishes of the defendant (*Rosc. Am.* 129). Similarly in defence of Milo, he makes an appeal to the jury's pity, although his client is unwilling to make such a plea himself (*Mil.* 92). Kennedy, 'The Rhetoric of Advocacy', 431–2 notes the opportunities offered by such a distinction between client and advocate. In the present case Cicero also exploits this distinction in making his virulent attacks upon Cluentius' mother, Sassia: it would perhaps have appeared less acceptable if the son had been making these criticisms in person. At *Amic.* 57 Cicero explicitly recognizes this greater licence when acting on behalf of one's friends.

[40] This was originally a Gracchan law which sought to punish senators who tried to frame innocent individuals rather than one simply directed against jurors taking bribes. See D. Stockton, *The Gracchi* (Oxford, 1979), 122–6 and U. Ewins, 'Ne Quis Iudicio Cicumveniatur', *JRS* 50 (1960) 94–107. [41] *Clu.* 149.

[42] Cicero's modern biographers also tend to give particular weight to this section of the speech, emphasizing that it enabled the orator to set out his own patronage of the *equites*, whilst hinting for the first time at his idea of a *concordia ordinum* between the senate and *equites* (§ 152): see E. Rawson, *Cicero* (London, 1975) 53–4; M. Gelzer, *Cicero: ein biographischer Versuch* (Wiesbaden, 1969) 58; and D. Stockton, *Cicero* (Oxford, 1971) 62. However this broader motivation, if it does represent Cicero's own thinking, does not detract from the significance of the manner in which he presents his role as an advocate in the present case.

The legal aspect, as I said before, is of concern to me personally, and the sort of point that I must mention out of duty to the Roman people. For the life I lead is such that I have dedicated all my care and efforts to the defence of men subjected to peril.[43]

Cicero proceeds to assert that he will personally defend anyone else who, as a non-senator, is unfairly charged under this law. This is an impressive pledge for an advocate to make since it suggests that he is a true servant of other citizens who are struggling to achieve justice. Unlike modern barristers there was no obligation for Roman advocates to take on any briefs which they received, but Cicero's promise does approach the idea that the advocate owed some duty to his fellow-citizens.[44] The pledge also serves the rhetorical needs of Cicero's argument since, by a kind of *praeteritio*, it allows him to make the legal point while distancing Cluentius from it, but that does not detract from the point that he feels able to make the promise. Moreover Cicero is better able to make it because he does appear regularly in court, offering his rhetorical services to those who approach him.[45]

But more specifically than a general duty towards individual citizens, Cicero can attach himself very closely to the service of the law itself. This issue is raised in his impassioned defence of the principle of law in sections 146–7. Magistrates are ministers of the law, judges its interpreters and all its slaves ('servi sumus'). Advocates, like judges and the clerks of the court are the visible apparatus of the law: 'I repeat that all the activity of this court is controlled and guided by the law, as if by a mind.'[46] While this certainly does not amount to the duty towards a court, which a modern barrister owes, it approximates to the idea that, out of public interest, the advocate must act as 'a helper in the administration of justice', as Lord Justice Singleton put it.[47] In the light of the fact that Cicero feels able to

---

[43] *Clu.* 157.

[44] The idea that a modern barrister must accept any brief for which he or she is competent is referred to as the 'cab-rank rule'. R. Du Cann, *The Art of the Advocate* (London, 1993) 37: 'The barrister is bound to accept any brief which will take him into the courts in which he professes to practise'. See also Pannick, *Advocates*, 135–7. On Cicero's readiness to defend all his fellow-citizens, compare the opening of *Rab. Perd.* where he claims that he did not need to justify taking on cases (although he proceeds to explain his decision to defend Rabirius).

[45] We might also compare the way in which he had taken up the brief of Scamander, when, according to Cicero, he was responding to pressure from Fabricius' fellow-townsmen of Aletrium (*Clu.* 49–50). But it is important to note that even Antonius in the *De Oratore* is made to excuse his defence of his friend Norbanus by using an *a fortiori* argument, which depends on the fact that he too had represented men previously unknown to him: he asked that he should be permitted to defend a close friend as an advocate who 'was on many occasions considered to have been the saviour of complete strangers, so long as they were citizens' (2.200).   [46] *Clu.* 147.

[47] Lord Justice Singleton in *Beevis v. Dawson* (1957) in *Law Reports 1: Queen's Bench Division* 195.

make these arguments, Crook perhaps goes too far in insisting that the Roman advocate spoke only for one master, the client.[48]

Cicero's assistance to the process of law and his self-presentation as a protector of his fellow-citizens can be employed not only in the courts, but in pursuit of his political career as well. In the *De Officiis* Cicero is clear about the gratitude and reputation that can be won by a pleader offering himself as a guardian for the needier members of society, who can see the advocate as a champion of their cause.[49] But a more striking testimony is provided in the Sixth Philippic, delivered before the people during Cicero's final crisis against Antony: the orator refers to his continued forensic practice as a token of his goodwill towards the people: he has expended the same labour in the Forum, after his honours were won, as he did when seeking them. How could he display greater gratitude towards the people than this?[50]

It would be impossible for Cicero to make this appeal to the Roman people, if they saw his forensic practice merely as an extension of the personal relationships of traditional patronage. I do not wish to deny the continued existence of this type of advocacy–enough of it is visible in Cicero's own speeches–nor do I wish to represent Roman advocates as the exact equivalents of modern barristers. However the arguments which Cicero deploys in the *Pro Cluentio* do depend for their efficacy upon the perceived existence of a skilled, pseudo-professional, group of advocates.[51]

It is important to recognize that these arguments, in the same way as those which suggest the more traditional type of advocacy, are usually introduced as the particular circumstances of Cicero's case demand. Indeed, the very fact that he develops at such length these arguments about the orator's role implies that the precise nature of the advocate's role was constantly being renegotiated. As in his defence of Caelius, Cicero could exploit his relationship with the client in order to emphasize his role as patron and draw upon his own authority for the client's benefit; but on

[48] Crook, *Legal Advocacy*, 163.

[49] *Off.* 2. 70: 'si opulentum fortunatumque defenderis, in uno illo aut, si forte, in liberis eius manet gratia; sin autem inopem, probum tamen et modestum, omnes non improbi humiles, quae magna in populo multitudo est, praesidium sibi paratum vident' ('If you defend a wealthy and fortunate man, you will receive gratitude from him alone, or perhaps from his children, but if you defend a needy but upright and modest man, all lowly and decent men, of which there are many among the people, see that there is a protection prepared for them').   [50] *Phil.* 6. 17.

[51] My use of the term 'pseudo-professional' is intentional, and I do not wish to suggest that Roman advocates collectively formed a profession in any narrowly defined sense of the word. The word 'professional' also raises the issue of payment, and here the *lex Cincia* of 204 BC was explicit in outlawing advocates' fees and gifts above a certain limit. However, there is agreement that these prohibitions could have easily been evaded, especially by means of legacies (J. A. Crook, *Law and Life of Rome* (London, 1967) 90–1), and men such as the Caepasii may have depended upon some form of payment for their livelihood.

other occasions, particularly when no such ties existed, he could stress a more disinterested professionalism. It was on the basis of this profession-alism that Cicero, and perhaps other advocates, did seek to establish an independent authority centred upon their contribution to the fair working of the Roman law and the legal rights of individual citizens. In turn they could deploy this authority both in their legal practice, and, in Cicero's case, even in political life.

I2

Literature and Persuasion in Cicero's Pro Archia

D. H. Berry

Pro Archia has been described as 'undoubtedly the least typical speech of the Ciceronian corpus.'[1] Cicero's client is not, as so often, a prominent Roman aristocrat accused of violence, bribery, or extortion, but a Syrian poet whose claim to Roman citizenship was disputed. In Tacitus' *Dialogus de Oratoribus*, one of the speakers, Maternus, is made to remark, 'It is not, I take it, the speeches which Demosthenes composed against his guardians that make him famous, nor is it Cicero's defences of P. Quinctius or Licinius Archias that make him a great orator: it was Catiline and Milo and Verres and Antony who covered him with glory' ('Non, opinor, Demosthenen orationes inlustrant quas adversus tutores suos composuit, nec Ciceronem magnum oratorem P. Quinctius defensus aut Licinius Archias faciunt—Catilina et Milo et Verres et Antonius hanc illi famam circumdederunt', *Dial.* 37.6). In *Pro Archia*, then, we are not spectators of one of the great oratorical clashes which signalled the imminent fall of the Republic; instead, the case is a more small-scale affair, involving a defendant who was, by himself, of no political or social importance whatsoever.

A second factor which makes *Pro Archia* untypical is that the greater part of it (§§ 12–30) consists of an encomium of literature which, while

The following items of bibliography may be found useful: Albrecht, M. von, 'Das Prooemium von Ciceros Rede pro Archia poeta und das Problem der Zweckmäßigkeit der *argumentatio extra causam*', *Gymnasium* 76 (1969), 419–29; Berry, D. H., *Cicero: Defence Speeches* (Oxford, 2000); Gotoff, H. C., *Cicero's Elegant Style: an Analysis of the Pro Archia* (Urbana, Ill., 1979); Husband, R. W., 'The prosecution of Archias', *CJ* 10 (1914), 165–71; Orban, M., 'Le *Pro Archia* et le concept Cicéronien de la formation intellectuelle', *LEC* 25 (1957), 173–91; Porter, W. M., 'Cicero's *Pro Archia* and the responsibilities of reading', *Rhetorica* 8 (1990), 137–52; Reid, J. S., *Cicero: Pro Archia*, 2nd edn. (Cambridge, 1883); Sternkopf, W., 'Die ökonomie der Rede Ciceros für den Dichter Archias', *Hermes* 42 (1907), 337–73; Taylor, J. H., 'Political motives in Cicero's defense of Archias', *AJP* 73 (1952), 62–70; Vretska, H. and K., *Cicero: Pro Archia* (Texte zur Forschung 31; Darmstadt, 1979); Wallach, B. P., 'Cicero's *Pro Archia* and the topics', *RhM* 132 (1989), 313–31; Wiseman, T. P., '*Pete nobiles amicos*: poets and patrons in late republican Rome', in B. K. Gold (ed.), *Literary and Artistic Patronage in Ancient Rome* (Austin, 1982), 28–49.

[1] H. C. Gotoff, *Cicero's Elegant Style: an Analysis of the* Pro Archia (Urbana, Ill., 1979) 81.

making for agreeable reading, nevertheless appears at first sight to have little connection with the point at issue.[2] Of course, there is nothing un-Ciceronian about a lengthy *digressio* (as I shall term this passage);[3] but here the subject of the digression, the status of literature, is one so far removed from the normal concerns of a Cicero speech as to constitute a striking oddity. It is the encomium of literature, however, for which *Pro Archia* is read and remembered, and which makes this speech a particular favourite among readers for whom the cut and thrust of late Republican politics is not a primary concern.

In this chapter I shall briefly review the historical circumstances of Archias' trial, and then discuss the speech itself and some of the issues it raises, especially that of why the encomium of literature is included, and how it contributes to the defence.

Our information about Archias derives almost exclusively from Cicero's speech. He was born at Antioch in Syria, probably in the mid-120s, and at an early age became famous throughout the East as a professional poet.[4] It is likely that at around this time some of his poems were anthologized by Meleager for his *Garland*, and the *Greek Anthology* contains thirty-seven epigrams attributed to a poet with the name 'Archias'. In some cases, however, the ascriptions read not just 'Archias' but 'Archias the *grammatikos*', 'Archias of Macedon', 'Archias of Byzantium', 'Archias of Mytilene', and 'Archias the younger'. There could therefore be as many as six Archiases, and we have no way of knowing for certain which of the epigrams in the *Greek Anthology* are the work of our poet.[5] Cicero tells us that Archias travelled to southern Italy (he was probably doing a round of festivals),[6] and was granted honorary citizenship by some of the cities he visited. He finally arrived at Rome in 102, when C. Marius and Q. Lutatius Catulus were consuls. Catulus was an enthusiast for Greek culture, and admitted Archias to his circle. It has been conjectured that it was Archias who first brought Meleager's *Garland* to Rome and thus introduced the Romans to Greek epigram: we have two Latin epigrams by Catulus, one of which is a translation of an epigram of

[2] Cf. Lord Brougham's often-quoted pronouncement: 'Cicero's speech for Archias, which is exquisitely composed, but of which not more than one-sixth is to the purpose, could not have been delivered in a British court of Justice' (*Eloquence of the Ancients*).

[3] See H. V. Canter, '*Digressio* in the Orations of Cicero', *AJP* 52 (1931), 351–61.

[4] On Greek professional poets see A. Hardie, *Statius and the Silvae: Poets, Patrons and Epideixis in the Graeco-Roman World* (Liverpool, 1983) 2–36.

[5] See A. S. F. Gow and D. L. Page (eds.), *The Greek Anthology: The Garland of Philip and Some Contemporary Epigrams* (Cambridge, 1968) ii. 432–5. It may be that all or most of the epigrams attributed to 'Archias' without qualification are the work of our poet. Several of these poems are imitations of Leonidas of Tarentum, and Professor F. Cairns has suggested to me the possibility that they were composed by our Archias during his stay in that city (§§ 5, 10) as a compliment to his hosts.

[6] See E. D. Rawson, *Intellectual Life in the Late Roman Republic* (London, 1985), 32.

Callimachus in the *Greek Anthology*, and the *Garland* appears also to have been imitated by other contemporary Roman poets (Gel. 19.9.10–14 (19.9.14: cf. Callim. *Anth. Pal.* 12.73); Cic. *Nat. D.* 1.79).[7] The other consul, Marius, though reputedly uninterested in Greek culture, approved of Archias' poem on Marius' own defeat of the Cimbri in 101 (§ 19).

At Rome, Archias was accepted into the household of the Luculli. The head of the family, L. Licinius Lucullus, went into exile, probably in 102, after being convicted of misconduct in Sicily the previous year, but he had two teenage sons at home, Lucius and Marcus, and Archias no doubt assisted with their education. His connections were not, however, limited to the Catuli and the Luculli. Cicero says that he attracted the attention of the Metelli Numidicus and Pius, M. Aemilius Scaurus, and L. Crassus, and also that he was on close terms with M. Livius Drusus (the tribune of 91), the Octavii, Cato (the father of Uticensis), and the Hortensii (§ 6).[8] During this period the young Cicero also received instruction from Archias (§ 1): Archias was presumably his Greek *grammatikos.*[9]

Some time later, Archias accompanied M. Lucullus on a visit to Sicily, and on their return journey Lucullus arranged for him to be granted honorary citizenship at Heraclea in Lucania. He continued, however, to live in Rome. After the Social War, citizenship was granted to the allies by the *lex Iulia* in 90, and this was followed in 89 by a further measure, the *lex Plautia Papiria*, which among other provisions extended the citizenship to honorary citizens of federate states not resident in those states but nevertheless resident in Italy, provided that they reported to one of the praetors at Rome within sixty days.[10] As an honorary citizen of Heraclea, which had been allied to Rome since 278, and being long resident in Rome, Archias duly reported to the praetor Metellus Pius within the specified period. Thus he became a Roman citizen, calling himself, in the Roman fashion, A. Licinius Archias, the *nomen* Licinius being adopted out of respect for his patrons the Luculli.

He continued to live with the Luculli, accompanying L. Lucullus to the East in the 80s and again during the Third Mithridatic War (73–63 BC), in the period when Lucullus was in command of the Roman forces (73–67). Lucullus' command proved to be highly successful in the early stages of the war, but after pursuing Mithridates into Armenia in 69 he began to lose the

---

[7] See A. A. Day, *The Origins of Latin Love-Elegy* (Oxford, 1938) 102–4; A. Cameron, *The Greek Anthology from Meleager to Planudes* (Oxford, 1993) 51–6.

[8] On the nature of Archias' relationship with these men see T. P. Wiseman, 'Pete Nobiles Amicos: Poets and Patrons in Late Republican Rome', in B. K. Gold (ed.), *Literary and Artistic Patronage in Ancient Rome* (Austin, Tex., 1982) 31–4.

[9] See M. L. Clarke, 'Cicero at School', *G&R* 15 (1968), 18–20. Conceivably this might explain 'Archias the *grammatikos*' in the *Greek Anthology.*

[10] On this law see A. N. Sherwin-White, *The Roman Citizenship*, 2nd edn. (Oxford, 1973) 150–2.

support of his troops; when his subordinate C. Valerius Triarius was heavily defeated in 67, he was relieved of his command, and Pompey was appointed the following year to bring the war to a successful conclusion. We know that Archias wrote, in Greek, a historical poem in several books on the Mithridatic War (§21). Cicero claims that this covered the war 'in its entirety' ('Mithridaticum vero bellum...totum ab hoc expressum est', §21), but in view of the great hostility which had arisen between Lucullus and Pompey this must be an exaggeration: the poem was a commission from the Luculli (*Att.* 1.16.15), and will obviously have stopped short of Pompey's appointment. It was no doubt publicly performed at Lucullus' triumph in 63.[11]

In 65 the tribune C. Papius had carried a law expelling from Rome all non-citizens who did not have a fixed residence in Italy: residents of Rome, therefore, who could not prove themselves Roman citizens, were liable to be prosecuted under the law and expelled from the city. In 62 Archias was prosecuted under this law. The prosecutor, Grattius, is not otherwise known, but in view of the hostility between Lucullus and Pompey he is usually assumed to have been one of Pompey's supporters, and the prosecution is therefore interpreted as an attack by a supporter of Pompey on the protégé of Pompey's enemy Lucullus.[12] This seems plausible: it is difficult to see why anyone should otherwise have wished to call into question Archias' citizenship, which had gone unchallenged for twenty-seven years. But Archias was only a poet, and it would be too much to suppose that the trial had any great political significance. It is perhaps most likely that Grattius was acting on his own initiative to avenge an imagined slight to his patron (who was still away in Asia)–the slight being simply that Archias had given Lucullus extravagant praise in his poem on the Mithridatic War.

Cicero's reasons for undertaking the defence are apparent from the speech. First there is the genuine sense of gratitude he felt towards his old teacher (§1), a factor which should not be cynically denied. As M. L. Clarke has pointed out, Archias was not the only one of Cicero's boyhood teachers whom he went out of his way to help: he had Diodotus to live in his house after he had become old and blind (*Brut.* 309; *Luc.* 115; *Tusc.* 5.113), and it was partly for Phaedrus' sake that he intervened with C. Memmius to prevent him from demolishing Epicurus' house in Athens (*Fam.* 13.1.4).[13] Secondly, Cicero had high hopes that Archias would immortalize his suppression of the Catilinarian conspiracy in Greek verse (§§28, 31), just as he had immortalized the achievements of Lucullus. Whether this reason or his

---

[11] See Wiseman (cited n. 8) 33.

[12] See e.g. E. S. Gruen, *The Last Generation of the Roman Republic* (Berkeley, Calif., 1974) 267 f. For a contrary view see D. L. Stockton, *Cicero: A Political Biography* (Oxford, 1971) 154.

[13] Clarke (cited n. 9) 21.

desire to protect his old teacher weighed more heavily with him it would
be foolish to speculate.[14] A third reason not explicitly mentioned in the
speech but quite clear from it is that Cicero wished to oblige the Luculli.
Plutarch tells us that Cicero was a good friend of L. Lucullus (*Luc.* 41.3, 42.4),
and in politics they shared the same conservative outlook. Lucullus must
have helped to bring about Cicero's election to the consulship, and in
July 63 Cicero in return had enabled Lucullus to celebrate his long-delayed
triumph (Cic. *Luc.* 3). Again, Lucullus had helped Cicero during the
Catilinarian conspiracy (ibid.), and Cicero had set aside time during it to
defend a relation of Lucullus' (*Att.* 13.6.4), L. Licinius Murena, the consul-
elect. By the end of 63, it was already clear that Cicero would be open to
attack for his execution of the conspirators, and it was therefore useful to
him to remain closely allied with the conservative elements in the Senate,
who would (at least until the formation of the 'First Triumvirate') be in a
position to protect him. But the connection brought social advantages too.
It was in 62 that Cicero sought to improve his social position (*Att.* 1.13.6)
by purchasing from Crassus a grand house on the Palatine overlooking the
Forum. This was a suitable house for a member of the nobility, as Cicero now
was, and it would, incidentally, have been one of the ones frequented by
Archias in the 90s, having been the residence then of M. Drusus (Vell. 2.14.3).
But the Luculli were aristocrats in the fishpond class (*Att.* 1.19.6, 1.20.3; cf.
Macrob. *Sat.* 3.15.6), and we have from Plutarch the attractive story of how
Pompey and Cicero invited themselves round to Lucullus' house for dinner,
and how he tricked them into thinking that he dined on the most lavish
scale even when eating alone (*Luc.* 41.3–6). Clearly Cicero would not have
jeopardized his relationship with such a family by refusing to defend their
poet. From every point of view, then, it would have been unthinkable for
him not to take on Archias' defence.

Archias was acquitted, as he surely deserved to be: of Cicero's clients,
Archias is one of those of whom we can say with most certainty that he
was innocent of the crime with which he was charged.[15] We hear of him
again in 61, presumably still living in Rome, and contemplating writing a
poem for the Metelli (*Att.* 1.16.15). It was Metellus Pius who had enrolled
him as a citizen and whose careful records provided the documentary evidence that he needed to establish his claim to citizenship. Metellus had died
by the time of the trial, but Cicero talks in § 26 of Metellus' concern to have

---

[14] Cf. W. M. Porter, 'Cicero's *Pro Archia* and the Responsibilities of Reading', *Rhetorica* 8 (1990)
143: 'We are left with the suspicion that the entire speech is little more than a product of Cicero's
vanity.' This seems harsh and unfair.

[15] Cf. E. Badian, 'Marius' Villas: The Testimony of the Slave and the Knave', *JRS* 63 (1973) 129:
'For once there can be no doubt that the prosecution was a piece of mere chicanery, and that
Cicero's client was as innocent as his counsel claimed.'

his achievements immortalized in verse, and it seems that Archias put his obligation to that family before his obligation to Cicero. This is understandable in view of the higher social status of the Metelli. But the poem on Cicero's consulship seems never to have been written, a strange omission on Archias' part, since he had a clear duty to provide it. Perhaps the project was opposed by one of Archias' noble patrons; or one could speculate that this may have been a commission made impossible by the enthusiasm of the client. Or perhaps Archias had simply grown tired of praising the Romans, and felt confident that Cicero would forgive him if he failed to oblige. In any case, Archias is mentioned once more by Cicero, in a philosophical treatise of 44, with affection (*Div.* 1.79).

So much for the historical circumstances; I now turn to examine the speech itself. The structure is, in its main divisions, extremely straightforward. There is an *exordium* (§§ 1–4a), then a *narratio* (§§ 4b–7) outlining Archias' career and the process by which he became a Roman citizen. There is then a *confirmatio* (§§ 8–11), which consists of arguments based on the facts as given in the *narratio*. At this point there is nothing further that Cicero can say that is directly relevant to the legal issue, and so the *digressio* (§§ 12–30), consisting of the encomium of literature, intervenes. The speech is rounded off with a brief *conclusio* (§§ 31–2). There is no *partitio*,[16] and no *reprehensio* (unless §§ 10–11 are viewed as *reprehensio*).

The speech begins (§ 1):

Si quid est in me ingeni, iudices, quod sentio quam sit exiguum, aut si qua exercitatio dicendi, in qua me non infitior mediocriter esse versatum, aut si huiusce rei ratio aliqua ab optimarum artium studiis ac disciplina profecta, a qua ego nullum confiteor aetatis meae tempus abhoruisse, earum rerum omnium vel in primis hic A. Licinius fructum a me repetere prope suo iure debet.

If I have any natural talent, members of the jury—and I am aware how limited it is; or if I have any experience in public speaking—in which I do not deny that I am moderately well practised; or if there is any technical skill in my oratory which has been derived from application and training in the liberal arts—and I admit that I have never at any period of my life been averse to such training: if I do have any of these capabilities, then A. Licinius here is entitled almost as of right to be among the very first to claim from me the benefits which they may bring.

This sentence, with its elegant series of carefully balanced clauses, immediately raises the question of the style of the speech: with the exception, naturally, of the *narratio*, the speech is pitched at a higher stylistic level than is normal in Cicero. We should therefore begin by asking what it was

---

[16] P. MacKendrick takes § 4a as a *partitio* (*The Speeches of Cicero: Context, Law, Rhetoric* (London, 1995) 110). As regards the content of 4a this would be correct; but 4a cannot easily be separated from 3, and in any case the *partitio*, if included, ought to occur *after* the *narratio*.

about this particular case that led Cicero to adopt such a style.[17] The question is especially pertinent in the context of the *exordium*, since stylistic brilliance was normally to be avoided in this part of the speech (*Inv.* 1.25; Quint. *Inst.* 4.1.54–60).

I suggest three reasons. First, Archias was a literary man, a poet, and this is a factor which was potentially prejudicial to the defence. Cicero cannot conceal or explain away Archias' occupation, and so he has no choice but to make a virtue of it. What he does, in fact, is to base his defence upon a positive, robust view of literature (as we shall see below), and in this strategy the style of his speech, as displayed initially in the *exordium*, plays an integral part. The style marks the speech as being a self-consciously literary product, and thus cleverly reinforces Cicero's contention that literature can be directed towards useful, practical ends, and is therefore something of value to society.

The high stylistic level, secondly, serves to establish an atmosphere of culture and sophistication, and this too is something that was best done right from the start. Cicero immediately takes us into a world of intelligent culture in which he and Archias play a part, and in which the jury are flattered into fancying that they also belong. The technique is similar to that employed the previous year in *Pro Murena* (*Mur.* 61):

Et quoniam non est nobis haec oratio habenda aut in imperita multitudine aut in aliquo conventu agrestium, audacius paulo de studiis humanitatis quae et mihi et vobis nota et iucunda sunt disputabo. (one sentence)

Now since I am not making this speech before an ignorant rabble or before some gathering of rustics I shall be a little more bold in discussing those cultural studies with which you and I are so familiar, and which we find so agreeable.

In both speeches Cicero encourages the jury to feel that they possess the cultural knowledge which will entitle them to pronounce on intellectual questions (and in both speeches he is extremely careful to place only minimal demands on that supposed cultural knowledge). It is only in *Pro Archia*, however, that the style is made to play an active part in the process (§3):

... quaeso a vobis ut in hac causa mihi detis hanc veniam accommodatam huic reo, vobis, quem ad modum spero, non molestam, ut me pro summo poeta atque eruditissimo homine dicentem hoc concursu hominum litteratissimorum, hac vestra humanitate, hoc denique praetore exercente iudicium, patiamini de studiis humanitatis ac litterarum paulo loqui liberius, et in eius modi persona quae propter otium ac studium minime in iudiciis periculisque tractata est uti prope novo quodam et inusitato genere dicendi.

... I beg of you that you will grant me an indulgence in this trial which is appropriate to this defendant here, and, I trust, not disagreeable to you–that you will

---

[17] Cf. Gotoff (cited n. 1) 81; Porter (cited n. 14) 144 f.

allow me, speaking as I am on behalf of an eminent poet and a most learned man and before this crowd of highly educated people, this civilized jury, and such a praetor as is now presiding, to speak rather more freely on cultural and literary matters, and, as befits the character of a man who because of his life of seclusion and study has had very little to do with the hazards of the courts, to employ a somewhat novel and unconventional manner of speaking.

In this passage (which comprises less than two-thirds of the Latin sentence) the atmosphere of high culture is conveyed not only by what Cicero is saying but very largely by the sophisticated way in which the clauses are accumulated and integrated.

The third reason for the high stylistic level may be stated more briefly. In §1, Cicero claims that he owes his skill in speaking to Archias. A show of stylistic brilliance on Cicero's part will therefore reflect creditably on the man who taught him. Archias must indeed be a teacher of genius, the jury will conclude, if he taught Cicero to speak like this.

Let us now turn to the argument of the opening sections; this is also revealing of Cicero's techniques. Cicero begins by explaining to the jury why he is obliged to defend Archias (or A. Licinius, as he prefers to call him at important moments in the speech). Stripped to its essentials, the argument runs as follows: 'If I have any talent, experience in speaking, or technical skill in oratory derived from training in the liberal arts, then Archias has a strong claim on it. This is because he was my teacher. He trained my voice, which I have used to save people on trial. I therefore have a duty to save him' (§1). This argument, understood literally, does in fact have some validity. If Archias was Cicero's *grammatikos*, he would have taught him to recite Homer and other Greek poets, and the vocal training that this involved may genuinely have helped him on his way to becoming a great orator. But the argument is nevertheless misleading because it leaves the impression, for example by the reference to 'technical skill in oratory' ('huiusce rei (referring to *exercitatio dicendi*) ratio'), that Archias actually taught Cicero rhetoric. If Cicero had wished to be less ambiguous he could have said: 'When I was a child, Archias was my tutor in Greek poetry, and I benefited from his teaching. Now that I have become a famous advocate, I feel that I have a duty to defend him.' But this would of course be much less neat rhetorically, and would also make Cicero's obligation appear much less pressing. For the argument to be effective, Cicero has to imply that it was Archias who made him the great orator he has become; this then demands an element of vagueness as to precisely what Archias' contribution was. There is also a further consideration. Throughout the speech Cicero wishes to show that Archias is someone who is useful to society. If he can somehow imply that Archias trains advocates, then that will give a much more favourable impression than saying that he merely provides instruction in Greek poetry.

In §2 Cicero decides to meet head-on the objection that Archias is not a *rhetor*:

Ac ne quis a nobis hoc ita dici forte miretur, quod alia quaedam in hoc facultas sit ingeni neque haec dicendi ratio aut disciplina, ne nos quidem huic uni studio penitus umquam dediti fuimus. Etenim omnes artes quae ad humanitatem pertinent habent quoddam commune vinclum et quasi cognatione quadam inter se continentur.

But in case anyone is surprised to hear me say this, given that my client's talents lie not in the theory and practice of oratory but in another direction, I should point out that I have never devoted myself exclusively to this one art. For all branches of culture are linked by a sort of common bond and have a certain kinship with one another.

If this argument too is put another way, its weakness will be apparent: 'You may be surprised to hear me attributing my success in the courts to a poet rather than a rhetorician, but rhetoric is not the only subject I have studied, and in any case rhetoric and poetry are really the same sort of thing.' The main value of this argument, however, is that it introduces the idea of the 'common bond' (*commune vinclum*) by which Cicero claims all branches of culture are linked. This is a convenient idea for Cicero because it will allow him, later in the speech, to widen his discussion to include other disciplines of more obvious practicality or value. It will also give him a much larger pool of examples on which to draw, including the actor Q. Roscius Gallus (§17), the rhetorician L. Plotius Gallus (§20), and the historian Theophanes of Mytilene (§24), none of whom would otherwise be relevant to his argument.

The *exordium* ends (§4a) with a statement of what Cicero intends to prove: (i) that Archias is a Roman citizen, and (ii) that, were he not a citizen, he ought to be one (and ought therefore to be acquitted). This twofold pattern of argument is a common one in Cicero, and is found most famously in *Pro Milone*: 'Milo did not set out deliberately to kill Clodius; but had he done so, it would have been justified.'[18] In *Pro Archia*, the first stage of the argument (*enstasis*) occupies §§4b–11, while the encomium of literature, occupying §§12–30, is formally the second stage (*antiparastasis*). The fact that the encomium of literature is flagged in the *exordium* in this way helps to bind it more tightly into the overall structure of the speech.

The legal argument, that Archias is a Roman citizen, is divided into two roughly equal halves, the *narratio* (§§4b–7) and the *confirmatio* (§§8–11). In the *narratio*, the facts are very simply stated. Archias' career is recounted up as far as his arrival in Rome in 102; Cicero impressively manages

---

[18] Cf. D. H. Berry and M. Heath, 'Oratory and Declamation', in S. E. Porter (ed.), *Handbook of Classical Rhetoric in the Hellenistic Period 330 BC–AD 400* (Leiden, 1997) 403, 410–11, 417.

to connect him with both the consuls of that year, Marius and Catulus.
Then (§ 5):

Statim Luculli, cum praetextatus etiam tum Archias esset, eum domum suam
receperunt.

The Luculli straight away received Archias into their house, although even at this
time he was still of the age when the toga of boyhood is worn.

There are two pieces of misrepresentation in this sentence. First, Cicero
must be exaggerating Archias' youth: he has just told us that the people of
Tarentum, Rhegium, and Neapolis had honoured him with their citizenship,
and it is inconceivable that they should have done this if he was still a boy.
But more fundamentally, Cicero's words convey the impression that Archias
was already a Roman citizen. In reality Archias, if he ever wore a toga at all,
which is doubtful, would not have done so until 89, by which time he had
been settled in Rome for thirteen years. Cicero is not, however, attempting
to predate Archias' acquisition of the citizenship: he is simply encouraging
the jury to think of Archias in terms appropriate to a Roman citizen.

Persuasion of a different kind occurs in the next section (§ 6):

Erat temporibus illis iucundus Q. Metello illi Numidico et eius Pio filio, audiebatur
a M. Aemilio, vivebat cum Q. Catulo et patre et filio, a L. Crasso colebatur,
Lucullos vero et Drusum et Octavios et Catonem et totam Hortensiorum domum
devinctam consuetudine cum teneret, adficiebatur summo honore . . .

Back in those days Archias was regarded with affection by the famous Q. Metellus
Numidicus and his son Pius; his recitations were attended by M. Aemilius; he was
constantly in the company of Q. Catulus and his son; his friendship was cultivated
by L. Crassus; and as for the Luculli, Drusus, the Octavii, Cato, and the entire family of the Hortensii, he was on the closest terms with all of them and was treated
by them with the greatest respect . . .

In one sentence Cicero mentions ten consuls, the entire political establishment of the previous generation: this is name-dropping on the grandest
scale imaginable. The effect on the jury of this roll-call of aristocratic
names must have been considerable: it would make it abundantly clear
that Archias, even allowing for some exaggeration on Cicero's part,
enjoyed the patronage and favour of Rome's leading families. At the same
time the names confer legitimacy and respectability not only on Archias,
but on the world of intelligent culture to which he belongs.

The *narratio* concludes with the vital facts relating to Archias' acquisition of the citizenship. First, M. Lucullus arranged for him to be granted
honorary citizenship at Heraclea. Later, in 89, the *lex Plautia Papiria* was
passed, and Cicero quotes the clause which covered Archias' case: persons
would be granted Roman citizenship if (*a*) they had previously been
enrolled as a citizen of a federate state, (*b*) they had had a fixed residence

in Italy at the time when the law was passed, and (*c*) they declared themselves before a praetor within sixty days (§ 7). As an honorary citizen of Heraclea, Archias satisfied condition (*a*), and as a long-standing resident of Rome he satisfied condition (*b*). He therefore declared himself before his friend the praetor Q. Metellus Pius and obtained Roman citizenship.

Cicero now moves on to the *confirmatio*, which, because of the simplicity of the case, is almost as brief as the *narratio*. He does not have documentary proof that Archias is a citizen of Heraclea, he says, because the public record office at Heraclea was burnt down in the Social War and all the records destroyed;[19] but he can nevertheless produce M. Lucullus as a witness to Archias' enrolment, and an official deputation has been sent from Heraclea with a written statement confirming Archias' claim. As for his declaration before the praetor Metellus, Cicero produces the citizen lists which Metellus compiled, argues for their accuracy, and points to the name of A. Licinius.

Several more arguments follow, but they are of little practical value since Cicero has already proved his case. The Romans seem to have found it advantageous to make use of every argument at their disposal, not merely the decisive ones: this can be observed not only in oratory but also for example in Lucretius. Here, however, Cicero does need to explain briefly why Archias was never included in a census: that of 89 was abandoned, and when censuses were held in 86 and 70 he was each time accompanying L. Lucullus on campaign in the East. Cicero does not bother to mention the further censuses of 65 and 64, since the jury would be aware that they too had been abandoned.

The legal argument now being triumphantly concluded, it might be assumed that Cicero's defence is over. Instead of a *conclusio*, however, we now have a *digressio* which accounts for significantly more than half the speech (§§ 12–30). I should like therefore to pause at this point and consider what are Cicero's reasons for including this digression, and for allowing it so to dominate the speech.

The first point to bear in mind, then, is that this passage is, formally at least, the second stage of Cicero's argument as announced at § 4a. There he said that he intended to prove first that Archias is a Roman citizen, and secondly that, were he not a citizen, he ought to be one. By now Cicero may or may not have persuaded the jury of Archias' legal claim. If he has not, then the further argument is obviously required. But even if he has, the jury may still feel reluctant to acquit Archias, because they are prejudiced against him. It is this potential prejudice that Cicero has to overcome in the remainder of the speech.

---

[19] R. W. Husband notes that if the lack of public records at Heraclea were to count against Archias then none of the citizens of Heraclea would qualify as Roman citizens ('The Prosecution of Archias', *CJ* 10 (1914) 169).

Archias was not the sort of person that a Roman juror would necessarily have considered desirable as a member of the Roman citizen body. To begin with, he was a Syrian by birth, a Greek-speaker from the eastern edge of the Empire. It is clear from *Pro Flacco* that the sort of unremarkable, upper-class men who for the most part constituted Roman juries cannot have had any great respect for the Greek nation. In that speech Cicero is able to characterize the Greeks as clever talkers, certainly, but also deceitful, dishonest, fickle, and brazen, and motivated by a hatred of the Romans. He does, it is true, make an exception for the Greeks of Achaea, who could point to a more distinguished, if remote, past, and lived closer to Rome. But the Asiatic Greeks (and it was the Asiatic part of the Greek world from which Archias originated) are presented in uniformly negative terms. Such a characterization could not have been employed by Cicero unless the jury already held, or at least were disposed to hold, a similar view themselves. Clearly, then, in attempting to persuade a jury that Archias deserved to be a Roman citizen, Cicero faced an uphill struggle. The extent of upper-class Roman prejudice regarding a man's place of origin is revealed by the fact that, in the year before Archias' trial, Cicero himself had been described in the Senate by one patrician as an 'immigrant citizen' ('inquilinus civis', Sal. *Cat.* 31.7). Catiline would presumably not have made such a remark unless he expected it at least to carry some weight with some of the senators.

Secondly, Archias was not just a Greek, but a Greek poet. Poets (at least good ones) were of course highly esteemed by cultured Romans such as the Catuli, the Luculli, and Cicero himself, but such men were a minority. A typical juror–one of a panel of seventy-five[20]–would have taken an entirely different view. We can infer this from the reticent tone Cicero feels it necessary to adopt in other speeches when he is discussing subjects with any kind of intellectual content. In the *Fourth Verrine*, for example, when he is dealing with Verres' theft of art treasures, he affects to be unable to recall the name of the famous sculptor Polyclitus (*Verr. II* 4.5; cf. Quint. *Inst.* 9.2.61–2). In *Pro Lege Manilia*, admittedly a speech to the people, he pretends to be only vaguely aware that Athens was once a great sea power (*Leg. Manil.* 54). Again, in outlining the content of Plato's *Phaedo* in *Pro Scauro*, he implies that he has not read the work, and adds, for the jury's benefit, that Plato was a great philosopher (*Scaur.* 4). When he does choose to discuss an intellectual subject at length, in *Pro Murena*, he begins, as we have seen, by flattering the jury on their erudition, and then proceeds to describe the Stoic school of philosophy in a way which first of all

---

[20] This seems to have been the usual number: see A. H. M. Jones, *The Criminal Courts of the Roman Republic and Principate* (Oxford, 1972) 69 f.

assumes no prior knowledge whatsoever, not even the name of the founder, and secondly serves merely to reinforce, for his own ends, the jury's anti-intellectual prejudices.[21] Cicero was to admit, many years later, that the jury that heard Murena's case were an ignorant lot (*Fin.* 4.74), and there is no reason to suppose that the one that heard Archias' the following year was any different. The view it would have taken of sophisticated Greek poetry can easily be surmised. A large part of Archias' output, and his entire output before he attracted Roman patronage, would doubtless have consisted of poems on typical Hellenistic themes (the epigrams in the *Greek Anthology* which may be his include erotic poems, dedications to a god, epitaphs, and poems on a work of art). Such poetry was unfamiliar to most Romans, and had not yet been widely imitated in Latin. It would have seemed entirely alien to Archias' jury, who would have regarded it not just with the suspicion they directed at all intellectual subjects, but would have seen it as frivolous, effeminate, and even immoral. It was, in short, beneath the consideration of a Roman.

This, then, is the attitude with which Cicero, himself derided as a 'wee Greek' ('Graeculus') by his detractors (Dio 46.18.1; cf. Plut. *Cic.* 5.2), has to contend. He does so by presenting poetry in a particular way likely to appeal to his audience. He makes it out to be not an exclusive or intellectual subject, but something practical and useful to society. Archias' poetry, according to Cicero, is serious historical poetry, written to celebrate the glorious exploits of Rome's generals and statesmen and make them known throughout the world—a large part of which, he adds, speaks only Greek. This type of poetry, he says, provides patterns of excellence for men to imitate, while the prospect of being immortalized in verse spurs men on to perform heroic deeds in the service of the state. By this line of argument, Archias, though Greek, is turned into someone who helps to promote Roman values and bolsters Roman authority and tradition.[22] He therefore has an important part to play in Roman society, and hence deserves his place within it as a Roman citizen.

So the necessity to present Archias and his poetry in a favourable light is Cicero's main reason for including a lengthy *digressio* in his speech. But there are other reasons too which should be mentioned. First, whatever the jurors' private views on poetry and culture, it is nevertheless flattering

---

[21] On the hostility of the late-Republican Roman ruling class to Greek philosophy (and to the Greek language) see H. D. Jocelyn, 'The Ruling Class of the Roman Republic and Greek Philosophers', *BRL* 59 (1976–7), 323–66 (esp. 359 f. on the attitude adopted by Cicero in his speeches towards philosophy and other intellectual subjects).

[22] G. Williams, *Tradition and Originality in Roman Poetry* (Oxford, 1968) 31–3, contrasts Archias with his younger contemporary Catullus, whose poetry undermined Roman authority and tradition. Catullus' poetry, however, was written some years after Archias' trial, and so would not have been a factor prejudicing the jury.

for them to be treated as intellectuals, as a select group of people who are well educated and superior to the common herd (cf. *Mur.* 61, already quoted). If they condemn Archias, then they will also be rejecting this flattering picture of themselves. But Cicero's technique is not simply one of flattery. Treating the jury as intellectuals also serves to reduce the apparent cultural distance separating them and Archias: during the trial, Cicero, Archias, and the jury will all be literary men together.

Secondly, the *digressio* is an enjoyable diversion for the jurors (and also an intellectually undemanding one, despite Cicero's flattery). Cicero was always aware of the importance of entertaining and amusing his audiences, and he won them over partly by providing them with passages they would derive pleasure from listening to. In *Pro Murena* and *Pro Caelio*, for example, this is done with humour. Here it is done with charm. The *digressio*, then, is not simply an instrument of persuasion, it is also an elegant essay that would have been as appealing to its original audience as it has been to readers down the ages.

Finally, the *digressio* performs an important function in diverting attention from the political aspect of the trial. The prosecution of Archias was probably undertaken, as we have seen, by a supporter of Pompey, and was directed not so much against Archias as against his patron L. Lucullus. Cicero, for his part, had no wish to become embroiled in this conflict between Pompey and Lucullus, and was anxious to remain on friendly terms with both men;[23] although the speech contains much praise of Lucullus, the one reference that there is to Pompey is highly complimentary (§ 24). Cicero in fact knew well how to serve one side without offending the other: he had done it before in *Pro Lege Manilia* (66 BC), in which praise for Pompey is combined with a generous appreciation of Lucullus' achievements. In *Pro Archia*, then, it is partly in order to minimize the political element that Cicero places so much emphasis on literary questions.

Let us turn now to the *digressio* itself. The structure of this passage is difficult to analyse. W. M. Porter divides it into three parts, §§ 12–16 covering the benefits afforded by the study of poetry, §§ 17–19 covering the intrinsic virtues of poets, and §§ 20–30 covering the relationship of the poet and his poetry to the state. P. MacKendrick, on the other hand, divides it into four parts, §§ 12–17a, 17b–22, 23–7, and 28–30.[24] Without wishing to dispute either of these schemes, I prefer myself to divide the passage into just two basic parts. In the first, §§ 12–17 (Porter and MacKendrick also agree on a break at

---

[23] In addition to defending Archias at this time, he also undertook the defence of Pompey's brother-in-law P. Sulla. *Fam.* 5.7 (April 62 BC) shows him seeking to form closer ties with Pompey. On the political aspect see further Gruen and Stockton (cited n. 12), the former making too much of and the latter too little of the trial's political significance.

[24] Porter (cited n. 14) 140 f.; MacKendrick (cited n. 16) 110 f.

around § 17), Cicero discusses literature in general rather than specifically poetry (here I do disagree with Porter), and provides a series of arguments to show that literature is useful, or at least not harmful. In the second part, §§ 18–30, he turns from literature to poetry and brings Archias into the discussion (Archias is not referred to at all in §§ 13–17), arguing that poetry, and *a fortiori* Archias, is useful to society. This second part can be subdivided in several ways (MacKendrick identifies the decisive breaks), but for the most part the transitions are gradual and one point merges into the next.

First, then, let us review §§ 12–17. The *digressio* begins as if in anticipation of a question from the prosecutor (§ 12): 'You will no doubt ask me, Grattius, why I am so delighted with this man' ('Quaeres a nobis, Gratti, cur tanto opere hoc homine delectemur'). Grattius, of course, has already delivered his speech, and has not asked such a question, but the question gives Cicero an excuse to embark upon his digression and, later, to parade Archias' virtues. He starts by saying that Archias enables him to unwind after a busy day in the courts (the jury will sympathize), but he then immediately broadens the discussion from poetry to literature in general, and he will stick firmly to literature in general until § 18. Literature, he says, provides him with material for his speeches: it is therefore useful (this argument incidentally helps to reinforce the impression, given in the *exordium*, that Archias has in some way played a part in Cicero's rhetorical training). A distinction is then made between those like Cicero who study literature and apply it to a useful end, such as defending people in court, and those who study it but make no practical use of it; the latter category, Cicero says, should be ashamed of themselves. In § 13 he contrasts his own study of literature with the frivolous amusements of others: if others devote their spare time to the games, to parties, and dice, why should he not devote his to a pursuit which, he repeats, enables him to defend people in court? In § 14 he introduces a new idea, that literature inspires men to perform acts of self-sacrifice for the state. Were it not for his study of literature, he says, he would never have stood up to Catiline. He continues (§ 14):

Sed pleni omnes sunt libri, plenae sapientium voces, plena exemplorum vetustas; quae iacerent in tenebris omnia, nisi litterarum lumen accederet. Quam multas nobis imagines non solum ad intuendum verum etiam ad imitandum fortissimorum virorum expressas scriptores et Graeci et Latini reliquerunt! Quas ego mihi semper in administranda re publica proponens animum et mentem meam ipsa cogitatione hominum excellentium conformabam.

But all books, all the words of the wise and all history are full of examples which teach this lesson—examples which would all be lying in obscurity, had not the light of the written word been brought to them. How many finely executed portraits of the most valiant men have the Greek and Latin writers left us, and not only for our contemplation but for our emulation! Indeed, I myself, when serving as a magistrate, have always kept these men before my eyes, and have modelled myself on them, heart and mind, by meditating on their excellences.

Clearly Cicero is not thinking only of poetry at this point: 'scriptores et Graeci et Latini' ('the Greek and Latin writers') would apply equally to prose historiography or biography, genres which some members of the jury may personally have considered more valuable and worthwhile, or less reprehensible, than poetry. At the same time he is also alluding to the uniquely Roman custom whereby nobles kept wax masks (*imagines*) of their ancestors who had held curule office within the *atria* of their houses. In a possible reminiscence of this passage, Sallust tells us that Q. Fabius Maximus Verrucosus and the elder Scipio were said to have been spurred on to virtuous deeds by contemplating the masks of their ancestors (*Jug.* 4.5);[25] Cicero's claim here is that works of literature, whether Greek or Latin, have the same salutary effect.

In §§ 15–16 Cicero considers the objection that many of the great Romans of old were not themselves lovers of literature. He gracefully concedes the point, but then goes on to instance some outstanding Romans who did study literature (§ 16):

Ex hoc esse hunc numero quem patres nostri viderunt, divinum hominem, Africanum, ex hoc C. Laelium, L. Furium, moderatissimos homines et continentissimos, ex hoc fortissimum virum et illis temporibus doctissimum, ⟨M.⟩ Catonem illum senem; qui profecto si nihil ad percipiendam colendamque virtutem litteris adiuvarentur, numquam se ad earum studium contulissent.

There were examples of this in our fathers' time, the younger Africanus, a godlike man, and C. Laelius and L. Furius, men of the greatest moderation and self-control, also the elder M. Cato, a most valiant man and the most learned of his day. These great men would surely never have taken up the study of literature had it not been of help to them in attaining and practising excellence.

The authority of these great Romans (all were consuls and two were also censor) wins Cicero his point after all; the technique is the same as that used at § 6. It would appear in fact that this argument has been introduced primarily in order to provide a context for the famous names, since it is the names that carry the main persuasive force.[26]

After this, § 16 closes with the argument that literature is inherently pleasant. The sententious and lyrical language in which the point is made effectively proves the point (§ 16):

Nam ceterae neque temporum sunt neque aetatum omnium neque locorum; at haec studia adulescentiam acuunt, senectutem oblectant, secundas res ornant, adversis perfugium ac solacium praebent, delectant domi, non impediunt foris, pernoctant nobiscum, peregrinantur, rusticantur.

---

[25] Cf. Polyb. 6.53.9–10; Cic. *Phil.* 2.26; Val. Max. 5.8.3. I am grateful to Professor A. J. Woodman for drawing my attention to the Sallust passage. [26] Porter (cited n. 14) 145 f.

For other forms of mental relaxation are in no way suited to every time, age, and place. But the study of literature sharpens youth and delights old age; it enhances prosperity and provides a refuge and comfort in adversity; it gives enjoyment at home without being a hindrance in the wider world; at night, and when travelling, and on country visits, it is an unfailing companion.

Such language does not occur often in Cicero's speeches, at least after the earlier ones:[27] as we have already observed, the style of this speech is pitched at a higher level than normal.

The passage on literature in general ends with § 17. The argument here runs as follows: (i) even if we are not interested in literature, we should admire those who have literary talent; we admired the talent of the actor Q. Roscius Gallus; (and equally we should admire that of Archias); (ii) we loved Roscius merely because of the movements of his body; we should therefore respond to the movements of (Archias') mind. The argument itself is feeble (if rhetorically neat) and requires no further comment. What is interesting, however, is the way Cicero brings in a popular celebrity who has little or nothing to do with Archias and blatantly capitalizes on his star status and the affection in which he was held. Roscius and Archias were artists of quite a different kind: Roscius was a Roman *eques*, now dead, who had acted in plays before large audiences; Archias was a Syrian immigrant who wrote poetry in Greek for a small number of aristocratic families. Just about all that the two men had in common was that they were both at some point represented in court by Cicero (they were also linked by the fact that Archias, like his patron Catulus (*Nat. D.* 1.79), wrote a poem on Roscius (*Div.* 1.79)). But Roscius was a figure who was familiar to the jury and entirely acceptable to them (partly, perhaps, on account of his high social status, unusual for an actor): Cicero now hopes that he can lay claim to that acceptance for Archias too.

At § 18 Cicero moves to the second part of the *digressio*. In this part he turns his attention specifically to poetry and to Archias, and argues that both are useful to society. The transition is made by mentioning Archias (not referred to since § 12, or named since § 9) and marvelling at his ability both to improvise (cf. Quint. *Inst.* 10.7.19, based on this passage) and to produce written compositions. He is represented as a genius, and as equalling the 'ancient writers' ('veterum scriptorum')–a phrase which leaves it conveniently vague whether we are to think of Greeks (Homer) or Romans (Ennius). After this, Cicero goes on to declare that poets are divinely inspired, and hence sacred. The testimony of Ennius (which can hardly be considered impartial!)[28] is cited in support of this view; at § 31 Cicero will go

---

[27] Cf. M. Winterbottom in *Éloquence et rhétorique chez Cicéron* (Fondation Hardt *Entretiens* 28; 1982) 260–1.   [28] Porter (cited n. 14) 141.

further and claim that 'everyone' ('apud omnis') has always held poets to be sacred. The argument reaches a climax at the beginning of §19:

Sit igitur, iudices, sanctum apud vos, humanissimos homines, hoc poetae nomen quod nulla umquam barbaria violavit. Saxa atque solitudines voci respondent, bestiae saepe immanes cantu flectuntur atque consistunt; nos instituti rebus optimis non poetarum voce moveamur?

So let the name of poet, gentlemen, which no barbarian race has ever treated with disrespect, be a sacred name among you, the most enlightened of men. Rocks and deserts respond to the poet's voice; ferocious wild animals are often turned aside by singing and stopped in their tracks: shall we, then, who have been brought up to all that is best, remain unmoved by the voice of a poet?

Here again we find the elevated and lyrical style used earlier at §16; the opinion of some scholars[29] that this passage is 'turgid' is refuted by Quintilian, who cites it, sometimes with explicit approval, no fewer than six times (*Inst.* 5.11.25, 8.3.75, 9.4.44, 11.1.34, 11.3.84, 11.3.167).

Cicero's next argument begins with a rhetorical and effective (if not very logical) comparison between Archias and Homer: various Greek cities vie for the honour of having numbered Homer among their citizens, so Rome should be grateful that Archias belongs to her. The important point is then made that Archias' poetry celebrates the military glory of the Roman people: his poem on the war against the Cimbri actually won the approval of Marius. The reason for this, Cicero continues, is that there is no one who is unwilling to have his own deeds immortalized in verse (this was indeed true in his own case, as he will later reveal). Themistocles is cited as an example, but then we have the surprising sentence (§20): 'It was for the same reason that Marius was so fond of L. Plotius: he thought that his achievements could be made famous by Plotius' talent' ('Itaque ille Marius item eximie L. Plotium dilexit, cuius ingenio putabat ea quae gesserat posse celebrari'). Now Plotius was not a poet but a rhetorician, and if he praised Marius he would have done so in a Latin speech, not a Greek poem. He is therefore a poor example to cite. But for Cicero, the opportunity to make play with Marius' name a third time was too tempting to pass up.

The next paragraph takes us from the war against the Cimbri to the Third Mithridatic War, about which Archias had also written (and at much greater length). Cicero's main point here is that Archias' poem honours not just Lucullus but the Roman people as well: this is meant to show that Archias is useful to the Roman people, and so ought to be cherished by them. Cicero also wants to see that Archias is firmly set within the serious, masculine, and Roman context of warfare, rather than in the frivolous and

---

[29] MacKendrick (cited n. 16) 122; cf. J. S. Reid, *Cicero: Pro Archia*, 2nd edn. (Cambridge, 1883) 18 f.

self-regarding world of Greek poetry. But while the Roman people are honoured, Lucullus too is given a full share of the glory (§ 21):

Nostra semper feretur et praedicabitur L. Lucullo dimicante, cum interfectis ducibus depressa hostium classis est, incredibilis apud Tenedum pugna illa navalis, nostra sunt tropaea, nostra monumenta, nostri triumphi.

That astonishing naval battle off Tenedos, when L. Lucullus killed the enemy commanders and sank their fleet, will always be spoken of and proclaimed as ours: ours are the trophies, ours the monuments, ours the triumphs.

Cicero seeks to maximize Lucullus' glory, since Lucullus' authority is an important factor in Archias' defence.[30] He has, however, taken some liberty in this regard: we are told by Memnon, a second-century AD historian of Heraclea Pontica, that the naval battle off Tenedos was in fact won not by Lucullus himself but by his subordinate Triarius (*FGrH* III B, 361 (33.1)).

The idea that poets who honour great men honour the Roman people at the same time is continued in § 22, but with Ennius as the example: Ennius praised the elder Scipio, the elder Cato, Q. Fabius Maximus Verrucosus, M. Claudius Marcellus, and M. Fulvius Nobilior, and was rewarded with Roman citizenship. Rome should therefore be grateful that Archias already belongs to her (the argument concludes in the same way as the argument from Homer at § 19). The comparison with Ennius is a useful one for Cicero, since Ennius was Rome's great national poet and would have been fully acceptable to the jury. Both poets were befriended by a leading family at Rome (Ennius by the Fulvii Nobiliores), taken on campaign by them, and granted citizenship through their influence; unlike Archias, however, Ennius was from Italy and wrote in Latin.

The comparison with Ennius at last brings Cicero to answer the objection that Archias writes in Greek (§ 23). This is done in the briefest way possible: Cicero simply says that Greek is spoken virtually everywhere whereas Latin is not, and it is desirable that all the nations that Rome has conquered should be able to read of her glory. After this he quickly moves on to less controversial territory. Literary commemoration, he says, incites men to undertake dangerous and heroic deeds. The two examples he mentions here are Alexander the Great and Pompey the Great (§ 24); the comparison is highly complimentary to the latter. First we have Alexander at Sigeum, desiderating

---

[30] C. Damon, *The Mask of the Parasite: A Pathology of Roman Patronage* (Ann Arbor, Mich., 1997) 268–76, argues, if I understand correctly, that Cicero plays down Lucullus' role and declines to make use of his authority because it would harm Archias if he were to be seen as Lucullus' parasite. But Cicero does make use of Lucullus' authority, and his emphasis on the Roman people is entirely appropriate in a citizenship trial. Much is made of Lucullus' supposed absence from the trial; but no ancient evidence is cited to support this.

a Homer who could write of his achievements. This is a fair parallel, since
Homer and Archias were both Greek poets who produced poems narrating
the exploits of military leaders. The next example, however, is that of Pompey
giving Roman citizenship to Theophanes of Mytilene.[31] This parallel is less
valid since Theophanes was not a poet but a prose historian (*scriptorem*,
'writer', is the ambiguous word Cicero uses). Theophanes is, nevertheless, a
good example for Cicero to cite, not only because he was a Greek who was
given the citizenship, but because he was given it by Pompey. If Archias'
accuser is indeed connected with Pompey, as seems likely, then the reference
has added point: in seeking to deprive Lucullus' man of his citizenship,
Grattius is ignoring the precedent set by his own patron.

The arguments that follow continue the close connection of poetry with
military affairs. If Archias had not already possessed Roman citizenship,
Cicero says, he could easily have obtained it as a favour from some general such as Sulla, or from his friend Metellus Pius (§§ 25–26a). Metellus,
we learn, was anxious for his deeds to be immortalized in verse, and this
leads Cicero back to a theme he has touched on earlier (at § 20), the desire
of all great men to be praised. After a brief hit at philosophers for their
hypocrisy in writing their names on the books they have written, we are
back with Roman generals once again: D. Junius Brutus Callaicus inscribed
his monuments with poems by Accius, and M. Fulvius Nobilior dedicated
his spoils of war to the Muses (§§ 26b–27).

The *digressio* concludes (§§ 28–30) with Cicero's admission that he too
wishes to be immortalized in verse; as he has demonstrated, there are many
honourable precedents for this. Without praise, he explains, men would
have no incentive to perform great deeds (the point is repeated from § 23).
All good men wish their name to live on for ever after their lives are over;
and whether or not Cicero, after his death, will have any awareness of his
posthumous fame, he at least derives pleasure at this moment from the
thought that his achievements will be remembered. The tone of the passage
is philosophical; but it is popular philosophy of a straightforward nature,
designed to reassure rather than intimidate the jury.

The *conclusio* (§§ 31–2) recapitulates the main points of the case, and contains no emotional appeal. It ends with a curious reference to the praetor in
charge of the court (§ 32):

... quae a foro aliena iudiciialique consuetudine et de hominis ingenio et communiter
de ipso studio locutus sum, ea, iudices, a vobis spero esse in bonam partem accepta,
ab eo qui iudicium exercet certo scio.

... as for the part of my speech which was out of keeping with the Forum and the
tradition of the courts—when I discussed my client's talents and literary studies in

---

[31] Scholars all give the date as 62, citing our passage; but our passage is not so specific.

general–I hope that this has been received in good part by you, gentlemen, as I know it has been by the man who is presiding over this court.

Even if we had not been informed by the scholia (175 Stangl), we would, I think, have been able to tell that the praetor in question is Cicero's brother Quintus. H. C. Gotoff asserts that the reference is 'either jocular or tasteless', and adds: 'Perhaps the best way to understand the reference to his brother . . . is to take it together with Cicero's decision to speak in a style more epideictic than usually deemed effective in the law courts, and to assume that the orator had reason to be confident from the start in the outcome of the trial.'[32] This suggestion cannot be accepted, because a praetor in charge of a court had no means of determining or influencing a jury's verdict; this is why in his speeches Cicero addresses himself to the jury, and generally ignores the praetor. It is therefore impossible that Quintus should have assured Cicero in advance that an epideictic style would be well received or that Archias would be acquitted. I suggest that, on the contrary, Cicero's defence is wholly unaffected by the fact that he is speaking before his brother, and that the reference at the end of the speech is no more than a friendly nod to someone who, until this moment, he has had to treat exactly as he would any other praetor.

Pro Archia, then, is genuinely, all of it, an exercise in persuasion. The jury must be persuaded both that Archias is a Roman citizen and that he deserves to be one. From the persuasive point of view, it is the second of these questions that is the more difficult, and therefore the more interesting. Here Cicero was confronted by a marked xenophobic and anti-intellectual prejudice, one with which he and his brother had no sympathy, but which was prevalent among the jury. His method of dealing with this prejudice is to include a lengthy passage on literature which presents Archias and his poetry in terms which the jurors will find unobjectionable, and perhaps even praiseworthy. Consequently this passage, though it might formally be termed *digressio*, is, like other digressions in Cicero's speeches, central to the case. It is not a passage that could not be included were it not for the presence of a sympathetic praetor. For centuries it has been seen as a charming encomium of literature, and it would be wrong to deny that it is that. But if Cicero had written a treatise on literature for an educated readership outside the courtroom, we can be certain it would have had little resemblance to the version which was offered to Archias' jury.

---

[32] Gotoff (cited n. 1) 211, 212–13 (cf. 81).

13

De Domo Sua: *Legal Problem and Structure*

WILFRIED STROH

The Problem

On 29 September,[1] 57 BC, before the Roman college of priests, Cicero won his reinstatement into his house and grounds which had in part been dedicated to the gods by P. Clodius Pulcher. Cicero himself regarded the speech delivered on that day (*De domo sua*)[2] as an outstanding example of his own passionately inspired 'power of eloquence' ('vis dicendi'), a masterpiece which he 'must not keep the young waiting for' any longer, i.e. had to publish as soon as possible in written form: 'si umquam in dicendo fuimus aliquid aut etiam si numquam alias fuimus, tum profecto doloris magnitudo[3]

---

[1] So according to Cic. *Att.* 4.2.2: *prid. Kal. Oct.*, not '30 September', as occasionally stated (most recently by P. MacKendrick *The Speeches of Cicero: Context, Law, Rhetoric* (London, 1995) 147), which would be correct only after Caesar's calendar reform of 46 BC.

[2] Of more recent editions and commentaries the most important are: *M. Tulli Ciceronis orationes*, vol. 5, ed. G. Peterson (Oxford, 1911 repr.); *M. Tulli Ciceronis De Domo Sua ad pontifices oratio*, ed. R. G. Nisbet (Oxford 1939) reproduces the Oxford text; commentary esp. on linguistic points; *M. Tulli Ciceronis scripta*, fasc. 21 (*Red. Sen., Red. Quir., Dom., Har. Resp.*) ed. T. Maslowski (Leipzig, Teubner, 1981), the standard edition today; see also *M. Tullius Cicero: Sämtliche Reden*, introd., tr., and comm. by M. Fuhrmann (Zurich and Munich, 1970–82) v.195–279, 484–95 ('Über das eigene Haus', without Latin text); *Cicero Back from Exile: Six Speeches upon his Return*, tr. with introd. and notes by D. R. Shackleton Bailey (Chicago, 1991) 37–101, without Latin text, but with excellent short notes. The fullest interpretative study of the whole work in recent times is that of C. J. Classen, *Recht–Rhetorik–Politik: Untersuchungen zu Ciceros rhetorischer Strategie* (Darmstadt, 1985) 218–67; less important, P. MacKendrick (cited n. 1) 147–76; C. Bergemann, *Politik und Religion im spätrepublikanischen Rom*, Palingenesia 38 (Stuttgart, 1992) (=Diss., Technische Universität Berlin 1989), also gives a commentary on almost the whole speech. A new commentary would be very desirable.

[3] Shackleton Bailey (in the Teubner edn., Stuttgart 1987) reads with other editors (following Gulielmius) *dolor et ⟨rei⟩ magnitudo*–the paradosis is not clear–which fits the hyperbole in the speech itself (*Dom.* 1 'quod si ullo tempore magna causa') better than the more sober tone of the letter. In any case, the basis of this is the well-known idea that strong emotion or grief makes one eloquent; in Cicero: *Brut.* 93 (concerning Galba) 'naturalis quidam dolor dicentem incendebat'; ibid. 278 (from a speech against Calidius) 'ubi dolor, ubi ardor animi, qui etiam ex infantium ingeniis elicere voces et querelas solet?'; *Or.* 130 'ut viderer excellere non ingenio sed dolore adsequebar' (on this antithesis: D. R. Shackleton Bailey, *Propertiana*, Cambridge, 1956, 21); cf. *De Or.* 2.188 ff.; also Quint. *Inst.* 6.2.26; 10.7.15; Juv. 1.79.

vim quandam nobis dicendi dedit: itaque oratio iuventuti nostrae deberi non potest' (*Att.* 4.2.2). Posterity has not always followed Cicero's self-assessment without hesitation. Admittedly, in Germany at least, the title of the speech (in the version 'Pro domo',[4] by which is meant 'speech on one's own behalf') has today become almost as popular and proverbial[5] as that of the (second) 'Philippic' (i.e. a 'dressing-down'). On the other hand, in literary criticism it has been regarded as agreed for quite some time that *De domo sua* is rather inferior in rhetorical quality. As late as the sixteenth century, the humanist Corradus had extolled it as 'prope omnium pulcherrimam',[6] but then Jeremias Markland (1745) and above all Friedrich August Wolf (1801) wished to reject it, together with several other speeches, as unworthy of Cicero;[7] and even now that its genuineness has again been generally recognized, it is still usually held that Cicero went too far in spiteful polemics against his enemies and unscrupulous glorification of himself, or, at any rate, that he went a great deal further than he needed to in order to win the case. After all, only a relatively small part of the speech (104–41) is obviously devoted to the substantive problem, and only a few paragraphs (127–37) to the central legal point which was relevant for the priests;[8] everything seems overgrown by a

---

[4] As Klaus Bartels (*Veni vidi vici: geflügelte Worte aus dem Griechischen und Lateinischen*, 8th edn., Zurich and Munich, 1990) correctly notes, 'Pro domo' is the title in older editions, demonstrable approximately up until the complete edition of Cicero by Chr. G. Schütz, Leipzig 1814–23 (according to Engelmann–Preuss, *Bibl. Script. Class.* II 128); it is based after all on two manuscripts, yet our oldest manuscript has 'De domo sua', as do the grammarians' testimonia (according to statements in Maslowski's apparatus). Its use as a cliché in the sense customary today, which must necessarily be older, is noted for instance in L. Herhold, *Lateinischer Wort- und Gedankenschatz* (Hanover, 1887) 206 and in G. Büchmann, *Geflügelte Worte*, 31st edn. (Berlin, 1964) 504, but it is not found in R. Tosi, *Dizionario delle sentenze latine e greche*, 21st edn. (Milan, 1996) or in J. R. Stone, *Latin for the Illiterati* (New York and London, 1996).

[5] Even commercial advertising has taken hold of it; a brand of coffee popular in Germany is called 'prodomo'; and Cicero's supposed title could also have had an effect on semibarbaric or pseudo-Latin names like 'Pro musica' or 'Pro musica antiqua' (for music ensembles) or 'Pro familia' (for an advice centre for family planning or abortion). Just in the last few years various German companies, clubs, and projects have followed their example: 'Pro Seniore', 'Pro infante', 'Pro Liberis', 'Pro Christo', 'Pro Animale' [!] etc., and of course also 'Pro Lingua Latina'.

[6] Quoted in F. A. Wolf (ed.), *M. Tulli Ciceronis quae vulgo feruntur orationes quatuor . . . recognovit animadversiones integras I. Marklandi et I. M. Gesneri suasque adiecit F. A. W.* (Berlin, 1801) at p. 131 (in the introduction to the speech).

[7] Cf. n. 6. The denial of authorship extended to all four *post reditum* speeches, on which Eduard Meyer, *Caesars Monarchie und das Principat des Pompejus*, 3rd edn. (Stuttgart and Berlin, 1923, repr. 1964) 123 was still ready to pronounce judgement: they 'belong to the most objectionable products of this whole literature, which is in itself already so unedifying through its mendacity and affected moral pose'. Bibliography on the problem of authenticity is recorded in Classen (cited n. 2) 221–2; even more detail in C. Rück, *De M. Tulli Ciceronis oratione de domo sua ad pontifices*, Progr. Gymnasii Guilielmini Monacensis, 1881, 3–7; further details in Classen 220–1 on the reputation of the speech from antiquity to the early modern era.

[8] This was apparently first recognized correctly by Ferratius (*Epistolarum libri sex*, 1738 (title quoted by Nisbet, cited n. 2)), whose explanations, which are still worth reading, are quoted in detail in Wolf (cited n. 6) 135–7.

luxuriant mass of exposition which is as self-satisfied as it is off the point, and–a still more serious criticism–was at the time uncalled for.[9]

Thus, to quote just a few more recent opinions, Pierre Wuilleumier regarded the speech as 'trop long et mal équilibré';[10] Matthias Gelzer noted with dismay the contradiction (obvious also to contemporary listeners) between Cicero's 'heroic pose' and the 'well-known reality';[11] Manfred Fuhrmann counts it among 'the weaker achievements of the great orator ... because of the self-glorification and ... far too great detail';[12] and when Carl Joachim Classen raises the question how it was 'to be explained ... that this speech could be praised just as much as it could be sharply criti-cised',[13] after a wide-ranging interpretation, he finds the latter decidedly easier to explain. He, too, sees 'a weakness' in the fact that 'in this speech Cicero's psychological state itself plays an important role' (apparently he means by this that Cicero here no longer has his feelings completely under control); indeed, because of this he even issues a stern warning to modern orators not 'to follow ancient models in every respect'; and when he then sets against this that of course Cicero's 'statements about himself and the injustice done to him also contribute to his success here', this remains an assertion which lacks the argument needed to make it plausible.[14]

Yet the question raised by Classen allows a clear answer. I think that Cicero was right to place a high value on his speech, because he was conscious of the embarrassing difficulty with which he had had to struggle. The speech is today underestimated because scholars no longer properly recognize this

[9] W. Jeffrey Tatum at least judges differently in an article both original and full of ideas ('The lex Papiria de dedicationibus', *CPh* 88 (1993) 319–28), which unfortunately became known to me only shortly before the manuscript was finished. For his view cf. below, p. 327 and nn. 75, 79.

[10] *Cicéron, Discours*, vol. 13, Budé edn. (Paris, 1952) Introd., p. 27.

[11] M. Gelzer, *Cicero: ein biographischer Versuch* (Wiesbaden 1969) 154–5.

[12] Fuhrmann (cited n. 2) 200–1.

[13] Classen (cited n. 2) 222; the following two quotations are on pp. 266 and 255.

[14] Ibid. 266. For the main problem as to why Cicero says so little to the point, Classen briefly offers three alternative answers (265) without himself deciding between them. Classen's well-known book offers much useful explanatory material for the speeches, but hardly ever a key to the understanding of the conception of a given speech as a whole, since the speeches are described as a series of individual tactical tricks rather than anything else. In the case of *De domo sua* it is particularly unhelpful that Classen neither reconstructs Clodius' speech nor goes into the question of the priests' *responsum* (which is of decisive importance for the understanding of the speech), nor into all the events after the trial; in the light of Cicero's letter to Atticus 4.2.2 ff. (cf. below pp. 324; 330–1) his statement (255) is frankly unbelievable: 'It is not known how the pontifices reacted to Cicero's expositions. Perhaps [!] they really let themselves be impressed by the arguments selected and by their presentation'. Exemplary interpretations of Cicero speeches, such as Friedrich L. Keller and Richard Heinze once presented (cf. W. Stroh, *Taxis und Taktik: die advokatische Dispositionskunst in Ciceros Gerichtsreden*, Stuttgart 1975, 1–2) are also rare today. (M. Fuhrmann, 'Die Tradition der Rhetorik-Verachtung und das deutsche Bild vom 'Advokaten' Cicero', in *Ciceroniana* 6 (1988), 19–30, esp. 28 ff., comes to a slightly different judgement on German scholarship since C. Neumeister's certainly important book, *Grundsätze der forensischen Rhetorik, gezeigt an Gerichtsreden Ciceros* (Munich 1964)).

very difficulty: namely the fact that Cicero's claim to his house could not really be justified from the point of view of sacral law, which was supposed to be all that mattered to the pontifices.[15] Though his deadly enemy P. Clodius Pulcher[16] had performed the dedication in question with definitely spiteful intent, still, as we shall see, it was performed in a legally correct, binding, and, according to Roman conceptions, irreversible manner. So Cicero certainly had good reason to divert attention from the salient point through irrelevant polemics, and to mobilize the full power of his emotions on his own behalf (*pro domo*). This is what I aim to demonstrate in what follows. First, however, it is of course necessary to deal with the factual basis of the dispute, about which many erroneous ideas still prevail.

The Legal Dispute about Cicero's House

As is well known, the tribune of the people Clodius in 58 BC drove his opponent Cicero into exile and took away his house, grounds and other property, by means of two laws.[17] With the so-called *lex de capite civis*

---

[15] K. Latte at least (*Römische Religionsgeschichte* (Munich, 1960) 201), without giving a reason, had already written of Cicero's 'legally extremely questionable position'. Tatum also has reservations (cited n. 9).

[16] His enmity towards Cicero (since the Bona Dea affair of the year 62) belongs to the few constants in the confusing politics of the popular 'jack-in-the-box' Clodius, who, like Antonius later, did not avoid the scandalous but–something which above all apparently infuriated Cicero who was himself so much in need of recognition–actually strove for it (cf. C. Meier, *Caesar* (Berlin, 1982) 266 ff.). On the contradictory image of Clodius prevalent today cf. now esp. H. Benner, *Die Politik des P. Clodius Pulcher*, Hermes Einzelschriften 50 (Stuttgart, 1987) 17–18. Older literature on Clodius can also be found in Classen (cited n. 2) 218 n. 1; some more recent information in J. Spielvogel, 'P. Clodius Pulcher–eine politische Ausnahmeerscheinung der späten Republik?', *Hermes* 125 (1997) 56–74 and W. Will, '[I.4] C(lodius) Pulcher, P.', *Der Neue Pauly* 3 (1997), 37–9, who however misjudges Cicero (col. 39): 'The invectives [sc. against Clodius] in Cicero's speeches consist only of an accumulation of all those commonplaces which he always lavished on his opponents (even more, for example, on Calpurnius Piso or A. Gabinius).' In fact Cicero's character-presentation was capable of very sharp distinctions even in invective: cf. now C. Klodt, 'Prozessparteien und politische Gegner als dramatis personae: Charakterstilisierung in Ciceros Reden', in: B.-J. Schröder and J.-P. Schröder (eds.), *Studium declamatorium: Untersuchungen zu Schulübungen und Prunkreden von der Antike bis zur Neuzeit* (Munich and Leipzig, 2003) 35–106 and Craig in this volume.–Inaccessible to me: W. J. Tatum, *The Patrician Tribune: Publius Clodius Pulcher* (Chapel Hill, 1999)

[17] Summaries of the events have been most recently provided especially by O. Seel, *Cicero: Wort–Staat–Welt*, 3rd edn. (Stuttgart, 1967) 116 ff. (ingenious, not always reliable); R. E. Smith, *Cicero, the Statesman* (Cambridge 1966) 155 ff.; P. Grimal, *Études de chronologie cicéronienne (années 58 et 57 av. J.-C.)* (Paris 1967) (up to the return to Rome); M. Gelzer, *Cicero: ein biographischer Versuch*, (Wiesbaden, 1969) 135 ff. (rich source references); D. Stockton, *Cicero: A Political Biography* (Oxford, 1971) 188 ff.; D. R. Shackleton Bailey, *Cicero* (London, 1971) 61 ff.; E. L. Grasmück, 'Ciceros Verbannung aus Rom', *Bonner Festgabe Johannes Straub* (Bonn 1977) 165–177; popular account in M. Fuhrmann, *Cicero und die römische Republik* (Munich and Zurich, 1989) 129 ff.;

Romani which had already been promulgated in January (Vell. 2.45.1: QVI CIVEM ROMANVM ⟨IN⟩DEMNATVM INTEREMISSET EI AQVA ET IGNI INTER- DICERETUR[18]), which was aimed at Cicero (because of the execution of the Catilinarians in December 63) but still without naming him,[19] he suc- ceeded in intimidating him to such an extent that he, after a few futile demonstrations—a tactical mistake, as he later realized (*Att.* 3.15.5)[20]—at the beginning of March, left Rome on the day of the plebiscite[21] in order to escape the consequences of proscription. To prevent Cicero from escaping these consequences, and to cut him off from return once and for all, Clodius as a counterattack immediately promulgated a second so-called *lex de exilio*[22]—sc. Ciceronis[23]—in which it was said expressly VT M. TVLLIO AQVA ET IGNI INTERDICTVM SIT (according to *Dom.* 47), for which the following,

C. Habicht, *Cicero der Politiker* (Munich, 1990) 62 ff. (succinct, excellent); T. N. Mitchell: *Cicero, The Senior Statesman*, (New Haven and London, 1991) 132 ff. (giving access to more recent literature); T. P. Wiseman, 'Caesar, Pompey and Rome, 59–50 BC', in *CAH*² 9 (Cambridge, 1994) 368–423, esp. 380 ff.; F. Millar, *The Crowd in Rome in the Late Republic* (Ann Arbor, 1998) 124–166 (on the first half of the 50s). On the speeches of Cicero from 57–52 BC cf. now A. M. Riggsby, 'The Post Reditum Speeches', in: J. M. May (ed), *Brill's Companion to Cicero: Oratory and Rhetoric* (Leiden etc., 2002) 159–95 (without much historical detail). Of older accounts the following are still valuable: L. Lange, *Römische Alterthümer* (Berlin, 1871) iii.292 ff.; W. Drumann–P. Groebe, *Geschichte Roms in seinem Übergange von der republikanischen zur monarchischen Verfassung*, 2nd edn. (Berlin and Leipzig, 1899–1929, repr. 1964) ii.208 ff.; v.628 ff.; E. Ciaceri, *Cicerone e i suoi tempi* (Milan 1930) ii.49 ff.; E. Meyer, *Caesars Monarchie und das Principat des Pompejus*, 3rd edn. (Stuttgart and Berlin, 1923, repr. 1964) 95 ff. remains especially worth reading.

[18] The precise wording was therefore probably: QVI CIVEM ROMANVM INDEMNATVM INTEREMIT INTEREMERIT EI AQVA ET IGNI INTERDICATVR. The rest of the sources are to be found in G. Rotondi, *Leges publicae populi Romani* (1912; repr. Hildesheim 1966) 394–5, where, however, not all the passages are relevant; this is also true of the references in T. R. S. Broughton, *The Magistrates of the Roman Republic* (New York 1952) ii.196.

[19] Since W. Sternkopf ('Ueber die "Verbesserung" des Clodianischen Gesetzentwurfes de exilio Ciceronis', *Philologus* 59 [1900] 272–303, esp. 272) scholars have tended to call this law, since it is supposed to have been intended to renew the right of *provocatio*, 'Provocationsgesetz' (thus most recently especially J. Bleicken, *Lex publica: Gesetz und Recht in der römischen Republik* (Berlin, 1975) 207: 'lex Clodia de provocatione'; W. Nippel, *Aufruhr und "Polizei" in der römischen Republik* (Stuttgart, 1988) 115; cf. Will (cited n. 16) 38, where the proscription is erroneously equated with *relegatio*). This is not a very fortunate expression, since *provocatio*, formerly overrated in its import- ance by Mommsen, (see especially W. Kunkel *Untersuchungen zur Entwicklung des römischen Kriminalverfahrens in vorsullanischer Zeit* (Munich, 1962) 24 ff., cf. 89 on the execution of the Catilinarians) does not figure as a term in the sources.

[20] But this does not in any way imply that, as Gelzer (cited n. 11) 136 seems to assume against all ancient authorities, the law was not aimed individually at Cicero.

[21] This appears clearly from Cic. *Sest.* 53; accordingly Dio 38.17.6, and datings in more recent research following Dio, need to be corrected.

[22] The name is misleading since the law without doubt did not decree Cicero's exile (*Dom.* 51 'ne id quidem scriptum est ut exirem'; 82 'nihil de me tulisti quominus essem . . . in civium numero'; cf. 83), but, treating Cicero so to speak as someone who has already been exiled, later—just as after condemnation in a criminal trial—pronounced the proscription; cf. below, p. 335 with n. 108.

[23] On this in most detail P. Moreau, 'La *lex Clodia* sur le bannissement de Cicéron', *Athenaeum* NS 65 (1987) 465–92 (with older lit.); of earlier work that of Sternkopf (cited n. 19) is particularly important; cf. Rotondi (cited n. 18) 395–6.

probably among other things, was indicated as a reason:[24] QVOD M. TVLLIVS FALSVM SENATVS CONSVLTVM RETTVLERIT (*Dom.* 50).[25] The proscription (in other cases customary after capital sentencing in criminal trials[26]) was not restricted to Italy but was supposed to be valid for a further 400–500 miles beyond;[27] it was combined (in this respect, too, harsher than in a capital sentence[28]) with the confiscation of his property[29] and thus in particular of the imposing house on the Palatine (which in 62 he had acquired with a large loan and not without public displeasure,[30] and the loss of which affected him more than other things[31]). Even before the proposal for the second law of Clodius had been decided on,[32] this very house was apparently plundered and burnt down by the outraged mob.[33]

[24] That the 'killing of Roman citizens without trial and conviction' would also have been mentioned in this law (as in the first one), seems factually plausible and is without exception assumed as obvious by scholars (most recently especially Moreau (cited n. 23) 473; but it is not really proved either by the passages quoted by W. Drumann (Drumann–Groebe (cited n. 17) ii.219 n. 7) or by Cic. *Pis.* 72 (where QVOD VINDICARIT cannot possibly be a quotation, as is clear from the commentary of R. G. M. Nisbet (Oxford, 1961) ad loc. and Moreau (cited n. 23) 484) or [Livy] *per.* 103 (to which passages Gelzer (cited n. 11) 140 n. 68 refers). But perhaps the law did imply that Cicero by his departure had confessed himself to be guilty of the killing of uncondemned Roman citizens and thereby condemned himself.

[25] Through this accusation, through which the allegation made earlier that Cicero had falsified the Senate records (*Sull.* 40–1) was intensified into the realm of the outrageous, Clodius apparently intended to exonerate the Senate, and to stop them from feeling or declaring any solidarity with Cicero (correctly Habicht (cited n. 17) 131 n. 41).

[26] Cf. W. Kunkel, 'quaestio', *RE* XXIV (1963), 720–86, at 766–7; in very great detail: G. Crifò, '*Exilica causa, quae adversus exulem agitur*: problemi dell' *aqua et igni interdictio*', in: Y. Thomas et al., *Du châtiment dans la cité* (Rome, 1984) 453–497. In Cicero's case it was an exacerbating factor that the law with the penalty of proscription also forbade anyone to receive him as a guest.

[27] Thus (after Plutarch, *Cic.* 32.1) convincingly Sternkopf (cited n. 19), especially 291 ff., most recently Moreau (cited n. 23) 475 (with bibliography).

[28] Cf. M. Fuhrmann, 'publicatio bonorum', *RE* XXIII 2 (1959) 2484–2515, esp. col. 2495 (on Cicero: col. 2497).

[29] Cf. especially Moreau (cited n. 23) 476 and the references quoted in Gelzer (cited n. 11) 140 n. 69 which are significant to different degrees. From *Dom.* 108 and 116 it can be concluded that Cicero's personal property was also sold.

[30] Nippel (cited n. 19) 116–17 is informative on this.

[31] Characteristic: Cic. *Att.* 3.15.6 (Aug. 58): 'quid de bonis? quid de domo? poteritne restitui? aut si non poterit, egomet quomodo potero?' 3.20.2 'nihil malo quam domum'; cf. *Fam.* 14.2.3. Therefore it is true what Cicero says in *Dom.* 147. Cf. especially B. Berg, 'Cicero's Palatine Home and Clodius' Shrine of Liberty: Alternative Emblems of the Republic in Cicero's *De Domo Sua*', in: C. Deroux (ed.), *Studies in Latin Literature and Roman History* VIII (Brussels, 1997) 122–43, esp. 122–3.

[32] This timing emerges from *Dom.* 62; from *Red. Sen.* 17–18 and *Sest.* 54 it is even probable that the burning of the house immediately followed Cicero's departure, as for instance Gelzer (cited n. 11) 139, Nisbet (cited n. 2) 206 and Berg (cited n. 31) 129 indicate.

[33] Cicero was so successful in conveying his hatred of Clodius to his readers that one reads everywhere (already in Plutarch, *Cic.* 33.1) that Clodius himself had set fire to Cicero's house or made someone do so (thus for instance Drumann–Groebe (cited n. 17) ii.228 and most recently especially Nippel (cited n. 19) 116, cf. also Bergemann (cited n. 2) 75), although in fact not even Cicero himself dares claim this: he merely regards him as the secret (!) instigator and, apart from this, protests against the consuls who had not done anything against the blaze kindled by *furiae Clodianae* (*Pis.* 26) but had even enriched themselves while it happened (cf. also *Sest.* 54). Asconius

The building projects on and in the vicinity of Cicero's confiscated plot which were now arranged or planned by Clodius (or merely attributed to him) are not clear in every respect, and for our purpose their details do not need to be discussed, any more than the general layout of housing on the Palatine, which is still disputed among scholars.[34] It seems clear, at least, that Clodius rebuilt in his own name the colonnaded hall[35] of Catulus, which was built on top of the destroyed house of the popular rabble-rouser M. Fulvius Flaccus[36] and decorated with the trophies of the Cimbrian war (*Dom.* 102; 114). This adjoined Cicero's house and grounds, and was rebuilt in such a way that it henceforth encroached on the latter–even though only on a tenth part of it (*Dom.* 116).[37] It is clear, also, that he set up, as part of the colonnaded hall,[38] if not indeed identical

(*In Pisonianam* 26) cannot in my opinion be right when he understands the burning down of the house as a consequence of a *publicatio bonorum* which had already happened after Cicero's departure, cf. previous note (this seems to have impressed Fuhrmann (cited n. 28) 2497 and Nippel loc. cit. 118 for instance): Cicero could not say specifically: 'domus ardebat in Palatio non fortuito sed oblato incendio' (*Dom.* 62) if the blaze had virtually resulted from an official act; he wants to intimate here that the supposedly spontaneous wrath of the people in reality was controlled by Clodius.

[34] In addition to Appendix V in Nisbet (cited n. 2) 206–9, cf. especially W. Allen, 'Cicero's house and Libertas', *TAPA* 75 (1944), 1–9 (with reference to earlier works by Allen); B. Tamm, *Auditorium and Palatium* (Stockholm, 1963) (not yet available to me); G.-C. Picard, 'L' Aedes Libertatis de Clodius au Palatin', *REL* 43 (1965) 229–37; A. Carandini, '*Domus* e *insulae* sulla pendice settentrionale del Palatino', *Bull. Comm.* 91 (1986) 263–78; id., *Schiavi in Italia* (Rome, 1988) 359–87 (including the excavation results in the discussion); M. Royo, 'Le quartier républicain du Palatin, nouvelles hypothèses de localisation', *REL* 65 (1987) 89–114 esp. 101–7; E. Papi, 'Domus: P. Clodius Pulcher', in: E. M. Steinby (ed.), *Lexicon topographicum urbis Romae* (Rome, 1993–9) ii.85–6; id. 'Domus: M. Tullius Cicero (1)', ii.202–4; id.: 'Libertas (1)', iii.188–9.; id., 'Porticus (Monumentum) Catuli', iv.119 (in each case with further bibliography); most recently S. M. Cerutti, 'The Location of the Houses of Cicero and Clodius and the Porticus Catuli on the Palatine Hill in Rome', *AJP* 118 (1997) 417–26, as well as the work by Berg (cited n. 31). For valuable, especially archaeological, references I thank my former pupil Dr Johanna Fabricius.

[35] It is called *porticus* (*Dom.* 102; 103; 114; 116), besides also *ambulatio* (116; 121); Cerutti (cited n. 34) 420 wrongly wishes to distinguish between the two.

[36] Berg's (cited n. 31, at 127–8) view that only a small part of the destroyed house of Flaccus was used in building the *porticus Catuli*, and that Clodius had taken possession of the remainder, is for the second part without foundation in the text and for the first is based on a wrong interpretation of *Dom.* 102: 'meam domum cum Flacci domo coniungebat' does not, as the context shows, mean that a connection was built between Cicero's house and a still extant ruin of Flaccus but that through the encroachment of the new *porticus* (which had been built on top of the *domus* Flacci) on the plot of Cicero's house the latter visibly suffered the same fate as that of the state enemy Flaccus. Thus I cannot follow Berg's further topographical considerations either.

[37] A different view is apparently taken by Tamm (cited n. 34) 36 ff.

[38] That the shrine cannot have been an independent building as is normally assumed (most recently Shackleton Bailey (cited n. 2) p. 37 and Cerutti (cited n. 34) 420; especially misleading here are K. Ziegler, 'Palatium', *RE* XVIII 2b (1949) 44–5 and Classen (cited n. 2) 219) but belonged to the rebuilt *porticus* can be concluded from *Har. Resp.* 33 alone where it is said about the statue of Libertas: ' . . . ereptum ex meretricis sepulchro 〈in〉 imperatoris monumento [which can only be the *porticus* of Catulus] conlocaras.' *Dom.* 121 is also unambiguous where it is said about the dedication of the shrine of Libertas: 'postem teneri in dedicatione oportere videor audisse templi' [Cicero affects ignorance of the precise sacred legal regulations]; 'ibi enim postis est ubi templi aditus

with it,[39] a shrine[40] of the goddess Libertas with an appropriate statue and, enlisting a pontifex, his brother-in-law L. Pinarius Natta, 'dedicated' it, i.e. transferred it from human into divine ownership.[41] The intention was unmistakable: Cicero was supposed to be branded through this 'memorial' (*monumentum*, as Clodius probably said)[42] as a state enemy (like Flaccus) and an expelled *rex* or *tyrannus* (probably like Tarquin);[43] and at the same time it was supposed to be made impossible ever to remove the new *porticus Clodii* again.[44] Even if Cicero, in spite of the second *lex Clodia*, which was directed against him (and which went so far as to forbid a trial of his case) were ever to regain possession of his plot or house, substantially undiminished by the rebuilding,[45] he would then of course have had to endure, as a neighbour or fellow occupant on the area that had formerly belonged to

---

et valvae: ambulationis postes nemo umquam tenuit in dedicando.' As especially the plural *postes* shows, this is supposed to mean that during a dedication there could never have been a touching of the door post of an *ambulatio* since of course the latter is without a door properly so called, as Gesner (in Nisbet (cited n. 2) ad loc.) correctly says: 'ambulatio ubique patet, tota porta est' (so Cicero intends to indicate that the dedication cannot have been quite correct formally). This clearly presupposes a certain identity of the Libertas sanctuary and the colonnaded hall. In my view this passage is completely misunderstood by Picard (cited n. 34) 236, who in connection with Libertas envisages an independent round temple like a mausoleum which did not have a door—for which reason then the priest had to hold the door post of the *ambulatio* as a substitute! Picard's claim (cf. p. 229) that the dedication was annulled by the pontifices because of this formal mistake (cf. also Papi (cited n. 34), iii. 189) stands in crass contradiction to the terms of their decree (see below).

[39] This is probably supported by *Dom.* 103: 'quam porticum . . . si opus esset, manibus vestris disturbare cuperetis–nisi quem forte . . . superstitiosa dedicatio deterret.' According to Nisbet (cited n. 2) 208 this point of view was already held by Ferratius (1738).

[40] Probably also so as not to enhance the status of the latter, Cicero avoids the word *templum* (only generally: *Dom.* 121, but cf. *Leg.* 2.42 'templum Licentiae'!) and only once talks about *delubrum* (*Dom.* 132).

[41] That this dedication did not happen until later when Cicero's return was in prospect is a hypothesis of Berg (cited n. 31) 133, cf. already Nisbet (cited n. 2) 207, Moreau (cited n. 23) 480 and Bergemann (cited n. 2) 76, which is implicitly refuted by the present reconstruction of the legal position.

[42] *Dom.* 51 'hoc ipsum quod nunc apud pontifices agis: . . . te monumentum fecisse in meis aedibus . . .'; 100 'sin mea domus . . . monumentum praebet inimico doloris mei, sceleris sui, publicae calamitatis'; 146 'non monumentum sed vulnus patriae'; cf. 112 'in eo monumento'. That Clodius really spoke about a 'memorial (of liberty?)' is suggested especially by *Dom.* 115 ('monumentum iste umquam . . . excogitavit?') and 116: 'causa ['a mere pretext'] fuit ambulatio et monumentum et ista . . . Libertas.'

[43] Cf. especially the essay by Allen (cited n. 34), Nippel (cited n. 19) 117, 119; and recently B. Liou-Gille, 'La consécration du Champ de Mars et la consécration du domaine de Cicéron', *MH* 55 (1998) 37–59, esp. 54 ff. (less helpful for the understanding of Cicero's speech).

[44] Cerutti's assumption (cited n. 34) 420 that Clodius himself had in mind a later 'deconsecration' of the sanctuary—which is of course absolutely out of the question–is erroneous.

[45] In fact, as the events around the sale already show, even if the dedication was valid, the larger part (nine tenths) of Cicero's plot would have been at his disposal to be built on again. This is hardly taken into consideration in scholarly literature on the speech, because Cicero intentionally always talks in general terms about the dedication of his *domus* or his *aedes* as though the whole were meant (which is not the case)–a turn of phrase which already Dio Cassius 39.11.1 and after him most recent scholarship has taken over.

him, that very Libertas who had just moved in to show contempt for him
and who could no longer be evicted! Clodius was not mistaken when he
regarded this as impossible. Besides, a buyer called Scato[46] was found for
the part of Cicero's confiscated house or plot which was situated higher
up; Clodius is supposed to have 'allocated' the remaining part, which was
situated lower down, to the gens Clodia (*Dom.* 116)–it is not clear for what
purpose.[47]

So much for the events during Cicero's 'exile', which need not detain us
longer here. When on 4 August the people passed the law drafted by Pompey
to recall Cicero, the reinstatement into his house (and–it goes without
saying–the rest of his property) was also stipulated in it: 'eandem domum
populus Romanus, cuius est summa potestas omnium rerum, comitiis
centuriatis omnium aetatum ordinumque suffragiis eodem iure esse iussit quo
fuisset' (*Har. Resp.* 11).[48] The house and villas, the Senate decided, were to
be rebuilt at public expense.[49] But in that case, if one did not want to have
Cicero cohabiting with the offending Libertas, the question arose of the
validity of the dedication performed by Clodius. This question must soon
have concerned the Senate too, and–though scholars seem to have overlooked this almost without exception–the pontifices, even before the trial
de domo on 29 September. *Dom.* 69 mentions a *senatusconsultum*, passed on
the proposal of M. Bibulus, that the pontifices had to 'decide' about Cicero's
house (after 4 August, as can be concluded from *Har. Resp.* 11 'postea');
what was meant by this, as Mommsen already clearly emphasized,[50] was

---

[46] One should not repeat the allegation by Cicero, who does not give any proof of this
(*Dom.* 116), that Scato in the context of Clodius' building plans was a mere 'front man' (thus most
recently for instance Bergemann (cited n. 2) 75 and Cerutti (cited n. 34) 419); the view which is
quite frequently found, that at the time of Cicero's return Clodius through the negotiation of this
sham buyer was already the owner of Cicero's plot (thus for instance Classen (cited n. 2) 219 and
Nippel (cited n. 19) 119) or that he had even set up a 'magnificent building' already (Classen, similarly Ziegler (cited n. 38)), is completely groundless. What would Cicero have made out of such
facts! He implies (*Dom.* 115–16) merely that Clodius originally had the intention through the connection of his own house with those of Seius (which he indeed bought) and of Cicero (which he
is supposed to have secured through the aforementioned intermediary) to want to produce
a colossal building in which then, if I understand correctly–but this is uncertain–the converted
porticus Catuli would also have been included as a colossal *peristylium* which virtually belonged to
the house (*Dom.* 116). Conversion and (partial?) dedication of the *porticus* would therefore be a
pretext (*Dom.* 116 *causa*) for these plans whose existence was merely inferred by Cicero, and which
were by no means obvious, let alone already realized.
[47] Cf. most recently Moreau (cited n. 23) 478 n. 95 and Cerutti (cited n. 34) 419 (with reference
to Marquardt) but who has completely erroneous ideas on the chronology of the events.
[48] Interestingly enough this important statement is not to be found in the *De domo*. Since it matters to Cicero there to make the second *lex Clodia* appear as not legally valid, he avoids any unnecessary reference to the *lex de reditu* through which it was rescinded, and acts as if *de iure* he had
never lost anything.   [49] Thus Plut. *Cic.* 33. 4.
[50] T. Mommsen, *Römisches Staatsrecht*, 3rd edn. (Leipzig, 1887–8) ii.49–50. On the senate's
competence for religious matters cf. M. Beard: 'Priesthood in the Roman Republic', in M. Beard
and J. North, *Pagan priests* (Ithaca and New York, 1990) 19–48, at 30–34.

a juridical report (*responsum*) which at least formally left the actual decision to the Senate. This decree had not been drawn up by 8 September; Cicero knew this, and therefore in the Senate meeting on this day had to be careful not to offend any of the pontifices present (*Att.* 4.1.7). But probably there had been a hearing by the pontifices before, because later Cicero spoke about a 'causa ... duobus locis dicta' (*Har. Resp.* 12)[51] and on 29 September, the day of the final trial, Clodius said (quoted in *Dom.* 4): 'fuisti (inquit) *tum* apud pontifices superior, sed iam, quoniam te ad populum contulisti [through his behaviour especially on 7 September], sis inferior necesse est'–here the indication of a preceding trial date is as good as certain.[52] When Cicero, before this, protestingly reproaches his opponent (*Dom.* 3) with the question how it came about 'ut hos talis viros ... aliud de summa religione hoc tempore sensuros ac *me absente* senserint arbitrere', then it seems reasonable to assume that this earlier hearing is to be dated while Cicero was still absent from Rome:[53] so probably before 4 September, and certainly, as stated earlier, after 4 August. By a fortunate coincidence, we can even guess who spoke on Cicero's behalf at that time: Quintilian (*Inst.* 10.1.23) knows a speech de domo Ciceronis delivered by M. Calidius,[54] who, as praetor in the year 57, had also on other occasions supported Cicero's recall. Apparently he, whom Cicero clearly regarded highly as an intelligent and astute orator (*Brut.* 274–8), but who (he interestingly enough thought) lacked precisely the emotional effectiveness, the appeal to the emotions ('vis atque contentio') which would be decisive for victory, did not succeed in winning the pontifices over to give a report favourable to Cicero. So the matter was adjourned in order to arrange after Cicero's return a trial in the presence of the two parties to the dispute, indeed even–strangely enough for a committee of experts–with these as oratorical protagonists:[55] Also, the presence of a large

---

[51] Gelzer (cited n. 11) 154 n. 249 conjecturally interprets this expression to mean 'that the college examined matters itself on the spot'. But such an examination could not be described by *causam dicere.*

[52] From the commentary by G. Long (*M. T. Ciceronis Orationes* (London 1856) iii.353), which Carl Joachim Classen generously made available to me, I gather that this view was already taken by Garatoni and Klotz.

[53] It would at best be conceivable that Cicero had to stay away from the trial, as Bergemann (cited n. 2) 43 must obviously assume, if she has the trials take place 'on two consecutive days'.

[54] The fact that Quintilian mentions this speech together with the speech by Brutus *Pro Milone* also makes it clear that Calidius spoke for, not against, Cicero; that Brutus's speech is expressly described as a mere written practice exercise implies that this was precisely not true of that of Calidius.–Classen (cited n. 2) 219 n. 8 would prefer this speech of Calidius also to have been delivered at the sitting on 29 September; but he himself notes the strangeness of the fact that, if this were the case, Cicero does not then, as on other occasions when he speaks together with others, make an explicit separation of roles between himself and his fellow-speaker(s). In view of the proof of the existence of the earlier sitting, further debate is superfluous.

[55] In fact it made sense that Clodius should have made a statement, since of course as performer of the dedication he was also its first witness. Only the fact that he could be regarded as biased in his own cause could justify bringing in Cicero as well. But to arrange a veritable oratorical *agon*, as it were, in front of the judges in this case, was bold, and proves the pleasure which the Romans, too, took in the dramatic side of legal debates.

crowd of listeners[56] on 29 September revealed that here a kind of trial *de domo Ciceronis* was supposed to take place, a trial during which for the first time in his advocate's career the occasion would offer itself to Cicero–as once to Demosthenes in his famous speech *De Corona*[57]–to speak on his own behalf, in fact (as is still said in Germany) 'pro domo'.

It was probably not difficult to see that altogether he enjoyed a certain degree of favour from the pontifices who, for the most part senators, had already voted for his return.[58] Apart from the *pontifex maximus* Caesar, who fortunately was preoccupied with Gaul–for he had Clodius' plebeian adoption and thus indirectly all the acts of his tribunate on his conscience–precisely the one pontifex who had participated in the dedication, the still quite youthful L. Pinarius Natta, was absent. Perhaps he had been given an appropriate hint, so that Cicero could be unpleasant to him without overmuch consideration, indeed could insinuate at least conjecturally that he had committed some formal errors (117–21; esp. 138–41).[59] Perhaps it was also significant that the tactically disadvantageous part of the plaintiff who spoke first was allocated to Clodius. But was that enough to induce the priests for the first time in Roman history, as far as is known, to deconsecrate a place which had been dedicated 'through'[60] one of them, in fact to dispossess the gods? And this in favour of the *homo novus* Cicero, who after all had always seemed to have been living beyond his means in the magnificent house on the Palatine?

The Legal Problem: Clodius Authorized for Dedication?

As we know, the judgement or decree which concluded the 'trial' did indeed amount to a decision in Cicero's favour. The pontifices manifestly upheld the argument which, when we read the speech, seems to us too to be the decisive one: that the dedication had taken place without the authorization by law

[56] *Har. Resp.* 12: the augurs, even though not entitled to vote, were present perhaps even in an official capacity (*Dom.* 34; cf. 39); M. Bibulus is mentioned as an example of a senator interested in the matter (*Dom.* 39). The presence of Pompey is important above all (*Dom.* 25), cf. below, p. 346.

[57] On the *De Corona* as a model cf. below, n. 192.

[58] Cicero gives the exact list of the priests in *Har. Resp.* 12; it is prosopographically annotated by L. R. Taylor, 'Caesar's Colleagues in the Pontifical College', *AJP* 63 (1942) 385–412 (esp. 389–400) and Bergemann (cited n. 2) 25–35. Most of these were conservative–optimate politicians who more or less without exception reach the consulate or at least the praetorship (for the exception cf. below, n. 59), although among the more recent members there are naturally also some Caesarians (cf. also Bergemann (cited n. 2) 48–9).

[59] That later he was the only one of the pontifices not to have a public career (cf. above, n. 58) should not necessarily make us conclude that he died early (thus Bergemann (cited n. 2) 32); because of his commitment to Clodius the senatorial aristocracy may have dropped him.

[60] According to Roman linguistic usage the dedication was performed *per pontificem* by the person authorized to carry it out, cf. on this esp. G. Wissowa, 'Dedicatio', *RE* IV 2 (1901) 2356–9, esp. 2358.

or plebiscite[61] demanded by the *lex Papiria* (otherwise not known to us).[62] One should compare Cicero's comments (*Dom.* 127): 'video . . . esse legem veterem tribuniciam quae vetet iniussu plebis aedis, terram, aram consecrari'[63] and (*Dom.* 128): 'lex Papiria vetat aedis iniussu plebis consecrari' with the decree in Cicero's favour (in Cic. *Att.* 4.2.3): 'si neque populi iussu neque plebis scitu is qui se dedicasse diceret nominatim ei rei praefectus esset, neque populi iussu aut plebis scitu id facere iussus esset, videri posse sine religione eam partem areae mihi restitui'. So the pontifices, in their official statement at any rate, left unconsidered Cicero's detailed explanations according to which the so-called *lex de exilio* which decreed the confiscation of his property for very varied reasons had not been a legally valid law at all (*Dom.* 43–103 or rather 34b–103); which of course seems appropriate and sensible. For, on the one hand, the Senate had already in principle acknowledged the legal validity of this *lex Clodia*, precisely through the fact that it had it specially rescinded through the new law *de reditu* (and not, as had also at least been proposed, silently annulled it[64]); on the other hand, it would have been strange to refer specially to the invalidity of the *lex* if, as is generally assumed today, Clodius was not able to rely on it at all in so far as it did not in fact authorize him to perform the disputed dedication. Indeed one continues to wonder why–and with this we state more precisely the question we asked at the beginning–Cicero then went into these matters in such detail at all, matters which were not supposed to be, and did not have to be, decisive for the pontifices.

It was the *Gymnasium* teacher Ludwig Schaum from Mainz who in 1889 (in a *Schulprogramm*[65] whose value has recently been acknowledged again by D. R. Shackleton Bailey[66]) pointed out the fact that Cicero's comments

---

[61] Ferratius was the first to claim this categorically; repeated in Wolf (cited n. 6) p. 134, whose opinion in this respect has since then rightly remained uncontroverted.

[62] Apart from Mommsen, *Staatsrecht* (cited n. 50) iii.2.1050 and Rotondi (cited n. 18) 234–5 (with reference to the work of P. Willems, *Le sénat de la république romaine* (Louvain, 1885) ii. 307–9 which is rich in material) see most recently esp. the work by Tatum (cited n. 9), A. Ziolkowski, *The Temples of Mid-Republican Rome and their Historical and Topographical Context* (Rome, 1992) 219–34 (with lit.) and E. M. Orlin, *Temples, Religions and Politics in the Roman Republic* (Leiden, etc., 1997) 163–71; this law can hardly (as Ziolkowski most recently argued) be identical with the law of 304 BC mentioned in Livy 9.46.7. The cases mentioned by Cicero of its application from the years 154 and 123 BC (*Dom.* 130; 136) seem to give a *terminus ante quem* (even though they might not actually have had anything to do with the *lex Papiria*); the *terminus p. q.* is disputed (cf. Orlin 166–7 n. 13 and Bergemann (cited n. 2) 51).

[63] Cicero admittedly suggests that in this law private houses were not originally envisaged; but he does not assert, as Bergemann (cited n. 2) 51 implies that he does, 'that such dedications as such were not permitted'.

[64] Cf. the voices of influential politicians quoted in Habicht (cited n. 17) 131 (= n. 43 to p. 63).

[65] 'De consecratione domus Ciceronianae', *Progr. des Großherzoglichen Gymn. zu Mainz*, 1889, 3–8: In the ensuing account I do not follow Schaum who has merely drawn attention to the conflict between sections 106–10 and 127–9.

[66] Shackleton Bailey (cited n. 2) 38, in the introduction to the speech.

about the relation of the *lex* to the dedication of the Libertas sanctuary—there are four passages in total, of which the latter two are connected—appear inconsistent, indeed actually contradictory. In the statements of the main section on the dedication (*Dom.* 127–37) (which was apparently decisive for the *responsum*) one gets, as was said earlier, the impression that Cicero wants flatly to deny an authorization through the *lex*.

Passage I: *Dom.* 127 'quis eras tu qui dedicabas?' [imperfect, *trying* to dedicate] '. . . ubi te isti rei populus Romanus praefecerat?'

Passage II (*a*): *Dom.* 128 'sed quaero quae lex lata sit ut tu aedis meas consecrares, ubi tibi haec potestas data sit, quo iure ⟨tu⟩⁶⁷ feceris . . . ' (*b*): 'unum ostende verbum consecrationis in ipsa tua lege, si illa lex est ac non vox sceleris et crudelitatis tuae.' But previously we had read something different:

Passage III: *Dom.* 51: (Cicero protests against the law being a *lex per saturam*, i.e. that it contained an illegal variety of contents) 'quid? hoc ipsum quod nunc apud pontifices agis: te meam domum consecrasse, te monumentum fecisse in meis aedibus, te signum dedicasse eaque te ex una rogatiuncula fecisse—unum et idem videtur esse atque id quod de me ipso nominatim tulisti?' [sc. *ut M. Tullio aqua et igni interdictum sit* etc.] From this alone it follows unambiguously that, at least according to Clodius' statement, the dedication of the 'house' (referred to in general terms) and the statue of Libertas took place according to the second *lex Clodia*. And even if this does not matter for Cicero's argument at this point, it is nevertheless surprising that, since he mentions this at all, he does not at least in passing contradict such an assertion which is fatal for his case.

Passage IV: *Dom.* 106 (where the legal validity of the dedication is directly dealt with) seems even less comprehensible: 'quae tua fuit consecratio? "tuleram," inquit, "ut mihi liceret".'⁶⁸ Instead of directly and energetically denying this, as one would have expected after the (later) paragraphs 127–8, Cicero silently concedes its accuracy by giving merely a weakly protesting reference to the usual exception formula: 'quid? non exceperas ut, si quid ius non esset rogari, ne esset rogatum?' Doubt seems hardly possible: *tulit*

---

⁶⁷ For the insertion see below, n. 76.

⁶⁸ Bergemann (cited n. 2) 75, toning it down, paraphrases to the effect that Cicero had 'seen also a *consecratio* implied [!] in his law', but then Cicero would be able to argue differently. Classen (cited n. 2, at 257–8 with n. 123) incredibly even thinks that here Clodius is 'reproached with *licentia*' or 'capriciousness' and that the *ut* is purely one of purpose in the sense of 'I had introduced (this law) so that [!] I would be allowed', but the usage of *ferre ut* (Hey, *TLL* VI.1.547.77 ff.; *OLD* s. v. *fero* 28a) is unambiguous, cf. *Dom.* 51, 'tulisti de me, ne reciperer' ('you decreed by law about me that I should not be received', not 'you introduced the law so that . . . not'!).

Clodius, ut sibi liceret. The law must have authorized him to perform the dedication. But how can Cicero later deny precisely this?

Schaum, the clear-sighted discoverer of the contradiction (which Mommsen, to name no others, had completely overlooked in his *Römisches Staatsrecht*)[69] tried a genetic hypothesis according to which Cicero had carelessly mixed up different drafts. He had, Schaum argues, to a large extent drafted his speech in written form as early as his return journey from 'exile', at a time when, still without precise knowledge of the wording of the so-called *lex de exilio*–(as if that could be imagined)–he had thought Clodius had been authorized through it to perform the dedication; having been informed otherwise at Rome, he emphasized in the spoken version only the lack of authorization, but included the earlier draft in the written version. Such an explanation not only contradicts what we know about the working method of Cicero, who nearly always writes down his speeches for publication only after delivery: it is inconceivable also in itself. If Schaum thinks that the contradictions discovered by him had been unreasonable for every listener–'quis credat res tantopere secum repugnantes easque ad argumentandum gravissimas, mentes eorum qui audirent, fugisse?' (p. 8)–then this must of course a priori be valid for readers who, like us, can examine Cicero's words at leisure.

Even less credible is the explanation which Philippe Moreau, who saw the problem apparently without knowing Schaum's work, tried to give in passing in 1987.[70] According to him the original of the law had been lost[71]– a bold assumption–so that now only private copies of it existed; and that therefore Cicero and Clodius were arguing about whether originally an authorization clause had existed in it. So: 'tuleram ut mihi liceret' [= No. IV] would describe 'Clodius' thesis': 'The clause existed'; 'unum ostende verbum consecrationis' [= No. II] would according to Cicero mean: 'The clause did not exist'. No! Not one syllable in Cicero's argumentation points

---

[69] In *Staatsrecht* (as above, n. 50) ii.1.50 n. 1 he wrote about the conditional form of the pontifical decree (*si neque populi etc.*): 'Notorisch war ein solcher Volksschluss nicht ergangen, ja dessen Vorhandensein gar nicht behauptet [!]; aber die gutachtende Behörde lässt, wie billig, die Thatfrage dahingestellt.' On the other hand, in the same work, iii.1.335 with n. 4, it is said to clarify the 'inviolability of the *res sacrae*': 'Dahin gehört die durch Clodius in Gemässheit eines Mandats der Gemeinde [!] vollzogene Dedication des Hauses Ciceros (*de domo* 40, 106 [= above, no. IV]). Es wurde geltend gemacht, dass das Gesetz über dessen Rückkehr wie jedes andere die Rechte der Götter ausgenommen habe und er also insoweit nicht in seine früheren Rechte restituirt sei.' The meaning of the latter argument is correctly grasped by Mommsen.

[70] In the essay quoted above, n. 23, at p. 468, Moreau surprisingly does not make any reference here to scholarship on *De domo sua*.

[71] Moreau wishes to understand this, at least for the year 55, from Cic. *Pis.* 72 'at hoc nusquam opinor scriptum fuisse [!] in illo elogio quod te consule in sepulcro rei publicae incisum est' [meaning the second *lex Clodia*]; but *scriptum fuisse*, which indeed stands out, results from the fact that the 'sepulcrum rei publicae' was removed through Cicero's return or that the law became invalid on this account.

to the law having been lost or its wording being disputed. Under the assumption made by Moreau, it would have to look completely different.

Similar objections can also be made to a hypothesis recently (1993) put forward by W. Jeffrey Tatum,[72] although it seems to come very much closer to the right answer. According to it Clodius would have had himself authorized in his *lex* only for the building, but not for the dedication of the Libertas sanctuary. An obstacle to this is not only the phrase 'tuleram ut mihi liceret', sc. *consecrare* (No. IV) which is mentioned from time to time and, as said before, left uncontradicted by Cicero, but above all else also that clearer traces would surely have been left in Cicero's reply by the argumentation we would in that case have to infer for Clodius, according to which the one authorization would implicitly be included in the other–according to ancient rhetoric a case of the 'status' *scriptum et voluntas*.

On the other hand his line of argumentation becomes completely clear and comprehensible when, with *Dom.* 51 and 106 (No. III and IV)[73]–against the *communis opinio* which is as good as unanimous[74]–we start out from the assumption that Clodius was indeed authorized to perform the dedication through his law, but that there still remained in it certain formal errors that could be demurred to. Cicero emphasizes these with all possible vigour in *Dom.* 127–8. (Nos. I and II), the passage which was ultimately decisive for the decree: (1) Clodius had not been authorized by name to perform the dedication. (2) The term used in his law was not *consecrare*, but *dedicare*. On these assumptions it will then also become clear for the first time why Clodius was able, after the issue of the priests' decree, to claim–something which until now has mostly been judged as sheer madness–that it had been issued in his favour, and, furthermore, how by means of this claim he even succeeded in delaying the Senate's decision by a day (Cic. *Att.* 4.2.3–5). We shall take these points in order.

The *lex Papiria* in its precise wording (*Dom.* 128 'vetat aedis iniussu plebis consecrari')–the *argumentum ex silentio* is totally certain here–did not say anything about an individual authorization by name being necessary[75] and

---

[72] See above, n. 9. Tatum's view (for this cf. also below, n. 79) seems, even though with somewhat unclear phrasing, to be followed by Orlin (cited n. 61) 169–70 n. 22.

[73] Section 69 also gives a telling reference to this, cf. below, p. 355.

[74] Thus most recently for instance Nippel (cited n. 19) 122 with n. 166, Berg (cited n. 31) 133 and Liou-Gille (cited n. 43) 58 n. 112.

[75] Erroneously therefore Tatum (cited n. 9) 323: 'clearly the terms of the *Lex Papiria* required popular authorization that explicitly enabled an individual to perform a dedication'. When G. Wissowa asserts that 'only a magistrate who through his office was automatically authorized [i.e. someone with imperium] or through a special order (*nominatim*) had been designated for the task by the people' was authorized to dedicate state property ('Consecratio', *RE* IV.1 (1900) 896–902, at 897) he does not, as Cicero does, refer to the *lex Papiria* (which he conjecturally refers to 'dedications of private property') but only to the pontifical decree of the year 154 (see below) which Cicero himself produced, and the decision of the pontifices in Cicero's own case. But it is surely problematic to adopt Cicero's biased legal standpoint on such a difficult issue without even acknowledging Cicero's reasoning.

so Clodius could, without thinking twice about it, regard himself as authorized through his law to perform the dedication (IV: 'tuleram ut mihi liceret'). But Cicero, since he cannot deny the authorization, insists on precisely the fact that no individual has been named. One has only to emphasize the personal pronouns in the relevant sentences to bring out their full meaning, even if one assumes a general authorization to perform the dedication: (*Dom.* 127 = I) 'quis eras *tu* qui dedicabas?' (*Dom.* 128 = IIa): 'sed quaero quae lex lata sit ut *tu* aedis meas consecrares, ubi *tibi* haec potestas data sit, quo iure ⟨*tu*⟩[76] feceris . . .'. And even if there was no law, there was, however, at least an earlier decree–Cicero had probably had it leaked to him by one of the pontifices–in which the requirement of the plebiscite in accordance with the *lex Papiria* had been linked with authorization by name, which was not demanded by the *lex*. In the year 154 BC, the following decree had been issued by the *pontifex maximus* to the censor C. Cassius (Longinus)[77] for the planned dedication of a statue of Concordia (*Dom.* 136): ' . . . nisi eum populus Romanus *nominatim* praefecisset atque eius iussu faceret, non videri eam posse recte dedicari.' Admittedly, this was not a perfect precedent. First, of course, all that was in question at that time was that the order by name was made a prerequisite of an intended dedication.[78] There was no question of a dedication already performed being annulled because the order had been lacking. Second, this was not about a plot of land at all but about a statue, which was not actually covered by the *lex Papiria*.[79] However, what was lacking here could at least be partly supplied by relying on the case of the Vestal Virgin Licinia from the year 123 BC (also in *Dom.* 136), where indeed a dedication of altar and sanctuary had once been declared invalid– it is true that this was only because of the lack of a plebiscite, not because the name had not been mentioned (so this additional example did not help Cicero's case quite so much[80]). It was in essence the decree for Cassius, not

[76] The supplement suggests itself not only for the sake of concinnity but also to improve the rhythm of the clausula (double cretic instead of hypodochmius).

[77] Broughton (cited n. 18) i.449; F. Münzer, 'Cassius' No. 55, *RE* III.2 (1899) 1726 (mistakenly omitting to mention this matter).

[78] From Cicero's wording we cannot infer conclusively that the dedication should on this account have been prevented according to the intention of the priests, even though de facto it apparently did not take place after all; the former is the general view; cf. in T. Hölscher, 'Homonoia/Concordia', *LIMC* V.1 (1990) 488 (cf. 493, no. 111) the works by Skard and Scullard which are quoted with further literature; most recently esp. Bergemann (cited n. 2) 50 and F. Coarelli, 'Curia Hostilia', in Steinby (cited n. 34) i.331, with very strange reasoning which departs from Cicero's line of argument.

[79] Tatum (cited n. 9) 320 with n. 8 has emphasized this important point. He assumes rightly that Cicero falsifies when he suggests (only in *Dom.* 130, correctly in *Dom.* 136) that, at the same time as the statue, the temple also would be dedicated. But apart from this, *pace* Tatum, it does not seem at all certain to me but, rather, improbable that the pontifical decree concerning Concordia was issued with the *lex Papiria* in mind.

[80] It can also be concluded with certainty *ex silentio* that Licinia had not consulted a pontifex. Apparently Cicero does not have any other example of the later annulment of a temple dedication.

the *lex Papiria*, which made it possible for the pontifices to draw up a *responsum* favourable to Cicero: 'si neque populi iussu neque plebis scitu . . . *nominatim* ei rei *praefectus* esset neque populi iussu aut plebis scitu id *facere iussus esset*' etc. (the wording, as can be seen, was taken over almost verbatim).

The second of the two modest objections which Cicero was able to raise against Clodius' authorization (*Dom.* 128 = II b) proved to be less important: 'unum ostende verbum consecrationis in ipsa tua lege.' By this Cicero means that the word *consecrare*, used for the 'dedication' in the *lex Papiria* (*Dom.* 127, 128), is missing in Clodius' law. Why? Because at that time, Cicero says, Clodius had so many plans in his head which were malicious and hostile to the state that he and his adviser on legal drafting (Sex. Cloelius) could not concentrate sufficiently to express everything with the proper legal formulae, i.e. those of the *lex Papiria* ('verbis legitimis'). It is also quite clear here that Cicero would never have argued in this way if nothing at all had been said about dedication in the *lex Clodia*. On the other hand, his argument becomes easily comprehensible if Clodius used for the dedication the verb *dedicare* which is put into his mouth by Cicero (*Dom.* 125): ' "dedicatio magnam", inquit, "habet religionem".'[81] Of course from this 'mistake' one cannot exactly construct a knock-down argument. The words *dedicare* and *consecrare* are almost synonymous,[82] so that they are freely juxtaposed as synonyms;[83] what seems to make the most important difference–which Cicero also emphasizes earlier in a slightly different context (*Dom.* 125: 'an consecratio nullum habet ius, dedicatio est religiosa?'[84])–is that *dedicare* is

[81] In *Dom.* 127 Cicero first uses the word *dedicare* or *dedicatio* five times concerning Clodius' claim (cf. also already *Dom.* 118 'hanc tu igitur dedicationem appellas . . . ?'), then, beginning with the quotation of the *lex Papiria*, nine times in succession (up to the end of sect. 128) *consecrare* or *consecratio*. Also the pontifical decree enables Clodius to speak of *dedicare* (in Cic. *Att.* 4.2.3 [see above]: 'is qui se dedicasse diceret').

[82] Cicero himself in *Dom.* 137 uses first *consecrare*, then *dedicatio* about the dedication of the same altar.

[83] The passages are collected in Wissowa, 'Consecratio' (cited n. 75) 897, partly reproduced by Nisbet (cited n. 2) 209; he (as also Nisbet, with reservations) thought that *dedicare* negatively indicated the giving up of one's own property in favour of the deity, *consecrare* positively indicated the transfer into the deity's ownership (and through this the transformation into a *res sacra*) (cf. id., *Religion und Kultus der Römer*, 2nd edn. (Munich, 1912) 385–6 and now also e.g. J. Linderski, 'dedicatio', *OCD*³ 438); but this attempt at a distinction, which is clearly inspired only by the etymology of the prefixes *de-* and *con-*, is improbable already for the reason that instead of *dedicare* one can also say *dicare* with the same meaning (like *sacrare* instead of *consecrare*, see Wissowa 896), see *OLD* s.v. *dicare* IIa). Classen (cited n. 2) 257 n. 122 (with further lit.) seems to me to come closer to the truth.

[84] Here one thinks of two comprehensive *consecrationes bonorum* in the year of Clodius' tribunate (see below n. 105) and of the *dedicatio* of the Libertas sanctuary. One purpose of the wording seems to me, with regard to the later argumentation (*Dom.* 128–9) to suggest subliminally to the listeners that *dedicatio* and *consecratio* are rather different from each other. For this reason alone Fuhrmann's translation (cited n. 2) with which Bergemann (cited n. 2) 73 agrees, is perhaps not quite appropriate: 'Oder hat die Weihung durch einen Tribunen keinerlei Wirkung und begründet nur die Weihung durch einen Oberpriester religiöse Bindungen?'

used, above all, of temples, altars, and statues,[85] while the more comprehensive *consecrare* is used additionally of all forms of property and especially also of land.[86] That the *lex Papiria*, which was supposed to include all real estate (*aedes, terra, ara*), spoke about *consecrare* was therefore more or less a linguistic necessity; however, conversely, it also at least seemed reasonable that Clodius should use the word *dedicare* about his temple dedication. Cicero could not insist more firmly on this difference, which was irrelevant in terms of religious law, if he did not want to appear pedantic or even sophistic. But with this, apparently, every argument[87] that could immediately be brought forward against the authorization through the *lex Clodia* had been exhausted. One should observe that, in the part concerning Cicero's land and the disputed dedication, it is not quoted by him at any point. What would he, the master of juridical text exegesis, have done if the wording of the law had been favourable to his cause here!

The weakness of Cicero's legal standpoint is also illuminated by the events following his speech. Although of course the question whether a valid dedication had taken place or not was being dealt with, the pontifices did not give their *responsum* apodictically as in the parallel case of the Vestal Licinia (*Dom.* 136 'quod ... dedicasset, sacrum non viderier') but conditionally as in Cassius' case ('nisi eum populus Romanus nominatim praefecisset')–where, however, it had been about the permissibility of a future dedication; I reproduce the passage in part once again (Cic. *Att.* 4.2.3): 'si neque populi iussu neque plebis scitu is qui se dedicasse diceret nominatim ei rei praefectus esset ... videri posse sine religione eam partem areae ... restitui'. So it was apparently a matter of opinion whether the 'being ordered by name' had taken place through the *lex Clodia* or not; and

---

[85] It seems to be common to this group of things that one can attach to them as a sign of the dedication an appropriate inscription which each time 'declares' it or 'gives it out' (*dedicat*) as belonging to this or that god. This is perhaps why *dedicare* is also the technical term for the dedication of literary works.

[86] To my surprise I do not find this observation expressed anywhere else. On *dedicare*: Gudeman, *TLL* V.1.258.41–259.56; on *consecrare*: Lommatzsch, *TLL* IV. 379.71–381.40. Cicero in his speeches (except for *De domo sua*) and philosophical writings connects the (rarer) *dedicare* with *templum, delubrum, aedis, simulacrum;* the (far more frequent) *consecrare* also for instance with *ager, ara, insula, mons, manubiae, candelabrum* etc. (even the use of the word which is later applied to the apotheosis of emperors is prefigured in Cicero: *Att.* 12.18.1 'illam [sc. Tulliam] consecrabo').

[87] Or nearly every argument. When a year later Cicero once more comes to speak about the dedication of his house, he says (*Har. Resp.* 11): 'quam [sc. domum meam] primum inimicus ipse in illa tempestate ac nocte rei publicae ... ne una quidem attigit littera religionis'. So here he complains that in the law concerning the dedication his house or plot of land had not been mentioned (differently, in accordance with received opinion, J. O. Lenaghan, *A Commentary on Cicero's Oration De Haruspicum Responso* (The Hague and Paris, 1969) 80, ad loc.): Clodius could have had himself authorized for the rebuilding of the *porticus* and for the dedication of the Libertas sanctuary connected with it without the necessity that Cicero's property was explicitly mentioned at this point. This weak argument he left out of *De domo sua,* or at most suggested it through appropriate emphasis in *Dom.* 128 '... quae lex lata sit ut tu aedis meas consecrares.'

although, as Cicero reports, the decree was generally interpreted as favourable to him (loc. cit.: 'cum pontifices decressent ita, "si neque... restitui", mihi facta statim est gratulatio–nemo enim dubitabat quin domus nobis esset adiudicata'), Clodius was still able at a people's assembly convened immediately by his brother Appius to claim (loc. cit.) 'pontifices secundum se decrevisse, me autem vi conari in possessionem venire'–the people were supposed to follow him and Appius in order to defend 'their freedom'! Of course we do not know how precisely he argued, but we may assume that he believed that, at least in terms of the spirit of the law, he could read off from it a reference to an authorization by name or at least to an individual appointment.[88]

And so the controversy continues in the Senate (*Att.* 4.2.4). Marcellinus, consul designate and Cicero's supporter, asks the senatorial pontifices who are present: 'quid essent in decernendo secuti', i.e. what they 'had been driving at'[89] with their decree–which shows that this was in fact not yet clear–, whereupon M. Lucullus answers in the name of the priests' college: 'religionis iudices pontifices fuisse, legis esse senatum; se et collegas suos de religione statuisse, in senatu de lege statuturos cum senatu', in other words that the Senate had to decide about precisely how the *lex Clodia*[90] was to be interpreted, or whether the facts conditionally stated in the pontifical decree were given there or not.[91] The pontifices who are present then duly do this by each 'arguing much in favour of Cicero's cause', i.e. by interpreting the *lex Clodia* in a way favourable to him with regard to the decree. Nevertheless, Clodius defends his legal standpoint once more in a three-hour speech and finally, after turbulent scenes, the matter comes to an adjournment. This would all be incomprehensible if Clodius had not–broadly speaking–been authorized to perform the dedication through his law. The debate only concerned the interpretation of nuances in the wording. Cicero's victory in

---

[88] His brother-in-law Pinarius Natta could have let him have some material from the pontifical archives which–in this grey area of interpretation–would have been favourable for him; I am thinking in particular of cases where the ordering of a specific person for a dedication was to be understood from the general context of the relevant plebiscite.

[89] For the expression Drumann–Groebe (cited n. 17) ii.265 n. 7 (after Tunstall) compare Cic. *Att.* 8.11d.5 'nec, si ego quid tu secutus sis non perspicio, idcirco minus existimo te nihil nisi summa ratione fecisse'; more in Shackleton Bailey's commentary (Cambridge, 1965) on *Att.* 4.2.4. More distantly related are the examples given in the *OLD* s.v. *sequor* 10 b.

[90] Only it, and not the *lex Papiria*, can be meant; differently apparently J. Linderski ('The Libri Reconditi', *HSCP* 89 (1985) 214–26, at 217) who understands it thus: 'In the event the dedication should prove legally invalid, the pontiffs removed the *religio*; now it was the Senate's turn to decide whether the law was violated.' The *lex Papiria*, which the priests had very wisely left out of their decree (because of the missing *nominatim* clause), need not have been a topic of discussion in the Senate.

[91] Although Lucullus' antithesis corresponds to that of Cicero, *Dom.* 32–3, it is still hardly likely that he means that the question of the validity of the second *lex Clodia* should be negotiated once more in the Senate.

the end–the following day finally brought the desired decision of the
Senate–was hard-won. And not even conclusive: a whole year later a decree
of the Etruscan *haruspices* which complained of divine wrath about the prof-
anation of holy places (Cic. *Har. Resp.* 9, 'loca sacra et religiosa profana
haberi') got Cicero's house into great difficulty, and the *dedicatio* by Clodius
was again on the Senate agenda. Evidently it was not without reason that he
observed (*Dom.* 127): 'dedicatio magnam ... habet religionem'.

Clodius' Speech

A better understanding of the legal position also makes it easier for us to
reconstruct Clodius' speech[92] which was delivered on 29 September and
for which Cicero's opposing speech offers rich evidence. To put matters in
a nutshell, Clodius' legal position was as strong as his standing with the
public, which had by now turned against him, was weak. The construction
of the sanctuary of Libertas (like Cicero's 'exile' which was connected with
it) had, because of the execution order of 5 December, also been an affront
against the Senate, to which most of the pontifices belonged. So it had to
be Clodius' first task to break down this natural support for Cicero (for
which we have already given some evidence above), to mobilize old feelings of resentment, and to exploit for his own cause more recent feelings
of ill-will among the envious (those who, Cicero thought, 'had clipped his
wings' and now 'did not want them to grow again').[93] The fact that Cicero
had recently, as much to the joy of the people as to the chagrin of conservative senators, pronounced himself in favour of a five-year extraordinary
imperium for his benefactor Pompey to reorganize the grain supply,
offered a first, handy starting-point for this. Clodius openly gave people to
understand that he had hopes from this for a change of mood in comparison with that during the first hearing in Cicero's absence (see above, p. 322):
' "fuisti", inquit, "tum apud pontifices superior, sed iam, quoniam te ad
populum contulisti, sis inferior necesse est" ' (*Dom.* 4). Sheer mockery in
the mouth of the *popularis* Clodius, who with relish made the most of the
dilemma into which his opponent, in order to show his gratitude to as
many people as possible, had manoeuvred himself! He reproached Cicero

---

[92] It is missing (as are many other important speeches) in H. Malcovati (ed.), *Oratorum
Romanorum fragmenta*, 3rd edn. (Turin, 1953) (4th edn. 1976) where strangely enough (429)
Clodius' weakly documented Senate speech of 1 October has been included instead. The following
notes are intended as a provisional substitute for a collection of fragments.

[93] Cic. *Att.* 4.2.5 'illi, quos ne tu quidem ignoras, qui mihi pinnas inciderant, nolunt easdem
renasci.'

for the fact that on 7 September, a day of large demonstrations by the people, he had gone to the Capitol for the Senate session at all,[94] whereas nearly all the other consulars had stayed at home in order not to expose themselves to acts of violence and not to have to negotiate under pressure from the mob.[95] Of course, the hero of the rabble, whom the crowd called by name to action on Pompey's behalf,[96] naturally had nothing to fear. He was once again, as before in December of his year as consul, a *hostis Capitolinus* who was virtually fighting against the Roman state![97] Clodius was playing the part of the senator devoted to the *mos maiorum*, partly seriously, when in this case he declared himself against an extraordinary *imperium* for an individual,[98] but partly also with pure sarcasm when he, obviously parodying the topoi of Cicero's speeches of thanks *post reditum*,[99] contrasted the (oh! so hot) yearning of the Optimates for their Cicero with

[94] *Dom.* 5 ' "at enim in senatum venire in Capitolium turbulento illo die non debuisti." '

[95] *Dom.* 8 ' "at enim non nulli propter timorem, quod se in senatu tuto non esse arbitrabantur, discesserunt." . . . cur ego non timuerim quaeris?' *Dom.* 9 ' "at enim liberum senatus iudicium propter metum non fuit." ' Cic. *Att.* 4.1.6 'cum abessent consulares, quod tuto se negarent posse sententiam dicere, praeter Messallam et Afranium'. Of course these had not claimed that they had stayed away precisely for fear of Clodius, as Smith (cited n. 17) 166 strangely assumes.

[96] Cic. *Att.* 4.1.6 'multitudoque a me nominatim ut id decernerem postularet'; slightly distorted in *Dom.* 15 ' . . . in senatum nominatim vocabar'.

[97] *Dom.* 7 'hic tu me etiam, custodem defensoremque Capitoli templorumque omnium hostem Capitolinum appellare ausus es . . . ?' Cf. for the explanation in addition to Fuhrmann (cited n. 2) ad loc. ('that the special power for Pompey . . . was tantamount to a coup d'état') also the full Appendix I in Nisbet (cited n. 2, p. 198–9) where however the pointed allusion to the infamous occupation of the Capitol on 4 December 63 (Gelzer (cited n. 17) 275, with references) has not been taken into consideration properly; the displeasure aroused precisely by this was attested by Gabinius in the year 58 (Cic. *Sest.* 28, *Red. Sen.* 32) and still by Antonius in the year 44 (Cic. *Phil.* 2.16). This reproach of being a *hostis Capitolinus* becomes most pointed when Clodius reproaches Cicero with having used armed terror this time as well: this becomes probable from Cicero's comment (*Dom.* 6) which otherwise would be basically incomprehensible: 'postea quam mihi nuntiatum est . . . ministros . . . scelerum tuorum partim amissis gladiis, partim ereptis diffugisse, veni non solum sine ullis copiis ac manu' [Clodius' reproach is likely to have been precisely that], 'verum etiam cum paucis amicis' [i.e. with *only* a few friends]. Therefore it seems clear that on that turbulent day Cicero had a protective force with him; one could argue about how large and aggressive this was.–D. R. Shackleton Bailey 'On Cicero's Speeches', *HSCP* 83 (1979) 237–85, at 264) wants to read *hospitem Capitolinum* (in agreement Classen (cited n. 2) 225 n. 32) with allusion to the fact that Cicero was no longer a *civis Romanus*; but this destroys the evident antithesis to *defensorem Capitoli*.

[98] *Dom.* 18: 'negat oportuisse quicquam uni extra ordinem decerni'; cf. *Dom.* 20 (with cunning distortion) 'ut audeas dicere extra ordinem nihil cuiquam [!] dari oportere'; cf. *Dom.* 21, 26. Benner (cited n. 16) 125–7, who erroneously regards the second wording (*Dom.* 20) as authentic, apart from this shows well that this action against an *imperium extraordinarium* was not merely a tactical trick by Clodius. According to his idea the *cura annonae* should still be entrusted to Sex. Cloelius who had been ordered to do this through his *lex frumentaria* (*Dom.* 25, cf. esp. Benner 58–60, 119–20) (*Dom.* 26 'queritur etiam importuna pestis ex ore impurissimo Sex. Cloeli rem frumentariam esse ereptam summisque in periculis eius viri auxilium implorasse rem publicam a quo saepe se et servatam et amplificatam esse meminisset').

[99] This strangely enough never seems to have been noticed; yet at least Shackleton Bailey (cited n. 2) ad loc. notes: 'In Clodius' mouth these questions will have been put sarcastically, but Cicero pretends to take them seriously.'

the latter's despicable change of attitude[100] (*Dom.* 4): ' "tune es ille", inquit, "quo senatus carere non potuit, quem boni luxerunt, quem res publica desideravit, quo restituto senatus auctoritatem restitutam putabamus[101]– quam primum adveniens prodidisti!" ' Here Clodius was able to revive quite a few antipathies against Cicero, whose vainglory, even after his return, must again have got on the nerves of many contemporaries.

This, then, as we see, was the first part of his speech.[102] For the rest, the structure cannot be recovered, but only the content.[103] The central point of Clodius' speech was naturally the complete legal validity of his dedication which, according to him, could now no longer be annulled. He had in the correct manner enlisted a member of the pontifical college (*Dom.* 117): ' "pontifex", inquit, "adfuit" '; as was only natural, this was the one who was personally closest to him (*Dom.* 118): 'quis ergo adfuit? "frater", inquit, "uxoris meae." '[104] The latter had first recited to him the solemn dedicatory formulae (cf. *Dom.* 119; 121) and held the doorpost (*Dom.* 121: ' . . . pontificem postem tenuisse dixisti'). Clodius himself contrasted the dedication which in the case of Cicero's property he had performed ritually in full seriousness, with the *consecratio bonorum* with which he had also in the year of his tribunate dedicated to the gods the property of the consul Gabinius in front of the people's assembly,[105] which he had apparently only meant in jest (and which had been performed without a pontifex) (*Dom.* 126): 'iam fateor', inquit, 'me in Gabinio nefarium fuisse.' But above all, he said, he had safeguarded his dedication in the required way through plebiscite or law (*Dom.* 106): ' "tuleram", inquit, "ut mihi liceret" ' (cf. above p. 325 on *Dom.* 51). Admittedly, the law itself, he was able to argue, had been annulled by means of a new one; however, its irreversible consequences of course held good (*Dom.* 127): ' "dedicatio magnam", inquit, "habet religionem." '

---

[100] This is perhaps the first time that this reproach, which from now on runs through the polemics against Cicero (Ps.-Sall. *Inv. in Cic.* 5 'modo harum, modo illarum partium'), is raised.

[101] Cf. for instance Cic. *Red. Sen.* 34 'mecum leges . . . mecum senatus auctoritas . . . afuerunt. [39] . . . cum me vestra auctoritas arcessierit, populus Romanus vocarit, res publica implorarit, Italia cuncta paene suis umeris reportarit'. In this context, Clodius of course had to omit Cicero's inclusion of the *populus*.

[102] The structure as far as this comes to light from *Dom.* 3: 'sed quoniam ille demens, si ea quae per hos dies ego in senatu de re publica sensi vituperasset, aliquem se aditum ad auris vestras esse habiturum putavit, omittam ordinem dicendi meum.'

[103] But cf. below, n. 116.

[104] Liou-Gille's claim (cited n. 43) that the ceremony required at least three priests (p. 58 n. 112) is founded on a strange confusion; otherwise here she uncritically follows Cicero's partial account (without taking into consideration more recent research on the speech).

[105] On the peculiar *consecrationes bonorum* which were apparently without consequences, which Cicero mentions in this context (*Dom.* 123 ff.) cf. Nippel (cited n. 19) 119, Bergemann (cited n. 2) 63–4, most recently Liou-Gille (cited n. 43) 51–2 and esp. W. Kunkel and R. Wittmann, *Staatsordnung und Staatspraxis der römischen Republik*, 2: *Die Magistratur* (Munich, 1995) 173–4, 577–9.

Furthermore, we can also understand from Cicero's speech that Clodius did not content himself with demonstrating the formal correctness of his actions concerning his 'exile law', which of course could still appear as a piece of malicious chicanery. He wanted to be seen to have been in the right both substantively and morally as well. When he abused Cicero as *exsul* (*Dom.* 72: 'hunc tu etiam, portentosa pestis, exsulem appellare ausus es . . . ?'),[106] he probably meant by this less the proscription pronounced by means of his second law (which actually would not yet justify an *exilium*), but above all that Cicero himself had applied the first *lex Clodia* with its proscription threat to himself, and that through his departure–*Dom.* 95: 'obicitur mihi meus ille discessus'–he had admitted that he was guilty of having killed *cives Romanos indemnatos.*[107] His second law, Clodius was able to say, had only taken the logical step from this self-condemnation by Cicero who had personally stripped himself of his citizenship by leaving state territory.[108] And this loss of *civitas* (it seems that this was Clodius' argument, though it is certainly an excessively bold one) had not really been annulled even through the *lex de reditu* (*Dom.* 85): 'et tu unus pestifer civis eum restitutum negas esse [!] quem eiectum universus senatus non modo civem, sed etiam egregium civem semper putavit.' It is a pity that Clodius' argument here, which must have amounted to the idea that Cicero was still then virtually an *exsul*,[109] can no longer be reconstructed in more detail. At any rate, he was able to describe the dedication on Cicero's land of a sanctuary specifically of Libertas–*Dom.* 110: 'at quae dea est? . . . "Libertas", inquit, "est" ' –as a meaningful *monumentum*[110] of the liberty which had been won back after the expulsion of the *crudelis tyrannus* (cf. *Dom.* 75).[111] The Roman people, so he perhaps threatened (foreshadowing his later behaviour[112]) would, if need be, know in alliance with the immortal gods how to defend its *Libertas*.

From two comments of Cicero's we can infer that, and in what way, Clodius sought to safeguard himself against a counterargument which was

---

[106] *Dom.* 76 also refers to this: 'hoc genus totum maledicti . . . in isto tuo maledicto', 86 'calamitas . . . maledicti locum aut criminis obtinebit?' 88 'meum probrum'.

[107] In this trial Clodius no longer seems to have reproached Cicero with the execution of the Catilinarians itself; otherwise Cicero would hardly be able to say that even Clodius and his followers no longer dared to describe Cicero's 'exile' as the result of a *peccatum* (*Dom.* 72).

[108] Clodius probably understood his law in this way already at that time. In doing so, as Habicht (cited n. 17) 63 brilliantly expounds, he applies Cicero's own method against the Catilinarians to the man himself. Just as Cicero had once had them killed as manifest criminals without trial, in the same way he was now himself being proscribed as a confessed criminal: 'The main difference was that what had happened in December 63 could not be undone whereas Cicero's banishment could be revoked.'

[109] One should also note Cicero's wording in the passage quoted (*Dom.* 72): 'exsulem appellare ausus es', not for instance *exsulem fuisse* . . .   [110] Cf. above, n. 42.

[111] Cf. esp. Liou-Gille (as above, n. 43) 56–7.   [112] Cf. Cic. *Att.* 4.2.3 (see above); 4.3.2.

to be expected from Cicero. First *Dom.* 34: 'videsne me non radicitus evellere omnes actiones tuas' [sc. in the year of his tribunate 58] 'neque illud agere quod apertum est: te omnino nihil gessisse iure, non fuisse tribunum plebis, hodie esse patricium?' In order to declare invalid the so-called *lex de exsilio*, on which the dedication was based, Cicero–so Clodius apparently prophesied[113]–would try for reasons of religious law to contest his adoption into the family of a plebeian (which had been per-formed by Caesar) and with that to declare illegal all his actions as tribune of the plebs. Clodius could warn with justification that this argumentation should not be followed, since the Senate itself had treated the so-called *lex de exsilio* as legally valid (see above, p. 324), and since an annulment of his plebeian status by the pontifices would have virtually incalculable political consequences.

The second *praemunitio* comes to light from *Dom.* 92: '*hic* tu me etiam gloriari vetas: negas esse ferenda quae soleam de me praedicare ...'. Since in the preceding section (91) Cicero spoke about the motives for his *discessus*, it is to be assumed as probable that *hic* ('in this context') refers precisely to this. Already from the earlier speeches *post reditum* Clodius could foresee without difficulty that Cicero would describe his 'exile' as self-sacrifice for the common good (*Red. Quir.* 1,[114] this is done still more carefully in *Red. Sen.* 34) if not even as the second saving of the state;[115] and he makes fun in advance of the self-glorification which is to be expected, so that this is comparable with the ironical passage which can be inferred from *Dom.* 4 'tune es ille...' (see above pp. 333–4). This gave him the opportunity generally to pull Cicero's notorious vanity to pieces (*Dom.* 93 '... hoc rep-rehendis quod solere me dicas de me ipso gloriosius praedicare') and in doing so–this had nothing to do with the 'exile' any more–even to allude to a passage from the epic *De consulatu suo* where Cicero (boldly indeed!) had been his own Homer (*Dom.* 92, immediately after the passage quoted above): 'et homo facetus inducis etiam sermonem urbanum ac venustum: me dicere solere esse me Iovem eundemque dictitare Minervam esse sororem meam'. So now, just as after his year as consul, Cicero's vainglory was for a second time about to become tiresome to those around him.

---

[113] Shackleton Bailey however understands the passage differently; see below, n. 146.

[114] 'cum me fortunasque meas pro vestra incolumitate otio concordiaque devovi'; cf. on this the references in J. Graff, *Ciceros Selbstauffassung* (Heidelberg, 1963) 32–3 and esp. n. 58, 59, 63, 64, 65 (unfortunately Graff does not make any attempt to describe the gradual development of the topoi in terms of which Cicero interprets his *discessus*).

[115] This formula which became important later (Graff, cited n. 114) 33 with n. 67), which iron-ically goes back to the reviled consul Piso (Cic. *Pis.* 78 reports as Piso's remark: 'me posse rem publicam iterum servare, si cessissem'–treated there of course as pure cynicism by Cicero), can, if I am not overlooking anything, be first detected in *Dom.* 76, then above all *Dom.* 99 (see below p. 359), but could also perhaps have been used earlier by Cicero.

This is what we can infer of Clodius' speech with certainty.[116] It was possibly a milestone in the development of what Zielinski christened the 'Cicero caricature in antiquity'.[117] The reproaches of cruelty (*crudelitas*) and despotic rule (*regnum*) which were above all those which had been raised earlier, are now followed, and thus completed or replaced, by accusations of vanity and lack of principle (of which the former may well have existed before[118]); it is possible but cannot be proved that Clodius had also already included in his invective, with regard to the 'exile', Cicero's unmanliness in his grief[119] and, with regard to his self-portrayal, his all too effusive oratorical style (which was later reprimanded by the 'Atticists')–again we think of the passage in *Dom.* 4 quoted above. But these personal, polemical components of the speech must not make us forget that in its centre stood the religious appeal to the priests. This 'trial', according to Clodius' perfectly truthful description, was about a dedication performed correctly according to law and all the rules of the art, the annulment of which would necessarily draw down the wrath of the gods on Rome: 'dedicatio magnam habet

---

[116] After what we have seen, it could, in contrast to Cicero's speech, definitely have had the normal structure of a forensic speech, roughly as follows (I shall put thoughts which are not directly attested, but inferred or to be assumed, in angle brackets):

1. *Prooemium*: ⟨Greatness of the subject: first attempt in Roman history to annul a dedication performed by a pontifex.⟩

2. *Digressio*: Cicero now at a disadvantage in comparison with the earlier trial, since in the meantime he has stood up for Pompey; his behaviour on 7 September. Mocking of his change of attitude.

3. *Narratio*: ⟨Cicero's reaction to the *lex de capite civis Romani*: self-condemnation. Belated proscription through second *lex Clodia* as ratification of actual exile.⟩ Proper confiscation and dedication of the *aedes Libertatis* with legal authorization, and with pontifical assistance in accordance with the ritual.

4. *Propositio*: The dedicated part of Cicero's house is *res sacra* which in no case can be restored.

5. *Argumentatio* I = *Probatio*:
   ⟨(*a*) Annulment of the second *lex Clodia* through the *lex de reditu* strictly speaking cannot annul Cicero's self-condemnation:⟩ Cicero is and remains an *exsul*.
   ⟨(*b*) *lex de reditu* cannot by any means cancel dedication.⟩ *dedicatio magnam habet religionem* ⟨and is fundamentally irreversible⟩.

6. *Argumentatio* II = *Refutatio* (or *Praemunitio*):
   (*a*) against the appeal to the invalidity of the adoption which is to be expected
   (*b*) against Cicero's description of his exile and his intolerable self-glorification

7. *Peroratio*: ⟨No law can annul sanctity of a pontifical dedication: Just as the people will defend their *Libertas* so the gods will not give up their property unavenged.⟩

[117] *Cicero im Wandel der Jahrhunderte*, 3rd edn. (Leipzig and Berlin, 1912) 280–8 (where this speech is not dealt with in detail).

[118] According to Plut. *Cic.* 24 and Quint. *Inst.* 11.1.24 (only with reference to the poems) the way in which Cicero spoke about his suppression of Catiline's coup was already tiresome to his contemporaries (cf. Graff (cited n. 114) 77–80: 'Cicero's self-praise'). But as far as I remember there is no immediate evidence of this from the years 63 to 58.

[119] Against this reproach which above all Petrarch takes up later Cicero defends himself in *Dom.* 97–8 (where, however, he merely ascribes it to others in the past 'qui me animo nimis fracto esse atque adflicto loquebantur'.

religionem'. We see in Clodius, through Ciceronian spectacles, only the reckless libertine of the Bona Dea scandal. But on this 29 September, he must have appeared as a conservative and devout Roman, reminding the pontifices of their responsibility and their duty to leave to the gods what belonged to them. There were other sites for Cicero to build on.

General Plan and Structure of Cicero's Speech

Any objection that Cicero was able to put forward against this in terms of religious law, as we have seen, was weak; other possible legal arguments (e.g. concerning the invalidity of the adoption or of the second *lex Clodia*) had little prospect of success, for political reasons which are well known and without doubt were rehearsed by Clodius. So if Cicero wanted to get the pontifices to clutch at the straw offered by the *lex Papiria* and above all by the decree issued to Cassius (with its *nominatim* clause, which at any rate was useful), in the hope of obtaining a decree which it would be almost against their professional ethic to grant, and so to clear the way for a deconsecration, then almost the only thing which remained for him was the appeal to the emotions. It was not sufficient that the college of priests generally was well disposed towards him, and remained so in spite of the dissatisfaction regarding Pompey. The pontifices had to be made to feel as painfully indignant as he himself did that a demagogue's statue of Liberty should be allowed to stand in triumph on the land of the man who had fought and suffered for the authority of the Senate as no other had done. And they, doubtless more than Cicero himself, had to be convinced that something like that simply could not be the will of the immortal gods.

These considerations are reflected in the at first sight confused,[120] but at least as far as the essential features are concerned, very simply calculated structure of *De Domo Sua*. In the first part of the speech (32–103), after the *prooemium* and the necessary introductory remarks (1–31) Cicero tries, above all with the help of old feelings of resentment, to fan the flames of the indignation against Clodius and his actions and thus to provoke the desire to remove the new *porticus* with its Libertas; the second part (104–41) with the epilogue (142–7) is then supposed to remove the pontifical inhibitions which stand in the way of the satisfaction of this desire and of Cicero's final return home. This structure (of desire and fulfilment

---

[120] Thus Wolf (cited n. 6) 131 complains: 'Summam eius [sc. orationis Pro domo] persequi difficile est propter miram varietatem rerum quae in ea perplexius confusae sunt'; whereupon he gives a purely linear structure (following Manutius) in which, however, (following Ferratius) the most important argument seems to have been overlooked!

so to speak) expresses itself manifestly in the two sentences which conclude respectively the first part and the whole speech. In section 103, the true hinge and central point of the speech, it is said: 'quam porticum, pro amore quem habetis in rem publicam et semper habuistis, non modo *sententiis*, sed, si opus esset, *manibus vestris* disturbare cuperetis–nisi quem forte illius castissimi sacerdotis superstitiosa dedicatio deterret.' In the (passionately serious) main clause Cicero describes the result he desires from the first part; in the (sarcastically mocking) conditional clause, added as an afterthought, he mentions the obstacle which will have to be removed in the second part. After carrying out this task, too, he can finally plead at the end (147): '. . . quaeso obtestorque vos, pontifices, ut me, quem auctoritate studio *sententiis* restituistis, nunc, quoniam senatus ita vult, *manibus* quoque *vestris* in sedibus meis conlocetis.' After the first part the pontifices wish 'to tear down' Clodius' building 'not only with their votes but with their own hands'; after the second part they may just as once they 'led' Cicero 'back with their votes' so now 'place' him 'back into his house with their own hands'.

This is the real large-scale plan of this speech, which, with all its subtlety of argumentation, is still throughout orientated to the emotions. Cicero did not set it out explicitly, at least no more clearly than emerges from the remarks just quoted. According to his principle that the orator should rather conceal the aim of stirring the emotions in favour of the supposed aim of providing factual information (*De Orat.* 2.310), generally speaking, in his speeches he frequently places the individual parts under titles or headings other than those which would correspond to their true function; indeed, he even sometimes deliberately obscures the structure and articulation. In the present case, one might say that both these things are done. For in the first part, looking at it from the outside, (i.e. apart from what may be called the overall emotional strategy) Cicero speaks above all about questions of public or state law (32 f. *ius publicum; ius rei publicae*); on the other hand, in the second part he speaks about questions of religious law (32 *ius religionis*),[121] and one could say to a certain extent that in the first part he tries to prove the nullity of the dedication by showing the invalidity of the *lex Clodia* (according to *ius publicum*), in the second by showing the invalidity of the *dedicatio* itself (according to *ius religionis*). Now, it is true that Cicero himself introduces these two very notions in sections 32-3 which form a kind of *propositio*,[122] and at the place where he again leaves the *ius religionis* he at least marks the transition as

---

[121] MacKendrick's division (cited n. 1, at pp. 147-57) into 3b-99 'Narratio', 100-41 'Argumentatio' is not worth discussing.

[122] Sect. 32 'quae [sc. causa cognitioque vestra] cum sit in ius religionis et in ius rei publicae distributa'. This is possibly the first prefiguring of the modern *ius utrumque* (secular and religious law).

such (142): '... revocate iam animos vestros ab hac subtili [!] nostra disputatione ad universam rem publicam'; but in the *propositio* mentioned he conceals this division by mischievously denying that he proposes to speak about *ius religionis* at all (32): 'sed hoc [sc. *quod multa dixi extra causam*] compensabo brevitate[123] eius orationis quae pertinet ad ipsam causam cognitionemque vestram; quae cum sit in *ius religionis* et in *ius rei publicae* distributa, religionis partem, quae multo est verbosior, praetermittam,[124] de iure rei publicae dicam.' Cicero justifies this restraint on the ground of his modesty which, he says, prevents him from wanting to instruct the specialists in religious matters when he is a layman (33 'quid est enim ... tam adrogans quam de religione ... pontificum conlegium docere conari ... ?'), and this may be not just an effective argument[125] but also to a certain extent[126] true, but on its own it does not yet exactly explain the obfuscation (which becomes evident in retrospect). Only in so far as Cicero hardly goes into the details of the dedication ritual–which doubtless nobody would have expected him to–can it be said that he restrains himself concerning the *ius religionis*; in other respects, it would be difficult to state which aspect of this allegedly *res multo verbosior* he would have omitted. Cicero himself finally admits this when he says towards the end of the second main part (138): 'dixi a principio [32–3] nihil me de scientia vestra, nihil de sacris, nihil de abscondito pontificum iure dicturum; quae sunt adhuc a me de iure dedicandi disputata non sunt quaesita ex occulto aliquo genere litterarum, sed sumpta de medio, ex rebus palam per magistratus actis ad collegiumque delatis, ex senatus consulto, ex lege.'[127] So Cicero does not deny here that he has dealt with (and is still dealing with) the *ius dedicandi* which without doubt belongs to religious law; but instead he acts as if by *ius religionis* he had exclusively meant the religious law which drew on inaccessible sources, not religious law in general. Different again is section 33, where Cicero admittedly also understands by *ius religionis* the arcane special knowledge of the priests, but in addition to that above all the more general questions *de religione, de rebus*

---

[123] All the same, another 115 paragraphs follow!

[124] Classen (cited n. 2) 233, like other interpreters, believes this: the 'discussion' of the *ius religionis* would 'doubtless have been rhetorically unproductive'.

[125] Especially if one assumes that Clodius somewhat exaggerated his role as champion of Roman religion–Cicero's speech seems to lead in this direction in other places as well (cf. esp. 127).

[126] The manner in which for instance in sect. 121 he exaggerates his ignorance of the dedication rites recalls the manner in which elsewhere in law court speeches he plays down his knowledge of Greek art or philosophy; thus Gesner in Wolf (cited n. 6) ad loc.

[127] Of the three parts introduced with *ex* which (contrary to Behaghel's principle) decrease in extent while their factual importance increases–the deletion of *ex senatus ... lege* by Maslowski and others destroys an artistic effect–the first refers to the cases of Cassius and Licinia, the second only of Licinia, the third to the *lex Papiria* as the alleged legal basis.

divinis, caerimoniis, sacris. And so the question remains why at the beginning Cicero claims to leave aside the treatment of the *ius religionis*.

I see two reasons. First: while claiming that he wants to deal only with the *ius publicum* anyway, Cicero gives the impression that this point alone (in respect of which he is indeed on firmer ground) could be sufficient to decide the case. This corresponds to the thought which he expresses in the *prooemium* (this will be discussed in a moment); and it is expressed explicitly in the effectively decisive final part of the speech (after cursory treatment of a detail of religious law concerning the dedication), sect. 122: 'quamquam quid ego de dedicatione loquor, aut quid de vestro iure et *religione* contra quam proposueram [32–3] disputo? ego vero, si omnia sollemnibus verbis, veteribus et traditis institutis acta esse dicerem, tamen me *rei publicae* iure defenderem.'

But a second point is perhaps even more important. It cannot escape more exact examination that in the proof which is decisive for the final verdict, Cicero has to rely on a piece of extremely specialized *ius pontificium*, namely the decree issued to Cassius which came from the pontifical archive,[128] which Cicero can only have found out with expert help[129]–in complete contradiction to his statement (section 33) that it was foolish '. . . si quis quid in vestris libris invenerit, id narrare vobis.'[130] Cicero now tries to give more weight to this modest precedent which only partially covers the same ground (see above p. 328) by presenting it as a definitive interpretation of the *lex Papiria*–which is naturally of incomparably higher authority–which of course according to Cicero is supposed to invalidate Clodius' dedication and in doing so without doubt constitutes a fully valid item of *ius publicum*. He emphasizes precisely this, by more or less expressly reverting to sections 31–2, at the place where he first emphatically asks about Clodius' personal authorization, section 128: 'neque ego nunc de religione sed de bonis omnium nostrum, nec de *pontificio* sed de iure *publico* disputo' (Cicero stresses emphatically that he is relying on the law, not, as it would have been correct for him to say, on the decree); then, where he himself

---

[128] Since Cicero (who otherwise pretends to have only superficial knowledge of religious law) specially points out this fact (136 'habetis in commentariis vestris C. Cassium censorem de signo Concordiae dedicando ad pontificum conlegium rettulisse eique M. Aemilium pontificem maximum pro conlegio respondisse') the assumption suggests itself that this decree is not known to most of the priests before Cicero's speech. Cf. Linderski (cited n. 90) 215 n. 41 (against G. Rohde).

[129] Linderski (cited n. 90) 215 ff. (with older lit.) draws from Cicero's statements a different conclusion: that the *commentarii pontificum* containing the decrees were collected in a form which was accessible to the public or at least to senators, and therefore did not belong to the *occultum genus litterarum* (according to sect. 138) which only the priests have at their disposal (more carefully p. 222 where he assumes a literary work as the source). But then Cicero would, according to the drift of his entire argument, have to stress the non-esoteric character of the Cassius decree.

[130] Linderski (cited n. 90) 220 very artificially wants to understand by this ' "scholarly" studies written by various learned pontiffs'.

introduces the decree, section 136 'sed ut revertar ad ius *publicum* dedicandi (quod ⟨id⟩[131] ipsi pontifices semper non solum ad suas caerimonias sed etiam ad populi iussa adcommodaverunt) ... '. Here, the decree, since it is supposed to have been issued in accordance with the *lex*, itself becomes an item of *ius publicum*, and as such is enhanced in status. Particularly with regard to this testimony which was the most important for his argument, it made sense for Cicero from the beginning to give the impression that he wanted to stay exclusively in the sphere of *ius publicum*, and in doing so also to distract attention from the fact that in the decisive point he even had to rely on some quite remote specialist pontifical knowledge.

So far only the basic features of the plan of Cicero's speech have become clear to us. He uses the part of his speech concerned with state law, which deals above all with the second *lex Clodia*, in order to stir up displeasure against Clodius, which he needs so that in the part concerning religious law–which is neither expressly divided off nor correctly signposted–he will be able to dispel reservations about the annulment of the dedication. To understand further aspects of this, it is necessary to examine, at least in outline, the individual parts of the speech.

Introduction: *Prooemium* (1–2) and *Digressio* (3–31)

Already in the *prooemium* (1–2) the relation between state and religion (a fundamental topic of the speech) is dealt with. Cicero's position in terms of religious law was weak, as we have learnt. So he explains to the pontifices, to whose religious responsibility Clodius must only just have appealed, that it was particularly wise of the ancestors not to isolate the class of priests as a caste but through a prudent personal union of pontifex and politician–here a peculiarity of Roman religion[132] is put into words perhaps for the first time–to ensure that decisions about religious matters were never made without also considering the interests of the state. In this case–now Cicero exposes the pious speeches of his predecessor–it was

---

[131] My supplement. The transmitted text, with the rightly undisputed correction *dedicandi* instead of *iudicandi* and with *quod* as relative, seems to say that the priests always adapted the *ius publicum* also to the *populi iussa*, which is incomprehensible. With the addition of ⟨*id*⟩, the *quod*-clause, now causal, explains why it is correct to speak of *ius publicum* in connection with dedication.

[132] According to G. J. Szemler ('Priesthood and Priestly Careers in Ancient Rome', *ANRW* II.16.3 (1986) 2314–31, at 2316) it is an established result of prosopographical research 'that in Rome the religious establishment was identical with the political establishment'.

a matter of preventing unscrupulous magistrates in the future from being allowed to use religion, on top of everything else, as a weapon. As a Roman conscious of tradition Clodius had urged that religion must remain holy. Cicero urges, almost like a philosopher of the Enlightenment, that religion must not be instrumentalized for unholy purposes. Otherwise, he says, it would be better to look for new cults and new priests! (The degree of passion to which the *prooemium* already soars at this point, probably inspired by the preceding emotionalism of Clodius, is astonishing.) On the other hand–Cicero now pours oil on the waters of his indignation–if the priests were to do justice to their task as statesmen, then the wisdom of the ancestors would have proved its worth. Thus in this *prooemium*, taken, according to his own prescription elsewhere, completely *ex ipsis visceribus causae* (*De Orat.* 2.318), he succeeds with a few purposeful sentences in himself regaining the conservative's role usurped by Clodius, and in hurling back at his opponent a certain accusation of impiety.

Through his attack on Cicero's action on Pompey's behalf, Clodius had tried to ingratiate himself with the priests (3 'aliquem se aditum ad auris vestras esse habiturum putavit,' cf. above, pp. 332–3), and in doing so can hardly have been unsuccessful. Cicero has to counter this in a *digressio* (3b–31), which is required by the situation in order to create any foundation at all for his counterattack on Clodius. Since this passage, in the context of the whole speech, is in fact somewhat exceptional (32 'extra causam'), it cannot be treated in as much detail as it would really merit because of its unsolved historical problems. As Classen already saw,[133] Cicero keeps back the crucial point, namely the statement specifically in favour of Pompey. He begins, in a truly ingenious manner, with the most vulnerable of his opponent's points, by indignantly interpreting Clodius' confidence that the pontifices have changed their attitude towards Cicero to imply precisely that accusation of fickleness (4 'quod in imperita multitudine est vitiosissimum ... hoc tu ad hos transferas ... !')–which had of course been raised against Cicero himself, and which he immediately repels ('tune es ille ... '; the passage has been quoted already). So the pontifical listeners appear to be associated with Cicero from the beginning as it were in a shared destiny with regard to the common enemy Clodius; then immediately a first furious attack on the ground of Cicero's expulsion (5a) is launched against him, in a markedly sharp contrast to the frivolous irony of the quote from Clodius. After that Cicero tries to justify his behaviour on 7 September by blaming for the turmoil Clodius' faction (and not for instance the Pompeians in the crowd, who had obviously been more conspicuous)

---

[133] Classen (cited n. 2) 225, cf. 226.

(5b–8).[134] He first deals with his proposal for Pompey's exorbitant command which he now has to justify (9–26) by almost euphemistically avoiding mention of the person concerned (whose name had been mentioned only once, in section 3, until it finally reappears in section 16);[135] and in doing this Cicero acts as if–against the historical truth which is still recognizable for us–the people had not actually asked for Pompey but for Cicero himself as a tried and trusted helper[136] and as if he had on his own

---

[134] The unrest of that day is wrongly conflated by historians (with the exception of P. Stein, *Die Senatssitzungen der Ciceronischen Zeit (68–43)* (Münster, 1930 (diss. 1928)) 34 with n. 186, quoted by Nisbet (cited n. 2) p. 76 on sect. 11 line 2, and of Wiseman (cited n. 17) 389 note 77) with the more violent riots which Cicero deals with in sections 11–14 and during which a *lapidatio* took place (cf. most recently esp. Mitchell (cited n. 17) 158 with n. 50, taking issue with Shackleton Bailey in his commentary (Cambridge, 1965) on *Att.* 4.1.6, who, also incorrectly, dates the *lapidatio* to 6 September). The Senate session in the Temple of Concordia mentioned there which had been convened by Metellus–on 7 September there was a session on the Capitol, so probably in the Temple of Jupiter (cf. Mommsen, *Staatsrecht* (cited n. 50) iii.928)–took place much earlier, at the beginning of the difficulties with the supply ('cum ingravescerat annona'), therefore not in August either (as Stein and Wiseman assume, see above) but still before the Senate session in July during which Cicero's return was decided (cf. for instance Mitchell (cited n. 17) 155 with n. 39) and following which grain prices sank rapidly again (sect. 14); this is confirmed by Asconius on Cic. *Mil.* 38 (p. 48.20 Clark) who dates a grain riot on the *ludi Apollinares* (6–13 July) (thus B.A. Marshall, *A Historical Commentary on Asconius* (Columbia, Mo., 1985) 200, who like Shackleton Bailey dates the *lapidatio* on 5 or 6 September and concludes from this that Asconius confused the *ludi Apollinares* with the *ludi Romani* which took place in September, is incorrect). Cicero mentions these earlier brawls in which two notorious Clodians, Sergius and Lollius, had participated, above all to show that now (at the beginning of September)–when of course visibly the Pompeians were dominating in public–Clodius had again been on the point of exploiting the food shortage to stir up the people (so that 'the torch of rebellion might take hold' (sect. 13)). So Cicero can say about the recent danger with regard to the earlier events (sect. 11): 'neque id [sc. *periculum*] coniectura prospiciebamus, sed iam experti videbamus'. Precisely the content of that *iam experti* is explained in what follows. Cicero's apparent lack of chronological clarity did not of course exist for his listeners at that time.

[135] According to the set of alternatives presented in sect. 10 (functioning as a *partitio* for this section) the following must be dealt with: (1) whether the crisis necessitated new measures (10–13), (2) whether Cicero had a special part to play in this (14–16a), (3) whether the action taken and the choice of Pompey in particular was right (16b–30). Through this arrangement the thought cannot even arise that the reason for Cicero's activity was the debt of gratitude which he owed to Pompey–in fact this was doubtless the case. In the decisive place where he first gives reasons for the choice of Pompey (16), mentioning of course the latter's competence and good luck, he protests not against the idea that he wanted to get his friend a position of power, but that he wanted to load a burden on to him!

[136] This demand by the people (15 'a populo Romano universo . . . in senatum nominatim vocabar'; more clearly 16 'flagitabar bonorum expostulatione') according to Cicero's intention has to be distinguished from the malicious choruses of the Clodians (16 'improborum convicia') who had already much earlier (during the *lapidatio*, cf. above, n. 134) blamed Cicero for the shortage (14 'annonam praestare oportere dicebant'; cf. about this esp. Wiseman (cited n. 17) 389) and who were now calling his name as that of the guilty person (15 'ab operis tuis impulsu tuo nominabar'; cf. *Att.* 4.1.6 'cum . . . homines . . . impulsu Clodi mea opera frumenti inopiam esse clamarent', whereby apparently it was insinuated that Cicero had a culpable intention); Nisbet (cited n. 2) p. 79 on sections 14–24 is unclear, MacKendrick (cited n. 1) 148 is wrong, Classen (cited n. 2) 227 is confusing: 'So it was not Cicero who bore the responsibility, he only did what the general public demanded' (as Cicero's statement, whose meaning remains incomprehensible anyway in Classen's rendering of sections 14–18).

initiative 'delegated' the matter to his 'friend with greater resources' (16 'delegavi amico locupletiori').[137] The reason for this surprising falsification (which of course paradoxically even exaggerates Cicero's action on Pompey's behalf) seems at first to be that before the pontifices he wants to be regarded still as a Pompeian rather than as a populist. Incidentally, Clodius' statement against an *imperium extra ordinem*[138] (which was not to the liking of the pontifices) at least gives a welcome opportunity to castigate his *inconstantia* (18–24) (with which of course he for his part had reproached Cicero) and in doing so recalling his outrageous behaviour towards Cato (20–2) as well as of the shameful distribution of the consular provinces in the year 58 (23–4).

But the manner in which Cicero then in the end not only justifies but in fact praises his commitment to an extraordinary imperium specifically for Pompey can hardly be explained by the intention of his speech and his consideration for the pontifices who are to issue the *responsum*. Whereas at first he had of course done everything to justify his proposal purely from practical necessity, and without consideration of his personal relationship to Pompey,[139] he now at the end of the digression makes an extremely surprising, unadorned confession of this friendship[140]–as he says, a 'collaboration in the interests of good government' (28 'hanc conspirationem in re publica bene gerenda'). Nobody should hope to be able to turn him and Pompey against each other once more (for instance by insinuating to Cicero (29) that Pompey had deserted him at that time when he had to leave Rome)![141] He knew what Pompey had achieved for his recall and was now happy to be able to reconcile the welfare of the state with his own debt of gratitude. Even if he can always count on forbearance, even affection, for his action on behalf of his *amicus*, Cicero is well aware that with such an enthusiastic emphasis he must offend priests hostile to Pompey.[142] Fortunately at the beginning of this final passage, he has given

---

[137] In Cic. *Att.* 4.1.6 it is said clearly that the people had *nominatim* demanded of him the support for the proposal on Pompey's behalf ('ut id decernerem', cf. Shackleton Bailey (comm. ad loc.); in *Dom.* 15 this becomes a 'calling into the Senate *nominatim*'–a considerable difference!

[138] Here Cicero falsifies the opinion of Clodius who had not rejected such an *imperium* on principle but only for this case; see above, n. 98.   [139] Cf. above, n. 135.

[140] After the depiction of the regime of terror of Clodius and his companions, who like pirates steer the captured ship of state whose crew has gone overboard (sect. 24), Pompey is introduced as a saviour in time of greatest affliction; the associative manner in which this is done is brilliant (25). In the same way, Cicero suggests, he will be the saviour now as well.

[141] It is well known that Cicero himself knew that this was true: *Q. fr.* 1.4.4 'subita defectio Pompeii'. What he suggests in *Dom.* 30 about the men behind his expulsion and its true originators ('utile est, quorum id scelere conflatum sit, me occultare et tacere')–since Clodius, Piso and Gabinius are openly abused–can really only refer to Caesar; differently Shackleton Bailey (cited n. 2) ad loc. (p. 51).

[142] Cf. 31 (referring to the Senate motion): 'si cuius forte pontificis animum, quod certo scio aliter esse [!], mea sententia offendit'.

us, his readers, an indication of his motive: Pompey, who on 8 September
had appointed him the first of the fifteen legates who had been allowed
him and in doing so–in the Roman Senate!–had described him as his
future *alter ego*,[143] had on the 29th personally appeared for the trial before
the pontifices (25 'dicam ipso audiente quod sensi et sentio') in order thus
to speak up for his friend with his authority. In this situation Cicero's
confession of loyalty, although damaging rather than anything else at that
moment, was a sheer obligation of gratitude, a piece of *amicitia* in practice
(cf. just here sect. 27 'remuneratio benevolentiae') and of a policy which
goes beyond the moment. Only now do we also understand completely
why Cicero did not want to give the impression that the proposal on
Pompey's behalf had been made by the people but that it had been his
own idea (cf. above, pp. 344–5). Cicero, even speaking on his own behalf,
pro domo, was not just an advocate.

The Overall Plan of the *Argumentatio* (32 ff.) and the *Praeteritio: de iure adoptionis* (34–42)

After the passage which has been described as *extra causam* (32) we now
come to what Cicero regards as the real 'matter'. In order now to be able
to understand more precisely the structure of this main part of the speech
which until now we have looked at only with regard to its general psychological strategy (above, pp. 338–9) we shall have once again to recall
systematically the three lines of argument against the validity of the dedication which are in principle possible:

1. 'The dedication as such was invalid because of serious procedural
   errors.' This argumentation from the point of view of religious law
   would be the strongest with regard to the point to be proved, but since
   Clodius had been very circumspect during the dedication, this could be
   carried out only with difficulty (see above pp. 327ff.).

---

[143] The formula coined by Aristotle (*EN* 1166a31: 'the friend is another self') and Zeno (Diog.
Laert. 7.23: 'another I') had probably still hardly been introduced in Rome (it is probably first used
by Cicero in *Att.* 3.15.4; classic then in *Lael.* 80, cf. J. G. F. Powell's commentary (Warminster,
1990), 91) on *Lael.* 23). Pompey could in any case want to suggest that his relationship with Cicero
went even beyond the end-directed Roman *amicitia* (impressively described in Cic. *Dom.* 27); but
to begin with he apparently meant that Cicero, although only his legate, was supposed to be
everywhere (*ad omnia*) his equal in terms of authority in the future (*fore!*), not: '(that) Cicero
was [!] in every respect his other I', as F. Lossmann (*Cicero und Caesar im Jahre 54* (Wiesbaden,
1962) 46), who incidentally gives much valuable material on the history of the phrase, imprecisely
translates. According to him 'in political language the topos had long become a well-worn coin
and been degraded to a catchword' (p. 47).

2. 'The law on which the dedication was based was invalid because of its content or how it was passed.' This constitutional argument, which indirectly serves to prove the point, could in itself (at least before senatorial judges) be carried through more easily, but it was politically dubious, since of course the validity of the second *lex Clodia* had in the meantime been implicitly acknowledged by the Senate as well (see above p. 324).

3. 'The law was invalid for the reason that its originator was not authorized to introduce it.' This even more indirect argument from the illegality (according to religious law) of Clodius' adoption, which of course was what made his tribunate of the people, and with that his legislation, possible at all, was admittedly the most appropriate as far as the facts were concerned, but politically it was completely inopportune. Since it had been Caesar who, allying himself with the people's favourite, Pompey, had contrived Clodius' adoption, this act, like all the legally dubious *acta Caesaris*, could not in the present political situation be annulled (cf. above p. 338).[144]

As may be noticed immediately, Cicero uses all these three possibilities for proof in the *argumentatio* of his speech, and in fact in a sequence which goes from the indirect to the direct and in doing so also roughly corresponds to chronology (adoption–law–dedication); but he uses them in a very varied manner which has been precisely adapted to political expediency. As will be noticeable immediately, he brings forward the argument which is first in the speech (above, no. 3: adoption, sections 34–42) only in the form of a *praeteritio*, i.e. with the declared intention that he does not want to rely on it. He does indeed set out the second (above, no. 2: *lex Clodia*) without reservation and lengthily (43–103) but then again still in a strangely cautious and in the end indecisive way, namely by nowhere drawing the decisive conclusion and the one which is really required by the matter in hand: 'So, since the *lex Clodia* is invalid, then also the dedication must be void.' Why? Surely because of the political dubiousness which had to prevent the pontifices from founding a decree favourable to Cicero precisely on this tricky point, but probably also for the other reason that this conclusion, if it were drawn explicitly rather than vaguely before the mind, almost inevitably would include the admission that through his law Clodius was authorized to perform the dedication—something which Cicero in the end still in fact wants to deny. Thus this large part, too, which embraces nearly half the speech, with all its subtlety of argumentation by which Clodius as legislator is put in the wrong, at the end still serves to stir up the emotions rather more than anything else, as was already stated in general terms above (p. 339). Only the third and last part (above, no. 1: dedication, 104–42), factually weak as it may be, can, since it is

---

[144] The attacks on Caesar remain hidden because Cicero needs to show consideration for the presence of Pompey and for Caesarians among the pontifices; cf. Bergemann (cited n. 2) 48–9.

politically safe, give the pontifices a reasonably useful basis for their decree. Thus by and large one can observe in this speech the paradox that the arguments admittedly become weaker and weaker from a factual point of view, but at the same time also less and less harmful, and, with regard to the pontifical decision, more and more significant. Let us now again go into detail!

So now, after an appeal to the priests to make a strictly objective decision, an appeal which concludes the preceding digression (31), there follows the *propositio* which we have already dealt with, in which Cicero claims that he wants to speak only about *ius publicum* (32–3) by which, de facto, he tries to clear the way for his first grand invective against Clodius (whom the preceding speeches of thanks before the Senate and the people had strangely spared[145]). The superficially juridical discussion of Clodius' adoption offered rich material to recall to mind the old resentment against this enemy of the Senate, Clodius, who had only just at that very moment effected a rapprochement with the optimate majority. Cicero had obviously planned to begin with this illegal and sacrilegious adoption in the year of Caesar's consulship, which made Clodius' tribunate invalid; and even after Clodius, as we have seen, had predicted this line of argument and warned about it (above pp. 335–6), Cicero of course did not fail to take advantage of material which was so rewarding and so effective, especially before priests. He only slightly changes the order of presentation by at first announcing the point which, in practice, he intends to deal with only later (43 ff.): that the *lex Clodia* with its proscription of Cicero pronounced without a court verdict had on principle been unconstitutional (33 'nego potuisse iure publico . . . ' etc.); but only in order to claim triumphantly that he therefore does not at all wish to prove that Clodius was not a plebeian, and therefore not a tribune of the people either (34 init.: see above),[146] and then to furnish precisely this proof after all, only not *suo nomine* but, so to speak, in the form of a *praeteritio* or *occultatio*:[147] 34 'dico apud pontifices, augures adsunt: versor in medio iure publico'. This difficult sentence can hardly be meant in any other way than giving a reason for what

---

[145] This is particularly noticeable because of the contrast to the merciless polemics against the two consuls of the year 58: perhaps immediately after his return Cicero was still hoping that Clodius could abandon the acts of hostility concerning the house if he was not provoked. In our speech he uses from the beginning, in fact quite pointedly *at* the beginning, the sharpest vocabulary of invective (2 'illa labes ac flamma rei publicae', 3 'a te homine vesano ac furioso', 4 'funesta rei publicae pestis').

[146] Differently Shackleton Bailey ('On Cicero's Speeches', *HSCP* 83 (1979) 237–85, at 264–5), according to whom Cicero first (sect. 33) showed 'that the confiscation of his property was contrary to Roman law' (which strictly speaking is not correct, since this is not shown until later), then that it was 'invalid for a different reason' (namely because of the invalidity of the adoption): '*videsne* sqq. is not to say that Cicero *will* not take this second line of argument; it calls on Clodius to note that he has not yet reached it.' This is not comprehensible to me: who would announce a second point which is to be dealt with in such a strange way?

[147] Nisbet (cited n. 2) on sect. 34 line 24 recognized this correctly (but also cf. already Rück (cited n. 7) 62); he refers to the definition of *occultatio* in *Rhet. Her.* 4.27.37: 'cum dicimus nos praeterire aut non scire aut nolle dicere id quod nunc maxime dicimus'.–Dio Cassius 39.11.2-3 paraphrases incorrectly.

came before.[148] Apparently Cicero wants to say that before the pontifices and the *augures* he does not need to demonstrate the illegality of the adoption at all since thanks to their specialized knowledge this is self-evident to them anyway (cf. earlier, section 33: 'neque illud agere quod apertum est'), and that because of this–if the text is really correct here[149]–he is able to restrict himself to the *ius publicum*. With 'quod est, pontifices, ius adoptionis? nempe ut is . . .' etc., this point which is self-evident to the experts is then brought into consciousness: namely that there had not been a satisfactory reason for this 'simulata adoptio' (36) through a considerably younger man (as Cicero emphasizes with special indignation) (34–37a), and that if such adoptions became rampant this would threaten the continued existence of the patrician *gentes* as well as that of those priesthoods which could only be filled with patricians (37b–38). These are impressive arguments for the ears of pontifices who must have been all the more annoyed by the event at that time, in that the *pontifex maximus* Caesar–criticism of him should be read between the lines–had apparently not consulted them but had quite contemptuously disregarded religion and *mos maiorum*. It was extremely clever of Cicero to begin with precisely this point in order to undermine Clodius' reputation as champion of Roman religiosity.[150]

The next argument against the legality of the adoption, as Cicero gives to understand, is directed at the *augures*–Caesar had had the relevant *lex curiata*, like other laws (as is well known), passed with cheeky disregard for the law of auspices.[151] The last argument is then finally derived from the

---

[148] In Peterson (cited n. 2) this sentence concludes the preceding paragraph; Shackleton Bailey (cited n. 2, see n. 146) makes the following one begin with it: Maslowski (cited n. 2), who begins the new paragraph already with *Videsne* etc., divides more correctly than either. Nisbet's paraphrase (cited n. 2, on sections 32–4) seems to me completely inappropriate: 'I do so though I am addressing a religious court' etc. (but against this, Classen (cited n. 2) 234, n. 63).

[149] *versor in medio iure publico*, accepted by all editors, causes difficulty because it precedes a passage which expressly deals with *ius pontificium* with reference to the knowledge of the pontifices, if only in the form of a *praeteritio* (cf. 36 'dico apud pontifices: nego istam adoptionem pontificio iure esse factam'; similarly 38 'dixi apud pontifices istam adoptionem . . . contra omne ius pontificium factam'). Probably *iure publico* should be deleted; *versor in medio* then means: I am not dealing with any remote specialist knowledge but only with items of the *ius pontificium* which are more generally known; similarly 138 'quae sunt adhuc a me de iure dedicandi disputata, non sunt quaesita ex occulto aliquo genere litterarum, sed sumpta *de medio*'; similar in sense (but not expression) is sect. 39, cf. esp. *De Orat.* 1.12 'dicendi autem omnis ratio in medio posita' (in contrast to other disciplines with their sources which can only be accessed with difficulty). Numerous references for this and similar usages of *in medio* in Bulhart, *TLL* VIII 594, 30–72.

[150] Cicero saves up for later the Bona Dea scandal which was of course even more appropriate for this (see below pp. 360–1).

[151] As Cicero without doubt truthfully explains, Clodius himself had already at the end of the year of his tribunate demanded the annulment of the consular *acta Caesaris*, giving this reason (Benner (cited n. 16) 56–7, cf. 134–5, gives a good explanation: Clodius in a purely populist manner went along with the radically changed mood). When he said that under this condition he was prepared to carry Cicero home on his shoulders this was not supposed to mean that he no longer hated Cicero but merely that for the moment the new enmity was more important to him than the old one; besides, with this he probably implied that it was above all Caesar who had wanted Cicero's banishment.

genuine *ius publicum* and concerns the fact that the promulgation period
had not been observed for this law. All these objections to the adoption–
section 42 gives an *enumeratio: sacra, auspicia* and *leges*–are in themselves
convincing; yet Cicero again makes it clear that he does not propose to
rely on them at all (42 'at ego hoc totum non sine causa relinquo')–the
praeteritio is thus marked once more at its end–, because certain *principes
civitatis*,[152] for all their sympathy for Cicero, would still have accepted
Clodius as a legitimate tribune. The passage has after all been sufficiently
effective for the propaganda against Clodius (and secretly above all against
his former protector Caesar[153]).

The *Probatio* in the First Main Part of the *Argumentatio*: Invalidity of the *lex Clodia* (43–71)

And thus Cicero now comes to the main part of his speech which was
announced in section 33–and which does indeed concern the *ius publicum*–
in which he tries to explain the illegality of the *lex Clodia*, which was
directed against him, and on which of course the dedication in turn was
based (43–103,[154] cf. above p. 339). In order to understand the strange
course of Cicero's argument–something which can be done here only in
a general survey–we shall have to recall once more that Clodius, if we have
reconstructed his thought correctly, in order to justify his law which was
indeed outrageous, through which a Roman citizen was proscribed without a court trial, had appealed to Cicero's own behaviour in the matter (see
above, p. 335). The latter was the only person who had taken the first *lex
Clodia* to refer to himself, though it still mentioned nobody by name; in
fact the whole Senate could have felt threatened by it (A). Through his
departure he had declared himself guilty and proscribed (B), so that the
second law had, so to speak, merely confirmed the self-condemnation (C).
Through it alone Cicero was *exsul* (D). It would have been extremely inad-
visable for Cicero to get involved with this argument, which basically

[152] Suggested names are: Cato, Bibulus, Marcellus (see Nisbet (cited n. 2) ad loc.) and Curio
(Classen (cited n. 2) 238 n. 69). But in fact one should think above all of Pompey, who could not
accept a questioning of the *acta Caesaris*.

[153] The third point (promulgation period) served above all to make Clodius' adoption appear as
an expression of Caesar's annoyance–hardly veiled through the nebulous formulation at section 41
'ad quosdam viros fortis'–about Cicero. Cicero's concealed sneering remarks against the *pontifex
maximus*, since he utters them in Pompey's presence, allow us to assume that already at this time
he secretly hopes to be able to alienate Pompey from Caesar. Cf. below, n. 155.

[154] When looked at superficially, this is the topic only of sections 43–71; but, as will emerge
below, sections 72 ff. belong closely to this.

followed the chronology of events, since there was not much that could be raised in objection to the first law, and it was difficult not to interpret the *discessus* in connection with this law as an expression either of feelings of guilt, as Clodius wanted, or (which would to a large extent have been true) of the fear of death, but to pass it off as a vicarious sacrifice for the general public threatened by civil war,[155] as Cicero had tried to do from the time of his return (see above p. 336). Only with Cicero's departure, and above all in the context of the endeavours for his recall, did Clodius begin to use terrorist violence; the extremely popular laws from the beginning of his tribunate (to which also the first so called *lex de capite civis Romani* belonged)–as Wilfried Nippel has aptly emphasized[156]–he got through effortlessly without violence; nor is an incitement of the people directed against Cicero actually mentioned in the sources for this time.[157] It was difficult for Cicero to establish his account of the *discessus*, on whose interpretation indeed everything here depended, in opposition to Clodius, who had probably reminded his audience of the events very precisely.

As often in a difficult position, he worked by means of a restructuring which partly also confuses the chronology, but which in doing so superficially corresponds to the traditional division into *probatio* (43–71) and *refutatio* (72–99).[158] A coherent *narratio* of the events is missing, not without reason. Cicero, completely neglecting the first law (A),[159] immediately attacks the second as illegal (C): 43–55; 66–71. Only in this context does he give reasons for and justify his *discessus* (B) which can now be presented in a completely different light (56–65), and–with this the *refutatio* begins–from

---

[155] But this version which today is mocked by historians was not completely wrong after all, since Caesar up until Cicero's departure at any rate (or the passing of the first *lex Clodia* which happened at the same time) stayed outside the city and Clodius appealed to his support (cf. Meyer (cited n. 17) 100 and the references most recently collected by Mitchell (cited n. 17) 136 n. 113 which have hardly been appreciated for instance by Gelzer (cited n. 11) 137 with n. 24): there should at least have been fear that Caesar could summon his troops (Cic. *Sest.* 41 'erat ad portas, erat cum imperio; erat in Italia eius exercitus', cf. 52 and esp. *Har. Resp.* 47) and become a second Sulla. (That Cicero speaks so little and with such restraint about this decisive point [cf. sect. 131!] is easily explained by his consideration for Pompey; but cf. also n. 153.)

[156] Nippel (cited n. 19) 114 with n. 81, cf. esp. 120 ff.

[157] At any rate Cicero hints (54) that some friends of his, according to *Sest.* 27 young Roman *equites*, who publicly interceded for him, had been driven apart by Clodius (or his supporters) *manibus, ferro, lapidibus*, in sect. 110 he speaks about violence against an unnamed consular who was present (in view of *Mil.* 37 one could think of Hortensius). Only in Plutarch (*Cic.* 30.7) is this turned into a daring gang with which Clodius surrounds himself, which goes into action against Cicero, mocks him and by throwing dirt and stones prevents his attempts to gain a hearing with the people (similarly Appian who is particularly badly informed here, *B.C.* 2.15): Cicero's silence speaks against this later evidence.

[158] Also in the *probatio* Cicero refers to statements by Clodius (51, 57), but not in order to refute them; cf. on the other hand in the *refutatio* esp. 72, 85, 92, 93, 95.

[159] Already Sternkopf (cited n. 19) 276 finely observed that Cicero avoids 'drawing this popular law into the debate' and, where he cannot avoid it, uses 'an ambiguous, veiled manner of representation'.

this position deals with the reproach that he is *exsul* (D) (72–90). A second justification of the *discessus* (B) concludes the section (91–9). Thus we have the sequence: C–B–C–D–B. Even in a brief survey, the well-calculated effectiveness of his method can be recognized.

Cicero tries to demonstrate the illegality of the law (C) with five arguments (arranged according to the so called *Homerica dispositio*[160]): (1) since it was directed against a person it was an inadmissible *privilegium*, basically a *proscriptio* through which one appropriated someone else's property without a court trial[161] (43–47a: here Cicero plays with the fears of all who own property); (2) that it was formulated nonsensically (47b–50a),[162] and in fact (3) in such a way that it rendered itself void (50b);[163] (4) that it was an improper *lex per saturam* (50c–53a).[164] But then the last argument, viz.

---

[160] Cf. Quint. *Inst.* 5.12.14 (after Hom. *Il.* 4.297 ff.) and the parallels (e.g. Cic. *De Or.* 2.314) in L. Calboli Montefusco (ed.): *Consulti Fortunatiani Ars rhetorica* (Bologna, 1979) 426–7 (on Fortun. 3. 2): the orator places the most effective arguments at the beginning and at the end as the commander places the strongest units of the troops on the wings.

[161] Cicero's argument has been controversial until the present day; cf. J. Bleicken, *Lex publica: Gesetz und Recht in der römischen Republik* (Berlin, 1975) 198 ff., Bergemann (cited n. 2) 69–72 and the literature quoted in Classen (cited n. 2) 239 n. 72.

[162] Cicero's seemingly pedantic protest against VT INTERDICTVM SIT instead of the 'correct' VT INTERDICATVR (on the linguistic aspect cf. Nisbet (cited n. 2), Appendix IV, 204–5; Classen (cited n. 2) 241 is incomprehensible) is not unfounded. With VT INTERDICATVR the proscription would only have resulted through the second law; INTERDICTVM SIT conveyed that it had been pronounced already through the first law and therefore now had only to be confirmed. Consequently the latter recorded that Cicero had been proscribed through a genuine, viz. a general *lex*, not (as he now tries to present it) through an illegal *privilegium* which had been aimed specifically at him. So it also makes sense that Cicero at first protests against the *privilegium* of the second *lex* (which he treats as the effective source of the proscription) and only then against the wording of this *lex* (from which it is evident that this is not in fact so).

[163] The argument (which is to my mind wrongly judged by Classen (cited n. 2) 242) is purely sophistic or paralogistic. Even if it was indeed correct that Cicero had not falsified a Senate decree, which (*pace* Classen) was confirmed impressively by the behaviour of the Senate at Cicero's expulsion and especially his return, the law was of course not annulled by this means: QVOD [!] M. TVLLIVS FALSVM SENATVS CONSVLTVM RETTVLERIT (on the subjunctive of inner dependence correctly Nisbet (cited n. 2) ad loc., differently Moreau (cited n. 23) 473 n. 51) does not specify a condition for the validity of the law but gives a reason why it was passed; scarcely with justification Fuhrmann (cited n. 2) translates *quod* with 'in view of the fact', cf. Moreau 473.

[164] In sect. 51 Cicero does not at all protest against the fact that Clodius 'let the supervision of public works and the putting up of an inscription . . . turn into a plundering of Cicero's house' (thus strangely enough Classen (cited n. 2) 242–3 with note 83, which fundamentally refutes Classen's view). He means, rather, that these things should not be allowed to stand in a *lex de exilio* (but, with Shackleton Bailey ('More on Cicero's Speeches (Post Reditum)', *HSCP* 89 (1985) 141–51, at 143) *non aliud* or possibly ⟨*u*⟩*num* ⟨*an*⟩ *aliud* should be read instead of *num aliud*). Nor does he attack Clodius there because the latter (Classen loc. cit. 243) 'had derived the measures with which this trial deals, the dedication of the house, the building of a small temple . . . and the dedication of a statue, from the so hotly debated second law', but because these measures were likewise not identical either with that 'quod de me ipse nominatim tulisti' (52 fin.), i.e. the proscription. Here Classen (like MacKendrick (cited n. 1) 150 on sections 50b–51: 'The bill . . . did not entitle him to despoil Cicero's property') allowed himself to be confused by Nisbet's (cited note 2) supplement in sect. 51 line 15–until that point the latter is correct–and did not take note

that (5)[165] the law had been passed by means of violence (53b ff.) is decisive for the rhetorical plausibility of the whole passage (43–103).

Admittedly Cicero has to concede that the vote itself went peaceably (according to section 53b there were no stones thrown nor was there any other violence) but in a truly masterly suggestive description (which also had to convince his listeners, who were well informed since they were contemporary witnesses) he succeeds in again calling to mind the atmosphere of fear, terror, and latent violence which must have prevailed at the time after the promulgation of the first *lex Clodia*.[166] Cicero's own *discessus*, which here at first is justified almost in passing and from a different perspective (57–8)– for this is about the legality of the decisive *lex Clodia*–appears, not completely without justification, as proof of the intimidating power which Clodius was able to exert at that time through the recruiting of paramilitary *collegia*, through visible arms transports and above all through the threatening intervention against all demonstrations on Cicero's behalf (which was covered, indeed supported, by the bribed consuls) (54–5). Then, gradually and hardly perceptibly, after the argument presented in section 58 that he fled not from a trial but from the physical attacks on his life which were to be expected during it,[167] Cicero leaves on one side the alleged point to be proved (viz. that the second *lex Clodia* could only have been passed using violence): he describes the cruelty (*crudelitas*[168]) of his enemies who even after the *discessus* had let themselves go in attacking his family (59) and his house (60–1), not out of acquisitiveness but out of sheer hatred (61)–here

of the fact that the whole passage 50c–53 concerns the contravention of the *lex Caecilia et Didia* i.e. the prohibition on laws which, by combining unconnected items, illegally restrict the voters' freedom of decision (brilliantly elucidated by Cicero in sect. 53a). In that way one could, for instance, construct the hypothesis that someone agreed to Cicero's proscription but would disapprove of e.g. the building of the Libertas sanctuary. Also the example which is fictitiously thought up by Cicero himself (52 'quid? si eidem . . .' etc.) is meant merely to set forth 'the illegality of every collective law' (thus correctly Classen 243), not at all 'to prompt the politically interested contemporary to all sorts of speculation' (thus incorrectly Classen ibid.). With these objections Cicero wants neither to protest against the content of the law nor against the way it has been applied but just to illuminate the sloppiness of its drafting. But this is definitely a relevant point, and we really cannot talk about 'discussions which become ever more long-drawn-out' or the danger 'of becoming boring or annoying through all too detailed digressions' (Classen ibid.).

[165] Sect. 50c 'quot modis doceo legem istam, quam vocas, non esse legem?' connects the four preceding arguments with the new one; incorrectly Classen (cited n. 2) 242 n. 80.

[166] Classen (cited n. 2) 245 simplifies too strongly: 'Cicero, however, has to owe us the proof that this law also was carried with the use of violence; but he can hope that this will escape his listeners . . .'.

[167] Instead of the senseless *an, si ego praesens . . . ?*–a question introduced with *an* would have to give reasons for the preceding sentence (Fuhrmann and Shackleton Bailey (cited n. 2) translate differently, the latter suppressing *an* completely)–we should read *at, si* (with Lehmann); at the end of the sentence, perhaps *consulum ⟨num⟩ corpori meo pepercissent?*

[168] The carefully chosen word–for in the polemics against Cicero his behaviour with regard to the Catilinarians was described as *crudelitas*–appears five times in sections 58–62.

the original point to be proved is still vaguely in mind[169]–and the magnanimity of precisely this *discessus*, through which Cicero as representative victim or scapegoat had drawn onto himself the brunt of his enemies' attack and, instead of falling with the state, had through his departure saved it the otherwise inevitable bloodshed (62-5).

One has to realize that this passage (62-5), so to speak under the wrong heading,[170] contains the real response to Clodius' representation of the 'exile' (a representation which in Cicero's speech here never becomes clear, not even as an object of refutation).[171] For Clodius, Cicero's departure, which he described as a reaction to his first *lex*, was a confession of guilt by a manifest criminal. For Cicero, who suppresses this *lex* and instead of it describes an atmosphere of increasing violence, it represents a sacrificial act by the saviour of the state, comparable to the *devotio* of the Decii (64). And just as Clodius was able to derive from his version the moral right to carry out the disputed dedication, so Cicero, through his, asserts the right to his house of which he has been shamefully robbed. It was not without reason that he ornamented this decisive part of the speech in particular with the most beguiling features of his oratorical art, which had at its command all the colours of *evidentia* and all the tricks of emotional psychagogy. In the background of this scene, he paints the consuls feasting in the bright glow of the conflagration of his house, and indulging in reminiscences of Catiline (62); in the foreground he represents himself, as he leaves the city like a holy martyr or man of sorrows, drawing to himself the torches and arrows of the wicked (63). The scene belongs among the most grandiose he ever spoke and wrote.

When Cicero in what follows shows by way of a hint how the *furor* and *vis* of the wicked had lost some of their force through the crime of his expulsion (thus expressly 64 fin.[172]), this stands almost in direct contradiction to the original point to be proved, according to which of course it would have to be shown that the second *lex Clodia* (which was passed a considerable time after

---

[169] 58 fin.: the *crudelitas* of the enemies after Cicero's departure suggests that their previous readiness for violence was all the greater.

[170] Only the keyword *vis*, which from 53 to 68 is again and again carefully repeated, creates a vague impression of logical rigour and conceals the irrelevance especially of 62-4. Classen (cited n. 2) 247 already makes the generally correct point about these sections: 'Clodius' law seems to have been forgotten'.

[171] Looked at in terms of content it would belong in the *refutatio*, but precisely this fact is concealed: Cicero follows his principle, which can be detected elsewhere as well, of concealing the fact that he is dealing with a particular point before he comes to discuss it explicitly.

[172] Cato (sect. 65) is removed through a sham honour, not, like Cicero, through sheer intimidation; as far as Pompey is concerned (66-7), the *caedes* and *lapidationes* which still take place are the result of a *vis . . . distracta et exstincta* which earlier as *oriens et congregata* had been much more powerful. Classen (cited n. 2) 247 oversimplifies: 'that Clodius . . . everywhere strung one act of violence onto another' (as far as Cato is concerned, this is quite wrong).

the *discessus*) was pushed through by *vis*. Only with the description of the events which follow 1 January 57 (68 ff.)–the chronological description which was avoided at the beginning proves itself favourable after all from the *discessus* onwards–does Cicero steer the thought back to the starting point. During all the negotiations in the Senate–which of course took place contrary to the ban of the second *lex Clodia* (68; 70–1)–it had always been clear that the law was to be regarded as null and void; also the consultation of the pontifices concerning the dedication, which had been decided on for reasons of expediency and security, had not implied its legality (69)! This thought which has been expressed deliberately in vague terms[173] which like a spotlight once again gives us a reference to the fact that Clodius through his *lex* was indeed authorized to perform the dedication,[174] at the same time again also shows most clearly how small must be the factual relevance of all Cicero's explanations on the invalidity of the 'exile law' (43–7; taken more broadly, 43–103). Of course the Senate, as is already clear through its resolution specifically to pass a *lex de reditu*,[175] and also through the fact that it requested a decree by the pontifices about Cicero's house at all, had in a certain way recognized this law. At any rate, if the law was invalid, the Senate could itself more easily have pronounced the annulment of the dedication; if, however, it regarded the law as valid, then one was indeed left with the problem of religious law which came within the remit of the priests, i.e. the question whether the dedication could be pronounced invalid in spite of the *lex*. Nevertheless, as we have seen, this passage was of decisive importance for Cicero in order to justify the deeper, in fact the moral, claim to his house: his *discessus*, through which he had lost the house, was, as he had shown, not a confession of guilt, but a sacrifice for the sake of the general public. The public should restore to him what he had given up for its sake.

The *Refutatio* in the First Main Part of the *Argumentatio*: Justification of the *discessus* and Interior Epilogue (72–103)

We cannot completely appreciate Cicero's ensuing detailed reply (72–99) to the reproach raised by Clodius of being an *exsul*–in Rome of course

---

[173] 'non quo dubitaret quin ab isto nihil legibus, nihil religionibus, nihil iure esset actum'; Cicero does not dare to say after all what would actually be required by logic: 'quin illa lex nulla esset'.

[174] If this were not the case, it could not of course be seen why Cicero makes this assurance at all.

[175] Cicero, who does not allow this thought to come up explicitly, tries to counteract it through the subtle linguistic argument that it had not been decreed in the *lex de reditu* (71) 'ut mihi Romam venire liceret'–this according to Cicero would have meant an admission of legality–but 'ut venirem'. The subtle conclusion of an ultimately hardly tenable argument!

indeed a term of abuse[176] in spite of Cicero's subtle remark (72) 'ipsum per se nomen calamitatis, non turpitudinis'–for the reason that Clodius' argument here is for us only partly recognizable. We can take it as certain that he derived the reproach from the *discessus* (and not for instance from the 'exile law'); it remains unclear how far or on what more precise grounds (in spite of the *lex de reditu*) he treated Cicero as someone who was still *exsul*, i.e. had lost his Roman civil rights (*civitas*) and with that also the claim to his property (see above p. 335).[177] At any rate, if one disregards the context of Clodius' argument which of course never became visible in Cicero's representation of it, the reproach can to some extent be refuted. Cicero does this with dialectical subtlety: that *exsilium* is either *poena peccati*–which in his case (he says) is refuted through the honourable decisions of Senate, people etc. on his return (73–6)[178]–or, alternatively, *poena damnati* or *iudicii*:[179] but for this to be the case there would have to have been a legal proceeding against Cicero (77), followed (in case of condemnation) by the voluntary surrender of civil rights, linked with the assumption of a different citizenship, which was performed *vertendi soli causa* (78). On principle, he says, a loss of civil rights could not be effected against the will of the person concerned,[180] not even through plebiscite (78–81), to say nothing of Clodius' law which had not even decreed Cicero's exile (82). Cicero backs up his astute explanations through examples of historical personalities, who in a situation comparable to his had either never been described as *exsules* at all, or after an honourable return had no longer been called by this term of abuse (83–7).[181] In his own case, given that Clodius had mobilized hired mercenaries and violent criminals against

---

[176] Cf. above, n. 106.

[177] So it is probably not just the case that Cicero 'feels that he has been affected particularly badly and effectively lowered in the eyes of the public' through Clodius' reproach, as assumed by Classen (cited n. 2) 251, who is surprised by the detail of Cicero's explanations on this point (p. 252: 'long-winded and unproductive').

[178] In sect. 76 fin. the *discessus* is once more extolled briefly with the thought set out in 62 ff., and at the same time the motif of the *patria bis servata* (cf. p. 359 on sect. 99), which will later be brought out triumphantly, is already casually introduced.

[179] 'at fuit iudicii' (77) is Cicero's fictitious objection which results from the *partitio* in sect. 72; this is hardly, as Classen (cited n. 2) 251 assumes, an 'enemy's objection': Cicero does not suggest in any way that Clodius had interpreted his second *lex* as a court judgement about Cicero (although such an argument might perhaps be conceivable).

[180] This is, however, doubted by today's scholars of Roman law (cf. the literature quoted in Classen [cited n. 2] 250 n. 103) and seems to contradict above all the case reported in Cic. *De Or.* 1.181.

[181] What in this context is said virtually in passing (87), 'afui simul cum re publica', gives an interesting reference to how Cicero–typically enough only *post reditum* (first in *Red. Sen.* 17, 'ego una cum re publica')–gets hold of the idea of identifying himself with the state (cf. Habicht [cited n. 17] 65, cf. 119), for then he could not, as Clodius alleged, have been *exsul* at all, since he had of course taken the state along with him. (But the genesis and the history of this idea, which is of course more complex, would have to be dealt with in more detail.)

him, there could be no question of an expulsion by the People themselves: they had always been on his side (88–90).

However, this now leads up to a renewed justification of the *discessus*, but one which at first seems to turn out to be strangely feeble (91–92a), for Cicero, continuing by association what came before, says that at the time he himself had been able to lean on the people's support against Clodius, and that only the opposition of the two consuls as well had prevented him from resisting. Incidentally: 'erant eo tempore multa etiam alia metuenda . . .'. Why does he speak so timidly about an event which he has previously already compared to the sacrificial death of the Decii? I answer: (a) because the true glorification of the *discessus* is still to come; (b) Cicero wants to wait for his opponent to supply the cue for it.

Clodius had teased Cicero with sarcastic remarks about his 'intolerable self-satisfaction' concerning the 'exile' (see above, p. 354). Cicero, who now, not unnaturally, at this point comes to speak about this (92 ff.)–was not the extremely modest tone of his preceding remarks enough to provide a refutation of the accusation of *gloriari* made by Clodius?–Cicero claims that it is only under compulsion and in self-defence (93 'coactus ac necessario') that he praises himself[182] concerning the year of his consulship (where he had been reproached with *crudelitas*: 94) as well as with regard to the *discessus* with which he had just been reproached. To neither of these could he reply 'sine mea maxima laude' (95). When Cicero now once again passes in review the possible explanations of his *discessus* which he rejects and pronounces absurd, for the first and only time for a moment the version appears on which Clodius must himself have relied and which also was behind his accusation of being *exsul*: 'quid enim, pontifices, debeo dicere? peccatine conscientia me profugisse?' To which Cicero replies no more than this: 'at id quod mihi crimini dabatur non modo peccatum non erat, sed erat res post natos homines pulcherrima.' And then after an even shorter refutation of the alternatives already dealt with (fear of trial? lack of support? fear of death?) he now for the second time, but this time at the logically correct place–for from this point on it is indeed the *discessus*, not the legal validity of the second *lex Clodia*, which is under discussion (cf. above p. 354 on sections 62–4)–gives the grounds for his departure, which at the same time represents a classic example of the self-glorification which has just been reprehended by Clodius (observing the good oratorical rule by countering irony with complete seriousness, indeed here

---

[182] Classen (cited n. 2) 253–4 does not realize that this thought runs through right up to the end of sect. 99 ('he believes that he can easily push aside the reproach of self-praise') so that the inner connection of the passage, which he treats as a more or less arbitrary series of retorts, escapes him.

with particular emphasis[183]). When in him and through him, he says, all the forces which were sustaining the state were fatally threatened, he left Rome because a possible defeat of the *boni* in the otherwise inevitable civil war would have meant the end of the state (96).

This passage is an intentional duplicate of the preceding justification of the *discessus* as a vicarious sacrifice (62–4), a doublet also in so far as it powerfully aims at an emotional effect on the listeners. But whereas there the admiration for Cicero's heroic greatness which drew the forces of evil on itself, and even drew them into exile with him, stood in the foreground, now it is the intensity of his suffering, the violence of his grief for what he has lost in and with his home, which asks for sympathy and pity (97): 'accepi, pontifices, magnum atque incredibilem dolorem, non nego;[184] neque istam mihi adscisco sapientiam quam non nulli in me requirebant, qui me animo nimis fracto esse atque adflicto loquebantur.' If not exactly weeping, at least still close to tears, Cicero, who here indeed almost anticipates Ovid's famous farewell to Rome,[185] continues to speak in these terms: 'an ego poteram, cum a tot rerum tanta varietate divellerer, quas idcirco praetereo quod ne nunc quidem sine fletu commemorare possum, infitiari me esse hominem et communem naturae sensum repudiare?' A few lines later Cicero's favourite word, *humanitas*,[186] which is here already in the mind, is uttered. In this context, for once, completely without any humanist overtones, it describes nothing other than human existence in all its weakness. Since one can hardly arouse admiration of bravery and pity for grief of mind to the same degree at the same time, the doublet was almost necessary.[187] There, virtue demanded its prize; here, above all, *humanitas* demands its damages. And it is now also clear why Cicero moves particularly the second, 'more human' version into this second place: because here it was necessary to show also, against Clodius, that Cicero himself was not unrestrained in his self-glorification, that he

---

[183] Sect. 96 'quam possum maxima voce dico' presumably means that Cicero wants to be heard not only by the pontifices but by the entire crowd of spectators (see above, pp. 322–3). Such descriptions of delivery could possibly have been inserted only afterwards for the benefit of young people who are studying and also want to learn something about Cicero's *actio*.

[184] Also for rhythmic reasons–'atque incredibilem dolorem' would be a hipponacteus at the end of the sentence–this punctuation seems to me more natural than that of the editors.

[185] *Trist.* 1.3.1–4: 'Cum subit illius tristissima noctis imago, | quod mihi supremum tempus in urbe fuit, | cum repeto noctem, qua tot mihi cara reliqui | ' (cf. 'cum a tot rerum . . .') 'labitur ex oculis nunc quoque gutta meis.' Cf. E. Doblhofer, *Exil und Emigration: Zum Erlebnis der Heimatferne in der römischen Literatur* (Darmstadt, 1987) 74–5 (referrings to further parallels between Cic. *Dom.* 97–8 and *Trist.* 1.3).

[186] This is appreciated in a nice summary by O. Hiltbrunner, 'Humanitas', *Reallexikon für Antike und Christentum* 16 (1994), 711–52, at 726–30.

[187] So Classen (cited n. 2) 254 wrongly speaks of an 'explanation in which nothing appears to be new': Cicero (he says) would have to give it at this place 'since he now wants to attend to the problems of his house'.

was prepared even to admit weaknesses. In moving phrases, Cicero, who here more or less counts his human sensitivity as a virtue–for only grief for what has been lost turns renunciation into merit (97, 98)–describes the pain of his *discessus* in phrases which could almost form the conclusion of a tragedy, ending with the sudden fall and departure of the hero (98): ' . . . ea quae capta urbe accidunt victis stante urbe unum perpeti et iam se videre distrahi a complexu suorum, disturbari tecta,[188] diripi fortunas, patriae denique causa patriam ipsam amittere,[189] spoliari populi Romani beneficiis amplissimis, praecipitari ex amplissimo dignitatis gradu, videre praetextatos inimicos nondum morte complorata arbitria petentis funeris: haec omnia subire conservandorum civium causa atque id dolenter, cum sis[190] non tam sapiens quam ii qui nihil curant,[191] sed tam amans tuorum quam communis humanitas postulat, ea laus praeclara atque divina est'. The certainly vain-glorious last words at the same time also form a transition to the formula with which Cicero summarizes his statesmanlike achievement, with sharp, Demosthenic polemics[192] against the mocking Clodius–who of course (as he says) has forced him into this vaingloriousness in the first place–(99): 'qua re dirumpatur licet ista furia atque ⟨pestis patriae⟩, audiet haec ex me, quoniam lacessivit: bis servavi ⟨rem publicam⟩, qui consul togatus armatos vicerim, privatus consulibus armatis cesserim.'

With this second glorification of his *discessus*, which supplements and outdoes the first, Cicero's speech seems to have come to its end, and one can say that henceforth, in summarizing and appealing to the judges, he is virtually simulating a grandiose *peroratio* (100–3). In their hands, he says, now lies the decision about whether his achievement will indeed find its due recognition, whether his *reditus* which was decided by the people and the Senate is a real and final one. If he had to tolerate on his own estate the colonnade with the name of Clodius and his sanctuary of Libertas, an eternal *monumentum* of his grief (100, 103)–which of course he has just described–then his return would be a mere *poena sempiterna*, then it would be better to emigrate and to become an exile in reality and not just be mockingly so called by Clodius (100): 'demigrandum potius aliquo est quam habitandum in ea urbe in qua tropaea de me et de re publica videam

---

[188] The destruction of the house above (62) was not the trigger of the grief but an indication of the extent of the *vis* which Cicero drew onto himself.

[189] One of the rare phrases where Cicero already anticipates the pointed, paradoxical style of the Augustan age or the early Empire.

[190] According to my own, highly uncertain conjecture: the transmitted text is *atque ita cum dolenter adsis*.

[191] Probably a side-swipe at the Stoics' *apatheia*, with Peripatetic metriopathy in mind; cf. below p. 370.

[192] Cf. Dem. *De Cor.* 21 (A. Weische, *Ciceros Nachahmung der attischen Redner* (Heidelberg, 1972) 81). Generally, imitation of Demosthenes, particularly in this speech, (cf. above p. 323) still plays a strikingly small part.

constituta.'[193] But Cicero believes that he knows that, like himself, so also the pontifices desire to tear down the ill-omened colonnade with their own hands (103): 'You can do it, not with your hands, but certainly with your courageous decision!'–we expect this sentence as a final aphorism, for Cicero has given the impression as if now everything important had already been said. But the ending does not come, as we have already seen (see above p. 339); the coda was, as musicians say, a false one: Cicero must lead up to that which in factual terms is the decisive point, but for him of course the most awkward, embarrassing one: the validity of the dedication performed by Clodius according to legal authorization.

The Second main Part of the *Argumentatio*: The Invalidity of the Dedication (104–141)

Only when one has recognized the feebleness of Cicero's legal claim (for what more did he have to go on, apart from the very highly contestable precedent of the dedication which had been refused to Cassius in the year 154 (see above pp. 328, 341–2) can one appreciate the brilliance of his oratorical art, which triumphs precisely at its weakest point. Just as previously he had postponed the question of the dedication itself in the general plan of the speech (in order first to arouse the listeners' sympathy for his own policy, and antipathy towards his opponent's), so now his guiding principle is not immediately to deploy the decree on Cassius either, as the modest trump card in his hand, but first of all to stir up displeasure about Clodius' performance of the dedication. It is quite amazing that Cicero, in spite of all the emotionalism of the speech, managed with cunning economy of means to save up precisely this event, which is, indeed, not only factually the most important but also the one which affected him most deeply in person, until section 103,[194] where it suddenly appears in the last clause like a last trick with which Clodius wants to save his machinations from the workings of justice: the 'castissimi sacerdotis superstitiosa dedicatio'. In order to appreciate this phrase, which is dripping with sarcasm, one should remember Clodius' unctuous profession of Roman religion which preceded the speech.

Cicero immediately sets against this, and against the dedication, what is in this context the most serious reproach of all which he has in reserve

---

[193] The variation of a motif from the *prooemium* (see above, pp. 342–3) is here taken up again in an apparent ring composition.

[194] The casual mention in sect. 51 does not count here. This one example should already give us cause to reconsider the common judgement, according to which Cicero in *De Domo Sua* allows himself to be dominated by his feelings (cf. above, p. 315).

against Clodius: his sacrilege[195] in the house of the *pontifex maximus* at the time of the Bona Dea scandal of December 62 BC, where only a bribed court had been able to save him from condemnation. In order not to shoot his bolt prematurely, he had very wisely also almost completely left this out of the speech until now;[196] but now he introduces it with sarcastic mockery (104): 'Publiusne Clodius, qui ex pontificis maximi domo religionem eripuit, is in meam—intulit!'[197] huncine vos, qui estis antistites caerimoniarum et sacrorum, auctorem habetis et magistrum publicae religionis?' And as a sign of extreme, even holy indignation he uses—this also for the first time at this point in the speech—an apostrophe[198] in the form of a prayer (which very appropriately opens this last section, where the subject matter is *de iure religionis* and the tone rises commensurately): 'o di immortales—vos enim[199] haec audire cupio—P. Clodius vestra sacra curat, vestrum nomen horret, res omnis humanas religione vestra contineri putat!'[200] This again must be a sarcastic echo of Clodian phrases: Clodius *cannot* be champion of religion; his concern for the sanctity of the dedication is only the feigned *anilis superstitio* of a deeply impious person (104–5).[201] So what can the appeal" to the *lex Clodia*, made briefly and flatly (' "tuleram," inquit, "ut mihi liceret," ' 106)

---

[195] The *nefas* had been detected at the time by the reporting pontifices (*Att.* 1.13.3). On the whole affair cf. for instance Drumann–Groebe (cited n. 17) ii. 176–85; most recently H. H. J. Brouwer, *Bona Dea*, (Leiden etc. 1989) 144 ff. (with commentary on the evidence in Cicero), 363 ff.; Mitchell (cited n. 17) 83–6 (with literature).

[196] Compare at any rate the scanty allusions in sections 77 and 80 (on the trial); not relevant is sect. 35, cited by Brouwer (cited n. 195) 158 (who does not seem to know Nisbet's commentary). The later side-swipe at the beginning of sect. 110 is brilliant.

[197] The rhythm of the clausula suggests that before *intulit*, which constitutes the main point, Cicero makes a small pause and thus at any rate avoids the synaloepha *me(am) intulit* (which would result in a hypodochmius).

[198] The next apostrophes are directed at Q. Catulus junior (113: once a highly favoured candidate in the election for Pontifex Maximus) and his father (114: builder of the now altered *porticus*), both already deceased, so that the tone is appropriately elevated. The last apostrophes are contained in the prayer to the Capitoline Triad, the Penates and Vesta (associated with the *pontifex maximus*) (144).

[199] *enim* probably indicates the loudness of delivery. The parenthesis incidentally gives us an explanation of why the normally postponed vocative is regularly put first in prayers and hymns: the purpose is first of all to open the channel of communication to the gods (who are absent and do not listen right from the outset).

[200] The tricolon brilliantly describes the quintessence of what religiousness amounts to in Rome: (1) correct cult, (2) fear of the gods (or *deisidaimonia*, Polybius 6.56.7), (3) belief in divine omnipotence. Cf. *Har. Resp.* 19 'pietate' (1), 'religione' (2) 'atque hac una sapientia quod deorum numine omnia regi gubernarique perspeximus' (3).

[201] In the centuries-old quarrel reported in the commentary by Nisbet (cited n. 2) on sect. 105 ('monete eum modum quendam esse religionis: nimium esse superstitiosum non oportere') about whether Cicero could consider a certain degree of 'superstition' as permissible, it does not seem to be properly taken into consideration—cf. at any rate Wolf (cited n. 6) 251—that the passage is meant sarcastically. According to Cicero Clodius is of course neither *religiosus* nor even *superstitiosus* but he behaves as if he were, and so the priests—pure sarcasm on Cicero's part and/or theirs—are supposed to remind him that 'excessive superstition' is not even in accordance with their wishes; i.e., leaving irony aside, that they have seen through him as a hypocrite.

mean in the mouth of such a man? This alleged authorization, Cicero thinks–not as a serious argument but as a means of heightening indignation–had already been annulled through the exception clause: 'si quid ius non esset rogari, ne esset rogatum' (106);[202] it could not possibly have been in accordance with the will of the gods, who did not want to move into Cicero's house at all (107–9)–even less so since the *Libertas* which had been erected,[203] about whose origin Cicero claims to have made thorough investigations, was the statue from the grave of a Greek prostitute (110–14). At this point, indignation that religion is here unscrupulously degraded into a tool of personal revenge is not enough: in pre-Christian times revenge is after all legitimate.[204] So Cicero next provides a second, more ugly motive: ultimately what is behind the dedication is only excessive ambition for luxurious building and lifestyle[205] on the part of Clodius, who wanted to impress the Roman public from the most beautiful spot on the Palatine (Cicero here uses against his enemy the envy which was otherwise directed against himself, sections 115–16). No wonder that only the youngest and least experienced member of the college of priests allowed himself to be involved in such an obvious abuse of religion[206] (117–21)–an abuse which, just as in the case of the *consecratio* of Gabinius' property, was not taken seriously either by Clodius himself or by others (122–6).

All these arguments, presented by Cicero with a beautiful mixture of sarcasm and passion, show more or less plausibly that Clodius' conduct is determined by quite unreligious, selfish motives. They must make the pontifices increasingly eager to strip his house of its *religio*. But they still do not give a legal justification for this, especially when one considers the character of Roman religion, which was strictly formalistic and concerned about flawless ritual. The notorious invalidity of earlier confiscations of property–certainly the most serious argument–after all still means little, since these, as religious improvisations so to speak, had been performed without the priestly assistance which ensured the correct procedure. As mentioned, only the decree regarding Cassius from the pontifical archives can, if the word *nominatim* is stressed appropriately, provide the desired precedent (above, p. 328). Cicero introduces it with a long, delaying digression by at

---

[202] According to Cic. *Caec.* 95 this clause, which one should hardly refer just to the prevention of unwitting 'impiety' (Strachan-Davidson in Nisbet (cited n. 2) on *Dom.* 106 line 25) was written in all Roman laws.

[203] According to the needs of the argument in each case, it is–according to Clodius' wish, of course–the (undefined) gods who are supposed to move into Cicero's house (107), or *Libertas* who, once she has moved in, drives out Penates and even Lares (108).

[204] The fine passage *Red. Quir.* 22–3 on his renunciation of revenge is striking.

[205] Cf. above p. 321 with n. 46.

[206] This notion of abuse of religion, introduced in the *prooemium*, then suspended together with the whole topic of religion in the first part, now becomes the dominating topic of the last section.

first putting in the mouth of Clodius, who in the meantime has apparently been unmasked as a reckless Tartuffe, the sentence which is indeed important and central for the legal case: ' "dedicatio magnam", inquit, "habet religionem" ' (127: in the tone of voice of a pompous lecturer). After a brief mockery of this new 'teacher of religion' and 'Numa'—through which what was said before is recapitulated, and, while this is done, there is a retrospective glance also at the adoption, which was against religious principles—Cicero asserts that he will prove the invalidity of the sentence quoted for this case according to all the rules of the art: here certainly of his own dialectic,[207] not of pontifical discipline: 'quid? in dedicatione nonne et quis dedicet et quid et quo modo quaeritur?' So, to look at this critically in slow motion, without allowing ourselves to be bluffed by Cicero's sleight of hand, the points to be proved would be: (1) whether Clodius was qualified for the dedication, (2) whether the site could legally be dedicated, (3) whether the dedication was performed correctly (cf. the interior recapitulation in section 138). Let us here, even more carefully than elsewhere, keep an eye on the master of oratorical trickery!

Cicero seems to begin with the question of the person (no. 1): 127 '*quis eras tu* qui dedicabas?' At the same time, he hints obscurely at the idea that Clodius had not been authorized by name. We have partly looked at this passage already (above, p. 328): 'quo iure? qua lege? quo exemplo? qua potestate?' So far, the impression is at first given only vaguely that we are dealing with an unprecedented, outrageous procedure contrary to tradition. But the last of the four cola then leads up to that point of Cicero's which is ultimately decisive: 'ubi *te* isti rei populus Romanus praefecerat?' Now Cicero would really have to prove that the man dedicating would only be authorized to perform the dedication through personal authorization in a plebiscite. He does not dare to derive such a claim from just the one, remote decree on Cassius. More impressive is the *lex Papiria* which is now solemnly summoned against Clodius as an 'old tribunician law' and which in general—modern scholarship has followed Cicero here—seems to be the basis of the line of argumentation in the ensuing section. The fact that the decisive *nominatim* is of course now missing from it (above, p. 327) is not allowed properly to come into the listener's consciousness; and so the point about the personal nomination, which with the emphasized *te* has only been touched on briefly, is dropped again for the time being, and instead suddenly the *quid* of the object to be dedicated (above, no. 2) is made the focus of the argument. The *lex Papiria* (Cicero argues) had not been intended for the dedication of private houses at all, but for state property, above all for spoils

---

[207] According to *Orator* 16 (cf. ibid. 116 and W. Kroll (comm., 1913) ad loc.) the orator must be an expert in the dialectic art of *tribuere in partes*.

of war (128). But this argument too, which is possible, though weak–and which could easily be deployed against Cicero himself[208]–is only hinted at, not set out: Cicero acts as if he were generously conceding Clodius the right to appeal to the *lex Papiria* at all (which in all probability he never actually did[209]) and asks again, even though again only by way of a hint, about the personal authorization (quoted above, p. 328): '... quae lex lata sit, ut tu aedis meas consecrares,' etc. The wording of the *lex Papiria* of course provides no ground for following up this particular thought; and so, after a renewed affirmation that he is moving within the sphere of *ius publicum*,[210] and after a renewed *concessio*, he bends the argument for the time being in a different direction (129): that Clodius in his *lex* had not even used the legitimate word *consecrare* (we know the passage, above, pp. 329–30) which makes possible a sharp side-swipe at the circumstances of the legislation. So up to now, through the jumping to and fro of Cicero's argument, the only impression that could arise is the still somewhat indefinite one that there was a conflict between the *lex Papiria* and Clodius' dedication; but the decisive proof of the latter's invalidity does not yet seem to have been offered.

Cicero's most subtle trick follows, and with it he has of course fooled scholars up to the present day. Instead of correctly admitting that the *lex Papiria* according to its wording does not require an authorization by name, but that the latter had been required for this by the pontifices who once passed a decree in the roughly similar case of Cassius–which would be the precedent to be acted upon here–instead of this certainly not very impressive argument, from a precedent in which there was not even an annulment of the dedication (see above p. 328)–Cicero uses every device to understand the *lex Papiria* itself in the light of the decree, to interpret authorization as authorization by name. Immediately the introductory

---

[208] Correctly Classen (cited n. 2) 262, n. 139, and after this Bergemann (cited n. 2) 50: One could argue the other way round 'that this law was not applicable in his case and therefore the dedication could be valid even without the consent of the people'.

[209] The following points speak against this: (1) the way in which Cicero introduces the law (127 'video enim esse ...'); (2) the expression (128) 'quae si [!] tu interpretaris de nostris aedibus atque agris scripta esse ...' (if Clodius had said this, Cicero would say *quod* rather than *si*), (3) that Clodius, for his part, had no reason at all to refer to a law which he had of course complied with, (4) that precisely for this reason he could not foresee Cicero's argumentation with the *lex Papiria* either. Possibly he and perhaps also the priests were not familiar with the *lex* at all, so that Cicero (who never quotes it verbatim!) could all the more easily twist its meaning in the desired direction. In any case, Cicero now profits from the fact that Clodius no longer has an opportunity to correct him.

[210] 'neque ego nunc de religione sed de bonis omnium nostrum, nec de pontificio sed de iure publico disputo'. The first part of the sentence, where the antithesis does not appear very logical, is probably meant to hint that the strict standards of religion cannot be valid where the latter is being mobilized against private property in a way such as to constitute a public danger; on the second part see above pp. 341–2. Perhaps Cicero also wants to intimate here that, though *consecrare* and *dedicare* admittedly do not make a difference according to *ius pontificium*, a *lex* according to *ius publicum* demands the *verba legitima*.

sentence does not leave any doubt that in the following narrative the meaning of the *lex Papiria* would come to light (130): 'at videte quanta sit vis huius Papiriae legis in re tali ⟨etiam honesta⟩,[211] non qualem tu adfers sceleris plenam et furoris!' Then of course Cicero is careful not to deploy immediately the decree which will later be decisive for the pontifices; instead he postpones it and initially uses the story of the censor C. Cassius who in the year 154 wanted to dedicate a statue of Concordia, to make a detailed *comparatio* of the dedication which was planned at that time with the one which has been performed now, in order to castigate the outrageousness of the present temple dedication, through which of course the saviour of the state was supposed to be annihilated and to which only one single, inexperienced pontifex had been enlisted (130–34a)–does one not have to assume that the young priest, forced into this sin, under this psychological strain, committed the gravest formal errors against the dedication? (134b–35)[212] Only now, after five long paragraphs, which will have increased the displeasure against Clodius as much as they caused the audience to forget the wording of the *lex Papiria* with its bare phrase *iniussu plebis*, does this item from the pontifical archives follow which is so valuable to Cicero, during which in accordance with the tactics already adopted in sections 32–3, he does not neglect to present precisely this pronouncement of the high priest M. Aemilius as one which had its roots entirely in the *ius publicum*, in which alone, of course, Cicero claims to be competent (136, see above pp. 341–2): 'sed ut revertar ad ius publicum dedicandi . . .' etc. There is no doubt, Cicero suggests, that this was the intention of the *lex Papiria*. And the example of the Vestal Virgin Licinia, which has quickly been added (see above p. 328), is supposed to demonstrate that this *lex* was also already once used for the annulment of dedications; this is underlined by a *senatus consultum* which is read out verbatim.[213] A passionate short recapitulation of the *comparatio* between former religiousness and contemporary abuse of religion (137) concludes this section, which is at the same time factually the most important, in terms of argument the weakest, and linguistically perhaps the most polished one of the speech.

This juridical sleight of hand is followed by theological mesmerism which Cicero achieves here (138–41) with a virtuosity found elsewhere only in *Pro Milone* (85–6). After the proof that neither *quis* nor *quid*–the

---

[211] With the brilliant *exempli gratia* completion by Shackleton Bailey (cited n. 164) 145.

[212] Cicero is particularly crafty, in that he formulates this extremely sharp criticism of Pinarius Natta (whom he does not name either in order to protect him further) as homage to the latter's political sense of shame: his noble nature had prevented him from doing his duty correctly according to the rules when such a hero was suffering (134).

[213] Cf. the correct constitution of the text in Maslowski (cited n. 2), essentially after Lambinus.

second was always mentioned only by the way–satisfy the conditions of the dedication now (according to the *partitio* of section 127), only the *quo modo* would have to be dealt with: '... quid me attinet iam illud tertium quod proposueram docere, non iis institutis ac verbis quibus caerimoniae postulant dedicasse?' Cicero counts these things among the arcana of pontifical law, in which, as a layman (according to 32–3), he claims not to be competent; but he claims that of course he too heard this, that, as the young priest had reeled off his form of words in a state of panic (139 'quod ... mente ac lingua titubante fecisse dicatur', cf. 134–5), so Clodius in the consciousness of his crimes is supposed all the more to have got into a muddle and to have committed grave errors of ritual and procedure (140 'quem ad modum iste praeposteris verbis . . . omnia aliter ac vos in monumentis habetis et pronuntiarit et fecerit'). This is even supposed–here an augur's smile might have flashed across the face even of the pontifices–to have been on every-one's lips (140); and yet without doubt it originated in Cicero's creative imagination. In a magnificent final painting which unites and outdoes all the religious tones or colours from section 104 onwards, he describes (141) how during the dedication Clodius can no longer utter any *verbum sollemne* (cf. 140) because the gods themselves, who refuse to move into Cicero's house (cf. 107), are confusing his mind, and because the *Res publica* per-sonified, although driven abroad with Cicero (cf. 137), like a Fury, haunts the mind of its undoer even from afar–a last stylistic highlight of the speech. The mockery Cicero experienced about the appearances of gods in his epic did not take away his enjoyment of poetic invention[214] which here wonderfully suits the religious theme, and removes the last scruples as regards the annulment of the dedication.

Thus the actual *peroratio* (142–7), which with an appeal to the will of the gods (143) and a great final prayer to them (144–5) takes up the solemn tone of the preceding passage, can bring the thought of the interior *peroratio* which had earlier petered out in a false ending (100–3, see p. 360) to a successful conclusion. Since without the restitution of his house Cicero's actual return home to Rome was impossible (143, 146, cf. 100), let him be permitted to beg the pontifices, mindful of their political responsibility (142, cf. sect. 1) to remove the *vulnus patriae* which grieved him more than oth-ers (146, cf. 103[215]) '... that as for me, whom you have brought back with your influence, your intervention and your votes, now that the Senate

---

[214] Here one thinks already of the appearance of *Roma* in Lucan 1.185 ff. (cf. the interesting parallels in the edition by G. Viansino (Milan, 1995) i. 9 n. 20); but most likely he has a scene from a tragedy in mind.

[215] 'calamitatis rei publicae ... indicium'. Cicero's identification of self with the state (see above, n. 181) also serves the purpose that his listeners are supposed to feel his pain as their own.

wants it thus [!]²¹⁶ you should also restore me to my dwelling place with your own hands.'²¹⁷

These final passages are typical of almost the whole speech: effusive in tone, extravagant in verbal richness, powerful in passion. Not everybody even in Rome liked this style. It was probably soon after *De Domo Sua* that criticism of Cicero's grandiose oratorical style began.²¹⁸ But at any rate nothing at all in this speech is superfluous or inappropriate. For all its variety of tones—among which above all the religious pathos stands out as relatively new in Cicero²¹⁹—it is sustained by a generally aggressive vigour; and it follows a well-calculated plan in which every part, even every seemingly spontaneous emotional outburst, fulfils its function, although the latter is not always recognizable at first sight, and often is not even supposed to be recognizable at all. Of course if the issue had been as simple as scholarship has hitherto assumed, i.e. if Clodius had indeed not had authorization to perform the disputed dedication through a plebiscite, then Cicero could have delivered a speech which would have been considerably more simple, more transparent and—in the sense of the rhetorical pattern prescribed for legal or court cases—more in accordance with the rules.²²⁰ Nothing would have prevented him, after the *prooemium* (let us say about the dangers of the abuse of religion) and the *digressio* about Pompey (which was certainly necessary) from describing in a *narratio* how the villain Clodius with his gangs had driven him out, but while doing this, in the overenthusiasm of his spitefulness, had neglected to have himself authorized through the law to perform the intended dedication. The *propositio* would have defined the point to be proved or the actual point

---

²¹⁶ So Cicero dares at the end to interpret the request for a decree: if gods and Senate want the same thing, what is left for the priests to do?

²¹⁷ Here as elsewhere Cicero suggests that there is only one alternative, either to tear down Clodius' building in favour of Cicero or to leave it there. This is dramatically pushed too far: in *Att.* 4.1.7 (mid-September) he assumes that even if the decision of the pontifices does not go in his favour the building will be removed and replaced with a new building (with a temple presumably of Libertas, of course) (cf. Shackleton Bailey's commentary ad loc., p. 169). The *religio* of the dedication apparently attaches to the site, not to the building.

²¹⁸ Viz. with the Roman *Attici*; on their beginnings in the 50s see most recently especially J. Wisse, 'Greeks, Romans, and the Rise of Atticism', in *Greek Literary Theory after Aristotle* (Amsterdam, 1995) 65–82 (with lit.), M. Hose, 'Die zweite Begegnung Roms mit den Griechen oder: Zu politischen Ursachen des Attizismus', in G. Vogt-Spira and B. Rommel (eds.), *Rezeption und Identität* (Stuttgart, 1999) 274–88, at 278–80, and W. Stroh, 'Declamatio', in Schröder (ed.), *Studium declamatorium* (cited n. 16), 5–34, at 25–6.

²¹⁹ Individual instances of this kind can already be found in the Verrines and the Catilinarian speeches; but here, before the pontifices to whose ears Cicero adapts his tone right from the beginning—*divinitus* (instead of e.g. *egregie*) is the third word of the speech—he achieves an intensity of religious atmosphere also in larger passages which is unique and also, as far as I remember, without parallel in the Attic orators.

²²⁰ As an attempt was made to reconstruct it for Clodius above (n. 116). On the relationship of Cicero's court speeches to rhetorical theory, cf. esp. the books by Neumeister and Stroh (cited n. 14).

at issue, for instance: *Ciceronis domum sacram* (or *rite consecratam*) *non esse* or *utrum Ciceronis domus sacra sit necne*, and then in the *probatio*, in order to prove the point *sacram non esse*, the *lex Papiria* would have had to be quoted. Here it would above all have been important to demonstrate why the legislator had taken such special precautions for the dedication particularly of plots of land or real estate–a rewarding topic concerning which one could have brought forward many plausible arguments. In the *refutatio*, against the possible claim by Clodius that a ritually performed dedication was valid under all circumstances (because the gods paid attention to the religious formulas and sacrifices, not to any preceding plebiscite) Cicero would have quoted a case like that of the Vestal Virgin Licinia; to the reproach of being an *exsul* he could have replied among other things that this, even if it were correct, would not make the dedication any more valid. If Cicero then finally, for instance in an ensuing passage *extra causam*, had still castigated Clodius' whole behaviour at his expulsion, even this would not have impaired the comprehensibility and the clarity of the speech.

We see that Cicero did not write or deliver such a regularly laid-out speech. We know the main reason for this and, looking back on the speech which was actually delivered, we can still to some extent follow his tactical considerations in detail. A coherent *narratio* of the events was ruled out, not only because during it attention would necessarily be drawn also to the first *lex Clodia*, a mention of which Cicero of course avoids because of his embarrassing mistake in reacting to it which Clodius has deployed against him (see p. 351) but above all also because he could hardly have avoided mentioning that Clodius had had himself authorized by plebiscite to perform the dedication.[221] The pontifices of course know this, and Cicero knows that they do; but it was still better to keep this point far away from their consciousness for as long as possible–in our speech, until section 103–and to occupy their minds with other things.

More surprising than this absence of a comprehensive *narratio*, which of course is not to be found in every instance elsewhere in Cicero's court speeches,[222] is the absence of a *propositio*. Cicero never states what he actually wants to prove; he only makes clear his desire to be allowed to return to his house (100 and 143–7). As we have already recognized in passing, this, too, is connected with the feebleness of his legal standpoint. If Cicero at the beginning of his speech had set out the *propositio* according to the rules, he would have had to relate the parts of the speech to this stated point to be proved,

---

[221] It is different in *Pro Sestio* where Cicero for the first and only time gives a complete, chronologically structured narration of his *discessus* (*Sest.* 15 ff.). Since there he is not under compulsion to defend himself against Clodius' influential account of the matter, which described his first *lex* as harmless and Cicero's departure as a confession of guilt, he can without inhibitions speak about this *lex* as promulgated *de mea pernicie* (25); the second *lex Clodia* only needs to be mentioned briefly (65), and the dedication is not spoken about at all.

[222] Cf. Stroh (cited n. 14) esp. 212–13 with reference to Cic. *Inv.* 1.30.

and so would above all have had to say clearly that the first main part, which contained far more than a third of the speech (43–71), together with the appendix belonging to it (72–99) where the illegality of the second *lex Clodia* is proved, was intended in addition to demonstrate the invalidity of the authorization to dedicate which was contained in the *lex*; but in doing this he would have practically already admitted the authorization (see above) which of course he wants to contest later, and he would have had to put his money exclusively on the annulment of the *lex*, which politically had been impossible for a long time. But on the other hand it was also impractical completely to do without or to relegate into an appendix this passage, which of course could so splendidly stir up public opinion against Clodius, arouse sympathy for Cicero and above all justify his *discessus*. Cicero looks for a middle course, which is logically as weak as it is tactically prudent. He leaves the argumentative status of this entire passage, so to speak, in the balance,[223] and thus leaves it to the individual pontifex to decide whether, secretly convinced of the illegality of the whole *lex*, he wants, for instance under the title of a formal defect in the wording of the law, to provide Cicero with satisfaction for the insult he suffered. But then the second main part of the *argumentatio* (104–41), also for this reason, could no longer be clearly delimited in its function (cf. above, pp. 338 ff.). In Cicero's actual speech, in contrast to the first part of the *argumentatio*, it has only one topic (the dedication), and no stated thesis, at least not an explicitly stated one. Lovers of neatly structured school exercises and of a concluding 'Quod erat demonstrandum' cannot derive pleasure from this speech, which is cautious, often imprecise, and disguises its own intention; this does not prevent it from being a masterpiece in its own kind.

But we do not do justice to the speech, either, if we appreciate it only as a trick of clever and tactical cunning to establish an ultimately untenable legal standpoint. Cicero put down its effectiveness, its success—which, probably because he knew some hard-boiled formalists among the pontifices, did not by any means seem certain to him[224]—ultimately to his *vis dicendi* which originated from the *doloris magnitudo* (above, pp. 313–14: to the ability by virtue of one's own pain–'si me vis flere, dolendum est | primum ipsi tibi' (Horace, *AP* 102–3)–to move others; and he is probably right in this. Just as Demosthenes' speech *De Corona*, with which it invites comparison as a speech 'pro domo', does not derive its power from the craftiness with which

---

[223] When Cicero in sect. 122 once says that, even if the dedication had formally been entirely correct, he could defend himself *rei publicae iure* (cf. above p. 341) then, according to the context, he does not mean the previously claimed invalidity of the second *lex Clodia* in terms of public law (or even the *lex Papiria*, which has not even yet been mentioned) but much more generally that the enemy of the state is not allowed to use religion against the state (cf. 137), or still more generally (139): 'in scelere religio non valeret'. Even such thoughts, which are vaguely in the mind, create a certain linkage between the two parts.

[224] In *Att.* 4.1.7 Cicero reckons with the possibility that the pontifices may decide against him (see above, n. 217).

Demosthenes plays down the juridical arguments which speak against him[225] but from the power of emotion, the irresistible pathos of the hero who also in the face of his political failure insists on the idea that he has done what is right and correct for the people and with the people who followed him,[226] so also Cicero's *De Domo Sua* lives not through the ingenious economy of its argumentation, which in a hopeless situation still manages to secure by cunning a favourable verdict, but from the all-pervading ardour of its passion. Of course it is not the 'heroic pose', mocked by Gelzer and others, of the man who claims of his own free will to have sacrificed himself for his people and to have saved the state not once but twice which ultimately moves one–it probably displeased his contemporaries as well. But we are indeed moved by Cicero's sheer pain over his expulsion, the treatment of his family and, above all, the loss (connected with this) of his house which he loved and which, looking over the city from the Palatine and itself seen from everywhere (100, 146), was a manifest symbol of the position achieved by the *homo novus*, and with the conflagration and disgraceful dedication of which his existence seemed visibly destroyed. In this respect he himself confessed at one place in *De Domo Sua* (97–8), as we have seen, to have failed when compared with the strictest heroic standards, and, without the mental *apatheia* demanded by others,[227] to have paid tribute to 'common humanity' (see above, pp. 358–9). Perhaps he speaks even more beautifully, more simply and more movingly at the end of the speech where at any rate, but only just for a moment, he throws himself into the pose of a rigorous Stoic despiser of the world and of fortune who dismisses all outward goods as *fortunae et temporum munera* but then, more modestly, takes the one house which is indispensable for him out of the series of these *adiaphora*[228] and, before the final appeal in the closing sentences, makes the confession (147): 'But my house which was criminally taken away from me, occupied through robbery, built through the power of religion even more despicably than it was destroyed, this I cannot forgo, without the greatest disgrace of the general public, without my own humiliation and pain.' The immortal gods too, whom after all he deprived of their property with this speech, seem to have been moved and turned a blind eye.

---

[225] In the speech *De Corona*, too, the legal position of the opponent was incomparably better; cf. for instance H. Wankel (comm.), *Demosthenes Rede für Ktesiphon über den Kranz*, (Heidelberg, 1976) i.16 ff., 44.

[226] Dem. *De Cor.* 199 ff., esp. 207 (like Cicero, but very much more modestly, Demosthenes identifies himself with his city); cf. Wankel (cited n. 225) 62.

[227] On the latent anti-Stoic attitude of section 97, Wolf (cited n. 6) rightly referred to what the Academic Crantor (whom Cicero later follows in the *Consolatio*), quoted in Cic. *Tusc.* 3.12, says about *indolentia*.

[228] The passage, which appears highly philosophical, may also be taken in a banal sense: Cicero wishes to make the value of the financial compensation planned by the Senate for Cicero, in case the pontifical decision was unfavourable (*Att.* 4.1.7), appear irrelevant. Money belongs to the 'caduca . . . et mobilia' (146): Cicero will accept only 'immoveable' property.

14

The Dilemma of Cicero's Speech for Ligarius

Jeffrey P. Johnson

In this chapter I will assess Cicero's forensic strategy in his speech for Ligarius. Because of the difficulties of this speech, that strategy is not readily apparent. Through a close reading of the text, however, we can perceive that Cicero's goal was to refuse admitting his client's guilt but also to dress his speech in the language of a plea for mercy, thus catching Caesar on both horns of a good dilemma.

Pro Ligario is a fascinating speech, admired since Quintilian, who quotes from it copiously,[1] and in modern times the subject of a great deal of speculation. This is one of the reasons the speech is so interesting; we know only the barest circumstances of the trial–many questions remain unanswered, such as: what was the charge, why was the charge brought, why did Cicero take the case, why did Caesar hear the case, and why did Ligarius get off?

Kumaniecki sums up many of the problems when he writes:

This lack of clarity arises partly from the fact that only Cicero's defence speech survives in full, while we know Tubero's prosecution speech only from a few fragments handed down to us by Quintilian. On the other hand, the defence speech of Pansa,

This chapter was delivered in previous incarnations at the Baylor University Academic Honors Week and also at a Durham University graduate seminar. I owe thanks to both audiences. I would also like to thank R. Alden Smith, Timothy S. Johnson, Stephen R. Todd, C. F. Konrad, J. L. Moles, D. S. Levene, A. J. Woodman, Robert Kaster, Elaine Fantham, Andrew Feldherr, Paolo Asso, and especially J. J. Paterson and J. G. F. Powell for their helpful comments. I would like to extend a sincere and respectful thanks to Oxford University Press's anonymous referee, whose criticisms allowed me to clarify and strengthen several points. I owe a most profound thanks to Christopher Craig for originally setting me to this speech and reading my conclusions in an earlier draft. He has shown me every kindness, and where I depart from him, I hope it is only to affirm the spirit of his work on Cicero. H. C. Gotoff, 'Cicero's Caesarian Orations' in J. M. May (ed.) *Brill's Companion to Cicero* (Leiden 2002) 219–71 reaches some conclusions similar to mine, but appeared too late for me to take it into account.

[1] *Inst.* 4.1.39, 4.1.67, 4.1.70, 4.2.51, 4.2.108, 4.2.109, 4.2.110, 4.2.131, 5.10.93, 5.11.42, 5.13.20, 5.13.31, 5.14.1.

who spoke before Cicero, is completely unknown to us. Moreover it is still unclear whether Tubero came forward with a charge from a personal motive on his own or if he allowed himself to be guided somewhat by Caesar's inspiration. It is also unclear whether the acquittal was agreed on from the start and whether Cicero, when he undertook the defence, allowed himself to be misused as a tool of Caesar's policy, or whether he followed his own policy in opposition to the dictator.[2]

Indeed, even more than this is unclear. Before examining some of the difficulties and attempting to sort them out, we must consider the historical background.

i

Quintus Ligarius had gone to Africa in 50 BC as legate to the governor C. Considius Longus before the outbreak of open hostility between Caesar and Pompey. The governor left the province and returned to Rome at the end of 50 to stand for the consulship. Ligarius, meanwhile, stayed on and against his will (as Cicero tells it) legally assumed his superior's duties. Not long after, civil war broke out, and the former governor of the province (P. Attius Varus) arrived at Utica, took over, and raised two legions. As far as we can tell, Ligarius acted in no way to prevent Varus from doing this. Ligarius served under Varus, and at one point prevented from landing L. Aelius Tubero (who had been appointed by the Senate to succeed C. Considius Longus) and Tubero's son Quintus, who was ill aboard ship. In fact, Ligarius had even refused the Tuberones water replenishments.

After Pharsalus, Ligarius remained in Africa and continued fighting, as did some other Pompeians. He probably fought against Curio in 49 and Caesar in 46,[3] but after the battle of Thapsus he was pardoned by Caesar, though not allowed to return home.

After Caesar's return to Rome and the celebration of his fourfold triumph, Cicero was doing what he could to intervene on behalf of Pompeians still in exile. One of the men Cicero sought to help was Quintus

---

[2] 'Diese Unklarheiten ergeben sich teils aus der Tatsache, daß sich nur die Verteidigungsrede Ciceros in ihrem vollen Wortlaut erhalten hat, während wir die Anklagerede Tuberos nur aus einigen, uns von Quintilian überlieferten Fragmenten kennen, dagegen ist uns die Verteidigungsrede von Pansa, der vor Cicero sprach, überhaupt nicht bekannt. Außerdem ist für uns immer noch unklar, ob Tubero mit einer Anklage hervortrat, bei der er sich durch persönliche Beweggründe oder etwa durch Caesars Inspirationen leiten ließ. Auch ist nicht bekannt, ob der Freispruch von vornherein ausgemacht war und ob Cicero, als er die Verteidigung übernahm, sich als Werkzeug der Politik Caesars mißbrauchen ließ, oder ob er dem Diktator gegenüber seine eigene Politik verfolgte' (K. Kumaniecki, 'Der Prozess gegen Q. Ligarius', *Hermes* 95 (1967) 434–57 at 434).

[3] See C. P. Craig, 'The Central Argument of Cicero's Speech for Ligarius', *CJ* 79 (1984) 193–9 at 194, and W. C. McDermott, 'In Ligarianam', *TAPA* 101 (1970) 317–47 at 321.

Ligarius, whose brothers, Caesarians themselves, were also at work petitioning Caesar for Ligarius' return. We have two letters from Cicero to Ligarius.[4] In them Cicero strikes a hopeful note, but sticks to the facts. (As Kumaniecki notes of the first, 'this letter does not contain concrete promises.'[5]) If we believe Cicero, it was just beginning to seem that Ligarius might be in the clear. At this point, however, charges were brought against Ligarius by Quintus Tubero, the same Tubero who had been ill, had tried to land, and was refused by Ligarius. So the charges by Tubero (who himself had been a Pompeian) were apparently recompense for this unkindness. The main difference between Tubero's situation, indeed between the situation of most Pompeians to this point, and that of Ligarius, lay in the fact that Ligarius had continued to fight after Pharsalus.

After Pompey's defeat Caesar acquired a number of powers in the city of Rome. One of these was the right to hear and decide judicial cases, and one of the first cases he decided to hear was that of Quintus Ligarius.[6] Cicero had just delivered his fulsome *Pro Marcello* in the Senate chamber. According to Plutarch, the day arrived and events transpired thus:

It is also said that when Quintus Ligarius was on trial because he had been one of Caesar's enemies, and Cicero was defending him, Caesar said to his friends: 'What is stopping us from hearing Cicero speak after all this time, since the fellow has long ago been judged a criminal and enemy?' But when Cicero began to speak and moved him tremendously, and the speech, as it proceeded, was both varied in emotion and wonderful in charm, Caesar let many shades of emotion show on his face and was quite clearly experiencing all the changing emotions of the soul, and finally, when the orator tackled the struggles at Pharsalus, he [sc. Caesar] became completely overcome by emotion—his body shook and he let some of his documents fall from his hand. At any rate he acquitted the man of the charge under compulsion.[7]

Because such controversy surrounds *Pro Ligario*, I will briefly survey some of the scholarship, which will give an idea how the difficulties have been handled, and then consider the text itself.

ii

Following Drumann,[8] some scholars have tended to take an unfavourable view of *Pro Ligario*. They see the trial as staged, Cicero's pleading as rather

---

[4] *Fam.* 6.13 (August or September 46) and 6.14 (24 September 46).

[5] 'Wie wir sehen, enthält dieser Brief keine konkreten Versprechungen'. Kumaniecki, 'Der Prozess', 438.

[6] Dio Cassius, 42.19–20.   [7] Plut. *Cic.* 39.6–7, tr. J. L. Moles.

[8] W. Drumann and P. Groebe, *Geschichte Roms in seinem Übergange von der republikanischen zur monarchischen Verfassung*, 2nd edn. (Berlin and Leipzig, 1899–1929) 232–5 and 635–8.

pitiable, and the whole affair as a low point in Cicero's life. In his history of Latin literature, Gian Biagio Conte deems none of the Caesarian speeches worthy of individual comment, and of the three together he says only, 'Cicero probably fell short of his full dignity; it is rather difficult to accept the sincerity of the Caesarian speeches, which abound in praise for Caesar.'[9] Conte has summed up what for many is a stumbling block: reconciling praise for Caesar with what we know from Cicero's letters were his true sentiments.

Among the speech's detractors is W. C. McDermott, who reads the speech as a simple *deprecatio*. Because Cicero mentions Corfidius (who was dead) as being present at the trial,[10] McDermott concludes that Cicero must not have been intimate with the Ligarii, and only became involved in the case at the behest of Brutus. On this view, Cicero had never intended to defend Ligarius in court, but once he became involved found himself drawn deeper and deeper into the case. Cicero also would have found it difficult to plead against the Tuberones given that 'Q. Tubero was *propinquus* and his father Lucius was *adfinis* and *necessarius*'.[11] Because Cicero did not become involved in the case by design, Tubero could not have known Cicero would be his opponent at the bar, so Tubero would have felt that he could gain a conviction.[12] The charge would have been *perduellio*, the defence and prosecution colluded before the trial (and before Cicero joined the defence), and Caesar intended the condemnation of Ligarius to be a stern warning to the Pompeians still fighting in Spain. Nevertheless, McDermott admits that 'any effect of his conviction on the Pompeiani in Spain was problematical'.[13] Therefore Caesar, originally having intended to convict Ligarius, acquitted him to effect a settlement with Cicero. (What this settlement was or why it was necessary are not made clear.) This speech is not among Cicero's best, McDermott says, and Cicero knew it. (McDermott does not address the question this raises of why Cicero published the speech so quickly if he was not proud of it.) Quintilian's quotations from it tend to fall in clusters, so Quintilian must have memorized the speech simply for use in the classroom but not because of its quality. Thus McDermott cautions against saying that Quintilian admired the speech for any greatness of its thought. Quintilian certainly understood *Pro Ligario* as a *deprecatio*, and in his day this sort of speech before an absolute ruler would have been much more common, thus guaranteeing the speech greater popularity than it deserved. Finally, McDermott labours to point out how Caesar courted Cicero, and even goes so far as to

---

[9] Gian Biagio Conte, *Latin Literature: A History*, tr. Joseph B. Solodow (Baltimore, 1994) 184.
[10] *Lig.* 33, but see *Att.* 13.44.3, where Cicero attempts to correct this mistake.
[11] McDermott, 'In Ligarium', 323.   [12] Ibid. 325.   [13] Ibid. 326.

conjecture that Caesar may have offered Cicero the position of *magister equitum* in 47, which seems highly doubtful.

Also in this group of critics are Drumann, Walser, and Kumaniecki. Like McDermott, they see the trial as a put-up job, but where McDermott sees a thwarted conviction, they see an intended pardon. Their accounts differ from one another in the details,[14] but the result of these accounts is basically the same: Cicero, whether through accident or cynical cooperation, served Caesar's purposes. Walser, for example, believes that because Cicero had such connections with the Tuberones, because Ligarius was a far less prominent figure than Marcellus, and because Cicero must have possessed some strong reason to throw his whole weight behind the case of a relatively unknown figure, the cause can only have been instigation by Caesar. For Walser the trial is a peace proposal from Caesar to the remaining Pompeians in Spain, a proposal similar to the one he made before the battle of Pharsalus.[15] The whole episode, writes Walser, is an example of Cicero's blindness and hubris: he knew the goals of Caesar's propaganda and he accepted Caesar's offer just the same.[16] Drumann at least makes some room for Cicero's dignity: 'Ligarius was acquitted and Cicero praised and admired in more than one sense: Caesar had Rome, but he [Cicero] had overcome Caesar; the bad speech of his opponent was used as a foil for his own; he published this in the following year, and soon everyone read it.'[17]

Christopher Craig seems to take a middle view, viewing Cicero as not essentially independent but neither completely manipulated. He accepts that Caesar had decided beforehand to acquit Ligarius, and that Cicero cooperated in a staged trial which was merely an advertisement for Caesar's *clementia*. Based on the testimony of Quintilian,[18] Craig agrees that the charge would certainly have been *perduellio* and Craig offers the innovative solution that, generically speaking, *Pro Ligario* is a sort of mixture of *deprecatio* and *purgatio*.[19] Cicero was given the task of advertising Caesar's *clementia* and therefore had to walk a delicate tightrope, admitting the *perduellio* so that Caesar would have something to pardon and denying the *perduellio* so that Caesar would not seem unjust. Yet these conflicting

---

[14] Drumann, for instance, sees the trial as a general set piece for Caesar's *clementia*, while Walser and Kumaniecki see it as more intended for the Pompeians still fighting in Spain.

[15] G. Walser, 'Der Prozess gegen Ligarius im Jahre 46 v. Chr.', *Historia* 8 (1959) 90–6 at 95.

[16] 'Auch der Ligariusprozeß ist ein Beispiel von Ciceros Blindheit und Selbstüberschätzung: Er erkannte Caesars Propagandaabsicht und ging trotzdem auf das heikle Angebot Caesars ein, die alte forensiche Beredsamkeit auch unter der Diktatur fortzusetzen' (Ibid. 96).

[17] 'Ligarius wurde freigesprochen und Cicero in mehr als einer Hinsicht bewundert und gepriesen; Caesar hatte Rom, er hatte Caesar überwunden; die schlechte Rede des Gegners diente der seinigen zur Folie; er machte diese im folgenden Jahre bekannt, und bald las sie jedermann' (Drumann–Groebe, *Geschichte Roms*, 638).   [18] Quint. *Inst.* 11.1.78.

[19] Craig, 'Central Argument', 196 n. 9. See also Lausberg, §§ 187–90.

purposes raise difficulties in Craig's interpretation. Craig (p. 195) writes that the 'role of fair judge is, strictly speaking, incompatible with that of benevolent and forgiving victor. This incompatibility makes cohesive argumentation impossible.' This incompatibility–the difficulty of pleading to two different aspects of Caesar simultaneously–could certainly, as Craig reasons, have led Cicero to plead Ligarius' innocence in the less-noticed middle of the speech, having been given and having accepted an impossible task from the dictator. But if the dictator was interested in staging a trial, would he not have been able to realize the conflicting nature of the task which he set before Cicero?[20] Put another way, if the trial would not have been a good vehicle by which to advertise *clementia*, it may be possible that in fact this purpose is not the reason the trial was held. In addition, Cicero had just given *Pro Marcello*, a piece of eloquent testimony to Caesar's *clementia*. What would have occasioned the need for new testimony? And would not an outright pardon instead of a staged trial have served such purposes better? On Craig's interpretation, Cicero walked this tightrope by placing his weakest argument–that Ligarius is not guilty–in the middle of the speech, thus following his own rhetorical advice.[21] Cicero dealt with the difference between Ligarius and the Pompeians who quit fighting after Pharsalus either by ignoring it or by making Ligarius' pertinacity seem no worse than the deeds of the Tuberones.[22] This blurring allows Caesar to pardon while still seeming just. For Craig it would seem that the trial of Ligarius, while no means a moral high point in Cicero's advocacy, at least allowed him to show his oratorical prowess again near the end of his career.

Harold C. Gotoff has offered a reading of the speech which gives more latitude to Cicero's advocacy. Gotoff believes that the charge against Ligarius cannot be known with certainty, but that *perduellio* seems too archaic.[23] He cautions that Plutarch's account of Caesar's reaction should not be so quickly rejected as it is by most scholars. Gotoff argues that scholars overlook some facts in assuming Ligarius' acquittal was a foregone conclusion in order to provide a dashing piece of praise for the policy of *clementia*.[24] As already noticed, such a piece had already been provided by *Pro Marcello*. If political expediency were the only concern, what about the expediency of offending Caesarians eager for vengeance? And what about the expediency of offending the Tuberones by rigging a trial in

---

[20] As Craig, 'Central Argument', 195 n. 6, acknowledges, things might not have been presented to Cicero in such a way, but the difficulty remains. Assuming a put-up job, the problem would no doubt have been left to Cicero to work out, but it still inheres in the situation, and one wonders whether so clever a politician as Caesar could have missed it.

[21] Craig, 'Central Argument', 193.   [22] Ibid. 196.

[23] H. C. Gotoff, *Cicero's Caesarian Speeches: A Stylistic Commentary* (Chapel Hill, NC, 1993), p. xxxiii.   [24] Ibid., pp. xxxiv–xxxv.

which they had no fair chance? We cannot know all of Caesar's reasons for acquitting Ligarius, but there is no reason to assume the cynical view that the speech was merely a show.[25]

James May likewise gives a sympathetic reading to *Pro Ligario* and observes how Cicero's customary rhetoric of character–the character of the defence advocates, the prosecution, and the defendant–has been adapted for this trial. In unusual circumstances Cicero must rely on unusual tactics. Normally, May points out, Cicero would pit the character of the defendant and patron against that of the prosecution. Here, however, no one's character can seem to outweigh that of Caesar.[26] Therefore Cicero carefully measures his praise of himself and his client, and frames his criticisms of the prosecution in reference to the dictator. Ligarius longed for peace, and Tubero inhumanly clamours for judgement. But Caesar, in contrast to Tubero, is clement. And Ligarius is of the same stock as his Caesarian brothers. By grounding the defence in the good character of Caesar and painting Tubero so darkly, Cicero has given Caesar a simplified, reductionistic choice: Tubero is bad, and clemency is good. How, May seems to wonder (p. 148), is there a choice at all?

Irony is one of the most commented upon features of *Pro Ligario*, and one on which the article of Holly Montague sheds much light. Montague follows Craig in tracing the contradictions of Cicero's position, and argues that Cicero sends powerful messages to Caesar about the value of courts and advocacy, while keeping everything safe by cloaking his defence of Ligarius in contradictory rhetoric. Montague argues that the charge would have been collusion with Juba, putting Ligarius in a different category from other Pompeians and also in significant legal jeopardy. For Montague, the brilliance of Cicero's speech is that it allows him to indulge in obfuscation of the particular charge, and at the same time to please Caesar with a performance of verbal virtuosity which, in the end, amounted to no argument, no statement, nothing more than 'verbal sophistry' and 'formal perfection'. Montague concludes that 'the speech goes beyond irony to the sort of ambiguity which is often associated with Augustan poetry'.[27]

In an unpublished dissertation Charles Ramos argues that Cicero was not subservient or obsequious in this speech, but rather clever and even critical of Caesar's regime. Ramos reads Cicero's praise as prescriptive, and argues that the speech contains outright criticism of the dictator. Ramos grounds his argument on the idea of *emphasis* or figured speech, which he defines as

[25] Ibid., p. xxxvii.
[26] J. M. May, *Trials of Character: The Eloquence of Ciceronian Ethos* (Chapel Hill, NC, and London, 1988) 141.
[27] H. W. Montague, 'Advocacy and Politics: The Paradox of Cicero's Pro Ligario', *AJP* 113 (1992) 559–74, at pp. 573–4.

'the purposeful insertion of hidden meanings in a statement which the reader or listener must dig out'.[28] He examines the discussions of Quintilian and Demetrius concerning this sort of speech, which Frederick Ahl calls 'the art of safe criticism'.[29] By using subtle language that could be understood by orator and tyrant, but might also be interpreted differently, the speaker could be as critical as he desired and yet present his criticisms in a way more likely to be appreciated by a tyrant than would be unqualified opposition. Cicero must have known of figured speech, and although he may never have had a chance to apply it previously, the Caesarian speeches represent such an opportunity. On Ramos's view, the weight of figured speech rests with every use of *clementia* in the Caesarian speeches.[30] Through an analysis of Cicero's letters Ramos argues that *clementia* would have held negative connotations for Republicans and former Pompeians, would have already taken on positive shades for many Caesarians, but would have been avoided by Caesar, who was aware of its potential to arouse resentment. Ramos points out that modern critics when they assess some of Cicero's praise as distasteful or excessive, must bear in mind that these criticisms themselves are after all only statements of taste, and one must be careful not to impose modern assumptions and sensibilities on the ancient Roman. Rather, Cicero's praise must be measured against his praise elsewhere and against his own and his contemporaries' views concerning what is rhetorically appropriate.

Ramos is not the first to view *Pro Ligario* as figured speech. Ten years earlier Claude Loutsch made the same suggestion. As Loutsch points out, Cicero very quickly gives up the irony of the *exordium*, until he comes in the speech to ask not for freedom from guilt, but pardon for error. According to Loutsch, this is the point in the speech where Cicero makes his *deprecatio* clear, and Loutsch's hypothesis is that Cicero 'uses the irony solely to prepare the listener to accept this unusual way of pleading without taking offence'.[31] Like Craig, Loutsch sees the central paragraphs of the speech as placed there according to rhetorical theory, 'in a place where the so-called Homeric disposition places the arguments most difficult to make the listeners accept'.[32] The irony of the speech also allows Cicero to

[28] C. F. Ramos, 'Politics and Rhetoric: Studies in Cicero's Caesarian Speeches', Ph.D. diss. (University of Texas at Austin, 1994) 7. See also sects. 905–6 in H. Lausberg, *Handbuch der literarischen Rhetorik* (Munich, 1960).

[29] F. Ahl, 'The Art of Safe Criticism in Greece and Rome', *AJP* 105 (1984) 174–208.

[30] For a thorough but concise discussion of the term *clementia*, see S. Weinstock, *Divus Julius* (Oxford, 1971) 233–43.

[31] 'l'orateur se sert de l'ironie uniquement pour préparer l'auditeur à accueillir cette façon insolite de plaider sans s'offusquer' (C. Loutsch, 'Ironie et Liberté de parole: remarques sur l'exorde *ad principem* du Pro Ligario de Ciceron', *REL* 62 (1984) 98–110 at 106).

[32] 'en un endroit où la disposition dite homérique place les arguments les plus difficiles à faire accepter aux auditeurs' (Ibid. 107).

refuse admitting the legitimacy of the suit, or to solve a merely political problem on judicial grounds. Why did this strategy not hurt the cause of Ligarius? Since Cicero couches his arguments in irony and figured speech, Caesar cannot be displeased, because this is a sign that Cicero 'bows before his authority and recognizes implicitly that he no longer has the right to criticize freely and overtly'.[33]

Recently Paola Gagliardi has written on *Pro Ligario* in a very similar vein. Like Ramos and Loutsch, she sees *Pro Ligario* as figured speech. According to Gagliardi, the charge was *perduellio* by collusion with King Juba of Numidia.[34] Like many before her, Gagliardi tells us the speech is a put-up job, footnoting Walser and Kumaniecki.[35] She has no doubt that the speech is a *deprecatio*,[36] and that it thus anticipates in many ways the oratory of imperial Rome. But by reading *Pro Ligario* as *deprecatio* coupled with figured speech, Gagliardi sees a certain 'doubleness' in the speech, worked out with multiple layerings: 'this "doubleness" is reflected in the audience (Caesar and his enemies), in the purposes (admonishment to the first one and indignation for the second), and in the levels of reading (literal and ironic); not by chance will its success be double, in the Caesarian and anti-Caesarian spheres.'[37] For her this ironic bundle is a brilliant construction on Cicero's part, and it allows Cicero to point up the inherent hypocrisy and weakness of Caesar's position. If the charge had to do with Juba and with bearing arms against the Roman state, then how does Caesar deal with the tension created by his own actions at the start of the Civil War? Cicero's ironic praise of Caesar's *clementia*, on Gagliardi's reading, serves not so much to point up the goodness of *clementia* as the necessity of it, just as the fact that Caesar must listen to men like Cicero praise Pompey is a sign that Caesar still needs the former Pompeians. Gagliardi does not want to read part of the speech as ironic and part as straightforward, but rather wishes to see the ironic *duplicità* working throughout the oration, start to finish.[38]

Sabine Rochlitz has also written about *Pro Ligario* with a view to more subtle messages and more clever positioning on Cicero's part. She too sees the speech as *deprecatio*, although *deprecatio* with potential dangers because

---

[33] 'Cicéron s'incline devant son autorité et reconnaît implicitement qu'il n'a plus le droit de le critiquer librement et ouvertement' (Ibid. 108).

[34] P. Gagliardi, *Il dissenso e l'ironia: per una rilettura delle orazione 'cesariane' di Cicerone* (Naples, 1997) 26.   [35] Ibid. 29.

[36] Ibid. 49–50.

[37] 'E questa "duplicità" si riflette nella destinazione (a Cesare e ai suoi nemici), negli scopi (ammonimento al primo ed indignazione per i secondi), nei livelli di lettura (letterale ed ironico); non a caso duplice sarà pure il suo successo, in ambienti cesariani e anticesariani' (Ibid. 51).

[38] Ibid. 50.

of its inadmissibility in court.[39] Rochlitz is interested in the shifting network of political catchwords that appear in the Caesarian speeches, such as *clementia, misericordia,* and *sapientia.* In *Pro Ligario, sapientia* ('political savvy'[40]) moves aside from the prominent position it held in *Pro Marcello* to make room for an overriding concern with *clementia.* This does not mean for her that Cicero undercuts Caesar's *sapientia,* but rather it reflects a difference in purposes: political savvy, broadly conceived in relation to Rome's future, was the subject of *Pro Marcello,* while in *Pro Ligario* the pardon of one particular individual is the goal, pursued through *deprecatio.* Ligarius' position was already subordinate to Caesar's before the trial was ever conceived, and so it makes sense to speak of *clementia* extended to a lesser individual, while in the case of the more prominent Marcellus, the idea of *sapientia* had to be employed. Still, Rochlitz ends her discussion with the idea that *Pro Ligario* marks a shift in tone for Cicero:

On the other hand, one could interpret Cicero's words also as sign of an increasing pessimism, as signs that he has again given up the hope of constructing the state under a *Caesar sapiens,* even if he keeps up the fiction of a *res publica* at some places in his speech. This is probably so that he could make his entreaty rather than that he maintains any self-deception. In any case, the speech lacks the careful optimism of the *Pro Marcello*–on the contrary, bitter irony often sounds through.[41]

One can see that scholarship over *Pro Ligario* tends to argue a good deal about what Cicero's motivations might have been and what Caesar may have wished. If nothing else, a survey of scholarship reveals just how much is still in dispute. Following Drumann, many scholars have tended to assume the trial was staged. While it is important to look at all the evidence, it seems to me that the place to begin is the text of the speech itself, keeping in mind the salutary caution that we owe almost everything we know about Ligarius and his case to Cicero's speech and to a few fragments from the prosecution of Tubero, and that both these sources are biased and unobjective.[42]

---

[39] 'Das gleiche bezweckt wohl die von Cicero gewählte Form der "Verteidigung", die *deprecatio,* eine Gattung, die es vor Gericht nicht gibt, da sie keine objektiven Entscheidungskriterien voraussetzt' (S. Rochlitz, *Das Bild Caesars in Ciceros Orationes Caesarianae: Untersuchungen zur 'clementia' und 'sapientia Caesaris'* (Frankfurt am Main, 1993)). [40] Ibid. 127.

[41] 'Auf der anderen Seite könnte man Ciceros Worte auch als Zeichen eines zunehmenden Pessimismus deuten, daß er die Hoffnung, unter einem Caesar sapiens den Staat aufzubauen, wieder aufgegeben hat, auch wenn er an einigen Stellen seiner Rede die Fiktion einer res publica aufrecht erhält. Dies wohl eher, um sie zu beschwören, als daß er sich irgendwelchen Selbsttäuschungen hingab. Der Rede fehlt jedenfalls der vorsichtige Optimismus der Marcellus-Rede, es klingt im Gegenteil oft bittere Ironie durch' (Ibid. 128).

[42] 'Die Schwierigkeit besteht darin, daß wir nahezu alles, was wir über Ligarius und seine Sache wissen, der Rede Ciceros und einigen wenigen Fragmenten der Anklagerede Tuberos verdanken, diese beiden Quellen aber voreingenommen sind, also nicht objective sein können' (Kumaniecki, 'Der Prozess', 434).

Before I advance to the text, however, I should like to make clear how I take a number of issues external to the speech, some of which I will not examine in closest detail because it seems to me that they do not affect our interpretation of Cicero's forensic strategy.

First, why did Cicero take the case? As I hope the foregoing discussion will have shown, this is a question we must stop asking, not because it is unimportant, but simply because we do not have the evidence to supply a trustworthy answer. We have the speech and the letters to Ligarius, but Cicero never explicitly tells why he took the case, and to guess at a reason involves relying too much upon impressions of Cicero and Caesar, surely an unreliable method. In addition, Cicero's connections with Tubero will always be inconclusive. He may have taken the case in spite of connections with Tubero, knowing somehow that he would not cause offence or could overcome any offence. But there is also the possibility that he was sought out for the defence because he was in a particularly good position, by playing the avuncular role that he did with Atratinus in *Pro Caelio*, to reprove Tubero without incurring offence. It may well be that Cicero had secondary reasons: if Ligarius' family was not important, perhaps the case touched him in some way we cannot guess. Today, it is impossible to know. Moreover, how would it change our understanding of the strategy even if we did know why Cicero originally took the case? Regardless of Cicero's first motivation, he seems to operate under a rhetorical strategy which we can discern in the text of *Pro Ligario*.

Second, I will not be treating Plutarch's account with very much credulity. Most scholarship has not regarded it highly, and for good reason. Gotoff does not wish to reject it out of hand, but only McDermott takes it to be truly reliable. George Kennedy sums up the objections well:

It was *not* a very long time since Caesar had heard Cicero, for the speech for Marcellus had been delivered the same month. Nor from Cicero's letters does it appear that Ligarius had in fact 'long ago' been condemned in Caesar's mind, rather the opposite. Further, Plutarch fails to mention that Cicero was the second of two advocates for Ligarius, as appears from the beginning of the speech. C. Pansa had already spoken on Ligarius' behalf.[43]

Kennedy decides that if Plutarch's account is genuine, it was a jest overheard by an ignorant bystander. Most scholars also object to the extreme emotionalism Caesar seems to show in Plutarch's description. D. T. Benedikston in 1989 advanced the hypothesis that this passage describes Caesar experiencing an epileptic seizure,[44] which might explain the apparent emotionalism. *Pro Ligario* scholarship has not considered this possibility, but intriguing as it is,

---

[43] G. A. Kennedy, *The Art of Rhetoric in the Roman World* (Princeton, 1972), 261.
[44] Abstract in *Ploutarchos* November 1989. The idea may have been current in scholarly circles earlier, but this abstract is the only application of it to *Pro Ligario* I can find.

even if true it would not necessarily show that Plutarch's account of the verdict should be decisive. In addition, those who would use Plutarch as evidence for *Pro Ligario* must remember that his account of the speech does not stand alone, and cannot be isolated from its context. Plutarch writes with his own programme in mind, and at 39.6–7 his aim is to show Cicero back from retirement and speaking well. As John Moles has written, 'Plutarch only guarantees the last sentence of this suspect anecdote, but creates an effect of the tremendous power of Cicero's oratory at its best, reactivated after so long an absence, soon to fall silent again.'[45] In general, Plutarch uses 'it is said' to introduce three sorts of accounts: one probably true, one probably untrue, and one the truth of which Plutarch will not judge but which he will use for the purposes of his narrative. This passage is of the third type.[46] If Plutarch himself will not vouch for the accuracy of this testimony it seems imprudent to trust it as evidence for our own understanding of *Pro Ligario*. In the same manner as he seeks to heighten the power of the *Pro Ligario* vignette, Plutarch at section 35 in his *Cicero* distorts Cicero's miserable performance in delivering *Pro Milone* to serve the dramatic movement of the narrative.[47] Given an author with these artistic purposes, one must approach him carefully as an historical source.

I will not attempt to answer the question of Caesar's involvement in the genesis of this trial, again because of the paucity and inconclusiveness of the evidence. Apart from whatever clues we can glean from Cicero's speech, which will be few, I would like to suggest that these questions also are better left untouched, once again, not because they are unimportant, but because we have no evidence. Any attempt to answer this question is bound completely to its assumptions, such as George Kennedy's: 'It is unlikely Pansa would have wanted or been allowed to defend in public a man whom Caesar had determined to convict.'[48] Perhaps this is true. And perhaps, as Walser would have it, Pansa wanted to defend Ligarius because Caesar wanted to acquit Ligarius. We simply do not have enough evidence to say. Whatever the case, encouragement from Caesar cannot be proven; but even if it could be, it still would not show with what aim Caesar had the trial in mind—that is, whether to convict or acquit. Most important, regardless of whether Caesar instigated the proceedings or what verdict he had in mind, one can still postulate an independent strategy on Cicero's part.

The question of the charge might seem to illuminate our understanding of Cicero's rhetorical strategy, but this issue is difficult. We may guess what the charge was, but the evidence is conflicting. The charge might stem from four sources: that Ligarius refused to yield the province to the elder

[45] J. L. Moles (ed., tr., and comm.) *Plutarch: The Life of Cicero* (Warminster, 1988) 188.
[46] Ibid. 147 n. 1.1. For a more general discussion of historicity in Plutarch's *Cicero*, see Moles, 32–53.   [47] Ibid. 183–4.
[48] Kennedy, *Art of Rhetoric*, 261.

Tubero, the duly appointed new governor; that Ligarius had failed to render aid to a Roman citizen in distress, that is, the younger Tubero who was ill; that Ligarius fought against Caesar in Africa in the civil war; or more specifically, that Ligarius fought against the Roman state by allying himself with King Juba of Numidia after the battle of Pharsalus. Or perhaps, with Bauman, we might take all these together and believe Cicero when he says that *in Africa fuisse* was the indictment against Ligarius.[49] If so, this phrase was the prosecution's method of conveniently rolling all four of the previous indictments into one and thus clearing the way for multiple lines of attack. We simply do not know. Even worse, we do not know whether the charge was *maiestas* or *perduellio*. If the charge was *maiestas*, and if there was no special praetor for hearing cases of *maiestas* at this time, then Caesar hearing the case alone in the Forum would make good procedural sense.[50] *Perduellio* might have seemed archaic, and it also involved the full procedure of a public trial before the *comitia*. It was last used in prosecution of a crime committed fifty-four years earlier.[51] On the other hand, Tubero seems to want the death penalty, which makes *perduellio* seem more probable than *maiestas*; and Quintilian reports the charge as *perduellio*. Many scholars agree with Quintilian, but again our evidence is thin. George Long imagines that there may not have been any charge at all, and that Caesar simply considered the case through his power as dictator to exclude dangerous individuals from Rome.[52] In any case, I will argue that Cicero treats the charge as though it stemmed from Ligarius' continued fighting in Africa after Pharsalus. If this actually was the charge, no difficulty troubles Cicero's handling of it; if the charge was something different, then we must conclude Cicero side-stepped it. Because the evidence is so thin, however, it will not help us much in understanding Cicero's rhetoric.

iii

Here I would like to examine the speech itself. The *exordium* (1–2) has often been noted for its irony:

Novum crimen, C. Caesar, et ante hanc diem non auditum propinquus meus ad te Q. Tubero detulit, Q. Ligarium in Africa fuisse, idque C. Pansa, praestanti vir ingenio, fretus fortasse familiaritate ea, quae est ei tecum, ausus est confiteri: itaque quo

---

[49] R. A. Bauman, *The Crimen Maiestatis in the Roman Republic and Augustan Principate* (Johannesburg, 1967), 144–6. Cicero himself uses the idea of being 'in Africa' to distinguish between pre- and post-Pharsalus Pompeians in *Fam.* 4.7.3.

[50] G. M. Long, *M. Tulli Ciceronis Orationes* (London, 1856–8) 399, paraphrasing Halm.

[51] *Pro Rabirio Perduellionis.* Cicero was the advocate in this case as well, and Caesar one of the judges.   [52] Long, *M. T. Ciceronis Orationes*, 400.

me vertam nescio. Paratus enim veneram, cum tu id neque per te scires neque audire aliunde potuisses, ut ignoratione tua ad hominis miseri salutem abuterer; sed quoniam diligentia inimici investigatum est quod latebat, confitendum est, opinor, praesertim cum meus necessarius Pansa fecerit, ut id integrum iam non esset, omissaque controversia omnis oratio ad misericordiam tuam conferenda est, qua plurimi sunt conservati, cum a te non liberationem culpae, sed errati veniam impetravissent. Habes igitur, Tubero, quod est accusatori maxime optandum, confitentem reum, sed tamen hoc confitentem, se in ea parte fuisse, qua te, qua virum omni laude dignum, patrem tuum. Itaque prius de vestro delicto confiteamini necesse est, quam Ligarii ullam culpam reprehendatis.

A new charge, Gaius Caesar, and before this day unheard of, is the one my kinsman Quintus Tubero brings to you, namely that Ligarius was in Africa. Gaius Pansa, a man with outstanding natural ability, has dared to confess this, strengthened perhaps by intimacy with you. And so I don't know where to turn. For because you could not have known anything about the case on your own nor could you have heard about it from another, I had come prepared to take advantage of your ignorance to save a wretched man. But now that what was hidden has been discovered by the diligence of a personal enemy, it must be confessed, I suppose. This is especially true now that my colleague Pansa has left us no option. The whole controversy put aside, all my speech must be directed at your compassion, by which many have been saved, since they have obtained from you not freedom from guilt but pardon for an error. So you have, Tubero, what every prosecutor especially hopes for, a confessing defendant; but for all that, one confessing this: he was on the same side as you and as your father, a man completely worthy of praise. And thus it is necessary that you confess to your own offence before you find fault with any defect of Ligarius.

If, as Cicero intimates, Ligarius is accused of no more than being physically present in Africa, then this is truly a new charge. Unfortunately, we have no contemporary record of the charge except this. Pansa's appearance in the *exordium* is remarkable, and I will come to it below. Here I would like to draw attention to the fact that this is not a repentant or sincere way to begin a *deprecatio*.

In this entire *exordium*, Cicero makes virtually no simple or straightforward statement. Caesar surely would have known more about Ligarius than Cicero here implies. After Thapsus he had pardoned Ligarius (though he had not allowed him to return to Rome) and therefore must have known something of the case. In addition, this was the first trial to be held in Rome in quite some time, not some mundane civil affair that would be passed unnoticed by the city. Moreover, Cicero himself had already attended two audiences with Caesar to discuss the situation, as he says in his letters to Ligarius. It would be absurd to suppose that Cicero came to the Forum expecting Caesar to be uninformed about the case. Irresistible, then, is the false naivety of *itaque quo me vertam nescio*, with the comic, unbelievable image of the orator out of his depth, incapable of facing an unexpected situation and cross at the idea of not being able to use his prepared speech.'[53] There is also a level of irony operating in the very use of this oratorical *topos*.[54] Confessing oneself to be at a loss is rhetorically called for in certain situations, but one can only believe that Cicero uses it here wryly.

Furthermore, Cicero is not about to pass over a proper defence of Ligarius with 'omissa . . . controversia', nor does he direct his entire speech to Caesar's compassion. In fact, just after this *exordium* Cicero will launch into a vigorous defence of Ligarius' actions in the Civil War. The only parts of the speech which can be said to be directed to Caesar's compassion might be §§ 6–8 and 31–8. Apart from these few paragraphs, the preponderance of the speech is a proper defence. Moreover, Cicero makes clear that even the parts of the speech which might appeal to Caesar's compassion do not claim that Ligarius has any *culpa*, but only an error.

Next come the first lines of § 2. Here the irony is made truly explicit and any abject spirit from the first paragraph is undermined. To say, 'Yes, we confess' may sound penitent, but to say 'Yes, we confess to something that certainly is no crime and which praiseworthy men have done' is rather different. Hence Cicero will be able to argue from here to § 29 that Ligarius is innocent. The irony amounts to saying, 'Of course he's guilty . . . guilty of being innocent!'

After §§ 2–5 establish the facts of Ligarius' involvement in Africa, Cicero moves on in §§ 6–8 to praise Caesar's past clemency quite effusively. Cicero then sets this clemency against the bloodthirstiness expressed by Tubero on account of a personal grudge (§§ 9–16). According to Cicero, the Tuberones wanted exactly the same thing that Ligarius enjoyed and for which they now bring charges. But not only that, by demanding death Tubero betrays himself as very un-Roman. Cicero then takes the argument one step more (§ 14) and calls him not only un-Roman, but downright inhuman. In contrast to Caesar's *clementia*, it is the basest sort of revenge which Tubero seeks. This is very clever: if Caesar is moved to condemn Ligarius by inhuman and savage arguments, what does that make Caesar? At the end of § 16 Cicero expands on this point again: 'suam citius abiciet humanitatem quam extorquebit tuam' ('he will sooner throw away his own humanity than wrest yours away'). This is a masterful castigation of Tubero (the kind which Cicero, through his seniority, is in a position to carry out, just as with Atratinus in *Pro Caelio*: cf. Quint. *Inst.* 11.1.68) and a compliment to Caesar in the same stroke. It is through a fault of his own character that Tubero will throw away the very feeling which makes

---

[53] 'Irresistibile, poi, la falsa ingenuità di *itaque quo me vertam nescio*, con la comica, incredibile immagine dell'oratore spaesato, incapace di fronteggiare la situazione imprevista e contrariato all'idea di non poter sfruttare il discorso preparato' (Gagliardi, *Il dissenso*, 62).

[54] See Montague, 'Advocacy and Politics', 563 ff., on the irony of the *exordium*.

him human, but it is the strength of Caesar's character which keeps that feeling intact. Once again, if this is a convincing argument, Caesar is in a difficult position to condemn Ligarius. The implication is that a Caesar who would condemn Ligarius is a Caesar whose very humanity is more easily wrenched away than Cicero had thought. Accordingly, Cicero's praise of Caesar in §§ 6–8 is not a simple and straightforward panegyric. Quite the opposite: it is very conditional praise, and it also serves a rhetorical function over against Cicero's description of Tubero.

We come now to §§ 17–19, which Craig calls the weakest part of the speech. On the contrary, I believe these paragraphs are the hinge and moral underpinning of the speech. It seems to me that one of Cicero's aims in *Pro Ligario* is to obscure distinctions between pre- and post-Pharsalus Pompeians, and perhaps at a later time to argue from Ligarius' case that other post-Pharsalus Pompeians should be forgiven.[55] It may or may not have been the prosecution's charge that Ligarius continued fighting after Pharsalus. But in any case, that does not really matter. The point is the vision Cicero casts–that is, the construction he puts upon the facts as he reports them. As Gagliardi observes, 'not by chance will the protagonists be the same Caesar, the Tuberones, and Cicero, while Ligarius, perpetually in the shade, remains a marginal figure.'[56] I cannot agree with Gagliardi wholeheartedly (it is precisely from Ligarius' case that Cicero argues for principles, and so he hardly remains marginal), but her observation gets at an important point: Ligarius is never as visible in the speech as one would expect a defendant to be in a defence; Cicero constructs his argument around issues external to Ligarius' case.

Near the beginning of § 17 I follow the reading of the Oxford text:

Ac primus aditus et postulatio Tuberonis haec, ut opinor, fuit, velle se de Q. Ligari scelere dicere. Non dubito quin admiratus sis, vel quod nullo de alio quisquam, vel quod is, qui in eadem causa fuisset, vel quidnam novi sceleris adferret.

Now in his preliminary application for leave to bring this suit Tubero stated, I believe, that he wished to speak concerning the crime of Quintus Ligarius. I do not doubt but that you should be surprised, either because about no other did anyone wish to speak, or because this man who was a partisan on the same side wished to speak, or as to what sort of new charge he was bringing.

---

[55] It must be noted that Cicero does not use the term 'Pompeian' in this speech as I have used it here. Cicero speaks of those who fought under Pompey at Pharsalus and those who fought on after his death, and thus, by eliminating the dynastic element, perhaps affirms in a subtle way that Caesar was an enemy of Republican *libertas*. To avoid awkward repetition, I will use 'pre- and post-Pharsalus Pompeian' to designate 'those who fought under Pompey at Pharsalus and those who fought on after his death'.

[56] 'non a caso i protagonisti saranno Cesare stesso, i Tuberoni, Cicerone, mentre Ligario, perennemente nell'ombra, resta una figura marginale' (Gagliardi, *Il dissenso*, 51).

Mommsen thought *quisquam* should be removed here. On the reading of the Oxford text, however, the argument coheres better: is it not unusual that the only post-Pharsalus Pompeian to be charged with anything should be the one whose sole distinguishing mark is that he once wronged Tubero? The point is not that Tubero would have prosecuted someone other than Ligarius by now, but that someone, anyone, would surely by now have prosecuted some other post-Pharsalus Pompeian if the charge really stood up. The generalization is stronger than the specific instance of Tubero.

In § 18 Cicero continues to deconstruct the distinction between pre- and post-Pharsalus Pompeians. It is hardly conceivable that Tubero would have charged Pompey himself with an indictment, yet because of Cicero's eloquence one almost feels that Tubero would. This is precisely Cicero's point: Caesar might as well convict Pompey and many others if he insists on Ligarius' being a criminal.

At the end of § 18 Cicero cleverly links the character of the Pompeians with that of Caesar. Cicero suggests that Caesar surely would not have attempted to negotiate peace with Pompey and his followers if they had been wicked citizens. Finally, in § 19 Cicero says that both sides wanted the best for the state and both strayed from the common good. The Pompeians were guilty of no crime, or if they were, then so were the Caesarians. This is hardly a subservient or obsequious argument.

To sum up, it was clearly a civil war, not a war against a foreign enemy, and the combatants all deserve honour alike, regardless of side. Each believed his course to be for the welfare of the Republic. Cicero says that no one so far has called it a crime merely to have fought against Caesar. Surely the dead and fallen were not criminals? And though he does not explicitly mention the post-Pharsalus Pompeians, their innocence follows by logical implication. If the first set of Pompeians are guilty of no crime by virtue of the fact that they were engaged in civil war, then are they not also innocent who finished off that conflict? Caesar always held the struggle to be a rebellion, not a war. Has it suddenly become something different now that it is almost over? This section is short, but it is the key to the speech. One of the reasons why it could not for Cicero be the weakest part of the speech is that it implies a very serious objection to any view of the Civil War which took it to be dynastic. If the conflict amounted to nothing more than dynasts fighting over personal grievances, then by all accounts the post-Pharsalus Pompeians (as I am calling them) certainly should have stopped fighting. If the war was fought over the Roman constitution and fundamental questions of governance, then it really did not matter whether Pompey led the fight, some other person, or no designated leader at all. This is one reason why Cicero must place the argument in a less noticeable location: not that it is weak, but that it is dangerous. He might be viewed as effectively saying to Caesar, 'We were not mere dynasts; I still think we were right.' Cicero hedges, then, at the end of the paragraph, and admits that Caesar's cause was the right one, but only from the vantage-point of the present, and only because the gods, in the providence of choosing Caesar the winner, have left him no choice.

In §§ 20–9, Cicero returns to his indictment of the prosecution. If being a participant in the Civil War was a crime, then Tubero is just as guilty. Instead, Caesar's generosity in allowing it to be called a civil war allows the particip-ants even now to applaud Pompeian actions or condemn Caesarian ones. Tubero surely had no good designs for Africa. But most important, through use of words like *constantia* and *patientia* (§ 26), Cicero seems to obliterate any distinction between those fighting before and after Pharsalus. If the crime was zealousness for the cause, the Tuberones certainly outstrip Ligarius.[57] They went to Pompey after being turned away by their own allies at Utica. To remain loyal after being rejected by one's own must certainly show greater devotion than Ligarius had. According to Cicero, it is no crime that Ligarius continued fighting after Pharsalus, because the Tuberones con-tinued fighting after Utica. Each in his own way demonstrates a certain zeal for the cause of Pompey. Tubero shows the same constancy with which, according to Cicero, he charges Ligarius. Neither deserves punishment. But Tubero certainly deserves blame for manipulating the situation for personal motives, a tactic that is more threatening because it endangers not only Ligarius but also the principle of Caesar's *clementia* generally.

The passage from the middle of § 29 to the end of § 30 is one of the most striking in *Pro Ligario*, and has caused scholars no small amount of trouble. Read through it quickly and it will seem merely an extension of the *deprecatio* that Cicero appeared to start in § 1. A closer examination is called for, however.

Itaque num tibi videor in causa Ligarii esse occupatus? Num de eius facto dicere? Quidquid dixi, ad unam summam referri volo vel humanitatis vel clementiae vel misericordiae. Causas, Caesar, egi multas, equidem tecum, dum te in foro tenuit ratio honorum tuorum, certe numquam hoc modo: 'Ignoscite, iudices, erravit, lapsus est, non putavit, si umquam posthac . . . ' . Ad parentem sic agi solet; ad iudices: 'Non fecit, non cogitavit; falsi testes, fictum crimen.' Dic te, Caesar, de facto Ligarii iudicem esse, quibus in praesidiis fuerit quaere; taceo, ne haec quidem conligo quae fortasse valerent etiam apud iudicem: 'Legatus ante bellum profectus, relictus in pace, bello oppressus, in eo ipso non acerbus, totus animo et studio tuus.' Ad iudicem sic, sed ego apud parentem loquor: 'Erravit, temere fecit, paenitet; ad clementiam tuam confugio, delicti veniam peto, ut ignoscatur oro.' Si nemo impetravit, adroganter; si plurimi, tu idem fer opem qui spem dedisti.

---

[57] C. P. Craig, 'The Accusator as Amicus: An Original Roman Tactic of Ethical Argumentation', *TAPA* III (1981) 31–7 at 36.

And thus I don't seem to be occupied in the defence of Ligarius, do I? I don't seem to be speaking of his deed, right? Anything I have said, I wish to be referred to one heading: either your humanity or your clemency or your compassion. Many cases indeed have I pleaded with you when the nature of your career kept you in the Forum. But I never pleaded in this way: 'Forgive, judges! He made a mistake, he slipped, he didn't mean it! If ever again . . . ' One speaks with a parent like that. But to judges one says, 'He didn't do it; he didn't intend it! The witnesses are false and the charge is made up!' Say, Caesar, that you are a judge in Ligarius' case, and investigate in which camp he was. I am silent! Indeed I do not assemble arguments which might perhaps be strong even before a judge: 'He set out before the start of war, he was left there in peace-time, he was surprised by the war, and in the war itself he was not keen; and now he is completely yours in heart and zeal.' That's how you would plead before a judge. But I am pleading before a parent. 'He made a mistake, he did it rashly, it grieves him. I throw him on your mercy, I seek pardon for his mistake, I ask he be forgiven.' If no one has succeeded in that kind of plea, then I am using it presumptuously. But if very many, then grant help in the same way you've granted hope.

This is a tightly packed argument that requires some untangling before we can grasp its significance. Cicero first asks whether he does not seem to be occupied with the specific case of Ligarius. The particle *num*, appearing twice in this question, expects the answer 'no'. ('I don't, do I?') Here again we have deep irony, and even sarcasm. The answer to Cicero's question is, 'But yes, you do!' However, Cicero wishes whatever he has said to be referred back to the heading of Caesar's clemency. This is a very curious desire. Nothing in the *narratio* admits of any crime that would require mercy. At § 9 Cicero asks, 'Quis putat esse crimen fuisse in Africa?' ('But who thinks it a charge that he had been in Africa?') And Cicero makes the same point again at § 17: 'Scelus tu illud vocas, Tubero? Cur? Isto enim nomine illa adhuc causa caruit' ('You call it a crime, Tubero? Why? Up to now this sort of case has been free of such labels'). Elsewhere Cicero defends Ligarius with arguments from necessity. It is an odd thing that such arguments be put under the heading of an appeal to Caesar's compassion. To acquit because the charge wasn't a crime or because it was an unavoidable crime is to decide on legal grounds, not on clemency.

Cicero next says that although he has pleaded with Caesar before, he has never pleaded as one would before a parent. He has always pleaded as one would before a judge. 'He didn't do it; he didn't think it. The witnesses are false and the charge is made up!' But now comes the most curious part of all: 'Dic, te, Caesar . . . iudicem esse' ('Say you're a judge, Caesar'). What can this mean? Was Caesar not *iudex* proper in this case?[58] If so, does Cicero here mean to imply that his status as *iudex* is illegitimate? It is also curious

---

[58] Unfortunately, we do not know under what formal *aegis* this trial took place.

what comes next. Having advised what the proper method of pleading is before judges and parents, Cicero proclaims that *if* Caesar is a judge in this case, Cicero will not plead as before a judge (and through clever *praeteritio* makes plain exactly what arrows he has in his quiver, and indeed which he has used already[59]). Although Caesar is judge, Cicero will plead as he would before a parent. But Cicero does not imply that this is the only line of defence open to Ligarius. Rather, he uses this defence because it works: 'Si nemo impetravit, adroganter; si plurimi, tu idem fer opem qui spem dedisti' ('If no one has succeeded in this kind of plea, then I use it presumptuously. But if very many, then grant help in the same way you've granted hope').

So although Cicero has set out a defence of his client, he tosses that aside now to plead before Father Caesar. This is rather startling in its implications. One possibility is that Cicero does not have the evidence to prove his client's case and simply must fall back upon *deprecatio* as the last line of defence. But Cicero has just used *praeteritio* to show the evidence he could lay out if he wished, as he has done several times already. There are two other possibilities. One is that Cicero wishes to deny the validity of Caesar to sit as judge, and that this passage is actually an example of figured speech or *emphasis*. We have seen that Ramos takes *Pro Ligario* in this way.[60] On this reading the implication is, 'Let's assume for the moment you are a judge (even though we all know you are not).' Another possibility for reading figured speech in this passage is to say that Cicero tosses aside a defence of Ligarius because he knows that a defence before a dictator like Caesar would simply be unsuccessful. Gagliardi points out that

at paragraph 29, at the beginning of the *peroratio*, the affirmation *quidquid dixi, ad unam summam referri volo vel humanitatis vel clementiae vel misericordiae* picks up again the concept of the *exordium*, and by means of the rapid *climax* of publicized virtues of the dictator, it exposes them to indignation as the characteristics of a

---

[59] This *praeteritio*, by the way, undermines one of the central points of departure for Kumaniecki and Walser, who argue that Cicero never uses the strongest line of defence for Ligarius, which was his subordinate role: 'W[alser] hebt mit Recht hervor, daß der neuzeitliche Leser mit Verwunderung fragen kann, warum in Ciceros Verteidigungsrede der stärkste Entlastungsbeweis für die dem Ligarius zur Last gelegten Handlungen, die er in Verbindung mit seiner Tätigkeit in Afrika begangen haben soll, fehlt, nämlich der Hinweis auf die durchaus untergeordnete und selbständige Rolle, die er dort spielte' (Kumaniecki, 'Der Prozess', 434). And yet Cicero here mentions exactly that fact: *Legatus ante bellum profectus, relictus in pace, bello oppressus.* It is not that Cicero wishes to avoid these arguments (in which case he would not have included them), but that he constructs a defence with greater tensions, centered here not around Ligarius but around the difficulty of Caesar's position. See Montague, 'Advocacy and Politics', 562, for a brief statement of Cicero's 'normal forensic strategies' in the speech.

[60] Montague, 'Advocacy and Politics', 573, also appears to accept that Cicero denies Caesar's status as a judge, which calls into question her argument about the relative safety of *Pro Ligario*. R. R. Dyer, 'Rhetoric and Intention in Cicero's Pro Marcello,' *JRS* 80 (1990) 17–30, argues in a similar manner for *Pro Marcello* as well.

sovereign, connecting them to the idea of the uselessness, by now, of republican trials in the face of the will of an individual (see the very indicative phrase *ad unam summam*).[61]

Figured speech is hard to prove precisely because, if present, it admits of a different interpretation, and the secondary meaning is aimed at a narrow audience. In this respect figured speech is very like irony, concerning which Gagliardi observes:

On these premises, it becomes an even more difficult proposition to interpret a text in ironic terms, because problems arising from the slippery nature of irony are added to the subjectivity of the interpretation. Moreover, it is inherently impossible to establish if a text is ironic or not, since the irony, to be such, needs a cover of literal seriousness; when it is revealed as irony, it loses its more intimate status of ambiguity[62]

This text is certainly a good candidate for figured speech (especially given the oddity of 'Dic, te, Caesar ... esse iudicem'). The tone is startling, and Cicero, in making his plea for mercy, says a number of things that are simply untrue–indeed almost sarcastic–such as 'taceo, ne haec quidem conligo, quae fortasse valerent etiam apud iudicem' ('I am silent, and I do not assemble arguments which would perhaps be strong even before a judge').

A third possibility in resolving the difficulty at § 30, and the one I prefer, is that Cicero denies not the legitimacy of Caesar as judge, but the status of the charges as criminal. In fact, this view coheres better with the logical argument Cicero has constructed. He has said several times that Tubero should never have brought the case to trial, and he has constructed a defence that rests upon the legitimacy of both sides having followed their consciences during the Civil War. To plead Ligarius' case in a normal manner would be an admission, if not of Ligarius' guilt, then at least of the legitimacy of the charges. Cicero, however, denies this legitimacy. His plea for mercy here is constructed upon a moral principle, not a purely legal one. To sum up, Cicero's argument in § 30 is not 'I wouldn't normally plead this way', but rather 'I wouldn't normally plead this way for an innocent man'.

---

[61] 'Al par. 29, all'inizio della *peroratio*, l'affermazione *quidquid dixi, ad unam summam referri volo vel humanitatis vel clementiae vel misericordiae* riprende il concetto dell'esordio, e con la rapida climax delle virtù propagandate del dittatore, le addita all'indignazione come caratteristiche di un sovrano, collegandole all'idea dell'inutilità, ormai, dei processi repubblicani, di fronte all'arbitrio di un singolo (quanto mai indicativo *ad unam summam*)' (Gagliardi, *Il dissenso*, 74–5).

[62] 'Su queste premesse, a maggior ragione diventa ardua una proposta di ripensamento di un testo in chiave ironica, perché alla soggettività dell'interpretazione si aggiungono i problemi dati dalla natura sfuggente dell'ironia. Intanto, è constituzionalmente impossibile stabilire se un testo è ironico o no, giacché l'ironia, per essere tale, ha bisogno di una copertura di serietà letterale; quando si rivela come ironia, perde il sua status più intimo di ambiguità' (Gagliardi, *Il dissenso*, 7).

It should be noted moreover that a double defence, or an oscillation between various lines of defence, is not uncommon in Cicero.[63] In *Pro Cluentio*, for instance, Cicero does not get around to the specific charges against his client until §§ 143 and following of that speech. At § 144, Cicero says that he would have liked to argue the case merely on the legal grounds that the statute in question does not apply, but his client, crying, begged him to try the case on its merits and not on a legal argument. Cicero constructs his cases as the client wishes: 'In hominis honesti prudentisque iudicio non solum meo consilio uti consuevi, sed multum etiam eius, quem defendo, et consilio et voluntati obtempero' ('In trials of upright and prudent men I have not been accustomed to be guided by my own counsel alone, but I defer much also to the counsel and wishes of him whom I am defending'). And so, one is to believe, Cicero will not plead the legal argument. But quite the contrary, Cicero spends §§ 145–60 constructing a highly elaborate and technical legal argument against the charges facing Cluentius. How he does this and at the same time avoids contravening his client's wishes is not complicated: he merely assigns the legal argument to himself as an attorney wishing to establish a point of law quite distinct from his client's case.[64]

In *Pro Rabirio Perduellionis Reo* Cicero uses the same combination of practical arguments with theoretical arguments as in *Pro Cluentio*. There, in §§ 26–30, Cicero argues that it is theoretically wrong to bring charges against Rabirius, because the best men of Rabirius' age would be affected. But Cicero overrides this argument almost immediately in §§ 31–2, where he argues that regardless of legal theory, the man who committed the crime was already recognized, and it was not Rabirius.

For an interesting parallel to the sort of irony Cicero employs in § 2 of *Pro Ligario*, we might go to *Pro Milone* § 38, where Cicero says that even if Milo had killed Clodius on any of the occasions when he could have, 'cuncta civitas eam laudem pro sua vindicaret' ('the whole state would have claimed that praise as their very own'). How convincing this sort of argumentation would be in regard to Milo is another matter. The point is the same as Cicero makes in *Pro Ligario*: even if he did it, there is nothing

[63] C. P. Craig, 'The Structural Pedigree of Cicero's Speeches *Pro Archia, Pro Milone* and *Pro Quinctio*', *Classical Philology* 80 (1985), 136–7, calls attention to this strategy as found in *Pro Archia, Pro Milone*, and *Pro Quinctio*. Specifically, Craig is interested in cases in which Cicero argues 'that (*a*) his client's case satisfies the strict legal requirements for judgment in his favor, and that (*b*) even if his client's case failed to satisfy these requirements, judgment should still be in his favor'. Craig cites examples of this form from Gorgias, Antiphon, Lysias, Isaeus, Demosthenes, and Herodotus, but reveals Cicero to innovate in being the first 'to organize an entire *argumentatio*' around this device.

[64] *Clu.* 149: 'Est enim quiddam in hac causa quod Cluentius ad se, est aliquid quod ego ad me putem pertinere . . . Non enim mihi haec causa sola dicenda est' ('For there is something about this case that Cluentius thinks to pertain to himself, and something about it I think pertains to me . . . For this is not the only case which I must plead').

wrong with it. In both cases, Cicero is concerned with the status or quality of the deed.

Pro Caelio affords another example of Cicero's double defence. There, he offers almost contradictory arguments in rapid sequence about how the jury should take into account Caelius' youth. In § 28 of that speech, Cicero implies that the jury should forgive Caelius for any youthful indiscretions, because many people indulge in youthful indiscretions and go on to live perfectly upright lives: 'Datur enim concessu omnium huic aliqui ludus aetati, et ipsa natura profundit adulescentiae cupiditates' ('for by the consent of all a little playing around is given to that time of life, and nature herself pours into the heart the desires of young manhood'). So, one seems to think, Caelius is to be excused because everyone sows wild oats (with the implication that Caelius does too), and most end up just fine. But in § 29, Cicero says that the prosecution spoke against vices so successfully 'quod uno reo proposito de multorum vitiis cogitabamus' ('because, although only one defendant was brought forward, we were thinking of the vices of many'). One must not condemn Caelius because of the vices common to his age; so Cicero argues in § 30. Don't assume Caelius sows wild oats just because everyone else does! We could turn to other examples in other speeches; Cicero was in the habit of offering multiple lines of defence, and the presence of one within a speech does not necessarily invalidate another.

Having now offered a double defence for Ligarius, Cicero gives in §§ 31–7 the usual parade of distraught kinsmen and neighbours, and he asserts that Ligarius' pardon is not only good for these people, but also good for the state. In the closing section of §§ 37–8, Cicero once more highlights the absolute importance of Caesar's clemency. But the last line of the speech is key:

Quare cum utilius esse arbitrer te ipsum quam aut me aut quemquam loqui tecum, finem iam faciam; tantum te admonebo, si illi absenti salutem dederis, praesentibus te his daturum.

Wherefore since I think it more useful that you yourself speak than that I or anyone else speak to you, I will now close. Only I will advise you, that if you grant safety to the absent [Ligarius], you will be granting safety to all these men who are present.

Here Cicero recalls §§ 17–19, and ties the case to the larger cause of the Pompeians and, ultimately, of the state. If Caesar chooses to condemn, he will establish a precedent that affects not only Ligarius, still in exile, but also everyone standing in the Forum that day. If he acquits, he will preserve the safety not only of one exiled Pompeian, but also the safety of everyone who fought in the Civil War.[65]

---

[65] Montague, 'Advocacy and Politics', 569, in reference to the *argumentatio*, observes: 'Cicero deals not with Ligarius' circumstances, but with the question of what it means to have been a Pompeian, and with Caesar's postwar image.'

iv

With only one or two exceptions, the virtually unanimous judgement has been that this speech is a straightforward *deprecatio*. I would like to suggest that *Pro Ligario* is not a *deprecatio*, or that if it is, it is so only in the most restricted and technical sense.

One indication of this strategy might be Pansa's appearance in the *exordium*. Following a close reading of the first paragraph, one might be led to believe that Pansa and Cicero did not make a coordinated defence. One sometimes gets the impression, as for instance in *Pro Caelio*, that Roman defence teams coordinated their speeches and would perhaps have dealt with different areas of the defence. But it is noteworthy that Cicero does not make reference to task-sharing here, nor does he take up just one element of the defence. Cicero includes a *narratio* in *Pro Ligario*, although the *narratio* was often given by Cicero to another counsel for the defence so that he would be free to deal with other matters.[66]

On this reading, Cicero may have wished to offer his client a vigorous defence, or might have wished to pursue some other line of defence than *deprecatio*. But Pansa spoke first, and once he had laid out his confession, Cicero had no choice but to follow suit in some manner. So, he chose to give a *deprecatio*, but one wholly specious and insincere. We can detect a note of exasperation, or pretended exasperation, in Cicero's tone at § 1. Pansa has dared to confess, strengthened perhaps by familiarity with Caesar, and he has left the case *non integrum*. Cicero is too clever to be backed into a defence, and so he offers a speech which both is *deprecatio* but more truly is not. This reading does not require us to imagine Cicero blindsided at the bar by his fellow defence counsel (although that is one possibility). Perhaps it is Cicero who does the blindsiding. If I wished to follow scholars who view the speech as a put-up job, then I might imagine Cicero using an ironical *deprecatio* in order to get around Caesar. Nor must we imagine that this rhetorical confession of *aporia* be taken at face value; it may be a highly ironic (and therefore safer) way of registering dissent in the handling of the case. The point is that Cicero will not be forced into a defence, but will construct one according to the situation.

The only three parts of the speech which can plausibly be read as *deprecatio* are the *exordium*, which we have shown is highly ironic; § 30, which is either figured speech or, more likely, a denial that the allegations are

---

[66] Rhetorical theory calls for leaving out the *narratio* in a weak case and peppering the facts throughout the speech so as to put the best possible face on things (*Inv.* 1.30), and yet Cicero takes pains to give a clear *narratio* in *Pro Ligario*. On possible implications of the formal structure, see Montague, 'Advocacy and Politics', esp. 559–60, 562 ff., and 564–6 on the *narratio*.

a matter to be tried in court; and finally the pitiful parade of weepy kinsmen and neighbours at §§ 32-6. This last section, in particular, certainly contains elements which one might expect in a *deprecatio*.[67] The *topos* is hardly unusual, however, and similar rhetoric can be found at *Pro Caelio* 79-80, *Pro Fonteio* 45-6, *Pro Flacco* 106, *Pro Cn. Plancio* 102, *Pro Archia Poeta* 31, *Pro Murena* 88-90, *Pro Rabirio* 48, and *Pro Sulla* 89. A careful reading of these passages will show that there is not a single element in the *topos* as it appears in *Pro Ligario* which does not occur in one of these other speeches. So, although §§ 32-6 are clearly meant to arouse pity, there is nothing unique in them to *deprecatio*. Moreover, the key element of a *deprecatio* is the admission of guilt,[68] and this is an admission Cicero makes only ironically.

Must we deny that *Pro Ligario* can plausibly be read as *deprecatio*? This is not necessary. Many scholars who place the speech as *deprecatio* (not least Quintilian!) are perceptive and have said much to illuminate understanding. Quintilian is a trustworthy critic and he classes the speech as *deprecatio* (although it must be pointed out that he was in a historical situation more likely to see *deprecatio*). In fact, he places the speech in his section on *deprecatio* even despite the obviating defence which Cicero mounts, and which Quintilian notices:

Quamquam illae quoque apud C. Caesarem et triumviros pro diversarum partium hominibus actiones, etiamsi precibus utuntur, adhibent tamen patrocinia; nisi hoc non fortissime defendentis est dicere, Quid aliud egimus, Tubero, nisi ut, quod hic potest, nos possemus? Quodsi quando apud principem aliumve, cui utrum velit liceat, dicendum erit, dignum quidem morte eum, pro quo loquemur, clementi tamen servandum esse vel talem, primum omnium non erit res nobis cum adversario sed cum iudice, deinde forma deliberativae magis materiae quam iudicialis utemur.

---

[67] P. MacKendrick, *The Speeches of Cicero: Context, Law, Rhetoric* (London, 1995) scoffs at the idea that *Pro Ligario* is not a *deprecatio* (425), citing this passage *inter alia*. Montague, 'Advocacy and Politics', 562 n. 14, sees *deprecatio* only in the *exordium* and *conclusio*.

[68] MacKendrick, *The Speeches of Cicero*, 425. See also *Her.* 2.25: 'Deprecatione utemur cum fatebimur nos peccasse, neque id inprudentes aut fortuito aut necessario fecisse dicemus, et tamen ignosci nobis postulabimus' ('We will use the *deprecatio* when we confess that we did the wrong, do not say we did it from ignorance, chance, or necessity, and still beg for pardon'). Confessing the wrong is the very first condition of this plea. See also Lausberg, *Handbuch*, §§ 192-204, and especially the criteria in § 192: '*Deprecatio* . . . constitutes the weakest level of defence since both the unlawfulness of the deed (as in the whole of *concessio* . . .) and the wrongful intent of the perpetrator are here admitted (whereas in *purgatio* it was still possible to defend the culprit's *voluntas* . . .).' *Purgatio* admits the deed but denies intent or guilt, and Craig, 'Central Argument', 196 n. 9, sees that at least the wrongful intent is denied in this speech, so he suggests the generic category of *purgatio*. This does not seem a very promising line to me, since Cicero attempts to argue that there is no criminal deed at all. For a detailed treatment of *purgatio* see Lausberg, sections 187-90. As I emphasize, neither the unlawfulness of the deed nor the wrongful intent is admitted in this speech. It is not just that Ligarius did something wrong and didn't mean it (a position Cicero uses only hypothetically), but that he in fact did nothing wrong (a position Cicero makes clear through irony again and again).

Even those speeches delivered before Gaius Caesar and the triumvirs on behalf of members of the opposite party, although they do employ such pleas for mercy, also make use of the ordinary methods of defence. For I think you will agree with me that the following passage contains arguments of a strongly defensive character: 'What was our object, Tubero, save that we might have the power that Caesar has now?' But if, when pleading before the emperor or any other person who has power either to acquit or condemn, it is incumbent upon us to urge that, while our client has committed an offence which deserves the death penalty, it is still the duty of a merciful judge to spare him despite his sins, it must be noted in the first place that we have to deal, not with our adversary, but with the judge, and secondly that we shall have to employ the deliberative rather than the forensic style.[69]

Nevertheless, while admitting that *deprecatio* is a plausible reading, we must insist that Cicero undermines this reading. It would be convenient for Cicero if some of the speech's audience saw his remarks as straightforward praise, or perceived him to be throwing Ligarius on the mercy of the court, but the fact remains that Cicero never admits guilt, which even Quintilian above ('dignum quidem morte eum') seems not to notice.

It is important to note that this question of *deprecatio* is not mere quibbling over an item of rhetorical jargon.[70] Whether or not one admits guilt or culpability in a judicial proceeding is one of the most significant and elementary decisions in the formulation of any defence. This fact is true today just as it was in ancient times. In order better to understand what Cicero accomplishes through denying guilt, it will be useful to pose some hypothetical questions.

Under what circumstances might we imagine Cicero making a pure *deprecatio* to Caesar in a similar case? Perhaps Cicero might have done this if he had nothing to gain from detailing the reasons for Ligarius' innocence. What were the benefits of detailing this innocence? Cicero would not want a client to seem too guilty when making a *deprecatio*, because if there is too much guilt, what right has a judicial figure to let off the criminal? So, as Craig argues, Cicero simply inserts a rather flimsy defence in the middle where it will attract notice but not too much attention.[71] Perhaps better, however, if Ligarius' case has parallels with other potential cases, then there may be some benefit in detailing the reasons for Ligarius' innocence, even if Cicero feels that a simple *deprecatio* would do for gaining acquital. One does not want to set precedents so that similar cases require *deprecatio*.

---

[69] *Inst.* 5.13.5, tr. H. E. Butler.

[70] I am indebted to Oxford University Press's anonymous referee, who raised this issue and pressed me to clarify it.

[71] The problem here is that, as I have shown, Cicero does not simply insert a flimsy defence in the middle. The defence is carefully woven all through the speech. So, on the contrary, one might almost say he inserts flimsy elements of *deprecatio*.

Likewise, under what circumstances might we imagine Cicero making a more adversarial or forthright defence? Perhaps he would make such a defence if there were no need whatsoever to be conciliatory towards Caesar. This would be the case, for instance, if Cicero and Ligarius are more eager to establish a matter of principle than to secure Ligarius' return, or if Cicero is certain that he can prove Ligarius' innocence of the crimes with which he was charged so clearly that the judge has no choice but to acquit. If Cicero could do this, then a guilty verdict on Caesar's part would have been a scandal and in clear opposition to the clemency he sought to establish with the verdict on Marcellus.

In a sense these hypothetical questions constitute another version of Cicero's own difficulty. Is Caesar Judge or Father? If the former, only innocence will work as a defence. If the latter, there is no point in protesting legal innocence because the political offence against Caesar remains; one must appeal to Caesar's better nature. Either of these lines of defence alone is risky, because Caesar might respond by switching roles. The line of defence Cicero follows in *Pro Ligario*, however, catches Caesar both ways, as a good dilemma should. It points up a contradiction within Caesar's position and turns it to Ligarius' advantage.[72]

Is this contradiction in Caesar's position inherent or is it a construction of Cicero's rhetoric? The answer is not simple, but the contradiction exists. The paradox of Caesar's position must have been apparent, but it is both masterful and also bold for Cicero to point out that this paradox demands an acquittal. How might we understand Caesar's position without the *Pro Ligario*, or with a *Pro Ligario* that framed the case in different terms?[73] What could Caesar have meant this affair to be? If it was to be a proper trial, then *deprecatio* is hardly appropriate.[74] Therefore, if the speech is a *deprecatio*, it is no compliment to any revival of the courts. The *genre* itself poses dangers for Caesar:

The same formal choice of the *deprecatio* acquits at least two ironic functions: in the first place, denunciation of the overthrow in an autocratic sense of trials in Rome, now subordinate to the unilateral whim of the tyrant.... In the second place, it sets in prominence that attitude, flattering to excess, which, according to Aristotle, has the power to provoke indignation simply through the image of the

---

[72] Thanks are due to J. G. F. Powell for expansion of the ideas in this paragraph and suggestions of diction.

[73] Montague, 'Advocacy and Politics', 571, quite rightly points out that a *deprecatio* is not a formal necessity when pleading before a person who is both judge and dictator, concerned, as Craig argues, with both justice and *clementia*. Cicero performs that operation in *Pro Rege Deiotaro* without *deprecatio*.

[74] See *Rhet. Her.* 1.24 (cf. *Inv.* 2.104), which is at pains to make clear a *deprecatio* was inadmissible in court.

orator (in our case, a man of high social and intellectual intelligence) forced in humiliation to blandish a tyrant.[75]

Given these functions, why would Caesar demand a *deprecatio* or Cicero choose to plead one? On the other hand, if this speech was to be a plea before a general, then a proper defence is hardly appropriate. Our very confusion is the result of Cicero's construction. The orator adapts his arguments to Caesar's position and not only refuses to gloss over the difficulties of it, but offers alternative readings of this position which only serve to heighten its tension. By his formal choice, he invests his own argument with a sense of rigour, and diverts attention from its (perhaps disingenuous) assumptions.[76]

On the horns of this dilemma, Cicero gives Caesar the power to choose his role. The major premise is that Ligarius did nothing wrong. If Caesar is a judge, then he must not condemn a man who has committed no crime. But if Caesar would condemn Ligarius out of personal enmity or as an offended parent, then Cicero asks for mercy. If Caesar chooses to be a parent, however, he must also remember what that choice entails. As father, Caesar risks the associations of seeming to be a *paterfamilias*, treating the entire state as his house.[77] Caesar was given the title *parens patriae* by 45 or 44,[78] and certainly there may have been hints or discussions of such an honour as early as the time of this speech in 46. Weinstock writes of this new title:

The consequences were far-reaching. His relation to his fellow citizens was completely changed. They all were now bound to him, like the son to his father, by *pietas*, began to pray for his welfare and to swear by it, to worship his Genius as if it were their own. And conversely those who had broken this bond and were excluded from the community, the exiles, were not allowed to show themselves in his presence, just as a banished son was not allowed to return to the house of his father. It was the first step towards the introduction in Rome of a relationship which existed in the Greek world between the ruler and his subjects.

If Caesar chooses to act as father, Cicero has constructed an argument that shows Caesar using *patria potestas*, making the *res publica* his own household, pardoning and forgiving as he chooses.[79] The fact that such an honour had not yet been formally ceded presents no difficulty; given an atmosphere in

---

[75] 'La stessa scelta formale della deprecatio assolve ad almeno due funzioni ironiche: in primo luogo, denuncia l'involuzione in senso autocratico dei processi a Roma, ora subordinati alla sola volontà del tiranno.... In secondo luogo, pone in risalto quell'atteggiamento adulatorio fino all'eccesso, valido, secondo Aristotele, per provocare indignazione con la sola immagine dell'oratore (nel nostro caso, un uomo di alta levatura sociale ed intellettuale) costretto all'umiliazione di blandire un tiranno' (Gagliardi, *Il dissenso*, 54–5).

[76] C. P. Craig, *Form as Argument in Cicero's Speeches: A Study of Dilemma* (Atlanta, 1993) 171.

[77] See Weinstock, *Divus Julius*, ch. 10, 'Parens Patriae'.   [78] Ibid. 200.

[79] Thanks are due to Elaine Fantham for pointing me in the right directions with regard to Caesar as *paterfamilias*.

which the honour soon will be formalized, Cicero's construction can only be provocative.

We might also say that with this dilemma, Cicero gives Ligarius the power to choose. Marcellus was pardoned but had no desire to come home. There was clearly the potential to offend the pardoned simply by the act of pardoning, as Gagliardi notes: 'Grace is also then an action of deep contempt for the exile, which he will show himself to have understood fully, accepted unwillingly and interpreted in the correct sense of an affirmation of the absoluteness of Caesarian power and of a benefit granted unilaterally from a sovereign to a subject.'[80] Cicero had a difficult time convincing Marcellus to return,[81] but what if he could have created room for multiple interpretations of the judgement? In constructing his dilemma Cicero seems to allow Ligarius exactly this choice: to decide under which terms he wants to return.

Craig's typology of Ciceronian dilemma indicates dilemma aimed at the audience, the opponents, the client, and even Cicero himself.[82] Here we have an innovation: a dilemma aimed at the judge, and extending throughout the entire speech. In *Pro Ligario*, Cicero gives a double defence that is at once a way for his client to save face, a dilemma aimed at forcing Caesar into an acquittal, and a brilliant and independent piece of rhetoric.

---

[80] 'La grazia, poi, è anche un atto di profondo disprezzo per l'esule, che quegli mostrerà di aver compreso pienamente, accettandola malvolentieri e intendendola nel giusto senso di affermazione dell'assolutezza del potere cesariano e di beneficio concesso unilateralmente da un sovrano ad un suddito' (Gagliardi, *Il dissenso*, 21). [81] *Fam.* 4.9.

[82] Craig, *Form as Argument*, 179.

15

Epilogue: Cicero and the Modern Advocate

John Laws

In everything that follows there are connections, similarities, and differences between the courts of Cicero's Rome and the practice of the advocate's profession in modern England. I am mostly interested in comparisons, not judgements. Only an unintelligent reader (and, of course, there will be none) will be bothered if he finds anachronisms.

i. The Ethics of the Advocate

In the first century BC the background to the practice of the law by advocates in the courts of Rome was one of violence and intimidation; they had come to be included in the armoury of political activity. The tribune Tiberius Sempronius Gracchus had been murdered by senators and their friends in 133 BC. His brother Gaius was killed twelve years later. The disastrous Social War, in which Cicero served, followed in the early years of the first century (91–89). Then there was the dictatorship of Sulla, who in 82, according to Plutarch (*Sulla* 4), 'now devoted himself entirely to the work of butchery'. Sherwin-White says:

Cicero's writings reveal the ambiguous and contradictory attitudes towards the concepts of law and self-help to which he and other Romans were reduced when they found themselves in the no-man's land where the city-state fails to control partisan violence.[1]

So in the case which made Cicero an immediate reputation, the defence of Sextus Roscius of Ameria in 80 BC on a charge of parricide, Cicero explained that 'notable orators and eminent citizens' remained 'firmly rooted in their seats' and, though sympathetic, did not undertake the

---

[1] A. N. Sherwin-White, review of A. W. Lintott, *Violence in Republican Rome*, *JRS* 59 (1969) 286.

defence of Roscius 'owing to the hazardous times in which we live' (*propter iniquitatem temporum*). Fascinating and alien to the modern advocate is the fact that Cicero thought it necessary or desirable to go on to explain to the judges his own motives for taking the brief:

You may well ask, then, my real motive in undertaking this defence of Sextius Roscius, which the others were so reluctant to touch. Well, my motive was this. These men I am speaking of are important, authoritative figures. Now, if any of them had made a statement, if anything in this statement had possessed political implications–a thing which would have been inevitable in a case like the present one–then people would have made out that he was meaning a great deal more than he had actually intended to. But I, on the contrary, can say every single thing that needs to be said, and say it with the most complete freedom, without there being the slightest question of my speech becoming known or achieving publicity to anything like the same degree. . . .

And another reason why I accepted the commission is this . . . the approach to myself came from men whose friendship I regard as carrying enormous weight; I cannot forget all the services I have received from them, not to speak of the high positions they occupy in the state. The kindness they have done me, as well as the importance of their rank, seemed to me too great to disregard; and so I felt that I could not possibly ignore their wishes.

Those are the reasons why I agreed to undertake Roscius' defence. It is not a question of having been singled out as the most talented pleader.[2]

No barrister in an English court (at least, no competent one) would expatiate on why he had taken the brief, and if he did so the court would regard it as unprofessional and inappropriate. He takes the brief because he is obliged to do so by the 'cab-rank' rule: that is, he is required by his profession's rules of conduct to take any case that comes his way if it is within his field of expertise, unless he is otherwise engaged or would be professionally embarrassed, and the case is offered at a proper fee. He may welcome it; he may not.

The culture of the English Bar,[3] and the value attributed to it, rests largely on its independence, in particular its independence from the State. This is very real. Daily in the High Court counsel appear to advance arguments to the effect that the executive government has arrived at an unlawful decision in such sensitive fields as immigration and political asylum.

---

[2] *Rosc. Am.* 1–5. The translation is Michael Grant's, published in *Cicero, Murder Trials* (Harmondsworth, 1975). The Introduction to the volume is a very useful *vade mecum* to the context of Cicero's defence speeches in homicide cases, and I acknowledge, with pleasure, the extent to which I have drawn on it.

[3] The extension of rights of audience to solicitors in the higher courts in England has been very contentious, but does not, I think, affect what I have to say; and nothing I have written in this chapter implies any views about it.

Defendants accused of horrific terrorist offences are represented in the Crown Court before judge and jury by leading and junior counsel at the public expense. There is no question of counsel being criticized for doing so. We take all this for granted. None of it was true in Cicero's time. If an advocate then was prepared to stand up for his client in the face of hostile vested interests, where to do so might risk his own advancement or even his personal safety, he might do it out of duty to a patron, or (most likely) the allure of some yet greater interest of his own, or out of his own courage and conscience; or any combination of these. It would not be because, simply, that was what was expected and required of him by his profession, by the court, and by the public. And the Roman advocate's motives, no doubt, were not unaffected by the fact that he was forbidden to accept fees for his services. Moreover the possibility of the advocate's acting with anything like what we would regard as independent professional judgement was further undermined by the circumstance that prosecutions were not undertaken by a public authority whose duty before the case was launched was to consider objectively whether there was sufficient evidence to offer a likelihood of conviction and whether it was in the public interest to proceed.[4] In Cicero's Rome prosecutions were brought by private individuals. Wolfgang Kunkel says:

Every citizen of good reputation was, in principle, permitted to initiate a prosecution (except in the case of the procedure before the *quaestio de iniuriis*) ... The motives of the prosecutors were naturally very varied. Besides an injured party's thirst for vengeance ... enmities which had nothing to do with the crime in question played a great part; and so, above all, did greed for money, for the criminal statutes promised rewards of considerable size for the victorious prosecutor: indeed, in the case of capital condemnation the prosecutor actually received a proportion of the confiscated property. Without doubt there were many people who made a business of instituting prosecutions, and very few who in instituting them thought only of the public interest.[5]

While in the United Kingdom we are right to be proud of our powerful tradition of independent advocacy, it is easy to forget that much of its strength rests on the fact of its general acceptance; no one—at least no one sensible—disapproves of it. In particular *government* does not disapprove of it—quite the reverse. In the criminal courts, as I have said, the defendants charged with grave offences are regularly represented by leading and junior counsel at the public expense. I am not here concerned with the arrangements under which they are paid out of legal aid. What I am at pains to

---

[4] This is, I hope, a fair summary in very short form of the duty of the Director of Public Prosecutions and the Crown Prosecution Service in England.
[5] W. Kunkel, *An Introduction to Roman Legal and Constitutional History* (Oxford, 1966) 64.

emphasize is the cultural, endemic nature of the legal profession's independence. No one raises an eyebrow when a QC who not long before was briefed to defend an accused on a terrorist murder charge is raised to the High Court bench. And it is generally regarded as a virtue for barristers in criminal practice to take briefs both for prosecution and defence;[6] it tends to enhance objective judgement, and to discourage the vice of the advocate falling in love with his cause–a vice which Cicero and his contemporaries would simply not have seen as such. Indeed he and they would be likely to accept a case *precisely because* of their connections with the client.[7]

In the British jurisdictions[8] there is nothing dishonourable for counsel to take a brief in the most unpopular cause imaginable; indeed, other things being equal, it is his *duty* to do so. His client may be as morally repulsive as you could suppose; the case against him, on an objective view of the evidence, may seem insuperable; but he is obliged by his very profession of barrister to run his client's case as tenaciously as he can, however unpromising it is, restricted only by his duty to the court. That is an over-riding duty: he must not deceive the court, either as to the evidence or the law. This was not the culture of Cicero's Rome.

I may enter a parenthesis here about the old chestnut–a favourite open-ing gambit at a drinks party, where someone asks a barrister how he can defend someone he knows to be guilty. Quite sophisticated people seem to have difficulty with this, yet the answer is perfectly simple. Dr Johnson had it right in 1773:

A lawyer has no business with the justice or injustice of the cause which he under-takes, unless his client asks his opinion, and then he is bound to give it honestly. The justice or injustice of the cause is to be decided by the judge.[9]

The underlying principle, of course, is that every man is entitled to have his case, criminal or civil, tried by an impartial court with the benefit of

---

[6] However, there are certainly members of the criminal Bar who only defend or only prose-cute. At the Central Criminal Court (the Old Bailey) there is a *cadre* of barristers who only prosecute. They are known as Treasury Counsel (not to be confused, confusing though it is, with the office of First Junior Counsel to the Treasury, to which I will refer shortly). I understand this to be justified, or sought to be justified, by the needs of the Director of Public Prosecutions to have uninterrupted access to a team of high quality specialist prosecuting counsel, having regard to the unremitting stream of very heavy cases at the Old Bailey, not a few of which are of particular pub-lic importance or attract an especially heightened glare of publicity. I believe there are some bar-risters who only defend because of their personal views about authority or the establishment, call it what you will; if there are, I think it is a breach of the cab-rank rule. Of course a barrister may rightly get a name as a formidable defender, as did Sir Edward Marshall Hall KC, of whom more later. [7] Cf. *Off.* 2.51 (cited below, p. 407).

[8] That is: England and Wales; Scotland; Northern Ireland. These are all separate jurisdictions.

[9] R. W. Chapman (ed.) *Johnson's Journey to the Western Islands of Scotland and Boswell's Journal of a Tour to the Hebrides with Samuel Johnson, LL.D.* (Oxford, 1924) 175.

counsel. If counsel were allowed to refuse the brief because the evidence against the client appeared so strong that he and any other reasonable man–including, it may be, anyone else in the Temple to whom the brief was returned–were driven to believe that the client was going to lose, he would be deprived of a trial in which he was properly represented; he would end up represented, if at all, by the incompetent or the unscrupulous, or the briefless barrister to whom any case is a blessing.[10] That would be barbarous.

In the field of civil cases, the institutional independence of the advocate's profession in England is perhaps clearest in the context of judicial review litigation, in which executive decisions taken by government ministers or in their name are challenged every day in the court calendar. Counsel appearing in court against the government in such cases are judged solely by their professional competence. They are so judged by the court itself, which *expects* a good point to be taken against the government if there is one. They are also so judged by the government itself. A very considerable proportion of the heaviest government litigation is taken by First Junior Counsel to the Treasury, which is a misleading (though historically hallowed) title for the barrister appointed by the Attorney General to conduct the leading cases in which the government appears as a party in the higher courts and in the European Court of Justice at Luxembourg. But there is so much government work that the Treasury Junior can by no means do all of it. Some government cases are conducted by silks–Queen's Counsel; much is done by junior barristers (that is, not silks) appointed by the Attorney General to one of three panels of counsel whom government departments are authorized to instruct. Unlike the Treasury Junior, silks and the members of the panels briefed by the government are not restricted to Crown work.[11] They may regularly be instructed against the government, and just as often on its behalf.[12] Junior Counsel not yet on a

---

[10] What may in short be called rights of due process are guaranteed by Article 6 of the European Convention on Human Rights and Fundamental Freedoms, incorporated into the law of the United Kingdom by the Human Rights Act 1988: 'In the determination of his civil rights and obligations or of any criminal charge against him, everyone is entitled to a fair and public hearing within a reasonable time by an independent & impartial tribunal established by law.'

[11] The Treasury Junior takes no private, that is non-government, clients. This is an exception to the cab-rank rule, justified and accepted by the profession on the grounds of necessity. First, he may be called on at any time to give urgent advice or appear in court for the government at extremely short notice, so that it would be unfair to the private client if he had to drop the latter's case at the last minute; and the pressure of government work, to which he is obliged to give priority, is so great that he could not do justice to his private client's interests. Secondly, he is privy to some of the inner workings of government and to what is sometimes extremely confidential information, knowledge of which would put him in an impossible position if he were obliged to accept briefs against the Crown. What is important for present purposes is that the exception to the cab-rank rule *needs* to be justified.

[12] It is true that some sets of barristers' chambers have a name as 'establishment' sets, and others as 'anti-establishment' sets. The reasons are not straightforward, but it is a very bad thing.

panel, who come to the notice of the Treasury Solicitor because of the quality of their work *against* the government, may be considered for, and offered, a panel appointment for that very reason.

I may add a word about my own experience as Treasury Junior for seven years between 1984 and 1992. Over that period the work involved an increasing majority of public law cases, brought by judicial review or similar proceedings, in which actions or decisions of government were challenged by affected parties as being unlawful. I had not infrequently to give advice to government departments in cases of considerable political sensitivity, as my predecessors and successors in the office must also have done. There was not a single occasion on which any pressure of any kind was put upon me to give what might be seen as convenient advice, or to conduct a case in court other than in accordance with the Bar's strictest professional standards. If any such suggestion had even been hinted at, it would have been regarded as entirely outrageous; it would also have been so regarded by the Law Officers and by the Lord Chancellor, and by the senior judiciary if they heard of it. Of course no such suggestion was made, and it never occurred to me or, I am sure, to anyone else that it might be. All the government was concerned with was my competence at the work (as to which, were I Cicero, I would no doubt roundly disavow any claim).

In the same vein, I recall some occasions on which the applicant for relief against the government was incompetently represented, and if I thought he had a point but had not seen it, I put it to the court myself, even though I was acting for the respondent government department. I claim no credit whatever for this; it was what the court expected, and it was what *my clients expected*. It required no courage on my part, nor any unlooked-for independence. It is merely a function of the legal culture to which court, government, and advocate are alike committed.

The virtue of all this is an institutional virtue; it is not a virtue of particular individuals, though individuals have certainly contributed to it over time. It is too easy to forget the demands of personal courage and determination exacted of an advocate—and, indeed (and perhaps especially), the judges—in the courts of a place where the culture promotes no such ideal. Across the world there are nowadays lamentable instances of that very thing. It is not for us to sit back in cosy self-congratulation; the independence of Bar and Bench has been given to us, we have not in this generation created it. It is certainly our duty to defend it without compromise if it is threatened, but it is also our duty to lend support, wherever it is proper and legitimate to do so, to the legal professions in places where it has to be fought for.

All this brings me back to Cicero. It is interesting he always preferred to defend in criminal cases, although, of course, he had a spectacular success as a prosecutor against Verres (70 BC). In his defence of Roscius he expresses this preference with an insouciant hypocrisy which, as so often with Cicero, is maddening but engaging for its sheer *chutzpah*:

If I enjoyed being an accuser, there are other people I should prefer to accuse, engaging in cases that would advance my career. But this I have decided not to do, as long as the option remains open to me. For real respect is earned by improving one's reputation by one's own merits, not by climbing upon the distresses and disasters of someone else.[13]

In the Roscius case Chrysogonus, the man behind the prosecution, was a favourite freedman of the dictator Sulla. I think it is not too romantic a view to regard Cicero's defence as an instance of courage displayed by the independent advocate in the face of the State's power, even though it is true that Cicero was very careful to mount no attack on Sulla himself.

In the treatise *De Officiis*, written much later, Cicero offered a longer explanation of his preference for defending:

There is no need ... to have any scruples about occasionally defending a person who is guilty–provided he is not really a depraved or wicked character. For popular sentiment requires this; it is sanctioned by custom, and conforms with human decency. The judges' business, in every trial, is to discover the truth. As for counsel, however, he may on occasion have to base his advocacy on points which *look like* the truth, even if they do not correspond with it exactly ... the greatest renown, the profoundest gratitude, is won by speeches defending people. These considerations particularly apply when as sometimes happens, the defendent is evidently the victim of oppression and persecution at the hands of some power and formidable personage. That is the sort of case I have often taken on. For example, when I was young, I spoke up for Sextus Roscius of Ameria *against the tyrannical might of the dictator Sulla* (my emphasis).[14]

Perhaps all men embroider history when they write about themselves. But the passage is more interesting than its somewhat loaded recall of Roscius' case. It shows very clearly that the Roman advocate regarded his client's merits as highly relevant to his decision to take the case.

The modern advocate's ethics, however, are by no means only concerned with the virtues of courage and independence and the cab-rank rule. I have mentioned his duty to the court, which in our jurisdiction is a permanent obligation. Cicero would not have recognized such a duty as we now conceive it. Quintilian said, 'Cicero boasted that he had thrown dust in the eyes of the jury in the case of Cluentius'.[15] It has a modern ring.

---

[13] *Rosc. Am.* 83 (Grant's translation). Cf. *Off.* 2.48 ff. One can perhaps see why Peter Green, *Classical Bearings* (London, 1989) 149 referred to Cicero as 'that stupefyingly respectable bourgeois politician'; but he was so much more than that.

[14] *Off.* 2.51. Translation by Michael Grant, *Cicero, The Good Life* (Harmondsworth, 1971).

[15] *Inst.* 2.17.21: 'tenebras se offudisse iudicibus'. Cluentius was charged with murder. Pliny the Younger (of whom more below) regarded this as the best of Cicero's speeches (*Ep.* 1.20.4).

There are some present-day English barristers who might make the same boast of their latest triumph down at the Old Bailey. But not the best ones. You must not deceive the court; you must not misrepresent the law, or the evidence. The principle is easy enough to apply when the case is heard by a professional judge without a jury. Apart from anything else, most judges' eyes are, I hope, immune to the throwing of dust. But what price the throwing of dust before a jury of laymen?

Juries' common sense and powers of concentration are, I think, much underestimated. But because they try all cases where the defendant is arraigned in the Crown Court and pleads not guilty, their remit includes complex frauds; and in such cases the defence advocate's best weapon can be the sheer scale and detail of the case. The jury may simply be worn down by it. Counsel for the defence, while behaving perfectly properly and honourably, may require the Crown to spend an unconscionable welter of time in proving a range of facts and matters which are not at the centre of the dispute, which, in the end, as likely as not, will simply be whether the defendant had acted dishonestly. The way in which these cases ought best to be managed is the subject of current discussion. There is, I think, a question in cases of this kind as to the relation between the advocate's duty to the court and his duty to his client.

However that may be, the duty to the court is generally clear. I think Cicero would at least have recognized one of its pragmatic features: if you deceive the court, and are found out, it will not trust you next time.

ii. The Art of the Advocate

The art of advocacy is, of course, the art of persuasion. Cicero's spectacular success depended on a mixture of flattery, emotional appeal, and the force of argument. In the *De Optimo Genere Oratorum* 1.3 he said:

The best of orators is one who by his speech informs, entertains, and persuades the minds of his audience. It is his duty to educate; his privilege to entertain; and of necessity he must persuade.

In 70 BC Cicero undertook the prosecution of Verres for extortion in Sicily. The defence brief was held by his senior Hortensius, who was then preeminent at the Roman Bar. According to the usual account, Verres gave up after the *actio prima* of Cicero's presentation, and went into exile. There were still five speeches to come, and which have come down to us, in the *actio secunda*. Verres' flight after the *actio prima* puts me in mind of a nice story of a great leader of the North-East Circuit, Henry Scott QC, who sometime in the 1960s had the brief to prosecute a serious charge in which until the trial the defendant had vigorously contested the accusation. Scott delivered his opening speech–*actio prima*–to the jury. There was then the lunchtime adjournment; the defendant went to see his lawyers, indicated his intention to change his plea to guilty, and said, 'I am not now so convinced of my innocence as I was before I heard Mr Scott's speech.' Cicero, perhaps, lacked the gift of brevity, which to the modern English judge, required to listen to arguments good and bad, is a prince among the advocate's virtues. In another case in which he was prosecuting, Scott QC came to make his closing speech to the jury after all the evidence was over including that of the defendant who gave a full account of himself, protesting his extremely improbable innocence. Usually Crown counsel at this stage analyses the evidence, often in some detail, exposing the points which might fairly lead the jury to convict the defendant. Not Scott. He said, 'Members of the jury, are there fairies at the bottom of your garden?' and sat down. The jury convicted.

The art of persuasion is not single, uniform. Some advocates are wonderful with the facts, others with the law (some are bad at both, and they should not be in practice; some are good at both). In the British jurisdiction the former will generally find their successes in the first instance courts, and in particular before juries. The latter are more likely to flourish in the appellate courts; and appellate advocacy is a distinct form of the art. In Cicero's Rome there was not the hierarchy of appeals we possess, and records of his cross-examination of witnesses–often the stuff of first instance trials–have, perhaps inevitably, not come down to us. He was clearly a master of the facts, as the cases of Roscius, Cluentius, Verres, and others amply demonstrate.

For the barrister interested in his own posterity (and it has always been a profession of prima donnas) in one sense advocacy is a melancholy art. Its brilliance fades as soon as the words are spoken. Its red blood is in the seduction of the tribunal, judge or jury, then and there. If you try to recall its tinder and its sparks, you hear an echo, not a voice. The British advocate has to improvise; especially at the appeal level, he is likely to be interrupted, closely questioned, his arguments tested, by the judge or judges. There is no modern practice of publishing speeches after the event, 'written up' (*confecta*), as Cicero did.[16] Indeed, the dialectical nature of live advocacy would make it almost impossible. The nearest we get is the account of counsel's arguments which appear in the official Law Reports, but these make pretty dry reading, however good the advocate. However, this is very much the common law tradition;

---

[16] *OCD* 3rd edn. (Oxford, 1996) 156.

in the civil law systems the bulk of the argument is presented in written briefs, and the role of oral submissions is distinctly subordinate. Counsel's address to the court is frequently severely time-limited. I have heard it said that whereas the English advocate expects to be interrupted and questioned by the court (indeed, if he is good at his job he may welcome it, for it can help him drive home his case), the French advocate would regard it as an insult. When I first appeared in the European Court of Justice at Luxembourg [17] in the early 1980s, I was greatly struck by the court's lack of response to argument; there seemed to be very little debate. The Advocate General and the *Juge Rapporteur* assigned to the case (his principal task is the drafting of the judgement) would ask some questions; they would generally do it in the decorous Continental manner, at the end of counsel's speech. And the speech was limited to thirty minutes, unless you made a justified request for further time, and I have the impression that that was rather frowned on. By the time I last went there as an advocate in 1991, there had been a significant change. The time limit remained, but I was questioned quite freely, as I recall, both during, as well as after, my thirty minutes. By this time the United Kingdom had been a Member State of the European Community (as it still was) for very nearly twice as long as when I first appeared at the Court of Justice. Many lawyers with much greater experience of practice at that court than I had would, I think, agree that the court had been influenced by the common law tradition. They were presented with advocates who were used to being interrupted, whose stock in trade was thinking on their feet, and they found it of considerable assistance.[18]

Cicero's speeches have of course come down to us in the versions which he worked up. We do not know how often he was likely to be interrupted when actually addressing the court. I have found one instance, recounted

---

[17] This is the court of the European Union and is not to be confused with the European Court of Human Rights at Strasbourg, established under the auspices of the Council of Europe, a body altogether different from the European Union. I mention this wholly elementary fact of current affairs only because the newspapers get it wrong all the time.

[18] One of the stresses and strains arising from the enlarged membership of the Union, which will become more acute with its present enlargement, concerns what one may call the language problem. The text of Community legislation in each of the languages is equally authentic. The resources of time, money, and expertise spent on the task of translation is enormous. The answer is a common official Community (or Union) language for legislation and court proceedings, which, for the avoidance of obvious national sensitivities and associated political difficulty, ought, if other things are equal, plainly to be Latin. But other things are not equal. Far too few people have the good fortune to have been taught Latin (let alone Greek).

by R. G. M. Nisbet. It concerns Cicero's description in the *Pro Milone* of the beginnings of Milo's fatal encounter with Clodius on the Appian Way. After citing a passage from the speech Nisbet says:

Cicero . . . is trying to put the murder a little later than it actually occurred, and so to suggest that Clodius had no reason for travelling. We are told that when he was pressed in court to give the time when Clodius was killed, he retorted 'sero'; the word can mean both 'late' and 'too late' (Quintilian 6.3.49).[19] However, in the published version of the speech one misses such spontaneous strokes of wit.[20]

Interrupted or not when they were delivered, Cicero's speeches as we have them are surely an echo not a voice. The written word cannot convey the power of their delivery in court. I forget who first said that history is the desire to hear the dead speak (I know the phrase from the distinguished church historian, Professor Eamon Duffy). Would there had been tape recorders in ancient Rome.

Pliny the Younger, however, entertained quite different views about the relation between a speech as delivered and its reduction to writing. In the same letter as he commended Cicero's speech in the Cluentius case, he said this (writing, of course, 150 years after Cicero):

Then it is argued that there is a great difference between a speech as delivered and the written version. This is a popular view I know, but I feel convinced (if I am not mistaken) that, though some good speeches may sound better than they read, if the written speech is good it must also be good when delivered, for it is the *model and prototype for the spoken version.* That is why we find so many rhetorical figures, apparently spontaneous, in any good written speech, even in those we know were published without being delivered; for example, in Cicero's speech against Verres: 'An artist—now who was he? Thank you for telling me; people said it was Polyclitus.'[21] It follows then that the perfect speech when delivered is that which keeps most closely to the written version, so long as the speaker is allowed the full time due to him; if he is cut short it is no fault of his, but a serious error on the part of the judge. The law supports my view, for it allows speakers any amount of time and recommends not brevity but the full exposition and precision which brevity cannot permit, except in very restricted cases. [My emphasis.][22]

---

[19] It is not however clear from Quintilian whether the response 'sero' is to be attributed to Cicero or to Milo. The ambiguity of the word puts me in mind of a peculiarity of Modern Greek. The expression 'parapoly' may mean 'too much' or 'very much'. I have a guidebook, translated from the Greek, which describes the beautiful Vikos Gorge in northern Greece as 'much too interesting'.   [20] In T. A. Dorey (ed.), *Cicero* (London, 1965) 70.
[21] The reference is to *Verr. II* 4.3. It is very arch; Cicero writes it as if he were responding to an interchange with his audience, but of course there was no audience, according to the usual view.
[22] *Ep.* 1.20, written to Tacitus. Translation by Betty Radice, *The Letters of the Younger Pliny* (Harmondsworth, 1963).

In the same letter, there shortly follows this passage:

Regulus once said to me when we were appearing in the same case: 'You think you should follow up every point, but I make straight for the throat and hang on to that.' (He certainly hangs on to whatever he seizes, but he often misses the right place.) I pointed out that it might be the knee or the heel he seized when he thought he had the throat. 'I can't see the throat,' I said, 'so my method is to feel my way up and try everything—in fact I "leave no stone unturned" ... When I am making a speech I scatter various arguments around like seeds in order to reap whatever crop comes up.'

This is interesting and *dreadful*. Pliny's view that the written speech is the template for the delivered oration hopelessly demotes the immediacy of the spoken word, of which we may be sure Cicero was a master. Aside from that, Pliny clearly thinks it good advocacy to take as long as possible and to develop every conceivable point. Nothing could be worse. His job as an advocate—it is every advocate's job—was 'to seize the throat' and sink his teeth in it. It is precisely what the worst advocates cannot do. There are not many cases with more than two or three good points in them (some, of course, have none), and the barrister who persists in ploughing through fifteen bad ones is the judge's nightmare and a menace to his client. If that is what Pliny did, I hope Regulus beat him every time. I do not care that he sat at the feet of Quintilian, whom the Emperor Vespasian had appointed as a salaried professor of rhetoric, or that he was consul at thirty-nine.

The art of advocacy is by no means all rhetoric; though even nowadays, you can get a long way with charm and a natural persuasive talent. I recall once appearing against a very senior QC in a case of some complexity. He opened his case by announcing to the judge that he was going to 'paint with a very broad brush', and addressed the court for a little under an hour, blithely eliding the technical (and undoubtedly tedious) points upon which the case actually turned. The judge was clearly impressed and I had a good deal of difficulty regaining ground. I think Cicero, admiring the rhetoric, would have been on the QC's side, and so, in a sense, am I. The best advocates (and here I will be anachronistic) are cavaliers, not roundheads.

But in a case of any real complexity—and in truth in any case—there is no substitute for painstaking preparation. You have to be absolute master of your brief. Nowadays many prosecutions brought by the Serious Fraud Office are necessarily larded with so much detail that they take weeks of preparation time by lawyers on both sides. It is painstaking, difficult, and often dreary. The task is lightened by the division of responsibility between solicitor and barrister: the former collects and assimilates the evidence, the latter turns it into a form which he can present to the court, in the first place (if he is the prosecutor) by his opening speech to the jury. The Verres case was very like a SFO prosecution. There was an enormous amount of detail. But Cicero had to act both as solicitor and barrister. As Palmer Bovie says:

Cicero was allowed one hundred and ten days in which to prepare his case, but with dispatch and energy completed the gathering of evidence and examination of witnesses in Sicily in fifty days, and returned home with the documentary proof he need to support his charges.[23]

So far as Cicero took oral testimony in Sicily, the procedure may be compared with the convenient practice in the English courts of having witnesses examined 'on commission' before the trial and at a different location. Nowadays witnesses may be questioned over a video link; as a first instance judge in one case I heard video evidence given live by an Australian witness, from Australia, while I and counsel sat in the London offices of one of the parties' solicitors. Cicero's fifty days was a remarkable feat.

Like every art, the art of advocacy is subject to changes of style. In England before the current debilitating forms of mass entertainment were available, the leading barristers were pop stars. Chief among them were great figures such as Sir Edward Marshall Hall KC, who died in 1927, F. E. Smith, who as Lord Birkenhead held office as Lord Chancellor between 1919 and 1922, and Norman Birkett KC who participated in the Nuremberg trials and was a much better advocate than a judge. The people crowded into court to watch their cases. Marshall Hall was florid, demonstrative, emotional; his appeal was nakedly to the jury's sentiment. But the style has changed: good advocacy now is much more clinical. In Cicero's case, his own style changed. As the *Oxford Classical Dictionary* has it:

As he himself observed, in his youth he had a tendency to exuberance . . . best exemplified in the *Pro Roscio Amerino* . . . this was later tempered by increasing maturity and by a change in oratorical fashion.[24]

Tempered also, I venture to think, by his studies in Athens and Rhodes from 79 to 77 BC. There he worked at philosophy, as well as oratory, and was all his life a student of philosophy; in his later years–seeking consolation for the death of his daughter Tullia–he wrote much on the subject. His substantive place as a philosopher is outside my remit, but his intellectual vigour as an advocate, and the refinement of his style, must have been fuelled by the instruction he received in his youth variously from Phaedrus the Epicurean, Philo the chief of the New Academy, and Diodotus the

---

[23] *Cicero: Nine Orations and the Dream of Scipio* (London, 1967) 18.
[24] *OCD* 3rd edn. (Oxford, 1996) 1560.

Stoic. So he brought to his practice at the Bar the breadth of mind that comes with an education not limited to the law. In recent years a remarkable proportion of talented beginners at the English Bar have graduated in subjects other than Law, which is very heartening. It has bucked the trend for training before education. However, Peter Birks, the present Professor of Civil Law in the University of Oxford, would disagree with this. I do not know whether he is acquainted with the details of Cicero's career. In the United States, law is always a postgraduate qualification; its students must generally first acquire a degree in the liberal arts. It was Sir Walter Scott who said:

A lawyer without history or literature is a mechanic, a mere working mason: if he possesses some knowledge of these, he may venture to call himself an architect.

So also if he possesses some philosophy. Law is a workhorse discipline; as an education it falls between the rigour of logic and mathematics, and the cultural wealth of the classics, history, or literature. So it needs both. Its necessary medium is language; elegance is, therefore, its virtue and handmaiden. It is as true in English as in Latin. Cicero understood much better than many modern English lawyers the delicate balance between art and logic which law and its medium constitute.

But practising lawyers also need legal academics. Until relatively recently there was an unhealthy tradition in the English legal world, whereby the practitioners–the barristers and judges–looked on academic lawyers, not to put too fine a point on it, as a lower form of life. There was even a convention (still just about current when I was called to the Bar in 1970) that the works of an academic writer could not be cited in court as possessing any authority until the author was *dead*. Similar contempt for the academic law expert existed in Cicero's Rome and he was prepared to exploit it, when it served his purpose, in his debunking of Servius Sulpicius Rufus, in the *Pro Murena*.[25] Yet it is clear that Sulpicius also remained a life-long, admired friend. Indeed, it was in Cicero's lifetime that the opinions of jurists were first to have an impact on the development of the law.[26] The modern Continental lawyers did not understand the attitude of the English legal world; indeed it is inherent in the civil law systems, derived of course from Roman law, that the work of jurists, scholarly legal writers, is an important source of legal principle. The genesis of this peculiar English tradition lies, however, in the very nature of the common law. The common law is made and evolved by the judges. The only other source of law is legislation. Academic writing is not a source of law. This certainly

---

[25] *Mur.* 28–9.
[26] See B. W. Frier, *The Rise of the Roman Jurists* (Princeton, 1985).

remains the constitutional position; but, very obviously, it has never justified the *de haut en bas* attitude towards academics which at one time prevailed. Fortunately, that is all gone. Distinguished lawyers in the universities have in recent years had enormous, and manifestly beneficial, influence on the law's development. I might (without being invidious) name two in particular, whose fields have been particular disciplines with which I am more familiar than others. They are Professor Sir William Wade QC and Professor Sir John Smith QC. Sir William's contribution to our public law has been spectacular,[27] and recognized as such in decisions of the House of Lords. No less Sir John's contribution to the criminal law.

It is interesting that Pliny, as good at gossip as he was unsound on the theory of advocacy, has a passage which across the centuries reflects what has sometimes been the successful barrister's patronizing attitude to the academic. Writing to Cornelius Mucianus he says:

> Have you heard that Valerius Licinianus is teaching rhetoric in Sicily? The news has only just come so I doubt if it will have reached you yet. It is not long since this senator of praetorian rank was considered one of the best advocates in Rome. Now he has sunk to his present position—the senator is an exile and the orator a teacher of rhetoric.[28]

The barrister's art, practised at its best, involves an alchemy; an alchemy in which intellect and personality, logic and style, combine to persuade what may be a reluctant, sceptical, or sometimes downright hostile court—or at least it offers the best possible shot. It has some connections with political speech, though in modern Britain they are indirect and sometimes do not apply at all. Cicero, who of course was at least as much a politician as a lawyer, would, I think (given the *milieu* of first-century BC Rome), not have seen much difference between these two forms of the advocate's art. But he would have recognized, must have experienced, the heady moment when you can feel the court turning in your favour. He had logic and style to the full. Budding advocates (and mature ones) should read him. Better if they can do so in Latin.

It was Cicero's misfortune to live in an extremely turbulent era; the Roman Republic, which he loved and defended, was in truth in terminal decline when he was assassinated in 43 BC on the orders of Mark Antony, Octavian, and Lepidus, the Second Triumvirate. He paid with his life for the majestic fourteen Philippics delivered against Antony. He could be forgiven for agreeing with the deeply untrue *dictum* attributed to Confucius, that it is a curse to live in interesting times. He was by nature reflective,

---

[27] As witness the 8th edition of his majestic *Administrative Law* (Oxford, 2001), written with Dr Christopher Forsyth of Robinson College, Cambridge.

[28] *Ep.* 4.11, Betty Radice's translation.

peaceable, conservative, and no doubt very self-satisfied. He had a lot to be self-satisfied about: he was a very great intellect and a very great advocate. And in the end, and I think at the beginning, he was courageous. Like many with what the Scots call 'a good conceit of themselves', he would not have wished to let himself down.

APPENDIX

Chronological List of Cicero's Known Appearances as an Advocate

This list is meant for quick reference. Further details and discussion may be found in editions of the published speeches, in Jane W. Crawford, *M. Tullius Cicero: The Lost and Unpublished Orations* (Göttingen, 1984) and *M. Tullius Cicero: The Fragmentary Speeches*, 2nd edn. (Atlanta, 1994), and in Michael C. Alexander, *Trials in the Late Roman Republic 149 B.C. to 50 B.C.* (Toronto, 1990). Titles of Cicero's extant speeches are printed in bold type.

Date (BC)   *Details of Advocacy*

81   **Pro Quinctio.** On behalf of a claim for restitution of property by
               P. Quinctius against S. Naevius. Result unknown (successful?).[1] Cicero
               mentions in the *Pro Quinctio* that he had appeared in other cases
               before this one, but we have no details.

80 or 79   On behalf of a claim to freedom by a woman of Arretium; successful
               on second hearing. *Pro Caecina* 97.[2]

80   **Pro Sex. Roscio Amerino.** Defence of Sextus Roscius of Ameria
               before a *quaestio* (with a jury of senators only) on a charge of mur-
               dering his father. Successful (*Off.* 2.51).

?79   On behalf of Titinia, wife of Cotta, in a private suit against Ser.
               Naevius.[3] Result unknown, but probably successful: the opposing
               counsel Curio lost his grip on the case. *Brutus* 217; cf. *Orator* 129.

?77   On behalf of C. Curtius, who sought restitution after the Sullan pro-
               scriptions; it is not however clear that this was a formal court appear-
               ance. *Fam.* 13.5.2–3.

?77–76   Defence of L. Varenus on murder charges under the *lex de sicariis*.
               Unsuccessful, but the speech was circulated and is quoted several
               times by Quintilian. Crawford, *Fragmentary Speeches*, 7–18.

---

[1] In this instance, early in Cicero's career, success would provide an obvious motive for publication which otherwise would be lacking. T. E. Kinsey in his edition (Sydney, 1971), followed by
Alexander (*Trials in the Late Roman Republic*, 65) suggests that Cicero lost, but gives no clear
evidence to prove this.

[2] Cicero's opponent was C. Aurelius Cotta; it is generally supposed that Cotta claimed ownership of the woman as a slave.

[3] It is stated quite clearly by Cicero that this was a private suit, but the issue is not specified.
Pace Crawford, there is no indication that it was a poisoning case; the reference to *veneficium* was
merely a heavy joke by Curio to explain his loss of memory.

?76–68   **Pro Q. Roscio comoedo**. On behalf of Q. Roscius the comic actor, in a financial claim (*condictio certae pecuniae*).

75   Defence before the governor of Sicily of unnamed noble Roman youths accused of cowardice and insubordination. Successful. Plutarch, *Cicero* 6.

74   Defence of Scamander on a poisoning charge. Unsuccessful. *Pro Cluentio* 49–55.

73   On behalf of C. Mustius against a substantial monetary claim. Successful. *Verr. II* 1.139 and schol. ad loc. (252 St.)

72   On behalf of Sthenius of Thermae for a claim to residence in Rome, before the college of Tribunes of the Plebs. Successful. *Verr. II* 2.100.

72–71   **Pro M. Tullio**. On behalf of M. Tullius (otherwise unknown; not necessarily a relative), before a jury of *recuperatores*, in a claim for damages against a neighbour for murder of his slaves. There were two hearings; the incomplete surviving speech relates to the second of them.

70   **Divinatio in Caecilium; In Verrem Actio Prima; In Verrem Actio Secunda** (divided into five 'books'). Prosecution of Verres for extortion and misgovernment in Sicily, before the *quaestio de repetundis* (senatorial jury). Successful; Verres withdrew into exile before the conclusion of the trial.

?69   **Pro M. Fonteio** (incomplete). Defence of M. Fonteius, governor of Gallia Narbonensis, for extortion, before the reformed *quaestio de repetundis* (senators, equestrians and '*tribuni aerarii*'). Probably successful (if the M. Fonteius of *Att.* 1.6.1 is the same man).

69   Defence of P. Oppius on charges relating to military offences. Crawford, *Fragmentary Speeches*, 23–32.

?69   **Pro A. Caecina**. On behalf of Aulus Caecina of Volaterrae, in a claim for restitution of property before a jury of *recuperatores*. Almost certainly successful.[4]

67   On behalf of D. Matrinius in a complaint of unfair dismissal from the post of *scriba aedilicius*, before two praetors and the two curule aediles. *Pro Cluentio* 126.

66   **Pro A. Cluentio**. On behalf of A. Cluentius Habitus of Larinum on charges of either judicial corruption or poisoning or both. Almost certainly successful.[5]

66–65   Defence of C. Manilius: the sources (for which see Crawford, *Fragmentary Speeches*, 39–41) are clear that Cicero as praetor in 66 undertook to defend Manilius at the end of the latter's term of office as tribune; the trial, early in 65, was disrupted by Manilius' gangs. The defendant was brought to trial a second time, unusually with both consuls presiding (Asc. *In Cornelianam* 60 C.); this time he offered no

---

[4] See B. Frier, *The Rise of the Roman Jurists: Studies in Cicero's* Pro Caecina (Princeton, 1985) 231–2.

[5] Cf. Cicero's triumphant comment quoted by Quint. *Inst.* 2.17.21: 'tenebras se offudisse iudicibus'.

defence and was condemned *in absentia*. The nature of the charges is unclear (*repetundae* according to Plutarch, *maiestas* according to the Scholia Bobiensia–both equally unreliable sources for this kind of information). A speech *pro Manilio* is quoted once by the lexicographer Nonius Marcellus.[6]

66–65   Defence of C. Fundanius (unknown charge). Successful. [Q. Cicero] *Comm. Pet.* 19. The speech was in circulation and is quoted a number of times by Quintilian and the grammarians; see Crawford, *Fragmentary Speeches*, 57–64.[7]

65   Defence of C. Cornelius on a charge of *maiestas*, for illegal promulgation of a bill to the popular assembly in defiance of a fellow-tribune's veto. Successful. Cicero's defence lasted four days, and the material of the defence was digested into two published speeches (Asc. *In Cornelianam* 62 C.). The prosecution speech of P. Cominius was also published (ibid.). The speeches were famous in antiquity and form the subject of a commentary by Asconius; this and other sources preserve eighty fragments. See Crawford, *Fragmentary Speeches*, 65–144.

65   Defence of C. Orchivius (unknown charge). Successful. [Q. Cicero] *Comm. Pet.* 19.

?65–4   Defence of Q. Mucius Orestinus on a charge of theft; case settled out of court. *In Toga Candida* fr. 6.

64   Defence of Q. Gallius on a charge of electoral bribery. Successful. Asc. *In Tog. Cand.* 88 C.; [Q. Cic.] *Comm. Pet.* 19. The speech was in circulation and a few fragments survive; one of them, describing a drunken party with 'the ground muddy with wine, covered with faded garlands and fishbones', is quoted in several places and was evidently famous, while another mocks the soporific and unconvincing style of the prosecuting counsel M. Calidius. See Crawford, *Fragmentary Speeches*, 145–58.

63   **Pro C. Rabirio perduellionis reo**. Defence of Gaius Rabirius on a charge of high treason (*perduellio*) before the Comitia Centuriata. Trial abandoned before a verdict was reached.

---

[6] The issues surrounding this trial or trials are complex: see the discussions in Crawford, *Lost and Unpublished Orations*, 64–9 (difficult to follow at some points) and *Fragmentary Speeches*, 33–41 (clearer and largely plausible). There has been doubt about the 'pro Manilio' referred to by Nonius, but there is no serious problem in supposing that it was Cicero's speech in defence of Manilius at the first trial; presumably Manilius' gangs would not have interrupted his own defence counsel. It can hardly be from the second trial, as Asconius tells us that Manilius did not answer the charges against him; there is no need to suppose, as Crawford does, that Cicero declined to defend him the second time, as it looks as though he did not get the opportunity to do so.

[7] This trial was the occasion for some characteristic Ciceronian witticisms. Quint. *Inst.* 1.4.14 records a joke at the expense of a Greek witness for the prosecution who could not pronounce the sound F at the beginning of Fundanius' name; and, since we happen to know (from Priscian) that Sextus Villius Annalis appeared in this trial, this may have been the occasion for the anecdote recorded in Quint. *Inst.* 6.3.86 in which Cicero, pressed to respond to the testimony of Sextus Annalis, quoted from the sixth book of Ennius' Annals (*de sexto annali*) the opening line 'quis potis ingentis causas evolvere belli?'–'Who can unfold the cause of mighty war?'

63	**Pro L. Murena**. Defence of L. Licinius Murena on a charge of electoral bribery, before the *quaestio de ambitu* under a statute passed by Cicero himself. Successful.
63	Defence of C. Calpurnius Piso before *quaestio de repetundis* on charge of unlawful execution of a provincial. Successful. *Pro Flacco* 98 (cf. Sall. *Cat.* 49).
62	**Pro P. Sulla**. Defence of P. Cornelius Sulla on a charge of implication in the Catilinarian conspiracy. Successful.
62	**Pro Archia**. Defence of the poet (A. Licinius) Archias on a charge of falsely assuming Roman citizenship. Successful.
60	Defence of Q. Caecilius Metellus Pius Scipio on charge of electoral bribery; successful. *Att.* 2.1.9.
59	Defence of C. Antonius (Cicero's consular colleague) on charges related to his government of Macedonia. Unsuccessful; Antonius was exiled. Evidence in Crawford, *Lost and Unpublished Orations*, 128–31.
59	Defence of (Minucius) Thermus in two trials; both successful. *Pro Flacco* 98.
59	**Pro L. Flacco**. Defence of L. Valerius Flaccus before the *quaestio repetundarum*. Successful.
Before 58	Appearance against M. Cispius and family in a private suit (*Red. Sen.* 21).
58–56	Defence of L. Calpurnius Bestia in six trials; successful in all but the last. *Philippic* 11.11. A trial of Bestia on 11 February 56 on a bribery charge, probably the fifth of the six, is mentioned in *Q. Fr.* 2.3.6; see also *Pro Caelio* 16, 56, 76, 78 (Caelius was the prosecutor both in February 56 and in the subsequent trial in which Bestia was convicted).
57	**De Domo Sua**. In person, before the College of Pontifices in a claim for restitution of the part of his house that had been 'consecrated' by Clodius. Successful.
?57–56	Defence of M. Cispius on bribery charge. Unsuccessful. *Pro Plancio* 75–7 and schol. (165 St.).
56	**Pro P. Sestio**. Defence of P. Sestius before the *quaestio de vi*. Successful (*Q. Fr.* 2.4.1). Also from this trial is the published **Interrogatio in P. Vatinium testem** (*In Vatinium*), the only example we have of an *interrogatio*, i.e. a speech cross-examining a hostile witness.
56	Defence of P. Asicius on charge of murdering the Alexandrian ambassador Dio. Successful. *Pro Caelio* 23–4.
56	**Pro M. Caelio**. Defence of M. Caelius Rufus before the *quaestio de vi publica*. The main charges related to public disturbances and attacks on the Alexandrian ambassadors, including the murder of their leader Dio. Successful.
56	**Pro L. Balbo**. Defence of L. Cornelius Balbus on a charge of unlawfully exercising the rights of a Roman citizen. Successful.

?56–52   Defence of T. Munatius Plancus Bursa (unknown charges). Successful.
          Fam. 7.2.3; Plutarch *Cicero* 25.[8]
55   Defence of L. Caninius Gallus (unknown charge). Probably unsuc-
          cessful (unless Caninius' conviction, Val. Max. 4.2.6, was in a later
          trial). *Fam.* 7.1.4.
?55   Defence of T. Ampius Balbus (unknown charge). *Leg.* 2.6.
54   Defence of P. Vatinius on charges of electoral bribery under the *lex
          Licinia de sodaliciis* of 55 BC Testimonia in Crawford, *Fragmentary
          Speeches*, 307–8 (no genuine fragments survive).
54   **Pro Cn. Plancio**. Defence of Gnaeus Plancius under the *lex de
          sodaliciis*. Successful.
54   On behalf of the town of Reate, objecting to a proposal by the town
          council of Interamna to block the outflow from Lake Velinus. Before
          the consuls and ten *legati*. Successful. *Att.* 4.15.5, *Pro Scauro* 27.[9]
54   Defence of C. Messius under the *lex de sodaliciis*; probably successful.
          Att. 4.15.9.
54   Defence of M. Livius Drusus on a charge of *praevaricatio*. *Att.* 4.16.5,
          4.15.9. Successful (*Att.* 4.17.5); Drusus was acquitted by four votes
          (*Q. Fr.* 2.16.3).
54   **Pro M. Scauro** (fragmentary). Defence of M. Aemilius Scaurus
          before the *quaestio de repetundis*. Successful.
54–52   Defence of M. Scaurus on a bribery charge. Scaurus was accused in
          54 (*Q. Fr.* 3.2.3) and (according to Appian *BC* 2.24) eventually con-
          victed and exiled in 52. It seems that the accusation of 54 was for
          some reason suspended and then renewed in 52; but it is also possible
          that there were two separate trials. Cicero's notes of the case were
          available to Quintilian (*Inst.* 4.1.69).
54   ?Defence of M. Valerius Messalla Rufus on a bribery charge; the evid-
          ence from Cicero's letters (Crawford, *Lost and Unpublished Orations*,
          186–7) does not sufficiently indicate whether Cicero actually spoke as
          an advocate at this trial. Messalla was acquitted.
54   Defence of A. Gabinius before the *quaestio de repetundis*. Unsuccessful.
          Rab. Post. 19; 33.[10]
54–53   **Pro C. Rabirio Postumo**. Defence of C. Rabirius Postumus on a
          charge of receiving money unlawfully extorted by Gabinius.[11]

[8] According to Plutarch, Cicero made the same comment about befogging the jury to Plancus
after this trial as, according to Quintilian, he made after the trial of Cluentius. It is more than likely
that either Plutarch or Quintilian confused the two occasions.
[9] Cicero's conscientiousness as an advocate is illustrated in the *Pro Scauro* passage by the fact
that he went in person to see the site.
[10] For the evidence on the two trials see Crawford, *Lost and Unpublished Orations*, 188–97; see
further Introd., p. 21, n. 81.
[11] There is some doubt as to the result of this case. Suet. *Claudius* 16 suggests that Postumus was
found guilty; but M. Siani-Davies, *Marcus Tullius Cicero Pro Rabirio Postumo* (Oxford, 2001) 82–4
argues that Suetonius' evidence may be confused and that Cicero may after all have succeeded in
securing an acquittal.

52   **Pro Milone**. Defence of T. Annius Milo for the murder of Clodius, before a special court set up under a law proposed by Pompey. Unsuccessful.

52   Defence of M. Saufeius in two separate trials, first under Pompey's law and secondly under the older *lex Plautia de vi*, for his involvement in the murder of Clodius. Successful in both trials, in the first by one vote, in the second by a decisive majority of 30 to 19. Asconius *In Milonianam* 54–5 C.[12]

52   Defence of P. Sestius on a bribery charge. *Att.* 13.49.1, *Fam.* 7.24.2.

?52   Defence of P. Cornelius Dolabella (unknown charges). *Fam.* 3.10.5.

52   Prosecution of T. Munatius Plancus Bursa under *lex Pompeia de vi.* Successful (Plancus was unanimously convicted, *Phil.* 6.10). *Fam.* 7.2.2; Plutarch, *Pompey* 55.4–6; Dio 40.55.4.

46   **Pro Q. Ligario**. Defence of Q. Ligarius before Caesar, sitting in public as sole judge, on a charge of *perduellio*. Successful.

46   **Pro Rege Deiotaro**. Defence of King Deiotarus of Galatia before Caesar sitting in private, on a charge of attempting to murder Caesar. Successful.

Appearances of Unknown Date:

(before 48)   Defence of C. Popillius Laenas on a charge of parricide, at the request of M. Caelius. Successful. Val. Max. 5.3.4, Plutarch *Cicero* 48.1, Sen. *Contr.* 7.2.1, etc.

(before 44)   Defences of one Acilius in two capital trials. Successful. *Fam.* 7.30.3.

---

[12] Cicero's appearance and success in the two trials of Saufeius is noteworthy after the failure of his defence of Milo. Clearly he had not lost credit as a defence advocate. It would be interesting in the highest degree to know what Cicero's line of argument was in the defence of Saufeius, given that (according to Asconius) he had a worse case than Milo. But the speeches were apparently not circulated; one may presume the reason to be that Saufeius was too unimportant a client for his successful defence to do Cicero any credit at this stage in his career—or else that Cicero did not believe in his own arguments.

LIST OF WORKS CITED

ACHARD, G., *Pratique rhétorique et idéologie politique dans les discours "optimates" de Cicéron* (Leiden, 1981).

ACHESON, G. J., *The Caesarian Orations* (Johannesburg, 1965).

ADAMIETZ, J. (ed.), *Marcus Tullius Cicero Pro Murena*. Mit einem Kommentar herausgegeben. Texte zur Forschung 55 (Darmstadt, 1989).

ALBRECHT, M. VON., 'Das Prooemium von Ciceros Rede pro Archia poeta und das Problem der Zweckmäßigkeit der *argumentatio extra causam*', *Gymnasium* 76 (1969) 419–29.

ALEXANDER, M., 'Repetition of Prosecution, and the Scope of Prosecutions, in the Standing Criminal Courts of the Late Republic', *CA* 1 (1982) 141–66.

ALEXANDER, M. C., 'Hortensius' Speech in Defense of Verres', *Phoenix* 30 (1976) 46–53.

— 'Repetition of Prosecution, and the Scope of Prosecutions, in the Standing Criminal Courts of the Late Republic', *CA* 1 (1982) 141–66.

— '*Praemia* in the *Quaestiones* of the Late Republic' *CPh* 80 (1985) 20–32.

— *Trials in the late Roman Republic 149 B.C. to 50 B.C.* (Toronto, 1990).

— *The Case for the Prosecution in the Ciceronian Era* (Ann Arbor, 2002).

ALLEN, W. (ed.), *Tacitus: The Annals, Books I–VI* (Boston, 1890).

ALLEN, W., Jr., 'Cicero's House and Libertas', *TAPA* 75 (1944) 1–9.

— 'Cicero's Conceit', *TAPA* 85 (1954) 121–44.

ATHERTON, C., 'Hand over Fist: The Failure of Stoic Rhetoric', *CQ* 38 (1988) 392–427.

— *The Stoics on Ambiguity* (Cambridge, 1993).

AURIGEMMA, S., and SCACCIA SCARAFONI, G., 'Atina (Frosinone)–Scoperta di un pavimento in mosaico', *NSc* 4 (1950) 108–15.

AUSTIN, R. G., *M. Tulli Ciceronis Pro M. Caelio Oratio*, 2nd edn. (Oxford, 1952).

BADIAN, E., 'Marius' Villas: the Testimony of the Slave and the Knave', *JRS* 63 (1973) 129.

— 'E.H.N.L.R.', *Mus. Helv.* (1988) 203–17.

BARTELS, K., *Veni vidi vici: geflügelte Worte aus dem Griechischen und Lateinischen*, 8th edn. (Zurich and Munich, 1990).

BAUMAN, R. A., *The Crimen Maiestatis in the Roman Republic and Augustan Principate* (Johannesburg, 1967).

— *Lawyers in Republican Politics*, Münchener Beiträge zur Papyrusforschung und antiken Rechtsgeschichte 75 (Munich, 1983).

BEARD, M., 'Priesthood in the Roman Republic', in M. Beard and J. North, *Pagan Priests* (Ithaca and New York, 1990).

BECKETT, J. V., *The Aristocracy in England 1660–1914* (Oxford, 1988).

BENNER, H., *Die Politik des P. Clodius Pulcher*, Hermes Einzelschriften 50 (Stuttgart, 1987).

BERANGER, E., and SORRENTINO, A., *La cinta muraria di Atina* (Sora, 1980).

BERG, B., 'Cicero's Palatine Home and Clodius' Shrine of Liberty: Alternative Emblems of the Republic in Cicero's *De domo sua*', in C. Deroux (ed.), *Studies in Latin Literature and Roman History*, viii (Brussels, 1997) 122–43.

BERGEMANN, C., *Politik und Religion im spätrepublikanischen Rom* (Stuttgart, 1992).

BERGER, D., *Cicero als Erzähler* (Frankfurt am Main, 1978).

BERRY, D. H., 'Pompey's Legal knowledge–or lack of it: Cic. *Mil.* 70 and the date of *Pro Milone*', *Historia* 42 (1993) 503–4.

— 'Cicero's Masterpiece?', *Omnibus* 25 (1993) 10.

— *Cicero Pro P. Sulla Oratio*, Cambridge Classical Texts and Commentaries 30 (Cambridge, 1996).

— and HEATH, M., 'Oratory and Declamation', in Stanley E. Porter (ed.), *Handbook of Classical Rhetoric in the Hellenistic Period 330 B.C.–A.D. 400* (Leiden, 1997) 393–407.

BIRKETT, N., Lord. *Six Great Advocates* (Harmondsworth, 1961).

BIRKS, P., Review of Frier 1985, *Oxford Journal of Legal Studies* 7 (1987) 444–53.

BLEICKEN, J., *Lex publica: Gesetz und Recht in der römischen Republik* (Berlin, 1975).

BONNER, R. J., *Lawyers and Litigants in Ancient Athens* (Chicago, 1927).

BOVE, L., *Documenti processuali dalle Tabulae Pompeianae di Murecine* (Naples, 1979).

BOVIE, P., *Cicero: Nine Orations and the Dream of Scipio* (London, 1967).

BRADLEY, G., *Ancient Umbria. State, Culture and Identity in Central Italy from the Iron Age to the Augustan Era* (Oxford, 2000).

— and LOMAS, K., 'Regio V: Introduction', in T. J. Cornell and K. Lomas (eds.), *Cities and Urbanisation in Ancient Italy: An Archaeological Encyclopaedia* (Leiden, forthcoming).

BRAUND, D. C., '*Cohors*. The Governor and his Entourage in the Self-Image of the Roman Republic', in R. Laurence and J. Berry (eds.), *Cultural Identity in the Roman Empire* (London, 1998).

BRINGMANN, K., 'Der Diktator Caesar als Richter? Zu Ciceros Reden "Pro Ligario" und "Pro Rege Deiotaro"' *Hermes* 141 (1986) 72–8.

BRINK, C. O., *Horace on Poetry*, i: *Prolegomena to the Literary Epistles* (Cambridge, 1963).

BROUGHTON, T. R. S., *The Magistrates of the Roman Republic* (New York, 1952).

BROUWER, H. H. J., *Bona Dea* (Leiden, etc., 1989).

BROWN, G., and YULE, G., *Discourse Analysis* (Cambridge, 1983).

BRUNT, P. A., *The Fall of the Roman Republic* (Oxford, 1988).

BÜCHMANN, G., *Geflügelte Worte*, 31st edn. (Berlin, 1964).

BUFFA GIOLITO, M. F., 'La retorica degli inizi a proposito di Cic. Pro. Lig. 1–2', in *Cultura e scuola* (1996) 117–27.

BUSH, M. L., *The English Aristocracy: A Comparative Synthesis* (Manchester, 1984).

BUTLER, S., *The Hand of Cicero* (London, 2002).

CALBOLI MONTEFUSCO, L. (ed.), *Consulti Fortunatiani Ars rhetorica* (Bologna, 1979).

— *Exordium Narratio Epilogus* (Bologna, 1988).

— 'Cicerone, De oratore: la doppia funzione dell'ethos dell'oratore', *Rhetorica* 10 (1992) 245–59.

CALHOUN, G. M., *Athenian Clubs in Politics and Litigation*, Bulletin of the University of Texas 262 (Austin, Tex., 1913).

CAMERON, A., *The Greek Anthology from Meleager to Planudes* (Oxford, 1993).

CAMODECA, G., *L'Archivio Puteolano dei Sulpicii* (Naples, 1992).
— *Tabulae Pompeianae Sulpiciorum*, Vetera 12 (Rome, 1999).
CAMPBELL, B., *The Writings of the Roman Land-Surveyors* (London, 2000).
CANTER, H. V., 'Digressio in the orations of Cicero' *AJP* 52 (1931) 351–61.
CAPLAN, H., (ed., tr.), *[Cicero]: Ad C. Herennium de ratione dicendi*, Loeb Classical Library (Cambridge, Mass., 1954).
CARANDINI, A., '*Domus e insulae* sulla pendice settentrionale del Palatino', *Bull. Comm.* 91 (1986) 263–78.
— *Schiavi in Italia* (Rome, 1988) 359–87.
CARCOPINO, J., *Sylla ou la monarchie manquée* (Paris, 1947).
CERUTTI, S. M., *Cicero's Accretive Style: Rhetorical Strategies in the Exordia of the Judicial Speeches* (Lanham, Md., New York, and London, 1996).
— 'The Location of the Houses of Cicero and Clodius and the Porticus Catuli on the Palatine Hill in Rome', *AJP* 118 (1997) 417–26.
CIACERI, E., *Cicerone e i suoi tempi*, 2 vols. (Milan, 1930).
CINGOLI, A., and CINGOLI, G., *Da Interamnia a Teramo* (Teramo, 1978).
CIULEI, G., *L'Équité chez Cicéron* (Amsterdam, 1972).
CLARIDGE, A., *Rome: An Oxford Archaeological Guide* (Oxford, 1998).
CLARK, A. C. (ed.), *M. Tulli Ciceronis Pro T. Annio Milone ad iudices oratio*. Edited with introduction and commentary (Oxford, 1895).
— (ed.), *M. Tulli Ciceronis Orationes*, ii, OCT (Oxford, 1901).
CLARK, D. L., *Rhetoric in Greco-Roman Education* (New York, 1957).
CLARKE, M. L., 'Cicero at School', *G&R* 15 (1968) 18–22.
— *Rhetoric at Rome*, rev. D. H. Berry, 3rd edn. (London and New York, 1996).
CLASSEN, C. J., 'Cicero, the Laws and the Law-Courts', *Latomus* 37 (1978) 579–619.
— *Recht–Rhetorik–Politik* (Darmstadt, 1985).
COARELLI, F., *Lazio*. Guide Archeologiche Laterza (Bari, 1982).
— *Il foro romano: periodo repubblicano e augusteo* (Rome, 1985).
COLEMAN, J., *A History of Political Thought: From Ancient Greece to Early Christianity* (Oxford, 2000).
CORBEILL, A., *Controlling Laughter: Political Humor in the Late Republic* (Princeton, 1996).
COURTNEY, E., *A Commentary on the Satires of Juvenal* (London, 1980).
CRAIG, C. P., 'The Accusator as Amicus: An Original Roman Tactic of Ethical Argumentation', *TAPA* 111 (1981) 31–7.
— 'The Central Argument of Cicero's Speech for Ligarius', *CJ* 79 (1984) 193–9.
— 'The Structural Pedigree of Cicero's Speeches *Pro Archia*, *Pro Milone* and *Pro Quinctio*', *Classical Philology* 80 (1985) 136–7.
— *Form as Argument in Cicero's Speeches: A Study of Dilemma* (Atlanta, 1993).
CRAWFORD, J. W., *M. Tullius Cicero: The Lost and Unpublished Orations*, Hypomnemata 80 (Göttingen, 1984).
— *M. Tullius Cicero: The Fragmentary Speeches. An Edition with Commentary*, APA American Classical Studies 33, 2nd edn. (Atlanta, 1994).
CRAWFORD, M. (ed.), *Roman Statutes*, BICS Suppl. 64 (London, 1996).
CRIFÒ, G., '*Exilica causa, quae adversus exulem agitur*: problemi dell' *aqua et igni interdictio*', in Y. Thomas et al. (eds.), *Du châtiment dans le cité* (Rome, 1984) 453–97.

CROOK, J. A., *Law and Life of Rome* (London, 1967).
— *Legal Advocacy in the Roman World* (London, 1995).
D'ARMS, J. H., *The Romans on the Bay of Naples* (Cambridge, Mass., 1970).
— 'Upper Class Attitudes towards *viri municipales* and their Towns in the Early Roman Empire', *Athenaeum* 62 (1984) 440–67.
DAMON, C., *The Mask of the Parasite: A Pathology of Roman Patronage* (Ann Arbor, 1997).
DAVID, J.-M., *Le Patronat judiciaire au dernier siècle de la république romaine* (Rome, 1992).
DAY, A. A., *The Origins of Latin Love Elegy* (Oxford, 1938).
DE FELICE, E., *Larinum*, Forma Italiae 36 (Florence, 1994).
DE STE CROIX, G. E. M., *The Class Struggle in the Ancient Greek World* (London, 1981).
DE WITT, H. M., 'Quo Virtus: The Concept of Propriety in Ancient Literary Criticism', unpub. diss. (Oxford, 1997).
DEGRASSI, A., 'Quattuorviri in colonie Romane e in municipi retti da duoviri', *Mem. Linc.* 8.2 (1950) 281–344.
DENIAUX, E., *Clientèles et pouvoir à l'époque de Cicéron* (Rome, 1993).
DI NIRO, A., *Necropoli archaiche di Termoli e Larino* (Termoli, 1981).
DI TOMASSI, A., *Guida di Amelia* (Terni, 1936).
DOBLHOFER, E., *Exil und Emigration: Zum Erlebnis der Heimatferne in der römischen Literatur* (Darmstadt, 1987).
DONNELLY, F. P., *Cicero's Milo: A Rhetorical Commentary* (New York, 1935).
DOUGLAS, A. E., *M. Tulli Ciceronis Brutus* (Oxford, 1966).
— *Cicero*, Greece & Rome New Surveys in the Classics 2 (1968) 39.
DRUMANN, W., rev. P. GROEBE, *Geschichte Roms in seinem Übergange von der republikanischen zur monarchischen Verfassung*, 2nd edn. (Berlin and Leipzig, 1899–1929; repr. 1964).
DU CANN, R., *The Art of the Advocate* (London, 1980).
DUNKLE, J. R., 'The Greek Tyrant and Roman Political Invective of the Late Republic', *TAPA* 98 (1967) 151–71.
DYCK, A. R., 'Narrative Obfuscation, Philosophical *Topoi*, and Tragic Patterning in Cicero's *Pro Milone*', *HSCP* 98 (1998) 219–41.
— 'The "Other" *Pro Milone* Reconsidered', *Philologus* 146 (2002) 182–5.
— 'Evidence and Rhetoric in Cicero's *Pro Roscio Amerino*: The Case against Sex Roscius', *CQ* 53 (2003) 235–46.
ENKVIST, N. E., 'Connexity, Interpretability, Universes of Discourse', in S. Allén (ed.), *Possible Worlds in Humanities, Arts and Sciences* (Berlin, 1989) 162–86.
— 'On the Interpretability of Texts in General and of Literary Texts in Particular' in R. D. Sell (ed.), *Literary Pragmatics* (London, 1991) 1–25.
ENOS, R. L., *The Literate Mode of Cicero's Legal Rhetoric* (Carbondale, 1988).
EPSTEIN, D. F., *Personal Enmity in Roman Politics 218–43 B.C.* (London, 1987).
ÉVRARD, E., 'Le *Pro Sestio* de Cicéron: un leurre', in *Filologia e forme letterarie: studi offerti a Francesco della Corte*, ii (Urbino, n.d.), 223–34.
EWINS, U., '*Ne Quis Iudicio Circumveniatur*', *JRS* 50 (1960) 94–107.
FABBRI, P., 'De humanitate Ciceronis erga Provinciales in Verris crimine Lampsaceno describendo', *Atti del I congresso internazionale di studi Ciceroniani* (Rome, 1961).
FANTHAM, E., 'Ciceronian *conciliare* and Aristotelian Ethos', *Phoenix* 27 (1973) 262–75.

FERGUSON, R. A., 'Untold Stories in the Law', in P. Brooks and P. Gewirtz (eds.), *Law's Stories: Narrative and Rhetoric in the Law* (New Haven, 1996) 84–98.

FEY, G., *Das ethische Dilemma der Rhetorik in der Theorie der Antike und der Neuzeit* (Stuttgart, 1990).

FREESE, J. H., *M. Tullii Ciceronis Pro L. Murena Oratio ad Iudices* (London and New York, 1894).

FRIER, B. W., *The Rise of the Roman Jurists: Studies in Cicero's Pro Caecina* (Princeton, 1985).

FUHRMANN, M., 'Publicatio bonorum', *RE* XXIII.2 (1959) 2484–515.

— (transl., comm.) *M. Tullius Cicero: Sämtliche Reden* (Zürich and Munich, 1970–82).

— 'Techniche Narrative nella Seconda Orazione contra Verre', *Ciceroniana, Atti del IV Colloquium Tullianum* (Rome, 1980) 27–42.

— 'Die Tradition der Rhetorik-Verachtung und das deutsche Bild vom "Advokaten" Cicero', *Ciceroniana* 6 (1988) 19–30.

— *Cicero und die römische Republik* (Munich and Zurich, 1989).

— 'Mündlichkeit und fiktive Mündlichkeit in den von Cicero veröffentlichen Reden', in G. Vogt-Spira (ed.), *Strukturen der Mündlichkeit in der römischen Literatur* (Tübingen, 1990) 53–62.

GABBA, E., 'Le città italiche del I sec. a.C. e la politica', *Rivista Storica Italiana* 93 (1986) 653–63.

GAGGIOTTI, M., et al. *Umbria-Marche*. Guide Archeologiche Laterza (Bari, 1980).

GAGGIOTTI, M., and SENSI, L., 'Ascesa al senato e rapporti con i territori d'origine Italia: Regio VI Umbria', *Atti del Colloquio Internazionale AIEGL su epigraphie e ordine senatorio, Roma, 14–20 maggio 1981*, ii (Rome, 1981) 245–74.

GAGLIARDI, P., *Il dissenso e l'ironia: per una rilettura delle orazioni 'cesariane' di Cicerone* (Naples, 1997).

GASTI, F., *Marco Tullio Cicerone: Orazioni Cesariane*, Biblioteca Universale Rizzoli (Milan, 1997).

GEFFCKEN, K., *Comedy in the Pro Caelio*, Mnemosyne Suppl. 30 (Leiden, 1973).

GELZER, M., *Cicero: ein biographischer Versuch* (Wiesbaden, 1969).

GIAMMARCO, E., 'Per la storia linguistica di Interamna e di Teate', *Abruzzo* 21 (1983) 159–68.

GIDDENS, A., *The Constitution of Society* (Berkeley, Calif., 1984).

GILBERT, M., *The Oxford Book of Legal Anecdotes* (Oxford, 1986).

GILL, C. J., 'The Question of Character-Development: Plutarch and Tacitus', *CQ* 33 (1983) 469–87.

GIULIANI, C. F., and VERDUCHI, P., *L'area centrale del foro romano* (Florence, 1987).

GLINISTER, F., 'Volaterrae', in T. J. Cornell and K. Lomas (eds.), *Cities and Urbanism in Ancient Italy: An Archaeological Encyclopaedia* (Leiden, forthcoming).

GLUCKER, J., 'Chapter and Verse in Cicero', *Grazer Beiträge* 11 (1984) 103–12.

GONZALEZ, J., 'Lex Irnitana', *JRS* 76 (1986) 147–243.

GOTOFF, H. C., *Cicero's Elegant Style: An Analysis of the Pro Archia* (Urbana, Ill., 1979).

— 'Cicero's analysis of the prosecution speeches in the *Pro Caelio*: an exercise in practical criticism', *CPh* 81 (1986) 122–32.

— *Cicero's Caesarian Speeches: A Stylistic Commentary* (Chapel Hill, NC, 1993).

— 'Oratory: The Art of Illusion', *HSCP* 95 (1993) 288–313.

GOTZES, P., *De Ciceronis Tribus Generibus Dicendi in Orationibus pro A. Caecina, de imperio Cn. Pompei, pro C. Rabiro perduellionis reo adhibitis* (Rostock, 1914).

GOW, A. S. F., and Page, D. L. (eds.), *The Greek Anthology: The Garland of Philip and Some Contemporary Epigrams* (Cambridge, 1968).

GRAFF, J., *Ciceros Selbstauffassung*, diss. (Heidelberg, 1963).

GRANT, M. (tr.), *Cicero, On The Good Life* (Harmondsworth, 1971).

— (tr.), *Cicero, Murder Trials* (Harmondsworth, 1975).

GRASMÜCK, E. L., 'Ciceros Verbannung aus Rom', *Bonner Festgabe Johannes Straub* (Bonn, 1977) 165–77.

GREEN, P., *Classical Bearings* (London, 1989).

GREENIDGE, A. H. J., *The Legal Procedure of Cicero's Time* (London, repr. New York, 1971) 1901.

GRIMAL, P., *Études de chronologie cicéronienne années 58 et 57 av. J.C.* (Paris, 1967).

GRUBE, G. M. A., 'Theodorus of Gadara', *AJP* 80 (1959) 337–65.

GRUEN, E. S., *Roman Politics and the Criminal Courts, 149–78 B.C.* (Cambridge, Mass., 1968).

— 'The Trial of C. Antonius', *Latomus* 32 (1973) 301–10.

— *The Last Generation of the Roman Republic* (Berkeley, Calif., 1974).

HABICHT, C., *Cicero der Politiker* (Munich, 1990).

HALLIWELL, F. S., 'The Tradition of Greek Conceptions of Character', in C. Pelling (ed.), *Characterization and Individuality in Greek Literature* (Oxford, 1990).

HANDS, A., 'Postremo Suo Tantum Ingenio Utebatur', *CQ* 24 (1974) 312–17.

HARDIE, A., *Statius and the Silvae: Poets, Patrons and Epideixis in the Graeco-Roman World* (Liverpool, 1983).

HARRIS, W. V., *Rome in Etruria and Umbria* (Oxford, 1971).

HAURY, A., *L'Ironie et l'humour chez Cicéron* (Leiden, 1955).

HAÜSSLER, R., *Tacitus und das historische Bewusstsein* (Heidelberg, 1965).

HEAD, B. V., *Historia Nummorum*, 2nd edn. (Oxford, 1911).

HEINZE, R., '*Fides*', in E. Burck (ed.), *Vom Geist des Römertums*, 3rd edn. (Darmstadt, 1960) 70–3.

— 'Ciceros politische Anfänge' (1909), in E. Burck (ed.), *Vom Geist des Römertums*, 3rd edn. (Darmstadt, 1960) 87–140.

HEITLAND, W. (ed.), *M. T. Ciceronis Oratio Pro Murena* (London, 1876).

HELLEGOUARC'H, J., *Le Vocabulaire latin des relations et des partis politiques sous la république*, 2nd edn. (Paris, 1972).

HERHOLD, L., *Lateinischer Wort- und Gedankenschatz* (Hannover, 1887).

HILTBRUNNER, O., 'Humanitas', *Reallexiikon für Antike und Christentum* 16 (1994) 711–52.

HINARD, F., '*Paternus inimicus*. Sur un expression de Cicéron', *Mélanges de littérature et d'épigraphie latines, d'histoire ancienne et d'archéologie: Hommages à la mémoire de Pierre Wuilleumier* (Paris, 1980) 202 ff.

HÖEG, C., 'The Second Pleading of the Verres Trial', in ΔΡΑΓΜΑ *Martino P. Nilsson . . . dedicatum* (Stockholm, 1939) 264–79.

HOEY, M., *Patterns of Lexis in Text* (Oxford, 1991).

HOFFMANN, H., 'Morum tempora diversa', *Gymnasium* 75 (1968) 220–50.

HOHTI, P., 'Aulus Caecina the Volaterran: Romanization of an Etruscan', in P. Bruun (ed.), *Studies in the Romanization of Etruria* (Rome, 1975).

HÖLSCHER, T. H., 'Homonoia/Concordia' *LIMC* V.1 (1990).

HOPKINS, K., *Conquerors and Slaves* (Cambridge, 1978).

HOSE, M., 'Die zweite Begegnung Roms mit den Griechen oder: Zu politischen Ursachen des Attizismus' in: G. Vogt-Spira and B. Rommel (eds.) *Rezeption und Identität* (Stuttgart, 1999) 274–88.

HUBBELL, H. M., 'Cicero on Styles of Oratory' *YCS* 19 (1966) 171–86.

— (ed., tr.), *Cicero: De Inventione, De Optimo Genere Oratorum, Topica*, Loeb Classical Library (Cambridge, Mass., 1976).

HUMBERT, J., *Les Plaidoyers écrits et les plaidoiries réelles de Cicéron* (Paris, 1925).

HUMPHREYS, T., *Criminal Days* (London, 1946).

HUSBAND, R. W., 'The Prosecution of Archias', *CJ* 10 (1914) 137–52.

HUTCHINSON, G. O., *Cicero's Correspondence* (Oxford, 1998).

INGHIRAMI, P., 'Il teatro romano di Volterra', *Rassegna Volterrana* 40–1 (1977) 31–47.

INNES, D., and WINTERBOTTOM, M., *Sopatros the Rhetor, BICS* Supplement 48 (London, 1988).

JOCELYN, H. D., 'The Ruling Class of the Roman Republic and Greek Philosophers', *BRL* 59 (1976–7) 323–66.

JOHNSON, W. R., *Luxuriance and Economy: Cicero and the Alien Style* (Berkeley, Los Angeles, and London, 1971).

JONES, A. H. M., *The Criminal Courts of the Roman Republic and Principate* (Oxford, 1972).

JOUFFROY, H., *La Construction publique en Italie et dans L'Afrique romain* (Strasbourg, 1986).

KASTER, R. A., *C. Suetonius Tranquillus: De Grammaticis et Rhetoribus* (Oxford, 1995).

KELLY, J. M., *Roman Litigation* (Oxford, 1966).

— *Studies in the Civil Judicature of the Roman Republic* (Oxford, 1976).

— 'Comment Ciceron mystifia les juges de Cluentius', *REL* 16 (1938) 275–96.

KENNEDY, G. A., *The Art of Persuasion in Greece* (Princeton, 1963).

— 'The Rhetoric of Advocacy in Greece and Rome', *AJP* 89 (1968) 419–36.

— (trans., comm.) *Quintilian* (New York, 1969).

— *The Art of Rhetoric in the Roman World* (Princeton, 1972).

KINSEY, T. E., 'A Dilemma in the *Pro Roscio*', *Mnemosyne* 19 (1966) 270–1.

— 'The Dates of the *Pro Roscio Amerino* and the *Pro Quinctio*', *Mnemosyne* 20 (1967) 61–7.

— (ed.) *Cicero: Pro Quinctio* (Sydney, 1971).

— 'Cicero's Case against Magnus, Capito and Chrysogonus in the *Pro Sexto Roscio Amerino* and its Use for the Historian', *Ant. Class.* 49 (1980) 173–90.

— 'The Case against Sextus Roscius of Ameria', *Ant. Class.* 54 (1985) 188–96.

— 'The Sale of the Property of Roscius of Ameria: How Illegal Was It?', *Ant. Class.* 57 (1988) 296–7.

KIRBY, J., *The Rhetoric of Cicero's* Pro Cluentio (Amsterdam, 1990).

KLODT, C., 'Prozessparteien und politische Gegner als dramatis personae: Charakterstilisierung in Ciceros Reden' in Schröder and Schröder (eds., 2003).

KOSTER, S., *Der Invektive in der griechischen und romischen Literatur*, Beiträge zur klassischen Philologie 99 (Meisenheim an Glan, 1980).

KROLL, W. (ed.), *M. Tulli Ciceronis Orator* (Berlin, 1913, repr. 1958).

— 'Ciceros Rede für Plancius', *RhM* 86 (1937) 127–39.

KUMANIECKI, K., 'Der Prozess gegen Q. Ligarius', *Hermes* 95 (1967) 434–57.

KUNKEL, W., *Untersuchungen zur Entwicklung des römischen Kriminalverfahrens in vorsullanischer Zeit*, Abh. Bay. Ak. Wiss., phil.-hist. Kl., n.f. 56 (Munich, 1962).

— 'Quaestio', *RE* 24 (1963) 720–86.

— tr. J. M. Kelly, *An Introduction to Roman Legal and Constitutional History* (Oxford, 1966).

— and WITTMAN, R., *Staatsordnung und Staatspraxis der römischen Republik* (Munich, 1995).

LAFFI, U., 'I senati locali nell' Italia repubblicana' in M. Cébelliac-Gervasioni (ed.), *Les "Bourgeoisies" municipales italiennes au I^{me} et Ier siècles av. J.C.* (Paris and Naples, 1983) 59–74.

LANGE, L., *Römische Alterthümer*, vol. 3 (Berlin, 1871).

LATTE, K., *Römische Religionsgeschichte* (Munich, 1960).

LAURAND, L., *Cicéron*, 2nd edn. (Paris, 1933).

LAURENCE, R. M., *The Roads of Roman Italy: Mobility and Cultural Change* (London, 2000).

LAUSBERG, H., *Handbuch der literarischen Rhetorik* (Munich, 1960); Eng. tr. M. T. Bliss, A. Jansen, and D. E. Orton; ed. D. E. Orton and R. D. Anderson, *Handbook of Literary Rhetoric* (Leiden, 1998).

LAVENCY, M., *Aspects de la logographie judiciaire attique* (Louvain, 1964).

LEEMAN, A. D., *Orationis Ratio* (Amsterdam, 1963).

— 'The Technique of Persuasion in Cicero's Pro Murena', Fondation Hardt *Entretiens* 28 (1982) 193–228.

LENAGHAN, J. O., *A Commentary on Cicero's Oration De Haruspicum Responso* (The Hague and Paris, 1969).

LENEL, O., *Palingenesia Iuris Civilis* (Leipzig, 1889).

— *Das Edictum Perpetuum. Ein Versuch zu seiner Wiederherstellung* (Leipzig, 1927).

LEVENE, D. S., 'God and Man in the Classical Latin Panegyric', *PCPS* 43 (1997) 66–103.

LICORDARI, A., 'Ascesa al senato e rapporti con I territori d'origine Italia: Regio I Latium', *Atti del Colloquio Internazionale AIEGL su epigrafia e ordine senatorio, Roma, 14–20 maggio 1981*, ii (Rome, 1982) 9–57.

LINDERSKI, J., 'The Libri Reconditi', *HSCP* 89 (1985) 214–26.

— *OCD* s.v. 'dedicatio', 3rd edn. (Oxford, 1996).

LINTOTT, A. W., *Violence in Republican Rome*, 2nd edn. (Oxford, 1968).

— 'Provocatio. From the Struggle of the Orders to the Principate.', *ANRW* I. 2 (1972) 226–67.

— 'Cicero and Milo', *JRS* 64 (1974) 62–78.

— 'Cicero on Praetors who Failed to Abide by their Edicts', *CQ* 27 (1977) 184–6.

— 'The *Leges de Repetundis* and Associated Measures under the Republic', *ZSS* 98 (1981) 162–212.

— *Judicial Reform and Land Reform in the Roman Republic* (Cambridge, 1992).

— *Imperium Romanum: Politics and Administration* (London, 1993).

— *The Constitution of the Roman Republic* (Oxford, 1999).

LIOU-GILLE, B., 'La consécration du Champ de Mars et la consécration du domaine de Cicéron', *MH* 55 (1998) 37–59.

LLOYD, J. A., 'Pentri, Frentani and the Beginnings of Urbanisation c. 500–80 B.C.', in G. Barker (ed.), *A Mediterranean Valley: Landscape Archaeology and* Annales *History in the Biferno Valley* (London, 1995) 181–212.

LOB, M., *Cicéron, Discours: Pour Marcellus, Ligarius, le Roi Dejotarus* (Paris, 1952).

LOMAS, K., 'Roman Imperialism and the City in Italy', in R. Laurence and J. Berry (eds.), *Cultural Identity in the Roman Empire* (London, 1998) 64–78.

LONG, G. M., *M. Tulli Ciceronis Orationes* (London, 1856–8).

LOSSMANN, F., *Cicero und Caesar in Jahre 54* (Wiesbaden, 1962).

LOUTSCH, C., 'Ironie et Liberté de parole: Remarques sur l'exorde *ad principem* du Pro Ligario de Cicéron', *REL* 62 (1984) 98–110.

— *L'Exorde dans les discours de Cicéron*, Collection Latomus 224 (Brussels, 1994).

MA, J., 'Black Hunter Variations', *PCPS* 40 (1994) 49–80.

MCCARTHY, M., *Discourse Analysis for Language Teachers* (Cambridge, 1991).

MCDERMOTT, W. C., 'In Ligarianam', *TAPA* 101 (1970) 317–47.

MACK, D., *Senatsreden und Volksreden bei Cicero* (Würzburg, 1937; repr. Hildesheim, 1967).

MACKENDRICK, P., *The Speeches of Cicero: Context, Law, Rhetoric* (London, 1995).

MACMILLAN, H. P., 'The Ethics of Advocacy', in *Law and Other Things* (Cambridge, 1937).

MAGIE, D., *Roman Rule in Asia Minor*, 2 vols. (Princeton, 1950).

MALCOVATI, H. (ed.), *Oratorum Romanorum Fragmenta*, 3rd edn. (Turin, 1953; 4th edn., 1976).

MANCINI, G., 'Amelia', *NSc* (1920) 15 ff.

MARSHALL, A. J., 'Symbols and Showmanship in Roman Public Life: The Fasces', *Phoenix* 38 (1984) 120–41.

MARSHALL, B. A., *A Historical Commentary on Asconius* (Columbia, Mo., 1985).

— 'Excepta oratio, the Other *Pro Milone* and the Question of Shorthand', *Latomus* 46 (1987) 730–6.

MARTORANA, G., 'La *Venus* di Verre e le Verrine', *Kokalos* 25 (1979) [1981] 73–103.

MASLOWSKI, T. (ed.), *M. Tulli Ciceronis Scripta* fasc. 2, (Leipzig, 1981).

MAY, J. M., 'The Rhetoric of Advocacy and Patron–Client Identification: Variation on a Theme', *AJP* 102 (1981) 308–15.

— *Trials of Character: The Eloquence of Ciceronian Ethos* (Chapel Hill, NC, and London, 1988).

— 'Cicero and the Beasts', *Syllecta Classica* 7 (1996) 143–53.

— (ed.), *Brill's Companion to Cicero: Oratory and Rhetoric* (Leiden, 2002).

MAZZITTI, W., *Teramo archeologica. Ripertorio di monumenti* (Teramo, 1983).

MEIER, C., *Caesar* (Berlin, 1982).

MERRILL, N. W., *Cicero and Early Roman Invective*, Ph.D. diss. (University of Cincinnati, 1975).

METZGER, E., *A New Outline of the Roman Civil Trial* (Oxford, 1997).

MEYER, E., *Caesars Monarchie und das Principat des Pompejus*, 3rd edn. (Stuttgart and Berlin, 1923; repr. 1964).

MICHEL, A., *Rhétorique et philosophie chez Cicéron* (Paris, 1960).

— 'Lieux communs et sincérité chez Cicéron (Pro Milone, pro Marcello, pro Ligario)', *VL* 72 (1978) 11–22.

MIDDLETON, C., *The Life of Marcus Tullius Cicero* (London, 1810).

MIGLIORATI, L., 'Municipes et coloni. Note di urbanistica teramana', *Arch. Class.* 28 (1976) 242–56.

MILLAR, F., 'Some speeches in Cassius Dio', *Mus. Helv.* 18 (1961) 11–22.

—— *The Crowd in Rome in the Late Republic*, Jerome Lectures 22 (Ann Arbor, 1998).

MITCHELL, T. N. (ed., tr., and comm.), *Cicero, Verrines*. II.1 (Warminster, 1986).

—— *Cicero the Senior Statesman* (New Haven, 1991).

MOLES, J. L. (ed., tr., and comm.) *Plutarch: The Life of Cicero* (Warminster, 1988).

MOMMSEN, T., *Römisches Staatsrecht*, 3rd edn. (Leipzig, 1887).

—— *Römische Geschichte*, 8th edn. (Berlin, 1889).

—— *Römisches Strafrecht* (Leipzig, 1899).

MONTAGUE, H. W., 'Advocacy and Politics: The Paradox of Cicero's "Pro Ligario"', *AJP* 113 (1992) 559–74.

MOREAU, P., 'Structures de parenté et alliance à Larinum', in M. Cébelliac-Gervasioni (ed.), *Les "Bourgeoisies" municipales italiennes au I^{me} et I^r siècles av. J.C.* (Paris and Naples, 1983) 99–123.

—— 'La *Lex Clodia* sur le bannissement de Cicéron', *Athenaeum*, NS 65 (1987) 465–92.

MORLEY, N., *Metropolis and Hinterland: The City of Rome and the Italian Economy, 200 B.C.–A.D. 200* (Cambridge, 1996).

NARDUCCI, E., *Cicerone e l'eloquenza romana* (Rome, 1977).

—— '*Brutus*: The History of Roman Eloquence', in J. M. May (ed.), *Brill's Companion to Cicero: Oratory and Rhetoric* (Leiden, 2002), 401–25.

NEUHAUSER, W., *Patronus und Orator. Eine Geschichte der Begriffe von ihren Anfängen bis in die augusteische Zeit*, Commentationes Aenipontanae 14 (Innsbruck, 1958).

NEUMEISTER, C., *Grundsätze der forensischen Rhetorik, gezeigt an Gerichtsreden Ciceros* (Munich, 1964).

NICHOLAS, B., *An Introduction to Roman Law* (Oxford, 1962).

NICOLET, C., 'Arpinum, Aemilius Scaurus et les Tullii Cicerones', *REL* 45 (1967) 276–304.

NICOSIA, G., *Studi sulla 'Deiectio'* (Milan, 1965).

NIPPEL, W., *Aufruhr und Polizei in der römischen Republik* (Stuttgart, 1988).

—— *Public Order in Ancient Rome* (Cambridge, 1995).

NIPPERDEY, K. (ed.), *P. Cornelius Tacitus* (Berlin, 1915).

NISBET, R. G. (ed.), *M. Tulli Ciceronis De domo sua ad pontifices oratio* (Oxford, 1939).

NISBET, R. G. M. (ed.), *M. Tulli Ciceronis in L. Calpurnium Pisonem oratio* (Oxford, 1961).

—— 'The Speeches', in T. A. Dorey (ed.), *Cicero* (London, 1965) 47–80.

—— 'The Orator and Reader: Manipulation and Response in Cicero's Fifth Verrine', in A. J. Woodman and J. G. F. Powell (eds.), *Author and Audience in Latin Literature* (Cambridge, 1992) 1–17, repr. in his *Collected Papers on Latin Literature*, ed. S. J. Harrison (Oxford, 1995) 362–80.

NORDEN, E., *Die Antike Kunstprosa*, 2nd edn. (Leipzig and Berlin, 1909).

O'BANION, J. D., 'Narration and Argumentation: Quintilian on *narratio* as the Heart of Rhetorical Thinking', *Rhetorica* 5 (1987) 325–51.

OGILVIE, R. M., *A Commentary on Livy, Books 1–5* (Oxford, 1965).

OPELT, I., *Die lateinischen Schimpfwörter und verwandte sprachliche Erscheinungen: eine Typologie* (Heidelberg, 1965).

ORBAN, M., 'Le *Pro Archia* et le concept Cicéronien de la formation intellectuelle', *LEC* 25 (1957) 173–91.

ORLIN, E. M., *Temples, Religions and Politics in the Roman Republic* (Leiden, etc., 1997).

PAIRAULT, F.-H., *Recherches sur quelques séries d'urnes de Volterra à representátations mythologiques*, Collection de l'École Française de Rome 12 (Rome, 1972).

PANNICK, D., *Advocates* (Oxford, 1992).

PARKES, M. B., *Pause and Effect: An Introduction to the History of Punctuation in the West* (Aldershot, 1992).

PATERSON, J. J., 'Politics in the Late Republic', in T. P. Wiseman (ed.), *Roman Political Life 90 B.C.–A.D. 69* (Exeter, 1985) 23–7.

PETERSON, G. (ed.), *Cicero: Pro Cluentio* (London, 1899).

— (ed.), *M. Tulli Ciceronis orationes*, vol. 5, OCT (Oxford, 1911).

PETZOLD, P., *De Ciceronis detractoribus ac laudatoribus Romanis* (Leipzig, 1911).

PICARD, G.-C., 'L'Aedes Libertatis de Clodius au Palatin', *REL* 43 (1965) 229–37.

PLUCKNETT, T. F. T., *A Concise History of the Common Law* (London, 1940).

POCOCK, L. G., *A Commentary on Cicero In Vatinium* (London, 1926; repr. Amsterdam, 1967).

PORTER, W. M., 'Cicero's *Pro Archia* and the Responsibilities of Reading', *Rhetorica* 8 (1990) 137–52.

POWELL, J. G. F. (ed.), *Cicero, Cato Maior de senectute* (Cambridge, 1988).

— (ed., tr. and comm.), *Cicero: On friendship and The Dream of Scipio* (Warminster, 1990).

— *OCD* s.v. 'prose-rhythm, Latin', 3rd edn. (Oxford, 1996).

PUGLIESE CARRATELLI, G., 'Tabulae Herculanenses II', *Parola del Passato* 3 (1948) 165–84.

PURCELL, N., 'The *Apparitores*: A study in Social Mobility', *PBSR* 51 (1983) 125–73.

— 'The Roman Villa and the Landscape of Production', in T. J. Cornell and K. Lomas (eds.), *Urban Society in Roman Italy* (London, 1995).

RADICE, B., *The Letters of the Younger Pliny* (Harmondsworth, 1963).

RAMOS, C. E., 'Politics and Rhetoric: Studies in Cicero's Caesarian Speeches', Ph.D. diss. (University of Texas at Austin, 1994).

RAWSON, E. D., 'L. Crassus and Cicero: The Formation of a Statesman', *PCPS* NS 17 (1971) 75–88; repr. *Roman Culture and Society: Collected Papers* (Oxford, 1991) 16–33.

— 'The Ciceronian Aristocracy and its Properties', in M. I. Finley (ed.), *Studies in Roman Property* (Cambridge, 1971); repr., *Roman Culture and Society: Collected Papers* (Oxford, 1991) 204–22.

— *Cicero* (London, 1975).

— 'Caesar, Etruria and the *disciplina Etrusca*', *JRS* 68 (1978) 132–52; repr., *Roman Culture and Society: Collected Papers* (Oxford, 1991) 289–323.

— *Intellectual Life in the Late Roman Republic* (London, 1985).

REID, J. S., *Cicero: Pro Archia* (Cambridge, 1883).

RICHARDSON, J. S., 'The Administration of the Empire', *CAH* 9, 2nd edn. (Cambridge, 1994) 572–84.

RICOEUR, P., *Time and Narrative* (Chicago, 1984).

RIGGSBY, A., 'Did the Romans Believe in their Verdicts?', *Rhetorica* 15.3 (1997) 235–52.

— *Crime and Community in Ciceronian Rome* (Austin, Tex., 1999).

— 'The Post Reditum Speeches', in J. M. May (ed.) *Brill's Companion to Cicero* (Leiden, 2002).

RIMMON-KENAN, S., *Narrative Fiction: Contemporary Poetics* (London, 1983).

ROBINSON, O., *The Sources of Roman Law* (London, 1997).

ROCHLITZ, S., *Das Bild Caesars in Ciceros Orationes Caesarianae: Untersuchungen zur 'clementia' und 'sapientia Caesaris'* (Frankfurt am Main, 1993).

RODGER, A., 'The *Lex Irnitana* and Procedure in the Civil Courts', *JRS* 81 (1991) 74–90.

ROSS TAYLOR, L. H., 'Caesar's Colleagues in the Pontifical College', *AJP* 63 (1942) 385–412.

— *Party Politics in the Age of Caesar* (Berkeley, 1949).

ROTONDI, G., *Leges publicae populi Romani* (1912; repr. Hildesheim, 1966).

ROUSE, R. H., and REEVE, M. D., 'Cicero: Speeches' in L. D. Reynolds (ed.), *Texts and Transmission* (Oxford, 1983) 54–98.

ROYO, M., 'Le quartier républicain du Palatin, nouvelles hypothèses de localisation', *REL* 65 (1987) 89–114.

RUBINSTEIN, L., *Litigation and Co-operation: Supporting Speakers in the Courts of Classical Athens*, Historia Einzelschriften 147 (Stuttgart, 2000).

— 'Synêgoroi: their place in our reconstruction of the Athenian legal process', in G. Thür and F. J. Fernández Nieto (eds.), *Symposion 1999: Vorträge zur griechischen und hellenistischen Rechtsgeschichte* (Cologne, Weimar, and Vienna, 2003).

RÜCK, C., *De M. Tulli Ciceronis oratione de domo sua ad pontifices*, Progr. Gymnasii Guilielmini Monacensis (1881).

RUEBEL, J., 'The Trial of Milo in 52 B.C.: A Chronological Study', *TAPA* 109 (1979) 231–49.

RUSSELL, D. A. (ed., tr.) *Quintilian: The Orator's Education*, Loeb Classical Library, 5 vols. (Cambridge, Mass., and London, 2001).

RUTTER, N. K., *Historia Nummorum: Italy* (London, 2000).

SALMON, E. T., *Samnium and the Samnites* (Cambridge, 1965).

SALOMIES, O., 'Senatori oriundi del Lazio', in H. Solin (ed.), *Studi storico-epigrafici sul Lazio Antico* (Rome, 1996).

SANTALUCIA, B., 'Osservazioni sui Duumviri Perduellionis e sul procedimento duumvirale', in *Du Châtiment dans la cité: Supplices corporels et peine de mort dans le monde antique*, CEFR 79 (1984) 439–52.

— *Diritto e processo penale nell' antica Roma*, 2nd edn. (Milan, 1998).

SATRE, M., *L'Asie Mineure et l'Anatolie d'Alexandre à Dioclétian* (Paris, 1995).

— *Diritto e processo penale nell' antica Roma*, 2nd edn. (Milan, 1998).

SAVINI, F., 'Teramo. Scavi nel teatro romano', *NSc* 6.2 (1929) 391–402.

SCHAUM, L., 'De consecratione domus Ciceronianae', Progr. des Großherzoglichen Gymn. zu Mainz (1889).

SCHOFIELD, M., 'Cicero's Definition of *Res Publica*', in J. G. F. Powell (ed.), *Cicero the Philosopher* (Oxford, 1995) 63–84.

SCHÖLL, F., 'Zu Ciceros Ligariana', *RhM* 55 (1890) 489–500.

SCHRÖDER, B.-J., and SCHRÖDER, J.-P. (eds.), *Studium declamatorium: Untersuchungen zu Schulübungen und Prunkreden von der Antike bis zur Neuzeit* (Munich and Leipzig, 2003).

SEAGER, R., 'Iusta Catilinae', *Historia* 22 (1973) 240–8.

SEEL, O., *Cicero–Wort–Staat–Welt*, (Stuttgart, 1953; 3rd edn., 1967).

SETTLE, J. N., 'The Trial of Milo', *TAPA* 94 (1963) 268–80.

SHACKLETON BAILEY, D. R., *Propertiana* (Cambridge, 1956).

— (ed.), *Cicero's Letters to Atticus* (Cambridge, 1965).

— *Cicero* (London, 1971).

— 'On Cicero's Speeches', *HSCP* 83 (1979) 237–85.

— 'More on Cicero's Speeches Post Reditum', *HSCP* 89 (1985) 141–51.

— *Cicero Back from Exile: Six Speeches upon his Return* (Chicago, 1991).

SHERWIN-WHITE, A. N., Review of A. W. Lintott, *Violence in Republican Rome*, *JRS* 59 (1969) 286.

— 'The Roman Citizenship: A Survey of its Development into a World Franchise', *ANRW* I.2 (1972) 23–58.

— *The Roman Citizenship* (Oxford, 1973).

— 'The Political Ideas of C. Gracchus', *JRS* 72 (1982) 18–31.

SIANI-DAVIES, M., *Marcus Tullias Cicero Pro Rabirio Postumo*, trans. with introd. and comm. (Oxford, 2001).

SMITH, P., 'How Not to Write Philosophy: Did Cicero Get it Right?' in J. G. F. Powell (ed.), *Cicero the Philosopher* (Oxford, 1995) 301–23.

SMITH, R. E., *Cicero the Statesman* (Cambridge, 1966).

SOLMSEN, F., 'Aristotle and Cicero on the Orator's Playing upon the Feelings', *CPh* 33 (1938) 390–404.

SPENGEL, L., *Rhetores Graeci* (Leipzig, 1853).

SPIELVOGEL, J., 'P. Clodius Pulcher–eine politische Ausnahmeerscheinung der späten Republik?', *Hermes* 125 (1997) 56–74.

STANGL, T. (ed.), *Ciceronis Orationum Scholiastae* (Vienna, 1912; repr. Hildesheim, 1964).

STEEL, C., *Cicero, Rhetoric, and Empire* (Oxford, 2002).

STEIN, PAUL, *Die Senatssitzungen der ciceronischen Zeit 68–43.* (Münster, 1930; diss. 1928).

STEIN, PETER, 'The Place of Servius Sulpicius Rufus in the Development of Roman Legal Science', in *Festschrift F. Wieacker*, ed. O. Behrends et al. (Göttingen, 1978) 175–84.

STEINBY, E. M. (ed.), *Lexicon topographicum urbis Romae* (Rome, 1993).

STELLUTI, N., *Epigrafi di Larino e la bassa Frentania* (Campobasso, 1997).

STERNKOPF, W., 'Ueber die „Verbesserung" des Clodianischen Gesetzentwurfes de exilio Ciceronis', *Philologus* 59 (1900) 272–303.

— 'Die Ökonomie der Rede Ciceros für den Dichter Archias', *Hermes* 42 (1907) 337–73.

STOCKTON, D., *Cicero: A Political Biography* (Oxford, 1971).

— *The Gracchi* (Oxford, 1979).

STONE, A. M., 'Pro Milone: Cicero's Second Thoughts', *Antichthon* 14 (1980) 88–111.

STONE, J. R., *Latin for the Illiterati* (New York and London, 1996).

STRACHAN-DAVIDSON, J. L., *Problems of the Roman Criminal Law*, 2 vols. (Oxford, 1912).

STROH, W., *Taxis und Taktik. Die advokatische Dispositionskunst in Ciceros Gerichtsreden* (Stuttgart, 1975).

— 'Declamatio', in Schröder and Schröder (eds., 2003).

SÜSS, W., *Ethos: Studien zur älteren griechischen Rhetorik* (Leipzig, 1920; repr. Aalen, 1975).

SWARNEY, P. R., 'Social Status and Social Behaviour as Criteria in Judicial Proceedings in the Late Republic', in B. Halpern and D. Hobson (eds.), *Law, Politics and Society in the Ancient Mediterranean World* (Sheffield, 1993) 137–55.

SYME, R., *The Roman Revolution* (Oxford, 1939).

— 'Senators, Tribes and Towns', *Historia* 13 (1964) 105–24.

SZEMLER, G. J., 'Priesthood and Priestly Careers in Ancient Rome', *ANRW* II 16.3 (1986) 2314–31.

TAMM, B., *Auditorium and Palatium* (Stockholm, 1963).

TATUM, W. J., 'The lex Papiria de dedicationibus', *CPh* 88 (1993) 319–28.

— *The Patrician Tribune: Publica Clodius Pulcher* (Chapel Hill, 1999).

TAYLOR, J. H., 'Political Motives in Cicero's Defence of Archias', *AJP* 73 (1952) 62–70.

TAYLOR, L. R., 'Caesar's Colleagues in the Pontifical College', *AJP* 63 (1942) 385–412.

— *Party Politics in the Age of Caesar* (Berkeley, 1949).

TERRENATO, N., ' "Tam Firmum Municipium": The Romanization of Volaterrae and its Cultural Implications', *JRS* 88 (1998) 94–114.

— and SAGGIN, A., 'Ricognizioni archeologiche nel territorio di Volterra. La pianura costiera', *Arch. Class* 46 (1994) 465–82.

THIERFELDER, A., 'Über den Wert der Bemerkungen zur eigenen Person in Ciceros Prozessreden', *Gymnasium* 72 (1965) 385–415.

TORELLI, M., 'Senatori etruschi della tarda repubblica e dell'impero', *Dialoghi d' Archeologia* 3 (1969) 220–310.

— 'La situazione in Etruria', in *Atti del Colloquio Internazionale su epigraphia e ordine senatorio, Roma, 14–20 maggio 1981*, ii (Rome, 1982) 275–99.

TOSI, R., *Dizionario delle sentenze latine e greche* 21st edn. (Milan, 1996).

VASALY, A., 'The Masks of Rhetoric: Cicero's *Pro Roscio Amerino*', *Rhetorica* 3 (1985) 1–20.

— *Representations: Images of the World in Ciceronian Oratory* (Berkeley, Los Angeles, and Oxford, 1993).

— 'Cicero's Early Speeches', in J. M. May (ed.), *Brill's Companion to Cicero: Oratory and Rhetoric* (Leiden, 2002) 71–111.

VENTURINI, C., *Studi sul crimen repetundarum nell' età repubblicana* (Milan, 1979).

VETTER, E., *Handbuch der Italischen Dialekte* (Heidelberg, 1953).

VIANSINO, G. (ed.), *Lucano*, i (Milan, 1995).

VOLKMANN, R., *Die Rhetorik der Griechen und Römer in systematischer Uebersicht*, 2nd edn. (Leipzig, 1885; repr. Hildesheim, 1963).

VRETSKA, H., and VRETSKA, K., *Cicero: Pro Archia*, Texte zur Forschung 31 (Darmstadt, 1979).

WADE, W., and FORSYTH, C., *Administrative Law* (Oxford, 1997).

WAGENER, C., 'Zu Ciceros pro Ligario 1', *Philologus* 47 (1889) 551.

WALLACH, B. P., 'Cicero's *Pro Archia* and the topics', *RhM* 132 (1989) 313–31.

WALSER, G., 'Der Prozess gegen Ligarius im Jahre 46 v. Chr.', *Historia* 8 (1959) 90–6.

WALTON, D., *Ad Hominem Arguments* (Tuscaloosa, 1998).

WANKEL, H. (comm.), *Demosthenes Rede für Ktesiphon über den Kranz*, i (Heidelberg, 1976).

WATSON, A., 'Limits of Juristic Decision in the Late Roman Republic', *ANRW* I.2 (1972) 215–25.

— *Law-Making in the Later Roman Republic* (Oxford, 1974).

WEBB, R., 'Imagination and the Arousal of Emotions in Graeco-Roman Rhetoric', in S. M. Braund and C. Gill (eds.), *The Passions in Roman Thought and Literature* (Cambridge, 1997) 112–27.

WEBSTER, T. B. L. (ed.), *M. Tulli Ciceronis Pro L. Flacco Oratio*, ed. with introd. and notes (Oxford, 1931).

WEINSTOCK, S., *Divus Julius* (Oxford, 1971).

WEISCHE, A., *Ciceros Nachahmung der attischen Redner* (Heidelberg, 1972).

WIEACKER, F., *Cicero als Advokat*, Vortrag gehalten vor der Berliner Juristischen Gesellschaft am 29. April 1964 (Berlin, 1965).

WILL, W., *Der Neue Pauly* 3 (1997) s.v. 'Clodius Pulcher, P.'.

WILLEMS, P., *Le Sénat de la république romaine* (Louvain, 1885).

WILLIAMS, G., *Tradition and Originality in Roman Poetry* (Oxford, 1968).

WINTERBOTTOM, M., 'Cicero and the Silver Age', in *Éloquence et rhétorique chez Cicéron*, Fondation Hardt *Entretiens* 28 (1982) 237–74.

WISEMAN, T. P., *New Men in the Roman Senate* (Oxford, 1971).

— 'Cicero *Pro Sulla* 61–2', *LCM* ii (1977) 21–2.

— '*Pete Nobiles Amicos*: Poets and Patrons in Late Republican Rome', in B. K. Gold (ed.), *Literary and Artistic Patronage in Ancient Rome* (Austin, Tex., 1982) 28–49.

— '*Domi Nobiles* and the Roman Cultural Elite', in M. Cébeillac-Gervasoni (ed.), *Les "Bourgeoisies" municipales Italiennes aux IIme et Ier siècles av. J.-C.* (Paris, 1983), 299–307.

— 'Caesar, Pompey and Rome 59–50 B.C.', in *CAH* ix (1994) 368–423.

WISSE, J., *Ethos and Pathos from Aristotle to Cicero* (Amsterdam, 1989).

— 'Greeks, Romans, and the Rise of Atticism', in *Greek Literary Theory after Aristotle: Festschrift D. M. Schenkeveld* (Amsterdam, 1995) 65–82.

— 'The Intellectual Background of the Rhetorical Works', in J. M. May (ed.), *Brill's Companion to Cicero: Oratory and Rhetoric* (Leiden, 2002) 331–74.

WISSOWA, G., 'Consecratio', *RE* IV 1 (1900) 896–902.

— 'Dedicatio', *RE* IV 2 (1901) 2356–9.

— *Religion und Kultus der Römer*, 2nd edn. (Munich, 1912).

WOLF, F. A. (ed.), *M. Tulli Ciceronis quae vulgo feruntur orationes quatuor* (Berlin, 1801).

WOODMAN, A. J., 'Tacitus' Obituary of Tiberius', *CQ* 39 (1989) 197–205.

ZETZEL, J. E. G., Review of C. P. Craig, *Form as Argument in Cicero's Speeches*, BMCR 4 (1993) 450–1.

ZIEGLER, K., 'Palatium', *RE* XVIII 2b (1949).

ZIELIŃSKI, T., *Cicero im Wandel der Jahrhunderte*, 3rd edn. (Leipzig and Berlin, 1912).

ZIOLKOWSKI, A., *The Temples of Mid-Republican Rome and their Historical and Topographical Context* (Rome, 1992).

INDEX OF PASSAGES

GENERAL INDEX